Microsoft® Office Specialist
Study Guide—Office 2003 Edition

Online Training Solutions, Inc.

PUBLISHED BY
Microsoft Press
A Division of Microsoft Corporation
One Microsoft Way
Redmond, Washington 98052-6399

Library of Congress Cataloging-in-Publication Data pending.

ISBN 0-7356-2110-1

Printed and bound in the United States of America.

1 2 3 4 5 6 7 8 9   QWT   9 8 7 6 5 4

Distributed in Canada by H.B. Fenn and Company Ltd.

A CIP catalogue record for this book is available from the British Library.

Microsoft Press books are available through booksellers and distributors worldwide. For further information about international editions, contact your local Microsoft Corporation office or contact Microsoft Press International directly at fax (425) 936-7329. Visit our Web site at www.microsoft.com/learning/. Send comments to *mspinput@microsoft.com*.

Microsoft, Microsoft Press, ActiveX, AutoSum, Encarta, Hotmail, IntelliMouse, MSN, Outlook, PivotChart, PivotTable, PowerPoint, SharePoint, Verdana, Visual Basic, Visual FoxPro, Windows, and Wingdings are either registered trademarks or trademarks of Microsoft Corporation in the United States and/or other countries. Other product and company names mentioned herein may be the trademarks of their respective owners.

The example companies, organizations, products, domain names, e-mail addresses, logos, people, places, and events depicted herein are fictitious. No association with any real company, organization, product, domain name, e-mail address, logo, person, place, or event is intended or should be inferred.

This book expresses the author's views and opinions. The information contained in this book is provided without any express, statutory, or implied warranties. Neither the authors, Microsoft Corporation, nor its resellers or distributors will be held liable for any damages caused or alleged to be caused either directly or indirectly by this book.

Acquisitions Editor: Juliana Aldous
Project Editor: Laura Sackerman

Body Part No. X10-58409

Contents

Introduction xxi
    About Microsoft Office Specialist Certification xxi
    About This Book. xxii
    About the Book's CD-ROM xxiv
    How to Get Help. xxvi

Part I: **Microsoft Office Specialist Word 2003 Core Exam**

Knowledge You Need Before Studying for This Exam. 2

W03C-1   **Creating Content**   **4**
    W03C-1-1: Insert and Edit Text, Symbols, and Special Characters. 4
        Inserting Visible and Hidden Text 5
        Inserting Symbols and Special Characters. 7
        Editing and Deleting Text. 9
        Moving and Copying Text 10
        Checking Spelling and Grammar. 12
        Using the Thesaurus to Find the Best Word 15
    W03C-1-2: Insert Frequently Used and Predefined Text 15
        Using AutoCorrect. 16
        Using AutoText. 17
        Inserting the Date and Time 19
    W03C-1-3: Navigate to Specific Content 20
        Finding and Replacing Text. 20
        Jumping to a Specific Item 23
    W03C-1-4: Insert, Position, and Size Graphics 24
        Inserting, Positioning, and Sizing Graphics 24
        Inserting, Positioning, and Sizing Text Boxes 26
        Inserting, Positioning, and Sizing Shapes 27
    W03C-1-5: Create and Modify Diagrams and Charts 30
        Inserting and Formatting Organization Charts 30
        Inserting and Formatting Charts 33
    W03C-1-6: Locate, Select, and Insert Supporting Information 36
        Using the Research Service to Locate and Insert Information 36
    W03C-1 Review 38

Contents

W03C-2   **Organizing Content**   **39**

W03C-2-1: Insert and Modify Tables 39
    Inserting Tables 39
    Converting Text to Tables 41
    Changing Table Structure 43
    Formatting Tables Manually 46
    Applying Predefined Formats to Tables 49
W03C-2-2: Create Bulleted Lists, Numbered Lists, and Outlines 50
    Creating and Customizing Bulleted Lists 50
    Creating and Customizing Numbered Lists 52
    Creating Outlines 54
W03C-2-3: Insert and Modify Hyperlinks 57
    Inserting Hyperlinks to Documents, Web Pages, and E-Mail Addresses . . . 57
    Editing and Removing Hyperlinks 60
W03C-2 Review 61

W03C-3   **Formatting Content**   **62**

W03C-3-1: Format Text 62
    Applying Common Character Formatting 62
    Finding and Replacing Character Formatting 65
    Working with Styles 67
    Highlighting Text 70
    Applying Text Effects 70
    Modifying Character Spacing 71
W03C-3-2: Format Paragraphs 73
    Indenting, Spacing, and Aligning Paragraphs 73
    Applying Borders and Shading to Paragraphs 76
    Setting, Removing, and Modifying Tab Stops 78
W03C-3-3: Apply and Format Columns 81
    Setting Up Multiple Columns 81
    Formatting Columns 83
W03C-3-4: Insert and Modify Content in Headers and Footers 85
    Creating and Modifying Headers and Footers 85
    Inserting and Formatting Page Numbers 87
W03C-3-5: Modify Document Layout and Page Setup 89
    Inserting and Deleting Breaks 89
    Modifying Page Margins and Page Orientation 91
W03C-3 Review 93

W03C-4 **Collaborating**   **94**

W03C-4-1: Circulate Documents for Review 94
   Sending a Document for Review 94
   Sending a Document as an E-Mail Attachment 96
W03C-4-2: Compare and Merge Document Versions 97
   Comparing and Merging Documents 97
   Viewing Changes in a Merged Document. 98
W03C-4-3: Insert, View, and Edit Comments 99
   Inserting and Reviewing Comments 100
   Editing Comments. 101
W03C-4-4: Track, Accept, and Reject Proposed Changes 102
   Tracking Changes to a Document 102
   Locating and Managing Document Changes 103
W03C-4 Review 105

W03C-5 **Formatting and Managing Documents**   **106**

W03C-5-1: Create New Documents Using Templates 106
   Creating a New Document Based on a Template 106
W03C-5-2: Review and Modify Document Properties 109
   Reviewing and Modifying Summary Information. 109
   Checking Word, Paragraph, and Character Counts 111
W03C-5-3: Organize Documents Using File Folders 113
   Creating a Folder in Which to Store a Document. 113
   Renaming or Deleting a Document or Folder. 114
W03C-5-4: Save Documents in Appropriate Formats for Different Uses 115
   Saving a Document for Use in Another Program 115
   Saving a Document as a Web Page 116
W03C-5-5: Print Documents, Envelopes, and Labels 117
   Printing a Document 118
   Printing an Envelope or Label .119
W03C-5-6: Preview Documents and Web Pages 121
   Previewing a Document Before Printing. 121
   Previewing a Web Page for Publication 122
W03C-5-7: Change and Organize Document Views and Windows 123
   Switching Views 123
   Working in Print Layout View .124
   Working in Reading Layout View. 126
   Arranging and Splitting Windows 128
W03C-5 Review 130

Contents

Part II: **Microsoft Office Specialist Word 2003 Expert Exam**

Knowledge You Need Before Studying for This Exam. 132

W03E-1 **Formatting Content** **133**

W03E-1-1: Create Custom Styles for Text, Tables, and Lists 133
Creating Character and Paragraph Styles 133
Creating Table Styles 136
Creating List Styles. 137
W03E-1-2: Control Pagination 138
Controlling Orphans and Widows 139
Keeping Paragraphs Together .140
W03E-1-3: Format, Position, and Resize Graphics
Using Advanced Layout Features. 141
Sizing, Scaling, Cropping, and Rotating a Graphic 141
Controlling Contrast and Brightness. 142
Positioning a Graphic in Relation to the Surrounding Text 143
W03E-1-4: Insert and Modify Objects. 145
Inserting and Modifying a New Object 145
Inserting and Modifying an Object from a File 147
W03E-1-5: Create and Modify Diagrams and Charts
Using Data from Other Sources. 148
Importing Data to Create a Chart 149
Linking a Chart to Data from Another Source. 150
W03E-1 Review 152

W03E-2 **Organizing Content** **153**

W03E-2-1: Sort Content in Lists and Tables. 153
Sorting the Items in a List. 153
Sorting the Data in a Table 154
W03E-2-2: Perform Calculations in Tables. 155
Using a Formula in a Table 156
W03E-2-3: Modify Table Formats 157
Merging and Splitting Table Cells 157
Changing the Position and Direction of Cell Contents 158
Modifying Table Properties. 159
Inserting and Modifying Fields .160
W03E-2-4: Summarize Document Content Using Automated Tools 162
Summarizing a Document 162
Analyzing Content Readability .163

W03E-2-5: Use Automated Tools for Document Navigation. 164

    Inserting a Bookmark 165

    Using the Document Map and Thumbnails 166

W03E-2-6: Merge Letters with Other Data Sources 169

    Specifying the Data Source 169

    Preparing the Form Letter 172

    Merging the Data with the Form Letter 174

W03E-2-7: Merge Labels with Other Data Sources. 175

    Creating and Printing Mailing Labels 175

W03E-2-8: Structure Documents Using XML 177

    Creating an XML Document Based on a Schema 177

W03E-2 Review 182

W03E-3   **Formatting Documents**   **183**

W03E-3-1: Create and Modify Forms 183

    Setting Up a Form 183

    Modifying a Form 187

W03E-3-2: Create and Modify Document Background 188

    Changing the Background Color and Fill Effect 188

    Creating a Watermark 189

    Applying a Document Theme 191

W03E-3-3: Create and Modify Document Indexes and Tables. 192

    Creating an Index 192

    Creating a Table of Contents, a Table of Figures,
    or a Table of Authorities 195

W03E-3-4: Insert and Modify Endnotes, Footnotes, Captions,
and Cross-references 198

    Inserting and Formatting Footnotes and Endnotes. 198

    Inserting and Formatting Captions. 200

    Inserting Cross-References 201

W03E-3-5: Create and Manage Master Documents and Subdocuments 202

    Working with a Master Document and Subdocuments 202

W03E-3 Review 205

W03E-4   **Collaborating**   **206**

W03E-4-1: Modify Track Changes Options 206

    Setting Reviewer Options 206

    Setting Balloon Options. 208

W03E-4-2: Publish and Edit Web Documents in Word. 209

    Opening and Editing a Web Page .209

    Creating a Frames Page 211

W03E-4-3: Manage Document Versions. .212
    Creating and Managing Document Versions 212
W03E-4-4: Protect and Restrict Forms and Documents 213
    Protecting a Form 213
    Setting a Password 214
    Restricting Editing or Formatting. 216
W03E-4-5: Attach Digital Signatures to Documents 218
    Authenticating a Document with a Digital Signature. 218
W03E-4-6: Customize Document Properties 219
    Inserting and Editing Advanced Summary Information 219
    Inserting and Editing Custom Information 221
W03E-4 Review 222

W03E-5 **Customizing Word**   **223**
W03E-5-1: Create, Edit, and Run Macros 223
    Creating, Running, and Deleting a Macro 223
    Editing a Macro 226
W03E-5-2: Customize Menus and Toolbars. 227
    Creating a Custom Menu 227
    Customizing a Toolbar 230
W03E-5-3: Modify Word Default Settings. 232
    Changing Default File Locations .232
    Changing the Custom Dictionary 233
    Modifying Default Font Settings 234
W03E-5 Review 236

Part III: **Microsoft Office Specialist Excel 2003 Core Exam**

Knowledge You Need Before Studying for This Exam. 238
    Understanding Workbooks and Worksheets 238
    Selecting Ranges 239
    Completing entries 240
    Understanding How Excel Handles Long Entries 240

E03C-1 **Creating Data and Content**   **241**
E03C-1-1: Enter and Edit Cell Content. 241
    Entering Text, Numbers, and Symbols 241
    Entering Cell Content by Using the Fill Handle 245
    Editing and Clearing Cell Contents. 247

E03C-1-2: Navigate to Specific Cell Content 249
    Finding Cell Content or Formatting 249
    Navigating by Using the Go To Command 251
E03C-1-3: Locate, Select, and Insert Supporting Information 252
    Using the Thesaurus to Find the Best Word 252
    Using the Research Tool to Locate and Insert Supporting Information 253
E03C-1-4: Insert, Position, and Size Graphics 254
    Inserting and Positioning Graphics. 254
    Sizing Graphics 255
E03C-1 Review 257

E03C-2   **Analyzing Data**   **258**

E03C-2-1: Filter Lists Using AutoFilter 258
    Displaying Rows with a Specific Entry in a Specific Column 258
    Displaying Rows That Match Certain Criteria 260
E03C-2-2: Sort Lists 261
    Sorting on One Column. 261
    Sorting on Two or Three Columns 261
E03C-2-3: Insert and Modify Formulas 263
    Doing Simple Arithmetic 263
    Using a Function in a Formula 264
    Using Cell and Range References in a Formula 266
E03C-2-4: Use Statistical, Date and Time, Financial, and Logical Functions. 268
    Using Statistical Functions in Formulas 268
    Using Date and Time Functions in Formulas 269
    Using Financial Functions in Formulas. 269
    Using Logical Functions in Formulas. .270
E03C-2-5: Create, Modify, and Position Diagrams and Charts
Based on Worksheet Data. 271
    Creating, Modifying, and Positioning Diagrams 271
    Creating, Modifying, and Positioning Charts 273
E03C-2 Review 276

E03C-3   **Formatting Data and Content**   **277**

E03C-3-1: Apply and Modify Cell Formats .277
    Changing the Look of Cells and Cell Entries. 277
    Changing Cell Alignment. 280
    Applying an AutoFormat 281
    Changing the Format of Cell Entries. .282
    Copying Formatting. 284

E03C-3-2: Apply and Modify Cell Styles. .284
    Apply a Style 285
    Modify a Style 285
E03C-3-3: Modify Row and Column Formats 286
    Adjusting Column Widths and Row Heights 286
    Hiding and Revealing Columns and Rows 288
    Inserting and Deleting Columns and Rows 288
E03C-3-4: Format Worksheets 289
    Changing a Worksheet's Name, Tab, and Background 289
    Hiding and Revealing a Worksheet 290
E03C-3 Review 291

E03C-4   **Collaborating**   **292**

E03C-4-1: Insert, View, and Edit Comments. 292
    Attaching a Comment to a Worksheet Cell 292
    Editing or Deleting a Comment .293
E03C-4 Review 295

E03C-5   **Managing Workbooks**   **296**

E03C-5-1: Create New Workbooks from Templates 296
    Creating a Workbook Based on a Template 296
E03C-5-2: Insert, Delete, and Move Cells 297
    Inserting and Deleting Cells 298
    Copying and Moving Entries 299
    Controlling How Excel Pastes 301
E03C-5-3: Create and Modify Hyperlinks 302
    Inserting a Hyperlink 302
    Editing a Hyperlink 304
E03C-5-4: Organize Worksheets 304
    Inserting and Deleting Worksheets 304
    Moving a Worksheet 305
E03C-5-5: Preview Data in Other Views .306
    Previewing a Worksheet That Will Be Printed 306
    Previewing a Web Workbook. 307
E03C-5-6: Customize Window Layout 308
    Splitting a Window 308
    Freezing a Column or Row 309
    Arranging Windows. 309
    Hiding and Revealing Workbooks 310

E03C-5-7: Set Up Pages for Printing. .311
    Specifying a Print Area 311
    Controlling What Appears on Each Page 312
    Adding a Header or Footer. 315
E03C-5-8: Print Data 316
    Printing Selections, Worksheets, and Workbooks. 316
E03C-5-9: Organize Workbooks Using File Folders. 318
    Creating a Folder in Which to Store a Workbook. 318
    Renaming or Deleting a Workbook or Folder. 319
E03C-5-10: Save Data in Appropriate Formats for Different Uses 320
    Saving a Workbook for Use in Another Program 320
    Saving a Selection, Worksheet, or Workbook as a Web Page 321
E03C-5 Review 322

Part IV: Microsoft Office Specialist Excel 2003 Expert Exam

Knowledge You Need Before Studying for This Exam. 324

E03E-1 Organizing and Analyzing Data   325

E03E-1-1: Use Subtotals 325
    Calculating Subtotals 326
E03E-1-2: Define and Apply Advanced Filters. 327
    Creating a Criteria Range for Advanced Filtering 328
E03E-1-3: Group and Outline Data 329
    Outlining a Worksheet 329
E03E-1-4: Use Data Validation 331
    Avoiding Input Errors 331
E03E-1-5: Create and Modify List Ranges. 333
    Creating and Modifying a List .333
E03E-1-6: Add, Show, Close, Edit, Merge, and Summarize Scenarios 334
    Creating and Showing Scenarios. 334
    Merging Scenarios. 336
    Creating a Scenario Report 337
E03E-1-7: Perform Data Analysis Using Automated Tools 338
    Using the Analysis ToolPak 339
    Using Goal Seek 339
    Using a Data Table. 340
    Using Solver 343
E03E-1-8: Create PivotTable and PivotChart Reports. 345
    Creating a PivotTable Report .345
    Plotting a PivotTable as a PivotChart. 349

E03E-1-9: Use Lookup and Reference Functions .350
   Looking Up Information 350
E03E-1-10: Use Database Functions 352
   Creating Formulas That Use Database Functions 352
E03E-1-11: Trace Formula Precedents, Dependents, and Errors 354
   Fixing Errors 354
   Auditing a Worksheet 355
E03E-1-12: Locate Invalid Data and Formulas 356
   Using Error Checking 356
   Circling Invalid Data 357
E03E-1-13: Watch and Evaluate Formulas 358
   Watching a Cell 358
   Evaluating a Formula 359
E03E-1-14: Define, Modify, and Use Named Ranges 360
   Naming a Cell or Range 360
   Using a Name in a Formula 361
E03E-1-15: Structure Workbooks Using XML .362
   Adding and Deleting a Data Map 362
   Setting Up an XML Worksheet and Entering Data 364
E03E-1 Review 368

E03E-2   Formatting Data and Content   **370**

E03E-2-1: Create and Modify Custom Data Formats 370
   Creating a Custom Number Format 370
E03E-2-2: Use Conditional Formatting 372
   Monitoring a Worksheet with Conditional Formatting 372
E03E-2-3: Format and Resize Graphics 373
   Controlling the Contrast and Brightness of a Graphic 373
   Sizing, Scaling, Cropping, and Rotating a Graphic 374
E03E-2-4: Format Charts and Diagrams 376
   Formatting a Chart 376
   Formatting an Organization Chart 380
E03E-2 Review 382

E03E-3   Collaborating   **383**

E03E-3-1: Protect Cells, Worksheets, and Workbooks 383
   Preventing Changes to Cells, Worksheets, and Workbooks 383
E03E-3-2: Apply Workbook Security Settings .386
   Authenticating a Workbook with a Digital Signature 386
   Setting a Password 387
   Adjusting Macro Settings 388

E03E-3-3: Share Workbooks 390
   Creating a Shared Workbook. 390
   Using a Shared Workbook 391
E03E-3-4: Merge Workbooks. 393
   Comparing and Merging Workbooks 393
E03E-3-5: Track, Accept, and Reject Changes to Workbooks 394
   Tracking Changes to a Workbook .394
   Accepting and Rejecting Changes .395
E03E-3 Review 397

E03E-4   **Managing Data and Workbooks**   **398**

E03E-4-1: Import Data to Excel 398
   Importing Data from an External Data Source 398
   Importing Data from a Web Page .400
E03E-4-2: Export Data from Excel 401
   Exporting an XML Data File. 402
E03E-4-3: Publish and Edit Web Worksheets and Workbooks. 403
   Publishing a Worksheet as a Web Page 403
E03E-4-4: Create and Edit Templates .404
   Saving and Using a Custom Workbook Template. 405
   Editing a Workbook Template 406
E03E-4-5: Consolidate Data 406
   Consolidating Data from Two or More Worksheets. 407
E03E-4-6: Define and Modify Workbook Properties 408
   Viewing and Changing Workbook Properties. 408
E03E-4 Review 410

E03E-5   **Customizing Excel**   **411**

E03E-5-1: Customize Toolbars and Menus 411
   Customizing a Toolbar 411
   Creating a Custom Menu 413
E03E-5-2: Create, Edit, and Run Macros. 416
   Creating, Running, and Deleting a Macro 416
E03E-5-3: Editing a Macro 418
E03E-5-4: Modify Excel Default Settings 420
   Changing the Default Number of Worksheets, Font Settings,
   and File Locations 420
E03E-5 Review 421

Part V: Microsoft Office Specialist PowerPoint 2003 Exam

Knowledge You Need Before Studying for This Exam. 424
    Understanding PowerPoint's Normal View 424
    Selecting in PowerPoint. 425
    Moving Around a Presentation. 426

P03C-1   **Creating Content**   **427**

P03C-1-1: Create New Presentations from Templates 427
    Creating a Presentation by Using the AutoContent Wizard 427
    Creating a Presentation by Using a Design Template. 429
P03C-1-2: Insert and Edit Text-Based Content 430
    Adding and Editing Text 430
    Changing the Hierarchical Level of Text 433
    Importing Text from Other Sources 434
    Checking Spelling and Style 436
    Using the Thesaurus to Find the Best Word 438
P03C-1-3: Insert Tables, Charts, and Diagrams 438
    Creating Tables 439
    Creating Charts 442
    Creating Diagrams. 447
P03C-1-4: Insert Pictures, Shapes, and Graphics 449
    Adding Clip Art 449
    Adding Pictures 451
    Adding Shapes. 452
    Adding WordArt. 454
P03C-1-5: Insert Objects 458
    Inserting a Word Table 458
    Inserting an Excel Worksheet. 459
    Inserting a Media Clip. 460
P03C-1 Review 464

P03C-2   **Formatting Content**   **465**

P03C-2-1: Format Text-based Content .465
    Changing the Font, Size, and Font Style of Text. 465
    Modifying Text Colors. 468
    Changing Text Alignment. 470
    Finding and Replacing Fonts 471
P03C-2-2: Format Pictures, Shapes, and Graphics 472
    Sizing and Cropping Graphics 472

Adjusting the Color of Graphics 474
Aligning, Connecting, and Rotating Graphics 476
Adding Effects to Shapes 478
P03C-2-3: Format Slides 479
Coloring and Shading a Slide Background 480
Modifying the Slide Layout. .482
Using a Design Template to Make a Presentation Look Consistent 483
Setting the Slide Size and Orientation 484
P03C-2-4: Apply Animation Schemes 485
Animating Slides. 485
P03C-2-5: Apply Slide Transitions 486
Applying Transition Effects 486
P03C-2-6: Customize Slide Templates 487
Saving a Presentation as a Template 488
P03C-2-7: Work with Masters .488
Changing a Presentation's Masters. 489
Adding, Deleting, and Modifying Placeholders 491
Inserting Content in Headers and Footers. 493
P03C-2 Review 495

P03C-3   **Collaborating**   **496**
P03C-3-1: Track, Accept, and Reject Changes in a Presentation. 496
Viewing Tracked Changes. 496
Accepting and Rejecting Changes 498
P03C-3-2: Add, Edit, and Delete Comments in a Presentation 500
Adding Comments 500
Working with Comments 500
P03C-3-3: Compare and Merge Presentations 502
Comparing and Merging Presentations 502
P03C-3 Review 503

P03C-4   **Managing and Delivering Presentations**   **504**
P03C-4-1: Organize a Presentation 504
Working with Different Views .505
Organizing and Deleting Slides. 506
Adding and Viewing Notes. 507
Adding Hyperlinks. 508
P03C-4-2: Set Up Slide Shows for Delivery 510
Creating a Custom Slide Show .510
Working with Action Buttons. .511
Working with Hidden Slides 514

P03C-4-3: Rehearse Timing. .515
   Setting Slide Timings .515
   Rehearsing a Presentation 516
P03C-4-4: Deliver Presentations 518
   Delivering a Slide Show 518
   Using Tools for Emphasis 519
P03C-4-5: Prepare Presentations for Remote Delivery 521
   Packaging a Presentation for CD Storage 521
P03C-4-6: Save and Publish Presentations 522
   Saving an Entire Presentation or a Single Slide 523
   Saving and Publishing a Presentation as a Web Page 524
P03C-4-7: Print Slides, Outlines, Handouts, and Speaker Notes. 528
   Previewing a Presentation 528
   Printing a Presentation 530
P03C-4-8: Export a Presentation to Another Microsoft Office Program 532
   Sending a Presentation to Microsoft Word 532
P03C-4 Review 534

Part VI: **Microsoft Office Specialist Access 2003 Exam**

Knowledge You Need Before Studying for This Exam. 536

A03C-1   **Structuring Databases**   **539**

A03C-1-1: Create Access Databases. 539
   Creating a Database by Using the Database Wizard 539
   Creating a Blank Database 541
A03C-1-2: Create and Modify Tables 542
   Creating a Table by Using the Table Wizard. 542
   Creating a Table by Entering Data 544
   Creating and Modifying a Table in Design View 546
A03C-1-3: Define and Create Field Types 548
   Setting the Data Type and Size of a Field 548
   Creating a Primary Key Field 551
   Creating a Lookup Field. 552
A03C-1-4: Modify Field Properties. 554
   Setting Field Properties 555
   Using an Input Mask 557
A03C-1-5: Create and Modify One-to-Many Relationships 559
   Creating a Relationship Between Two Tables 560

A03C-1-6: Enforce Referential Integrity 562
   Setting Referential Integrity Rules 562
A03C-1-7: Create and Modify Queries .563
   Creating a Query by Using the Simple Query Wizard 564
   Modifying a Query in Design View. .565
   Creating a Crosstab Query 567
   Finding Duplicate Records 569
   Finding Unmatched Records 570
   Updating Information with an Action Query 572
A03C-1-8: Create Forms 574
   Creating an AutoForm 574
   Creating a Form by Using the Form Wizard. 575
A03C-1-9: Add and Modify Form Controls and Properties 577
   Setting Form and Control Properties 577
   Adding Controls to a Form 580
A03C-1-10: Create Reports. 583
   Creating a Report by Using the Report Wizard 583
   Creating Mailing Labels. 585
A03C-1-11: Add and Modify Report Control Properties. 587
   Setting Report and Control Properties. 587
   Adding Controls to a Report 591
A03C-1-12: Create a Data Access Page 593
   Creating and Modifying a Data Access Page 593
A03C-1 Review. 598

A03C-2 **Entering Data**   **600**

A03C-2-1: Enter, Edit, and Delete Records 600
   Entering Data in a Table's Datasheet. 600
   Deleting Records from a Table 602
A03C-2-2: Find and Move Among Records 603
   Navigating Among Records 603
   Finding a Specific Record 604
A03C-2-3: Import Data to Access 605
   Importing Objects from an Access Database 605
   Importing Data from Other Sources 606
A03C-2 Review. 608

Contents

A03C-3 **Organizing Data**   **609**

A03C-3-1: Create and Modify Calculated Fields and Aggregate Functions. 609
  Adding Calculated Fields to Queries. 609
  Calculating Totals in Queries .612
A03C-3-2: Modify Form Layout 613
  Setting Control Size, Alignment, and Spacing. 614
  Modifying Form and Section Layout. 615
A03C-3-3: Modify Report Layout and Page Setup 617
  Setting Control Size, Alignment, and Spacing. 617
  Modifying Report and Section Layout. 618
A03C-3-4: Format Datasheets 621
  Formatting a Datasheet. 622
A03C-3-5: Sort Records. 624
  Sorting Records in a Form or Datasheet. 624
  Sorting Records in a Report. 625
A03C-3-6: Filter Records 626
  Filtering Records for a Selected Value 627
  Filtering Records for Specified Values 628
A03C-3 Review. 630

A03C-4 **Managing Databases**   **631**

A03C-4-1: Identify and Modify Object Dependencies 631
  Identifying Object Dependencies .632
A03C-4-2: View Objects and Object Data in Other Views 633
  Using Print Preview and Layout Preview. 633
  Viewing PivotTables. 635
  Viewing PivotCharts. 637
A03C-4-3: Print Database Objects and Data 639
  Printing Objects and Data 639
A03C-4-4: Export Data from Access 640
  Exporting Data. 640
A03C-4-5: Back Up a Database 642
  Backing Up a Database 642
A03C-4-6: Compact and Repair Databases 643
  Compacting and Repairing a Database 643
A03C-4 Review. 644

Part VII: Microsoft Office Specialist Outlook 2003 Exam

Knowledge You Need Before Studying for This Exam 646

O03C-1 **Messaging** **651**

O03C-1-1: Originate and Respond to E-Mail and Instant Messages 651
    Addressing and Sending a New E-Mail Message 651
    Handling E-Mail Messages You Receive 653
    Sending and Replying to Instant Messages 655
O03C-1-2: Attach Files to Items 656
    Attaching a File to an E-Mail Message 657
    Sending a File Through an Instant Message 658
O03C-1-3: Create and Modify a Personal Signature for Messages 658
    Creating and Modifying an E-Mail Signature 659
    Specifying Unique Signatures for Multiple E-Mail Accounts 661
O03C-1-4: Modify E-Mail Message Settings and Delivery Options 662
    Flagging an E-Mail Message for Follow-Up 662
    Setting E-Mail Message Formats .664
    Setting E-Mail Message Importance, Sensitivity, and Delivery Options 666
O03C-1-5: Create and Edit Contacts .668
    Creating and Updating Contact Entries 668
    Creating Instant Messaging Contact Entries 671
O03C-1-6: Accept, Decline, and Delegate Tasks 672
    Handling Task Assignments 673
O03C-1 Review 675

O03C-2 **Scheduling** **676**

O03C-2-1: Create and Modify Appointments, Meetings, and Events 676
    Adding an Appointment or Event to the Outlook Calendar 676
    Inviting People and Resources to a Meeting 679
O03C-2-2: Update, Cancel, and Respond to Meeting Requests 682
    Responding to a Meeting Request 682
    Updating or Canceling a Meeting 686
O03C-2-3: Customize Calendar Settings 688
    Setting Your Outlook Calendar Options 688
    Defining Your Available Time 692
O03C-2-4: Create, Modify, and Assign Tasks 693
    Creating and Modifying a Task .694
    Assigning a Task 697
O03C-2 Review 698

O03C-3 **Organizing**   **699**

O03C-3-1: Create and Modify Distribution Lists 699
  Creating a Distribution List 699
  Modifying a Distribution List .702
O03C-3-2: Link Contacts to Other Items 703
  Linking an Outlook Item to a Contact Entry. 703
O03C-3-3: Create and Modify Notes 706
  Creating and Editing Notes. 706
O03C-3-4: Organize Items 707
  Adding and Deleting Fields from Folder Views 707
  Sorting Outlook Items. 709
  Filtering E-Mail Messages. 709
  Organizing Outlook Items by Using Colors 711
  Organizing E-Mail Messages by Using Rules 714
  Organizing Outlook Items by Using Views 716
O03C-3-5: Organize Items Using Folders 717
  Organizing E-Mail Messages in Folders 718
  Archiving Outlook Items 719
O03C-3-6: Search for Items 720
  Finding E-Mail Messages 720
  Using Search Folders 722
O03C-3-7: Save Items in Different File Formats. 724
  Saving E-Mail Messages in Other Formats. 724
O03C-3-8: Assign Items to Categories. 725
  Assigning Outlook Items to Categories 725
O03C-3-9: Preview and Print Items 726
  Previewing and Printing an E-Mail Message 726
  Previewing and Printing Your Outlook Calendar 728
  Previewing and Printing Contact Information. 730
O03C-3 Review. 733

Index   **734**

Introduction

Congratulations on taking the first step toward becoming certified as a Microsoft Office Specialist in one or more of the products in Microsoft Office System 2003. Buying this book shows that you are serious about adding this prestigious certification to your credentials.

About Microsoft Office Specialist Certification

You can get the latest information about Microsoft Office Specialist certification by visiting *www.microsoft.com/officespecialist*. On this website, you can learn about the exams themselves and locate the closest Authorized Testing Center.

Proving Yourself

Anyone can open a document or a spreadsheet, but today's employers want to know that candidates for jobs and promotions can leverage Microsoft Office programs in ways that contribute to the bottom line. By earning Microsoft Office Specialist certification you can identify yourself as an individual with proven expertise in Microsoft Office programs, including Microsoft Office Word, Microsoft Office Excel, Microsoft Office PowerPoint, Microsoft Office Access, and Microsoft Office Outlook.

Putting Microsoft on Your Résumé

In today's job market, it is not unusual for a single job posting to attract several hundred applicants. While that is good news for employers, it can be very discouraging for job seekers. Putting Microsoft Office Specialist certification on your résumé helps you stand out as a job candidate with the necessary computing skills to get the job done.

Earning College Credit

As an added benefit to certification, The American Council on Education (ACE) has issued a one-semester hour college credit recommendation for each Microsoft Office Specialist certification. This means it is now even easier to get recognized for your skills while reducing your class load and tuition bill. So get the credential that proves your skills in Microsoft Office programs. Become a Microsoft Office Specialist today.

"Microsoft Office Specialist certification was undoubtedly an essential step in my education and career."

Mark Turner
Graduate Business Student
Pepperdine University
Graziadio School of Business

About This Book

This *Microsoft Office Specialist Study Guide–Office 2003 Edition* includes step by step instructions for performing all the tasks likely to be tested in the Microsoft Office Specialist Office 2003 Editions certification exams. It assumes that you are already familiar enough with the program for which you are seeking certification to be able to carry out common tasks and create the types of Office files commonly used in a work environment.

Tip If you are a beginning user of Microsoft Office System 2003, you can get more in-depth information by reading the product-specific books in the Microsoft Learning *Step By Step* series. Each *Step by Step* course makes it easy to learn just what you need, just when you need it. Work through every lesson in the course, or choose your own starting point—with the modular *Step by Step* design, you drive the instruction.

Organization

The organization of this book parallels the exam, skill set, and skill standard organization outlined on the Microsoft Office Specialist Web site at *www.microsoft.com/learning/mcp /officespecialist/*. Specifically, the book's organization is as follows:

- *Exams:* The book is divided into seven parts, each of which focuses on one of the certification exams available for Word 2003, Excel 2003, PowerPoint 2003, Access 2003, and Outlook 2003.

- *Skill Sets:* Each exam is divided into three to five skill sets, which group together the skills needed to perform a particular category of tasks (such as formatting content or managing files). In this book, each skill set is identified by a number such as W03C-1, where *W03* means Microsoft Word 2003, *C* stands for core-level certification (*E* stands for expert-level), and *1* is the skill-set number. The number and name of each skill set is located at the top of each page to help you quickly locate the skill set you want to study.

- *Objectives:* Each skill set is divided into skill standards. In this book, we call these standards *objectives* and identify them by a number such as W03C-1-1. Within each objective, you will find one or more sets of instructions for performing tasks. Mastering these tasks demonstrates that you have the skills to meet that objective.

- *Practice Exercises:* Every objective has associated practice exercises that you use to prove to yourself that you know how to perform the task. Each practice exercise instructs you to carry out a task or set of tasks, but it does not provide step-by-step instructions for doing so.

This organization means that you have everything you need to prepare for a Microsoft Office Specialist certification exam in one convenient location. So where do you begin?

Recommended Strategy

We suggest that you first install the files you need to do the practice exercises, and then work through the practice exercises for your target exam.

See Also   For information about installing the practice files, refer to "Installing the Practice Files" on page xxv.

- If you can complete the exercise easily and are confident of your results, turn to the review table at the end of each skill set, and check off the corresponding item in the Mastered column. You have mastered this skill and can focus on other areas.

- If you can't complete the exercise or would like to reinforce your knowledge of the skills, work through the step-by-step instructions preceding the practice exercise. When you think you are ready, do the practice exercise again.

You can either apply this exercise-then-review strategy to each skill set in turn, or you can work through all the practice exercises for your target exam first, so that you can identify all your strengths and weaknesses before beginning your review.

Knowledge You Need Before Beginning This Book

The instructions in this book assume that you are already familiar enough with the program for which you are seeking certification to be able to carry out common tasks. Before you begin studying for any exam, you should make sure you have the skills you need to work in any program in Microsoft Office System 2003, such as:

- Giving instructions using menu bar commands, shortcut menus, and toolbar buttons
- Saving files
- Opening, activating, and closing files
- Working with wizards
- Getting help with the Office programs

Conventions

To help you follow along with the step-by-step instructions and do the practice exercises, we use **this font** for things you should click or select, and **this font** for things you need to type. Keys such as CTRL are shown in all CAPITALS, and key combinations (keys you need to press at the same time) such as CTRL+B are shown separated by plus signs.

Each set of step-by-step instructions is preceded by a paragraph like the one below, detailing the preparation necessary to complete the steps with your own file:

BE SURE TO open a document containing a graphic and to display the Picture toolbar before carrying out these steps.

Each practice exercise is preceded by a paragraph like the one below, telling you which of the installed practice files to use in conjunction with the exercise:

USE the *FindSubtotals* workbook in the *My Documents\Microsoft Press\MOS 2003 Study Guide\Excel \E03E-1-1* practice file folder.

About the Book's CD-ROM

The CD-ROM included with this book contains all the practice files you'll use as you work through the exercises in this book. In addition to the practice files, the CD-ROM contains this *Microsoft Office Specialist Study Guide* in e-book format, so if you prefer, you can prepare for your certification exam by using the book on your computer.

For information about how to redeem your free practice test, see the sticker on the inside back cover of the book or on the CD attached to the back cover.

Important The CD-ROM for this book does not contain the Microsoft Office System 2003 software. You should have purchased and installed that program before using this book.

Minimum System Requirements

To use this book, you will need:

- Computer/Processor

  Computer with a Pentium 133-megahertz (MHz) or higher processor

- Memory

  64 MB of RAM (128 MB recommended) plus an additional 8 MB of RAM for each Microsoft Office program (such as Word) running simultaneously

- Hard Disk

  245 MB of available hard disk space with 115 MB on the hard disk where the operating system is installed. An additional 67 MB of hard disk space is required for installing the practice files

  Hard disk requirements will vary depending on configuration; custom installation choices might require more or less hard disk space.

- Operating System

  Microsoft Windows 2000 with Service Pack 3 (SP3) or Microsoft Windows XP or later

- Drive

  CD-ROM drive

- Display

  Super VGA (800 × 600) or higher-resolution monitor with 256 colors

- Peripherals

  Microsoft Mouse, Microsoft IntelliMouse, or compatible pointing device

- Software

  Microsoft Office Word 2003, Microsoft Office Excel 2003, Microsoft Office Access 2003, Microsoft Office PowerPoint 2003, Microsoft Office Outlook 2003, and Microsoft Internet Explorer 5 or later

Important To complete some of the Access exercises in this book, you will need to install the Jet 4.0 Service Pack 7, which you can obtain from the Windows Update Web site at *windowsupdate.microsoft.com*.

Installing the Practice Files

You need to install the practice files on your hard disk before you can open them for use with the practice exercises. Follow these steps to copy the CD's files to your computer:

BE SURE TO turn on your computer, close any open files, and quit any running programs before carrying out these steps.

1   Insert the CD-ROM into the CD-ROM drive of your computer.

    An End User License Agreement appears. Follow the on-screen directions. It is necessary to accept the terms of the license agreement to use the practice files. After you accept the license agreement, a menu screen appears.

    Important   If the menu screen does not appear, start Windows Explorer. In the left pane, click the icon for your CD-ROM drive. In the right pane, double-click the StartCD executable file.

2   Click **Install Practice Files**.

3   Click **Next** on the first screen, select **I accept the terms in the license agreement**, and then click **Next**.

4   Click **Next** and then click **Install**.

5   After the practice files are installed, click **Finish**.

6   Close the CD window, remove the CD-ROM from the CD-ROM drive, and return it to the envelope inside the book.

    You now have a default installation folder on your hard disk, with subfolders for each exam and each objective in the book.

Uninstalling the Practice Files

After you finish working through this book, you should uninstall the practice files to free up hard disk space.

1   On the Windows taskbar, click the **Start** button, and then click **Control Panel**.

2   In Control Panel, click **Add or Remove Programs**, and then if necessary click **Remove a Program**.

3   In the list of installed programs, click **Microsoft Office Specialist Study Guide—Office 2003 Edition**, and then click the **Remove** button.

4   In the confirmation dialog box, click **Yes**.

5   After the files are uninstalled, close the Add or Remove Programs window and Control Panel.

    Important   If you need additional help installing or uninstalling the practice files, please see "Getting Help with This Book and Its CD-ROM," below. Microsoft Product Support Services does not provide support for this book or its CD-ROM.

How to Get Help

Every effort has been made to ensure the accuracy of this book and the contents of its CD-ROM. If you run into problems, please contact the appropriate source for help and assistance.

Getting Help with This Book and Its CD-ROM

If your question or issue concerns the content of this book or its companion CD-ROM, please first search the online Microsoft Learning Knowledge Base, which provides support information for known errors in or corrections to this book, at the following website:

www.microsoft.com/learning/support/search.asp

If you do not find your answer at the online Knowledge Base, send your comments or questions to Microsoft Learning Technical Support at:

mspinput@microsoft.com

Getting Additional Help

If your question is about a Microsoft software product and not about the content of this Microsoft Learning book, please search the appropriate product support center or the Microsoft Knowledge Base at:

support.microsoft.com

In the United States, Microsoft software product support issues not covered by the Microsoft Knowledge Base are addressed by Microsoft Product Support Services. The Microsoft software support options available from Microsoft Product Support Services are listed at:

support.microsoft.com

Outside the United States, for support information specific to your location, please refer to the Worldwide Support menu on the Microsoft Product Support Services website for the site specific to your country, which can be found at:

support.microsoft.com

Part I

Microsoft Office Specialist Word 2003 Core Exam

This part of the book covers the skills you need to have for certification as a Microsoft Office Specialist in Microsoft Office Word 2003 at the core level. Specifically, you will need to be able to complete tasks that require the following skills:

Skill Set Number	Skill Set
W03C-1	Creating content
W03C-2	Organizing content
W03C-3	Formatting content
W03C-4	Collaborating
W03C-5	Formatting and managing documents

You can use these basic skills to create the documents most commonly used in a business environment.

Knowledge You Need Before Studying for This Exam

We assume that you have been working with Word for a while and that you know how to carry out fundamental tasks that are not specifically mentioned in the Microsoft Office Specialist core-level objectives for Word 2003. Before you begin studying for this exam, you might want to scan this section to make sure you are familiar with this information.

Selecting Text

Before you can edit or format text, you need to select it. You can select text as follows:

- To select a word, double-click it. The word and the space following it are selected. Punctuation following a word is not selected.
- To select a sentence, click anywhere in the sentence while holding down the CTRL key. The first character in the sentence through the space following the ending punctuation mark are selected.
- To select a paragraph, triple-click it.

You can select adjacent words, lines, or paragraphs by positioning the insertion point at the beginning of the text you want to select, holding down the SHIFT key, and then pressing an arrow key or clicking at the end of the text that you want to select.

To select blocks of text that are not adjacent in a document, you select the first block, hold down the CTRL key, and then click to select the next block.

To select a block of text quickly, you can use the selection area—a blank strip to the left of the document's text column. When the pointer is in the selection area, it changes from an I-beam to a right-pointing arrow. You can use the selection area to quickly select these items:

- To select a line, click the selection area to the left of the line.
- To select a paragraph, double-click the selection area to the left of the paragraph.
- To select an entire document, triple-click the selection area.

To deselect text, click anywhere in the document window except the selection area.

Moving Around a Document

You can use the vertical and horizontal scroll bars to move around the active document. Using the scroll bars does not move the insertion point—it changes only your view of the document in the window. For example, if you drag the vertical scroll box down to the bottom of the scroll bar, the end of the document comes into view, but the insertion point does not move. Here are some other ways to use the scroll bars:

- Click the up or down scroll arrow on the vertical scroll bar to move the document window up or down one line of text.
- Click above or below the scroll box to move up or down one windowful.
- Click the left or right scroll arrow on the horizontal scroll bar to move the document window to the left or right several characters at a time.
- Click to the left or right of the scroll box to move left or right one windowful.

You can also move around a document by moving the insertion point. You can click to place the insertion point at a particular location, or you can press a key or a key combination to move the insertion point.

The following table shows the keys and key combinations you can use to move the insertion point quickly:

Pressing This Key	Moves the Insertion Point
LEFT ARROW	Left one character at a time
RIGHT ARROW	Right one character at a time
DOWN ARROW	Down one line at a time
UP ARROW	Up one line at a time
CTRL+LEFT ARROW	Left one word at a time
CTRL+RIGHT ARROW	Right one word at a time
HOME	To the beginning of the current line
END	To the end of the current line
CTRL+HOME	To the start of the document
CTRL+END	To the end of the document
CTRL+PAGE UP	To the beginning of the previous page
CTRL+PAGE DOWN	To the beginning of the next page
PAGE UP	Up one screen
PAGE DOWN	Down one screen

W03C-1
Creating Content

The skills tested by this section of the Microsoft Office Specialist Word 2003 Core Exam all relate to the creation of documents and the refinement of content. Specifically, the following objectives are associated with this set of skills:

Number	Objective
W03C-1-1	Insert and edit text, symbols, and special characters
W03C-1-2	Insert frequently used and predefined text
W03C-1-3	Navigate to specific content
W03C-1-4	Insert, position, and size graphics
W03C-1-5	Create and modify diagrams and charts
W03C-1-6	Locate, select, and insert supporting information

 Important Before you can do the practice exercises associated with this skill set, you need to install the practice files from the book's companion CD to their default location. See "Installing the Practice Files" on page xxv for more information.

Insert and Edit Text, Symbols, and Special Characters

W03C-1-1   The skills measured by this objective include the following:

- Inserting visible and hidden text
- Inserting symbols and special characters
- Editing and deleting text
- Moving and copying text
- Checking spelling and grammar
- Using the Thesaurus to find the best word

To be effective, a document must convey information in a way that is accurate and easy to understand. So your first task when you create any document is to make sure all its text is correct.

Inserting Visible and Hidden Text

Almost all Word documents contain visible text that you insert by typing. If you are creating a new document, you can simply start typing. If you want to insert new text in an existing document, you click to position the insertion point and then type the text. When the text you're typing goes beyond the right margin, Word "wraps" the text to the next line. Because of this word wrap feature, which is common in word-processing and desktop-publishing programs, you press ENTER only to start a new paragraph, not a new line.

Tip By default, Word is in Insert mode, and existing text to the right moves to accommodate the new text you type. If Word is in Overtype mode, each character you type replaces an existing character. To turn on Overtype mode, either double-click the letters *OVR* on the status bar or press the INSERT key. Repeat this action to switch back to Insert mode.

By default, the text you type is visible in the document, but you can also insert text that can be hidden. For example, you might want to include details that are hidden when you print a short form of a document but are shown when you print a longer version. You can type hidden text, and you can also select existing text and apply hidden formatting from the Font dialog box.

See Also For information about formatting text, refer to W03C-3-1, "Format Text."

You turn hidden text on or off by clicking the Show/Hide ¶ button on the Standard toolbar. When hidden text is visible, a dotted underline appears below it.

BE SURE TO open the document you want to work with before carrying out these steps.

To insert visible text:

1 Click to place an insertion point in the document.

2 Type the text.

To overtype text instead of inserting it:

1 On the status bar, double-click the letters **OVR** to turn on Overtype mode.

2 Type the text.

Each character you type replaces an existing character.

3 Double-click the letters **OVR** again to return to Insert mode.

To insert hidden text:

1 Click the location where you want to place the text in the document.

2 Press **CTRL+SHIFT+H** to turn on hidden formatting.

3 Type the text.

4 Press **CTRL+SHIFT+H** to turn off hidden formatting.

To hide/show hidden text:

Show/Hide

1 On the Standard toolbar, click the **Show/Hide ¶** button.

Word turns on this feature and shows non-printing characters and hidden text.

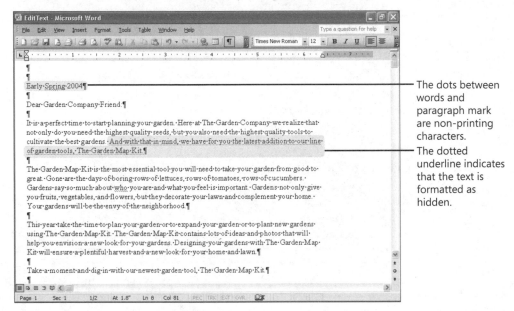

The dots between words and paragraph mark are non-printing characters.

The dotted underline indicates that the text is formatted as hidden.

2 Click the **Show/Hide ¶** button again to turn off this feature and hide hidden text.

Practice Exercise

In this exercise, you will enter visible and hidden text in a document.

USE the *EnterText* document in the *My Documents\Microsoft Press\MOS 2003 Study Guide\Word\W03C-1-1* practice file folder.

Open the *EnterText* document, and with the insertion point at the beginning of the document, type **Gardeners, Get Your Garden Tools Ready!** Press **ENTER** twice to insert a blank line below the heading. Then type **With spring just around the corner, let's start thinking flowers and vegetables. Let's start planning for this year's garden. Let's start celebrating blue-ribbon zinnias and zucchini. Let's get your garden tools ready.** Press **ENTER** two times to insert a blank line between paragraphs, and then type **Here at The Garden Company, we realize that you need the highest quality tools to cultivate the best gardens. And with that in mind, we have for you the latest addition in our line of garden tools, The Garden Map Kit.** Press **SPACE**, and then press **CTRL+SHIFT+H** to turn on hidden formatting. Type **On Saturday, March 6, be one of the first 25 customers to register for a training class or workshop, and receive this kit for free!** (The text will disappear as you type it.) Then press **CTRL+SHIFT+H** to turn off hidden formatting. On the Standard toolbar, click the **Show/Hide ¶** button to see what you have typed. Then close the *EnterText* document without saving it.

Inserting Symbols and Special Characters

You can insert some common symbols by holding down the SHIFT key and pressing the number keys on the top row of your keyboard. You can insert other characters by pressing keyboard shortcuts. For example, if you type two consecutive dashes followed by a word and a space, Word changes the two dashes to a professional-looking em-dash—like this one. (This symbol gets its name from the fact that it was originally the width of the character m.)

To insert other less-common symbols, you can select them in the Symbol dialog box, which lists all the characters you can enter in all the fonts installed on your computer. If you frequently use a particular symbol, you can select it in the Symbol dialog box and make a note of its shortcut key. Then if your keyboard has a numeric keypad, you can hold down the ALT key and press the corresponding numeric keypad numbers to insert the symbol without opening the dialog box. For example, you can enter the copyright symbol (©) by pressing ALT+0169.

BE SURE TO open the document you want to work with before carrying out these steps.

To insert a symbol from the Symbol dialog box:

1   Click the location where you want to insert the symbol in the text.

2   On the **Insert** menu, click **Symbol**.

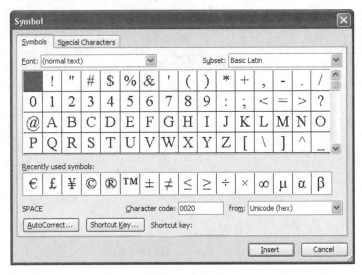

3   Scroll through the list of symbols, and click the one you want.

   Tip   If you don't see the symbol you want, you can switch to a different font by making a selection in the Font drop-down list.

4   Click **Insert**, and then click **Close**.

Word inserts the symbol in your document.

To insert a symbol by using a keyboard combination:

1   Click the location where you want to insert the symbol in the text.

2   On the **Insert** menu, click **Symbol**.

3   In the Symbol dialog box, click the symbol you want.

4   At the bottom of the dialog box, check whether this symbol can be entered with a keyboard combination, and if it can, make a note of it, and then close the dialog box.

5   Press the keyboard combination, using the numbers on the numeric keypad.

    Word inserts the symbol in your document.

To insert a special character from the Symbol dialog box:

1   Click the location where you want to insert the special character in the text.

2   On the **Insert** menu, click **Symbol**, and when the Symbol dialog box appears, click the **Special Characters** tab.

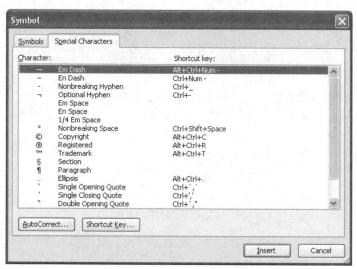

3   Scroll through the list, and click the one you want.

4   Click **Insert**, and then click **Close**.

    Word inserts the special character in your document.

Practice Exercise

In this exercise, you will insert a symbol in a document.

USE the *EnterSymbol* document in the *My Documents\Microsoft Press\MOS 2003 Study Guide\Word \W03C-1-1* practice file folder.

Open the *EnterSymbol* presentation, and click between the letter *t* and the period of the sentence that ends with *The Garden Map Kit*. Display the Symbol dialog box, and scroll until you can see ® (the registered symbol). Insert the symbol, and close the Symbol dialog box. Then close the *EnterSymbol* document without saving it.

Editing and Deleting Text

You will rarely write a perfect document that doesn't require any editing. You can edit a document as you create it, or you can write it first and then revise it. Or you might want to edit a document created for one purpose to create another document for a different purpose.

As you edit a document, Word keeps track of the changes you make so that you can easily reverse a change and restore your original text. If you undo an action, you can restore, or redo, the action, and you can undo and restore multiple actions at the same time.

Tip You cannot undo or redo any single action except the last one you performed.

If you make a change and you want to make the same change elsewhere in the text, you can position the insertion point or make a selection and then use the Repeat command or the F4 key to repeat your previous editing or formatting action.

BE SURE TO open the document you want to work with before carrying out these steps.

To replace selected text:

1 Select the text you want to replace.

2 Type the new text.

The first character you type replaces the entire selection, and subsequent characters are inserted in the usual way.

See Also For information about selecting text, refer to "Selecting Text" in "Knowledge You Need Before Studying for This Exam" on page 2.

To delete text:

1 Click to the left or right of the characters you want to delete.

2 Press the **DELETE** key to delete the character to the right, or press **BACKSPACE** to delete the character to the left.

To delete selected text:

1 Select the text you want to delete.

2 Press the **DELETE** or **BACKSPACE** key to delete the selection.

To undo and redo the previous editing action:

Undo

1 On the Standard toolbar, click the **Undo** button to reverse your previous editing action.

Redo

2 On the Standard toolbar, click the **Redo** button to restore your previous editing action.

Tip You can also click Undo or Redo on the Edit menu.

To undo and redo multiple editing actions:

Undo

1 On the Standard toolbar, click the **Undo** down arrow, and click the earliest of the actions you want to reverse.

Redo

2 On the Standard toolbar, click the **Redo** down arrow, and click the earliest of the actions you want to restore.

To repeat the previous editing action:

1 Position the insertion point or select the text on which you want to repeat the previous action.

2 Press the **F4** key.

Practice Exercise

In this exercise, you will edit text in the existing document. You'll change one paragraph and delete another, and then undo and redo the deletion.

USE the *EditText* document in the *My Documents\Microsoft Press\MOS 2003 Study Guide\Word\W03C-1-1* practice file folder.

Open the *EditText* document. Double-click the word *Early* at the top of the document to select it, and then press **ENTER** to delete the word and replace it with a new blank paragraph. Press **END** to move the insertion point to the end of the line, press **SPACE**, and then type **Has Arrived!** Select the first sentence of the first paragraph, and press **DELETE** to delete the sentence. On the Standard toolbar, click the **Undo** button to restore the deleted text. Then close the *EditText* document without saving it.

Moving and Copying Text

Although you can carry out simple editing by inserting and deleting text, more extensive editing often requires moving and copying chunks of text from one place to another in the same document or a different document. After selecting the text, you can move or copy it in the following ways:

- Use the Cut and Paste commands or buttons. Cut text disappears from the document but is temporarily stored in an area of your computer's memory called the Office Clipboard. You can then paste the text in its new location.

- Use the Copy and Paste commands or buttons. Text that is copied is stored on the Office Clipboard but also remains in its original location. You can then paste a duplicate in the new location.

- Use drag-and-drop editing, which does not involve the Office Clipboard. To move selected text, you simply point to it and drag it to its new location. To copy selected text, you hold down the CTRL key as you drag.

BE SURE TO open the document you want to work with before carrying out these steps.

To move text:

1 Select the text you want to move.

2 Do one of the following:

Cut

- On the Standard toolbar, click the **Cut** button.
- On the **Edit** menu, click **Cut**.
- Press **CTRL+X**.

The text is cut from the document and stored on the Office Clipboard.

3 Click the location where you want to paste the text.

4 Do one of the following:

Paste

- On the Standard toolbar, click the **Paste** button.
- On the **Edit** menu, click **Paste**.
- Press **CTRL+V**.

To copy text:

1 Select the text you want to copy.

2 Do one of the following:

Copy

- On the Standard toolbar, click the **Copy** button.
- On the **Edit** menu, click **Copy**.
- Press **CTRL+C**.

The text is copied and stored on the Office Clipboard.

3 Click the location where you want to paste the text.

4 Do one of the following:

Paste

- On the Standard toolbar, click the **Paste** button.
- On the **Edit** menu, click **Paste**.
- Press **CTRL+V**.

To drag and drop selected text:

1 Select the text you want to move or copy.

2 Point to the text, and do one of the following:

- If you are moving the selection, drag it to its new location.
- If you are copying the selection, hold down the **CTRL** key, drag the selection to its new location, and release the mouse button before releasing the **CTRL** key.

Practice Exercise

In this exercise, you will move and copy text.

USE the *MoveText* **document in the** *My Documents\Microsoft Press\MOS 2003 Study Guide\Word\W03C-1-1* practice file folder.

Open the *MoveText* document. Scroll the phrase *Happy Gardening!* into view, and select the entire line of text. Use the **Copy** button to copy the text, and then press **CTRL+HOME** to move to the beginning of the document. Paste the copied text into the document, select the new line, and click the **Cut** button. Press **CTRL+END** to move the insertion point to the end of the document, press **ENTER** to insert a blank line, and in the Clipboard task pane, click the **Happy Gardening!** item to paste it into the document. Close the Clipboard task pane, and scroll up to the paragraph that begins *The Garden Company welcomes your comments* if it is not in view. Triple-click anywhere in the paragraph to select it, hold down the **SHIFT** key, and press the **DOWN ARROW** key to add the blank paragraph mark below it to the selection. Drag the paragraph down to the blank space above *Happy Gardening!* Then close the *Move-Text* document without saving it.

Checking Spelling and Grammar

As you type the text of your document, by default Word underlines spelling and grammar errors with color-coded wavy lines:

■ A red line indicates that Word does not recognize the spelling of the word; that is, the word is not included in Word's online dictionary.

■ A green line indicates a possible grammar error.

To fix individual spelling and grammar errors quickly, you can right-click an underlined word to display a list of corrections from which you can choose.

Tip   To turn on grammar checking, click Options on the Tools menu, and on the Spelling & Grammar tab, select the "Check grammar as you type" check box.

In addition to correcting individual errors, you can check the entire document for spelling and grammar errors. Word then compares each word in the document with the words in its main dictionary and a supplemental dictionary containing words you have added. It also analyzes sentences for breaches of grammatical rules. Word displays the Spelling and Grammar dialog box with a list of potential replacements for any word it thinks is misspelled. If a sentence appears to break a grammatical rule, the Spelling and Grammar dialog box identifies the rule and lists suggestions for correcting the error. You can then tell Word how to handle the problem or whether to ignore this one instance or all instances in the document.

BE SURE TO open the document you want to work with before carrying out these steps.

To check the spelling of a single word:

1   Right-click a word that has a red wavy underline.

The shortcut menu lists possible correct spellings for this word, as well as actions you might want to carry out.

2 On the shortcut menu, click the correct spelling of the word you right-clicked.

Word removes the red wavy underline and inserts the correction.

To check the spelling of an entire document:

1 Press **CTRL+HOME** to move to the beginning of the document.

Tip You can also select a block of text to check the spelling of just that block.

Spelling and
Grammar

2 On the Standard toolbar, click the **Spelling and Grammar** button.

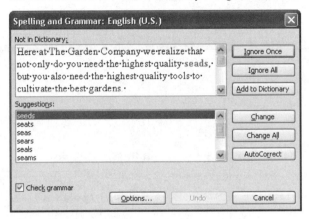

3 With the first problem highlighted, do one of the following:

- Click the document to eliminate an error by editing the document. The **Ignore Once** button changes to **Resume**. After you finish editing, click **Resume** to continue checking the document.

- Click **Ignore Once** to leave the highlighted error unchanged and find the next spelling or grammar error.

- Click **Ignore All** to leave all occurrences of the highlighted spelling error unchanged throughout the document and continue checking the document.

- Click **Change** to change the highlighted error to the word you select in the **Suggestions** box.

- Click **Change All** to change all occurrences of the highlighted error to the word you select in the **Suggestions** box and continue checking the document.

- Click **AutoCorrect** to add the spelling error and its correction to the **AutoCorrect** list so that Word corrects it the next time you type it.

See Also For information about AutoCorrect, refer to W03C-1-2, "Insert Frequently Used and Predefined Text."

- Click **Add to Dictionary** to add the selected word in the **Not in dictionary** box to the supplemental dictionary.

- Click **Undo** to undo the last spelling or grammar action you performed.

Tip   You can also click Options to open the Spelling and Grammar Options dialog box, where you can open a different custom dictionary or to change the rules that Word uses to check spelling and grammar.

4   When Word displays a message that there are no further errors in the document, click **OK** to end the spelling check.

To check the grammar of a single phrase:

1   Right-click a phrase that has a green wavy underline.

A shortcut menu lists possible replacements for the phrase, plus actions you might want to take.

2   On the shortcut menu, click the action you want to take.

Word removes the red wavy underline and inserts the correction, if any.

To check the grammar of an entire document:

1   Press **CTRL+HOME** to move to the beginning of the document.

Tip   You can also select a block of text to check the grammar of just that block.

Spelling and Grammar

2   On the Standard toolbar, click the **Spelling and Grammar** button.

3   With the first problem highlighted, do one of the following:

■ Click **Ignore Rule** to leave all occurrences of the highlighted grammar error unchanged throughout the document and continue checking the document.

■ Click **Change** to change the highlighted error to Word's suggestion.

■ Click **Next Sentence** to transfer to the document the corrections you've indicated and continue checking the document. This way you can fix grammatical errors without switching between the Spelling and Grammar dialog box and the document window.

4   When Word displays a message that there are no further errors in the document, click **OK** to end the grammar check.

Practice Exercise

In this exercise, you will check the spelling in the document and find, review, and correct a grammar error.

USE the *CheckSpelling* document in the *My Documents\Microsoft Press\MOS 2003 Study Guide\Word \W03C-1-1* practice file folder.

Open the *CheckSpelling* document, and right-click **bot**, the first word with a red wavy underline. On the shortcut menu, click **both**. Move to the beginning of the document, and click the **Spelling and Grammar** button. The Spelling and Grammar dialog box appears, highlighting *envrionmentally*, the first word that Word does not recognize. With *environmentally* selected in the **Suggestions** box, click **AutoCorrect** to add the misspelling and its correction to the **Auto-Correct** list. Change all instances of *harty* to *hearty*. Word then flags a possible grammar error and indicates that this text could be a sentence fragment; the sentence is missing a verb. In the **Fragment** box, click before the word *available*, type **are**, press **SPACE**, and then click **Change**. When Word displays a message indicating that it has finished checking the spelling and grammar of the document, click **OK**. Then close the *CheckSpelling* document without saving it.

Using the Thesaurus to Find the Best Word

Language is often contextual. The language you use in a letter to a friend is different from the language you use in business correspondence. To make sure you are using words that best convey your meaning in any given context, you can use Word's Thesaurus to look up alternative words, or synonyms, for a selected word.

BE SURE TO open the document you want to work with before carrying out these steps.

To replace a word with a synonym:

1   Select the word for which you want to find an alternative.

2   On the **Tools** menu, click **Language** and then **Thesaurus**.

    The Research task pane appears, listing synonyms for the word you selected.

3   Point to the word you want to use as an alternative to the selected word.

    Word surrounds the word with a box containing a down arrow.

4   Click the word's down arrow, and click **Insert** on the drop-down menu.

    Word substitutes this word for the selected word.

5   Close the Research task pane.

Practice Exercise

In this exercise, you will use the Thesaurus to replace one word with another.

USE the *UseThesaurus* document in the *My Documents\Microsoft Press\MOS 2003 Study Guide\Word \W03C-1-1* practice file folder.

Open the *UseThesaurus* document, and double-click the word **important** in the last line of the first paragraph. On the **Tools** menu, click **Language** and then **Thesaurus** to open the Research task pane, which displays a list of synonyms for the word *important*. Click the minus sign to the left of *significant* to close its list, bringing the synonym *valuable* and its list of synonyms into view. Click the plus sign to the left of *significant*, and then point to the word *significant* in the **Meanings** area just below it. Click the word's down arrow, and click **Insert** on the drop-down menu. Then close the Research task pane, and close the *UseThesaurus* document without saving it.

Insert Frequently Used and Predefined Text

W03C-1-2   The skills measured by this objective include the following:

■   Using AutoCorrect
■   Using AutoText
■   Inserting the date and time

Word includes several quick and easy ways to enter frequently used text in a document. Some types of text are predefined by the program, but you can define others to meet your needs.

Using AutoCorrect

If you type *teh*, Word changes it to *the* as soon as you press SPACE. This is a feature of AutoCorrect. Besides relying on this feature to correct misspelled words, you can also use AutoCorrect to insert a phrase when you type an abbreviation. You set up this type of replacement in the AutoCorrect dialog box.

When Word implements an AutoCorrect change, it displays a small blue rectangle near the changed text. Pointing to this rectangle displays the AutoCorrect Options button, and clicking this button displays a menu of choices. (You can also change AutoCorrect options in the AutoCorrect dialog box.)

BE SURE TO open the document you want to work with before carrying out these steps.

To create an AutoCorrect entry:

1   On the **Tools** menu, click **AutoCorrect Options**.

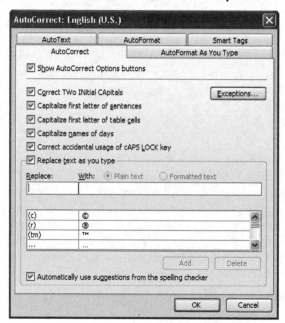

2   Click the **Replace** box, and type an abbreviation or a misspelled word.

3   Press the **TAB** key to move to the **With** box.

4   Type the word or phrase that the abbreviation represents, or the correct spelling for the word in the **Replace** box.

5   Click **Add** to add the entry to the correction list.

6   Click **OK** to close the AutoCorrect dialog box.

The text for the new AutoCorrect entry will now be inserted in a document each time you type the abbreviation or incorrect spelling and press SPACE.

To use an AutoCorrect entry:

1   Click the location where you want the AutoCorrect entry to appear.

2   Type the abbreviation of a word or phrase you added to the correction list, and then press **SPACE**.

    The abbreviation is replaced by the AutoCorrect word or phrase.

Practice Exercise

In this exercise, you will adjust the AutoCorrect settings and then add and use an Auto-Correct abbreviation.

USE the *UseAutoCorrect* document in the *My Documents\Microsoft Press\MOS 2003 Study Guide\Word \W03C-1-2* practice file folder.

Open the *UseAutoCorrect* document. Then display the **AutoCorrect** tab of the AutoCorrect dialog box, and clear the **Capitalize first letter of sentences** check box so that Word will not automatically capitalize a lowercase letter or word that follows a period. Then type **gc** in the **Replace** box, type **The Garden Company** in the **With** box, and click **Add** to add the entry to the correction list. Close the AutoCorrect dialog box, move to the end of the document, type **gc**, and press **SPACE**. Word replaces *gc* with *The Garden Company*. Close the *UseAuto-Correct* document without saving it.

Using AutoText

You can use the AutoText feature to save time and keep your documents consistent. Word comes with built-in AutoText entries for commonly used items, such as the salutations and closings for letters, and you can create your own AutoText entries for the words and phrases you use repeatedly, such as your name, address, company, and job title.

AutoText differs from AutoCorrect in that Word inserts an AutoText entry only when you tell it to. Thus you can use meaningful words as abbreviations without fear of inadvertent automatic replacements. For example, you can use *me* as the abbreviation for *Marketing Enterprises* without worrying that *me* will be replaced everywhere you use it in a document.

BE SURE TO open the document you want to work with before carrying out these steps.

To insert a predefined AutoText entry:

1   Click in the document.

2   On the **Insert** menu, click **AutoText**, a category of entries, and then the entry you want.

    Word inserts the entry at the location of the insertion point.

To create an AutoText entry and then insert it:

1   On the **Insert** menu, click **AutoText** and then **AutoText**.

2   In the **Enter AutoText entries here** box, type the text of the entry.

3   Click **Add**, and then click **OK** to close the AutoCorrect dialog box.

4   Back in the document, click the location where you want the text to appear, and then type the first few characters of the AutoText entry you just created.

A ScreenTip displays the entire entry, followed by *(Press ENTER to Insert)*.

5   Press the **ENTER** key to insert the full entry.

Practice Exercise

In this exercise, you will insert a predefined AutoText entry and then create and insert an AutoText entry of your own.

USE the *UseAutoText* document in the *My Documents\Microsoft Press\MOS 2003 Study Guide\Word \W03C-1-2* practice file folder.

Open the *UseAutoText* document, press **CTRL+END** to move to the end of the document, press **HOME** to move to the beginning of the line, and press **ENTER** to start a new paragraph. On the **Insert** menu, click **AutoText**, click **Closing**, and then click **Respectfully,** to insert this standard closing for a letter. Press **ENTER** four times to leave space for a signature, and then on the **Insert** menu, click **AutoText** and then **AutoText** to open the AutoCorrect dialog box with the **AutoText** tab active. In the **Enter AutoText entries here** box, type **Karen Berg**, click **Add**, and then click **OK**. Without moving the insertion point in the document, type **Kare**, press **ENTER** to insert the full name, and then press **ENTER** again. Then close the *UseAutoText* document without saving it.

Inserting the Date and Time

When you want to insert the date or time in a Word document, you don't have to look at a calendar or clock. You can insert a special code called a field that tells Word to insert the date or time recorded by your computer's internal calendar and clock. You can choose to have Word insert the current date or time or to have Word update the date and time whenever you open the document.

BE SURE TO open the document you want to work with before carrying out these steps.

To insert a date or time:

1   Click the location where you want the date or time to appear.

2   On the **Insert** menu, click **Date and Time**.

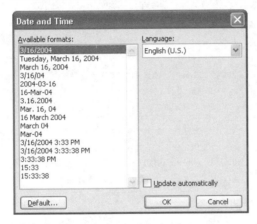

3   Click the date or time with the format you want.

4   Do one of the following:

- ■ To insert the date or time as ordinary text that can be edited, leave the **Update automatically** check box cleared.

- ■ To insert the date or time as a field so that Word inserts the current date or time whenever you open the document, select the **Update automatically** check box.

5   Click **OK**.

Tip   You can also insert date and time fields by clicking Field on the Insert menu. The Insert Field dialog box lists all the fields available for use in Word documents.

Practice Exercise

In this exercise, you will insert a time field in a document.

USE the *InsertTime* **document in the** *My Documents\Microsoft Press\MOS 2003 Study Guide\Word\W03C-1-2* practice file folder.

Open the *InsertTime* document. With the insertion point at the top of the document, open the Date and Time dialog box, and insert the current date and time with the format that shows seconds. Select the **Update automatically** check box, and close the dialog box.

Back in the document, click anywhere in the date and time Word inserted, and make a note of the time. Save the *InsertTime* document with the name **RightNow**, and then close the document. Use any method to open the *RightNow* document, and notice that the time has changed. Then close the *RightNow* document without saving it.

Navigate to Specific Content

W03C-1-3   The skills measured by this objective include the following:

- ■ Finding and replacing text
- ■ Jumping to a specific item

While creating a document, you might need to work with specific elements to ensure consistency and accuracy throughout. Word includes several methods for identifying and moving among specific text elements.

Finding and Replacing Text

If you want to find a specific word or phrase in a document, you can use the Find tab of the Find and Replace dialog box. After you enter the text in the "Find what" box, you can click the Find Next button to locate the next occurrence of that text.

You can also locate an occurrence of a word or phrase and replace it with a different one by using the Replace tab of the Find and Replace dialog box. After you enter the text you want to find in the "Find what" box and the text you want to substitute in the "Replace with" box, you can click buttons in the dialog box to control the substitution.

You can use other options in the Find and Replace dialog box to carry out more complicated searches. Clicking the More button expands the Find and Replace dialog box.

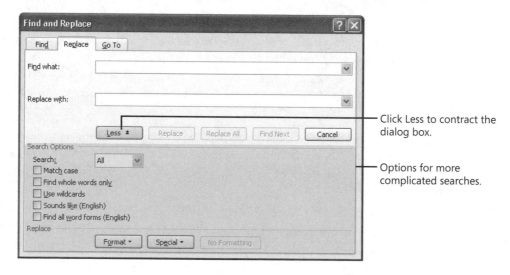

Click Less to contract the dialog box.

Options for more complicated searches.

The expanded dialog box includes the following options:

- Use the options in the Search drop-down list to guide the direction of the search.
- Select the "Match case" check box to match capitalization.
- Select the "Find whole words only" check box to find only whole-word occurrences of the "Find what" text.
- Select the "Use wildcards" check box to find words that are similar, such as *effect* and *affect*. Two common wildcard characters are ?, which stands for any single character in this location in the "Find what" text, and *, which stands for any number of characters in this location in the "Find what" text.
- Select the "Sounds like" check box to find occurrences of the search text that sound the same but are spelled differently, such as *there* and *their*.
- Select the "Find all word forms" check box to find occurrences of a particular word in any form, such as *plant*, *planted*, and *planting*.
- Locate formatting, such as bold, or special characters, such as tabs, by selecting them from the Format or Special drop-down list.

BE SURE TO open the document you want to work with before carrying out these steps.

To find a word or phrase by using the Find command:

1 With the insertion point at the beginning of the document, click **Find** on the **Edit** menu.

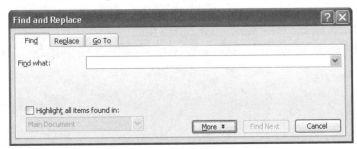

2 In the **Find what** box, type a word or phrase.

3 Click **Find Next** to jump from one occurrence of the text to another.

4 Click **Close** to close the Find and Replace dialog box.

To find all occurrences of a word or phrase by using the Find command:

1 With the insertion point at the beginning of the document, click **Find** on the **Edit** menu.

2 In the **Find what** box, type a word or phrase.

3 Select the **Highlight all items found in** check box, and click **Find All**.

Word finds and selects all the occurrences of the text in the document.

4 Click **Close** to close the Find and Replace dialog box.

To replace a word or phrase by using the Replace command:

1 With the insertion point at the beginning of the document, click **Replace** on the **Edit** menu.

2 In the **Find what** box, type a word or phrase.

3 In the **Replace with** box, type the replacement word or phrase.

4 Click **Find Next**, and then do one of the following:

- Click the **Replace** button to replace the selected occurrence and move to the next occurrence.

- Click the **Replace All** button to replace all occurrences.

- Click the **Find Next** button to leave the selected occurrence as it is and locate the next one.

When Word reaches the end of the document, it displays a message box indicating the number of replacements made.

5 Click **OK**, and then click **Close** to close the Find and Replace dialog box.

Practice Exercise

In this exercise, you will find a phrase and replace some instances of it, and then you'll replace one phrase with another one throughout the entire document.

USE the *ReplaceText* document in the *My Documents\Microsoft Press\MOS 2003 Study Guide\Word \W03C-1-3* practice file folder.

Open the *ReplaceText* document. With the insertion point at the beginning of the document, click **Find** on the **Edit** menu. In the **Find what** box, type **Garden Map Kit**, select the **Highlight all items found in** check box, and click **Find All**. Click the document behind the Find and Replace dialog box, and press **CTRL+HOME** to move to the beginning of the document. In the Find and Replace dialog box, click the **Replace** tab, type **Interactive Garden** as the replacement text, and replace the first occurrence. The replacement works as intended, so click **Replace All**. Then close the message that nine replacements were made, and close the Find and Replace dialog box. Finally, close the *ReplaceText* document without saving it.

Jumping to a Specific Item

If you want to move from one occurrence of a specific type of content to another, you can use two methods:

■ Clicking Go To on the Edit menu displays the Go To tab of the Find and Replace dialog box. You can then choose the content category, such as a page, and specify a specific instance of that type, such as 4 for *page 4*.

■ Clicking the Select Browse Object button at the bottom of the vertical scroll bar displays a palette of buttons. Clicking one of these buttons either moves you to the next instance of that type of content or displays a dialog box, where you can give more details about what you are looking for.

You can also move to specific sections of a document by using the Document Map in Normal view or thumbnails in Reading Layout view.

See Also For information about the Document Map and thumbnails, refer to W03E-2-5, "Use Automated Tools for Document Navigation."

BE SURE TO open the document you want to work with before carrying out these steps.

To navigate by using the Go To command:

1 With the insertion point at the beginning of the document, click **Go To** on the **Edit** menu.

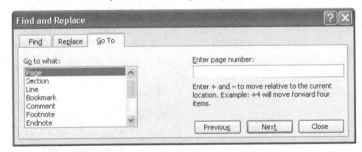

2 In the **Go to what** list, click the category of content you are looking for.

The name of the box to the right changes to reflect the kind of content you clicked.

3 If you want to find a specific instance, enter its information in the box to the right.

4 Click **Next**.

5 When you have finished the search, click **Close**.

To navigate by using the Select Browse Object button:

Select
Browse
Object

1 At the bottom of the vertical scroll bar, click the **Select Browse Object** button.

A palette of options appears.

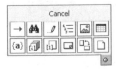

2   Move the pointer over the buttons on the palette.

The name of each object appears at the top of the palette as you point to it.

3   Click the button for the type of object you want to find.

4   If Word displays a dialog box, fill in specific information about the content you want to find, and click the appropriate button to close the dialog box.

If the specified content exists in the document, Word finds the first occurrence of it.

Next

5   To find its next occurrence of the same content, click the **Next** button at the bottom of the vertical scroll bar.

You can also click the Previous button to move back to an earlier occurrence.

Previous

Practice Exercise

In this exercise, you will jump to a specific page by using the Go To command and then jump from table to table by using the Select Browse Object button.

USE the *JumpItem* document in the *My Documents\Microsoft Press\MOS 2003 Study Guide\Word\W03C-1-3* practice file folder.

Open the *JumpItem* document. With the insertion point at the beginning of the document, click **Go To** on the **Edit** menu. In the **Go to what** list, click **Page**, type **3** in the **Enter page number** box, and click **Go To**. The insertion point moves from the beginning of page 1 to the beginning of page 3. Close the Find and Replace dialog box, and move to the top of the document. At the bottom of the vertical scroll bar, click the **Select Browse Object** button, and then click the **Browse by Table** button. When Word finds the first table in the document, click the **Next** button to move to the second table, and then click the **Previous** button to move back to the first. Close the *JumpItem* document without saving it.

Insert, Position, and Size Graphics

W03C-1-4   The skills measured by this objective include the following:

- ◼ Inserting, positioning, and sizing graphics
- ◼ Inserting, positioning, and sizing text boxes
- ◼ Inserting, positioning, and sizing shapes

You might want to insert graphics in a document to give it eye-appeal, convey facts at a glance, evoke a mood, or to visually reinforce an argument. For example, letters might display an organization's logo, or a brochure or newsletter might contain illustrations or photographs.

Inserting, Positioning, and Sizing Graphics

You can insert graphics from various sources in a document, including clip art provided with Office, graphics files created in other programs, images from a scanner or digital camera, and drawings that you create within Word. After inserting a graphic, you can move it within the document by dragging it, and you can adjust its size by dragging its sizing handles.

See Also   For information about adjusting the position and size of graphics more precisely, refer to W03E-1-3, "Format, Position, and Resize Graphics by Using Advanced Layout Features."

BE SURE TO open the document you want to work with before carrying out these steps.

To insert clip art from the collection that comes with Word:

1 Click the location where you want the graphic to appear.

2 On the **Insert** menu, click **Picture** and then **Clip Art**.

You can also click the Insert Clip Art button on the Drawing toolbar. The Clip Art task pane appears.

3 In the Clip Art task pane, click the piece of clip art you want to insert.

The picture is inserted into the document at the insertion point.

To search for a piece of clip art:

1 Click the location where you want the graphic to appear.

2 On the Drawing toolbar (not the Picture toolbar), click the **Insert Clip Art** button.

The Clip Art task pane appears.

Insert
Clip Art

3 In the Clip Art task pane, click the **Search for text** box, type a keyword that describes the type of picture you want to find, and then click **Go**.

The task pane displays graphics associated with the keyword you typed.

4 In the task pane, click the clip art you want to insert.

The graphic is inserted in the document, with circular handles surrounding its frame.

To insert a picture from a file on your hard disk, removable disk, or network:

1 Click the location where you want the graphic to appear.

2 On the **Insert** menu, click **Picture** and then **From File**.

You can also click the Insert Picture button on the Drawing toolbar.

3 Navigate to the picture you want to insert.

4 Double-click the picture.

The picture is inserted into the document at the insertion point.

To reposition a graphic visually:

1   Click the graphic to select it, if it is not already selected.

    When a graphic is selected, it is surrounded by handles.

2   Point to the graphic (avoiding its handles), and when the pointer changes to a four-headed arrow, drag the graphic to its new location.

To size a graphic visually:

1   Click the graphic to select it, if it is not already selected.

2   Point to the handle (the little black square) in the lower-right-corner of the graphic, and when the handle changes to a double arrow, drag diagonally until the graphic is the size you want.

Practice Exercise

In this exercise, you will insert a picture from a file and a piece of clip art.

USE the *InsertGraphic* document and the *GardenCo* file in the *My Documents\Microsoft Press\MOS 2003 Study Guide\Word\W03C-1-4* practice file folder.

Open the *InsertGraphic* document, and then open the Insert Picture dialog box, either by clicking **Picture** and then **From File** on the **Insert** menu, or by clicking the **Insert Picture** button on the Drawing toolbar. With your insertion point a the top of the document, find and insert the *Gardenco* picture file, and then make the graphic about 4.75 inches wide by 1.5 inches high. Move to the end of the document, and on the Drawing toolbar (not the Picture toolbar), click the **Insert Clip Art** button to display the Clip Art task pane. Search for clip art associated with the keyword **plant**, and insert the drawing of the green leaf. Make the graphic about 1/2 inch by 1/2 inch in size, and then move it so that it is centered at the bottom of the document. Close the *InsertGraphic* document without saving it.

Inserting, Positioning, and Sizing Text Boxes

Newsletter and magazine layouts often include text boxes that highlight a key concept or a quotation from an article or story to attract the attention of potential readers. You can include text boxes in Word documents, formatting the text in the boxes separately from the surrounding text to make it stand out. After inserting the text box and its text, you can position and size it just like any other graphic object.

BE SURE TO open the document you want to work with before carrying out these steps.

To insert a text box:

1   Click the location where you want the text box to appear.

2   On the Drawing toolbar (not the Picture toolbar), click the **Text Box** button.

Text Box

3   Move the pointer over the document, and drag diagonally down and to the right to create a box the size you want.

4   With the text box still selected, type the text you want the box to contain.

To reposition a text box visually:

1 Click the text box to select it, if it is not already selected.

When a text box is selected, it is surrounded by handles.

2 Point to the shaded area surrounding the text box (avoiding its handles), and when the pointer changes to a four-headed arrow, drag the box to its new location.

To size a text box visually:

1 Click the text box to select it, if it is not already selected.

2 Drag the handles surrounding the text box until the box is the size you want.

Practice Exercise

In this exercise, you will insert a text box, insert text, adjust the size of the box to fit the text, and then reposition it.

USE the *InsertTextBox* document in the *My Documents\Microsoft Press\MOS 2003 Study Guide\Word \W03C-1-4* practice file folder.

Open the *InsertTextBox* document, and make sure the Drawing toolbar is displayed. On the Drawing toolbar, click the **Text Box** button, and move the pointer over the document. Point to (but do not click) the lower-right corner of the inserted box, and drag diagonally down and to the right until the text box is about 2 inches high and 3 inches wide. Type **Dig in with our newest garden tool, The Garden Map Kit**, and then drag the handles of the text box until the box is just big enough to contain its text. Move the text box until it sits where you want it in the document. Close the *InsertTextBox* document without saving it.

Inserting, Positioning, and Sizing Shapes

You can use Word's drawing tools to add shapes to your documents. Popular shapes include ovals, rectangles, lines, and curves. You can also insert AutoShapes—more complex, pre-defined shapes such as stars and banners.

To insert a shape into a document, you click the corresponding tool on the Drawing toolbar and drag the pointer across a drawing canvas to create an object the size and shape you want. After creating a shape, you can change its size and shape by dragging its handles, or reposition it by dragging it or by nudging it into place. If you add multiple shapes to the same drawing canvas, you can size and move the drawing canvas to size and move the objects it contains as one unit.

BE SURE TO open the document you want to work with before carrying out these steps.

To insert a simple shape:

1 On the Drawing toolbar, click the button for the shape you want.

Word inserts a drawing canvas, and displays the Drawing Canvas toolbar.

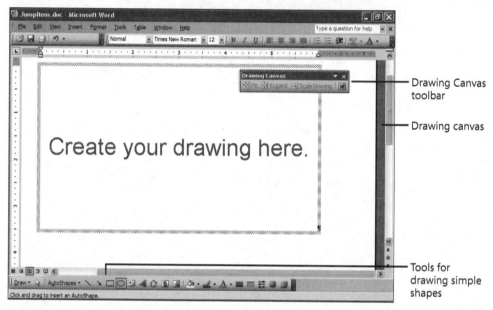

Drawing Canvas toolbar

Drawing canvas

Tools for drawing simple shapes

2 Point to the location where you want the shape to appear, and drag to create a shape the size you want.

Tip To draw shapes with equal heights and widths, such as a square or circle, hold down the SHIFT key while you drag.

To insert an AutoShape:

1 On the Drawing toolbar, click **AutoShapes**.

A menu of shape categories appears.

2 Click the category you want.

A palette of shapes in that category appears.

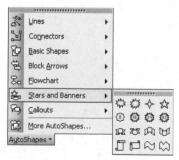

3   Click the button for the shape you want.

Word inserts a drawing canvas.

4   Point to the location where you want the shape to appear, and drag to create a shape the size you want.

To reposition a shape or AutoShape on the drawing canvas:

1   Click the shape to select it, if it is not already selected.

When a shape is selected, it is surrounded by handles.

2   Point to the shape (avoiding its handles), and when the pointer changes to a four-headed arrow, drag the shape to its new location.

To reposition the drawing canvas in the document:

1   Click a blank area of the drawing canvas to select the canvas without selecting any object.

2   Point to the canvas (avoiding its handles), and when the pointer changes to a four-headed arrow, drag the canvas to its new location.

The drawing canvas moves with the objects it contains.

To size a shape or an AutoShape manually:

1   Click the shape to select it, if it is not already selected.

2   Drag the handles surrounding the shape until it is the size you want.

To size a shape or an AutoShape by sizing the drawing canvas:

1   Right-click the drawing canvas, and click **Show Drawing Canvas Toolbar** on the shortcut menu.

2   Click a blank area of the drawing canvas to select the canvas without selecting any object.

3   On the Drawing Canvas toolbar (not the Drawing toolbar), click the **Scale Drawing** button.

> 🔲 Sca̲le Drawing

4   Point to the lower-right corner of the drawing canvas, and when the pointer changes to a double arrow, drag diagonally to increase or decrease the size of the canvas.

The shape shrinks in proportion to the canvas.

To group shapes so that they can be treated as a single unit:

1   Select the shapes you want to group by holding down the **SHIFT** or the **CTRL** key while clicking each object in turn.

2   On the Drawing toolbar, click **Draw** and then **Group**.

The selected objects are now surrounded by a single set of handles and can be positioned and sized as a unit.

Practice Exercise

In this exercise, you will insert a few shapes into a document and then position and size them.

USE the *DrawShape* document in the *My Documents\Microsoft Press\MOS 2003 Study Guide\Word \W03C-1-4* practice file folder.

Open the *DrawShape* document, and move to the end of the document. Display the Drawing toolbar, click the **Oval** button, and draw a balloon about 1 1/2 inches in diameter in the upper-left corner of the drawing canvas. Then draw another balloon in the upper-middle of the canvas and another in the upper-right corner. Use the **Line** tool to give each balloon a string. Then click the balloon on the left, hold down **CTRL**, and click its string. On the Drawing toolbar, click **Draw** and then **Group**. Drag this grouped object between the other two balloons, and then reduce its size so that it looks further away. Click a blank area of the drawing canvas to deselect the object, drag the drawing canvas to the center of the page below the document's last paragraph, and then click outside the drawing canvas to deselect it. (You might have to resize the drawing canvas so it will fit on the same page as the last paragraph.) Close the *DrawShape* document without saving it.

Create and Modify Diagrams and Charts

W03C-1-5   The skills measured by this objective include the following:

■ Inserting and formatting organization charts

■ Inserting and formatting charts

When you want to insert a diagram like an organization chart in a document, you can use the Office diagramming tool. You can also show numeric information visually by using Microsoft Graph, a program that comes with the Office suite, to insert a chart into a document.

Inserting and Formatting Organization Charts

To present hierarchical data or other types of information, you can create and insert diagrams in a document. A diagram is a relational representation of information. One common type of diagram is an organization chart. In addition to organization charts, you can create cycle diagrams, radial diagrams, pyramid diagrams, Venn diagrams, and target diagrams.

When you insert an organization chart into a document, the chart has placeholder text that you replace with your own. You can also move and change the chart's boxes and lines.

BE SURE TO open the document you want to work with and display the Drawing toolbar before carrying out these steps.

To insert an organization chart:

1   Click the location where you want the organization chart to appear in the document.

2   On the Drawing toolbar, click the **Insert Diagram or Organization Chart** button.

Insert
Diagram or
Organization
Chart

3 Click **OK**.

An organization chart is inserted into the document at the insertion point, and the Organization Chart toolbar appears.

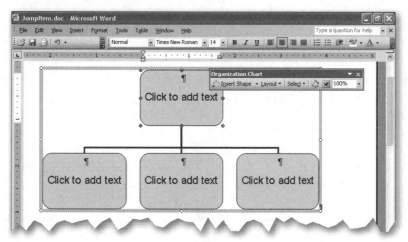

4 To customize the organization chart, click the boxes, and replace the placeholder text with your own information.

To quickly format an organization chart:

1 Click the organization chart to select it.

Autoformat

2 On the Organization Chart toolbar, click the **Autoformat** button.

The Organization Chart Style Gallery of predefined styles appears.

3 In the **Diagram Style** list, click the style you want, and then click **OK**.

The selected style is applied to your organization chart.

To modify the lines of an organization chart:

1 On the Organization Chart toolbar, click the **Select** down arrow, and then click **All Connecting Lines** on the drop-down menu.

All connecting lines in the organization chart are selected.

2   On the **Format** menu, click **AutoShape**.

3   In the **Line** area, click the **Color** down arrow, and click the color you want in the palette that appears.

4   In the **Arrows** area, click the **Begin style** down arrow, click the style you want, and click **OK**.

5   Click the blank area to the right of the organization chart to deselect it.

To size an organization chart:

1   Click the organization chart to select it.

2   Point to the handle in the lower-right-corner of the chart, and when the handle changes to a double arrow, drag diagonally until the chart is the size you want.

To position an organization chart:

1   Click the organization chart to select it.

2   Point to the shaded area surrounding the chart (avoiding its handles), and when the pointer changes to a four-headed arrow, drag the chart to its new location.

Practice Exercise

In this exercise, you will insert an organization chart into a document and then customize it.

USE the *InsertOrgChart* document in the *My Documents\Microsoft Press\MOS 2003 Study Guide\Word \W03C-1-5* practice file folder.

Open the *InsertOrgChart* document. Move to the end of the document, and use the **Insert Diagram or Organization Chart** button on the Drawing toolbar to add an organization chart to the document. Then type **Karen Berg** in the top box and **Kim Akers**, **David Ortiz**, and **Gordon Hee** in the boxes in the second row. On the Organization Chart toolbar, click the **Autoformat** button, and select the **Beveled** style. Select all the connecting lines, display the Format AutoShape dialog box, and change the color of the lines to red. Then attach arrows to the lines. Deselect the organization chart, and then close the *InsertOrgChart* document without saving it.

Inserting and Formatting Charts

To create a chart in a Word document, you start by using Microsoft Graph to insert a sample chart and a datasheet into the document. A datasheet looks similar to a table and displays data in rows and columns. The chart is linked to the datasheet and plots its data. While you are working with a chart in a Word document, the Microsoft Graph commands and buttons replace Word's on the menu bar and toolbars so that you can work with the chart and the datasheet directly in the document.

If the way a chart plots its underlying data doesn't suit you, change the chart type. Graph includes 18 different charts for presenting your data. Each type has both two-dimensional and three-dimensional variations. In addition to changing the chart type, you can change the formatting of the chart and its component objects. You start by selecting the object you want to modify, either by clicking the object itself or by clicking its name in the Chart Objects box on Graph's Standard toolbar. You can then move, size, or format the object.

BE SURE TO open the document you want to work with and display the Drawing toolbar before carrying out these steps.

To insert a chart in a document:

1 Click the location where you want the chart to appear in the document.

2 On the **Insert** menu, click **Picture** and then **Chart**.

A sample chart and datasheet appear.

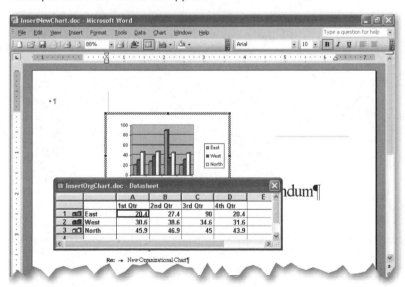

3 Click the **Select All** button in the upper-left corner of the datasheet, and then press the **DELETE** key.

The sample data and sample chart are deleted, leaving a blank datasheet and chart area.

4   Type row headings in the column to the left of column **A**, and type column headings in the row above row **1**.

> **Tip**   Press ENTER to move down in the same column and press SHIFT+ENTER to move up. Press TAB to move to the right in the same row and press SHIFT+TAB to move to the left. Or you can press the arrow keys to move up, down, left, or right a cell at a time.

5   Type data into each column of the chart's datasheet.

As you enter data, the chart changes to reflect what you type.

6   To make datasheet columns wider or narrower, drag the borders between column headings, or double-click a border to size the column to the left to fit its longest entry.

7   Click a blank area of the document to deselect the chart, hide the datasheet, and redisplay Word's menus and toolbars.

To change the chart type:

1   Double-click the chart to activate Microsoft Graph.

> **Tip**   Clicking the chart selects it for sizing or moving in the Word document. To activate Microsoft Graph, you have to double-click the chart.

The chart and datasheet appear along with Graph's toolbars and menus.

Chart Type

2   On the Standard toolbar, click the **Chart Type** down arrow.

The palette of chart types appears.

3   Click the button for the type of chart you want.

The chart is redrawn in the selected format, and the image on the Chart Type button changes to reflect the type of the chart you last selected.

To position a chart in a document:

1   Click a blank area of the document to make sure the chart is not active in Graph, and then click the chart once to select it in Word.

The chart object is surrounded by handles.

2   Point to the chart (avoiding the handles), and drag the chart to its new location.

To size an entire chart:

1   Click a blank area of the document to make sure the chart is not active in Graph, and then click the chart once to select it in Word.

2   Drag the chart's handles until the chart is the size you want.

To format the chart:

1   Double-click the chart to open it in Graph.

2   On Graph's Standard toolbar, click the **Chart Objects** down arrow, and click the part of the chart you want to format.

You can also simply click the part of the chart you want to work with to select it.

3   To reposition the selected object, simply drag it within the chart area.

4   To change the size of the selected object, drag its handles.

5   Use the buttons on Graph's toolbars to format the parts of the chart, or click the **Format** command for the object on the **Format** menu to open its dialog box and make changes there.

You can also right-click an object and then click its Format command on the shortcut menu.

6   Make any formatting adjustments you feel are necessary, and then click **OK**.

7   To work with optional chart objects, such as gridlines, titles, and the legend, click **Chart Options** on the **Chart** menu.

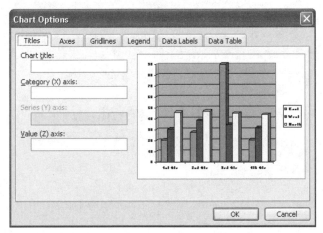

8   Make any adjustments you want on the tabs of this dialog box, and then click **OK**.

Practice Exercise

In this exercise, you will insert a chart. You will then modify the appearance of a chart by changing the chart type, the size, the color of the plot area, and the legend.

USE the *InsertChart* document in the *My Documents\Microsoft Press\MOS 2003 Study Guide\Word \W03C-1-5* practice file folder.

Open the *InsertChart* document. Move to the end of the document. Then insert a chart. Drag the title bar of the datasheet window so that the window is positioned below the sample chart. Then delete the contents of the datasheet. Type row headings for **Week 1** through

Week 4 and column headings for **Morning**, **Early Afternoon**, and **Evening**. Widen column **B** to fit its entry. Type the following data into the chart's datasheet:

		A Morning	B Early Afternoon	C Evening
1	Week 1	24	45	58
2	Week 2	29	69	99
3	Week 3	17	74	101
4	Week 4	32	78	167

On Graph's Standard toolbar, click the **View Datasheet** button to hide the datasheet. Then change the chart type to a line chart. Drag the chart area's handles so that its right frame roughly aligns with the 6-inch mark on the horizontal ruler and its bottom frame roughly aligns with the 7 1/2-inch mark on the vertical ruler. Click the plot area—the gray area of the chart—to select it, and use the **Fill Color** button on the Standard toolbar to change the background of the chart to light green. Remove the horizontal gridlines from the chart. Then give the chart the title **Customer Transactions**, and move the legend to the bottom of the chart area. Change the font size of the legend to **10 points**. Then put a border around the entire chart area, and make any other formatting adjustments you feel are necessary. Click outside the chart to deselect it, and after admiring your handiwork, close the *InsertChart* document without saving it.

Locate, Select, and Insert Supporting Information

W03C-1-6   The skills measured by this objective include the following:

- Using the Research Service to locate and insert information

For Word documents such as reports, research papers, and fact sheets, you might need to look up and insert information supporting a conclusion or underlining an assumption. For example, you might need a quotation; product specifications; or information about a person, place, or company. You can use the Research tool to access a wide variety of information in resources available via the Internet, such as Encarta, Factiva Search, MSN Search, Gale Company Profiles, and MSN Money Stock Quotes. You can also look up information in resources available on your own computer or on Web sites.

Using the Research Service to Locate and Insert Information

You can use the Research task pane to access a variety of informational resources, collectively known as the Research Service, from within Word. You can enter a topic in the "Search for" box and specify in the box below which resource Word should use to look for information regarding that topic. By clicking "Research options" at the bottom of the Research task pane, you can specify which of a predefined list of reference materials, such as Encarta and various Internet resources, will be available from a drop-down list, and you can also add your own reference-material sources.

BE SURE TO open the document you want to work with and display the Drawing toolbar before carrying out these steps.

To find information by using the Research Service:

1 Display the Research task pane by clicking **Research** on the **Tools** menu.

2 In the **Search for** box, type the topic you are interested in researching, and click the **Start searching** button.

Start searching

3 To specify or change the specific resource to search, click the box's down arrow, and click the resource you want to use to search for information.

As soon as you select a resource, the search automatically begins, and the search results are displayed in the task pane.

4 Click the plus sign to the left of a topic that interests you.

5 Click a hyperlink to a Web address to go to the Web to track down further information. Or click **Look Up** on the shortcut menu to research information about the selection.

To activate an installed resource in the Research Service:

1 At the bottom of the Research task pane, click **Research options** to display the Research Options dialog box.

2 Select one or more check boxes to activate additional research services, and click **OK**.

Tip   From the Research Options dialog box, you can also update or remove an installed service or apply parental controls.

To add a new resource to the Research Service:

1 At the bottom of the Research task pane, click **Research options** to display the Research Options dialog box.

2 Click **Add Services**, and in the **Address** box, type the URL of the new service.

To insert information located by the Research Service into a document:

1 Select all or part of a topic.

2 Right-click the topic, and click **Copy** on the shortcut menu.

3 Paste the selection into the document.

Practice Exercise

In this exercise, you will find and insert information in a document.

USE the *InsertInfo* document in the *My Documents\Microsoft Press\MOS 2003 Study Guide\Word\W03C-1-6* practice file folder.

Open the *InsertInfo* document. In the **Search for** box in the Research task pane, type **deer-proof plants**, and then specify **MSN Search** as the resource you want to search. If necessary, click the **Start searching** button to begin the search, When you see the search results displayed in the task pane, click the URL for an appropriate topic. Select part of the topic, right-click to display a shortcut menu, click **Copy**, and then paste the selection into your document. Close the *InsertInfo* document without saving it.

W03C-1 Review

Number	Objective	Mastered
W03C-1-1	Insert and edit text, symbols and special characters	
	Inserting visible and hidden text	❏
	Inserting symbols and special characters	❏
	Editing and deleting text	❏
	Moving and copying text	❏
	Checking spelling and grammar	❏
	Using the Thesaurus to find the best word	❏
W03C-1-2	Insert frequently used and predefined text	
	Using AutoCorrect	❏
	Using AutoText	❏
	Inserting the date and time	❏
W03C-1-3	Navigate to specific content	
	Finding and replacing text	❏
	Jumping to a specific item	❏
W03C-1-4	Insert, position, and size graphics	
	Inserting, positioning, and sizing graphics	❏
	Inserting, positioning, and sizing text boxes	❏
	Inserting, positioning, and sizing shapes	❏
W03C-1-5	Create and modify diagrams and charts	
	Inserting and formatting organization charts	❏
	Inserting and formatting charts	❏
W03C-1-6	Locate, select, and insert supporting information	
	Using the Research Service to locate and insert information	❏

W03C-2

Organizing Content

The skills tested by this section of the Microsoft Office Specialist Word 2003 Core Exam all relate to the organizing of content so that it is easy to access or interpret. Specifically, the following objectives are associated with this set of skills:

Number	Objective
W03C-2-1	Insert and modify tables
W03C-2-2	Create bulleted lists, numbered lists, and outlines
W03C-2-3	Insert and modify hyperlinks

Important   Before you can do the practice exercises associated with this skill set, you need to install the practice files from the book's companion CD to their default location. See "Installing the Practice Files" on page xxv for more information.

Insert and Modify Tables

W03C-2-1   The skills measured by this objective include the following:

- Inserting tables
- Converting text to tables
- Changing table structure
- Formatting tables manually
- Applying predefined formats to tables

You can use a table to make information in your document concise, consistent, and easy to read. A table organizes information neatly into rows and columns.

Inserting Tables

There are three ways to insert a table into a document:

- You can click the Insert Table button on the Standard toolbar and then select the number of rows and columns you want.
- You can click Insert and then Table on the Table menu to open the Insert Table dialog box, and then set the size of the table along with other options, such as table formatting.
- You can draw a table by using the Draw Table tool on the Tables and Borders toolbar.

After you create a table, you enter data by typing text or a number in each cell, which is the intersection of a row and a column. You press the ENTER key to move the insertion point from cell to cell down a column and the TAB key to move across a row. (If the insertion point is positioned in the rightmost cell in the last row of the table, pressing TAB adds another row to the bottom of the table.) You can also use the arrow keys, or you can simply click a cell to position the insertion point there.

BE SURE TO open the document you want to work with before carrying out these steps.

To insert a new table by using the Insert Table button:

1   Position the insertion point where you want the table to appear.

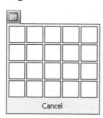
InsertTable

2   On the Standard toolbar, click the **Insert Table** button.

A grid of columns and rows appears.

3   Drag across the number of columns and down the number of rows you want.

A blank table with the specified number of columns and rows is inserted in the document, with the insertion point in the first cell.

To insert a new table by using the Insert/Table command:

1   Position the insertion point where you want the table to appear.

2   On the **Table** menu, click **Insert** and then **Table**.

3   Change the settings in the **Number of columns** and **Number of rows** boxes to suit your needs.

4   Click **OK**.

A blank table with your specifications is inserted in the document, with the insertion point in the first cell.

To insert a new table by using the Draw Table tool:

Tables and
Borders

Draw Table

1   Display the Tables and Borders toolbar by clicking the **Tables and Borders** button on the Standard toolbar.

2   On the Tables and Borders toolbar, click the **Draw Table** button.

   The pointer changes to a drawing tool in the shape of a pencil.

3   Point where you want the table to begin, and drag to create a row of the desired size.

4   Draw other rows where you want them.

5   Draw the number of columns you want.

6   Click the **Draw Table** button to deactivate the drawing tool.

   The table is now ready for you to type its data.

To enter text and other data in a table:

1   Click the cell in which you want to enter data.

2   Type the entry, and press the **TAB** key to move from cell to cell.

3   Continue making entries, pressing **TAB** or clicking cells to position the insertion point.

Practice Exercise

In this exercise, you will create one table by using the Insert/Table command and another by using the Draw Table tool.

USE the *CreateTable* document in the *My Documents\Microsoft Press\MOS 2003 Study Guide\Word \W03C-2-1* practice file folder.

Open the *CreateTable* document. Click the blank line below the *Please complete this form* paragraph to position the insertion point. Then display the Insert Table dialog box, check that the **Number of columns** box displays **5**, change the **Number of rows** setting to **3**, and click **OK**. In the second row, type these column headings: **Page #, Description, Quantity, Unit Price,** and **Total**. Then in the third row, type the following entries: **25, Lemon basil, 3, $2.29,** and **$6.87**. Click the **Draw Table** button on the Tables and Border toolbar, and draw an additional row at the bottom of the table. The use the Distribute Columns Evenly button to align the columns. In this row, type the following entries: **15, Borage, 4, $1.89,** and **$7.56**. Then close the *CreateTable* document without saving it.

Converting Text to Tables

A simple way to set up columns of information is to create a tabular list by typing entries separated by tabs. If you later want to convert the text to a regular table, you can select the tabbed paragraphs and use the Convert/Text to Table command. You can specify the number of columns and rows, the width of the columns, and whether an AutoFormat should be applied to the table.

See Also For information about setting tabs, refer to W03C-3-2, "Format Paragraphs." For information about AutoFormats, refer to "Applying Predefined Formats to Tables" later in this objective.

You can also use the Convert/Text to Table command to put existing plain text paragraphs into the first column of a table, or to put data that has been exported from a database as a comma-delimited file into a table.

BE SURE TO open a document containing tabular text before carrying out these steps.

To convert tabular text to a table:

1 Select all the paragraphs of tabular text.

2 On the **Table** menu, click **Convert** and then **Text to Table**.

3 If necessary, adjust the settings in the **Number of columns** and **Number of rows** boxes.

4 Make the appropriate selections in the **Autofit behavior** and **Separate text at** areas.

5 Click **OK** to close the Convert Text to Table dialog box.

The selected text appears in a table with specified number of columns and rows.

Practice Exercise

In this exercise, you will convert an existing tabulated list into a table.

USE the *ConvertText* document in the *My Documents\Microsoft Press\MOS 2003 Study Guide\Word \W03C-2-1* practice file folder.

Open the *ConvertText* document, and select the paragraphs that begin with *Order Amount* and end with *$15.95*. Display the Convert Text to Table dialog box, and specify that the new table should have two columns, that the columns should have automatically fixed widths according to their contents, and that the text should be separated on the tabs. When the selected text appears in a table with two columns and seven rows, close the *ConvertText* document without saving it.

Changing Table Structure

You can modify a table's structure at any time. To change parts of the structure, you must first use the following methods to select the part you want to change:

- ■ To select the entire table, click the Select Table button that appears above and to the left of the first cell in the table when you point to the table. Or on the Table menu, click Select and then Table.
- ■ To select a column or row, point to the top border of the column or the left border of the row, and when the pointer changes to an arrow, click once.
- ■ To select a cell, triple-click the cell.
- ■ To select multiple cells, click the first cell, hold down the SHIFT key, and press the arrow keys to select cells in a column or row.

Tip The Select Table button at the upper-left corner of the table and the table resize handle at the lower-right corner of the table can be used only in Print Layout view.

You can control some aspects of a table's structure in the Table Properties dialog box. On the Table tab, you can specify the preferred width of the entire table, as well as the way it interacts with the surrounding text. On the Row tab, you can specify the height of each row, whether a row is allowed to break across pages, and whether a row of column headings should be repeated at the top of each page. On the Column tab, you can set the width of each column, and on the Cell tab, you can set the preferred width of cells and the vertical alignment of text within them.

BE SURE TO open a document containing a table before carrying out these steps.

To insert a row or column:

1. Click anywhere in a row or column adjacent to the location where you want to make the insertion.
2. On the **Table** menu, click **Insert** and then **Rows Above**, **Rows Below**, **Columns to the Right**, or **Columns to the Left**.

Tip If you select more than one row or column and use an Insert command, Word inserts that number of rows or columns in the table.

To delete a row or column:

1. Click anywhere in the row or column.
2. On the **Table** menu, click **Delete** and then **Rows** or **Columns**.

To merge cells so that they span columns:

1. Select the cells you want to merge.
2. On the **Table** menu, click **Merge Cells**.

For example, to center a title in the first row of a table, you can create one merged cell that spans the table's width.

To split a merged cell into its component cells:

1 Select the cell you want to split.

2 On the **Table** menu, click **Split Cells**.

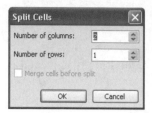

3 In the **Number of columns** and **Number of rows** boxes, enter the number of rows and columns you want.

4 Click OK.

To merge and split cells by using the table drawing tools:

Eraser

1 On the Tables and Borders toolbar, click the **Eraser** button.

2 With the tip of the eraser, point to the border between the cells you want to merge, and click.

   The border is removed, merging the cells.

3 Click the **Eraser** button to turn it off.

4 On the Tables and Borders toolbar, click the **Draw Table** button.

Draw Table

5 Draw a line where you want to split the cells.

6 Click the **Draw Table** button to turn it off.

To size an entire table:

1 Point to the table.

2 Drag the resize handle that appears in the lower-right corner of the table until the table is the size and shape you want.

   Tip To make finer adjustments, hold down the ALT key while you drag. Be careful to hold down the mouse button and not click it, because ALT+CLICK opens the Research task pane.

To change the width of a column or height of a row:

1 Point to the right border of a column or the bottom border of a row.

2 When the pointer changes to a resize pointer, drag the column border to the left or right, or drag the row border up or down.

To adjust the width of a column to fit its longest entry:

1 Point to the right border of the column.

2 When the pointer changes to a resize pointer, double-click to make the column just wide enough to hold the longest entry in the column.

To move a table:

1 Select the table.

2 Drag the table to its new location.

Tip When you hold down the ALT key while you drag, you can move the table in small increments.

You can also use the Cut and Paste commands to move the table.

To adjust table properties:

1 On the **Table** menu, click **Table Properties**.

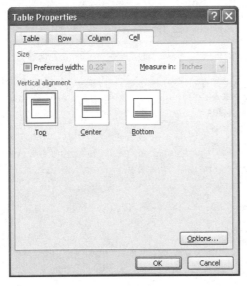

2 Click the tab of the table element whose properties you want to adjust.

3 Make changes to the properties as necessary.

4 Click **OK**.

Practice Exercise

In this exercise, you will add rows, merge cells, adjust column widths, and change the size and position of a table.

USE the *ChangeTable* document in the *My Documents\Microsoft Press\MOS 2003 Study Guide\Word \W03C-2-1* practice file folder.

Open the *ChangeTable* document, and select the first row. Merge the cells in the first row into one cell, and then type **The Garden Company Herb Plant Order Form**. Select the last two rows, and use the **Insert/Rows Below** command to add two new rows. Select the first four cells in the last row, and merge them. Then type **Subtotal**, and press **TAB** twice to add a new row with the same structure to the bottom of the table. Type **Add shipping/handling fee**, press **TAB** twice to add a new row, and then type **Add special delivery fee**. Add another new row, and type **Total**. Click anywhere in the table to deselect the cells, point to the right edge of the table, and when the pointer changes to a resize pointer, double-click to make the right column just wide enough to hold its longest entry. Select the special delivery table, and drag the table up and to the right of the shipping and handling fees table to create one combined table. Resize the columns, hold down the **ALT** key, and adjust the position of the right side until it aligns with the order form above it. Close the *ChangeTable* document without saving it.

Formatting Tables Manually

To enhance the appearance of a table, you can format its text by using the buttons on the Formatting toolbar, just as you would to format any text in a Word document. You can apply character formatting such as font styles and font effects, and you can apply paragraph formatting such as alignment and indenting.

You can emphasize the relationships within your table by adding borders and shading. For example, you might want to shade heading columns or rows or surround columns or rows containing totals with a thicker border.

BE SURE TO open a document containing a table before carrying out these steps.

To apply character formatting to an entry:

1   Select the cell or the part of the entry you want to format.

    You can also apply character formatting to multiple cells or to an entire column, row, or table.

2   On the Formatting toolbar, click the appropriate character formatting buttons.

    You can also click Font on the Format menu and make your selections in the Font dialog box.

To apply paragraph formatting to an entry:

1   Click the cell you want to format.

    You can also apply paragraph formatting to multiple cells or to an entire column, row, or table.

2 On the Formatting toolbar, click the appropriate paragraph formatting buttons.

You can also click Paragraph on the Format menu and make your selections in the Paragraph dialog box.

To add simple borders to a table:

1 Select the cells around which you want to put a border.

Border

2 On the Formatting toolbar, click the **Border** down arrow.

(The icon on this button changes to reflect the last border style you selected.) A palette of border options appears.

3 Click the button for the type of border you want to apply.

To add more complex borders to a table:

1 Select the cells around which you want to put a border.

2 On the **Format** menu, click **Borders and Shading**, and then click the **Borders** tab if it is not already displayed.

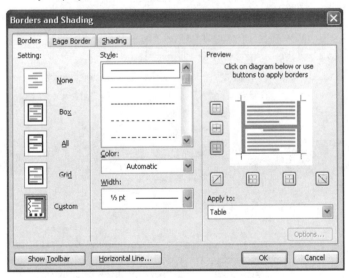

3 In the **Setting** area, click the icon representing the type of border you want.

4 In the **Style** list, click the line style you want.

5 Click the **Color** down arrow, and in the color palette, click the desired color.

6 Click the **Width** down arrow, and click the size you want.

7 Click **OK**.

Word applies the specified border to the selected cells.

Tip You can also display the Tables and Borders toolbar and use the toolbar's buttons to add borders of different styles, widths, and colors.

To add shading to cells:

1   Select the cells whose background you want to shade.

2   On the **Format** menu, click **Borders and Shading**, and then click the **Shading** tab if it is not already displayed.

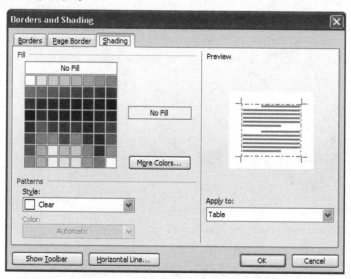

3   In the color palette, click the color box you want.

4   Click **OK** to close the Borders and Shading dialog box.

Word shades the background of the selected cell with the specified color.

Tip   You can also use the Shading Color button on the Tables and Borders toolbar to shade the background of selected cells.

Shading
Color

Practice Exercise

In this exercise, you will format the text in a table and add shading to a cell. You'll also add a border to a table.

USE the *FormatTable* document in the *My Documents\Microsoft Press\MOS 2003 Study Guide\Word \W03C-2-1* practice file folder.

Open the *FormatTable* document. Select the first row of the table, and change the font to **Arial** and the font size to **16**. Then expand your selection to include the second row, and make the headings bold and centered. Display the **Shading** tab of the Borders and Shading dialog box, and shade the background of the selected cells light yellow. Then select the third row of the table, and change the font style to italic and the text color to red. Select the last four rows in the order form table, and align the entries to the right. Move to the special delivery table, and surround it with a red double border. Then close the *FormatTable* document without saving it.

Applying Predefined Formats to Tables

Instead of applying formatting manually, you can quickly apply predefined sets of formatting to a table by using an AutoFormat. You can choose from numerous formats with a variety of borders, colors, and attributes to give your tables a professional look. If none of the AutoFormats meets your needs, you can create your own table styles.

See Also For information about table styles, refer to W03E-1-1, "Create Custom Styles for Text, Tables, and Lists."

BE SURE TO open a document containing a table before carrying out these steps.

To apply an AutoFormat to a table:

1   Click anywhere in the table you want to format.

2   On the **Table** menu, click **Table AutoFormat**.

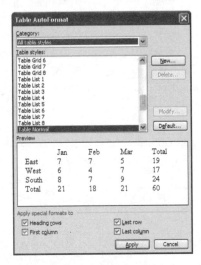

3   In the **Table styles** list, click an AutoFormat.

The preview box shows how that particular style will look when applied to the table.

4   When you find the style you want, click **Apply**.

Word formats the table according to the AutoFormat's specifications.

Practice Exercise

In this exercise, you will apply an AutoFormat to a table.

USE the *ApplyAutoFormat* document in the *My Documents\Microsoft Press\MOS 2003 Study Guide\Word \W03C-2-1* practice file folder.

Open the *ApplyAutoFormat* document, and click anywhere in the shipping and handling fees table. Display the Table AutoFormat dialog box, scroll through the **Table styles** list, and click **Table List 8**. Click **Apply**, admire the results, and then close the *ApplyAutoFormat* document without saving it.

Create Bulleted Lists, Numbered Lists, and Outlines

W03C-2-2   The skills measured by this objective include the following:

■ Creating and customizing bulleted lists

■ Creating and customizing numbered lists

■ Creating outlines

To organize information in a document, you might want to set it up in a bulleted or numbered list, such as a list of events, names, numbers, or procedures. In Word, you can also structure information in an outline format, and you can use the outline to organize the entire document.

Creating and Customizing Bulleted Lists

When you want to list items of information but the order of the items is not important, you can create a bulleted list. A bullet is a small graphic, such as a dot, that introduces each item in the list.

To create a bulleted list, you can type * (an asterisk) at the beginning of a paragraph, press SPACE or TAB, type the first item in the list, and press ENTER. Word formats the text as a bulleted list and inserts a bullet character at the beginning of the next paragraph. You can type the next item in the list or press ENTER or BACKSPACE to end the list.

For emphasis, you can change the bullet character to one of Word's predefined formats. For example, you can switch to a style that uses square bullets. You can also customize the list style or insert a picture as a bullet. Use the Bullets and Numbering dialog box to modify, format, and customize your list.

BE SURE TO open the document you want to work with before carrying out these steps.

To type a new bulleted list:

1   With the insertion point at the beginning of a new blank paragraph, type * (an asterisk), and then press **SPACE** or **TAB**.

2   Type the first item in the list, and press **ENTER**.

Word changes the formatting to a bulleted list, and inserts a bullet at the beginning of the next paragraph.

3   Type the next bulleted item, and press **ENTER**.

4   Continue typing items, or press **ENTER** or **BACKSPACE** to end the list.

To convert existing paragraphs to a bulleted list:

1   Select the paragraphs you want to convert into a list.

Bullets

2   On the Formatting toolbar, click the **Bullets** button.

Word applies its default bulleted list format to the selection.

Tip   To return a bulleted list to plain text paragraphs, you can select the list and click the Bullets button on the Formatting toolbar to turn it off.

To customize a bulleted list:

1 Select the bulleted paragraphs you want to customize.

2 On the **Format** menu, click **Bullets and Numbering**.

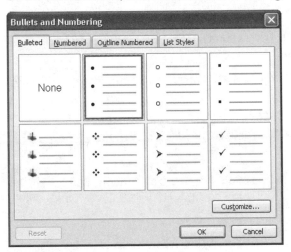

3 Click the style that most closely resembles the one you want.

4 If you want to refine the style, click the **Customize** button.

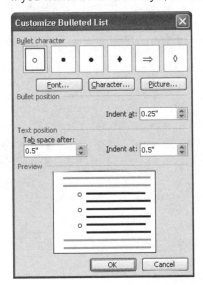

5   Make any necessary changes to the bullet character and position, and to the relationship of the bullet and the text of the item.

6   Click **OK**.

Practice Exercise

In this exercise, you will create a bulleted list and modify it by changing its bullet character and adjusting the indent of its text.

USE the *CreateBulletedList* document in the *My Documents\Microsoft Press\MOS 2003 Study Guide\Word \W03C-2-2* practice file folder.

Open the *CreateBulletedList* document, and drag through any part of the two paragraphs that start with *$10.00* and *$6.00*. Use the **Bullets** button to change the selected paragraphs to a bulleted list. Display the **Bulleted** tab of the Bullets and Numbering dialog box, and click the color bullet box in the second row of the first column. Then click **Customize**, and set the indent in the **Bullet position** area to **1.0** and the indent in both **Text position** areas to **1.35**. Click **OK**, check the results, and then close the *CreateBulletedList* document without saving it.

Creating and Customizing Numbered Lists

When you want to list items of information and the order of items is important, you can create a numbered list. Numbered lists are particularly useful for describing steps in a procedure or precise sequences of events.

To create a numbered list, you can type 1 at the beginning of a paragraph, press SPACE or TAB, type the first item in the list, and press ENTER. Word formats the text as a numbered list and inserts 2 at the beginning of the next paragraph. You can type the next item in the list or press ENTER or BACKSPACE to end the list. If you move, insert, or delete items in an existing numbered list, Word renumbers the list for you.

If you don't want to use Arabic digits as list numbers, you can change the numbering scheme of the list to another of Word's predefined formats. For example, you can switch to a style that uses Roman numerals (I, II, III, and so on) or letters (A, B, C, and so on). You can also customize the list style in the Bullets and Numbering dialog box.

BE SURE TO open the document you want to work with before carrying out these steps.

To type a new numbered list:

1   With the insertion point at the beginning of a new blank paragraph, type **1.**, and then press **SPACE** or **TAB**.

2   Type the first item in the list, and press **ENTER**.

Word changes the formatting to a numbered list, and inserts *2.* at the beginning of the next paragraph.

3   Type the next numbered item, and press **ENTER**.

4   Continue typing items, or press **ENTER** or **BACKSPACE** to end the list.

To convert existing paragraphs to a numbered list:

Numbering

1   Select the paragraphs you want to convert into a list.

2   On the Formatting toolbar, click the **Numbering** button.

Word applies its default numbered list format to the selection.

Tip   To return a numbered list to plain text paragraphs, you can select the list and click the Numbering button on the Formatting toolbar to turn it off.

To customize a numbered list:

1   Select the numbered paragraphs you want to customize.

2   On the **Format** menu, click **Bullets and Numbering**.

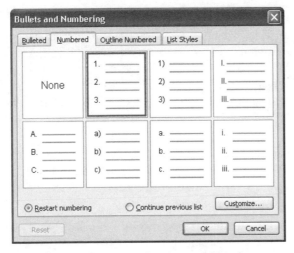

3   Click the style that most closely resembles the one you want.

4   If you want to refine the style, click the **Customize** button.

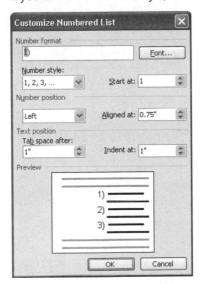

5   Make any necessary changes to the numbering scheme and position, and to the relationship of the number and the text of the item, and then click **OK**.

Tip   If the numbering sequence continues across lists instead of each list starting from 1, select the "Restart numbering" option in the Bullets and Numbering dialog box. To start at a number other than 1, use the "Start at" option in the Customize Numbered List dialog box.

Practice Exercise

In this exercise, you will create a numbered list and modify it by changing its numbering scheme and adjusting the indent of its text.

USE the *CreateNumberedList* document in the *My Documents\Microsoft Press\MOS 2003 Study Guide\Word \W03C-2-2* practice file folder.

Open the *CreateNumberedList* document. Scroll down the document, and drag through any part of the three paragraphs aligned with *Dates:*. Format the selected paragraphs as a numbered list. Display the **Numbered** tab of the Bullets and Numbering dialog box, and click the **A. B. C.** box in the second row of the first column to change the numbers to capital letters. Click the **Customize** button, and change the number alignment to **0.25** and the text indent to **0.5**. Click **OK** to see the results. Close the *CreateNumberedList* document without saving it.

Creating Outlines

In Word, it is easy to create an outline. You choose an outline style and then type the outline, pressing TAB and SHIFT+TAB to change outline levels. You can also turn a bulleted or numbered list into an outline by displaying the Outline Numbered tab of the Bullets and Numbering dialog box and selecting the outline style you want.

If you format a document with built-in heading styles that include outline levels, it is easy to view and organize the document in Outline view. You use this view to display only the headings of a document, level by level, and to rearrange the document without scrolling through all the pages. The indentations and symbols in Outline view indicate the level of a heading or paragraph in the document's structure and do not appear in the document when you print it.

See Also   For information about styles, refer to W03E-1-1, "Create Custom Styles for Text, Tables, and Lists."

BE SURE TO open the document you want to work with before carrying out these steps.

To type a new outline:

1   Click an insertion point at the beginning of a new blank paragraph.

2   On the **Format** menu, click **Bullets and Numbering**, and then click the **Outline numbered** tab.

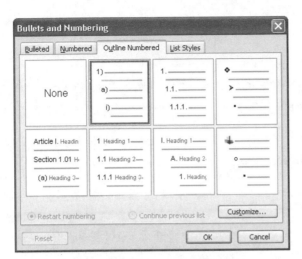

3 Click the outline style you want, and click **OK**.

4 Type the first item in the outline, and press **ENTER**.

Word changes the formatting to an outline and inserts the appropriate outline number style at the beginning of the next paragraph.

5 If you want the next item to be at a subordinate level, press **TAB**.

6 Type the next outline item, and press **ENTER**.

7 Continue typing items at this level, pressing **TAB** to move down a level, **SHIFT+TAB** to move up a level, or **ENTER** or **BACKSPACE** to end the list.

To convert an existing list to an outline:

1 Select the list you want to convert into an outline.

2 On the **Format** menu, click **Bullets and Numbering**, and then click the **Outline Numbered** tab.

3 Click the style that most closely resembles the one you want.

4 If you want to refine the style, click the **Customize** button.

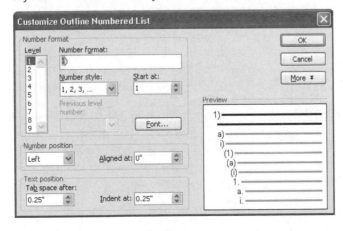

5   Make any necessary changes to the outlining scheme and position, and to the relationship of the outline number and the text of the item. Then click **OK**.

To organize a document in Outline view:

Outline View

1   In the lower-left corner of the document window, click the **Outline View** button.

The screen changes to display the document in Outline view, and the Outlining toolbar appears.

2   To organize the document, use the Outlining toolbar to do any of the following:

Show Level

■   Click the **Show Level** down arrow, and click the lowest heading level you want to see. Or click **Show All Levels** to see the entire document in Outline view.

Demote

■   To demote a heading level, click anywhere in the heading, and then click the **Demote** button.

Tip   When you restructure a heading in Outline view, the paragraphs below that heading are also restructured.

Promote

■   To promote a heading level, click anywhere in the heading, and then click the **Promote** button.

Move Up

■   To move a heading and its subordinate paragraphs up in the document, click anywhere in the heading, and then click the **Move Up** button.

Move Down

■   To move a heading and its subordinate paragraphs down in the document, click anywhere in the heading, and then click the **Move Down** button.

Expand

■   To display the headings under a selected heading, click the **Expand** button.

Collapse

■   To hide the headings under a selected heading, click the **Collapse** button.

3   To leave Outline view, click one of the other view buttons in the lower-right corner of the document window.

Practice Exercise

In this exercise, you will switch to Outline view, promote and demote headings, move headings, and expand and collapse the outline.

USE the *OutlineText* document in the *My Documents\Microsoft Press\MOS 2003 Study Guide\Word \W03C-2-2* practice file folder.

Open the *OutlineText* document, and switch to Outline view. Use the **Show Level** box on the Outlining toolbar to display only level 1 headings. Demote the **Hot or Cold?** heading to level 2, and then display all the level 1 and level 2 headings. Click anywhere in the **Composting DOs and DON'Ts** heading, and use the **Move Up** button to move the heading and its subordinate text above the *Compost and Soil* heading. Promote the **Hot or Cold?** heading to level 1, and then expand the heading to display all the paragraphs and headings under *Hot or Cold?*. Click the **Collapse** button to collapse the outline again, switch to Print Layout view, and then scroll through the document to see the effects of the reorganization. Close the *OutlineText* document without saving it.

Insert and Modify Hyperlinks

W03C-2-3   The skills measured by this objective include the following:

- ■ Inserting hyperlinks to documents, Web pages, and e-mail addresses
- ■ Editing and removing hyperlinks

Web pages use hyperlinks (links) as a quick way to perform tasks such as opening other Web pages, downloading files, or sending e-mail messages. You can insert hyperlinks into a Word document to accomplish the same tasks.

Inserting Hyperlinks to Documents, Web Pages, and E-Mail Addresses

To insert hyperlinks into a Web document or a regular Word document, you select the text or object you want to use as the link source and then specify the link's target, which can be another document or file, a Web page, another place in the same document (such as a heading or bookmark), or an e-mail address. You can control whether the link target appears in the same window, in a new window, or in a frame.

Text hyperlinks appear in Word documents as blue underlined text, which is similar to the way that they appear in most browsers. Graphic hyperlinks don't have any special identification, but the pointer does change to a hand when you point to them. You can jump to the target of a hyperlink in a Word document by holding down the CTRL key and clicking the link. If you subsequently save a Word document as a Web document, you can simply click the link in your browser to jump to the link's target.

See Also   For information about saving Web documents, refer to W03C-5-4, "Save Documents in Appropriate Formats for Different Uses."

BE SURE TO open the document you want to work with before carrying out these steps.

To insert a hyperlink to another file:

1   Select the text or click the graphic you want to use as the hyperlink source.

Insert
Hyperlink

2   On the Standard toolbar, click the **Insert Hyperlink** button.

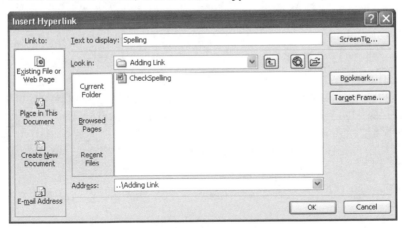

Tip You can also right-click the selection and click Hyperlink on the shortcut menu, or click Hyperlink on the Insert menu.

3 With the **Existing File or Web Page** button active on the **Link to** bar, use the **Look in** down arrow to navigate to the folder where the target file is stored.

4 Click (don't double-click) the target file.

The path to the target file is displayed in the Address box.

5 To add text that will display when someone points to the hyperlink in the document, click the **ScreenTip** button, enter the text in the **ScreenTip text** box, and click **OK**.

If you don't add anything, the ScreenTip shows the path to the hyperlink's target and information about how to follow the link in Word

6 Click **Target Frame**.

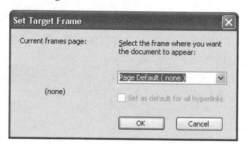

7 To change the type of frame the target file will appear in, change the **Page Default (none)** setting, and then click **OK**.

8 Click **OK** again to close the Insert Hyperlink dialog box.

9 In the document, point to the hyperlink.

Word displays either the ScreenTip you specified, or the path to the target file.

10 Test the link by holding down the **CTRL** key and clicking the hyperlink.

The target file is displayed in your Web browser window.

11 Close the browser window.

To insert a hyperlink to a Web page:

1 Select the text or click the graphic you want to use as the hyperlink source.

2 On the Standard toolbar, click the **Insert Hyperlink** button.

The Insert Hyperlink dialog box appears.

Insert
Hyperlink

3 With the **Existing File or Web Page** button active on the **Link to** bar, do one of the following:

■ Type the URL of the target Web page in the **Address** box.

■ Click the **Browse to Web** button, browse to the target Web page, and copy and paste the URL into the **Address** box.

Browse to
Web

4   Click **Target Frame**.

The Set Target Frame dialog box appears with Page Default (none) as the current frame setting.

5   If necessary, change the setting, and click **OK**.

6   Click **OK** again to close the Insert Hyperlink dialog box.

7   Test the link by holding down the **CTRL** key and clicking the hyperlink.

8   Close your Web browser window.

To insert a hyperlink to an e-mail address:

1   Select the text or click the graphic you want to use as the hyperlink source.

2   On the Standard toolbar, click the **Insert Hyperlink** button.

Insert
Hyperlink

3   On the **Link to** bar in the Insert Hyperlink dialog box, click the **E-mail Address** button.

The dialog box changes so that you can enter the information appropriate for an e-mail hyperlink.

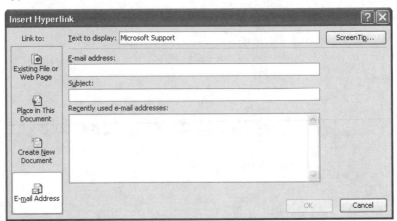

4   In the **E-mail address** box, type the target e-mail address.

5   In the **Subject** box, type the text that should appear on the Subject line of any e-mail generated from this link.

6   Click **OK**.

7   Test the link by holding down the **CTRL** key and clicking the hyperlink.

A message window appears with the e-mail address in the To box.

8   Close the message window.

Practice Exercise

In this exercise, you will insert and test a hyperlink.

USE the *InsertHyperlink* and *OtherLogos* documents in the *My Documents\Microsoft Press\MOS 2003 Study Guide\Word\W03C-2-3* practice file folder.

Open the *InsertHyperlink* document. Right-click **The Garden Company** logo, and click **Hyperlink** on the shortcut menu. In the list of folders and file names in the Insert Hyperlink dialog box, click (don't double-click) the **OtherLogos** file. Then click **Target Frame**, and click **OK** twice. Hold down the **CTRL** key, click the logo to display the *OtherLogos* file, and then close your browser window. Back in Word, zoom to **75%**, press **CTRL+END**, press **ENTER**, and center the new blank paragraph. Type **Contact us for more information**, select the text, and insert a hyperlink to the e-mail address **DavidO@gardenco.msn.com**. Test the hyperlink. Close the message window, and then close the *InsertHyperlink* document without saving it.

Editing and Removing Hyperlinks

To edit a hyperlink, you right-click it and then click one of the commands on the shortcut menu, which you can use to change the destination of the hyperlink, change the display text, or convert the hyperlink to regular text.

BE SURE TO open a document containing a hyperlink before carrying out these steps.

To edit a hyperlink:

1   Right-click the hyperlink, and click **Edit Hyperlink** on the shortcut menu.

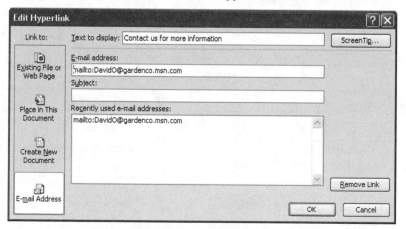

2   Edit the hyperlink as necessary, and click **OK**.

3   Hold down **CTRL**, and click the hyperlink to test it.

4   Close the browser or message window.

To remove a hyperlink:

● Right-click the hyperlink, and click **Remove Hyperlink** on the shortcut menu.
   The hyperlink is removed from the text or graphic.

Practice Exercise

In this exercise, you will modify a hyperlink and then remove it.

USE the *EditHyperlink* document in the *My Documents\Microsoft Press\MOS 2003 Study Guide\Word \W03C-2-3* practice file folder.

Open the *EditHyperlink* document, and scroll to the end of the document. Hold down **CTRL**, and click the centered hyperlink. Note the address in the **To** box, and close the message window. Then right-click the hyperlink, and click **Edit Hyperlink**. In the **E-mail address** box in the Edit Hyperlink dialog box, replace *DavidO* with **KimY**. Test the edited hyperlink, noting that the new e-mail address appears in the **To** box. Close the message window, and then close the *EditHyperlink* document without saving it.

W03C-2 Review

Number	Objective	Mastered
W03C-2-1	Insert and modify tables	
	Inserting tables	❑
	Converting text to tables	❑
	Changing table structure	❑
	Formatting tables manually	❑
	Applying predefined formats to tables	❑
W03C-2-2	Create bulleted lists, numbered lists, and outlines	
	Creating and customizing bulleted lists	❑
	Creating and customizing numbered lists	❑
	Creating outlines	❑
W03C-2-3	Insert and modify hyperlinks	
	Inserting hyperlinks to other documents and Web pages	❑
	Editing and removing hyperlinks	❑

W03C-3
Formatting Content

The skills tested by this section of the Microsoft Office Specialist Word 2003 Core Exam all relate to the formatting of documents and their contents. Specifically, the following objectives are associated with this set of skills:

Number	Objective
W03C-3-1	Format text
W03C-3-2	Format paragraphs
W03C-3-3	Apply and format columns
W03C-3-4	Insert and modify content in headers and footers
W03C-3-5	Modify document layout and page setup

Important Before you can do the practice exercises associated with this skill set, you need to install the practice files from the book's companion CD to their default location. See "Installing the Practice Files" on page xxv for more information.

Format Text

W03C-3-1   The skills measured by this objective include the following:

- Applying common character formatting
- Finding and replacing character formatting
- Working with styles
- Highlighting text
- Applying text effects
- Modifying character spacing

To vary the look of text, you can select the text and apply various attributes that are known collectively as character formatting. After you apply character formatting, it will also be applied to any text you type immediately after or within the formatted text.

Applying Common Character Formatting

The text you type in a document is displayed in a particular font. A font is a complete set of characters that all have the same design. You can vary a font's basic design by changing the following attributes:

- Almost every font comes in a range of font sizes. The font size is measured in points, with each point being equal to about 1/72 of an inch.

■ Almost every font comes in a range of font styles. The most common are regular (or plain), italic, bold, and bold italic.

■ A range of font colors is available in a standard palette, but you can also specify custom colors.

■ Fonts can be enhanced by applying font effects, such as underlining, small capital letters, and shadows.

After you have selected an appropriate font for an element of a document, you can use these attributes in different combinations to achieve different looks. You can apply character formatting to selected text by using the appropriate buttons and boxes on the Formatting toolbar or by changing settings in the Font dialog box.

While you are formatting a document, you might want to open the Reveal Formatting task pane. In this task pane you can display, change, or clear the formatting of selected text.

BE SURE TO open the document you want to work with before carrying out these steps.

To change the font:

1 Select the text whose font you want to change.

2 On the Formatting toolbar, click the **Font** down arrow.

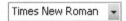

3 Scroll the list of available fonts, and click the font you want in the list.

The selected text now appears in the new font.

To change the size:

1 Select the text whose size you want to change.

Font Size

2 On the Formatting toolbar, click the **Font Size** down arrow.

3 Scroll the list of available sizes, and click the size you want in the list.

The selected text now appears in the new size.

To change the style:

1 Select the text whose style you want to change.

2 On the Formatting toolbar, click the appropriate style button:

Bold

■ To make the text bold, click the **Bold** button.

Italic

■ To make the text italic, click the **Italic** button.

Underline

■ To underline the text, click the **Underline** button.

The selected text now appears in the new style.

To change the color:

1 Select the text whose color you want to change.

Font Color

2   On the Formatting toolbar, click the **Font Color** down arrow.

3   On the color palette, click the box for the color you want.

The selected text now appears in the color you chose. (You'll need to deselect the text in order to see the color.)

Tip   To apply the most recently selected color to other text, select the word or phrase, and then click the Font Color button (not the down arrow). The color that appears on the Font Color button is applied to the selected text.

To change multiple combinations of character formatting at the same time:

1   Select the text whose formatting you want to change.

2   On the **Format** menu, click **Font**.

3   Make the desired font, size, style, or color changes.

4   Click **OK**.

To clear character formatting changes:

1   Select the text whose formatting you want to clear.

2   On the **Format** menu, click **Reveal Formatting**.

The Reveal Formatting task pane appears, displaying the formatting of the selected text.

3   At the top of the Reveal Formatting task pane, point to the **Selected text** box, click the down arrow, and then click **Clear Formatting**.

The formatting of the selected text is removed.

Tip   You can also select the text and press CTRL+SPACE to clear formatting.

To quickly apply the formatting of one block of text to another:

1   Select the text whose formatting you want to copy.

2   On the Formatting toolbar, click the **Format Painter** button.

3   Drag over the text to which you want to apply the formatting.

Format
Painter

Practice Exercise

In this exercise, you will format the text in a document by changing its font, font size, style, and color.

USE the *FormatText* document in the *My Documents\Microsoft Press\MOS 2003 Study Guide\Word \W03C-3-1* practice file folder.

Open the *FormatText* document, and select *The Lovely Lily*, the title at the top of the document. Change the font to **Monotype Corsiva**. (If Monotype Corsiva is not available, select a similar script-style font, such as Brush Script MT.) Change the size to **26** points. Open the Reveal Formatting task pane, and use the **Selected text** box to clear the formatting. Then undo this change to restore the formatting. Select the word **pinks** in the first sentence of the paragraph that begins *Lilies bloom*, and change its color to pink. (You'll need to deselect it to see the color.) Also change the color of the word *pink* at the bottom of the next paragraph to pink. Close the *FormatText* document without saving it.

Finding and Replacing Character Formatting

If you want to search for and replace one format with another, you can use the Find and Replace dialog box in much the same way you would to search for or replace words or phrases. You can also use the Reveal Formatting task pane to find all text that has a certain formatting and change all that formatting at once.

BE SURE TO open a document containing character formatting before carrying out these steps.

To find and change all text with similar formatting:

1   Select the text whose formatting you want to find.

2   On the **Format** menu, click **Reveal Formatting**.

3   In the Reveal Formatting task pane, click the **Selected text** down arrow, and then click **Select All Text With Similar Formatting**.

Any text with similar formatting is now selected.

4   In the **Font** area of the Reveal Formatting task pane, click the **Font** link to display the Font dialog box.

5   Make the necessary changes, and click **OK**.

All the selected text now reflects the changes you made.

To search for a specific format and replace it with a different format:

1   On **Edit** menu, click **Replace**.

The Find and Replace dialog box appears, displaying the Replace tab.

2   Click the **More** button to expand the dialog box.

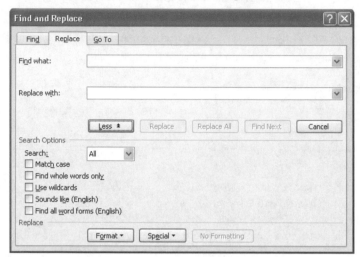

3   Click the **Format** button, and then click **Font**.

The Find Font dialog box appears. (You can also click Paragraph to search paragraph formatting or Style to search for paragraph or character styles.)

4   In the dialog box, click the font, size, style, or color you want to find (or a combination).

5   Click **OK**.

6   Click the **Replace with** box, click **Format**, and then click **Font**.

7   In the Replace Font dialog box, click the replacement font, size, style, or color (or a combination), and click **OK**.

8   Click **Find Next** to search for the next occurrence of the format, and then click **Replace** to replace that one instance or **Replace All** to replace every instance.

Practice Exercise

In this exercise, you will find and replace character formatting.

USE the *ReplaceFormatting* document in the *My Documents\Microsoft Press\MOS 2003 Study Guide\Word \W03C-3-1* practice file folder.

Open the *ReplaceFormatting* document. In the Reveal Formatting task pane, use the **Selected text** box to select all the pink text. Then make the selected text bold. Use the **Replace** tab of the Find and Replace dialog box to find all bold formatting and change it to bold italic formatting. Then close the *ReplaceFormatting* document without saving it.

Working with Styles

In Word, a style is a collection of character and paragraph formatting that can be saved. Instead of applying each format individually, you can apply all of them at once by using a style. Text styles come in two varieties:

- Character styles, which you use to format selected characters. You can apply character styles to a single letter, a word, a paragraph, or the entire document.

- Paragraph styles, which you use to format entire paragraphs. This type of style consists of indents, alignment, paragraph and line spacing, bullets or numbering, and tabs, as well as character attributes to be applied to the entire paragraph.

See Also For information about paragraph formatting, refer to W03C-3-2, "Format Paragraphs."

Text styles are stored in templates. By default, Word uses the Normal template for all new documents and applies the Normal style to all regular paragraphs. The Normal style formats paragraphs as 12-point, regular Times New Roman text that is left-aligned and single-spaced, with no extra space above or below it. To apply a different style, you can click it in the Style drop-down list on the Formatting toolbar, or you can use the Styles and Formatting task pane.

In addition to styles that can be applied to all text, Word has specialized styles for lists and tables that you can apply from the Bullets and Numbering dialog box and the Table AutoFormat dialog box.

BE SURE TO open the document you want to work with before carrying out these steps.

To see what style is applied to selected text:

1 Select the text whose style you want to investigate.

2 On the **Format** menu, click **Styles and Formatting**.

The Styles and Formatting task pane appears.

3 In the Styles and Formatting task pane, point to the **Formatting of selected text** box.

A ScreenTip appears, listing the formatting of the style applied to the selected text.

To apply a different style from the Style box:

1 Do one of the following:

- To apply a paragraph style, click anywhere in the paragraph.

- To apply a character style, select the text.

Style

2 On the Formatting toolbar, click the **Style** down arrow.

3 Scroll the list of available styles, and click the style you want in the list.

To apply a different style from the Styles and Formatting task pane:

1 Click anywhere in the paragraph, or select the text.

2 On the **Format** menu, click **Styles and Formatting** to open the Styles and Formatting task pane.

3 Scroll down in the **Pick formatting to apply** list, and click the style you want.

To change all text with one style to a different style:

1　Click any text to which the style you want to change has been applied.

2　On the **Format** menu, click **Styles and Formatting** to open the Styles and Formatting task pane.

3　In the Styles and Formatting task pane, click **Select All**.

　　Word selects all the text formatted with the style of the selected text.

4　In the Styles and Formatting task pane, click the new style.

　　Word applies the new style to all the selected paragraphs. A ScreenTip tells you the main characteristics of this style.

To change the style of a bulleted or numbered list:

1　Select any part of all the list paragraphs.

2　On the **Format** menu, click **Bullets and Numbering**, and then click the **List Styles** tab.

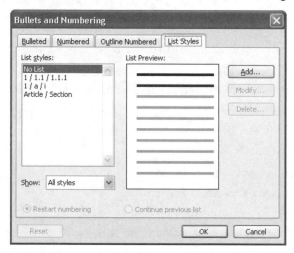

3　Click the style you want, and click **OK**.

　　The list is now formatted in the style you chose.

To clear the style from a list:

1　Select any part of all the list paragraphs.

2　On the **Format** menu, click **Bullets and Numbering**.

3　In the Bullets and Numbering dialog box, click the **List Styles** tab.

4　Click **No List**, and click **OK**.

　　The list is now reformatted as regular paragraphs.

To change the style of a table:

1　Click anywhere in the table to which you want to apply a style.

2 On the **Table** menu, click **Table AutoFormat**.

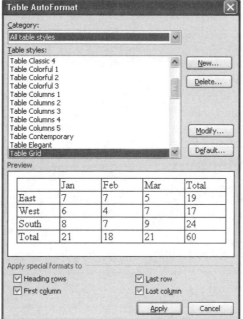

3 Scroll through the **Table styles** list, and click the style you want.

The Preview box displays a sample table with the selected style.

4 Click **Apply**.

The table is now formatted with the style you chose.

To clear the style from a table:

1 Click anywhere in the table whose style you want to clear.

2 On the **Table** menu, click **Table AutoFormat**.

3 In the **Table styles** list of the Table AutoFormat dialog box, click **Table Normal**.

4 Click **Apply**.

The table is now formatted in the default style.

Practice Exercises

In this exercise, you will apply text styles using both the Styles and Formatting task pane and the Style box.

USE the *FormatStyle* document in the *My Documents\Microsoft Press\MOS 2003 Study Guide\Word \W03C-3-1* practice file folder.

Open the *FormatStyle* document, and select the **History** paragraph. Open the Styles and Formatting task pane, and then point to the **Formatting of selected text** box to see the formatting of the style applied to the selected text. (In this case, the style is Normal.) Scroll down the document until you can see the *In the Garden* paragraph, hold down the **CTRL** key, and add the **In the Garden** paragraph to the existing selection. Then add the **Varieties** and **In the Kitchen** paragraphs. Apply the **Heading 2** style to all the selected paragraphs. Scroll to the top of the document, click anywhere in the **History** paragraph, and in the Styles and Formatting task pane, click **Select All**. Then on the Formatting toolbar, click the **Style** down arrow, and click **Heading 3**. Select any part of all of the three short list paragraphs under the *Varieties* heading. Display the **List Styles** tab of the Bullets and Numbering dialog box, and format the list by applying the 1/a/i style. Then clear the style by applying the **No List** style. Click anywhere in the **Currently in stock** table. Display the Table AutoFormat dialog box, and apply the **Table List 8** AutoFormat. Then clear the style by applying the **Table Normal** AutoFormat. Close the *FormatStyle* document without saving it.

Highlighting Text

One way to make text stand out is to highlight it. Just as you can use a highlighting pen to emphasize text in a paper document, you can highlight selected text in your electronic documents with a block of color.

BE SURE TO open the document you want to work with before carrying out these steps.

To highlight text:

Highlight

1   Select the text you want to highlight.

2   On the Formatting toolbar, click the **Highlight** down arrow.

3   On the color palette, click the box for the color you want.

The selected text now stands out from the rest of the document.

Tip   You can select a highlighting color from the color palette without first selecting text to change the mouse pointer into a highlighter. You can then drag across text to highlight it. Click the Highlight button again to turn it off.

Practice Exercise

In this exercise, you will format the text in a document by highlighting it.

USE the *HighlightText* document in the *My Documents\Microsoft Press\MOS 2003 Study Guide\Word \W03C-3-1* practice file folder.

Open the *HighlightText* document, and select the phrase **rich glow of gold** at the end of the second paragraph after the heading *The Lovely Lily*. Use the **Highlight** button on the Formatting toolbar to make the phrase yellow. Then close the *HighlightText* document without saving it.

Applying Text Effects

In addition to changing attributes such as color and style, you can enhance the appearance of text by applying animated text effects from the Font dialog box. Text effects are usually applied to headings, but they can also be used to draw attention to regular text, such as a date or important number in a report.

BE SURE TO open the document you want to work with before carrying out these steps.

To apply a text effect:

1   Select the text to which you want to add a text effect.

2   On the **Format** menu, click **Font**, and then click the **Text Effects** tab.

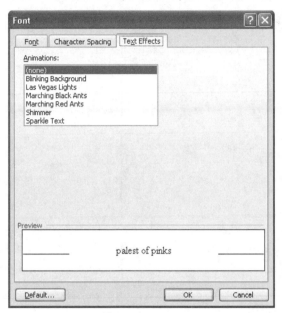

Tip   If the Reveal Formatting task pane is open, you can click the Font link instead.

3   In the **Animations** box, select the effect you want to apply.

The Preview box shows how the selected text will look with this effect applied.

4   Click **OK**.

Practice Exercise

In this exercise, you will format the text in a document by adding a text effect to it.

USE the *ApplyTextEffect* document in the *My Documents\Microsoft Press\MOS 2003 Study Guide\Word \W03C-3-1* practice file folder.

Open the *ApplyTextEffect* document, and select **The Lovely Lily**, the title at the top of the document. Open the Font dialog box, and display the **Text Effects** tab. Apply the **Shimmer** text effect to the title. Close the *ApplyTextEffect* document without saving it.

Modifying Character Spacing

You can alter the appearance of text quite dramatically by spreading out characters or by squeezing them together. You do this by telling Word to put more space between characters or to take space out. Usually changing character spacing is used only for headings, but sometimes you might want to add a line or lose a line from a paragraph by using this technique.

BE SURE TO open the document you want to work with before carrying out these steps.

To modify character spacing:

1   Select the text whose character spacing you want to change.

2   On the **Format** menu, click **Font**, and then click the **Character Spacing** tab.

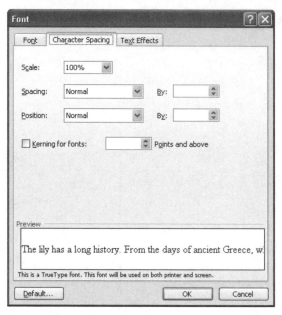

Tip   If the Reveal Formatting task pane is open, you can click the Font link instead.

3   Click the **Spacing** down arrow, and click **Expanded** or **Condensed**.

4   Click the **By** up or down arrow until the spacing is expanded or condensed by the desired amount.

5   Click **OK**.

The selected text appears with the spacing between the characters adjusted by the specified amount.

Practice Exercise

In this exercise, you will format the text in a document by changing its character spacing.

USE the *AdjustCharSpace* document in the *My Documents\Microsoft Press\MOS 2003 Study Guide\Word \W03C-3-1* practice file folder.

Open the *AdjustCharSpace* document, and select **The Lovely Lily**, the title at the top of the document. Open the Font dialog box, and display the **Character Spacing** tab. Expand the spacing of the selected text by **2 pt**, and click **OK**. Then close the *AdjustCharSpace* document without saving it.

Format Paragraphs

W03C-3-2   The skills measured by this objective include the following:

- Indenting, spacing, and aligning paragraphs
- Applying borders and shading to paragraphs
- Setting, removing, and modifying tab stops

In Word, a paragraph is any amount of text that ends when you press the ENTER key. You can vary the look of paragraphs by applying settings that are collectively known as paragraph formatting. To apply a paragraph format, you don't have to select the entire paragraph; you can simply click anywhere in the paragraph. After you apply the formatting, you can press ENTER to apply the same formatting to the next paragraph you type.

Tip   To apply the formatting to an existing paragraph, you can use the Format Painter button to quickly copy the formatting of one paragraph to another.

Indenting, Spacing, and Aligning Paragraphs

You control the width of paragraphs by setting the left and right margins, and you control the amount of text that will fit on a page by setting the top and bottom margins. After you've set up a document's margins, you can control the position of paragraphs within the margins by setting indents.

See Also   For information about setting margins, refer to W03C-3-5, "Modify Document Layout and Page Setup."

The horizontal ruler displays indent markers that control how text wraps on the left or right of each paragraph. You use these markers to indent paragraphs from the left or right margins.

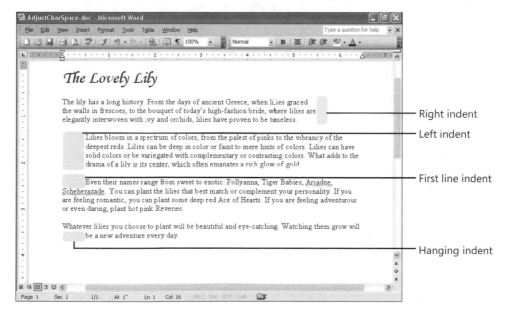

You can also control how text wraps within the document's margins by using the alignment buttons on the Formatting toolbar.

To add space between paragraphs, you can press the ENTER key to insert a blank line, or for more precise control, you can adjust the spacing before and after paragraphs. For example, instead of indicating a new paragraph by indenting the first line, you could use the Paragraph dialog box to add 12 points of blank space before a new paragraph.

You also use the Paragraph dialog box to adjust line spacing. You can select Single, 1.5 lines, or Double spacing; or you can enter a specific spacing in points.

BE SURE TO open the document you want to work with in Print Layout view before carrying out these steps.

To indent a paragraph from the left or right using the ruler:

1   Click anywhere in the paragraph you want to indent.

□
Left Indent

2   On the horizontal ruler, drag the **Left Indent** marker to the right.

The First Line Indent and Hanging Indent markers move with the Left Indent marker, and the entire paragraph is now indented from the left margin.

△
Right Indent

3   At the right end of the horizontal ruler, drag the **Right Indent** marker to the left.

The paragraph is now indented from the right margin.

Tip   You can also adjust the Left and Right settings in the Indentation area of the Paragraph dialog box.

To indent the first line of a paragraph:

1   Click anywhere in the paragraph you want to indent.

▽
First Line
Indent

2   On the horizontal ruler, drag the **First Line Indent** marker to the right.

The first line of text is now indented from the left margin.

Tip   In the Paragraph dialog box, you can also click "First line" in the Special drop-down list and adjust the By setting to the amount of the first-line indent.

To create a hanging indent:

1   Click anywhere in the paragraph where you want the second and subsequent lines to be indented more than the first.

△
Hanging
Indent

2   On the horizontal ruler, drag the **Hanging Indent** marker to the right.

The second and subsequent lines of text are now indented from the left margin.

Tip   In the Paragraph dialog box, you can also click Hanging in the Special drop-down list and adjust the By setting to the amount of indentation for the second and subsequent lines.

To change the alignment of text:

1   Click anywhere in the paragraph whose alignment you want to change.

2   On the Formatting toolbar, click one of the alignment buttons:

Align Left

■   To align the text at the left margin, click the **Align Left** button.

Center

■   To center the text between the left and right margins, click the **Center** button.

Align Right

■   To align the text at the right margin, click the **Align Right** button.

Justify

■   To align the text at both the left and right margins, click the **Justify** button.

To change the spacing above or below a paragraph:

1   Click anywhere in the paragraph whose spacing you want to change.

2   On the **Format** menu, click **Paragraph**.

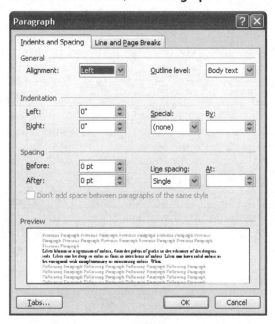

3   In the **Spacing** area, adjust the setting in the **Before** or **After** boxes.

4   Click **OK**.

The paragraph's position in relation to the one above or below it is adjusted accordingly.

75

To change the line spacing of a paragraph:

1   Click anywhere in the paragraph whose spacing you want to change.

2   On the **Format** menu, click **Paragraph**.

3   In the **Spacing** area of the Paragraph dialog box, adjust the setting in the **Line spacing** box.

4   If you selected **At least**, **Exactly**, or **Multiple**, change the setting in the adjacent **At** box as necessary, and click **OK**.

The paragraph's line spacing is adjusted accordingly.

Practice Exercise

In this exercise, you will change text alignment, indent a paragraph from the left and right margins, insert extra paragraph spacing, and modify line spacing.

USE the *FormatPara* document in the *My Documents\Microsoft Press\MOS 2003 Study Guide\Word \W03C-3-2* practice file folder.

Open the *FormatPara* document, and zoom the page to **75%**. Click immediately to the left of the word *for* in the title, hold down the **SHIFT** key, press the **ENTER** key, and then center the title. Justify the first paragraph below the title, and then indent the first line of text a half inch from the left margin. Indent the paragraph that starts *The description should explain* a half inch from both the left and right margins. Press **CTRL+HOME** to move the insertion point to the top of the document, open the Paragraph dialog box, and increase the space below the title by **12 pt**. Click the **Event Title** paragraph, and then use the Paragraph dialog box to add **12 pt** of space above and below that paragraph. Scroll to the bottom of the document, drag through any part of the last four paragraphs, and center them. Then use the Paragraph dialog box to increase the line spacing of the selected paragraphs to **1.5 lines**. Close the *FormatPara* document without saving it.

Applying Borders and Shading to Paragraphs

To set off a paragraph from the rest of the document, you can add borders and shading. For example, if you are sending a letter to customers advertising a spring sale, you might put a border around the paragraph you want customers to pay the most attention to. Alternatively, you might shade the background of the paragraph to create a subtler effect.

Tip   You can also put borders around all the pages in a document. On the Format menu, click Borders and Shading, click the Page Border tab, click the options you want, and click OK.

BE SURE TO open the document you want to work with in Print Layout view before carrying out these steps.

To create a border with default settings:

1   Click the paragraph around which you want to put a border.

If you want to put a single border around multiple paragraphs, drag to select any part of all of them.

Border

2 On the Formatting toolbar, click the **Border** down arrow.

A palette of button options drops down.

3 On the palette, click the type of border you want.

A border now surrounds the selected paragraphs.

To create a custom border:

1 Click the paragraph or paragraphs around which you want to put a border.

2 On the **Format** menu, click **Borders and Shading**.

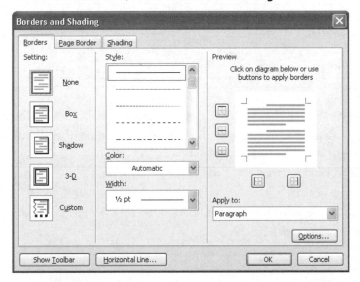

3 Do any of the following:

- In the **Setting**, **Style**, **Color**, and **Width** areas, click the options that will create the kind of border you want.

- If you want only one, two, or three sides of the paragraph to have a border, click the buttons surrounding the image in the **Preview** area.

- If you want to control the distance of the paragraph's text from its border, click the **Options** button, and adjust the **Top**, **Bottom**, **Left**, and **Right** settings.

4 Click **OK**.

A border with your custom specifications now surrounds the selected paragraphs.

To shade the paragraph background:

1 Click the paragraph or paragraphs whose background you want to shade.

2   On the **Format** menu, click **Borders and Shading**, and then click the **Shading** tab.

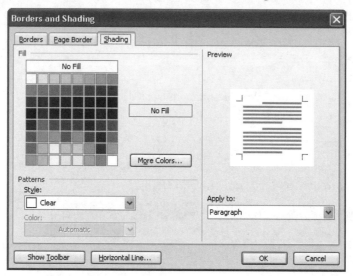

3   Do any of the following:

■   To create a solid background, click the color you want in the **Fill** area.

■   To create a patterned background, change the settings in the **Patterns** area to create the kind of shading you want.

The effect of your settings is shown in the Preview area.

4   Click **OK**.

The background of the paragraph is now shaded according to your specifications.

Practice Exercise

In this exercise, you will add borders and shading around paragraphs to make them stand out in the document.

USE the *AddBorder* document in the *My Documents\Microsoft Press\MOS 2003 Study Guide\Word\W03C-3-2* practice file folder.

Open the *AddBorder* document, scroll to the bottom of the document, and drag through any part of the last four paragraphs. Display the **Borders** tab of the Borders and Shading dialog box, and in the **Setting** area, click the **Shadow** icon. Then choose the settings necessary to create a fancy green border. Click the **Shading** tab, and shade the background of the selected paragraphs a light yellow. Close the *AddBorder* document without saving it.

Setting, Removing, and Modifying Tab Stops

Tab stops are locations across the page that you can use to align text. By default, left-aligned tab stops are set every half-inch, as indicated by gray marks below the ruler. To move the text to the right of the insertion point to the next tab stop, you press the TAB key.

If you want to set custom tab stops, you click the Tab button located at the left end of the ruler until the type of tab stop you want appears, as follows:

- A left tab (a capital *L*) aligns the left end of the text with the stop.
- A center tab (an upside-down *T*) aligns the center of the text with the stop.
- A right tab (a backward *L*) aligns the right end of the text with the stop.
- A decimal tab (an upside-down *T* with a decimal point) aligns the decimal point in the text with the stop.
- A bar tab (a bar) draws a vertical bar the length of the paragraph containing the insertion point.

After selecting the type of tab stop, you click the ruler where you want to set the tab stop. Word removes any default tab stops to the left of the one you set. Pressing TAB then aligns the text on the tab stop according to its type. You can drag the tab stop on the ruler to change its position, or you can fine-tune the position of tab stops in the Tabs dialog box. You might also open this dialog box if you want to use tab leaders—visible marks such as dots or dashes connecting the text before the tab with the text after it. To remove a tab stop, you simply drag it away from the ruler.

Tip   When you press ENTER at the end of a paragraph containing tab stops, the new paragraph contains the same tab settings as the previous paragraph.

BE SURE TO open the document you want to work with in Print Layout view before carrying out these steps.

To set a tab stop:

1   Click anywhere in the paragraph where you want to set a custom tab stop.
2   Click the **Tab** button at the junction of the two rulers until it shows the icon for the type of tab you want to set.
3   Click the ruler where you want to set the tab stop.

    Word inserts a custom tab stop and removes all the default tab stops to the left of it.

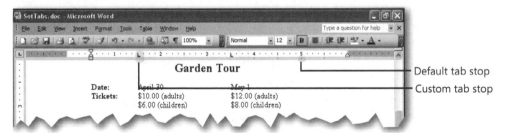

To fine-tune the position of tab stops or add tab leaders:

1   Click anywhere in the paragraph containing the custom tab stop you want to change.

2 On the **Format** menu, click **Tabs**.

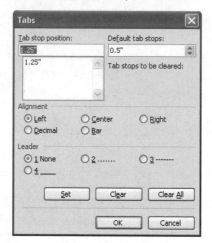

Tip You can also double-click any custom tab stop to display the Tabs dialog box.

3 In the **Tab stop position** list, click the desired tab stop, and adjust its setting as necessary.

4 In the **Leader** area, click the style of leader you want.

5 Click **OK**.

The modified tab stop adjusts its position, and if you have set a tab leader, a solid line or a line of dots or dashes now leads the eye to the tabbed text.

Tip You can also drag a tab stop on the ruler to adjust its position.

To adjust the interval between default tab stops:

1 Click any paragraph.

2 On the **Format** menu, click **Tabs**.

3 In the Tabs dialog box, adjust the setting in the **Default tab stops** box.

4 Click **OK**.

All the default tab stops adjust their positions to reflect the new setting.

To move text to a custom tab stop:

1 Click to the left of the text you want to move to the next tab stop.

2 Press the **TAB** key.

Word moves the text following the insertion point to the tab stop, aligning it according to its type.

To clear a custom tab stop:

1 Click anywhere in the paragraph containing the custom tab stop you want to remove.

2 Drag the tab stop away from the ruler.

> **Tip** You can also open the Tabs dialog box, click a tab stop in the "Tab stop position" list, and click Clear.

To clear all custom tab stops from selected paragraphs:

1   Click anywhere in the paragraph containing the custom tab stops you want to remove.

2   On the **Format** menu, click **Tabs**.

3   In the Tabs dialog box, click **Clear All**.

4   Click **OK**.

Practice Exercise

In this exercise, you will insert, modify, and remove two kinds of tab stops.

USE the *SetTabs* document in the *My Documents\Microsoft Press\MOS 2003 Study Guide\Word\W03C-3-2* practice file folder.

Open the *SetTabs* document, scroll down the page, and select the **Dates:** and **Tickets cost:** paragraphs. Set a left tab stop at the 1-inch mark on the ruler. Then click to the left of the word *Dates:*, and press the **TAB** key. Press **END** to move the insertion point to the end of the line, and press **ENTER** to create a new paragraph. Press **TAB**, and type **Times:**. Then press **ENTER** to create a new paragraph, press **TAB**, type **Location:**, press the **RIGHT ARROW** key to move the insertion point to the beginning of the next paragraph, and then press **TAB**. Drag through any part of the two paragraphs that start with *$10.00* and *$6.00*, and set a decimal tab stop at the 2.5-inch mark on the ruler. Click to the left of *$10.00*, and press **TAB**. Then click to the left of *$6.00*, and press **TAB** again. Select any part of the two paragraphs with dollar amounts, and on the horizontal ruler, drag the decimal tab stop from the 2.5-inch mark to the 2.0-inch mark. Close the *SetTabs* document without saving it.

Apply and Format Columns

W03C-3-3   The skills measured by this objective include the following:

■   Setting up multiple columns

■   Formatting columns

In Word, a column is a block of text that has its own margins. By default, Word displays text in one column, but you can specify that text be displayed in two, three, or more columns to create layouts like those used in newspapers and magazines.

Setting Up Multiple Columns

You can create a multi-column format in two ways:

■   By using the Columns command on the Format menu

■   By using the Columns button on the Standard toolbar

When you create multiple columns, the text flows, or "snakes," from the bottom of one column to the top of the next. You can insert a column break to force subsequent text to move to the next column.

BE SURE TO open the document you want to work with in Print Layout view before carrying out these steps.

To flow all existing text in multiple columns:

Columns

1   Click anywhere in the document.

2   On the Standard toolbar, click the **Columns** button.

Word displays a grid of columns.

3   Drag across the number of columns you want, and click the rightmost column.

The document is now formatted in the number of columns you specified. If you were working in Normal view, Word has switched to Print Layout view so that you can see the columns in place on the page.

To flow only part of the text in multiple columns:

Columns

1   Select the text you want to format in columns.

2   On the Standard toolbar, click the **Columns** button.

3   Drag across the number of columns you want, and click the rightmost column.

Word inserts section breaks above and below the selection and formats the selected text in the number of columns you specified.

See Also   For information about section breaks, refer to W03C-3-5, "Modify Document Layout and Page Setup."

To wrap text from one column to the next:

1   Click to the left of the text you want to appear in the next column.

2   On the **Insert** menu, click **Break**.

3   Select the **Column break** option, and click **OK**.

The text that follows the column break moves to the top of the next column.

Practice Exercise

In this exercise, you will flow part of the text in a document into three columns. You will then break the columns at specific locations instead of allowing the text to flow naturally from one column to the next.

USE the *CreateColumn* document in the *My Documents\Microsoft Press\MOS 2003 Study Guide\Word \W03C-3-3* practice file folder.

Open the *CreateColumn* document, and select the text from *Step 1* to the end of the document. Use either the **Columns** button on the Standard toolbar or the Columns dialog box to flow the text in three columns. Then click just to the left of *Step 4*, and insert a column break. Click at the end of the last column, and insert a continuous section break to balance the columns more evenly on the page. Close the *CreateColumn* document without saving it.

Formatting Columns

No matter how you set up the columns, you can change their width in the Columns dialog box or by dragging markers on the horizontal ruler. You can apply character and paragraph formatting to text in multiple columns just as you would to any other text. For example, you can change the indentation or the alignment of text in a column using the horizontal ruler or buttons on the Formatting toolbar.

BE SURE TO open a document that contains multiple columns in Print Layout view before carrying out these steps.

To change the width of columns visually:

1   Click anywhere in the column whose width you want to change.

     On the horizontal ruler, Word indicates the margins of the columns.

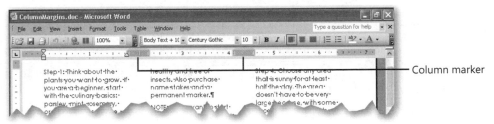

Column marker

2   On the horizontal ruler, point to the column's marker, and when the pointer changes to a double-headed arrow, drag the indicator to the right or left.

     Word adjusts the width of the column to reflect the new setting.

     Tip   Dragging the pointer to the right decreases the spacing between the columns, which decreases the amount of white space on the page. Dragging to the left increases the spacing, which increases the amount of white space.

83

To change the width of columns precisely:

1   Click anywhere in the column whose width you want to change.

2   On the **Format** menu, click **Columns**.

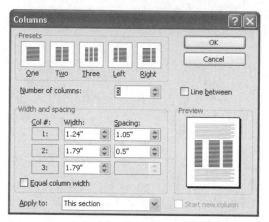

3   In the **Width and spacing** area, adjust the width of each column as necessary.

You can also adjust the spacing between columns in this area. The total width of all columns and the spaces between them cannot exceed the text width defined by the left and right margin settings.

4   Click **OK**.

The column widths are now adjusted according to your specifications.

To apply character or paragraph formatting to text in columns:

● Apply character and paragraph formatting as you would to regular text.

See Also   For information about formatting text, refer to W03C-3-1, "Format Text." For information about formatting paragraphs, refer to W03C-3-2, "Format Paragraphs."

Practice Exercise

In this exercise, you will reduce the amount of space between the columns, and indent column text.

USE the *FormatColumn* document in the *My Documents\Microsoft Press\MOS 2003 Study Guide\Word \W03C-3-3* practice file folder.

Open the *FormatColumn* document, select the text from *Step 1* to the end of the document, and justify the column text. Zoom to **75%**, and on the horizontal ruler, drag the **Right Margin** marker for the second column 1/8 inch (one tick mark) to the right. Click anywhere in the **NOTE** paragraph that appears after the *Step 3* paragraph, and on the horizontal ruler, drag the **Hanging Indent** marker 1/8 inch to the right. Click anywhere in the **NOTE** paragraph that appears after the *Step 4* paragraph, and press the **F4** key to apply the same formatting to this paragraph. Then close the *FormatColumn* document without saving it.

Insert and Modify Content in Headers and Footers

W03C-3-4   The skills measured by this objective include the following:

- Creating and modifying headers and footers
- Inserting and formatting page numbers

In a multi-page document, you might want to display repeating information such as a document title or date on each page. You might also want to display page numbers. You include repeating information in your documents by using headers or footers. You include page numbers either by using headers or footers or by using the Page Numbers command.

Creating and Modifying Headers and Footers

Headers and footers are areas at the top and bottom of a page that can be created and formatted independently. To make these areas active, you use the Header and Footer command. You can then enter information in the areas the same way you enter ordinary text. You can use the buttons on the Header and Footer toolbar to enter AutoText entries, sequential page numbers, the total number of pages in the document, and the date and time.

If your document contains section breaks, you can have different headers and footers for each section. You can also have a different header and footer on the first page, and different headers and footers on odd and even pages.

BE SURE TO open the document you want to work with before carrying out these steps.

To create a header or footer:

1   With the insertion point at the beginning of the document, click **Header and Footer** on the **View** menu.

   If another view is active, Word switches to Print Layout view. Then it outlines the header area at the top of the page, positions the insertion point in the header box, and displays the Header and Footer toolbar.

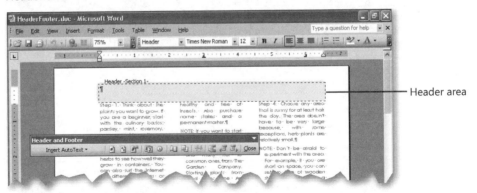

Header area

2   Type the text of the header, pressing the **TAB** key to position text in the center or on the right, and clicking buttons on the Header and Footer toolbar to insert special items.

3   Select the header text, and format it just as you would regular text.

See Also For information about formatting text, refer to W03C-3-1, "Format Text."

Switch
Between
Header and
Footer

4 On the Header and Footer toolbar, click the **Switch Between Header and Footer** button.

The insertion point is now positioned in the footer.

5 Enter and format the footer.

6 On the Header and Footer toolbar, click **Close** to return to the document.

In Print Layout view, the header and footer are now displayed in pale gray at the top and bottom of each page

To create a different header and footer for the first page:

1 With the insertion point to the beginning of the document, click **Header and Footer** on the **View** menu.

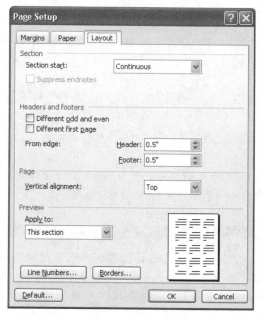

Page Setup

2 On the Header and Footer toolbar, click the **Page Setup** button, and in the Page Setup dialog box, click the **Layout** tab.

3 In the **Headers and footers** area, select the **Different first page** check box, and click **OK**.

4 Enter and format the header and footer, or leave them blank if you don't want a header or footer on the first page.

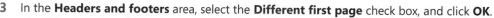

Show Next

5 On the Header and Footer toolbar, click the **Show Next** button.

Word moves to the header or footer for the second page of the document. By default, this header or footer is the same as the previous one.

Link to
Previous

6 On the Header and Footer toolbar, click the **Link to Previous** button to toggle it off.

7 Enter and format a different header and footer for subsequent pages of the document.

8 On the Header and Footer toolbar, click **Close** to return to the document.

To create a different header and footer for odd and even pages:

1   With the insertion point at the beginning of the document, click **Header and Footer** on the **View** menu.

Page Setup

2   On the Header and Footer toolbar, click the **Page Setup** button, and in the Page Setup dialog box, click the **Layout** tab.

3   In the **Headers and footers** area, select the **Different odd and even** check box, and click **OK**.

4   Enter and format the header and footer for the first (odd-numbered) page.

Show Next

5   On the Header and Footer toolbar, click the **Show Next** button.

Word moves to the header or footer for the second (even-numbered) page of the document. By default, this header or footer is the same as the previous one.

Link to Previous

6   On the Header and Footer toolbar, click the **Link to Previous** button to toggle it off.

7   Enter and format a different header and footer for the even-numbered pages of the document.

8   On the Header and Footer toolbar, click **Close** to return to the document.

Practice Exercise

In this exercise, you will add a header to the first page of a document and a footer containing the page number to subsequent pages.

USE the *InsertHeader* document in the *My Documents\Microsoft Press\MOS 2003 Study Guide\Word \W03C-3-4* practice file folder.

Open the *InsertHeader* document, and press **CTRL+HOME** to make sure the insertion point is at the beginning of the document. Display the first-page header, and type **The Garden Company**. Center the text, format it as 12-point bold Verdana, make it green, and expand the character spacing by 10 points. Then display the Page Setup dialog box, and specify that the header of the first page should be different from that of the remaining pages. Switch to the footer on the second page, tab to the right margin, and insert the page number. Select the number, and make it bold and green. Return to the *InsertHeader* document, and close it without saving it.

Inserting and Formatting Page Numbers

If you don't want to create headers and footers for a document but you do want to display page numbers, you can add them using the Page Numbers dialog box. By default, page numbers appear in the lower-right corner of each page, but you can change their position and alignment.

Page numbers inserted using the Page Numbers dialog box are inserted in the document's header or footer. When the header and footer areas are active, you can format the numbers directly by using buttons on the Formatting toolbar. However, to change the position or alignment of the numbers, or to change the style or starting number, you use the Page Numbers dialog box.

BE SURE TO open the document you want to work with before carrying out these steps.

To insert page numbers:

1 On the **Insert** menu, click **Page Numbers**.

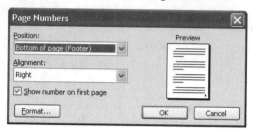

2 In the **Position** drop-down list, specify whether you want the numbers to appear at the top or bottom of the page.

3 In the **Alignment** drop-down list, specify whether you want the numbers to be left-aligned, centered, right-aligned, or on the outside or inside of a two-page spread.

4 If you don't want a page number to appear on the first page of the document, clear the **Show number on first page** check box, and then click **OK**.

Page numbers now appear as specified. (You need to be in Print Layout view to see them.)

To format page numbers:

1 On the **View** menu, click **Header and Footer**.

2 Display the header or footer box containing the page number, and use buttons on the Formatting toolbar to change its look.

3 On the Header and Footer toolbar, click the **Close** button.

To change the style or starting number of page numbers:

1 On the **Insert** menu, click **Page Numbers**.

2 In the Page Numbers dialog box, click the **Format** button.

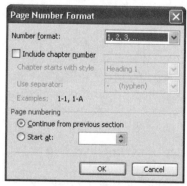

3 In the **Number format** drop-down list, specify the style you want for the numbers (such as 1, 2, 3 or A, B, C).

4 In the **Page numbering** area, specify whether you want the numbers to continue from the preceding section or to start at a particular number.

5   Click **OK** to close the Page Number Format dialog box, and click **OK** again to close the Page Numbers dialog box.

The page numbers now appear as specified.

Practice Exercise

In this exercise, you will insert and format page numbers in a document.

USE the *InsertPageNumber* document in the *My Documents\Microsoft Press\MOS 2003 Study Guide\Word \W03C-3-4* practice file folder.

Open the *InsertPageNumber* document, and display the Page Numbers dialog box. Do not show a page number on the first page, but specify that page numbers appear centered at the bottom of the rest of the pages. Then change the number format to **-1-, -2-, -3-**, and be sure that numbering starts at page 1. Display the header and footer areas, switch to the footer on the second page, make the page number appear in 10-point Arial, and change its color to 50% gray. Then close the *InsertPageNumber* document without saving it.

Modify Document Layout and Page Setup

W03C-3-5   The skills measured by this objective include the following:

- Inserting and deleting breaks
- Modifying page margins and page orientation

A pleasing page carefully balances text and white space, which is the area around the text. Too little white space results in pages that look crowded and content that looks hard to read. Too much white space results in pages that look vacant and content that looks lightweight. In addition to balancing text and white space, you might need to control the length of a document. You can juggle all these needs by adjusting the document's margins, orientation, and page breaks.

Inserting and Deleting Breaks

When you create a document that contains more than one page, Word paginates your document by inserting soft page breaks. If you want to control how pages break, you can insert manual page breaks. As you insert, delete, and move text, Word changes where it inserts soft page breaks. Word does not change the location of manual page breaks; you must do that yourself.

In addition to page breaks, you can insert section breaks in your documents. A section break identifies a part of the document to which you can apply page settings, such as orientation or margins, that are different from those of the rest of the document. Several types of section breaks are available:

- The "Next page" option starts the following text on the next page.
- The "Continuous" option creates a section break without affecting page breaks.
- The "Even page" option forces a break to the next even-numbered page.
- The "Odd page" option forces a break to the next odd-numbered page.

BE SURE TO open the document you want to work with before carrying out these steps.

To insert a page break:

1 If you see an awkward page break—for example, a break between a heading and its text—click where you want to rebreak the page.

2 Press **CTRL+ENTER**.

Word inserts a manual page break at the insertion point.

To insert a section break:

1 Click where you want to insert a section break.

If you want just part of an existing document to appear in a section of its own, select that part.

2 On the **Insert** menu, click **Break**.

3 In the **Section break types** area, click the type of section break you want, and then click **OK**.

If you clicked the document, a section break is created in the location of the click and subsequent text is contained in the new section. If you selected text, the selection appears in its own section, with different sections before and after it. Either way, you can now change the layout and page setup of the section without affecting other sections in the document.

To delete a break:

1 Switch to Normal view, and click immediately to the left of the break you want to delete.

2 Press **DELETE**.

If you delete a page break, Word repaginates the document from that point forward. If you delete a section break, the text formerly contained in the section assumes the layout and page setup of the preceding section.

Practice Exercise

In this exercise, you will check the page breaks in a document and insert manual page breaks. You will also push part of the document to the next page by inserting a section break.

USE the *InsertBreak* document in the *My Documents\Microsoft Press\MOS 2003 Study Guide\Word \W03C-3-5* practice file folder.

Open the *InsertBreak* document in Print Layout view, with the zoom level set to **100%**. Scroll through the document, noticing any bad page breaks. Then click to the left of the *Hot or*

Cold? heading, and insert a page break. Scroll down the document, and click to the left of the *Composting DOs and DON'Ts* heading. Insert a **Next page** section break to force the heading and its paragraphs to the next page. Scroll back up the document, switch to Normal view, click to the left of the page break preceding the *Hot or Cold?* heading, and press **DELETE**. Verify that the section that starts with *Composting DOs and DON'Ts* still appears on its own page. Close the *InsertBreak* document without saving it.

Modifying Page Margins and Page Orientation

You can change the margins of a document to fit more or less information on a page or to control where the information appears. You can adjust the margins either on the Margins tab of the Page Setup dialog box or by dragging markers on the rulers.

The way a page is laid out in a printed document is called the page orientation. The default orientation in Word is portrait. With this orientation, the page is taller than it is wide. You can also set the orientation to landscape, in which the page is wider than it is tall.

A document has only one set of margins and only one page orientation unless you divide your document into sections. Then each section can have its own margins and page orientation.

See Also   For information about sections, refer to "Inserting and Deleting Breaks" earlier in this objective.

BE SURE TO open the document you want to work with before carrying out these steps.

To change the page margins:

1   On the **File** menu, click **Page Setup**, and if another tab is displayed, click the **Margins** tab.

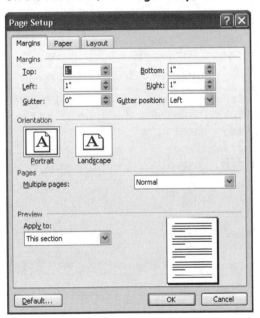

2   In the **Margins** area, change the values in the **Top**, **Bottom**, **Left**, and **Right** boxes as necessary, and then click **OK**.

The widths of the margins increase or decrease to reflect the new settings, and the text rewraps to fill the newly defined column width.

To change the page margins by using the rulers:

1   In Print Layout view, scroll the document until the upper-left corner of a page is visible.

2   To adjust the top or bottom margin, point to the top or bottom of the white section of the vertical ruler, and when the pointer changes to a two-headed arrow and you see a margin ScreenTip, drag the pointer up or down.

3   To adjust the left or right margin, point to the left or right end of the white section of the horizontal ruler, and when the pointer changes to a two-headed arrow and you see a margin ScreenTip, drag the pointer to the left or right.

The widths of the margins increase or decrease to reflect your changes, and the text rewraps to fill the newly defined column width.

To change the page orientation:

1   On the **File** menu, click **Page Setup**, and then if another tab is displayed, click the **Margins** tab.

2   In the **Orientation** area, click the **Portrait** icon for vertical pages or the **Landscape** icon for horizontal pages, and then click **OK**.

The pages of the document change to reflect the orientation you chose.

Practice Exercise

In this exercise, you will use the Page Setup dialog box to adjust all the margins of a document and change its orientation. Then you will adjust the top margin visually.

USE the *ChangeLayout* document in the *My Documents\Microsoft Press\MOS 2003 Study Guide\Word \W03C-3-5* practice file folder.

Open the *ChangeLayout* document in Print Layout view, and display the **Margins** tab of the Page Setup dialog box. Change all the margin settings to **1.5"**. Then change the orientation of the document to **Landscape**. With the top of a page visible, use the vertical ruler to decrease the top margin by about half an inch. Close the *ChangeLayout* document without saving it.

W03C-3 Review

Number	Objective	Mastered
W03C-3-1	Format text	
	Applying common character formatting	❏
	Finding and replacing character formatting	❏
	Working with styles	❏
	Highlighting text	❏
	Applying text effects	❏
	Modifying character spacing	❏
W03C-3-2	Format paragraphs	
	Indenting, spacing, and aligning paragraphs	❏
	Applying borders and shading to paragraphs	❏
	Setting, removing, and modifying tab stops	❏
W03C-3-3	Apply and format columns	
	Setting up multiple columns	❏
	Formatting columns	❏
W03C-3-4	Insert and modify content in headers and footers	
	Creating and modifying headers and footers	❏
	Inserting and formatting page numbers	❏
W03C-3-5	Modify document layout and page setup	
	Inserting and deleting breaks	❏
	Modifying page margins and page orientation	❏

W03C-4
Collaborating

The skills tested by this section of the Microsoft Office Specialist Word 2003 Core Exam all relate to the Word features that make it is easy to collaborate with other people on the creation and formatting of documents. Specifically, the following objectives are associated with this set of skills:

Number	Objective
W03C-4-1	Circulate documents for review
W03C-4-2	Compare and merge document versions
W03C-4-3	Insert, view, and edit comments
W03C-4-4	Track, accept, and reject proposed changes

Important   Before you can do the practice exercises associated with this skill set, you need to install the practice files from the book's companion CD to their default location. See "Installing the Practice Files" on page xxv for more information.

Circulate Documents for Review

W03C-4-1   The skills measured by this objective include the following:

- Sending a document for review
- Sending a document as an e-mail attachment

To make it easy to send documents to other people for review, you can access the Microsoft Office Outlook 2003 e-mail program from within Word.

Tip   You can use a different e-mail program to circulate documents for review. However, the steps for attaching and sending a message might vary from those given in the following sections.

Sending a Document for Review

You can quickly send a document through e-mail for review without having to start your e-mail program. The Send To submenu includes the Mail Recipient (for Review) command, which opens a message window with the current document as an attachment and the message *Please review the attached document.* All you have to do is enter the e-mail addresses of anyone you want to review the document and click Send. You can also send a document as the body of an e-mail message.

BE SURE TO open the document you want to work with before carrying out these steps. You will also need to have Outlook 2003 installed on your computer and an e-mail account set up.

To send a document for review:

1 On the **File** menu, click **Send To** and then **Mail Recipient (for Review)**.

A message window appears, with the document as an attachment.

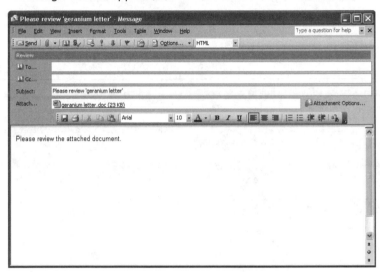

2 In the **To** box, enter the recipient's e-mail address.

3 Click **Send**.

To send a document in the body of an e-mail message:

E-mail

1 On the Standard toolbar, click the **E-mail** button.

A message window appears with the document as the text of the message.

2 In the **To** box, enter the recipient's address, and in the **Introduction** box, enter any notes for the recipient.

3 Click **Send a Copy**.

Practice Exercise

In this exercise, you will send a document for review in the body of an e-mail message.

USE the *SendDocument* document in the *My Documents\Microsoft Press\MOS 2003 Study Guide\Word \W03C-4-1* practice file folder.

Open the *SendDocument* document. On the Standard toolbar, click the **E-Mail** button, enter your own e-mail address in the **To** box, type **Here is a copy of the memo** in the **Introduction** box, and send the message. Then close the *SendDocument* document without saving it.

Sending a Document as an E-Mail Attachment

After you create a document, you can quickly send it as an e-mail attachment from within Word. You do not have to start your e-mail program. You simply use the Mail Recipient (as Attachment) command on the Send To submenu, and enter the e-mail addresses of anyone you want to receive the message and its attachment.

BE SURE TO open the document you want to work with before carrying out these steps. You will also need to have Outlook 2003 installed on your computer and an e-mail account set up.

To send a document as an e-mail attachment:

1 On the **File** menu, click **Send To** and then **Mail Recipient (as Attachment)**.

2 If the Choose Profile dialog box appears with information about your Internet or network profile, click **OK**.

The message window appears with the name of the document in the Subject line and the default message in the message pane.

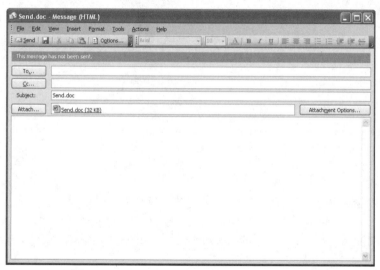

3 In the **To** box, type the e-mail address of the recipient. (Separate multiple addresses with semicolons.)

4 On the message window's toolbar, click the **Send** button.

The e-mail message with the attached documents is sent out for review.

Practice Exercise

In this exercise, you will attach three documents to an e-mail message so that you can send them for review.

USE the *AttachDocument, Attach1,* and *Attach2* documents in the *My Documents\Microsoft Press \MOS 2003 Study Guide\Word\W03C-4-1* practice file folder.

Open the *AttachDocument* document. Tell Word that you want to attach the open document to an e-mail message, and address the message to yourself. Then on the message window's toolbar, click the **Attach** button, navigate to the *My Documents\Microsoft Press \MOS 2003 Study Guide\Word\W03C-4-1* practice file folder, and add the *Attach1* and *Attach2* files as attachments. Click the **Send** button, and then close the *AttachDocument* document without saving it.

Compare and Merge Document Versions

W03C-4-2 The skills measured by this objective include the following:

- Comparing and merging documents
- Viewing changes in a merged document

After you send a document for review, you need a way to examine all the suggested changes. This task can be cumbersome, especially if you have asked several people to review the document. Word's Compare and Merge command simplifies the process.

Comparing and Merging Documents

Sometimes you might want to compare several versions of the same document. For example, if you have sent a document out for review by colleagues, you might want to compare their edited versions with the original document. Or you might want to compare an earlier version of a document with the current version. Instead of comparing multiple open documents, you can make this process much easier by using Word to compare the documents and merge the differences into one document as tracked changes that appear in comment balloons— text boxes that appear in the margin of the document.

See Also   For information about tracked changes, refer to W03C-4-4, "Track, Accept, and Reject Proposed Changes."

BE SURE TO open the document you want to work with and to have at least one other version of the document available before carrying out these steps.

To compare and merge documents:

1　On the **Tools** menu, click **Compare and Merge Documents**.

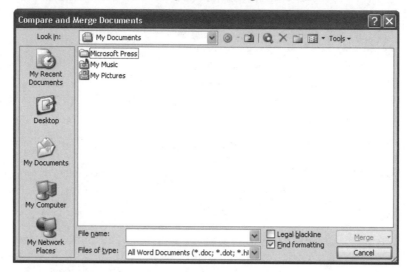

2　Navigate to the folder where the file you want to compare and merge with the original document is stored.

3　Click (don't double-click) the document, click the **Merge** down arrow, and then click **Merge into current document**.

The changes from the selected document are transferred to the open document.

4　Repeat steps 1 through 3 to merge the changes from any additional documents.

Practice Exercise

In this exercise, you will merge a document with two other versions of it.

USE the *CompareMerge, Merge1,* and *Merge2* documents in the *My Documents\Microsoft Press \MOS 2003 Study Guide\Word\W03C-4-2* practice file folder.

Open the *CompareMerge* document. Display the Compare and Merge Documents dialog box, navigate to the *My Documents\Microsoft Press\MOS Study Guide\Word\W03C-4-2* practice file folder, and merge the *Merge1* file into the open document. Repeat this process with the *Merge2* document, and scroll down the document to see all changes. Then close the *CompareMerge* document without saving it.

Viewing Changes in a Merged Document

When you compare and merge documents, Word shows the differences as tracked changes, even if the reviewers did not track their changes as they edited. If you merge several documents, each document's changes are shown in a different color.

BE SURE TO open the document you want to work with and ensure that Markup is active on the View menu before carrying out these steps.

> **Tip** When Markup is active, the icon to its left has a square blue border and appears on a tan background. The Reviewing toolbar is also displayed.

To hide formatting changes:

Show

1   On the Reviewing toolbar, click the **Show** down arrow, and click **Formatting**.

Only insertions and deletions, not formatting changes, appear in the document.

2   Click the **Show** down arrow, and click **Formatting** again to redisplay formatting changes.

To move from one change to the next:

Next

1   On the Reviewing toolbar, click the **Next** button to move forward through the document from change to change.

Previous

2   Click the **Previous** button to move backward from change to change.

To view the document with changes implemented:

1   On the Reviewing toolbar, click the **Display for Review** down arrow.

The changes are hidden so that the document looks the way it would if all the changes were accepted.

2   Click **Final**.

3   Click the **Display for Review** down arrow, and click **Final Showing Markup**.

The revision marks reappear.

Practice Exercise

In this exercise, you'll view the changes in a merged document in various ways.

USE the *ViewMerge* document in the *My Documents\Microsoft Press\MOS Study Guide\Word\W03C-4-2* practice file folder.

Open the *ViewMerge* document, and scroll down the document to see the product information. Then hide the document's formatting changes, and redisplay the changes of all the reviewers. Use the **Display for Review** box to hide all the tracked changes, and then scroll through the document, which now looks the way it would if all the changes were accepted. Then set the display to **Final Showing Markup** so that the tracked changes reappear. Then close the *ViewMerge* document without saving it.

Insert, View, and Edit Comments

W03C-4-3

The skills measured by this objective include the following:

- Inserting and reviewing comments
- Editing comments

Whether you are collaborating with several people or creating a document yourself, Word's Comments feature is a handy tool for keeping track of and clarifying information during the development process.

Inserting and Reviewing Comments

You might want to attach notes, or comments, to the text of a document to ask questions or explain suggested edits. Word puts colored brackets around commented text and displays the comment in the balloon in the margin of the document.

You click the Next and Previous buttons to move from one comment to another, reading the comments in their balloons. You can point to commented text to see a ScreenTip showing the name of the person who made the comment and when the comment was inserted.

BE SURE TO open the document you want to work with and ensure that Markup is active on the View menu before carrying out these steps.

Tip When Markup is active, the icon to its left has a square blue border and appears on a tan background. The Reviewing toolbar is also displayed.

To insert a comment in a document:

1   Select the text to which you want to attach the comment.

Insert
Comment

2   On the Reviewing toolbar, click the **Insert Comment** button.

Word surrounds the selected text with brackets and displays a new comment balloon in the right margin.

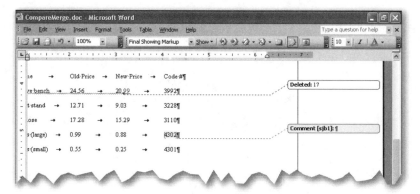

3   In the balloon, type your comment.

4   Click a blank area of the document to deselect the comment balloon.

To move from one comment to another:

Next

1   On the Reviewing toolbar, click the **Next** button until the next comment is visible.

The insertion point appears in the next comment balloon, and brackets surround the commented text. (If there are changes in the document, clicking Next also moves you from one change to the next.)

2   If the bottom of the comment balloon is not displayed, scroll downward.

3   If the right side of the comment balloon is not displayed, scroll to the right.

4   Point to commented text.

A ScreenTip displays information about who inserted the comment.

Previous

5   On the Reviewing toolbar, click the **Previous** button until the insertion point appears in the previous comment balloon.

To hide comments temporarily:

Show ▼
Show

1   On the Reviewing toolbar, click the **Show** down arrow, and then click **Comments**.

2   To redisplay the comments, click the **Show** down arrow, and click **Comments**.

Practice Exercise

In this exercise, you will insert a comment into a document and then review other comments.

USE the *InsertComment* document in the *My Documents\Microsoft Press\MOS 2003 Study Guide\Word \W03C-4-3* practice file folder.

Open the *InsertComment* document. Use the **Next** button to display the first comment in the document, and then scroll down to display the entire comment balloon. (If you can't read the comments in the right margin of the document, drag the horizontal scroll bar to the right.) Move to the next comment, and display its ScreenTip. Select the words *Garden hose* in the document, and insert a comment balloon that says **Preferred customers receive an extra 10% discount on hoses.** Then attach the comment **Kim, is this product code correct?** to *3992* in the decorative bench code. Click **Next** until you see the comment attached to small clay pots. Then close the *InsertComment* document without saving it.

Editing Comments

You can easily edit or delete a comment. You can also respond to a comment, either by adding text to an existing comment balloon or by adding a new comment balloon.

BE SURE TO open a document containing comments and ensure that Markup is active on the View menu before carrying out these steps.

Tip When Markup is active, the icon to its left has a square blue border and appears on a tan background. The Reviewing toolbar is also displayed.

To delete a comment:

● Right-click anywhere in the commented text, and click **Delete Comment** on the shortcut menu.

Word deletes the comment and its balloon.

To edit an existing comment:

1   Click the balloon whose comment you want to change.

2   Position the insertion point, and make edits in the usual way.

Tip You can also right-click the commented text and click Edit Comment on the shortcut menu.

To respond to an existing comment:

1 Right-click the commented text to which you want to respond, and click **Edit Comment** on the shortcut menu.

The insertion point appears at the end of the comment.

Insert
Comment

2 On the Reviewing toolbar, click the **Insert Comment** button.

A new comment balloon appears.

3 Type your response in the new comment balloon.

Practice Exercise

In this exercise, you will delete a comment that is no longer needed, edit an existing comment, and then respond to a comment.

USE the *EditComment* document in the *My Documents\Microsoft Press\MOS Study Guide\Word\W03C-4-3* practice file folder.

Open the *EditComment* document. Delete the comment attached to *Iron plant stand*. Click to the right of *intact* (the last word in the second comment), type your initials and a space, and then type **I'm not sure if there is enough shelf space.** Activate the comment attached to *Clay pots (small)*, and use the **Insert Comment** button to create a new comment balloon in response to the selected comment. In the new comment balloon, type **I checked with the shipping company. They are ready to go**. Then close the *EditComment* document without saving it.

Track, Accept, and Reject Proposed Changes

W03C-4-4   The skills measured by this objective include the following:

■ Tracking changes to a document

■ Locating and managing document changes

As the author of a document, you will probably not want other people to change it without your knowledge. Maintaining content control is particularly important with technical or legal documents, where edits such as reversing word order can change meaning.

Tracking Changes to a Document

When two or more people collaborate on a document, one person usually creates and "owns" the document and the others review it, suggesting changes to make it more accurate, logical, or readable. Reviewers can turn on the Track Changes feature so that the revisions they make to the document are recorded without the original text being lost. They then edit the text as usual.

Word shows changed text in a different color from the original text and uses revision marks, such as underlines, to distinguish the revised text from the original text. In Print Layout view, Word identifies the change and its type, such as a deletion, in a comment balloon and displays a vertical line in the margin to the left of any changed text to help you locate changes in the document.

BE SURE TO open the document you want to work with and ensure that Markup is active on the View menu before carrying out these steps.

> **Tip** When Markup is active, the icon to its left has a square blue border and appears on a tan background. The Reviewing toolbar is also displayed.

1 On the **View** menu, click **Toolbars** and then **Reviewing.**

The Reviewing toolbar appears.

Track
Changes

2 On the Reviewing toolbar, click the **Track Changes** button.

Any changes that you make will now be tracked.

> **Tip** When the Track Changes feature is turned on, the Track Changes button has a blue border, and the letters *TRK* on the status bar are black instead of gray. When change tracking is turned off, the Track Changes button has no border, and *TRK* is gray on the status bar.

3 Edit the document in the usual way.

Practice Exercise

In this exercise, you will turn on change tracking and make changes to the document.

USE the *TrackChanges* document in the *My Documents\Microsoft Press\MOS 2003 Study Guide\Word \W03C-4-4* practice file folder.

Open the *TrackChanges* document. Display the Reviewing toolbar, and turn on tracked changes. Scroll the document to see the product information, delete *20.17* (the new price for the decorative bench), and type **99**. Then replace the *29* in *$15.29* (the new price for the garden hose) with **99**. Point to *99* in the price for the decorative bench to display a ScreenTip that tells you who made the change, when the change was made, and the type of change. Then close the *TrackChanges* document without saving it.

Locating and Managing Document Changes

To help you manage changes that have been tracked in a document, you can turn on the Reviewing toolbar by right-clicking any visible toolbar and clicking Reviewing on the shortcut menu. You can then use the buttons on this toolbar to work with tracked changes in the following ways:

- If tracked changes are distracting, you can track changes without showing them on the screen. Word then shows the text as it would appear if you were making changes without tracking them.

- When changes are visible in the document, you can specify that only certain types of revisions be displayed.

- You can move from one change to another.

- You can incorporate a change into the document or delete it and restore the original text. You can also accept or delete all the changes at once.

BE SURE TO open a document containing tracked changes and ensure that Markup is active on the View menu before carrying out these steps.

> **Tip** When Markup is active, the icon to its left has a square blue border and appears on a tan background. The Reviewing toolbar is also displayed.

To hide or display tracked changes:

1 On the Reviewing toolbar, click the **Display for Review** down arrow.

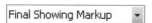

2 Click **Final**.

3 To display the changes again, click the **Display for Review** down arrow, and click **Final Showing Markup**.

To specify that only certain types of changes be displayed:

Show

1 On the Reviewing toolbar, click the **Show** down arrow.

2 Click the options you want on the drop-down menu.

To move among tracked changes:

Next

1 On the Reviewing toolbar, click the **Next** button to move to the next change.

Previous

2 Click the **Previous** button to move to the previous change.

To accept or reject a change:

1 Move to the change you want to accept or reject.

2 On the Reviewing toolbar, do one of the following:

Accept
Change

■ To incorporate the change, click the **Accept Change** button.

Reject
Change/
Delete
Comment

■ To disregard the change or comment, click the **Reject Change/Delete Comment** button.

> **Tip** To accept a change, you can also right-click the change and then click Accept Insertion or Accept Deletion on the shortcut menu.

To accept or reject all the changes at once:

● On the Reviewing toolbar, do one of the following:

Accept
Change

■ Click the **Accept Change** down arrow, and then click **Accept All Changes in Document**.

Reject
Change/
Delete
Comment

■ Click the **Reject Change/Delete Comment** down arrow, and then click **Reject All Changes in Document**.

Practice Exercise

In this exercise, you will move among suggested changes, and accept and reject them.

USE the *ManageChanges* document in the *My Documents\Microsoft Press\MOS 2003 Study Guide\Word \W03C-4-4* practice file folder.

Open the *ManageChanges* document. Display the Reviewing toolbar, and use the **Next** button to display the first tracked change in the document—the number *99* in the decorative bench price. Accept this change. Click **99** in the new garden hose price, and reject this change. Also reject the deletion of **29**. Then close the *ManageChanges* document without saving it.

W03C-4 Review

Number	Objective	Mastered
W03C-4-1	Circulate documents for review	
	Sending a document for review	❑
	Sending a document as an e-mail attachment	❑
W03C-4-2	Compare and merge document versions	
	Comparing and merging documents	❑
	Viewing changes in a merged document	❑
W03C-4-3	Insert, view, and edit comments	
	Inserting and reviewing comments	❑
	Editing comments	❑
W03C-4-4	Track, accept, and reject proposed changes	
	Tracking changes to a document	❑
	Locating and managing document changes	❑

W03C-5

Formatting and Managing Documents

The skills tested by this section of the Microsoft Office Word 2003 Specialist Exam all relate to working with entire documents, as opposed to working with their contents. Specifically, the following objectives are associated with this set of skills:

Number	Objective
W03C-5-1	Create new documents using templates
W03C-5-2	Review and modify document properties
W03C-5-3	Organize documents using file folders
W03C-5-4	Save documents in appropriate formats for different uses
W03C-5-5	Print documents, envelopes, and labels
W03C-5-6	Preview documents and Web pages
W03C-5-7	Change and organize document views and windows

Important   Before you can do the practice exercises associated with this skill set, you need to install the practice files from the book's companion CD to their default location. See "Installing the Practice Files" on page xxv for more information.

Create New Documents Using Templates

W03C-5-1   The skills measured by this objective include the following:

■   Creating a new document based on a template

The accuracy of the information in a document is essential, but the document's appearance is also important for effective communication. To help create visually appealing documents, you can use one of Word's professionally designed templates.

Creating a New Document Based on a Template

A template is a file that stores text, character and paragraph styles, page formatting, and macros as a pattern for creating other documents. Unless you specify otherwise, all new documents are based on the Normal template, which contains a minimum number of fairly plain styles, including the Normal style used for regular text paragraphs. Word also comes with templates for a variety of business and personal documents, including publications, reports, letters, faxes, memos, and Web pages.

To create a document based on one of Word's predefined templates, you select the template's location in the New Document task pane and then select the template you want. Some of the listed templates were installed on your computer during the program's installation; others are available on the Office Online Web site.

A document based on a Word template often displays formatted placeholders surrounded by square brackets—for example, *[Click here and type name]*. You can replace these placeholders with your own text, or if you don't need a placeholder, you simply delete it. After you have entered all the text you need for the document, you save it in the usual way. The changes you made affect the document, not the template it is based on, which remains available to help create other documents.

Tip After you make your changes, you can save the document as a template with a different name. The next time you need this template, you can use your modified version instead of the one included with Word.

BE SURE TO start Word before carrying out these steps.

To create a new document based on a Word template:

1   On the **File** menu, click **New**.

    The New Document task pane appears.

2   In the **Templates** area of the task pane, click **On my computer**.

    Word opens the Templates dialog box.

    Tip You can click Templates on Office Online to download a variety of ready-made templates from the Microsoft Office Online website.

3   Click the tab for the category of template you want to use.

4   Click (don't double-click) the icon for the desired template.

    The template appears in the Preview box.

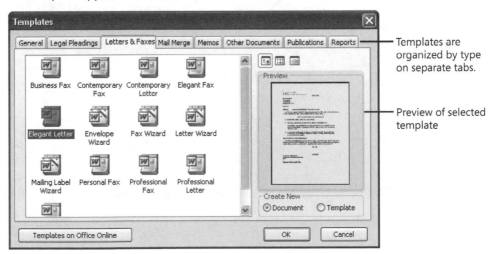

Templates are organized by type on separate tabs.

Preview of selected template

5 Click **OK**.

Word creates a new document based on the selected template, with placeholders for text you need to supply.

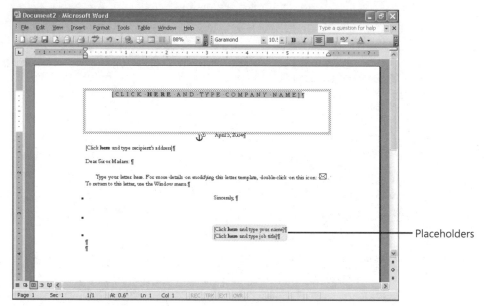

Placeholders

6 Replace all the appropriate placeholders with your own text, and select and delete any placeholders you don't need.

7 Save the document in the usual way.

Tip After you create a document, you can change its look by attaching a different template to it. (The new template must use the same paragraph and character style names as the existing template.) To attach a template, click Templates and Add-Ins on the Tools menu. In the Templates and Add-ins dialog box, click Attach, browse to the location of the template you want, and double-click it. Then make sure "Automatically update document styles" is selected, and click OK.

Practice Exercise

In this exercise, you will create a fax document based on a predefined Word template.

NO practice file is required for this exercise.

Open the New Document task pane, and in the **Templates** area, click **On my computer**. Display the **Letters & Faxes** tab of the Templates dialog box, and open a new document based on the **Contemporary Fax** template. At the top of the page, replace the *[Click here and type address]* placeholder with **The Garden Company**, press **ENTER**, type **1234 Oak Street**, press **ENTER**, and type **Seattle, WA 10101**. In the *To* line, replace the placeholder with **Flower Supplier**, and in the *From* line, replace the placeholder with **The Garden Company**. Type **1-800-555-0190** in the *Fax* line, **Order Confirmation** in the *Re* line, and **2** in the *Pages* line. In the *CC* line, delete the placeholder, and then scroll down and delete the paragraph that starts with *Notes: Select this text.* In its place, type **Please review this order and confirm that you will be able to deliver on time.** and press **ENTER**. Save the document with the name **FaxCover** in the *My Documents\Microsoft Press\MOS 2003 Study Guide\Word\W03C-5-1* practice file folder, and then close it.

Review and Modify Document Properties

W03C-5-2   The skills measured by this objective include the following:

■ Reviewing and modifying summary information
■ Checking word, paragraph, and character counts

Word stores information about each document as a set of properties. You can review all this information, and you can change some of it.

Reviewing and Modifying Summary Information

You can get summary information about any document by displaying its Properties dialog box. By default, the General tab displays the document's name, location, and size; and the dates of creation, modification, and last access. The Summary tab displays the title, subject, and author, as well as the category and any relevant keywords or comments. You enter this information so that you can see at a glance what the document is about.

Tip   If the document includes heading styles and you selected the "Save preview picture" check box on the Summary tab, the Contents tab displays an outline of the document.

You don't have to open a document and display its Properties dialog box to see a document's description. The author, title, subject, and first 126 characters of a comment entered on the Summary tab of the Properties dialog box is displayed in a ScreenTip when you point to the document in My Computer or Windows Explorer. If you have many Word documents stored on your computer, this information can help you find the one you need.

See Also   For information about the Statistics tab of the Properties dialog box, refer to "Checking Word, Paragraph, and Character Counts" later in this objective. For information about the Custom tab, refer to W03E-4-6, "Customize Document Properties."

BE SURE TO open the document you want to work with before carrying out these steps.

To review and modify summary information:

1   On the **File** menu, click **Properties**.

The General tab of the Properties dialog box appears. This tab displays information generated by Word.

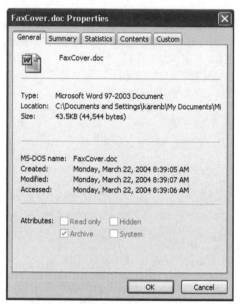

2   Click the **Summary** tab.

The Summary tab of the Properties dialog box displays information you can change.

3   Make any necessary adjustments to the title, subject, author, or comments, and click **OK**.

See Also   For information about assigning categories, keywords, and a hyperlink base, refer to W03E-4-6, "Customize Document Properties."

Practice Exercise

In this exercise, you will open a document's Properties dialog box and review and change some of its summary information.

USE the *ReviewSummary* document in the *My Documents\Microsoft Press\MOS 2003 Study Guide\Word \W03C-5-2* practice file folder.

Open the *ReviewSummary* document, and then open its Properties dialog box. Read the information on the **General** tab, and then click the **Summary** tab. In the **Subject** box, type **Composting**, and in the **Comments** box, type **An instructive overview of composting for the home garden**. Close the Properties dialog box, and then close the *ReviewSummary* document without saving it.

Checking Word, Paragraph, and Character Counts

You can check the number of pages, paragraphs, lines, words, and characters the document contains by opening the Properties dialog box and displaying the Statistics tab. This tab also tracks the number of times the document has been revised and the amount of time it has been open on the screen for editing.

Word, paragraph, and character counts are tracked in the Word Count dialog box. If you need to keep a close watch on the number of words or characters in a document as you edit text, you can display the Word Count toolbar.

BE SURE TO open the document you want to work with before carrying out these steps.

To display count information:

1 Do one of the following:

  ■ On the **File** menu, click **Properties**, and then click the **Statistics** tab.

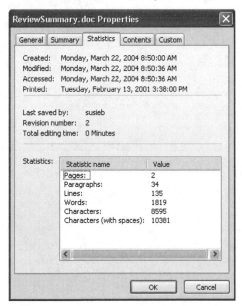

■ On the **Tools** menu, click **Word Count**.

2 Check the information you are interested in, and close the dialog box.

To track count information on the Word Count toolbar:

1 Right-click any toolbar, and click **Word Count** on the shortcut menu. The Word Count toolbar appears.

Tip You can also select the Show Toolbar check box in the Word Count dialog box or click Toolbars and then Word Count on the View menu to open this toolbar.

Recount

2 As you make changes to the document, click **Recount** on the Word Count toolbar to quickly update count information.

Practice Exercise

In this exercise, you will use three methods to check the word count of a document.

USE the *CheckCount* document in the *My Documents\Microsoft Press\MOS 2003 Study Guide\Word \W03C-5-2* practice file folder.

Open the *CheckCount* document, and then open the Word Count dialog box. Check the count information, and then select the **Show Toolbar** check box before closing the dialog box. Display the **Statistics** tab of the Properties dialog box, and compare the count information with that shown on the Word Count toolbar. Close the Properties dialog box. Delete several words from the document, and use the **Recount** button to update the information on the Word Count toolbar. Then close the *CheckCount* document without saving it.

Organize Documents Using File Folders

W03C-5-3   The skills measured by this objective include the following:

- ■ Creating a folder in which to save a document
- ■ Renaming or deleting a document or folder

When you are working in Word, you don't have to quit the program and use My Computer to create and manage the folders in which you store your files. You can perform most common organization tasks from within Word.

Creating a Folder in Which to Store a Document

To save a new document in Word, you click the Save button on the Standard toolbar or click the Save As command on the File menu. Either action displays the Save As dialog box, where you can name the file and indicate where you want to store it. To keep your documents organized and accessible, store related documents in a folder. You can create folders ahead of time in My Computer, or you can create them as you need them in the Save As dialog box.

Tip   You can also create and manage folders in the Open dialog box.

BE SURE TO open the document you want to work with before carrying out these steps.

To create a folder in which to save a document:

1   On the **File** menu, click **Save As**.

The Save As dialog box appears.

Tip   If this is the first time you have saved the document, you can also click the Save button on the Standard toolbar to display this dialog box.

Save

2   If you want to store the document in a subfolder of an existing folder, navigate to that folder and display its contents.

3   On the toolbar to the right of the **Save in** box, click the **Create New Folder** button.

Create New
Folder

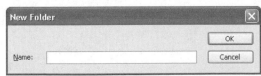

4 Type a name for the folder, and click **OK**.

Word makes the new folder the current folder.

5 Assign a name to the document, and click **Save**.

Practice Exercise

In this exercise, you will create a new folder while saving a document.

USE the *CreateFolder* document in the *My Documents\Microsoft Press\MOS 2003 Study Guide\Word \W03C-5-3* practice file folder.

Open the *CreateFolder* document, and then display the Save As dialog box. Navigate to the *My Documents\Microsoft Press\MOS 2003 Study Guide\Word\W03C-5-3* practice file folder, and create a new folder called **FirstFolder**. Back in the Save As dialog box, name the document **FirstSave**, and click **Save**. Then close the *CreateFolder* document.

Renaming or Deleting a Document or Folder

After creating a folder, you might decide that you want to change its name or that you no longer need it. Similarly, you might want to rename or delete a document. You can perform these organizational tasks from within Word in either the Save As or Open dialog box.

BE SURE TO start Word before carrying out these steps.

Tip To rename the current document, you use the Save As command on the File menu. You cannot use the following steps to rename or delete the current document or the folder containing the current document.

To rename a document or folder:

1 On the **File** menu, click **Open**.

The Open dialog box appears.

Open

Tip You can also click the Open button on the Standard toolbar to display this dialog box.

2 Navigate to the folder where the document or folder you want to rename is stored, and click it once.

3 On the toolbar to the right of the **Save in** box, click the **Tools** button, and then click **Rename** on the drop-down menu.

The document or folder is highlighted.

4 Enter the new name for the document or folder, and press **ENTER**.

To delete a document or folder:

1 On the **File** menu, click **Open**.

The Open dialog box appears.

2 Navigate to the folder where the document or folder you want to delete is stored, and click it once.

Tools ▾

3 On the toolbar to the right of the **Save in** box, click the **Tools** button, and then click **Delete** on the drop-down menu.

4 Click **Yes** to confirm deletion of the document or folder.

The document or folder is deleted.

Practice Exercise

In this exercise, you will rename a folder and delete the document it contains.

USE the *RenameFolder* folder and the *DeleteDocument* document in the *My Documents\Microsoft Press \MOS 2003 Study Guide\Word\W03C-5-3* practice file folder.

Display the Open dialog box, and navigate to the *My Documents\Microsoft Press \MOS 2003 Study Guide\Word\W03C-5-3* practice file folder. Click **RenameFolder** once in the list of documents and folders stored in the practice file folder, and change its name to **SecondFolder**. Then double-click **SecondFolder** to display its contents, and delete **DeleteDocument**. Confirm that you want to delete the document, and then close the Open dialog box.

Save Documents in Appropriate Formats for Different Uses

W03C-5-4   The skills measured by this objective include the following:

- ■ Saving a document for use in another program
- ■ Saving a document as a Web page

Because you might want to create a document in Word but be able to use it in another program, the Save As dialog box includes a "Save as type" setting that you use to easily change the document's file format.

Saving a Document for Use in Another Program

Being able to save a document in another file format is important if you share documents with people who use previous versions of Word (such as Word 6.0/95) or other programs (such as WordPerfect).

Tip   If you are not sure of the file format of a document, you can click Properties on the File menu and then click the General tab to display the format information.

BE SURE TO open the document you want to work with before carrying out these steps.

To save a document for use in another program:

1 On the **File** menu, click **Save As**.

The Save As dialog box appears.

2 In the **File name** box, type a new name for the document.

3 Click the **Save as type** down arrow, and click the file format you want to use.

4 Click **Save**.

Practice Exercise

In this exercise, you will save a document in Rich Text Format (*.rtf*), which can be read and interpreted by many popular programs.

USE the *SaveFormat* document in the *My Documents\Microsoft Press\MOS 2003 Study Guide\Word \W03C-5-4* practice file folder.

Open the *SaveFormat* document, and then open the Save As dialog box. Navigate to the *My Documents\Microsoft Press\MOS 2003 Study Guide\Word\W03C-5-4* practice file folder. Change **Save as type** to Rich Text Format, name the document **SaveRTF**, and click **Save**. Then close the *SaveRTF* document.

Saving a Document as a Web Page

You can save any Word document as a Web page so that it can be viewed in a Web browser such as Microsoft Internet Explorer. When you convert a document, most of the formatting is preserved, though some formatting, such as text wrapping around pictures and objects, is not converted and some features, such as table formatting, character formatting, page layout features, and security and document protection, are not supported by all Web browsers.

Tip If you know which Web browser people will use to view your Web page, it's a good idea to specify that browser and have Word disable any features that won't work.

By default, Word saves all items needed to create the Web page, such as graphics, in one file with the extension *.mht*. You can also save the Web page as a primary file with the extension *.htm* and a folder with the same name that holds all the items as separate files.

Tip If you move the Web page to another location, you must also move this folder; otherwise your Web browser won't be able to display the page.

BE SURE TO open the document you want to work with before carrying out these steps.

To specify a browser for the Web page:

1 On the **Tools** menu, click **Options**.

2 In the Options dialog box, click the **General** tab, and then click **Web Options**.

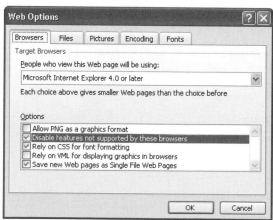

3   On the **Browsers** tab, click the **People who view this Web page will be using** down arrow, and then select the browser option you want.

4   In the **Options** list, verify that the **Disable features not supported by these browsers** check box is selected, and click **OK**.

5   Click **OK** to close the **Options** dialog box.

To convert a document to a Web page:

1   On the **File** menu, click **Save as Web Page**.

     The Save As dialog box appears.

2   Navigate to the location where you want to store the Web page.

3   Assign the page a file name.

4   To specify a Web page title that is different from the file name, click **Change Title**, type the title in the **Set Page Title** box, and click **OK**.

5   If you want to save the page as separate components instead of a single file, click the **Save as type** down arrow, and click **Web Page** in the drop-down list.

6   Click **Save**.

7   If a message tells you that some features in this document are not supported by the browser you specified, click **Continue**.

     The document appears in Word in Web Layout view.

Web Layout
View

     Tip   You can view a document in Web Layout view at any time by clicking the Web Layout View button in the lower-left corner of the document window, or by clicking Web Layout on the View menu.

Practice Exercise

In this exercise, you will set options for displaying a document in Microsoft Internet Explorer 5.0 or later. You will then save the document as a Web page.

USE the *CreateWeb* document in the *My Documents\Microsoft Press\MOS 2003 Study Guide\Word \W03C-5-4* practice file folder.

Open the *CreateWeb* document, and then display the Options dialog box. Click **Web Options**, and set the browser to **Microsoft Internet Explorer 5.0 or later**. Use the **Save as Web Page** command to open the Save As dialog box, navigate to the *My Documents\Microsoft Press \MOS 2003 Study Guide\Word\W03C-5-4* practice file folder, and name the Web page **WebDoc**. Change the page title to **The Garden Company**, and make sure the file format is **Web Page**. Click **Save**, and then click **Continue**. Scroll through the Web page to see the results, and then close it.

Print Documents, Envelopes, and Labels

W03C-5-5   The skills measured by this objective include the following:

■   Printing a document

■   Printing an envelope or label

Unless you are creating documents for electronic distribution, you will eventually want to print most documents. You can also print envelopes and labels for sending documents via the post office or a courier service.

Printing a Document

When you are satisfied with the way a document looks, you can print it by clicking the Print button on the Standard toolbar. Word then uses the settings specified in the Print dialog box and your computer's default printer to print the document. To view or change the print settings, open the Print dialog box, where you can change such settings as which printer to use, what to print, and how many copies to make.

BE SURE TO open the document you want to work with before carrying out these steps.

To print with custom settings:

Print

Tip If you want to use the default print settings, you can click the Print button on either the Standard or Print Preview toolbar.

1 On the **File** menu, click **Print**.

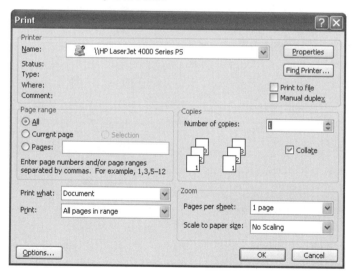

2 If you have more than one printer available to you and you want to switch printers, click the **Name** down arrow, and then click the printer you want in the drop-down list.

3 In the **Page Range** area, select the option you want.

Tip To print only specific pages of a document, select the Pages option, and then enter the page numbers you want to print, separated by commas.

4 In the **Copies** area, change the **Number of copies** setting appropriately.

5 Click **OK**.

Word prints the pages and number of copies you specified on the designated printer.

Practice Exercise

In this exercise, you will select a different printer and send the first page of a document to be printed.

USE the *PrintPage* document in the *My Documents\Microsoft Press\MOS 2003 Study Guide\Word\W03C-5-5* practice file folder.

Open the *PrintPage* document, and then open the Print dialog box. If you have more than one printer available to you, switch to a different one by clicking the **Name** down arrow and clicking the printer you want. Then select the **Current Page** option, set the number of copies to **2**, and click **OK**. Close the *PrintPage* document without saving it.

Printing an Envelope or Label

You can print an envelope or label using an address that you entered in a document. You can also enter the address directly in the Envelopes and Labels dialog box.

To provide a return address, Word uses the information that you entered when you installed Word. You can change that information on the User Information tab in the Options dialog box, which you open by clicking Options on the Tools menu.

BE SURE TO open a document containing the address you need before carrying out these steps.

To print an envelope using an address in a document:

1 Select the lines of the address.

Do not select any blank lines below the address.

2 On the **Tools** menu, click **Letters and Mailings** and then **Envelopes and Labels**.

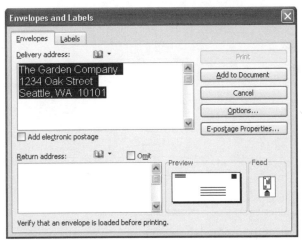

3 If you are using preprinted envelopes and don't want Word to print a return address, select the **Omit** check box.

4 Size 10 is the default envelope size. If you want to select a different envelope size, click **Options**, make your selection, and click **OK**.

5 Insert an envelope in the printer according to your printer manufacturer's directions.

6 Click **Print**.

To print an envelope from the Envelopes and Labels dialog box:

1 On the **Tools** menu, click **Letters and Mailings** and then **Envelopes and Labels**.

The Envelopes and Labels dialog box appears, with the insertion point in the "Delivery address" box.

2 Enter the address the way you want it to appear on the envelope.

3 In the **Return address** box, enter the address you want to appear, or select the **Omit** check box.

4 Click **Options**, and on the **Envelope Options** tab, select the envelope size and change the formatting as appropriate.

5 Click the **Printing Options** tab, and specify the method you are using to feed the envelope into the printer.

6 Click **OK**, and then click **Print**.

To print a label using an address in a document:

1 Select the lines of the address.

Do not select any blank lines below the address.

2 On the **Tools** menu, click **Letters and Mailings** and then **Envelopes and Labels**.

3 In the Envelopes and Labels dialog box, click the **Labels** tab.

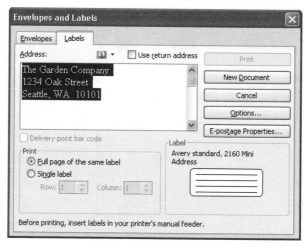

4 In the **Print** area, select the **Single label** option.

Row 1 and Column 1 appear under the "Single label" option.

Tip You can select "Full page of the same label" to print an entire sheet of labels using the same address.

5 Click **Options**, and enter information about the printer and type of labels you are using.

6 Click **OK**, and then click **Print**.

Practice Exercise

In this exercise, you will print an envelope based on an address entered in a document.

USE the *PrintEnvelope* document in the *My Documents\Microsoft Press\MOS 2003 Study Guide\Word \W03C-5-5* practice file folder.

Open the *PrintEnvelope* document. Select the customer address at the top of the letter, and display the Envelopes and Labels dialog box. Enter **The Garden Company, 1234 Oak Street, Seattle, WA 10101** as the return address. Change the font for both addresses to **Verdana**. Verify the printing options, and click **Print**. Close the *PrintEnvelope* document without saving it.

Preview Documents and Web Pages

W03C-5-6   The skills measured by this objective include the following:

- Previewing a document before printing
- Previewing a Web page before publishing

Before printing a document or publishing a Web page, you should verify that it looks the way you want. You can save time, money, and embarrassment by taking a few minutes to look over your work before setting it before the eyes of others.

Previewing a Document Before Printing

Print Preview shows you exactly how your text will be printed on each page. The Print Preview toolbar includes the tools to check the presentation of each page. You can change the layout by clicking the Page Setup button, and you can even change the text from this view.

BE SURE TO open the document you want to work with before carrying out these steps.

To preview a document before printing it:

Print
Preview

1   On the Standard toolbar, click the **Print Preview** button.

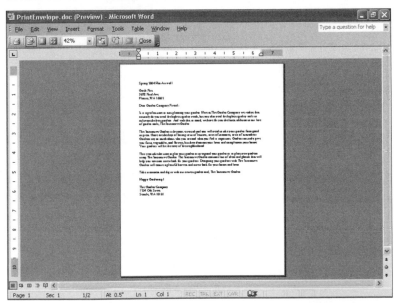

Multiple Pages

2 On the Print Preview toolbar, click the **Multiple Pages** button, and then click the box that represents the number of pages you want to see.

3 To zoom in, point to the page, and when the pointer becomes a magnifying glass, click. The Zoom percentage changes to 100%.

4 Click again to restore the original Zoom percentage.

5 Click the **Close Preview** button to return to the document.

Close Preview

Practice Exercise

In this exercise, you will preview a document before sending it to be printed.

USE the *ViewPages* document in the *My Documents\Microsoft Press\MOS 2003 Study Guide\Word\W03C-5-6* practice file folder.

Open the *ViewPages* document, and then open the Print Preview window. On the Print Preview toolbar, click the **Multiple Pages** button, and click the page box in the third column of the second row to display up to six pages. Point to the top of the first page of the document, and when the pointer becomes a magnifying glass, click to zoom to 100%. Click again to zoom back out, and then close Print Preview. Close the *ViewPages* document without saving it.

Previewing a Web Page for Publication

To see how a document will be displayed in a Web browser, you can preview it as a Web page.

Web Layout View

Tip While you are developing a document, you can also click the Web Layout View button in the lower-left corner of the document window to see how it will look.

BE SURE TO open the document you want to work with before carrying out these steps.

To preview a document as a Web page before publishing it:

1 On the **File** menu, click **Web Page Preview**.

The document is displayed in your Web browser as a Web page.

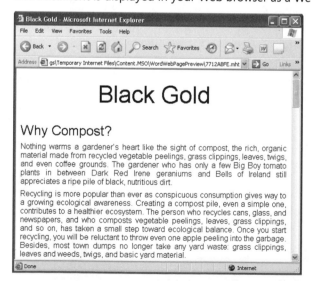

2   Test any hyperlinks by holding down the **CTRL** key and clicking the links.

3   Close the Web browser window.

Practice Exercise

In this exercise, you will preview a document as a Web page.

USE the *ViewWeb* document in the *My Documents\Microsoft Press\MOS 2003 Study Guide\Word\W03C-5-6* practice file folder.

Open the *ViewWeb* document, and click **Web Page Preview** to open it in your Web browser. Test the *entire stock* hyperlink, and then return to your original place in the document. Close the *ViewWeb* document without saving it.

Change and Organize Document Views and Windows

W03C-5-7   The skills measured by this objective include the following:

- ■ Switching views
- ■ Working in Print Layout view
- ■ Working in Reading Layout view
- ■ Arranging and splitting windows

To work efficiently in Word, it's a good idea to explore Word's views so that you have an idea of which one is most appropriate for which task. You can also manipulate the program window to set up the screen configuration that best suites your needs.

Switching Views

In Word, you can view a document in a variety of ways:

Print Layout View

- ■ Print Layout view displays a document on the screen the way it will look when printed.

Normal View

- ■ Normal view displays the content of a document with a simplified layout so that you can type and edit quickly.

Web Layout View

- ■ Web Layout view displays a document on the screen the way it will look when viewed in a Web browser.

Outline View

- ■ Outline view displays the structure of a document as nested levels of headings and body text, and it includes tools for viewing and changing its hierarchy.

Reading Layout

- ■ Reading Layout view displays as much of the content of the document as will fit on the screen at a size that is comfortable for reading.

You can easily switch from one view to another by clicking the view buttons in the lower-left corner of the document window or by clicking the corresponding command on the View menu.

123

Working in Print Layout View

In Print Layout view, you can see elements such as margins, page breaks, headers and footers, and watermarks as well as the text of the document. All formatting is displayed as it will be when printed, so you can accurately gauge the final effect.

When you are creating a document in Print Layout view, you might want to increase the magnification of the page by zooming in on a particular element, or you might want to decrease the magnification by zooming out. You might want to display hidden text and non-printing formatting characters to make it easier to position the insertion point while editing. You might also want to hide the white space between pages so that you can scroll through the document more quickly. However, you should turn off hidden text and non-printing formatting characters and restore the while space between pages so that you can check the document before you print it.

BE SURE TO open the document you want to work with in Print Layout view before carrying out these steps.

To compare Print Layout view and Normal view:

1 In the lower-left corner of the document window, click the **Normal View** button, or on the **View** menu, click **Normal**.

Normal View

2 Scroll through the document.

You can see the basic content of the document without any extraneous elements. The active area on the ruler indicates the width of the text column, dotted lines indicate page breaks, and scrolling is quick and easy.

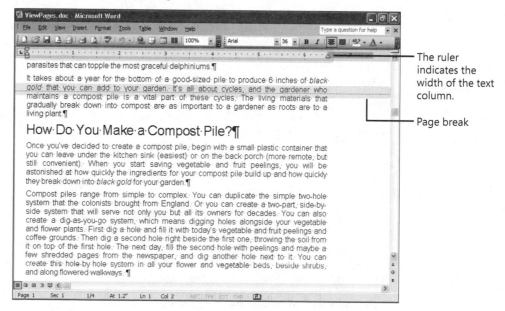

The ruler indicates the width of the text column.

Page break

Print Layout
View

3   In the lower-left corner of the document window, click the **Print Layout View** button, or on the **View** menu, click **Print Layout**.

4   Scroll through the document.

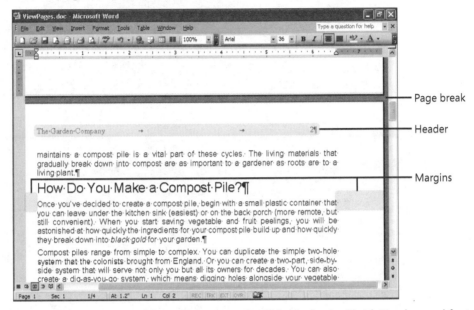

- Page break
- Header
- Margins

You can see the content of the document as it will look when printed. Headers and footers, footnotes, watermarks, and so on, are all shown in place.

To zoom in and out:

Zoom

1   On the Standard toolbar, click the **Zoom** down arrow, and click the percentage you want.

The screen changes to display the text of the document at the size you specified.

2   To zoom to a non-standard size, click the **Zoom** box, type the percentage you want, and press **ENTER**.

Tip   You can change the magnification in each view independently.

3   To return to the default percentage, click the **Zoom** down arrow, and click **100%**.

To reveal non-printing formatting characters and hidden text:

Show/Hide ¶

1   On the Standard toolbar, click the **Show/Hide ¶** button.

2   Click the **Show/Hide ¶** button again to turn off the display of these elements.

To hide or display white space between pages:

1   On the **Tools** menu, click **Options**.

2   On the **View** tab of the Options dialog box, clear the **White space between pages** check box.

3   Click **OK**.

125

The white space at the top and bottom of each page and the gray space between pages is hidden.

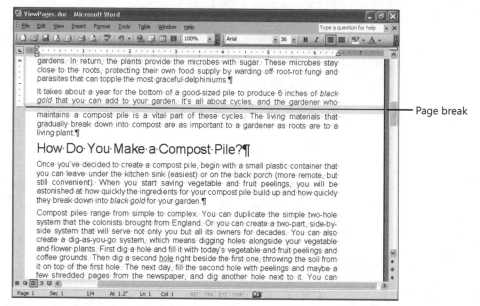

Page break

4   Restore the white space by clicking **Options** on the **Tools** menu, selecting the **White space between pages** check box, and clicking **OK**.

Tip   You can also show or hide the white space by pointing between the pages and clicking when a ScreenTip that says Show White Space or Hide White Space appears.

Practice Exercise

In this exercise, you will hide the white space between pages, reveal hidden text, and change the zoom percentage.

USE the *ViewDocument* document in the *My Documents\Microsoft Press\MOS 2003 Study Guide\Word \W03C-5-7* practice file folder.

Open the *ViewDocument* document. Display the **View** tab of the Options dialog box, and turn off the **White space between pages** option. Then turn on hidden text and non-printing formatting characters. Zoom the document to **200%**, and then zoom it to 40% by typing **40** in the **Zoom** box and pressing **ENTER**. Close the *ViewDocument* document without saving it.

Working in Reading Layout View

Reading Layout view is designed to make it easy to read documents on screens of all sizes, including those of hand-held e-book devices. In this view, you have access to the Reading Layout and Reviewing toolbars, which you can use to adjust the view, display page thumbnails, search the document, display the Document Map, and suggest changes.

See Also   For information about thumbnails and the Document Map, refer to W03E-2-5, "Use Automated Tools for Document Navigation."

BE SURE TO open the document you want to work with before carrying out these steps.

To use Reading Layout view:

Reading Layout

1   In the lower-left corner of the document window, click the **Reading Layout** button, or on the **View** menu, click **Reading Layout**.

Tip   You can also click the Read button on the Standard toolbar.

The screen changes to display the document in Reading Layout view, and the Reading Layout and Reviewing toolbars appear.

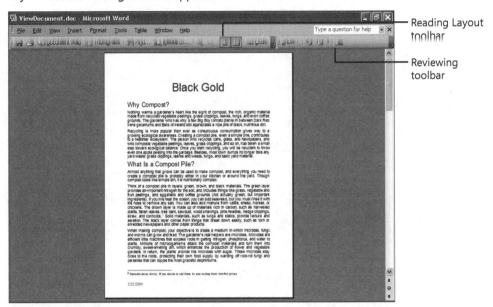

Reading Layout toolbar

Reviewing toolbar

Allow Multiple Pages

2   To see multiple pages, click all active buttons on the Reading Layout toolbar to toggle them off, and then click the **Allow Multiple Pages** button.

3   To see thumbnails of the pages, click the **Thumbnails** button.

4   To return to the previous view, click the **Close** button on the Reading Layout toolbar.

Practice Exercise

In this exercise, you will explore Reading Layout view by displaying the same document in various ways.

USE the *ReadDocument* document in the *My Documents\Microsoft Press\MOS 2003 Study Guide\Word \W03C-5-7* practice file folder.

Open the *ReadDocument* document, and switch to Reading Layout view. Click buttons on the Reading Layout toolbar, noticing each button's effect on your view of the document. Then close Reading Layout view, and close the *ReadDocument* document without saving it.

Arranging and Splitting Windows

When you open a document, a program button with the Word program icon and the document's name appears on the taskbar. You can have many documents open at the same time, but only one is the current or active document. To activate a different open document, you click its program button on the taskbar, or use the Window menu, which lists all open documents and indicates the active document with a check mark to the left of its name.

If you want to see parts of all the open documents at the same time, you can use the Arrange All command on the Window menu to arrange their windows on the screen. If you want to see different parts of the same document at the same time, you have two choices:

- Open the document in a new window, and then arrange the windows.
- Split the document window into panes that you can work in independently.

BE SURE TO open at least two documents before carrying out these steps.

To arrange the windows of all open documents:

1 On the **Window** menu, click **Arrange All**.

The windows of the open documents are sized and stacked one on top of the other. Each window has a menu bar, toolbars, and scroll bars, so you can work on each document independently.

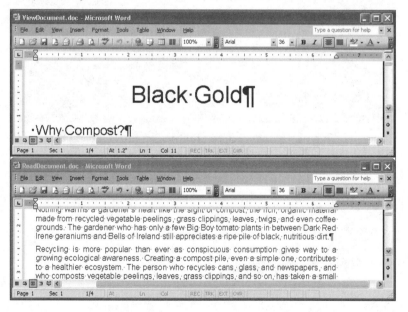

> **Tip**   The Arrange All command arranges all the open windows, so be sure to close any you don't want included in the arrangement before clicking the command.

Maximize

2   To view just one window again, activate the window you want to view, and click its **Maximize** button.

To open the active document in a new window:

1   On the **Window** menu, click **New Window**.

Word opens the document in a new window, with the name of the document followed by *:2* in the title bar.

2   To arrange the two document windows, click **Arrange All** on the **Window** menu.

To split the active document window:

1   On the **Window** menu, click **Split**.

The pointer becomes a split bar across the document window.

2   Move the mouse to position the split where you want it, and click to fix the bar's location.

Each pane of the window has its own set of scroll bars so that you can work on a different part of the document in each pane.

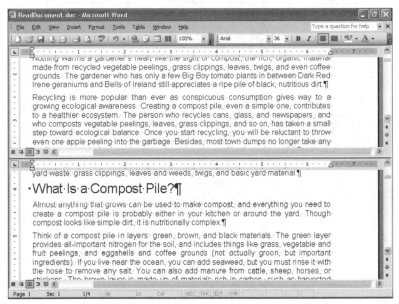

3   To remove the split and restore a single pane, click **Remove Split** on the **Window** menu.

Practice Exercise

In this exercise, you will open the same document in more than one window, arrange the open windows, and view parts of the same document in different panes.

USE the *ArrangeWindow1* and *ArrangeWindow2* documents in the *My Documents\Microsoft Press \MOS 2003 Study Guide\Word\W03C-5-7* practice file folder.

Open the *ArrangeWindow1* and *ArrangeWindow2* documents. With *ArrangeWindow1* active, open a new window for this document. Then arrange all three open windows. Activate and maximize *ArrangeWindow2*, and then split its window in half. Click the bottom pane, and press **CTRL+END** to scroll that pane to the end of the document. Then remove the split so that the document is displayed in a single pane again. Close the *ArrangeWindow1* and *ArrangeWindow2* documents without saving them.

W03C-5 Review

Number	Objective	Mastered
W03C-5-1	Create new documents using templates	
	Creating a new document based on a template	❏
W03C-5-2	Review and modify document properties	
	Reviewing and modifying summary information	❏
	Checking word, paragraph, and character counts	❏
W03C-5-3	Organize documents using file folders	
	Creating a folder in which to save a document	❏
	Renaming or deleting a document or folder	❏
W03C-5-4	Save documents in appropriate formats for different uses	
	Saving a document for use in another program	❏
	Saving a document as a Web page	❏
W03C-5-5	Print documents, envelopes, and labels	
	Printing a document	❏
	Printing an envelope or label	❏
W03C-5-6	Preview documents and Web pages	
	Previewing a document before printing	❏
	Previewing a Web page before publishing	❏
W03C-5-7	Change and organize document views and windows	
	Switching views	❏
	Working in Print Layout view	❏
	Working in Reading Layout view	❏
	Arranging and splitting windows	❏

Part II

Microsoft Office Specialist Word 2003 Expert Exam

This part of the book covers the skills you need to have for certification as a Microsoft Office Specialist in Microsoft Office Word 2003 at the expert level. Specifically, you will need to be able to complete tasks that require the following skills:

Number	Skill Set
W03E-1	Formatting content
W03E-2	Organizing content
W03E-3	Formatting documents
W03E-4	Collaborating
W03E-5	Customizing Word

You can use these more advanced skills to create almost any document used in a business environment.

Knowledge You Need Before Studying for This Exam

Before you begin studying for this exam, you should have mastered all the skills required for Microsoft Office Specialist certification in Word 2003 at the core level. You might want to review Part I: "Microsoft Office Specialist Word 2003 Core Exam" on page 1.

W03E-1
Formatting Content

The skills tested by this section of the Microsoft Office Specialist Word 2003 Expert Exam all relate to advanced formatting of documents and their content. Specifically, the following objectives are associated with this set of skills:

Number	Objective
W03E-1-1	Create custom styles for text, tables, and lists
W03E-1-2	Control pagination
W03E-1-3	Format, position, and resize graphics using advanced layout features
W03E-1-4	Insert and modify objects
W03E-1-5	Create and modify diagrams and charts using data from other sources

Important   Before you can do the practice exercises associated with this skill set, you need to install the practice files from the book's companion CD to their default location. See "Installing the Practice Files" on page xxv for more information.

Create Custom Styles for Text, Tables, and Lists

W03E-1-1   The skills measured by this objective include the following:

- Creating character and paragraph styles
- Creating table styles
- Creating list styles

Using styles is an efficient way of applying multiple formatting attributes at once and of maintaining formatting consistency. To give your documents a custom look, you can easily create your own styles.

Creating Character and Paragraph Styles

When Word's predefined styles don't quite meet your needs, you can create new ones in several ways:

- You can create a new style based on an existing one.
- You can format text the way you want it and then create a style that reflects the look of the text.
- You can define a style from scratch by using the New Style dialog box to specify the character and paragraph formatting for the style.

BE SURE TO open the document for which you want to create styles before carrying out these steps.

To create a new style based on an existing style:

1 Click a paragraph to which the style you want to modify is applied.

2 On the **Format** menu, click **Styles and Formatting**.

The Styles and Formatting task pane appears.

3 In the Styles and Formatting task pane, click **New Style**.

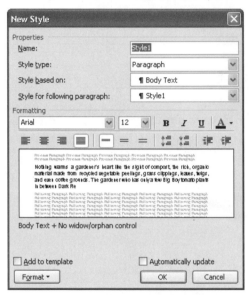

4 In the **Name** box, type a name for the new style.

5 In the **Formatting** area, change options to define the style.

6 Click **OK** to close the New Style dialog box.

The new style appears in the Styles and Formatting task pane, ready to be applied to other paragraphs.

To create a new style based on formatted text:

1 Select the formatted text on which the new style will be based.

2 On the **Format** menu, click **Styles and Formatting**.

The Style and Formatting task pane appears, with a blue box around the style of the selected text in the "Pick formatting to apply" box.

3   Point to the style, click its down arrow, and then click **Modify**.

4   In the **Properties** area, type a name for the new style, and click **OK**.

To create a new style from scratch:

1   On the **Format** menu, click **Styles and Formatting**.

The Styles and Formatting task pane appears.

2   In the Styles and Formatting task pane, click **New Style**.

3   In the **Properties** area of the New Style dialog box, type a name for the style.

4   In the **Formatting** area, select the character and paragraph formatting you want to be part of the new style.

5   Click the **Format** button, and click **Font**.

6   In the Font dialog box, make further refinements to the style.

   Tip   You can also add paragraph, numbering, and other formatting.

7   Click **OK**.

The new style appears in the Styles and Formatting task pane.

Practice Exercise

In this exercise, you will modify an existing style to create a new one, and then apply the new style to multiple paragraphs.

USE the *CreateStyle* document in the *My Documents\Microsoft Press\MOS 2003 Study Guide\Word \W03E-1-1* practice file folder.

Open the *CreateStyle* document. Select the **Why Compost?**, **What Is a Compost Pile?**, **How Do You Make a Compost Pile?**, **Hot or Cold?**, and **Compost and Soil** headings. Then open the Styles and Formatting task pane, and apply the **Heading 2** style to all the selected headings. Create a new style called **Heading 2 Plus** that is based on Heading 2 but is 16 points and blue. Apply the new style to the selected paragraphs. Then modify the **Heading 2 Plus** style by removing the **Italic** attribute, updating all the paragraphs to which the style is applied. Then close the *CreateStyle* document without saving it.

Creating Table Styles

You can easily change the appearance of a table by applying one of the many predefined table autoformats. As with styles, if you can't find exactly what you're looking for, you can easily modify an existing autoformat or create a whole new one.

BE SURE TO open a document containing a table before carrying out these steps.

To create a table style:

1   Click in the table for which you want to create a new table style.

2   On the **Table** menu, click **Table AutoFormat**.

3   In the Table AutoFormat dialog box, click **New**.

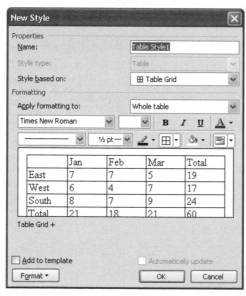

4   In the **Properties** area, type a name for your new style.

5 Click the **Style based on** down arrow, and click the autoformat on which you want to base the new style.

6 In the **Formatting** area, click the **Apply formatting to** down arrow, and select the area of the table to which you want to apply the style.

7 Change the formatting options to create the look you want, and click **OK**.

8 Preview your new style, and then click **Apply** to close the Table Autoformat dialog box.

The new style is applied to the table.

Practice Exercise

In this exercise, you will create and apply a new table style.

USE the *CreateTableStyle* document in the *My Documents\Microsoft Press\MOS 2003 Study Guide\Word \W03E-1-1* practice file folder.

Open the *CreateTableStyle* document, and with an insertion point in the first table, apply the **Table Classic 1** autoformat to the entire table. Modify the style so that the fill color in the header row is a pale green and the text in the Total row is red. Then close the *CreateTableStyle* document without saving it.

Creating List Styles

If none of the list styles in the Bullets and Numbering dialog box meets your needs, you can define a new style for a bulleted or numbered list by using the formatting options available through the Customize menu.

BE SURE TO open a document containing a list before carrying out these steps.

To create a list style:

1 Click anywhere in the list.

2 On the **Format** menu, click **Bullets and Numbering**, and then click the **List Styles** tab.

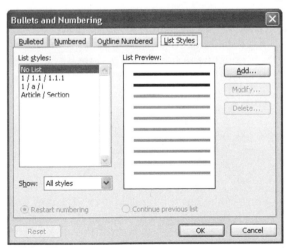

3   Click **Add**.

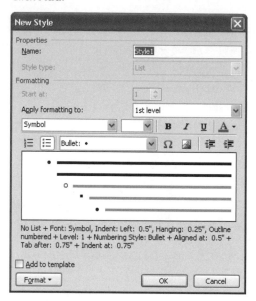

4   Name the new style, select the formatting you want to apply to each level of the list, and click **OK**.

5   View the format of your new style, then click **OK**.

The Bullets and Numbering dialog box closes, and the new style is applied to your list.

Practice Exercise

In this exercise, you will create and apply a new list style.

USE the *CreateListStyle* document in the *My Documents\Microsoft Press\MOS 2003 Study Guide\Word \W03E-1-1* practice file folder.

Open the *CreateListStyle* document, and click anywhere in the first bulleted item. Add a new list style named **Bullet2**. Change the bullet to a checkmark, the font to red, and the size to 18 points. Check how the first bullet item now looks, and then apply the new style to the remaining bullet items. Then close the *CreateListStyle* document without saving it.

Control Pagination

W03E-1-2   The skills measured by this objective include the following:

■ Controlling orphans and widows

■ Keeping paragraphs together

You can control pagination precisely by inserting manual page breaks. However, this process is tedious when working with longer documents, especially if editorial changes mean that page breaks constantly need to be relocated. You can avoid having to insert manual page breaks by setting options that more precisely control Word's pagination.

Controlling Orphans and Widows

Whether you allow Word to paginate your documents or you insert your own manual page breaks, you should make sure that the page breaks do not leave widows and orphans. Word defines a widow as the last line of a paragraph printed by itself at the top of a page and an orphan as the first line of a paragraph printed by itself at the bottom of a page.

See Also For information about manually breaking pages, refer to W03C-3-5, "Modify Document Layout and Page Setup."

BE SURE TO open the document in which you want to control pagination before carrying out these steps.

To control widows and orphans:

1 On the **Edit** menu, click **Select All**.

2 On the **Format** menu, click **Paragraph**, and then click the **Line and Page Breaks** tab.

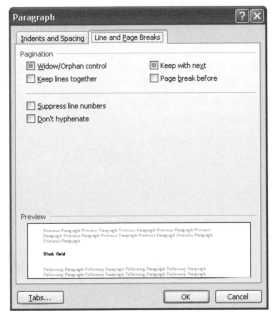

3 Select the **Widow/Orphan control** check box, and click **OK**.

Practice Exercise

In this exercise, you will ensure that Word prevents widows and orphans from occurring at the tops and bottoms of pages.

USE the *ControlWidow* document in the *My Documents\Microsoft Press\MOS 2003 Study Guide\Word \W03E-1-2* practice file folder.

Open the *ControlWidow* document, and scroll through the document, noticing any widows or orphans. Select the entire document, and then display the **Line and Page Breaks** tab of the Paragraph dialog box. Turn on widow and orphan control, and scroll through the document again. Then close the *ControlWidow* document without saving it.

Keeping Paragraphs Together

In addition to controlling widows and orphans, you can specify where page breaks are allowed in relation to a particular paragraph in a document:

- You can prevent a page break within a paragraph.
- You can prevent a page break between the selected paragraph and the following paragraph.
- You can tell Word to insert a page break before the selected paragraph.

  Tip You can apply the options in the Paragraph dialog box to individual paragraphs, or you can incorporate them into paragraph styles.

BE SURE TO open the document in which you want to control pagination before carrying out these steps.

To keep paragraphs together:

1 Click the paragraph for which you want to control page breaks.

2 On the **Format** menu, click **Paragraph**, and then click the **Line and Page Breaks** tab.

3 Do any of the following:

- To prevent a page break within the paragraph, select the **Keep lines together** check box.

- To prevent a page break between the selected paragraph and the following one, select the **Keep with next** check box.

- To force a page break before the selected paragraph, select the **Page break before** check box.

4 Click **OK**.

Practice Exercise

In this exercise, you will make sure that all the headings in a document appear on the same page as the paragraphs that follow them.

USE the *KeepParagraphs* document in the *My Documents\Microsoft Press\MOS 2003 Study Guide\Word \W03E-1-2* practice file folder.

Open the *KeepParagraphs* document, and select the **Why Compost?**, **What Is a Compost Pile?**, **How Do You Make a Compost Pile?**, **What's the Cost?**, **Hot or Cold?**, and **Compost and Soil** headings. Then display the **Line and Page Breaks** tab of the Paragraph dialog box, and select the **Keep with next** check box. Then close the *KeepParagraphs* document without saving it.

Format, Position, and Resize Graphics Using Advanced Layout Features

W03E-1-3   The skills measured by this objective include the following:

- Sizing, scaling, cropping, and rotating a graphic
- Controlling contrast and brightness
- Positioning a graphic in relation to the surrounding text

You can position graphics approximately by dragging them, and you can resize them visually by using their sizing handles. However, for more precise control over position, size, and other graphic attributes, you need to be familiar with the advanced options in the Format Picture dialog box.

Sizing, Scaling, Cropping, and Rotating a Graphic

After you insert any graphic into a document, you can click it to select it and then open the Format Picture dialog box, where you can make the following changes:

- You can change a graphic's size by entering either absolute dimensions or a scaling percentage.
- You can crop away parts of a graphic that you don't want.
- You can rotate a graphic.

BE SURE TO open a document containing a graphic before carrying out these steps.

To size a graphic:

1   Click the graphic to select it.

2   Point to one of the sizing handles, and when the pointer changes to a double arrow, drag until the graphic is the size you want.

To scale a graphic:

1   Click the graphic to select it.

2   Point to one of the corner sizing handles, and when the pointer changes to a double arrow, hold down the **CTRL** key while you drag to change the size of the graphic.

To crop a graphic:

1   Click the graphic to select it and to display the Picture toolbar.

   Tip   If the Picture toolbar doesn't appear, click Toolbars and then Picture on the View menu.

Crop

2   On the Picture toolbar, click the **Crop** button.

3   Use the cropping pointer to drag one of the cropping handles inward to crop away the part of the graphic you don't want.

4   Click outside the graphic to deselect it.

To rotate a graphic:

1   Right-click the graphic, click **Format Picture** on the shortcut menu, and if necessary, click the **Size** tab.

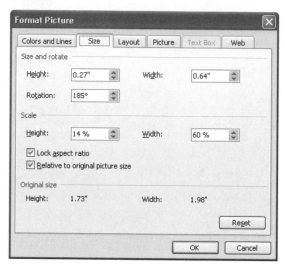

2   In the **Rotation** box, use the arrows to select the desired degree of rotation, and click **OK**. The graphic is rotated to the degree you selected.

Rotate

Tip   To rotate a graphic in 90-degree increments, you can use the Rotate button on the Picture toolbar.

Practice Exercise

In this exercise, you'll insert a piece of clip art, change its size, crop away parts of it, and rotate it to create the effect you want.

USE the *SizeClipArt* document in the *My Documents\Microsoft Press\MOS 2003 Study Guide\Word \W03E-1-3* practice file folder.

Open the *SizeClipArt* document. Use the **Insert Clip Art** button on the Drawing toolbar to search for clip art with the keyword **plant**, and insert the drawing of two brown leaves. With the graphic selected, hold down the **CTRL** key while dragging to scale the graphic to approximately 0.5" by 0.6". Then crop the bottom leaf away from the graphic, and use the **Rotate** button to rotate the graphic until the stem of the leaf is at the bottom of the picture. Display the **Size** tab of the Format Picture dialog box, and refine the degree of rotation to 185. Then drag the leaf graphic to the right of *Memorandum*. Close the *SizeClipArt* document without saving it.

Controlling Contrast and Brightness

Sometimes the colors in a graphic might be too bright or too muted for your document. Although you cannot make radical color changes to most graphics from within Word, you can manipulate their contrast and brightness by using buttons on the Picture toolbar.

BE SURE TO open a document containing a graphic before carrying out these steps.

To control contrast and brightness:

Color

1 On the Picture toolbar, click the **Color** button, and then click **Washout**.

The picture's colors decrease in intensity.

2 To control the brightness of the graphic, do one of the following:

Less
Brightness

■ To decrease the brightness, click the **Less Brightness** button on the Picture toolbar.

■ To increase the brightness, click the **More Brightness** button.

More
Brightness

3 To control the contrast of the graphic, do one of the following:

■ To decrease the contrast, click the **Less Contrast** button on the Picture toolbar.

Less
Contrast

■ To increase the contrast, click the **More Contrast** button.

More
Contrast

Tip Click the Reset Picture button on the Picture toolbar to restore the graphic to its original format. Any manual changes you have made will be lost.

Practice Exercise

In this exercise, you will experiment with the colors in a logo.

USE the *ColorGraphic* document in the *My Documents\Microsoft Press\MOS 2003 Study Guide\Word \W03E-1-3* practice file folder.

Open the *ColorGraphic* document. Click The Garden Company logo to select it, and make sure the Picture toolbar is displayed. Use the **Color** button to create a washout effect, and then reduce the logo's brightness and increase its contrast. Close the *ColorGraphic* document without saving it.

Positioning a Graphic in Relation to the Surrounding Text

After you insert a graphic into a document, you can use the Layout tab of the Format Picture dialog box to wrap text around it. There are seven different text-wrapping styles, and you can wrap text on both sides of a graphic, on one side of a graphic, or on the largest side of a graphic. In addition, you can set the distance between the edge of a graphic and the text itself.

You can specify that a graphic be positioned in one of two ways:

■ Absolutely, which positions the graphic according to measurements you set.

■ Relatively, which positions the graphic in relationship to another element of the document, such as the margin, the page, a column, or a particular character.

After you have positioned the graphic, adding text might upset the alignment. To prevent this, you can specify whether the graphic should remain anchored in its position on the page or should move with its related text. You can also specify whether the graphic should be allowed to overlap text.

BE SURE TO open a document containing a graphic before carrying out these steps.

To set the text-wrapping style:

Format
Picture

1 On the Picture toolbar, click the **Format Picture** button, and then the Format Picture dialog box appears, click the **Layout** tab.

2 Click **Advanced**.

3 Click a wrapping style.

4 In the **Wrap text** area, select the option you want.

5 Click **OK** to close the Advanced Layout dialog box, and then click **OK** again to close the Format Picture dialog box.

To align a graphic absolutely or relatively:

Format
Picture

1 On the Picture toolbar, click the **Format Picture** button, and click the **Layout** tab.

2 Click **Advanced**, and then click the **Picture Position** tab.

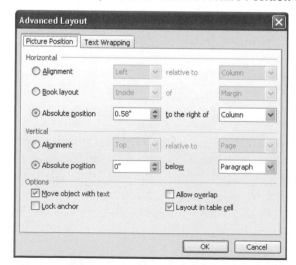

3   In the **Horizontal** area, do one of the following:

■ To position the graphic relatively, select the **Alignment** option, click the down arrow to its right, and then click the type of alignment you want. In the same area, click the **relative to** down arrow, and click the appropriate element in the drop-down list.

■ To position the graphic absolutely, select the **Absolute position** option, and type a measurement in the box to the right. In the same area, change the setting in the **to the right of** box to the appropriate element.

4   Repeat step 3 in the **Vertical** area.

The graphic is repositioned according to your specifications.

5   If you want the graphic to remain in place and not move with its associated text, select the **Lock anchor** check box in the **Options** area.

6   Click **OK** to close the Advanced Layout dialog box, and then click **OK** again to close the Format Picture dialog box.

Practice Exercise

In this exercise, you will modify the position and text-wrapping style of a graphic that has already been inserted into a document.

USE the *AlignGraphic* document in the *My Documents\Microsoft Press\MOS Study Guide\Word\W03E-1-3* practice file folder.

Open the *AlignGraphic* document, and click the logo for The Garden Company to select it. Display the **Layout** tab of the Format Picture dialog box, and then display the Advanced Layout dialog box. Wrap the text tightly on both sides. Then on the **Picture Position** tab, set the horizontal **Alignment** option to **Right** relative to **Margin**. Back in the document, click to the left of the word *The* at the beginning of the first paragraph, and press **ENTER**, noticing that the graphic moves with the text. Then close the *AlignGraphic* document without saving it.

Insert and Modify Objects

W03E-1-4   The skills measured by this objective include the following:

■ Inserting and modifying a new object

■ Inserting and modifying an object from a file

You can embed a variety of objects into a Word document including tables, charts, graphics, and sound or video clips. You can also create new objects on the fly while you are working on a Word document, or you can use existing files.

Inserting and Modifying a New Object

Sometimes you might want to use the tools available in other programs to create the object you need for a Word document. For example, you can perform simple calculations in a Word table, but if your table requires more complex calculations, you can create the table as an Excel worksheet object and take advantage of Excel's sophisticated functions.

BE SURE TO open the document in which you want to insert an object before carrying out these steps.

To insert a new object:

1 Click where you want to place the object.

2 On the **Insert** menu, click **Object**, and click the **Create New** tab.

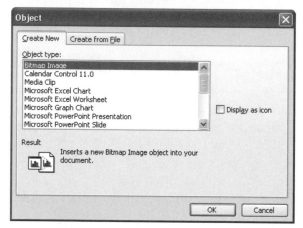

3 In the **Object type** list, click the type of object you want to embed.

4 Select the **Display as icon** check box if you want the embedded object to appear in the document as an icon.

5 Click **OK**.

Word opens the program you need to create the object within Word.

6 Create the new object, and then click a blank area of the document to deselect your object.

To modify an object you have created:

1 Double-click the object.

The object opens in the program in which you created it.

Tip You can also open the source program by right-clicking the object, clicking its type on the shortcut menu, and then clicking Edit.

2 Make any necessary changes, and then click outside the object to deselect it.

Practice Exercise

In this exercise, you will insert a new blank spreadsheet object into a document and then enter and edit data in it.

USE the *CreateObject* document in the *My Documents\Microsoft Press\MOS 2003 Study Guide \Word\W03E-1-4* practice file folder.

Open the *CreateObject* document, and add a blank line below the first full paragraph. Display the **Create New** tab of the Object dialog box, and select **Microsoft Excel Spreadsheet** as the object type. Starting in cell **A1** of the new worksheet, enter these headings in column **A: Order Amount, $15.00 and under, $16.00 to $50.00**, and **over $50.00**. Then starting in cell

B1, enter the following in column **B**: **Shipping Fees**, **$3.95**, **$4.95**, and **$6.95**. Size the worksheet so only the columns and rows with data are visible, and then click outside the object to deselect it. Double-click the object, change the heading in **B2** to **Shipping and Handling**, and resize the worksheet. In the document, press **ENTER** to add a blank line below the worksheet. Then close the *CreateObject* document without saving it.

Inserting and Modifying an Object from a File

When you need to use information that exists in another file in a Word document, you can create an object based on that file. There are two ways to insert an object that exists in another file into a Word document:

- You can create a link between the source file and the Word document. A linked object maintains a direct connection to the source file, and the Word file displays the data stored there. If you want to update the data, you do it in the source file. Then when you open the Word document, the linked object is updated.

- You can embed the source file in the Word document. The contents of the source file then exist as an object in the document, rather than as a separate file. If you want to update the data, you do it in the Word document, manipulating it with the program that you used to create the source file.

Whether you should link or embed an object depends on whether the information in the Word document must be synchronized with the information in the source file.

BE SURE TO open the document in which you want to work and have available a file that you want to insert as an object before carrying out these steps.

To insert an object from a file:

1   On the **Insert** menu, click **Object**, and then click the **Create from File** tab.

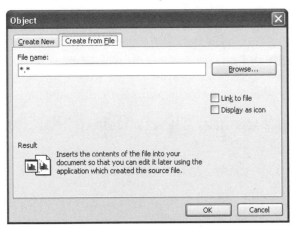

2   Click **Browse**, navigate to the folder where the file is stored, and then double-click the file. The file's name appears in the "File name" box.

3   If you want to maintain a link to the source file, select the **Link to file** check box.

4   If you want the object to be represented by an icon in the Word document, select the **Display as icon** check box.

5   Click **OK**.

The object appears in the document.

To modify a linked object:

1   Double-click anywhere in the object.

The object's source file opens in the program that created it.

2   Make the necessary changes.

3   Click outside the object to deselect it.

To modify an embedded object:

1   Double-click anywhere in the object.

The tools of the program that created the object become available from within Word.

2   Make the necessary changes.

3   Click the Word document to deselect and display the updated object.

Practice Exercise

In this exercise, you will embed an Excel worksheet in a Word document and then change the worksheet data.

USE the *InsertData* document and the *Worksheet* workbook in the *My Documents\Microsoft Press \MOS 2003 Study Guide\Word\W03E-1-4* practice file folder.

Open the *InsertData* document, and display the **Create from File** tab of the Object dialog box. Browse to the *My Documents\Microsoft Press\MOS 2003 Study Guide\Word\W03E-1-4* practice file folder, and double-click the **Worksheet** file. Back in the Object dialog box, make sure the **Link to file** and **Display as icon** check boxes are not selected, and click **OK**. Scroll up to see the beginning of the worksheet object, and double-click it. Click cell **B4**, type **10000**, and press the **ENTER** key. After Excel recalculates the data in the table to show the payment schedule for a $10,000 loan, click anywhere outside the Excel worksheet to display the updated table. Then close the *InsertData* document without saving it.

Create and Modify Diagrams and Charts Using Data from Other Sources

W03E-1-5   The skills measured by this objective include the following:

- ■ Importing data to create a chart
- ■ Linking a chart to data from another source

If the data you want to use in a chart or diagram already exists, you can recycle that data instead of having to create it from scratch.

Importing Data to Create a Chart

Instead of typing data in a datasheet to create a chart, you can enter data by importing it from another source, such as a Word table, a Microsoft Excel workbook, or a Microsoft Access database. You can create a new chart based on the imported data, or you can append the imported data to an existing datasheet to update a chart.

No link is maintained between imported data and its source file. If you want to modify a chart that is based on imported data, you activate the chart in Graph and edit the data in the datasheet as usual.

BE SURE TO open the document you want to work with before carrying out these steps.

Tip The import process varies depending on the type of data you are importing. The following steps assume you are importing data from an Excel worksheet.

To import chart data:

1   Click the location where you want the chart to appear in the document.

2   On the **Insert** menu, click **Picture** and then **Chart**.

A sample chart and datasheet appear.

Import File

3   In the datasheet, click the first cell in the first row, and on Graph's Standard toolbar, click the **Import File** button to open the Import File dialog box.

4   Navigate to the folder where the data you want to import is stored, and double-click the file.

The Import Data Options dialog box appears. In the case of an Excel workbook, the dialog box lists the worksheets in the workbook.

5   In the **Select sheet from workbook** box, click (don't double-click) the worksheet you want to import.

6   Select the **Range** option, and type the cell range in the adjacent box.

7   With the **Overwrite existing cells** check box selected, click **OK**.

Tip To append the imported data to existing data in a datasheet, clear the "Overwrite existing cells" check box.

8   The data from the Excel worksheet appears in the datasheet and is plotted in the chart.

To modify imported chart data:

View
Datasheet

1   Double-click the chart to activate it in Graph.

2   If the datasheet is not visible, click the **View Datasheet** button on Graph's Standard toolbar.

3   Edit the data in the datasheet to update the chart.

Practice Exercise

In this exercise, you will import data stored in a range of cells in an Excel worksheet into a chart in a Word document.

USE the *ImportData* document and the *Workbook* file in the *My Documents\Microsoft Press\MOS 2003 Study Guide\Word\W03E-1-5* practice file folder.

Open the *ImportData* document. Move to the end of the document, and then double-click the chart to activate it in Microsoft Graph. Move the datasheet upward, and then adjust its size until you can see about 18 rows. Click the first cell in row 9, and display the Import File dialog box. Navigate to the *My Documents\Microsoft Press\MOS 2003 Study Guide\Word\W03E-1-5* practice file folder, and double-click the **Workbook** file. In the **Select sheet from workbook** box, click (don't double-click) **weeks 9-12**. Then select the **Range** option, and type **A2:D5** in the adjacent box. Clear the **Overwrite existing cells** check box to add the incoming data to the existing chart data, and click **OK**. Adjust the chart as necessary to be able to clearly see the new data, and then close the *ImportData* document without saving it.

Linking a Chart to Data from Another Source

Instead of importing data for a chart, you might find that copying and pasting information from a data source into the chart's datasheet is easier. If you want to maintain a link between the chart and its data's source file, you have to use the Copy and Paste Link commands. Then when you update the data in its source file, the chart will be updated as well.

BE SURE TO open the document you want to work with before carrying out these steps.

To link a chart to data from another source:

1   Open the source file, and select the data on which you want to base the chart.

2   Right-click the selection, and click **Copy** on the shortcut menu.

3   In your Word document, click the location where you want the chart to appear.

4   On the **Insert** menu, click **Picture** and then **Chart**.

    A sample chart and datasheet appear.

5   Click the cell in which you want the copied data to begin, and on the **Edit** menu, click **Paste Link**.

    The linked data appears in the datasheet and is plotted in the chart.

To modify linked chart data:

1   Open the source file, edit the data on which the chart is based, and save and close the file.

2   In the Word document, check that the chart reflects the new source data.

To modify an object link:

1   Double-click the object to activate it in Graph.

2   On the Graph toolbar, click the **View Datasheet** button.

View
Datasheet

3   On the **Edit** menu, click **Links**.

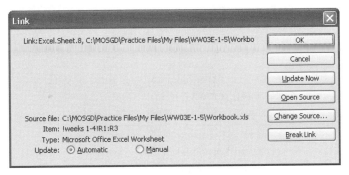

4   Make any changes to how the link operates, and click **OK**.

Tip   In the Links dialog box, you can switch between automatic and manual update mode, break the link, change the source, or open the current source.

Practice Exercise

In this exercise, you will link a chart to source data created in another program and then you'll update the data to test the link.

USE the *LinkData* document and the *SourceFile* workbook in the *My Documents\Microsoft Press \MOS 2003 Study Guide\Word\W03E-1-5* practice file folder.

Open the *SourceFile* workbook, copy the data in cells **A1:D5** of the **weeks 9-12** worksheet, and close the workbook. Then open the *LinkData* document, move to the end of the document, and double-click the chart to activate it in Graph. Click the first cell in the first row, and use the **Paste Link** command to paste in the data. After the chart is replotted, open the *SourceFile* workbook, change one of the values in the **weeks 9-12** worksheet, and save and close the workbook. Check that the chart in your Word document has been updated to reflect the edit, and then close the *LinkData* document without saving it.

W03E-1 Review

Number	Objective	Mastered
W03E-1-1	Create custom styles for text, tables, and lists	
	Creating character and paragraph styles	❏
	Creating table styles	❏
	Creating list styles	❏
W03E-1-2	Control pagination	
	Controlling orphans and widows	❏
	Keeping paragraphs together	❏
W03E-1-3	Format, position and resize graphics using advanced layout features	
	Sizing, scaling, cropping, and rotating a graphic	❏
	Controlling contrast and brightness	❏
	Positioning a graphic in relation to the surrounding text	❏
W03E-1-4	Insert and modify objects	
	Inserting and modifying a new object	❏
	Inserting and modifying an object from a file	❏
W03E-1-5	Create and modify diagrams and charts using data from other sources	
	Importing data to create a chart	❏
	Linking a chart to data from another source	❏

W03E-2

Organizing Content

The skills tested by this section of the Microsoft Office Specialist Word 2003 Expert Exam all relate to advanced tasks you can perform with document content. Specifically, the following objectives are associated with this set of skills:

Number	Objective
W03E-2-1	Sort content in lists and tables
W03E-2-2	Perform calculations in tables
W03E-2-3	Modify table formats
W03E-2-4	Summarize document content using automated tools
W03E-2-5	Use automated tools for document navigation
W03E-2-6	Merge letters with other data sources
W03E-2-7	Merge labels with other data sources
W03E-2-8	Structure documents using XML

 Important Before you can do the practice exercises associated with this skill set, you need to install the practice files from the book's companion CD to their default location. See "Installing the Practice Files" on page xxv for more information.

Sort Content in Lists and Tables

W03E-2-1   The skills measured by this objective include the following:

- Sorting the items in a list
- Sorting the data in a table

You can quickly and easily sort information in lists and tables by clicking Sort on the Table menu. The options available depend on the type of text you select before clicking the command.

Sorting the Items in a List

After you create a bulleted or numbered list, you can easily sort it in ascending or descending alphabetical order. If you sort a numbered list, Word renumbers the items sequentially after sorting them.

BE SURE TO open a document containing a bulleted or numbered list before carrying out these steps.

To sort the items in a list:

1 Select all the items in the list.

2 On the **Table** menu, click **Sort**.

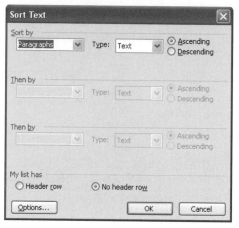

3 Select the **Ascending** or **Descending** option, and click **OK**.

The list changes to reflect the new sort order. If you are sorting a numbered list, the items are renumbered to reflect the new order.

Practice Exercise

In this exercise, you will sort the items in a bulleted list into alphabetic order.

USE the *SortList* document in the *My Documents\Microsoft Press\MOS 2003 Study Guide\Word\W03E-2-1* practice file folder.

Open the *SortList* document. Scroll down the document, and drag through the items in the bulleted list to select them. Display the Sort Text dialog box, make sure the **Ascending** option is selected, and click **OK**. Then close the *SortList* document without saving it.

Sorting the Data in a Table

You can use the Sort command on the Table menu to sort the rows in a table in ascending or descending order by the data in any column. For example, you can sort a table that has the column headings Name, Address, ZIP Code, and Phone Number on any one of those columns to arrange the information in alphabetical or numerical order. You can also sort on more than one column—for example, by name within ZIP Code.

BE SURE TO open a document containing a table before carrying out these steps.

To sort a table's data:

1 Click the first cell in the first row below the table's headings.

2 On the **Table** menu, click **Sort**.

3 Click the **Sort by** down arrow, and click the first column you want to use as the basis for the sort.

4 Click the first **Then by** down arrow, and click the second sort column.

5 Click the second **Then by** down arrow, and click the third sort column.

6 Select the **Ascending** or **Descending** option.

7 In the **My list has** area, make sure the **Header row** option is selected.

Selecting this option excludes the row of headings from the sort.

8 Click **OK**.

Word sorts the table in alphabetic or numeric order based on the three columns in turn.

Practice Exercise

In this exercise, you will sort the data in a table based on two of its columns.

USE the *SortTable* document in the *My Documents\Microsoft Press\MOS 2003 Study Guide\Word\W03E-2-1* practice file folder.

Open the *SortTable* document, and click the first cell in the first row below the table headings. Display the Sort dialog box, and specify **Furniture** as the **Sort by** column, **Unit Price** as the first **Then by** column, and **Ascending** as the order. Then close the *SortTable* document without saving it.

Perform Calculations in Tables

W03E-2-2 The skills measured by this objective include the following:

■ Using a formula in a table

You can perform certain calculations on numbers in a table using one of Word's built-in formulas.

Using a Formula in a Table

A formula is a mathematical expression that performs calculations, such as adding or averaging values. It consists of an equal sign followed by a function name, such as SUM, followed by the addresses, or references, of the cells on which you want to perform the calculation. Although many Word formulas refer to the cells above or to the left of the active cell, you can also reference a particular cell by typing the column letter and row number of the cell in parentheses after the function name. For example, the formula =SUM(b2, b4) totals the values in cells b2 and b4 and =SUM(b2:b4) totals the values in cells b2 through b4.

BE SURE TO open a document containing a table and display the Tables and Borders toolbar before carrying out these steps.

To quickly total a column or row of numbers:

1   Click the cell below or to the right of the column or row of values you want to total.

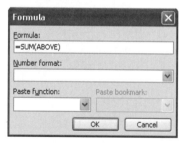

Σ

AutoSum

2   On the Tables and Borders toolbar, click the **AutoSum** button.

To use a function other than SUM:

1   Click the cell where you want to enter the formula.

2   On the **Table** menu, click **Formula**.

The Formula dialog box appears, with the Formula box showing the formula =SUM(ABOVE) or =SUM(LEFT), meaning that the formula will add the numbers in the cells above or to the left of the active cell.

3   Do any of the following:

■   To use a function other than SUM, delete the SUM function from the Formula box (but leave the equal sign), click the **Paste function** down arrow, and click the function you want in the drop-down list.

Tip   Word has 18 built-in functions, including functions to count (COUNT) the number of values in a column or row, and to find the maximum (MAX) or minimum (MIN) value in a series of cells.

■   To perform the calculation on cells other than those above or to the left, select **ABOVE** or **LEFT** in the formula's parentheses, and type the cell references, separating individual cells with commas (b2, b4) and ranges of cells with colons (b2:b4).

■   To specify the format for positive and negative results of the formula, click the **Number format** down arrow, and click the format you want.

4   Click **OK**.

Word calculates the formula and puts the result in the active cell.

Practice Exercise

In this exercise, you will add the numbers in a column of a table.

USE the *CalculateTable* document in the *My Documents\Microsoft Press\MOS 2003 Study Guide\Word \W03E-2-2* practice file folder.

Open the *CalculateTable* document, and click the lower-right cell of the furniture table (to the right of the cell containing *Total*). Display the Formula dialog box, and check that the **Formula** box shows the formula =SUM(ABOVE). Click **OK** to display the total cost of the furniture in the cell. Then close the *CalculateTable* document without saving it.

Modify Table Formats

W03E-2-3   The skills measured by this objective include the following:

■ Merging and splitting table cells

■ Changing the position and direction of cell contents

■ Modifying table properties

■ Inserting and modifying fields

When the needs of your data require more than a straightforward table structure, you can change the structure in a variety of ways to achieve just the effect you want.

Merging and Splitting Table Cells

You can create cells that span columns by merging them. For example, to center a title in the first row of a table, you can create one merged cell that spans the table's width. If you need to divide a merged cell into its component cells, you can split it.

BE SURE TO open a document containing a table and display the Tables and Borders toolbar before carrying out these steps.

To merge cells so that they span columns:

1   Select the cells you want to merge.

Merge Cells

2   On the Tables and Borders toolbar, click the **Merge Cells** button.

You can also click Merge Cells on the Table menu.

To split a merged cell into its component cells:

1   Select the cell you want to split.

Split Cells

2   On the Tables and Borders toolbar, click the **Split Cells** button.

You can also click Split Cells on the Table menu.

To merge and split cells by using the table drawing tools:

1   Select the cells you want to merge.

Eraser

2 On the Tables and Borders toolbar, click the **Eraser** button.

The pointer changes to an eraser tool.

3 Point to the table gridline between the cells you wish to merge, and click once.

The gridline separating the cells is erased, and the cells are merged into one.

4 Click the **Eraser** button again to turn it off.

> **Tip** The erased gridlines become paragraph marks. Delete or replace them with spaces, depending on how you want your table to look.

Draw Table

5 To split cells, click the **Draw Table** button on the Tables and Borders toolbar.

The pointer changes to a pencil tool.

6 Draw gridlines in the table wherever you want to split a cell.

7 Click the **Draw Table** button to toggle it off.

Practice Exercise

In this exercise, you will merge four cells into one and then add rows with the same structure to the bottom of a table.

USE the *MergeCells* document in the *My Documents\Microsoft Press\MOS 2003 Study Guide\Word \W03E-2-3* practice file folder.

Open the *MergeCells* document, and scroll down to the table. Select the first four cells in the last row, and merge them. Type **Subtotal**, and press **TAB** twice to add a new row with the same structure. Then type **Add shipping/handling fee**, press **TAB** twice to add a new row, type **Add special delivery fee**, press **TAB** twice, and then type **Total**. Then close the *MergeCells* document without saving it.

Changing the Position and Direction of Cell Contents

If your table has some columns with short cell entries and some with lengthy ones, reading across the rows can get difficult. You can improve the readability and looks of a table by centering the shorter entries on the longer entries.

When you need to enter headings for columns of numbers, the resulting column widths are often much wider than they need to be to accommodate the table's numeric data. This might result in readers having to scroll to see out-of-sight columns, or in a printed table spanning pages. To keep the column widths as narrow as possible, you can turn the headings sideways.

BE SURE TO open a document containing a table and display the Tables and Borders toolbar before carrying out these steps.

To change the position of text in a cell:

1 Select the cell(s) whose contents you want to reposition.

Align

2 On the Tables and Borders toolbar, click the **Align** down arrow, and select the position you want.

The Align button icon reflects your last alignment choice.

To change the direction of text in a cell:

1 Select the cell(s) you want to rotate.

2 On the **Format** menu, click **Text Direction**.

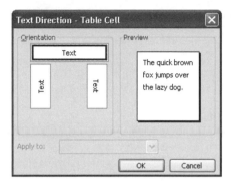

3 Click the orientation option you want.

4 Click **OK**.

Change Text
Direction

Tip To rotate the text 90 degrees to the right, you can click the Change Text Direction button on the Tables and Borders toolbar.

Practice Exercise

In this exercise, you will change the direction of column headings and the position of data in a table.

USE the *ChangeDirection* document in the *My Documents\Microsoft Press\MOS 2003 Study Guide\Word \W03E-2-3* practice file folder.

Open the *ChangeDirection* document, and select the first row. Center the **Customers** heading. Then rotate the headings in the second row so that they are at a 90 degree angle to the row below, and center the headings in their cells. Then close the *ChangeDirection* document without saving it.

Modifying Table Properties

You can control many aspects of a table by setting options on the tabs of the Table Properties dialog box. On the Table tab, you can specify the preferred width of the entire table, as well as the way it interacts with the surrounding text. On the Row tab, you can specify the height of each row, whether a row is allowed to break across pages, and whether a row of column headings should be repeated at the top of each page. On the Column tab, you can set the width of each column, and on the Cell tab, you can set the preferred width of cells and the vertical alignment of text within them.

BE SURE TO open a document containing a table before carrying out these steps.

To adjust a table's properties:

1 Click anywhere in the table, and on the **Table** menu, click **Table Properties**.

2 Click the tab of the table element whose properties you want to adjust.

3 Make adjustments to the properties as necessary.

4 Click **OK** to close the Table Properties dialog box.

Practice Exercise

In this exercise, you will specify that column headings should be repeated if the table breaks across pages. You'll also adjust the height of the heading row, and then apply a background pattern.

USE the *SetProperties* document in the *My Documents\Microsoft Press\MOS 2003 Study Guide\Word \W03E-2-3* practice file folder.

Open the *SetProperties* document, and in the Table Properties dialog box, set the first row to repeat at the top of each page. Specify the height of this row as **0.5″**, and then apply a 5% pattern to the table's background. Then close the *SetProperties* document without saving it.

Inserting and Modifying Fields

Just as you can insert fields in regular text to speed up text entry, you can insert fields in tables to insert program-generated items such as the date or time. After you insert a field, you cannot edit it in the usual way, but you can modify it by displaying the Field dialog box and changing its options.

See Also　For information about inserting date and time fields, refer to W03C-1-2, "Inserting Frequently Used and Predefined Text."

BE SURE TO open a document containing a table before carrying out these steps.

To insert a field:

1 Click the cell in which you want to insert a field.

2 On the **Insert** menu, click **Field**.

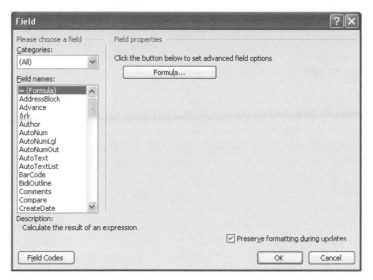

3 Click the **Categories** down arrow, and click the type of field you want.

4 In the **Field names** list, click the field you want, and then specify any additional information in the **Field properties** and **Field options** areas.

These areas change, depending on the field you choose.

5 Click **OK**.

Excel inserts the information required by the field in the table cell.

To update a field:

1 Click the cell whose field you want to update.

2 Press the **F9** key.

Practice Exercise

In this exercise, you will insert fields in a table and then update them.

USE the *InsertField* document in the *My Documents\Microsoft Press\MOS 2003 Study Guide\Word\W03E-2-3* practice file folder.

Open the *InsertField* document. Click the first cell in the table at the top of the document, and use the Field dialog box to insert an **AutoNum** field. Copy this field to the other cells in the table's first column. Then insert **NumChars**, **NumWords**, and **NumPages** fields in the last column of the table. Change the *Black Gold* title to **Creating Black Gold**, and insert a page break before the title. Update the fields, noticing the change in the number of words and number of pages. Then close the *InsertField* document without saving it.

Summarize Document Content Using Automated Tools

W03E-2-4   The skills measured by this objective include the following:

■ Summarizing a document

■ Analyzing content readability

Word includes built-in tools that take the work out of summarizing longer documents and assessing their readability.

Summarizing a Document

If you are concerned that people might be too busy to read a long and detailed document, you can use Word's AutoSummarize feature to extract the key points of the document. Auto-Summarize works best on well-structured documents with headings and subheadings, such as reports. The feature works by analyzing the document to determine which words are used frequently, and then assigning a score to each sentence based on the number of high-frequency words it contains. You determine what score is necessary for a sentence to be included in the summary, which can be inserted in the document as an executive summary or abstract that can be quickly scanned. You can also have Word copy the high-frequency words to the Summary tab of the Properties dialog box as keywords, and the high-scoring sentences as comments.

BE SURE TO open a longer document containing headings before carrying out these steps.

To summarize a document:

1   With the insertion point at the top of the document, click **AutoSummarize** on the **Tools** menu.

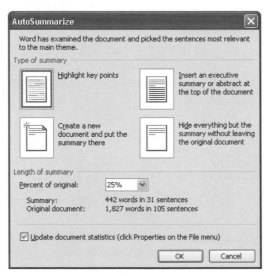

2   In the **Length of summary** area, click the **Percent of original** down arrow, and click a percentage in the drop-down list.

3   In the **Type of summary** area, select the type of summary you want, and click **OK**.

Tip If you entered keywords or comments on the Summary tab of the Properties dialog box, Word will replace them with its own information when you use the AutoSummarize feature. To prevent this, clear the "Update document statistics" check box in the Auto-Summarize dialog box.

Practice Exercise

In this exercise, you will first highlight the key points of a document and then insert the summary as an abstract at the beginning of the document.

USE the *SummarizeDocument* document in the *My Documents\Microsoft Press\MOS 2003 Study Guide \Word\W03E-2-4* practice file folder.

Open the *SummarizeDocument* document, and display the AutoSummarize dialog box. Set **Percent of original** to **25%** and **Type of summary** to **Highlight key points**. Scroll through the document, noticing what Word has highlighted. On the AutoSummarize toolbar, change **Percent of Original** to **10%**. Display the AutoSummarize dialog box, verify that **Percent of original** is set to 10%, and then set **Type of summary** to **Insert an executive summary or abstract at the top of the document**. Close the *SummarizeDocument* document without saving it.

Analyzing Content Readability

If you are writing for a specific audience, such as children, you might want to check the readability of your documents. On the Spelling & Grammar tab of the Options dialog box, you can tell Word to compile readability statistics for your documents by applying a couple of standard statistical tests. Then whenever you tell Word to check a document's spelling and grammar, it also displays such statistics as the average number of characters in a word, the average number of words in a sentence, and the reading level of the document (in terms of U.S. school grades 1 through 12).

BE SURE TO open the document you want to work with before carrying out these steps.

To analyze a document's readability:

1 On the **Tools** menu, click **Options**, and click the **Spelling & Grammar** tab.

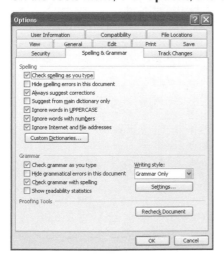

Spelling and
Grammar

2 In the **Grammar** area, select the **Show readability statistics** check box, and click **OK**.

3 On the Standard toolbar, click the **Spelling and Grammar** button, and check the spelling and grammar of the document.

See Also For information about checking spelling and grammar, refer to W03C-1-1, "Insert and Edit Text, Symbols, and Special Characters."

When Word finishes the spelling and grammar check, it displays the Readability Statistics dialog box, which summarizes the readability of the document.

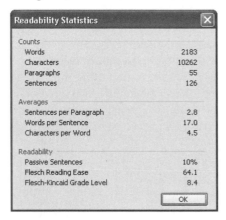

4 Click **OK** to close the summary.

Practice Exercise

In this exercise, you will check the readability of a document.

USE the *CheckReadability* document in the *My Documents\Microsoft Press\MOS 2003 Study Guide\Word \W03E-2-4* practice file folder.

Open the *CheckReadability* document. Display the **Spelling & Grammar** tab of the Options dialog box, and select the **Show readability statistics** check box. Then check the spelling and grammar of the document, clicking **Ignore Once** each time Word stops on a suspected error. When Word displays the Readability Statistics dialog box, check the readability statistics of the document, and then close the dialog box. Close the *CheckReadability* document without saving it.

Use Automated Tools for Document Navigation

W03E-2-5 The skills measured by this objective include the following:

■ Inserting a bookmark
■ Using Document Map and thumbnails

When working with longer documents, you often need to be able to jump from one place to another, either to access related material or to return to information you have flagged for future reference.

Inserting a Bookmark

Word includes several tools for navigating long documents, including bookmarks, with which you can jump easily to designated places. Like a physical bookmark, you can place a Word bookmark in a location you might want to return to later, but you do it electronically by marking a location in a document and naming it.

Tip   You can create bookmarks only to items within the same document, or within a master document and its subdocuments. If you want jump to a different document, you use hyperlinks instead.

See Also   For information about master documents, refer to W03E-3-5, "Create and Manage Master Documents and Subdocuments." For information about hyperlinks, refer to W03C-2-3, "Insert and Modify Hyperlinks."

BE SURE TO open the document you want to work with before carrying out these steps.

To insert a bookmark:

1   Click the location where you want to place a bookmark.

2   On the **Insert** menu, click **Bookmark**.

3   In the **Bookmark name** box, type a self-explanatory name for the bookmark.

Tip   Bookmark names cannot contain spaces. If you enter a space, the Add button will become inactive. To name bookmarks with multiple words, you'll need to run the words together, as in CompostAndSoil.

4   Click **Add**.

Although you can't see it, a bookmark is inserted into the document.

Tip   To delete a bookmark, click Bookmark on the Insert menu, click the bookmark's name, and then click Delete.

To jump to a bookmark:

1 On the **Edit** menu, click **Go To**.

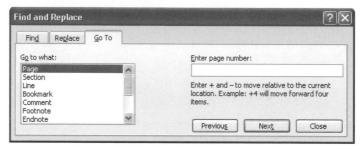

2 In the **Go to what** list, click **Bookmark**.

3 Click the **Enter bookmark name** down arrow, and click the bookmark you want to jump to.

4 Click the **Go To** button.

The insertion point moves to the location of the bookmark. The dialog box remains open in case you want to move somewhere else.

5 Click **Close** to close the Find and Replace dialog box.

Tip You can also click Bookmark on the Insert menu, click the bookmark's name in the Bookmark dialog box, and then click Go To.

Practice Exercise

In this exercise, you will insert a bookmark and jump to it in a document.

USE the *InsertBookmark* document in the *My Documents\Microsoft Press\MOS 2003 Study Guide\Word \W03E-2-5* practice file folder.

Open the *InsertBookmark* document. Scroll down to the last page in the document, and then click to the left of the *C* in *Composting DOs and DON'Ts* heading. Display the Bookmark dialog box, and add a bookmark called **DOs**. Move to the beginning of the document, and use the **Go To** tab of the Find and Replace dialog box to jump to the bookmark. Close the Find and Replace dialog box, and then close the *InsertBookmark* document without saving it.

Using the Document Map and Thumbnails

No matter which view you are working in, you can display a dynamic outline of the active document, called the Document Map, in a separate pane. When the Document Map is open, you can click a heading in its pane to jump directly to that heading in the document. If you make a change to a heading in the document, it is immediately reflected in the Document Map.

The outline level assigned to each paragraph determines whether that paragraph is displayed in the Document Map. You can set the outline level of any paragraph by clicking Paragraph on the Format menu and making a selection in the "Outline level" drop-down list. You can also set the outline level by applying a style that includes an outline level to the paragraph.

See Also   For information about outlines, refer to W03C-2-2, "Create Bulleted Lists, Numbered Lists, and Outlines." For information about styles, refer to W03C-3-1, "Format Text."

When you are working in Reading Layout view, you can display thumbnails of the document's pages in a separate pane. Clicking a thumbnail takes you to that part of the document.

See Also   For information about Reading Layout view, refer to W03C-5-7, "Change and Organize Document Views and Windows."

BE SURE TO open the document you want to work with before carrying out these steps.

To navigate by using the Document Map:

Document Map

1   On the Standard toolbar, click the **Document Map** button.

A pane appears to the left of the document.

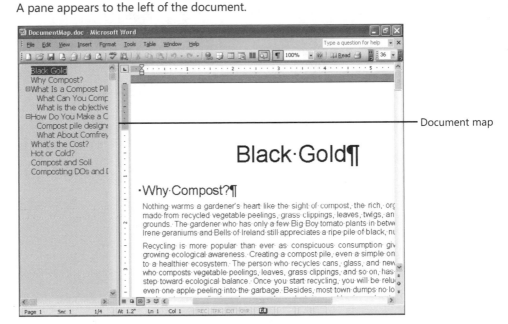

Document map

2   To see more or less of the heading text in the Document Map, drag the pane's right frame to right or left.

3   To jump to a heading in the document, and click that heading in the Document Map.

4   To expand or collapse the outline in the Document Map, click the minus or plus icons to the left of the headings.

5   On the Standard toolbar, click the **Document Map** button to close the document map.

Tip   You can also click Document Map on the View menu to turn its pane on or off.

To navigate by using thumbnails:

Reading
Layout

1 In the lower-left corner of the document window, click the **Reading Layout** button to switch to Reading Layout view.

Allow
Multiple
Pages

2 Make sure the **Allow Multiple Pages** button on the Reading Layout toolbar is turned off (not active).

3 On the Reading Layout toolbar, click the **Thumbnails** button.

Thumbnails

A pane appears on the left side of the screen showing each page of the document as a thumbnail image.

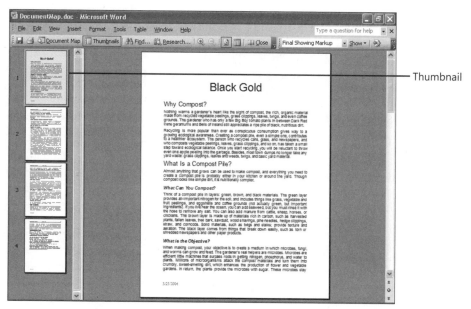

Thumbnail

4 In the left pane, click the thumbnail of the page you want to view.

Actual Page

5 To see the displayed section of text as it will look when printed, click the **Actual Page** button on the Reading Layout toolbar.

The thumbnails still appear in the left pane, but they change to represent the pages in the document in Print Layout view.

Practice Exercise

In this exercise, you will move around a document by using the Document Map.

USE the *UseDocumentMap* document in the *My Documents\Microsoft Press\MOS Study Guide\Word \W03E-2-5* practice file folder.

Open the *UseDocumentMap* document. With the insertion point at the beginning of the document, open the Document Map. If the left pane is not wide enough to show all the headings, drag the pane's right frame to the right. Click headings in the Document Map in the left pane to jump to the corresponding headings in the document in the right pane. Scan the headings in the Document Map, and notice that the capitalization of the fourth heading is inconsistent. Jump to the fourth heading in the document, and correct its capitalization. After the heading is updated in the Document Map, close the *UseDocumentMap* document without saving it.

Merge Letters with Other Data Sources

W03E-2-6   The skills measured by this objective include the following:

- Specifying the data source
- Preparing the form letter
- Merging the data with the form letter

The most common type of document used in the mail merge process is the form letter. The document typically contains merge fields for the name and address of each recipient, along with text that is the same in all the letters. The merge fields correspond to items of information in a data source.

Specifying the Data Source

Before you can create a form letter, you need to either specify an existing data source or create one. The data source consists of sets of information structured in columns called fields and rows called records. Each field is an item of information of a particular type, such as the first name of a customer, and is identified by its field name. Each record is all the items of information belonging to a set, such as the complete name and address of a customer.

Tip   Field names cannot contain spaces—for example, *FirstName* is an acceptable field name, but *First Name* is not.

You can use an existing database created in Microsoft Access, Microsoft Excel, Microsoft Visual FoxPro, or the Contacts list from Microsoft Outlook or Microsoft Outlook Express. You can also create a table in Word to use as a data source.

BE SURE TO open the document you want to work with and have a data source available before carrying out these steps.

To specify the data source:

1   On the **Tools** menu, click **Letters and Mailings** and then **Mail Merge**.

    The Mail Merge task pane appears, showing Step 1 of 6 of the wizard.

2   In the Mail Merge task pane, make sure the **Letters** option is selected, and then click **Next: Starting document** at the bottom of the pane.

    Step 2 appears in the Mail Merge task pane.

3   Make sure the **Use the current document** option is selected, and then click **Next: Select recipients** at the bottom of the pane.

    Step 3 appears.

4   Make sure the **Use an existing list** option is selected, and then click **Browse** to open the Select Data Source dialog box.

In the Select Data Source dialog box, you can select a Word document, an Excel spreadsheet, or an Access database as the data source.

5   Navigate to the folder on your hard disk where the data source is stored, and then double-click the file.

The Mail Merge Recipients dialog box appears, displaying the records contained in the data source.

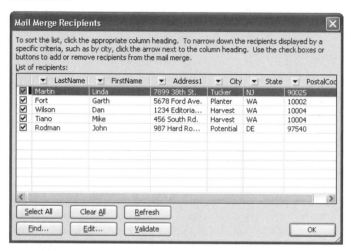

6   Click **OK** to close the Mail Merge Recipients dialog box.

To edit the data source:

1   Display the Mail Merge Recipients dialog box, and click **Edit**.

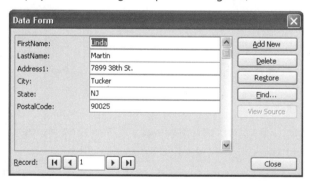

2   Move to the record you want to edit and make your changes, or click **Add New** and add a new record.

3   Click **Close** to close the Data Form dialog box.

The changes appear in the Mail Merge Recipients dialog box.

To sort the data source:

1 Display the Mail Merge Recipients dialog box, click the down arrow to the left of the field on which you want to base the sort, and click **Advanced**.

2 When the Query Options dialog box appears, click the **Sort Records** tab.

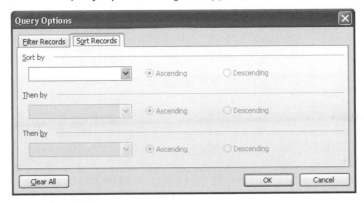

3 Click the **Sort by** down arrow, and click the field you want.

4 Select **Ascending** or **Descending**, and click **OK**.

The data is sorted on the specified field in the specified order.

To filter the data source:

1 Display the Mail Merge Recipients dialog box, click the down arrow to the left of the field you want to filter, and then click **Advanced**.

The Query Options dialog box appears, showing the Filter Records tab.

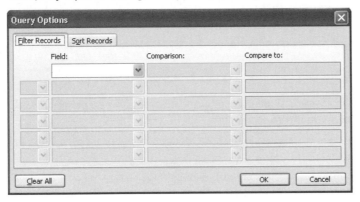

2 Click the **Field** down arrow, and then click the field you want.

Several other query options become available.

3 Click the **Comparison** down arrow, click the comparison operator you want, and in the **Compare to** box, type the comparison value.

4   Click **OK**.

The Mail Merge Recipients dialog box is updated to show only the records that meet your filtering criteria.

Practice Exercise

In this exercise, you will specify the data source (a mailing list), and then add a record to the data source. You will then sort the records by ZIP Code and create a simple query to select only the records for customers living in Washington State.

USE the *SpecifyData* and *Data* documents in the *My Documents\Microsoft Press\MOS 2003 Study Guide\Word\W03E-2-6* practice file folder.

Open the *SpecifyData* document, and display the Mail Merge task pane. Use the current document and an existing list (the *Data* file in the *My Documents\Microsoft Press\MOS 2003 Study Guide\Word\W03E-2-6* practice file folder). In the Mail Merge Recipients dialog box, add a new recipient with **Heidi** as the first name, **Steen** as the last name, **678 Pine St.** as the address, **Agriculture** as the city, **WA** as the state, and **19003** as the postal code. Sort the **PostalCode** field in **Ascending** order, and set the **State** field equal to **WA**. After the Mail Merge Recipients dialog box is updated to show only the four Washington State records in ascending ZIP Code order, close the Mail Merge Recipients dialog box. Then close the *SpecifyData* document without saving it.

Preparing the Form Letter

You can create a form letter in two ways: by inserting merge fields into an existing main document, or by creating a new main document as you work through the steps of the Mail Merge Wizard. In either case, you enter the text that will be common to all the letters and then insert the merge fields that will be replaced by the variable information from the data source. The merge fields appear in the main document surrounded by chevrons (« and »).

BE SURE TO open a document containing the text of a letter for which you have already specified the data source before carrying out these steps.

To prepare the form letter:

1   If the Mail Merge task pane is not already open, click **Letters and Mailings** and then **Mail Merge** on the **Tools** menu.

2   If Step 4 does not appear in the Mail Merge task pane, click the **Next** link until Step 4 appears.

Show/Hide¶

3   If non-printing characters are not visible on your screen, click the **Show/Hide ¶** button on the Standard toolbar to turn them on.

4   In the document window, click where you want to insert the merge fields for the address, and then in the Mail Merge task pane, click **Address block**.

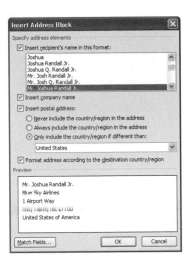

5   Make any necessary adjustments to the merge fields that will be included in the address, and click **OK** to insert the fields.

6   In the document window, click where you want to insert the greeting merge field, and in the Mail Merge task pane, click **Greeting line**.

7   Set up the greeting, and click **OK** to insert the fields.

Practice Exercise

In this exercise, you will modify an existing letter by adding merge fields for a standard inside address and informal greeting line.

USE the *PrepareLetter* document in the *My Documents\Microsoft Press\MOS 2003 Study Guide\Word \W03E-2-6* practice file folder.

Open the *PrepareLetter* document, and display Step 4 in the Mail Merge task pane. Turn on non-printing characters, and in the document window, click the second blank line under the date. In the Mail Merge task pane, click **Address block**, and accept the default settings. In the document window, click the second blank line after the «*Address Block*» merge field, and then in the Mail Merge task pane, click **Greeting line**. Set the second box in greeting line format to **Joshua**. Then close the *PrepareLetter* document without saving it.

Merging the Data with the Form Letter

After you set up a data source and enter merge fields in a letter, you are ready to merge them to create one merged document for each data source record used. You can either send the merged documents directly to the printer or you can merge them one after the other into a new document, separated by page breaks. You can edit the new document to personalize individual copies of the main document before sending them to the printer, and you can save it.

BE SURE TO open a form letter document for which a data source has been specified before carrying out these steps.

To merge the data with the form letter:

1 If the Mail Merge task pane is not already open, click **Letters and Mailings** and then **Mail Merge** on the **Tools** menu.

2 If Step 5 does not appear in the Mail Merge task pane, click the **Next** link until Step 5 appears.

The form letter is merged with the specified records in the data source, and the first personalized letter appears in the document window.

3 In the Mail Merge task pane, click the **Next Record** button.

The second personalized letter is displayed.

Tip You can exclude the displayed document from the merge process by clicking "Exclude this recipient" in the "Make changes" area of the Mail Merge task pane.

4 At the bottom of the Mail Merge task pane, click **Next: Complete the merge**.

You move to Step 6 of the wizard.

5 In the **Merge** area, do one of the following:

■ Click **Print** to send the form letters directly to the printer.

■ Click **Edit individual letters**, select the **All** option, and then click **OK**.

Word creates a new document called *Letters1* containing personalized copies of the form letter, one for each person in the data source. You can then save the document, edit it, and print it later.

Practice Exercise

In this exercise, you will review merged data and then merge letters into a new document containing one personalized copy of the letter for each recipient.

USE the *MergeLetter* document in the *My Documents\Microsoft Press\MOS 2003 Study Guide\Word \W03E-2-6* practice file folder.

Open the *MergeLetter* document, and display Step 5 in the Mail Merge task pane. Preview the letters, and then merge all the form letters into a new document. Review the document. Then close both the new document and the *MergeLetter* document without saving them.

Merge Labels with Other Data Sources

W03E-2-7   The skills measured by this objective include the following:

■ Creating and printing mailing labels

You can use a data source with more than one kind of form document. For example, the same data source you use to print form letters can be used to print sheets of mailing labels or envelopes.

Creating and Printing Mailing Labels

The mail-merge process for creating mailing labels is similar to the process for creating form letters. You start by selecting the brand and style of labels you plan to use, such as Avery standard 5159. Word then creates a full-page table with cells the size of the labels so that each cell will print on one label in a sheet. You specify the data source, and then insert merge fields into one cell as a template for all the other cells. When you merge the form document and the data source, you can print the labels or create a new label document that you can use whenever you want to send anything to the same set of people.

BE SURE TO open a blank document and have a data source available before carrying out these steps.

To create and print mailing labels:

1   On the **Tools** menu, click **Letters and Mailings** and then **Mail Merge**.

2   In the Mail Merge task pane, select the **Labels** option, and then click **Next: Starting document** to proceed to Step 2.

3   Select the **Change document layout** option, if necessary, and then click **Label options**.

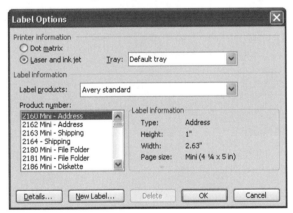

4   In the **Product number** list, select the type of label you want, and click **OK**.

Word inserts a table that fills the first page of the document with cells the size of the specified labels.

Tip   The document window might appear blank. However, the table with label-sized cells is there but not visible.

5   Click **Next: Select recipients**, and with **Use an existing list** selected, click **Browse**.

The Select Data Source dialog box appears.

6   Navigate to the folder on your hard disk where the data source is stored, and double-click the file.

The Mail Merge Recipients dialog box appears.

7   Sort and filter the data source as necessary, and click **OK**.

The «Next Record» merge field appears in all the labels in the main document.

8   Click **Next: Arrange your labels**, and with the insertion point positioned in the upper-left label in the document window, click **Address block** in the Mail Merge task pane, adjust the address fields as necessary, and click **OK**.

9   In the **Replicate labels** area of the Mail Merge task pane, click the **Update all labels** button.

The «AddressBlock» merge field is inserted in all the labels.

10   At the bottom of the Mail Merge task pane, click **Next: Preview your labels** to proceed to Step 5.

Word displays the labels as they will appear after the merge.

11   Click **Next: Complete the merge**.

The names and addresses from the data source appear in the mailing label document.

12   In the Mail Merge task pane, click **Print**.

13   Click **OK**.

The Print dialog box appears.

14   Check that the name of the printer you want to use appears in the **Name** box, and then click **OK** to print the labels.

Practice Exercise

In this exercise, you will create and print mailing labels.

USE the *CreateLabels* and *Data* documents in the *My Documents\Microsoft Press\MOS 2003 Study Guide\Word\W03E-2-7* practice file folder.

Open the *CreateLabels* document, and display the Mail Merge task pane. Select the **Labels** option, and specify **5159 – Address** as the label format. Specify **Data** as the data source, and when the Mail Merge Recipients dialog box appears, click **OK**. Insert the merge fields for the address in the upper-left label, and then update all the labels to reflect the first one. Complete the merge, and print the labels on regular paper on your default printer. Then close the *CreateLabels* document without saving it.

Structure Documents Using XML

W03E-2-8 The skills measured by this objective include the following:

■ Creating an XML document based on a schema

Web documents are coded with Hypertext Markup Language (HTML) so that they can be displayed in a Web browser, no matter what that browser might be. HTML is a small, fixed subset of the Standard Generalized Markup Language (SGML), a comprehensive system for coding the structure of text documents and other forms of data so that they can be used in a variety of environments. The Extensible Markup Language (XML) is another subset of SGML. However, instead of being fixed like HTML, XML can be customized (extended) to store data so that it can be used in many ways or in many environments—for example, as text, in a database or spreadsheet, or as a Web page.

Creating an XML Document Based on a Schema

To save a Word document in XML format, you need to attach an XML schema to it. This schema describes the structure allowed in the document, including the names of structural elements and what elements can contain what other elements. For example, a numbered list might be defined as an element that can contain only numbered items—no regular paragraphs, graphics, or sidebars. You designate the structure of each paragraph in the document from the XML Structure task pane. If the schema has defined attributes for any of its elements, you also assign the attributes from this task pane.

The power of XML is its adaptability. After you create an XML document, you can apply a transform to it to pull only the data you need, put it in the necessary format, and send it in different directions. For example, you could apply one transform to an XML document to extract and format information as a Web page for customers, and then apply a different transform that extracts and formats different information from the same XML document as a regular Word document.

Generally, companies employ a specialist with in-depth knowledge of XML to create custom schemas and transforms. However, after a schema is created, anyone can attach it to a Word document and convert it to an XML document. If you don't have a custom schema, you can still save a Word document as an XML document by using Word's built-in XML schema, which is called WordML.

BE SURE TO open the document you want to work with before carrying out these steps.

To add a schema to the Schema Library:

1   On the **Tools** menu, click **Templates and Add-Ins**, and then click the **XML Schema** tab.

2   Click **Schema Library**.

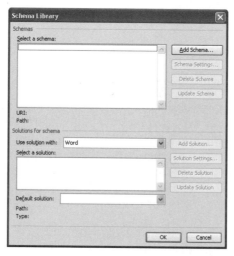

3   Click **Add Schema**, and when the Add Schema dialog box appears, navigate to the folder where the schema you want to use is located, and double-click the schema file.

The Schema Settings dialog box appears.

4   Make any adjustment you want, and click **OK**.

Word adds the schema to the Schema Library.

5   Click **OK** to close the Schema Library dialog box.

To attach a schema to a document and set XML options:

1   On the **Tools** menu, click **Templates and Add-Ins**, and click the **XML Schema** tab.

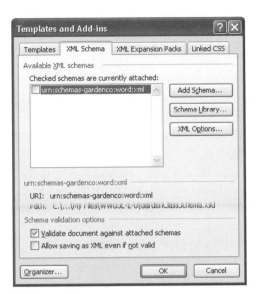

2 In the **Checked schemas are currently attached** box, select the check box of the schema you want to attach.

3 In the **Schema validation options** area, make sure the **Validate document against attached schemas** check box is selected.

4 Click **XML Options**.

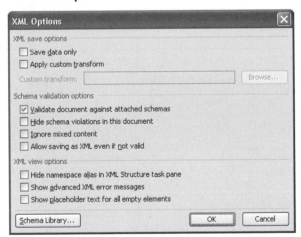

5 Set the options the way you want them. Typically, **Hide schema violations in this document** is cleared in the **Schema validation options** area, **Hide namespace alias in XML Structure task pane** is cleared, and **Show advanced XML error messages** is selected in the **XML view options** area.

6 Click **OK** to close the XML Options dialog box, and then click **OK** again to close the Templates and Add-ins dialog box.

The XML Structure task pane appears.

To apply XML structure to a document:

1   In the XML Structure task pane, make sure the **Show XML tags in the document** check box is selected.

2   Click anywhere in the document window. Then in the **Choose an element to apply to your current selection** box at the bottom of the XML Structure task pane, click the top-level element.

    Word asks whether you want to apply this element to the entire document.

3   Click **Apply to Entire Document**.

    Word selects all the text in the document, adds opening and closing XML tags at either end of the document to indicate that the entire document is now the specified element, and lists the element in the "Elements in the document" box in the XML Structure task pane.

4   Select text to which you want to apply the second-level element, and click that element in the **Choose an element to apply to your current selection** box.

    Tip   By default, the "List only child elements of current element" check box is selected. This simplifies the list of elements by showing only the ones that are valid in the current location.

5   Continue applying elements to text selections.

    As you tag each new element, Word adds that element to the growing structure in the "Elements in the document" box. A black X in a yellow diamond next to the class element tells you that the structure is not valid according to the schemas rules, and three dots under the classroom element tell you that the schema calls for an element that is missing. Pointing to one of these flags displays a ScreenTip that tells you the nature of the problem.

To assign an attribute to an element:

1   In the XML Structure task pane, right-click the element, and then click **Attributes**.

2   Select an attribute from the **Available attributes** box, and click **Add**.

3   Click **OK**.

To save a structured document as XML:

1   On the **File** menu, click **Save As**.

2   In the Save As dialog box, click the **Save as type** down arrow, and click **XML Document** in the drop-down list.

3   Click **Save** to save the XML document.

    Tip   If the "Allow saving as XML even if not valid" check box is cleared in the XML Options dialog box, Word will not allow you to save a document as XML unless the structure is valid. If Word tells you that it cannot save your document as XML because its structure violates the rules set by the schema, you have three choices: save the file as a Word document; click Cancel and change the option in the XML Options dialog box; or click Cancel and go back to the "Elements in the document" box of the XML Structure task pane and correct the structure of elements marked in red.

To use a transform:

1   Open the XML document you want to work with, and on the **File** menu, click **Save As**. The Save As dialog box appears.

2   In the **File name** box, type a name for the file.

3   Click the **Save as type** down arrow, and click **XML Document** in the drop-down list. The "Apply transform" check box appears to the right of the "File name" box.

4   Select the **Apply transform** check box, and then click **Transform**.

5   Navigate to the folder where the transform you want to apply is stored, and double-click the transform.

6   Click **Save**. Word warns you that saving a file through a transform without WordML could remove features such as formatting and pictures.

7   Do one of the following:

■   To save the file without WordML, click **Continue**.

■   To save the file with WordML, click **Keep WordML**.

Practice Exercise

In this exercise, you will attach a schema to a Word document and tag elements to create valid structure. Then you'll save the file as an XML document.

USE the *AttachSchema* document and the *GardenClassSchema* in the *My Documents\Microsoft Press \MOS 2003 Study Guide\Word\W03E-2-8* practice file folder.

Open the *AttachSchema* document, and display the **XML Schema** tab of the Templates and Add-ins dialog box. Add *GardenClassSchema* to the Schema Library. When the Schema Settings dialog box appears, assign **May Class Schema** as the schema's alias. Attach the **May Class Schema** in the **Checked schemas are currently attached** box. Then with **Validate document against attached schemas** selected in the **Schema validation options** area, display the XML Options dialog box. In the **Schema validation options** area, make sure the **Hide schema violations in this document** check box is cleared. Then in the **XML view options** area, make sure the **Hide namespace alias in XML Structure task pane** check box is cleared and that the **Show advanced XML error messages** check box is selected. Close both dialog boxes, and in the XML Structure task pane, make sure the **Show XML tags in the document** check box is selected. Apply the **classlist {May Class Schema}** element to the entire document. Then apply the **class** element to all the text from *Herb Gardening in Containers* down to *Check with Karen about fresh herbs for students to sample*. Apply the **title** element to *Herb Gardening in Containers* heading, and then select each of the next six paragraphs one at a time, and tag them in turn as **instructor, date, time, description, cost,** and **classroom**. Point to the X beside **class** to see the explanatory ScreenTip, and then select **Check with Karen about fresh herbs for students to sample.**—the only remaining untagged text in the class element (don't include the closing class tag). Apply the **notes** element to the selection. Apply the appropriate structural elements to the *All About Bulbs* class, and then point to the question mark in the **Elements in the document** box of the XML Structure task pane, which tells you

181

that the structure is incomplete. In the document window, click to the right of the **cost** end tag, press **ENTER**, type **classroom #2**, and apply the **classroom** element. Display the Save As dialog box, change the **Save as type** setting to **XML Document**, and save the *AttachSchema* XML document in the *My Documents\Microsoft Press\MOS 2003 Study Guide\Word\W03E-2-8* practice file folder. Then close the *AttachSchema* XML document.

W03E-2 Review

Number	Objective	Mastered
W03E-2-1	Sort content in lists and tables	
	Sorting the items in a list	❏
	Sorting the data in a table	❏
W03E-2-2	Perform calculations in tables	
	Using a formula in a table	❏
W03E-2-3	Modify table formats	
	Merging and splitting table cells	❏
	Changing the position and direction of cell contents	❏
	Modifying table properties	❏
	Inserting and modifying fields	❏
W03E-2-4	Summarize document content using automated tools	
	Summarizing a document	❏
	Analyzing content readability	❏
W03E-2-5	Use automated tools for document navigation	
	Inserting a bookmark	❏
	Using Document Map and thumbnails	❏
W03E-2-6	Merge letters with other data sources	
	Specifying the data source	❏
	Preparing the form letter	❏
	Merging the data with the form letter	❏
W03E-2-7	Merge labels with other data sources	
	Creating and printing mailing labels	❏
W03E-2-8	Structure documents using XML	
	Creating an XML document based on a schema	❏

W03E-3
Formatting Documents

The skills tested by this section of the Microsoft Office Specialist Word 2003 Expert Exam all relate to advanced formatting of documents. Specifically, the following objectives are associated with this set of skills:

Number	Objective
W03E-3-1	Create and modify forms
W03E-3-2	Create and modify document background
W03E-3-3	Create and modify document indexes and tables
W03E-3-4	Insert and modify endnotes, footnotes, captions, and cross-references
W03E-3-5	Create and manage master documents and subdocuments

Important Before you can do the practice exercises associated with this skill set, you need to install the practice files from the book's companion CD to their default location. See "Installing the Practice Files" on page xxv for more information.

Create and Modify Forms

W03E-3-1   The skills measured by this objective include the following:

- Setting up a form
- Modifying a form

A form is a document containing text instructions and questions, together with areas where users can enter their responses. These areas are form fields in which you can collect specific types of information in specific ways.

Setting Up a Form

To create a form, you type all the information that does not change from one form to the next as regular text, and you use the Forms toolbar to insert text form fields, check-box form fields, and drop-down form fields in which users supply their information. After you insert a form field, you can set form field properties, such as the type of text field, the maximum length of entries, and the options in a drop-down form field. The properties vary depending on the form field type.

W03E-3: **Formatting Documents**

BE SURE TO open a document containing the text of a form and to display the Forms toolbar before carrying out these steps.

To insert and format a text form field:

1 Click the location where you want to insert the field.

Text Form
Field

2 On the Forms toolbar, click the **Text Form Field** button.

Word inserts a text form field with the default text format.

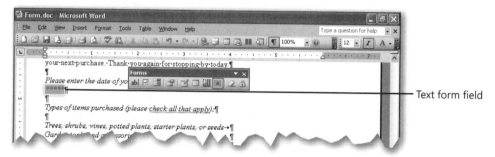

Text form field

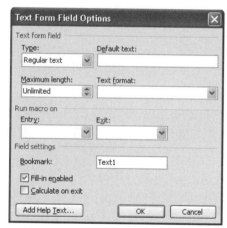

Form Field
Options

3 On the Forms toolbar, click the **Form Field Options** button.

4 In the Text Form Field Options dialog box, click the **Type** down arrow, and click the item you want.

5 Select any additional specifications for this type of text form field.

For example, you might specify a format for a date form field so that no matter how users fill in the field, the date will be displayed a certain way.

6 Click **OK** to close the Text Form Field Options dialog box.

To insert and format a set of check box form fields:

1 Click the location where you want to insert the field.

Check Box
Form Field

2   On the Forms toolbar, click the **Check Box Form Field** button.

Word inserts a check box form field.

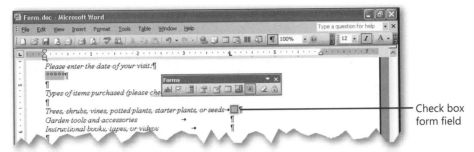

Check box
form field

Form Field
Options

3   On the Forms toolbar, click the **Form Fields Options** button.

Tip   You can provide instructions for filling out a field by adding help text to form fields. In any Form Field Options dialog box, click Add Help Text, select the "Type your own" option, type the instructions in the box, and then click OK.

4   Specify any formatting options you want for this form field.

Copy

5   On the Standard toolbar, click the **Copy** button.

The formatted check box is copied to the Office Clipboard.

Paste

6   Click the location where you want the second check box form field to appear, and on the Standard toolbar, click the **Paste** button.

7   Repeat step 6 for any additional check boxes.

Tip   You can also hold down the CTRL key and drag a copy of the selected check box.

To insert and format a drop-down form field:

1   Click the location where you want to insert the field.

Drop-Down
Form Field

2   On the Forms toolbar, click the **Drop-Down Form Field** button.

Word inserts a drop-down form field. (When users fill out the form, they will see a box with a down arrow.)

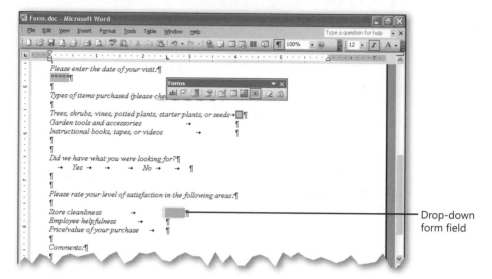

Drop-down
form field

Form Field
Options

3   On the Forms toolbar, click the **Form Fields Options** button.

4   In the **Drop-down item** box, type the first item in the list, and click **Add**.

This option is added to the "Items in drop-down list" box.

5   Repeat step 4 for each item you want to appear in the list.

6   To change the order of the items in the list, click an item, and then click the **Move Up** or **Move Down** arrow button.

7   Click **OK**.

Tip   You can copy and paste drop-down form fields using the same techniques you would use to copy regular text.

Practice Exercise

In this exercise, you will insert text form fields, check-box form fields, and drop-down form fields to create a form.

USE the *CreateForm* document in the *My Documents\Microsoft Press\MOS 2003 Study Guide\Word \W03E-3-1* practice file folder.

Open the *CreateForm* document, display the Forms toolbar, and display non-printing characters. Scroll down the document, click the blank line below *Please enter the date of your visit*, and insert a text form field. Display the Text Form Field Options dialog box, and specify **Date** as the type of text field and **MMMM d, yyyy** as its format. Move to the end of the document, and insert another text form field below the word *Comments*. Scroll up the document, click to the right of the Tab character after *Trees, shrubs, vines, potted plants, starter plants, or seeds*, and insert a check box form field. Set its size as **Exactly** and **12 pt**. Use any method to copy the check box to the right of the Tab characters after *Garden tools and accessories*, and *Instructional books, tapes, or videos*. Also copy it to the right of the Tab characters after *Yes* and *No*. Scroll down the document, click to the right of the Tab character after *Store cleanliness*, and insert a drop-down form field. Specify the following as the list's items: **Very Satisfied**, **Somewhat Satisfied**, **Satisfied**, **Very Dissatisfied**, and **Mildly Dissatisfied**. Then use the **Move Up** arrow button to move the *Mildly Dissatisfied* entry up in the list. Copy the drop-down form field to the right of the Tab characters after *Employee helpfulness* and *Price/value of your purchase*. Then close the *CreateForm* document without saving it.

Modifying a Form

You can enhance the look of a form by changing formatting and adding graphics just as you would in any other type of Word document. You can also modify form field properties to change the way the fields look and work.

BE SURE TO open a document containing a form and to display the Forms toolbar before carrying out these steps.

To format a form field:

1   Click the form field you want to format.
2   On the Formatting toolbar, click the appropriate buttons to format the field as you want.
3   Click a blank area of the document to deselect the form field.

To change a form field's properties:

1   Double-click the form field whose properties you want to change.
    The corresponding Form Field Options dialog box appears.
2   Modify the properties as you want.
3   Click **OK**.

To move or size a form field:

1   Click the form field you want to move or size.

Insert Frame

2   On the Forms toolbar, click the **Insert Frame** button.

The form field now has a frame, and handles around the frame indicate that this object can be moved or sized.

3   Drag the form field to the desired location, or drag the frame's sizing handles to increase or decrease its size.

Practice Exercise

In this exercise, you will format a text field, change the default value of a check box, change an item in a drop-down form field, insert a frame, and move and size a field.

USE the *ModifyForm* document in the *My Documents\Microsoft Press\MOS 2003 Study Guide\Word \W03E-3-1* practice file folder.

Open the *ModifyForm* document, and display the Forms toolbar. Scroll down the document, click the text form field below *Please enter the date of your visit*, and use the **Border** button on the Formatting toolbar to add a border to the field. Then double-click the check box to the right of *Yes*, and select **Checked** as the **Default value** option. Double-click the first drop-down form field, and remove **Mildly Dissatisfied** from the list. Add **Somewhat Dissatisfied**, and then move it up to where *Mildly Dissatisfied* was in the list. Repeat this step for the next two drop-down form fields. Click the text form field below the *Comments* heading, give it a frame, and then drag the text form field down about a quarter-inch to add space between it and *Comments*. Then make the frame about 6 inches wide and 1 1/2 inches high. Close the *ModifyForm* document without saving it.

Create and Modify Document Background

W03E-3-2   The skills measured by this objective include the following:

■ Changing the background color and fill effect

■ Creating a watermark

■ Applying a document theme

To ensure a consistent and polished look for a document, you can specify a background for its pages and a theme for its major elements.

Changing the Background Color and Fill Effect

If you are creating a document that will be published on the Internet and viewed in a Web browser, you can make your document stand out by adding a background color or pattern. This type of background is displayed only in Web Layout view and is not designed to be printed.

BE SURE TO open the document you want to work with in Web Layout view before carrying out these steps.

To change the background color:

1   On the **Format** menu, click **Background**.

A color palette appears.

2   Click the color box you want.

The background of the document changes to the selected color.

To change the background fill effect:

1   On the **Format** menu, click **Background**, and then click **Fill Effects** below the color palette.

2   When the Fill Effects dialog box appears, click the **Texture** tab.

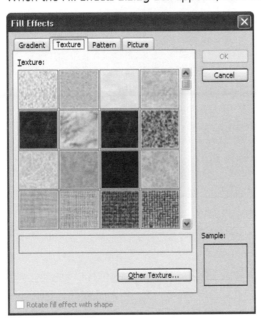

3   Click the fill effect you want, and click **OK**.

The background changes to display the effect.

Practice Exercise

In this exercise, you will apply a color and pattern to a document's background.

USE the *FormatBackground* document in the *My Documents\Microsoft Press\MOS 2003 Study Guide\Word \W03E-3-2* practice file folder.

Open the *FormatBackground* document, and switch to Web Layout view. Change the background color to **Light Green**. Then display the **Texture** tab of the Fill Effects dialog box, and change the background to the effect in the fourth column of the first row. Close the *FormatBackground* document without saving it.

Creating a Watermark

A watermark is a faint background image that is visible in a document but doesn't interfere with the readers' ability to view the document's main text. You can use words or a graphic as a watermark behind the text of a printed or online document.

BE SURE TO open the document you want to work with in Print Layout view before carrying out these steps.

To create a text watermark:

1   On the **Format** menu, click **Background**, and then click **Printed Watermark** below the color palette.

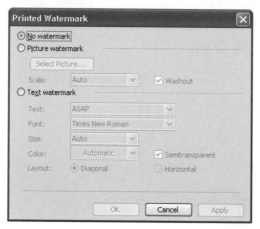

2   Select the **Text watermark** option.

3   Click the **Text** down arrow, and click the message you want in the drop-down list.

You can also type your own text.

4   Click the **Color** down arrow, and click the color you want for the watermark text in the palette.

5   Click **OK**.

To add a graphic watermark to every page of a document:

1   On the **Format** menu, click **Background**, and then click **Printed Watermark**.

2   In the Printed Watermark dialog box, select the **Picture watermark** option, and then click the **Select Picture** button.

3   In the Insert Picture dialog box, navigate to the folder where the graphic you want to use as a watermark is stored, and double-click the graphic file.

4   Click the **Scale** down arrow, and specify how big or small you want the watermark picture to appear in the document.

5   For a more vibrant picture, clear the **Washout** check box, and then click **OK**.

Practice Exercise

In this exercise, you will add a text watermark to a document.

USE the *AddWatermark* document in the *My Documents\Microsoft Press\MOS 2003 Study Guide\Word \W03E-3-2* practice file folder.

Open the *AddWatermark* document in Print Layout view. Display the Printed Watermark dialog box, select the **Text watermark** option, and click **URGENT** in the **Text** drop-down list. Change the watermark to **Bright Green**. To see the watermark, change the **Zoom** setting on the Standard toolbar to **Whole Page**. Close the *AddWatermark* document without saving it.

Applying a Document Theme

You can change the entire look of a document by applying one of Word's predefined themes. A theme is a unified look that incorporates heading styles, text styles formatted with font effects, lists with specially designed bullet characters, background colors, fill effects, and images. Each theme includes color schemes and graphical design elements that project a specific image or tone. You might want to use a theme when designing Web pages, reports, and presentations.

BE SURE TO open the document you want to work with before carrying out these steps.

To apply a theme:

1   On the **Format** menu, click **Theme**.

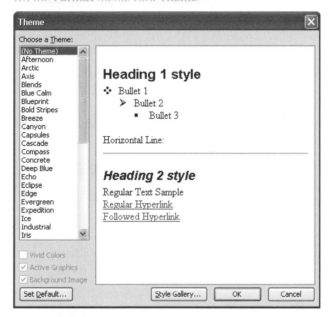

2   In the **Choose a Theme** list, click the theme you want to apply.

Tip   Some themes don't appear in the Theme dialog box until you install them. Word will display a message if you need to install the selected theme.

3   Click **OK** to apply the theme to the document.

Practice Exercise

In this exercise, you will apply a theme to an existing document.

USE the *ApplyTheme* document in the *My Documents\Microsoft Press\MOS 2003 Study Guide\Word \W03E-3-2* practice file folder.

Open the *ApplyTheme* document. Display the Theme dialog box, and apply the **Expedition** theme. Then display the Styles and Formatting task pane, and check out the formatting of the theme's styles. Close the task pane, and then close the *ApplyTheme* document without saving it.

Create and Modify Document Indexes and Tables

W03E-3-3   The skills measured by this objective include the following:

- Creating an index
- Creating a table of content, a table of figures, or a table of authorities

To make information in longer documents easy to find, you can include a table of contents at the beginning and an index at the end. You can also easily create a table of figures or a table of authorities.

Creating an Index

An index typically appears at the end of a document and alphabetically lists the main topics, names, and terms used in a document, along with the page numbers where they're located. The items in the list are called index entries. Before you can create an index, you must mark each index entry in the document. You can mark an entry for a word, phrase, or topic that appears on a single page or is discussed for several pages. You can also mark subentries, and you can create cross-reference entries that direct readers to related entries.

When you mark an index entry, Word inserts an index entry field that is formatted as hidden text. When the field is visible (that is, the Show/Hide ¶ button is active on the Standard toolbar), it appears in the document with a dotted underline.

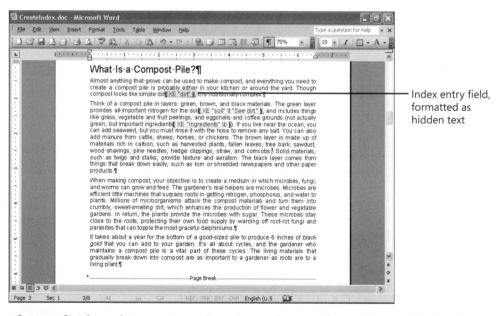

Index entry field, formatted as hidden text

After you finish marking entries, subentries, and cross-references, you click the document where you want the index to appear, and use the Index and Tables dialog box to tell Word to compile the index. You can control the style of the index and how page numbers appear. The index is inserted as a single field, but you can select and format its text as you would any other text. If you make changes to the document that affect its index entries or page numbering, you can easily update the index.

BE SURE TO open the document you want to work with and to display non-printing characters before carrying out these steps.

To mark an index entry:

1 Select the text you want to mark as an index entry.

2 On the **Insert** menu, click **Reference** and then **Index and Tables**, and then click the **Index** tab.

3 Click **Mark Entry**.

Tip You can also press ALT+SHIFT+X to open the Mark Index Entry dialog box without going through the Index and Tables dialog box.

4 Do one of the following:

- ■ To insert an index entry field adjacent to the selected text, click **Mark**.
- ■ To insert index entry fields adjacent to every occurrence of the selected text, click **Mark All**.
- ■ To adjust the entry, edit the text in the **Main entry** box, and click **Mark**.
- ■ To enter a subentry for this index entry, type the subentry in the **Subentry** box, and click **Mark**.

The Mark Index Entry dialog box remains open so that you can select a different word or phrase, activate the dialog box by clicking its title bar, and then mark the entry.

5 When you have finished marking entries, click **Cancel** to close the dialog box.

To format an index entry as you mark it:

1 Start the process of selecting and marking the index entry as usual.

2 In the **Page number format** area of the Mark Index Entry dialog box, select the check box for the format you want.

3 Complete the marking process.

When Word creates the index, it will show the page numbers for this entry in the format you specified.

To mark a cross-reference:

1   Start the process of selecting and marking the index entry as usual.

2   In the **Options** area of the Mark Index Entry dialog box, select the **Cross-reference** option.
    The insertion point moves to the space after the word *See* in the Cross-reference box.

3   Type the name of the entry you want to refer to.

4   Complete the marking process.

To compile the index on a separate page at the end of the document:

1   Press **CTRL+END** to move to the end of the document, and then press **CTRL+ENTER** to insert
    a new page.

Show/Hide ¶

2   On the Standard toolbar, turn off the **Show/Hide ¶** button to hide the index codes.
    If the index codes are visible, Word cannot paginate the document correctly.

3   On the **Insert** menu, click **Reference** and then **Index and Tables**.

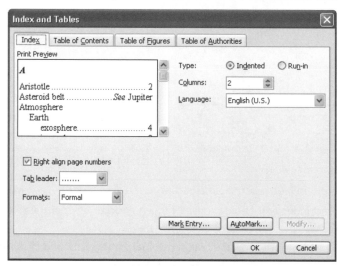

4   Click the **Formats** down arrow, and click the index style you want.

5   Make any other formatting adjustments.

6   Click **OK** to close the Index and Tables dialog box and create the index.

To update the index after editing the document:

1   In the document, add, edit, or delete index entries or other text as necessary.

2   Click anywhere in the index to select its field, and press the **F9** key.
    The index is updated to reflect your changes.

Practice Exercise

In this exercise, you will first mark a few index entries, subentries, and cross-references. Then you'll create and format an index.

USE the *CreateIndex* document in the *My Documents\Microsoft Press\MOS 2003 Study Guide\Word \W03E-3-3* practice file folder.

Open the *CreateIndex* document, and make sure non-printing characters are displayed. In the first sentence of the second paragraph below the *Why Compost?* heading, select the word *recycling*, display the **Index** tab of the Index and Tables dialog box, and click **Mark Entry**. In the Mark Index Entry dialog box, click **Mark All**. In the third line of the second paragraph on page 2, select the word *recycles*, and click the title bar of the Mark Index Entry dialog box to activate it. Change the entry to **recycling**, and click **Mark**. In the fourth line of the second paragraph on page 3, select the word *ingredients*, activate the Mark Index Entry dialog box, set the page number format to bold, and click **Mark All**. At the end of the first paragraph on page 3, select the word *dirt*, activate the Mark Index Entry dialog box, cross-reference this entry to **soil.** (including the period), and click **Mark**. Close the Mark Index Entry dialog box, move to the end of the document, and insert a new page. Type **Index**, press **ENTER** twice, and then make this heading bold and 18 points. Press **CTRL+END**, and turn off the **Show/Hide ¶** button. Display the Index and Tables dialog box, select **Formal** as the index format, clear the **Right Align Page Numbers** check box, and set the number of columns to **1**. Click **OK** to create the index, and then review the results. Close the *CreateIndex* document without saving it.

Creating a Table of Contents, a Table of Figures, or a Table of Authorities

A table of contents generally appears at the beginning of a document and lists headings and corresponding page numbers. To create and format a table of contents, you apply styles to the headings and then tell Word to compile the table. Word inserts the table at the insertion point as a single field. Each entry is hyperlinked to the heading it references, and you can hold down the **CTRL** key and click the entry to go to the corresponding heading.

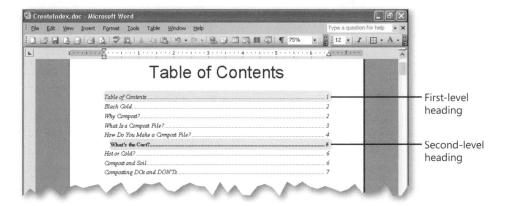

If a document includes figures or tables that have captions, you can tell Word to create a table of figures. If a legal document contains citations, you can tell Word to create a table of authorities. (You mark citations in much the same way that you mark index entries.)

See Also   For information about inserting captions, refer to W03E-3-4, "Insert and Modify Endnotes, Footnotes, Captions, and Cross-references."

You can tell Word which format to use when compiling a table, and you can edit and format a compiled table manually as you would any other text. If you create a table and later make changes that affect the table's entries or the document's pagination, you can update the table.

BE SURE TO open a document containing headings, figures with captions, or legal citations before carrying out these steps.

To insert a table of contents on a new page at the beginning of a document:

1   With the insertion point at the beginning of the document, press **CTRL+ENTER** to insert a new page, and then press **CTRL+HOME**.

2   On the **Insert** menu, click **Reference** and then **Index and Tables**, and then click the **Table of Contents** tab.

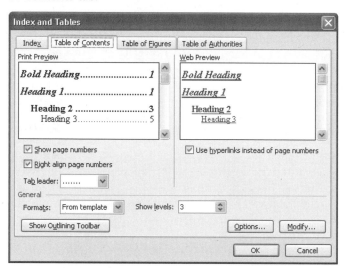

3   Click the **Formats** down arrow, and click the table style you want.

4   Click the **Tab leader** down arrow, and click the type of line you want to direct the eye to the page numbers, and then click **OK**.

Word inserts a table of contents with the formatting you specified.

To update the table of contents after editing the document:

1   In the document, add, edit, or delete headings or other text as necessary.

2   Click anywhere in the table of contents to select its field, and press the **F9** key.

3   In the Update Table of Contents dialog box, select whether you want to update page numbers only or update the entire table.

The table is updated to reflect your changes.

Tip   You can also use the Go to TOC and Update TOC buttons on the Outlining toolbar to work with the table of contents.

To insert a table of figures:

1   Click the location where you want to insert the table of figures.

2   On the **Insert** menu, click **Reference** and then **Index and Tables**, and then click the **Table of Figures** tab.

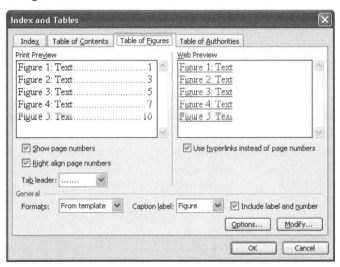

3   Click the **Caption label** down arrow, and click the type of caption you want.

4   Click the **Formats** down arrow, and click the format you want for the table.

5   Select any additional options you want, and click **OK** to insert the table of figures.

To insert a table of authorities:

1   Click the location where you want to insert the table of authorities.

2   On the **Insert** menu, click **Reference** and then **Index and Tables**, and then click the **Table of Authorities** tab.

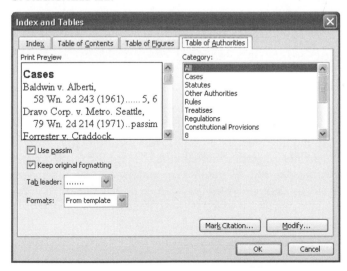

3   In the **Category** area, click the type of legal reference you want in your table of authorities, or click **All** to include all categories.

4   Select formatting options for the table, and click **OK**.

Word inserts the table of authorities in the specified format.

Practice Exercise

In this exercise, you will open a document that uses heading styles and create a table of contents. You will then change the document by inserting page breaks and update the table of contents.

USE the *CreateContents* document in the *My Documents\Microsoft Press\MOS 2003 Study Guide\Word \W03E-3-3* practice file folder.

Open the *CreateContents* document, insert a new page at the top, and move to the new page. Type **Table of Contents**, and press **ENTER**. Display the **Table of Contents** tab of the Index and Tables dialog box, set **Formats** to **Distinctive** and **Tab leader** to a dotted line, and click **OK**. After Word inserts the table, click to the left of the *What Is a Compost Pile?* heading on page 2, and press **CTRL+ENTER** to start a new page. Start another new page before the *How Do You Make a Compost Pile?* and *What's the Cost?* headings. Then change *What's the Cost?* to the **Heading 2** style. Move to the top of the document, click anywhere in the table of contents, and press the **F9** key to update the entire table. Then close the *CreateContents* document without saving it.

Insert and Modify Endnotes, Footnotes, Captions, and Cross-references

W03E-3-4   The skills measured by this objective include the following:

■ Inserting and formatting footnotes and endnotes

■ Inserting and formatting captions

■ Inserting cross-references

Longer documents such as research papers often include footnotes or endnotes to cite sources, and they commonly include graphics or tables with captions and cross-references from one part of the document to another.

Inserting and Formatting Footnotes and Endnotes

Footnotes and endnotes explain, comment on, or provide references for text in a document. Footnotes appear at the bottom of the page containing the associated text, whereas endnotes appear at the end of the document or at the end of a section in that document. Each footnote and endnote consists of a reference mark and note text. The reference mark is a number or symbol in the main text of the document that matches a number or symbol next to the footnote or endnote. By default, footnote reference marks are styled with a 1, 2, 3 format, and endnote reference marks are styled with a i, ii, iii format.

BE SURE TO open the document you want to work with in Print Layout view before carrying out these steps.

To insert a footnote or endnote:

1 Click the location where you want the reference mark to be.

2 On the **Insert** menu, click **Reference** and then **Footnote**.

3 In the **Location** area, select the **Footnotes** or **Endnotes** option.

4 In the **Format** area, click the **Number format** down arrow, and select a number format.

5 Click **Insert**.

Word inserts the reference mark in the document. The insertion point moves to an area at the bottom of the page or the end of the section. (If you are in Normal view, you type the note in a separate Notes pane.)

6 Type the note text.

To change the number format of existing footnotes or endnotes:

1 On the **Insert** menu, click **Reference** and then **Footnote**.

2 In the Footnote and Endnote dialog box, select the **Footnotes** or **Endnotes** option.

3 In the **Format** area, click the **Number format** down arrow, and click a new number format.

4 Verify that **Whole document** appears in the **Apply changes to** box, and then click **Apply**.

All footnotes change to the new number format.

To change the formatting applied to footnote or endnote reference marks:

1 Select the reference mark for the first footnote or endnote, and apply the character formatting you want.

2 Select another reference mark, and on the **Format** menu, click **Styles and Formatting**.

3 In the Styles and Formatting task pane, click **Select All** to select all the footnotes or endnotes in the document, and then in the **Pick formatting to apply** area, click **Footnote Reference**.

All the footnotes or endnotes now appear with the character formatting you applied in step 1.

Practice Exercise

In this exercise, you will insert footnotes and then change their format.

USE the *InsertFootnote* document in the *My Documents\Microsoft Press\MOS 2003 Study Guide\Word \W03E-3-4* practice file folder.

Open the *InsertFootnote* document in Print Layout view. Click to the right of the word *Ireland* in the first paragraph, and display the Footnote and Endnote dialog box. Specify that you want to insert footnotes with the default **1, 2, 3** style, and then type **Moluccella laevis** in the footnote area at the bottom of the page. Click to the right of the word *geraniums*, and create another footnote of the same style, typing **Pelargonium** as its text. Change the footnote numbering format of the whole document to **a, b, c**. Then close the *InsertFootnote* document without saving it.

Inserting and Formatting Captions

If a document includes figures, graphics, or tables that would benefit from numbers and captions, you can easily add them. Word keeps track of the numbers and updates them if you add or delete a caption.

BE SURE TO open a document containing figures, graphics, or tables before carrying out these steps.

To insert a caption:

1 Click the location where you want the caption to appear.

2 On the **Insert** menu, click **Reference** and then **Caption**.

3 In the Caption dialog box, click the **New Label** button, and when the New Label dialog box appears, type the default text for the caption (for example, **Figure**), and click **OK**.

4 In the Caption dialog box, click to the right of the label and its number in the **Caption** box, type the caption, and click **OK**.

The caption is inserted at the insertion point.

Practice Exercise

In this exercise, you will insert a caption in a document.

USE the *InsertCaption* document in the *My Documents\Microsoft Press\MOS 2003 Study Guide\Word \W03E-3-4* practice file folder.

Open the *InsertCaption* document. Click the graphic on page 3, and display the Caption dialog box. Create a new label that inserts the word *Graphic* and a sequential number. Then type **double-digging** as the caption, and insert the caption below the graphic. Close the *InsertCaption* document without saving it.

Inserting Cross-References

You can use cross-references to jump easily to associated information elsewhere in the document. To create cross-references, you need to mark locations in a document and name them. You can create cross-references to headings, figure captions, numbered paragraphs, endnotes, or any other text. If you later delete an item you have designated as the target of a cross-reference, you will need to update the cross-reference.

Tip You can create cross-references only to items within the same document, or within a master document and its subdocuments. If you want jump to a different document, you use hyperlinks instead.

See Also For information about master documents, refer to W03E-3-5, "Create and Manage Master Documents and Subdocuments." For information about hyperlinks, refer to W03C-2-3, "Insert and Modify Hyperlinks."

BE SURE TO open the document you want to work with before carrying out these steps.

To insert a cross-reference:

1 Type the lead-in for the cross-reference, such as **For more information, see**, and then press **SPACE**.

2 On the **Insert** menu, click **Reference** and then **Cross-reference**.

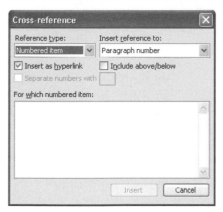

3 Click the **Reference type** down arrow, and click the type of item being referenced.

4 Click the **Insert reference to** down arrow, and click the element you want to appear in the cross-reference.

5 In the list box, click the cross-reference target.

6 Click **Insert**, and then click **Close**.

A hyperlinked cross-reference is inserted at the end of the lead-in text.

7 Hold down the **CTRL** key, and click the cross-reference to test it.

To update a cross-reference:

1 Select the text of the cross-reference (the hyperlinked text, not the lead-in).

2 Right-click the selected cross-reference, and on the shortcut menu, click **Update Field**.

Word updates the cross-reference to reflect any changes you made to the document.

3 Hold down the **CTRL** key, and click the cross-reference to test it.

Practice Exercise

In this exercise, you will insert a cross-reference, change the referenced item, and then update the cross-reference.

USE the *InsertReference* document in the *My Documents\Microsoft Press\MOS 2003 Study Guide\Word \W03E-3-4* practice file folder.

Open the *InsertReference* document. Click at the end of the first paragraph under the *What Is a Compost Pile?* heading, type **For more information, see**, and then press **SPACE**. Display the Cross-reference dialog box, set **Reference type** to **Heading**, set **Insert reference to** to **Heading text**, and in the **For which heading** list, click **Hot or Cold?**. Click **Insert**, and then close the dialog box. Hold down the **CTRL** key, and click the *Hot or Cold?* cross-reference to test it. With the insertion point to the left of the *Hot or Cold?* heading, type **Which Is Best,** and then press **SPACE**. Scroll up to the *What Is a Compost Pile?* section, and select the hyperlinked heading in the cross-reference. Right-click the selected cross-reference, and click **Update Field** to update the cross-reference to reflect the change you made to the heading. Then close the *InsertReference* document without saving it.

Create and Manage Master Documents and Subdocuments

W03E-3-5 The skills measured by this objective include the following:

■ Working with a master document and subdocuments

When a long document includes multiple sections, you can turn the document into a master document and subdocuments so that you can work on different parts independently.

Working with a Master Document and Subdocuments

A master document is structured like an outline, with hyperlinks to all its subdocuments. So before you can create a master document and subdocuments, you must switch to Outline view. If the headings in the document are not already assigned to specific heading levels, you can use the buttons on the Outlining toolbar to assign them. You can then break the document into subdocuments, or you can add existing documents to the master document as subdocuments.

After you create the master document, you can hide the subdocuments to make the master document easier to view and organize. You can see all the subdocument titles and simply drag them to reorder them. If you want to edit a subdocument, you can click its hyperlink to open it in a separate document window. (You can also open each subdocument in the usual way, without going through the master document.) If you want to work with the master document as a whole—for example, to check its spelling—you can click the Expand Subdocuments button to show the contents of all subdocuments. You can also use this view to create a table of contents, an index, cross-references, and headers and footers for the entire document.

BE SURE TO open a document containing headings that have been assigned to heading levels in Outline view before carrying out these steps.

To create the master document and subdocuments:

1   In Outline view, click the plus sign to the left of the heading whose text you want to turn into a subdocument.

Create
Subdocument

2   On the Outlining toolbar, click the **Create Subdocument** button.

The Subdocument icon appears in the left margin of the document, a light border surrounds the selected text, and the heading and its text become a subdocument of the master document.

3   Repeat steps 1 and 2 to turn each subsequent heading and its text into a subdocument.

Collapse
Subdocuments

4   On the Outlining toolbar, click the **Collapse Subdocuments** button.

Word prompts you to save changes to the master document before collapsing the subdocuments.

5   Click **OK**.

Word moves the heading and text of each subdocument to a separate file, saves the file with the heading as its name in the same folder as the master document, and then closes the subdocument. In the subdocument's place in the master document, Word inserts a hyperlink to the subdocument.

Hyperlink to subdocument

Tip   You can point to a hyperlink to see a ScreenTip with the complete path of the subdocument, including the file name.

To change the view of a master document:

Expand
Subdocuments

1 On the Outlining toolbar, click the **Expand Subdocuments** button.

The headings and text of all the subdocuments are displayed as part of the master document.

Show First
Line Only

2 On the Outlining toolbar, click the **Show First Line Only** button.

The subdocuments collapse to show just their first lines.

To remove a subdocument:

1 Click the plus sign to the left of the subdocument's heading in the master document.

Remove
Subdocument

2 On the Outlining toolbar, click the **Remove Subdocument** button.

The subdocument becomes part of the master document.

To make changes to a subdocument from the master document:

1 Hold down the **CTRL** key, and click the hyperlink of the subdocument you want to work with.

The subdocument opens in its own document window.

2 Edit and format the subdocument just as you would any other document.

3 Save the subdocument, and then close its window.

Practice Exercise

In this exercise, you will create a master document and a set of subdocuments. Then you will open and modify a subdocument and change the view of the master document.

USE the *CreateMaster* document in the *My Documents\Microsoft Press\MOS 2003 Study Guide\Word \W03E-3-5* practice file folder.

Open the *CreateMaster* document in Outline view, and save it as **CompostMaster**. Make sure the Outlining toolbar is displayed. Click the plus sign to the left of the *Why Compost?* heading to select the heading and its subordinate text, and click the **Create Subdocument** button on the Outlining toolbar. Repeat this step to turn each of the following headings and their text into subdocuments: *What Is a Compost Pile?*, *How Do You Make a Compost Pile?*, *Hot or Cold?*, and *Compost and Soil*. On the Outlining toolbar, click the **Collapse Subdocuments** button, and save the changes to the master document. Hold down the **CTRL** key, and click the hyperlink to open the *What Is a Compost Pile?* subdocument in its own document window. Scroll to the end of the document, and near the end of the third paragraph, make the words *black gold* bold so that they stand out. Save the subdocument, and close its window. On the Outlining toolbar, click the **Expand Subdocuments** button. Scroll to see the change you made to the *What Is a Compost Pile?* subdocument reflected in the master document, and then close the *CompostMaster* document without saving it.

W03E-3 Review

Number	Objective	Mastered
W03E-3-1	Create and modify forms	
	Setting up a form	❑
	Modifying a form	❑
W03E-3-2	Create and modify document background	
	Changing the background color and fill effect	❑
	Creating a watermark	❑
	Applying a document theme	❑
W03E-3-3	Create and modify document indexes and tables	
	Creating an index	❑
	Creating a table of content, a table of figures, or a table of authorities	❑
W03E-3-4	Insert and modify endnotes, footnotes, captions, and cross-references	
	Inserting and formatting footnotes and endnotes	❑
	Inserting and formatting captions	❑
	Inserting cross-references	❑
W03E-3-5	Create and manage master documents and subdocuments	
	Working with a master document and subdocuments	❑

W03E-4
Collaborating

The skills tested by this section of the Microsoft Office Specialist Word 2003 Expert Exam all relate to advanced Word features for collaborating with other people on the creation and formatting of documents. Specifically, the following objectives are associated with this set of skills:

Number	Objective
W03E-4-1	Modify track changes options
W03E-4-2	Publish and edit Web documents in Word
W03E-4-3	Manage document versions
W03E-4-4	Protect and restrict forms and documents
W03E-4-5	Attach digital signatures to documents
W03E-4-6	Customize document properties

Important   Before you can do the practice exercises associated with this skill set, you need to install the practice files from the book's companion CD to their default location. See "Installing the Practice Files" on page xxv for more information.

Modify Track Changes Options

W03E-4-1   The skills measured by this objective include the following:

- Setting reviewer options
- Setting balloon options

To make working with comments and tracked changes easier, you can customize the settings used to display them.

Setting Reviewer Options

Word assigns a different color to the tracked changes and comments made by each reviewer who works on a document. If you want your tracked changes and comments to always be in the same color, you can override Word's color assignments in the Tracked Changes dialog box.

Tip   You can also change the way Word marks insertions and deletions in this dialog box.

By default, the changes made by all reviewers are shown in the document. To make it easier to keep track of which reviewer made which change, you can view the changes made by one reviewer or a group of reviewers, hiding the changes made by other people.

BE SURE TO open a document containing tracked changes and to display the Reviewing toolbar before carrying out these steps.

To specify reviewer ink colors:

1 On the Reviewing toolbar, click the **Show** down arrow, and click **Options**.

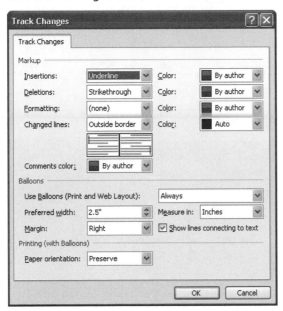

2 In the **Markup** area, click the **Color** down arrow for the item you want to change, click the desired color in the drop-down list, and then click **OK**.

Changes you make to the current document will now be tracked in your specified color.

To specify which reviewer's changes you want to see:

1 On the Reviewing toolbar, click the **Show** down arrow, click **Reviewers**, and then click the name of a reviewer whose changes you want to hide.

By default, all reviewers' changes are visible. You need to hide revisions you don't want to see.

2 Click the **Show** down arrow, click **Reviewers**, and then click **All Reviewers**.

The revisions made by all reviewers appear.

Practice Exercise

In this exercise, you will hide the changes made by one reviewer and then change the color used for your own changes.

USE the *SetReviewer* document in the *My Documents\Microsoft Press\MOS 2003 Study Guide\Word \W03E-4-1* practice file folder.

Open the *SetReviewer* document. Use the **Show** button on the Reviewing toolbar to hide the changes made by **Jill B**. Display the Track Changes dialog box, and change the **Color** boxes of both **Insertions** and **Deletions** to **Blue**. Delete the **Decorative bench** line item in the list, and notice that Word tracks the change in blue. Close the *SetReviewer* document without saving it.

Setting Balloon Options

By default, Word always shows tracked changes in balloons in the right margin of the document. Each balloon is 2.5 inches wide and has a connecting line to its text. In documents with many changes and comments, you might find comment balloons distracting or confusing. In these cases, you can turn off the balloons and instead review the changes and comments in a Reviewing pane at the bottom of the document window. You can also display only balloons for comments, and you can turn off the connecting lines.

BE SURE TO open a document containing tracked changes and comments and to display the Reviewing toolbar before carrying out these steps.

To turn balloons on or off:

1 On the Reviewing toolbar, click the **Show** down arrow, and then click **Options**.

Tip   You can also modify balloon settings by clicking Options on the Tools menu and clicking the Track Changes tab.

2 In the **Balloons** area, click the **Use Balloons (Print and Web Layout)** down arrow, and click the item you want.

3 Click **OK** to close the dialog box.

To view changes and comments in the Reviewing pane:

Reviewing
Pane

1   On the Reviewing toolbar, click the **Reviewing Pane** button.

The Reviewing pane appears at the bottom of the Word window.

2   To adjust the size of the pane, point to its top border, and when the pointer changes to a double-headed arrow, drag the border up or down.

3   To see a particular change or comment in the Reviewing pane, click the change or comment in the document.

Tip   You can view all of the comments and changes in a document by scrolling through them in the Reviewing pane.

4   On the Reviewing toolbar, click the **Reviewing Pane** button to close the pane.

Practice Exercise

In this exercise, you will turn off balloons and view changes and comments in the Reviewing pane.

USE the *SetBalloon* document in the *My Documents\Microsoft Press\MOS 2003 Study Guide\Word\W03E-4-1* practice file folder.

Open the *SetBalloon* document. Use the **Show** button on the Reviewing toolbar to hide comments. Then display the Track Changes dialog box, and turn off balloons altogether. Open the Reviewing pane to see the changes and comments in the document, and then close the pane again. Close the *SetBalloon* document without saving it.

Publish and Edit Web Documents in Word

W03E-4-2   The skills measured by this objective include the following:

■ Opening and editing a Web page
■ Creating a frames page

Word's Web capabilities are not limited to being able to save a document in HTML format. You can open and work with HTML documents in Word, and you can create fancy frames-based layouts.

Opening and Editing a Web Page

After you save a Word document as a Web page, you can open it in Word and edit it, just as you would a regular Word document. You can also use Word to open Web pages created in other programs and saved with a *.htm* or *.html* file name extension. Making changes can be as basic as replacing text and adjusting alignment or as advanced as inserting graphics. When you finish editing the document, you can save it as a Web page or as a regular Word document.

BE SURE TO start Word and have an HTML file available before carrying out these steps.

To open a Web page and modify it:

Open

1 On the Standard toolbar, click the **Open** button.

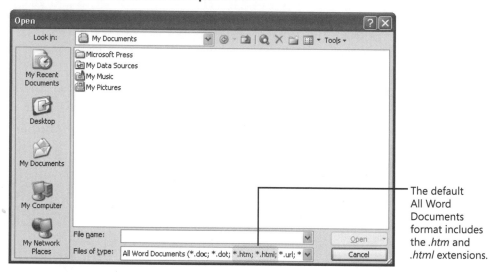

The default All Word Documents format includes the *.htm* and *.html* extensions.

2 Navigate to the folder where the Web page you want to open is stored, click the file name, and click **Open**.

3 If a message asks whether you want to make Word your default Web page editor, click **Yes** or **No** depending on your preference.

4 If a message asks whether you want to initialize ActiveX controls, read the information in the scrolling box, and click **Yes** or **No** depending on whether you trust the source of the document.

Tip ActiveX controls are software components that add interactivity and functionality to a Web page.

The Web page opens in Word. You can then edit and save it in the usual way.

Practice Exercise

In this exercise, you will open a Web page in word, edit it, and then save it.

USE the *OpenWeb* file in the *My Documents\Microsoft Press\MOS 2003 Study Guide\Word\W03E-4-2* practice file folder.

Use the Open dialog box to open the *OpenWeb* Web page in Word. Click **No** if you are asked whether you want to make Word your default Web page editor. Select the two paragraphs that have gray text, and change the font color to red. Then change the last two paragraphs to italics. Preview the page in your Web browser, and then close the browser. Use the **Save As** command to save the document with the name **WebPage**, and then close the *WebPage* document.

Creating a Frames Page

In Word, you can create Web pages that contain frames in which you can display documents, graphics, and other items of interest to create the types of layouts you see on Web sites. Because you can scroll the frames independently, the documents you display in frames can be any length.

BE SURE TO open Word in Web Layout view before carrying out these steps.

To create a frames page:

1 On the **Format** menu, click **Frames** and then **New Frames Page**.

Word opens a new document consisting of one area, or frame. Word also displays the Frames toolbar.

2 On the Frames toolbar, click **New Frame Left**.

A frame roughly half the width of the screen appears to the left of the existing frame.

3 To change the size of a frame, drag its borders.

4 Use the buttons on the Frames toolbar to add any other frames you want.

5 On the **File** menu, click **Save**.

6 In the Save As dialog box, type a name for the frames-page file, navigate to the folder in which you want to store the file, leave the file type as it is, and click **Save**.

To add content to a frames page:

1 Do one of the following:

■ Click a frame in which you want to enter text directly, and type the text. Then use the buttons on the Formatting toolbar to format the text any way you want.

■ Click a frame in which you want to display a document, and on the **Insert** menu, click **File**. Browse to the document you want to display, and double-click it to insert it.

Tip If the document you inserted is longer than the frame, you can scroll that frame without changing the view in adjacent frames.

2 Save the frames page.

The folder where the frames page is stored now contains an MHTML file for the frames page, and additional MHTML files that contain the information for the text typed directly in any frame and the documents inserted in any frame.

Practice Exercise

In this exercise, you will create a frames page, add text and a document to the page, and then save it.

USE the *InsertWeb* document in the *My Documents\Microsoft Press\MOS 2003 Study Guide\Word\W03E-4-2* practice file folder.

With all documents closed, create a frames page. Create a new frame to the left of the existing one, and then close the Frames toolbar. Make the frame on the left half its original width.

211

In the left frame, type **Check out The Garden Company's Children's Center!**, press **ENTER** three times, type **All activities are free to the public!**, and press **ENTER**. Select all the text in the left frame, and change its size to **26** and its color to **Orange**. Click the right frame, and insert the *InsertWeb* .htm file from the *My Documents\Microsoft Press\MOS 2003 Study Guide \Word\W03E-4-2* practice file folder. Scroll the document in its frame. Save the frames page with the name **FramesPage** in the *My Documents\Microsoft Press\MOS 2003 Study Guide \Word\W03E-4-2* practice file folder. Then close the *FramesPage* file.

Manage Document Versions

W03E-4-3   The skills measured by this objective include the following:

■   Creating and managing document versions

As documents evolve, you might want to keep track of various versions, either as an audit of changes or so that you can revert to an earlier version if necessary.

Creating and Managing Document Versions

If you want a record of changes made to a document, you can save different versions of it. Saving versions saves disk space because Word saves only the differences between versions, not an entire copy of each document. You can also have Word save a version of your document each time you close the document, which is useful when you need a record of who made changes and when, as in the case of a legal document.

After you've saved several versions of the document, you can review, open, print, and delete earlier versions.

BE SURE TO open the document you want to work with before carrying out these steps.

To create a document version:

1   On the **File** menu, click **Versions**.

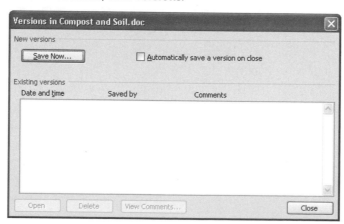

2   If you want Word to automatically save a new version of the document when you close it, select the **Automatically save a version on close** check box.

3   Click **Save Now**.

4   In the **Comments on version** box, type a suitable comment, and click **OK**.

Word closes the Versions dialog box and saves the current version of the document. A Versions icon appears on the status bar.

To view and delete document versions:

1   On the **File** menu, click **Versions**.

The "Existing versions" area of the Versions dialog box shows who saved the versions of the document.

Tip   You can also double-click the Versions icon on the status bar to open the Versions dialog box.

2   Do any of the following.

- ■ To open a previous version, click it in the **Existing versions** area, and click **Open**.
- ■ To delete a previous version, click it, and click **Delete**.
- ■ To view the comments assigned to a previous version, click it, and click **View Comments**.

3   Click the **Close** button to close the Versions dialog box.

Practice Exercise

In this exercise, you will create a second version of a document and then delete it.

USE the *CreateVersion* document in the *My Documents\Microsoft Press\MOS 2003 Study Guide\Word \W03E-4-3* practice file folder.

Open the *CreateVersion* document, and save a new version of it, entering **New price for decorative bench** as its comment. Then open the Versions in CreateVersion dialog box, and delete the new version. Close the dialog box, and then close the *CreateVersion* document without saving it.

Protect and Restrict Forms and Documents

W03E-4-4   The skills measured by this objective include the following:

- ■ Protecting a form
- ■ Setting a password
- ■ Restricting editing and formatting

Collaborating on documents with other people can lighten your load, but you might want to be able to control exactly who can work on a document. With Word, you can protect documents so that unauthorized people cannot open and change them.

Protecting a Form

After you finish a form but before you distribute it to users, you will want to protect it so that users can fill in the fields but not change the form itself. (In fact, you cannot use a form to gather electronic responses until you protect it.) If you need to change the layout or content of the form later, you will need to unprotect the form.

BE SURE TO open a document containing a form and to display the Forms toolbar before carrying out these steps.

To protect a form:

Protect
Form

1 On the Forms toolbar, click the **Protect Form** button.

Word locks all the non-field text and formatting of the form, protecting the form from changes other than to the form fields.

2 If you want to make further changes to the form, first turn off protection by clicking the **Protect Form** button.

Practice Exercise

In this exercise, you will turn on form protection.

USE the *ProtectForm* document in the *My Documents\Microsoft Press\MOS 2003 Study Guide\Word \W03E-4-4* practice file folder.

Open the *ProtectForm* document, and display the Forms toolbar. Click the **Protect Form** button to lock the document. Then close the *ProtectForm* document without saving it.

Setting a Password

If you want only certain people to be able to open a document, you can assign a password to it. Then to open the document, each user must enter the password exactly as it was set, including spaces, symbols, and uppercase and lowercase characters.

Tip If you want other people to be able to read or copy the document but not change it, you can make it read-only. You can also set the "Read-only recommended" option.

BE SURE TO open the document you want to work with before carrying out these steps.

To assign a password:

1 On the **Tools** menu, click **Options**, and click the **Security** tab.

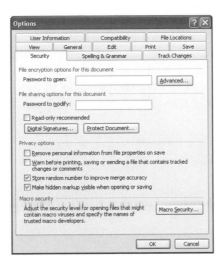

2   In either or both of the **Password to open** and **Password to modify** boxes, type the password(s).

To keep the password confidential, dots appear instead of the characters you type.

> **Tip**   Don't use common words or phrases as passwords, and don't use the same password for multiple documents. However, choose something you will remember. Word doesn't keep a list of passwords. If you lose or forget the password for a protected document, you will not be able to open it.

3   Click **OK** to close the Options dialog box.

Word asks you to confirm the password.

4   In the Confirm Password dialog box, type the same password.

5   Click **OK** to set the password.

To open a document to which a password is assigned:

Open

1   On the Standard toolbar, click the **Open** button.

2   In the Open dialog box, navigate to the folder in which the document you want to open is stored, and then double-click the file.

Because this document is protected by a password, the Password dialog box appears.

3   Do one of the following:

■ In the **Password** box, type the password, and click **OK**.

■ To open a read-only version of the document, click **Read Only**.

To remove a document's password:

1 On the **Tools** menu, click **Options**, and click the **Security** tab.

2 In the Options dialog box, select the contents of the **Password to modify** box, press DELETE, and then click **OK**.

The document's password protection is removed.

Practice Exercise

In this exercise, you will set a password for a document. You'll save and close the document, and then you'll test the document's security by entering an incorrect password. You will open a read-only version of the document and then reopen it with the correct password. Finally, you'll remove the protection from the document.

USE the *SettingPassword* document in the *My Documents\Microsoft Press\MOS 2003 Study Guide\Word \W03E-4-4* practice file folder.

Open the *SettingPassword* document. Display the **Security** tab of the Options dialog box, and set **tgc3** as the document's password. Confirm the password, and then save and close the document. Display the Open dialog box, navigate to the *My Documents\Microsoft Press \MOS Study Guide\Word\W03E-4-4* practice file folder, and then double-click the *SettingPassword* file. When the Password dialog box appears, enter **tgc1** as the password. When a message tells you that you typed an incorrect password, click **OK**, and then open a read-only version of the document. Close the document, and then reopen it, this time entering **tgc3** as the password. Close the document. Redisplay the **Security** tab of the Options dialog box, and delete the password. Save the *SettingPassword* document, and then close it.

Restricting Editing or Formatting

If you want people to be able to open and view a document but not make changes to it, you can use the Protect Document task pane's options to specify the types of changes that are allowed. You can specify that only comments can be inserted in the document, or you can require that only tracked changes can be made. To prevent anyone from introducing inconsistent formatting into a document, you can specify a selection of styles that must be used.

BE SURE TO open the document you want to work with before carrying out these steps.

To restrict editing and formatting changes:

1 On the **Tools** menu, click **Protect Document**.

2 In the **Formatting restrictions** area of the Protect Document task pane, select the **Limit formatting to a selection of styles** check box, and then click **Settings**.

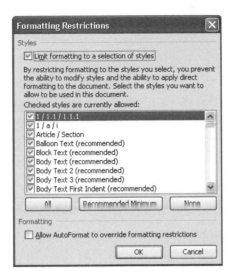

3 Scroll through the list of styles in the **Checked styles are currently allowed** box.

The styles reflect those in the template attached to the open document.

4 Click **Recommended Minimum**, and click **OK** to start implementing a restricted set of styles.

A message tells you that the document might contain direct formatting and asks whether you want it removed.

5 Click **Yes** or **No**, depending on whether you want to retain direct formatting.

6 In the **Editing restrictions** area of the Protect Document task pane, select the **Allow only this type of editing in the document** check box.

7 Click the down arrow to the right of the box below, and click the option you want in the drop-down list.

8 Click the **Yes, Start Enforcing Protection** button.

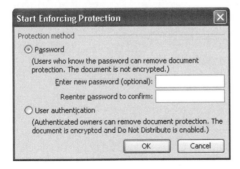

9 If you want only specific people to be able to turn off document protection, enter a password, and click **OK**.

With the exception of the Style box, the buttons on the Formatting toolbar are now unavailable.

To make exceptions to the restrictions:

1 On the **Tools** menu, click **Protect Document**.

2 In the **Exceptions** area of the Protect Document task pane, do any of the following:

- ■ To exempt a specific group of users from the restrictions, select the group's check box in the **Groups** box.

- ■ To exempt a specific user from the restrictions, click **More Users**, and in the Add Users dialog box, enter the user name, and click **OK**.

3 Click the **Yes, Start Enforcing Protection** button.

Tip You can limit the exceptions to certain areas of the document by selecting the text before creating the exception.

Practice Exercise

In this exercise, you will set editing and formatting restrictions for groups and individuals to selectively allow modifications to a protected document.

USE the *RestrictEditing* document in the *My Documents\Microsoft Press\MOS 2003 Study Guide\Word \W03E-4-4* practice file folder.

Open the *RestrictEditing* document. In the Protect Document task pane, limit the formatting allowed in this document to the recommended minimum group of styles, and remove any direct formatting. Then limit the editing to comments, but make an exception that allows anyone to make changes to the *Composting Dos and Don'ts* section. Start enforcing protection without entering a password. In the document, select the *Black Gold* heading, and click the **Format** menu, where most of the formatting commands are not available, indicating that the formatting restrictions are in effect. Then close the *RestrictEditing* document without saving it.

Attach Digital Signatures to Documents

W03E-4-5   The skills measured by this objective include the following:

- ■ Authenticating a document with a digital signature

Because of the proliferation of viruses and the ability to hide the true origins of a document, it is sometimes necessary to be able to guarantee a document's source.

Authenticating a Document with a Digital Signature

When you create a document that will be circulated to other people, you might want to attach a digital signature, which is an electronic stamp of authentication. Certified digital signatures can be obtained from companies such as VeriSign. The digital signature confirms the origin of the document and that no one has tampered with it since it was signed.

BE SURE TO open the document you want to work with and have a digital signature available before carrying out these steps.

To attach a digital signature to a document:

1   On the **Tools** menu, click **Options**, and then click the **Security** tab.

2   Click **Digital Signatures**.

3   In the Digital Signature dialog box, click **Add**.

4   In the Select Certificate dialog box, click a certificate in the list, and click **OK**.

5   Click **OK** twice to close the Digital Signature and Options dialog boxes.

    The word *(Signed)* now appears in Word's title bar.

6   On the Standard toolbar, click the **Save** button to save the document.

To view the digital signatures attached to a signed document:

1   On the **Tools** menu, click **Options**, and then click the **Security** tab.

2   Click **Digital Signatures**.

3   In the Digital Signature dialog box, check the signers and who issued their digital IDs.

4   Click **OK** twice to close the Digital Signature and Options dialog boxes.

Practice Exercise

Because you need an authentic digital signature to be able to carry out this task, there is no practice exercise for this topic.

Customize Document Properties

W03E-4-6   The skills measured by this objective include the following:

■   Inserting and editing advanced summary information

■   Inserting and editing custom information

A document's properties can include information that makes it easier to find and identify without having to read through the document's text.

Inserting and Editing Advanced Summary Information

The Summary tab of the Properties dialog box is most often used to record a document's title, subject, and author, and comments about the document. However, it can also store a category and relevant keywords. You enter this information so that when you use the Microsoft Windows XP search capabilities, you can locate all the documents belonging to a category or associated with a keyword.

You can also specify a hyperlink base on the Summary tab. A hyperlink base is the first part of a path that will be used for all hyperlinks on that path in the document. For example, you can specify a folder on a network server as the hyperlink base. Then when you insert a hyperlink to a document stored in that folder, only the part of the document's path to the right of the hyperlink base is displayed.

BE SURE TO open the document you want to work with before carrying out these steps.

To assign a category, keywords, and a hyperlink base to a document:

1   On the **File** menu, click **Properties**, and then click the **Summary** tab.

2   Do any of the following:

- In the **Category** box, type any categories to which you want to assign the document, separated by spaces.

- In the **Keywords** box, type any keywords you want to associate with the document, separated by spaces.

- In the **Hyperlink base** box, type the path of the location in which hyperlinked files will be stored.

3   Click **OK**.

Tip   The information you enter on the Summary tab of the Properties dialog box, including the keywords, can be entered as fields in the document. On the Insert menu, click Field, and set the Categories box to Document Information. In the "Field names" list, click the information you need, and click OK. Word inserts the information from the Summary tab of the Properties dialog box at the insertion point in your document.

To search by category or keyword:

1   On the Windows **Start** menu, click **Search**.

2   Specify that you want to search for a document, and display the advanced options.

3   In the **A word or phrase in the document** box, type the category or keyword.

4   Click **Search**.

Windows displays all documents whose text or Properties dialog box contains the word you typed.

Practice Exercise

In this exercise, you will insert a category and a keyword, search for a document by category, and then remove the summary information.

USE the *EditSummary* document in the *My Documents\Microsoft Press\MOS 2003 Study Guide\Word \W03E-4-6* practice file folder.

Open the *EditSummary* document, and then display the **Summary** tab of the Properties dialog box. Type **How-to** as the category and **Article** as a keyword. Save the document, and then close it. In Windows, search for the document by its *How-to* category, and double-click the file in the Search Results window to open it. Display the **Summary** tab of the Properties dialog box again, and delete the category and keyword. Then save and close the *EditSummary* document.

Inserting and Editing Custom Information

The Custom tab of the Properties dialog box lists custom properties you can associate with the document, together with the text you have entered. For example, you can enter a client's name or the document's status.

BE SURE TO open the document you want to work with before carrying out these steps.

To assign custom information to a document:

1   On the **File** menu, click **Properties**, and then click the **Custom** tab.

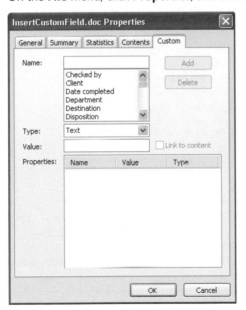

2   In the list box below the **Name** box, click one of the predefined custom fields.

Your selection is transferred to the Name box.

3   Select the field's type.

You can choose from Text, Date, Number, or "Yes or no."

4   Type a value for the field.

5   Click **Add**.

The custom field is now specified in the Properties box.

6   Click **OK**.

Practice Exercise

In this exercise, you will associate two custom fields with a document.

USE the *InsertCustomField* document in the *My Documents\Microsoft Press\MOS 2003 Study Guide\Word \W03E-4-6* practice file folder.

Open the *InsertCustomField* document, and then display the **Custom** tab of the Properties dialog box. Add a **Client** custom field with the value **Karen Berg**. Then add a **Disposition** custom field, with **Yes or no** as the type and **No** as the value. Close the Properties dialog box, and then close the *InsertCustomField* document without saving it.

W03E-4 Review

Number	Objective	Mastered
W03E-4-1	Modify track changes options	
	Setting reviewer options	❑
	Setting balloon options	❑
W03E-4-2	Publish and edit Web documents in Word	
	Opening and editing a Web page	❑
	Creating a frames page	❑
W03E-4-3	Manage document versions	
	Creating and managing document versions	❑
W03E-4-4	Protect and restrict forms and documents	
	Protecting a form	❑
	Setting a password	❑
	Restricting editing and formatting	❑
W03E-4-5	Attach digital signatures to documents	
	Authenticating a document with a digital signature	❑
W03E-4-6	Customize document properties	
	Inserting and editing advanced summary information	❑
	Inserting and editing custom information	❑

W03E-5
Customizing Word

The skills tested by this section of the Microsoft Office Specialist Word 2003 Expert Exam all relate to ways that you can tailor Word to make your working environment efficient and productive. Specifically, the following objectives are associated with this set of skills:

Number	Objective
W03E-5-1	Create, edit, and run macros
W03E-5-2	Customize menus and toolbars
W03E-5-3	Modify Word default settings

Important Before you can do the practice exercises associated with this skill set, you need to install the practice files from the book's companion CD to their default location. See "Installing the Practice Files" on page xxv for more information.

Create, Edit, and Run Macros

W03E-5-1   The skills measured by this objective include the following:

- Creating, running, and deleting a macro
- Editing a macro

To make repetitive tasks quick and easy, you can create a macro to perform a series of steps with a single click. You can also modify the macro as your needs change, and delete the macro when you are finished with it.

Creating, Running, and Deleting a Macro

A macro is a series of commands (keystrokes and instructions) that have been recorded so that you can repeat them with a single command. You can use macros to automate many tasks in Word, such as creating form letters, inserting AutoText entries, formatting text, creating tables, and turning command options on and off.

Macros are not separate files; they work only in conjunction with the document or template for which they were created. If you associate macros with the Normal template, they will be available to all new documents (unless you base the document on a different template). When you no longer need a macro, you can delete it from the document or template.

Tip Macros can contain viruses—destructive computer programs that can destroy information on your computer. If you frequently run macros created by other people, you should purchase and install anti-virus software. To further reduce the risk of virus infection in Word files, set your computer's macro security level to High or Medium by clicking Macro and then Security on the Tools menu, clicking the Security Level tab, and then setting the security level that you want.

BE SURE TO open the document from which you want to be able access the macro before carrying out these steps.

To record a macro:

1   Get ready to record the macro steps.

    For example, if you are going to insert an object, position the insertion point. Or if you are going to work with a text selection, select the text.

2   On the **Tools** menu, click **Macro** and then **Record New Macro**.

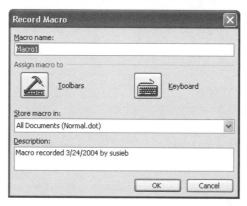

3   In the **Macro name** box, type a unique name for this macro.

4   If you want to store the macro with a template other than the Normal template or with a specific document, click the **Store macro in** down arrow, and make your selection.

5   Do one of the following:

    ■ Click the **Keyboard** button. Press **ALT** and a letter key to place that key combination in the **Press new shortcut key** box of the Customize Keyboard dialog box, click **Assign**, and then click **Close**.

    ■ Click the **Toolbars** button. Drag the new macro from the **Commands** area of the customize dialog box to the toolbar, and then click **Close**. (If the toolbar you want is not displayed, you can activate it from the **Toolbars** tab of the Customize dialog box.)

    Tip   You can assign a macro to a toolbar or menu before or after you record the macro.

    Word closes the dialog box and displays the Stop Recording toolbar, which has buttons that you can click to stop or pause the recording.

6   In the document, perform the steps of the task for which you are recording the macro.

7   On the Stop Recording toolbar, click the **Stop Recording** button.

Stop Recording

    The macro stops recording, and the Stop Recording toolbar closes.

To run a macro:

1   If necessary, get ready to run the macro.

    For example, if the macro inserts an object, position the insertion point. Or if the macro formats a text selection, select the text.

2   Do one of the following:

- ■ Press the macro's keyboard shortcut.

- ■ Click the macro's toolbar button.

- ■ On the **Tools** menu, click **Macro** and then **Macros** to display the Macro dialog box. Then in the list of macros, click the macro you want, and click **Run**.

To delete a macro:

1   On the **Tools** menu, click **Macro** and then **Macros.**

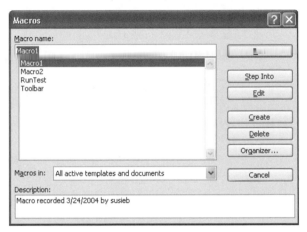

2   In the list of macros, click the macro you want to delete.

3   Click **Delete**, and when prompted to confirm the deletion, click **Yes**.

4   Click **Close** to close the Macros dialog box.

> **Tip**   If you delete a macro you assigned to a toolbar button or menu command, you can delete the macro's button or command by holding down the ALT key and dragging it into any blank space in the document window.

Practice Exercise

In this exercise, you will create a macro that formats the basic elements of a letter, and then you'll run the macro.

> **Tip**   If you cannot run the macro, your Security level is probably set to High. On the Tools menu, point to Macro, and then click Security to open the Security dialog box. On the Security Level tab, click Medium, and click OK. Then close and reopen the document, clicking Enable Macros when prompted. Be sure to return your security setting to High if you do not want to be able to run unsigned macros, which could contain viruses. (Unsigned macros do not have digital signatures that guarantee their source.)

USE the *RecordMacro* document in the *My Documents\Microsoft Press\MOS 2003 Study Guide\Word \W03E-5-1* practice file folder.

Open the *RecordMacro* document, and move to the end of the document. Display the Record Macro dialog box, name the new macro **Letter**, and store it in this document. If you want, assign the macro to a keyboard shortcut or toolbar button. At the top of the document, type **The Garden Company**, **1234 Oak Street**, and **Seattle, WA 10101** on three lines, and press **ENTER** three times. Type **To Whom It May Concern,** and press **ENTER** three times. Then type **Respectfully yours,** press **ENTER** three times, and type **Karen Berg**, **Owner**, and **The Garden Company** on three lines at the bottom of the document. Stop recording the macro. Then run the macro to insert placeholders for a second letter below the one you typed while recording the macro. Then close the *RecordMacro* document without saving it.

Editing a Macro

Sometimes a macro does not work as you expect, and you need to modify it. You can rerecord the macro to correct the problem, or because macros are instructions written in Microsoft Visual Basic for Applications (VBA), you can edit it in the Visual Basic Editor.

Word macros are stored in modules within a Visual Basic macro project that is stored in a document or template. To edit a macro, you display the Visual Basic Editor window, click the module you want to work on, and make changes.

BE SURE TO open a document containing the macro you want to edit before carrying out these steps.

To edit a macro:

1 On the **Tools** menu, click **Macro** and then **Macros**.

2 In the list of macros in the Macro dialog box, click the macro you want, and then click **Edit**. The macro's instructions are displayed in the Visual Basic Editor code window.

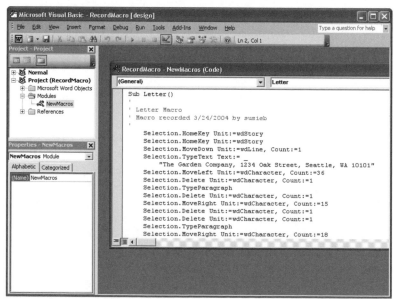

3   Scroll the window to find the section of code you want to edit.

4   Make the necessary changes.

> **Tip**   As you type new code, the Visual Basic Editor displays a menu of possible commands. You can click a command on the menu instead of typing the entire command. For information about inserting and editing macro commands in the Visual Basic Editor or about creating macros that perform tasks that cannot be recorded, use the Help menu in the Visual Basic Editor window.

5   On the **File** menu, click **Close and Return to Microsoft Word**.

The Visual Basic Editor closes, and the macro is saved with the change.

Practice Exercise

In this exercise, you will edit an existing macro to add character formatting.

USE the *ModifyMacro* document in the *My Documents\Microsoft Press\MOS 2003 Study Guide\Word \W03E-5-1* practice file folder.

Open the *ModifyMacro* document. Display the Macros dialog box, and open the **Letter** macro in the Visual Basic Editor window. Scroll to the bottom of the ModifyMacro - NewMacros (Code) window, click to the left of *Selection.TypeText Text:="Karen Berg"*, and press **ENTER** to insert a blank line before that instruction. On the blank line, type **Selection.Font.Bold = wdToggle** to tell Word that the following text should be displayed in bold. Close the Visual Basic Editor, and when you return to Word, move to the end of the document. Run the **Letter** macro, and then close the *ModifyMacro* document without saving it.

Customize Menus and Toolbars

W03F-5-2   The skills measured by this objective include the following:

- ■ Creating a custom menu
- ■ Customizing a toolbar

You might find that you use some menu commands and toolbar buttons frequently, and others almost never. Or you might need to create a custom toolbar or menu for a specific task. You can customize Word's menus and toolbars to better suit the way you work.

Creating a Custom Menu

If you want to control which commands appear on the menus, you can customize the menus. You can remove commands you never use and add commands you use often. For specialized tasks, you can even create new menus that can be attached to a template or specific document. For example, you might want to create a menu for a particular project and then delete it when you have finished.

BE SURE TO open the document from which you want to be able access the custom menu before carrying out these steps.

To create a custom menu:

1 On the **Tools** menu, click **Customize**, and then click the **Commands** tab if it's not already active.

2 Scroll down to the end of the **Categories** list, and click **New Menu**.

The New Menu appears in the Commands list.

3 Drag **New Menu** from the **Commands** list to the desired position on the menu bar.

Tip   If you later want to change the position of a menu, you can hold down the ALT key while you drag the menu to a new location.

4 On the menu bar, right-click **New Menu**, and then in the **Name** box on the shortcut menu, select the words **New Menu**, type a more specific name, and press **ENTER**.

5 In the **Categories** list of the Customize dialog box, click the name of the menu whose commands you want to add to the new menu.

6 In the **Commands** list, click the command you want.

7 Drag the command up to the menu bar and over the new menu, and when an empty menu appears, drag the command onto the menu, and release the mouse button.

The command appears on the menu.

Tip   You can also use this technique to add commands to Word's built-in menus.

8 Continue adding commands to the new menu.

9 Click **Close** to close the Customize dialog box.

To delete a custom menu:

1 Right-click any toolbar, and click **Customize** on the shortcut menu.

2 On Word's menu bar, right-click the custom menu, and then click **Delete**.

> **Tip** You can also hold down the ALT key and drag the custom menu into the document window.

To reset the menus:

1 On the **Tools** menu, click **Customize**, and then click the **Options** tab if it's not already active.

2 Click **Reset menu and toolbar usage data**, and then click **Yes**.

Word resets your menus and toolbars to their default settings so that they appear the way they did when you first started the program.

3 Click **Close** to close the dialog box and return to the document.

Practice Exercise

In this exercise, you will add and delete commands on Word's menus, create and then delete a custom menu, and then restore the original menu settings.

USE the *CustomizeMenu* document in the *My Documents\Microsoft Press\MOS 2003 Study Guide\Word \W03E-5-2* practice file folder.

Open the *CustomizeMenu* document. Display the **Commands** tab of the Customize dialog box, and then in the **Categories** list, click **Drawing**. Drag **WordArt Shape** to the **Format** menu, position the command below *Object* at the bottom of the menu, and then click the menu's name to close it. Create a new menu, drag it to the right of the **Help** menu on the menu bar, and name it **CustomMenu**. In the Customize dialog box, display the **Format** commands, and drag **Double Underline** onto the empty **CustomMenu** menu. Then drag **Word Underline** onto the menu, positioning it below *Double Underline*. Close the Customize dialog box. In the document window, select the **Preparation and Planting** heading, and on the **CustomMenu** menu, click **Double Underline**. Display the Customize dialog box, right-click the **CustomMenu** menu on the menu bar, and click **Delete** on the shortcut menu. Then delete the **WordArt Shape** command from the **Format** menu. Reset the menus to their default settings, and close the *CustomizeMenu* document without saving it.

Customizing a Toolbar

By default, the Standard and Formatting toolbars appear on one row at the top of the screen. When they occupy just one row, Word arranges the toolbars to show only the buttons you use most often. To see all the buttons associated with a toolbar, you can click the Toolbar Options button at the right end of a toolbar.

Tip To switch between displaying toolbars on one row and two rows, click the Toolbar Options button, and then click "Show Buttons on One Row" or "Show Buttons on Two Rows."

You can customize toolbars by adding, removing, and arranging buttons. You can also use the Customize dialog box to create a custom toolbar that displays the buttons you use most frequently. By using a custom toolbar, you can avoid having to jump between multiple menus or toolbars to complete your work.

BE SURE TO open the document from which you want to be able access the customized toolbar before carrying out these steps.

To display the Standard and Formatting toolbars on two rows:

Toolbar
Options

1 Click the **Toolbar Options** button on either toolbar.

2 Click **Show Buttons on Two Rows**.

3 To return to one row, repeat steps 1 and 2, clicking **Show Buttons on One Row**.

To display or hide toolbar buttons:

1 Display the toolbar you want to customize.

Toolbar
Options

2 At the right end of the toolbar, click the **Toolbar Options** button.

3 Click **Add or Remove Buttons**, and then click the toolbar's name.

Word displays a menu of all the buttons assigned to that toolbar. (The checked buttons are currently displayed on the toolbar.)

4 Do one of the following:

- Select the check boxes of any buttons you want to display.

- Clear the check boxes of any buttons you want to hide.

5 Click away from the menu.

The menu closes, and the toolbar is updated to reflect your changes.

To reset toolbar buttons:

Toolbar
Options

1 At the right end of the toolbar, click the **Toolbar Options** button.

2 Click **Add or Remove Buttons**, and then click the toolbar's name to display a menu of the buttons assigned to that toolbar.

3 On the menu, click **Reset Toolbar**.

The toolbar is restored to its default settings.

To create a custom toolbar:

1 Right-click any toolbar, click **Customize** on the shortcut menu, and click the **Toolbars** tab.

2   Click **New**.

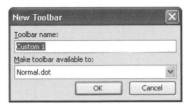

3   In the **Toolbar name** box, type a unique name for this toolbar.

4   If you want to change the template to which the new toolbar is attached, click the **Make toolbar available to** down arrow, and change the setting.

5   Click **OK**

A small, empty, floating toolbar called NewToolbar appears next to the Customize dialog box.

6   In the **Customize** dialog box, click the **Commands** tab.

7   In the **Commands** list, click the command you want, and drag it to the NewToolbar toolbar.

Tip   You can also use this technique to add buttons to Word's built-in toolbars.

8   Continue adding commands to the new toolbar.

9   Click **Close** to close the Customize dialog box.

10   Drag the new floating toolbar to dock it alongside the existing toolbars.

To delete a custom toolbar:

1   Right-click any toolbar, click **Customize** on the shortcut menu to open the Customize dialog box, and then click the **Toolbars** tab.

2   Scroll down the **Toolbars** list, click the toolbar you want to delete, and click **Delete**.

3   Click **OK** to confirm the deletion, and then click **Close** to close the Customize dialog box.

Practice Exercise

In this exercise, you will customize the Standard toolbar, and create a new toolbar.

USE the *CustomizeToolbar* document in the *My Documents\Microsoft Press\MOS 2003 Study Guide\Word \W03E-5-2* practice file folder.

Open the *CustomizeToolbar* document. Use the Standard toolbar's **Toolbar Options** button to hide the **Format Painter**, **Drawing**, and **Document Map** buttons. Then display the **Print** and **Envelopes and Labels** buttons with ellipses (...), which indicate that a dialog box will be displayed when the button is clicked. Restore the Standard toolbar to its default settings, and then display the **Toolbars** tab of the Customize dialog box. Create a new toolbar called **CustomToolbar** that is available only to the current document. Then add the **Grow Font**, **Shrink Font**, **Grow Font 1 Pt**, **Shrink Font 1 Pt**, and **Character Scaling** buttons from the **Commands** list for the **Format** category to the CustomToolbar toolbar. In the document window, select the **Preparation and Planting** heading, and use the **Grow Font 1 Pt** button to increase the font size by 2 points. Display the **Toolbars** tab of the Customize dialog box, and delete the CustomToolbar toolbar, confirming the deletion. Then close the *CustomizeToolbar* document without saving it.

Modify Word Default Settings

W03E-5-3 The skills measured by this objective include the following:

- Changing default file locations
- Changing the default dictionary
- Modifying default font settings

Word specifies certain default settings, but you can change many of these settings, including the default location where files are saved, the default dictionary, and the default font settings.

Changing Default File Locations

By default, Word stores templates in the *C:\Documents and Settings\[YourName]\Application Data\Microsoft\Templates* folder. If several people work with the same set of documents, everyone might want to change this default to the same agreed-upon location, so that the template doesn't have to be reattached every time the document is opened on a different computer.

Word also saves other types of documents in default locations. For example, it saves new Word documents in the *C:\Documents and Settings\[YourName]\My Documents* folder. You can also change these locations.

Important Before you modify any default setting, it is a good idea to make a note of the original setting in case you want to restore it later. Click the "Look in" down arrow, and write down the current location before you specify a new one.

BE SURE TO start Word before carrying out these steps.

To change the default location of a specific type of file:

1 On the **Tools** menu, click **Options** and then click the **File Locations** tab.

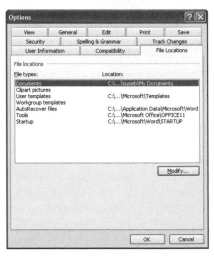

2   In the **File types** list, click the type of file whose default location you want to change.

3   Click **Modify**.

4   Navigate to the folder you want to make the default location.

5   Click **OK** to close the Modify Location dialog box, and then click **Close** to close the Options dialog box.

Practice Exercise

In this exercise, you will change the default location for templates.

USE the *ChangeLocation* document in the *My Documents\Microsoft Press\MOS 2003 Study Guide\Word \W03E-5-3* practice file folder.

Open the *ChangeLocation* document. Display the **File Locations** tab of the Options dialog box, and write down the current default location for **User templates**. Change the default to your *My Documents* folder, and then click **Cancel** to close the Modify Location dialog box without putting this change into effect. Close the Options dialog box, and then close the *ChangeLocation* document without saving it.

Changing the Custom Dictionary

If you work in an industry that uses terms not included in standard dictionaries, such as medicine or law, you can add a specialized dictionary to the supplemental dictionaries Word uses. That way, your industry terms will not be flagged as misspellings. (Supplemental dictionary files should have the file name extension *.dic*.) If you use this dictionary more than any other, you can make this dictionary the default supplemental dictionary.

BE SURE TO start Word before carrying out these steps.

To add a custom dictionary and make it the default supplemental dictionary:

1   On the **Tools** menu, click **Options**, and click the **Spelling & Grammar** tab.

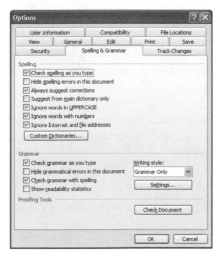

2   Click **Custom Dictionaries**.

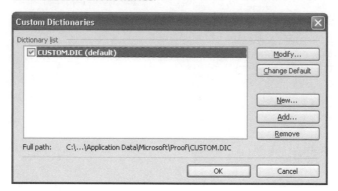

3   Click **Add**, navigate to the folder that contains the dictionary you want to use, and double-click the dictionary's file name.

Word adds the dictionary to the Dictionary list.

4   If the check box to the left of the dictionary's name is not selected, select the check box.

5   If you want this dictionary to be the default supplemental dictionary, click the **Change Default** button.

6   Click **OK** to close the Custom Dictionaries dialog box.

7   In the **Spelling** area of the Options dialog box, make sure that the **Suggest from main dictionary only** check box is cleared.

8   Click **OK** to close the Options dialog box.

Practice Exercise

In this exercise, you will make a custom dictionary available when checking the spelling of a document.

USE the *AddDictionary* document and the *Lilies.dic* dictionary file in the *My Documents\Microsoft Press \MOS 2003 Study Guide\Word\W03E-5-3* practice file folder.

Open the *AddDictionary* document, and notice the red wavy lines flagging possible misspellings in the document. Display the **Spelling & Grammar** tab of the Options dialog box, and add the *Lilies.dic* custom dictionary in the *My Documents\Microsoft Press \MOS 2003 Study Guide\Word\W03E-5-3* practice file folder to those to be used for checking this document. Use the **Spelling and Grammar** button to check the spelling of the document, noticing that Word no longer flags the names of the lilies as misspellings. Then close the *AddDictionary* document without saving it.

Modifying Default Font Settings

If you open a new blank document without specifying a template, Word applies the Normal template to the document and assigns the Normal style to all regular paragraphs. This style produces text in 12-point regular Times New Roman, with left alignment and single line spacing. You might prefer to create most of your documents in a different font or font size. Instead of manually adjusting the font or size in every document you create, you can simply set the font and font size in the Normal template to the setting you prefer.

BE SURE TO open a document to which the Normal template is applied before carrying out these steps.

To change the default font settings:

1   On the **Format** menu, click **Font**.

The Font dialog box appears, showing that the current font is Times New Roman, the font style is Regular, the size is 12, and the color is Automatic (meaning whatever is specified by the current template—in this case, black.)

2   Change the settings in the Font dialog box to create the look you want.

A sample of your font settings appears in the Preview box.

3   In the lower-left corner of the dialog box, click **Default**.

A message box asks you to confirm that you want to change the default font for new documents to the settings currently in the Font dialog box.

4   Click **Yes**.

Both the message box and the Font dialog box close, and the text of the open document changes to reflect the new default font.

Practice Exercise

In this exercise, you will modify the default font settings for documents that are based on the Normal template.

USE the *SetDefaultFont* document in the *My Documents\Microsoft Press\MOS 2003 Study Guide\Word \W03E-5-3* practice file folder.

Open the *SetDefaultFont* document, and display the Font dialog box. Change the **Font** to **Verdana**, the **Size** to **11**, and the **Font color** to **Dark Green**. Make the new settings the default for documents based on the Normal template. The text of the open document changes to reflect the new default font. Open a new document, and type a few words, noticing that they appear with the new default settings. Then return the default settings for the Normal template to **Times New Roman**, **Regular**, **12**, and **Automatic**. Close the *SetDefaultFont* document without saving it.

W03E-5 Review

Number	Objective	Mastered
W03E-5-1	Create, edit, and run macros	
	Creating, running, and deleting a macro	❏
	Editing a macro	❏
W03E-5-2	Customize menus and toolbars	
	Creating a custom menu	❏
	Customizing a toolbar	❏
W03E-5-3	Modify Word default settings	
	Changing default file locations	❏
	Changing the default dictionary	❏
	Modifying default font settings	❏

Part III

Microsoft Office Specialist
Excel 2003 Core Exam

This part of the book covers the skills you need to have for certification as a Microsoft Office Specialist in Microsoft Office Excel 2003 at the core level. Specifically, you will need to be able to complete tasks that require the following skills:

Number	Skill Set
E03C-1	Creating data and content
E03C-2	Analyzing data
E03C-3	Formatting data and content
E03C-4	Collaborating
E03C-5	Managing workbooks

You can use these basic skills to allow you to create the workbooks most commonly used in a business environment.

Knowledge You Need Before Studying for This Exam

We assume that you have been working with Excel for a while and that you know how to carry out fundamental tasks that are not specifically mentioned in the Microsoft Office Specialist core-level objectives for Excel 2003. Before you begin studying for this exam, you might want to scan this section to make sure you are familiar with this information.

Understanding Workbooks and Worksheets

A workbook is a file that consists of sheets on which you store data, perform calculations, and plot charts. By default, each new workbook contains three worksheets, named Sheet1, Sheet2, and Sheet3. However, a single workbook can contain up to 255 sheets. This format allows you to store related data on separate sheets but in a single workbook.

You can move from one sheet to another by clicking the sheet tabs at the bottom of the Excel window, but if you prefer to use the keyboard, here are some shortcuts:

Action	Keyboard Shortcut
Move to the next sheet	CTRL+PAGE DOWN
Move to the previous sheet	CTRL+PAGE UP
Select the current sheet and the one after it	CTRL+SHIFT+PAGE DOWN
Select the current sheet and the one before it	CTRL+SHIFT+PAGE UP

If you have many sheets in a workbook, some sheet tabs might not be visible. To activate a sheet whose tab is hidden, use the tab scrolling buttons. Click the First button (the left arrow with the bar) or Last button (the right arrow with the bar) to move to the first or last sheet, and use the Previous (left arrow) button or Next (right arrow) button to move backward or forward one sheet at a time.

Each worksheet is laid out in a grid of columns and rows. There are 256 columns, lettered A through IV, and 65,536 rows, numbered 1 through 65,536. The rectangle at the junction of each column and row is called a cell. To identify each of the more than 16 million cells on the worksheet, Excel uses an address, or reference, that consists of the letter at the top of the cell's column and the number at the left end of its row. For example, the reference of the cell in the upper-left corner of the worksheet is A1. The active cell-the one you're working with-is designated on the worksheet by a heavy border. Excel displays the cell reference of the active cell in the name box at the left end of the formula bar.

Selecting Ranges

To perform many tasks in a worksheet, you need to know how to select blocks of cells, called ranges. Selecting and working with a range saves you time because you can apply for mats to it or refer to it as a whole, instead of having to deal with each cell individually.

Any rectangular block or blocks containing more than one cell is a range. A range can include two cells, an entire row or column, or the entire worksheet. Range references consist of the address of the cell in the upper-left corner of the rectangular block and the address of the cell in the lower-right corner, separated by a colon. For example, A1:B2 identifies the range that consists of cells A1, A2, B1, and B2.

BE SURE TO display the worksheet you want to work with before carrying out these steps.

To select a range by dragging the mouse:

1   Point to the first cell you want to include in the range, hold down the left mouse button, and drag to the last cell you want to include in the range.

As you drag, the reference in the name box at the left end of the formula bar indicates the size of the range you are selecting. The selection's column and row headers—the gray boxes at the top of the columns containing letters and at the left end of the rows containing numbers—are shaded.

2   Release the mouse button.

Excel highlights the selected cells. The cell where you started the selection is white, indicating that it is the active cell in the range

To select an entire column or row:

●   Select a column of cells by clicking its header-the gray box at the top of the column containing the letter.

●   Select a row of cells by clicking its header-the gray box at the left end of the row containing the number.

To select an entire worksheet:

●   Click the gray box at the intersection of the column and row headers.

To select more than one range:

1   Select the first range.

2   Hold down the **CTRL** key, and select the subsequent ranges.

239

To select a range with the keyboard:

1   Select the first cell.

2   Hold down the **SHIFT** key, press the appropriate arrow keys, and release the **SHIFT** key.

Completing entries

You enter text or a number in a cell simply by clicking the cell and typing the entry. A Cancel (X) button and an Enter (check mark) button appear between the formula bar and name box, and the indicator at the left end of the status bar changes from *Ready* to *Enter*, because what you have typed will not be recorded in the cell until you "enter" it. You complete the entry by doing one of the following:

- Click the ENTER button to complete the entry and stay in the same cell.
- Press the ENTER or DOWN ARROW key to complete the entry and move to the next cell in the same column.
- Press the TAB or RIGHT ARROW key to complete the entry and move to the next cell in the same row.
- Press SHIFT+ENTER or the UP ARROW key to complete the entry and move to the previous cell in the same column.
- Press SHIFT+TAB or the LEFT ARROW key to complete the entry and move to the previous cell in the same row.

Understanding How Excel Handles Long Entries

A long text entry will overflow into an adjacent empty cell; Excel truncates the long entry only if the adjacent cell also contains an entry. However, unless you tell it otherwise, Excel displays long numbers in their simplest form, as follows:

- If you enter a number with fewer than 12 digits in a standard-width cell (which holds 8.43 characters), Excel adjusts the width of the column to accommodate the entry.
- If you enter a number with 12 or more digits, Excel displays it in scientific notation. For example, if you enter 12345678912345 in a standard-width cell, Excel displays 1.23457E+13 (1.23457 times 10 to the 13th power).
- If you enter a value with many decimal places, Excel might round it. For example, if you enter 123456.789 in a standard-width cell, Excel displays 123456.8.
- If you manually set the width of a column and then enter a currency value that is too large to be displayed in its entirety, Excel displays pound signs (#) instead of the value.

E03C-1

Creating Data and Content

The skills tested by this section of the Microsoft Office Specialist Excel 2003 Core Exam all relate to ways that you can enter content in an Excel worksheet. Specifically, the following objectives are associated with this set of skills:

Number	Objective
E03C-1-1	Enter and edit cell content
E03C-1-2	Navigate to specific cell content
E03C-1-3	Locate, select, and insert supporting information
E03C-1-4	Insert, position, and size graphics

 Important   Before you can do the practice exercises associated with this skill set, you need to install the practice files from the book's companion CD to their default location. See "Installing the Practice Files" on page xxv for more information.

Enter and Edit Cell Content

E03C-1-1   The skills measured by this objective include the following:

- Entering text, numbers, and symbols
- Entering cell content by using the fill handle
- Editing and clearing cell contents

One of the main purposes of building worksheets is to have Excel perform calculations for you. But before you can enter the formulas that will perform these calculations, you need to know how to enter and edit several different types of data.

Entering Text, Numbers, and Symbols

You enter text or a number in a cell simply by clicking the cell, typing the entry, and then completing it. You can enter text, numbers, dates and times, and symbols.

See Also   For information about completing entries, refer to "Knowledge You Need Before Studying for This Exam" on page 238.

When you type the first characters of a text entry that is already in that column, Excel's AutoComplete feature inserts the rest of the entry in the cell. If Excel's entry is correct, you can simply complete the entry without having to finish typing it.

Usually you want Excel to treat numbers used for identification, such as part numbers, as text. If the "number" includes not only the 0 through 9 digits but also letters and other characters (such as hyphens), Excel usually recognizes it as text. However, if it consists of only digits and you want Excel to treat it as text, you have to explicitly tell Excel to do so by preceding the number with an apostrophe.

Tip When you press ENTER after typing a number treated as text, Excel flags this entry as an error because the program expects all numbers to be entered as just numbers. You can ignore this flag.

When you enter a date or a time, you must type it in a format that Excel recognizes. Excel then displays the entry as you want it, but stores it as a value representing the number of days that have elapsed between the base date of January 1, 1900, which is assigned the value 1, and the date entered. Similarly, when you enter a time, it is internally recorded as a decimal value that represents the portion of the day that has elapsed between the base time of 12:00 midnight and the time entered. Excel stores dates and times this way so that you can perform calculations with them. For example, you can have Excel determine whether a payment is past due.

You can enter some common symbols from the keyboard, but to enter most symbols, such as the copyright or trademark symbol, you will need to use the Symbol dialog box.

BE SURE TO display the worksheet you want to work with before carrying out these steps.

To enter text or a number:

1 Click the cell in which you want to make an entry.

2 Type the text or number.

   As you type, the entry appears in both the cell and the formula bar, and a blinking insertion point in the cell tells you where the next character you type will be inserted.

3 Complete the entry.

   By default, Excel left-aligns a text entry and right-aligns a number entry.

To enter text by using AutoComplete:

1 Click the cell in which you want to make an entry, and type the first few letters of the entry.

   If these first few letters match those of text you have already entered in the same column, Excel's AutoComplete feature inserts the rest of the entry into the cell.

2 Do one of the following:

   ■ If Excel's entry is correct, complete it.

   ■ If it is not correct, continue typing the entry.

To enter a number as text:

1 Click the cell in which you want to type a number but have it treated as text.

2 Type an apostrophe (') and then the number.

3 Complete the entry.

   Because of the apostrophe, Excel recognizes the new entry as text and left-aligns it.

Tip   You can make Excel treat an existing number as text by selecting the cell containing the number, clicking Cells on the Format menu, and on the Number tab, selecting the Text format and clicking OK. You can also format numbers as ZIP codes, phone numbers, and social security numbers by selecting Special on the Number tab and then selecting the appropriate Type option.

To enter a date or time:

1   Click the cell in which you want to enter a date or time.

2   Type the date and/or time, using one of the following formats:

3/14	Mar-01	M	1:30 PM
3/14/01	March-01	M-01	13:30:55
03/14/01	March 14, 2001	3/14/2001	1:30:55 PM
14-Mar	3/14/01 1:30 PM	14-Mar-2001	30:55.4
14-Mar-01	3/14/01 13:30	13:30	37:30:55

3   Complete the entry.

Because dates and times are stored as numbers, Excel right-aligns the entry.

To enter a symbol:

1   Click the cell in which you want to enter a symbol.

2   On the **Insert** menu, click **Symbol**.

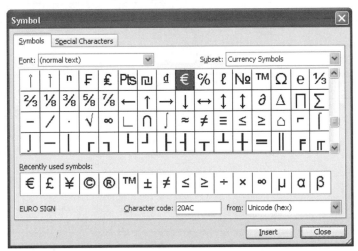

3   If you want to see the symbols from a different font, click the **Font** down arrow, and click the font you want.

4   Locate and click the symbol you want.

5   Click **Insert**, and then click **Close**.

Practice Exercise

In this exercise, you will enter text, numbers, and symbols.

USE the *EnterData* workbook in the *My Documents\Microsoft Press\MOS 2003 Study Guide\Excel\E03C-1-1* practice file folder.

Open the *EnterData* workbook. Starting in cell **A1**, enter the following headings, pressing **TAB** to move across row 1: **Date**, **Product Name**, **Customer Number**, and **Amount of Sale**. Enter **N-1000** in cell **B2** and **K-200** in cell **B3**. Then in cell **B4**, type **N**. Complete the entry Excel inserts for you. Then type the following product names, using the AutoComplete feature when appropriate.

B5	K-150	**B7**	N-3000
B6	K-150	**B8**	N-1000

In cell **C2**, enter **22869R**. (The R represents the accounts of retail stores as opposed to individual customers.) In cell **C3**, enter **'061333**. Then type the following account numbers, preceding those that contain only numbers with an apostrophe:

C4	'062031	**C7**	'082294
C5	60958R	**C8**	93069R
C6	'072956		

Complete the **Amount of Sale** column by typing the following amounts, pressing **ENTER** after each entry:

D2	3400.90	**D6**	450.80
D3	4560.85	**D7**	239.85
D4	1789.50	**D8**	2350.80
D5	6300.25		

To finish off the table, enter the following dates in the specified cells:

A2	Jan 5, 2004	**A6**	2/10/04
A3	1/9/04	**A7**	2/28/04
A4	25-Jan-04	**A8**	March 1, 2004
A5	Feb 7, 04		

In cell **E1**, type **Paid**, and press **ENTER** to move to cell **E2**. Display the Symbol dialog box, change the font to either **Wingdings** or **ZapfDingbats**, and insert a check mark symbol. Then close the *EnterData* workbook without saving it.

Entering Cell Content by Using the Fill Handle

When you want to copy the contents of a cell into the cells below or to the right, you can drag the small black fill handle in the lower-right corner of the selected cell. This simple mouse operation is called AutoFill.

Dragging the fill handle copies an entry exactly unless the cell contains a number that can be incremented or an entry from a custom list. If the cell contains a number that can be incremented, using AutoFill copies the entry and increments the number. If the cell contains an entry from a custom list, Excel fills the cells with sequential entries from that list.

Tip   If you want more control over how Excel copies entries, you can use the Fill command on the Edit menu.

BE SURE TO display the worksheet you want to work with before carrying out these steps.

To fill a range of cells:

1   Click the cell that contains the entry you want to copy.
2   Point to the fill handle in the lower-right corner of the cell, and when the pointer changes to a black cross, drag down or to the right to the last cell in which you want the entry copied.

    When you release the mouse button, Excel copies the entry into the selected cells. If the entry contains any numbers, Excel increments the first number by 1.

To enter a series of sequential numbers with an interval greater than 1:

1   Click the cell where you want to start the series, and type the first number.
2   Type the second number in the cell below or to the right.
3   Select the two cells.
4   Drag the fill handle through the appropriate number of adjacent cells.

    Excel calculates the difference between the first and second numbers and inserts entries incremented by that value across the selected range.

To enter a series of dates:

1   Click the cell where you want to start the series, and type the first date.
2   Type the second date in the cell below or to the right.
3   Select the two cells.
4   Drag the fill handle through the appropriate number of adjacent cells.

    Excel calculates the interval between the first and second dates and inserts entries incremented by that interval across the selected range.

To create and use a custom list:

1 On the **Tools** menu, click **Options**, and then click the **Custom Lists** tab.

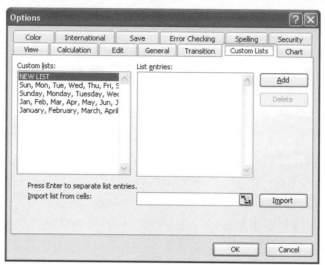

2 In the **Custom lists** box, select **NEW LIST**, and type the list's entries in the **List entries** box.

Tip If the list of entries already exists in the worksheet, you can click the "Import list from cells" box, select the range containing the entries, and click the Import button to import the entries as a list.

3 Click **OK** to close the dialog box.

4 Click the cell where you want the series of entries to begin, and type an item from a custom list.

5 With the cell still selected, drag the fill handle through the appropriate number of adjacent cells.

When you release the mouse button, Excel copies the subsequent entries from the list into the selected cells.

Practice Exercise

In this exercise, you will enter cell content by using the fill handle.

USE the *EnterFill* workbook in the *My Documents\Microsoft Press\MOS 2003 Study Guide\Excel\E03C-1-1* practice file folder.

Open the *EnterFill* workbook. Click cell **A13**, and drag its fill handle downward to cell **A16**. Then enter **3-Apr-04** in cell **A17** and **10-Apr-04** in cell **A18**, and insert a series of dates that are one week apart. Close the *EnterFill* workbook without saving it.

Editing and Clearing Cell Contents

You can correct most simple data-entry mistakes by using the BACKSPACE or DELETE key to erase errors and then retyping the entries. You can make this sort of change in either the formula bar or directly in a cell.

Using BACKSPACE or DELETE removes whatever entry is stored in the cell, but leaves any formatting or comments you might have applied to the cell. If you want to remove comments or formatting as well, you can use the Clear command instead.

If you want to replace an entry entirely, you can click its cell and type the new entry. If you have made the same mistake in several cells, you can use Excel's Find and Replace feature to replace cell entries (or parts of entries) without having to retype them over and over again. To reduce the likelihood of unexpected replacements, you can click the Options button in the Find and Replace dialog box and set options that make your Find and Replace entries more specific.

BE SURE TO display the worksheet you want to work with before carrying out these steps.

To change an existing entry in the formula bar:

1   Click the cell whose entry you want to change.

2   Click the formula bar where you want to make the change.

3   Use the **BACKSPACE** or **DELETE** key to delete the error, and retype the entry correctly.

4   Complete the entry.

To change an existing entry in its cell:

1   Double-click the cell whose entry you want to change, or click the cell and press the **F2** key to select the cell contents for editing.

2   Click the entry where you want to make the change.

3   Use the **BACKSPACE** or **DELETE** key to delete the error, and retype the entry correctly.

4   Complete the entry.

To replace an individual entry:

1   Click the cell whose entry you want to replace.

2   Type the new entry.

To replace all or part of multiple entries:

1   Select the cells in which you want to replace all or part of an entry, or click cell **A1** if you want to make changes throughout the worksheet.

2 On the **Edit** menu, click **Replace**.

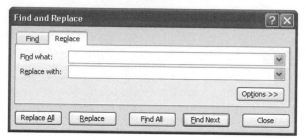

3 In the **Find what** box, type the text you want to replace.

4 In the **Replace with** box, type the replacement.

5 If you want to restrict the replacement, click the **Options** button.

The dialog box expands to include character, formatting, and workbook settings that you can use to make your Find and Replace entries more specific.

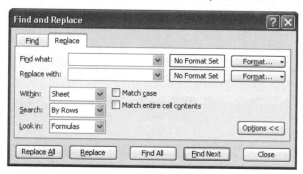

6 Make any necessary changes to the settings.

7 Do one of the following:

- To replace each instance of the **Find what** text individually, click **Find Next** and **Replace**.

- To replace all of the **Find what** instances at once, click **Replace All**.

8 When Excel tells you that the replacement is complete, click **OK**, and then click **Close** to close the Find and Replace dialog box.

To clear the contents of a cell:

1 Click the cell you want to clear.

2 Press the **BACKSPACE** or **DELETE** key.

To clear the formats or comments applied to a cell:

1 Click the cell you want to clear.

2 On the **Edit** menu, click **Clear**.

3 Do one of the following:

- ■ To clear all formats, contents, and comments from the cell, click **All**.
- ■ To clear only a specified element, select one of the three individual options: **Formats**, **Contents**, or **Comments**.

Practice Exercise

In this exercise, you will edit content and clear contents, formats, and comments from cells.

USE the *EditContent* workbook in the *My Documents\Microsoft Press\MOS 2003 Study Guide\Excel\E03C-1-1* practice file folder.

Open the *EditContent* workbook, and on **Sheet1**, select the contents of cell **D7** for editing. Delete the period to the left of the **8**, and insert a period between **8** and **5**. Complete the corrected entry. Display **Sheet2**, and select **A1:D13**. Clear all the contents, formats, and comments from this range. Display **Sheet3**, select **A1:D13**, and clear only its formats. Then close the *EditContent* workbook without saving it.

Navigate to Specific Cell Content

E03C-1-2   The skills measured by this objective include the following:

- ■ Finding cell content or formatting
- ■ Navigating by using the Go To command

A large Excel worksheet can contain dozens of columns and hundreds or even thousands of rows. When you need to find a specific entry or all cells with specific formatting, it's easier to rely on Excel's ability to quickly locate what you specify than to scan the entire worksheet yourself.

Finding Cell Content or Formatting

In addition to using Excel's Find and Replace feature to change cell entries, you can use it to find them. Clicking Find on the Edit menu displays the Find tab of the Find and Replace dialog box. You can look for cell contents or for cells formatted with a particular style or attribute.

BE SURE TO display the worksheet you want to work with before carrying out these steps.

To find specific cell content:

1 Select the cells you want to search, or click cell **A1** if you want to search the entire worksheet.

2 On the **Edit** menu, click **Find**.

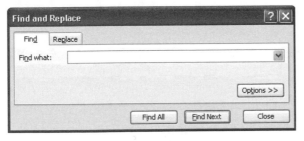

3 In the **Find what** box, type the text you want to find.

4 If you want to restrict the search, click the **Options** button, and make the necessary selections.

5 Click the **Find Next** button to find each instance of the **Find what** text.

6 When you have finished searching, click the **Close** button.

To find specific cell formatting:

1 Select the cells you want to search, or click cell **A1** if you want to search the entire worksheet.

2 On the **Edit** menu, click **Find**.

3 Click the **Options** button.

Excel expands the Find and Replace dialog box to display additional options.

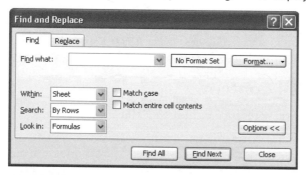

4 Click the **Format** button.

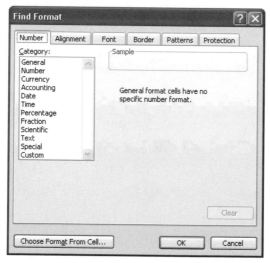

5 Change the settings on the tabs of the Find Format dialog box, and then click **OK**.

You can specify combinations of character and paragraph formatting by setting options on combinations of tabs.

6 In the Find and Replace dialog box, click the **Find Next** button to find the first instance of the formatting you specified.

7 When you have finished searching, click the **Close** button.

Practice Exercise

In this exercise, you will find cell contents with specific formatting.

USE the *FindContent* workbook in the *My Documents\Microsoft Press\MOS 2003 Study Guide\Excel\E03C-1-2* practice file folder.

Open the *FindContent* workbook, and display the expanded Find and Replace dialog box. Click the **Format** button, and specify that you want to find cells formatted in **Bold**. Then find the first couple of instances of this formatting. In the Find and Replace dialog box, click the **Format** down arrow, and click **Clear Find Format** on the menu. Display the **Number** tab of the Find Format dialog box, and specify that you want to find cells formatted as **Currency**. Then find all the cells with the specified formatting. Close the Find and Replace dialog box, and then close the *FindContent* workbook without saving it.

Navigating by Using the Go To Command

You can use the Go To command to move to a specific cell in a worksheet or selected range, or to select every cell in a worksheet or range with specific contents. You can accumulate a list of cell addresses that you go to frequently so that you can quickly jump to them at any time. You can also use the Go To Special dialog box to locate all cells that contain information such as comments, constants, or formulas. Other options include selecting blank cells or the last cell in a range or worksheet, going to only the visible cells in a range that includes hidden columns or rows, and going to objects, precedents, dependents, conditional formats, row differences, and column differences.

BE SURE TO display the worksheet you want to work with before carrying out these steps.

To go to a specific cell:

1 On the **Edit** menu, click **Go To**.

2 In the **Reference** text box, enter the address of the cell you want to find, and click **OK**.

To go to a specific kind of cell or information:

1 On the **Edit** menu, click **Go To**.

2   In the Go To diag box, click **Special**.

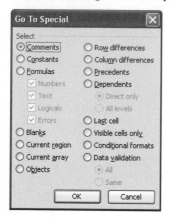

3   Select the option for where you want to go, and click **OK**.

Practice Exercise

In this exercise, you will navigate to specific cells by using the Go To command.

USE the *GoToContent* workbook in the *My Documents\Microsoft Press\MOS 2003 Study Guide\Excel\E03C-1-2* practice file folder.

Open the *GoToContent* workbook, display the Go To dialog box, and enter the cell reference **Jan04!D20** to go to cell D20 of the Jan04 worksheet. Display the Go To dialog box again, and then display the Go To Special dialog box. Jump to the last cell. Use the Go To Special dialog box to select all the cells that contain comments, and then use it again to select the current region. Close the *GoToContent* workbook without saving it.

Locate, Select, and Insert Supporting Information

E03C-1-3   The skills measured by this objective include the following:

■   Using the Thesaurus to find the best word
■   Using the Research tool to locate and insert supporting information

The Research tool provides access to information you might need as you create workbooks. It includes a dictionary, thesauruses for different languages, a translation service, and several research sites.

Using the Thesaurus to Find the Best Word

Although a worksheet is not a work of literature, it is still important for you to choose your words carefully to ensure that information is presented succinctly but correctly. Instead of laboring over important words, you can use the Research tool to suggest alternatives from the built-in Thesaurus.

BE SURE TO display the worksheet you want to work with before carrying out these steps.

To use the Thesaurus to find the best word:

1   Click the cell containing the word for which you want to find an alternative.

2 On the **Tools** menu, click **Research**.

3 In the Research task pane, click the **Reference** down arrow.

If you haven't used the Reference tool before, the Reference box contains the default All Reference Books option.

4 Click **Thesaurus: English (U.S.)** in the drop-down list.

5 If the word you want to replace does not already appear in the **Search for** box, type it there.

Start searching

6 Click the **Start Searching** button.

The results of your search appear in the Research task pane.

7 Point to the word you want to use, click its down arrow, and then click **Insert**.

The selected synonym replaces the entry in the cell.

Practice Exercise

In this exercise, you will use the Thesaurus to replace one word with another.

USE the *UseThesaurus* workbook in the *My Documents\Microsoft Press\MOS 2003 Study Guide\Excel\E03C-1-3* practice file folder.

Open the *UseThesaurus* workbook, and click cell **B2**, which contains the word *situation*. Display the Research task pane, and make sure **situation** appears in the **Search for** box. Set **Reference** to **Thesaurus: English (U.S.)**, and search for a synonym. When the results appear in the Research task pane, click the **state** down arrow, and look up synonyms for that word. In the second set of results, replace **situation** in cell B2 with **status**. Then close the *UseThesaurus* workbook without saving it.

Using the Research Tool to Locate and Insert Supporting Information

Sometimes you might need to look up and insert information supporting a conclusion or underlining an assumption. For example, you might need a stock quote or information about a particular company. Resources available through the Research tool include Encarta, Factiva Search, MSN Search, Gale Company Profiles, and MSN Money Stock Quotes.

BE SURE TO display the worksheet you want to work with before carrying out these steps.

To look up and insert information by using the Research tool:

1 Click the cell where you want to insert supporting information.

2 On the **Tools** menu, click **Research**.

3 In the Research task pane, click the **Reference** down arrow.

4 Click the name of a reference resource in the list.

Start searching

5 In the **Search for** box, enter your search criteria, and then click the **Start searching** button.

The results of your search appear in the Research task pane.

6 Do one of the following:

■ To insert a stock quote from MSN Money Stock Quotes, click the **Insert Price** button to insert the price into the selected cell.

■ To insert other types of information, type it directly in the cell.

Practice Exercise

In this exercise, you will use the Research tool to look up and insert a stock quote and review a company profile.

USE the *InsertInfo* workbook in the *My Documents\Microsoft Press\MOS 2003 Study Guide\Excel\E03C-1-3* practice file folder.

Open the *InsertInfo* workbook, and display the Research task pane. Set **Reference** to **MSN Money Stock Quotes**, and search for **Msft**. When the stock quote appears in the Research task pane, insert it into the worksheet. Then set **Reference** to **Gale Company Profiles**, and review the information about Microsoft Corporation. Copy the Microsoft Web address into cell **C2** of the worksheet, and then close the *InsertInfo* workbook without saving it.

Insert, Position, and Size Graphics

E03C-1-4   The skills measured by this objective include the following:

- Inserting and positioning graphics
- Sizing graphics

When inserting graphics into a worksheet, you will often need to change their position and size. Knowing how to manipulate a graphic after you have inserted it will ensure that the graphic enhances the worksheet without detracting from its usability.

Inserting and Positioning Graphics

You can insert graphics from several sources, including clip art images accessible through the Clip Art task pane, existing graphics files stored on your computer or a computer on your network, scanned pictures from your scanner, or digital photographs from your camera.

After you've inserted a graphic, you can move it to another location in the worksheet by dragging it to the desired spot or by nudging it using the keyboard.

BE SURE TO display the worksheet you want to work with before carrying out these steps.

To insert clip art in a cell:

1 Click the cell in which you want to insert the clip art.

2 On the **Insert** menu, click **Picture** and then **Clip Art**.

   The Clip Art task pane appears.

3 In the **Search for** box, enter a word or words describing the image you want to find.

4 If necessary, click the **Search in** down arrow to specify which collections to search, and click the **Results should be** down arrow to specify how the search should be limited.

5 Click **Go**.

   The results of the search appear in the Clip Art task pane.

6 Point to the image you want, click its down arrow, and then click **Insert**.

   The image appears in your worksheet, with its upper-left corner in the cell you selected.

To insert a graphic file in a cell:

1   Click the cell in which you want to insert the graphic.

2   On the **Insert** menu, click **Picture** and then **From File**.

3   Navigate to the folder in which the graphic you want to use is stored.

4   Double-click the graphic file.

    The graphic appears in the selected cell.

To position a graphic with the mouse:

1   If the graphic is not already selected (surrounded by handles), click it.

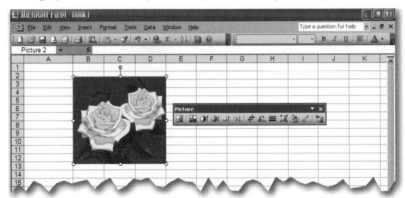

2   Drag the graphic (not a handle) where you want it to appear in the worksheet.

To position a graphic with the keyboard:

1   If the graphic is not already selected, click it.

2   Use the arrow keys to nudge the graphic in the desired direction.

Practice Exercise

In this exercise, you will insert a logo and then move it in the worksheet.

USE the *InsertGraphic* workbook and the *tgc_logo.gif* graphic file in the *My Documents\Microsoft Press \MOS 2003 Study Guide\Excel\E03C-1-4* practice file folder.

Open the *InsertGraphic* workbook, and use the Insert Picture dialog box to insert **tgc_logo.gif** in cell **F10**. Then move the graphic so that it sits over cell **A1**. Close the *InsertGraphic* workbook without saving it.

Sizing Graphics

You can size a graphic by selecting it and then dragging one of its handles to increase or decrease its height and width. If you want to control the size more precisely, you can enter absolute measurements in the Format Picture dialog box.

BE SURE TO display a worksheet containing a graphic before carrying out these steps.

To size a graphic visually:

1 If the graphic is not selected, click it.

2 Drag the appropriate handle in the direction in which you want to increase or decrease the graphic's size.

To size a graphic more precisely:

1 If the graphic is not selected, click it.

2 Right-click the graphic, click **Format Picture** on the shortcut menu, and then click the **Size** tab.

On this tab, the "Lock aspect ratio" check box is selected so that changing the size in one dimension also changes it proportionately in the other dimension.

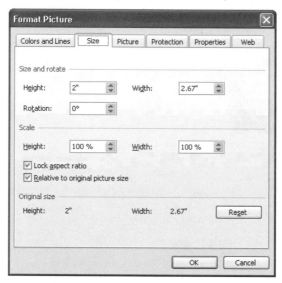

3 In the **Size and rotate** area, change the **Height** or **Width** setting by typing a new measurement, and then click **OK**.

The picture is resized, maintaining the original aspect ratio.

Practice Exercise

In this exercise, you will reduce the size of a graphic, first visually and then by entering measurements.

USE the *SizeGraphic* workbook in the *My Documents\Microsoft Press\MOS 2003 Study Guide\Excel\E03C-1-4* practice file folder.

Open the *SizeGraphic* workbook, and click the graphic to select it. Drag the sizing handles until the image is approximately **1.5** inches high and **5** inches wide. Then display the Format Picture dialog box, and if the settings in the **Height** and **Width** boxes in the **Size and rotate** area are not exactly **1.5** and **5**, change them. Close the dialog box, and then close the *SizeGraphic* workbook without saving it.

E03C-1 Review

Number	Objective	Mastered
E03C-1-1	Enter and edit cell content	
	Entering text, numbers, and symbols	❏
	Entering cell content by using the fill handle	❏
	Editing and clearing cell contents	❏
E03C-1-2	Navigate to specific cell content	
	Finding cell content or formatting	❏
	Navigating by using the Go To command	❏
E03C-1-3	Locate, select, and insert supporting information	
	Using the Thesaurus to find the best word	❏
	Using the Research tool to locate and insert supporting information	❏
E03C-1-4	Insert, position, and size graphics	
	Inserting and positioning graphics	❏
	Sizing graphics	❏

E03C-2

Analyzing Data

The skills tested by this section of the Microsoft Office Specialist Excel 2003 Core Exam all relate to ways that you can analyze data after you have entered it in an Excel worksheet. Specifically, the following objectives are associated with this set of skills:

Number	Objective
E03C-2-1	Filter lists using AutoFilter
E03C-2-2	Sort lists
E03C-2-3	Insert and modify formulas
E03C-2-4	Use statistical, date and time, financial, and logical functions
E03C-2-5	Create, modify, and position diagrams and charts based on worksheet data

Important   Before you can do the practice exercises associated with this skill set, you need to install the practice files from the book's companion CD to their default location. See "Installing the Practice Files" on page xxv for more information.

Filter Lists Using AutoFilter

E03C-2-1   The skills measured by this objective include the following:

- Displaying rows with a specific entry in a specific column
- Displaying rows that match certain criteria

Filtering is a technique for displaying the rows in a worksheet that you want to work with, while hiding the other rows. You can use filtering for tasks such as detecting patterns or comparing items.

Displaying Rows with a Specific Entry in a Specific Column

If a worksheet has column headings, you can zero in on the rows you want to see by using the AutoFilter tool. When you turn on AutoFilter, a down arrow appears in the heading cell of selected columns. Clicking the down arrow displays all the values in that column and three additional items: All, Top 10, and Custom. You can click a value to see only the rows with that value in the column, and you can click All to redisplay all the rows. If you want to display the rows for a range of values, you can click Top 10 to set up the filter you want.

Tip   After you have filtered out the rows you want, you can act on only those rows without affecting the rest of the worksheet. For example, you can create a graph using the filtered rows.

BE SURE TO display a worksheet containing column headings before carrying out these steps.

To display rows with a specific entry in a specific field:

1 Click any cell in the part of the worksheet containing entries.

2 On the **Data** menu, click **Filter** and then **AutoFilter**.

A down arrow appears at the right end of each heading cell.

3 Click the down arrow for the column on which you want to base the filter.

4 Click the value you want in the list.

Excel displays only the rows containing that value and changes the color of the down arrow of the filtered column.

5 To filter the visible records using a different column, click the down arrow for that column, and click the value you want.

To display rows with a range of entries in a specific field:

1 With AutoFilter turned on, click the down arrow for the column on which you want to base the filter.

2 Click **Top 10** in the list.

3 Do any of the following:

■ To display values from the bottom of the list instead of the top, click the first box's down arrow, and click **Bottom**.

■ To display fewer than 10 or more than 10 rows, use the down or up arrow to the right of the second box to specify the number.

■ To specify the value in the second box as a percentage, click the third box's down arrow, and click **Percent**.

4 Click **OK**.

To remove a filter without turning off AutoFilter:

1 Click the down arrow of the column on which you based the filter.

2 Click **All** in the list.

3 If you filtered on more than one column, repeat steps 1 and 2 for those columns as well.

Practice Exercise

In this exercise, you will use AutoFilter to filter the information in a list.

USE the *UseAutoFilter* workbook in the *My Documents\Microsoft Press\MOS 2003 Study Guide\Excel \E03C-2-1* practice file folder.

Open the *UseAutoFilter* workbook. Activate Excel's AutoFilter, and then use it to show only the rows with **Retail** in the **Type** column. Then show only the Retail records that have the ten largest amounts in the **Amount of Sale** column. One at a time, remove the filters you applied. Then turn off AutoFilter, and close the *UseAutoFilter* workbook without saving it.

Displaying Rows That Match Certain Criteria

If you want to display rows based on more complex criteria than a single value or range of values, you can use the Custom option in the filter list. By setting criteria in the Custom AutoFilter dialog box, you can display only rows containing values over a certain limit, for example, or rows containing either one value or another.

BE SURE TO display a worksheet containing column headings before carrying out these steps.

To display the records that match specified criteria:

1   With AutoFilter turned on, click the down arrow for the column on which you want to base the filter.

2   Click **Custom** in the list.

3   To change the operator, click the **equals** down arrow, and click the operator you want.

4   Press the **TAB** key to move to the adjacent box, and then do one of the following:

  ■ Type a value.

  ■ Click the box's down arrow, and click a value in the list.

5   To add a second set of criteria, select either the **And** or the **Or** option, and then specify the criteria in the boxes below.

6   Click **OK** to apply the filter.

Practice Exercise

In this exercise, you will filter a worksheet to display only the values for the first or second quarters that are over $4,000.

USE the *MatchCriteria* workbook in the *My Documents\Microsoft Press\MOS 2003 Study Guide\Excel \E03C-2-1* practice file folder.

Open the *MatchCriteria* workbook. Turn on AutoFilter, and then set up a custom filter to display only the records from **Quarter 1** and **Quarter 2**. Set up a second filter to display the records with values in the **Amount of Sale** column that are greater than $4,000. Then close the *MatchCriteria* workbook without saving it.

Sort Lists

E03C-2-2   The skills measured by this objective include the following:

- Sorting on one column
- Sorting on two or three columns

When you enter information in a worksheet, it is displayed in the order in which you entered it. However, you can sort the rows on any column to view the information in a different order.

Sorting on One Column

The simplest type of sort is based on only one column. You click a cell in the column Excel should use, and then rearrange the rows in either ascending or descending order based on that column. If your worksheet has column headings, Excel does not include the heading row in the sort operation.

BE SURE TO display the worksheet you want to work with before carrying out these steps.

To sort on one column by using toolbar buttons:

1   Click any cell in the column on which you want to base the sort.

2   On the Standard toolbar, do one of the following:

Sort
Ascending

- To sort the list starting with A (or the lowest digit), click the **Sort Ascending** button .

Sort
Descending

- To sort starting with Z (or the highest digit), click the **Sort Descending** button .

Practice Exercise

In this exercise, you will sort a worksheet based on one column and then on another column.

USE the *SortOne* workbook in the *My Documents\Microsoft Press\MOS 2003 Study Guide\Excel\E03C-2-2* practice file folder.

Open the *SortOne* workbook. Sort the worksheet in ascending order based on the **Product Name** column, and then change the sort to descending order. Then sort the worksheet by the **Type** column. Close the *SortOne* workbook without saving it.

Sorting on Two or Three Columns

If you want to sort on more than one column, you can use the buttons on the Standard toolbar, but you can also achieve the same effect by setting up a single sort operation in the Sort dialog box.

Before you sort any large worksheet, you might want to add a column of sort codes—a set of sequential numbers assigned to each row of entries. Then after you finish sorting the data, you can sort again based on the sort code column to put everything back where it was.

BE SURE TO display the worksheet you want to work with before carrying out these steps.

To sort on two or three columns:

1   Click any cell in the active area of the worksheet, or if you want to sort just part of the worksheet, select that part.

2   On the **Data** menu, click **Sort**.

3   Click the **Sort by** down arrow, and click the first column you want to sort by in the drop-down list.

4   To sort in descending order instead of ascending order (the default), select the **Descending** option.

5   To add a second sort column, click the first **Then by** down arrow, click the column you want, and select the **Descending** option if necessary.

6   If appropriate, add a third sort column.

7   If the data you are sorting does not have column headings at the top, select the **No header row** option in the **My data range has** area.

8   Click **OK** to sort the rows.

To add sort codes to a worksheet:

1   Set up a blank column immediately to the left or right of the data you want to sort.

2   If the data you want to sort has column headings, type **Sort Code** or something similar as the heading for the new column.

3   In the cell below the heading, type **1**, and complete the entry.

4   With the cell containing *1* selected, hold down the **CTRL** key, and drag the fill handle down the column to the last row containing data.

    Excel enters a series of sequential numbers that you can use to sort the data back into its original order.

Practice Exercise

In this exercise, you will add a sort column to a worksheet, sort the data on three columns, and then put it back in its original order.

USE the *SortTwo* workbook in the *My Documents\Microsoft Press\MOS 2003 Study Guide\Excel \E03C-2-2* practice file folder.

Open the *SortTwo* workbook. Add a sort column in column **G**. Sort the data by the **Type** column, then the **Product Name** column, and then by the **Amount of Sale** column. Use the sort column to return the data to its original order. Then close the *SortTwo* workbook without saving it.

Insert and Modify Formulas

E03C-2-3   The skills measured by this objective include the following:

- ■ Doing simple arithmetic
- ■ Using a function in a formula
- ■ Using cell and range references in a formula

When a cell contains a formula, its value is the result of the calculations performed by the formula. Those calculations can be simple arithmetic or complex expressions involving Excel's built-in functions and the values in multiple cells in the same worksheet or in other worksheets.

Doing Simple Arithmetic

In Excel, you begin a formula with an equal sign (=). In the simplest formulas, the equal sign is followed by values separated by one of four arithmetic operators (+, -, *, and /), which tell Excel to add, subtract, multiply, and divide. You can type the values, or you can tell Excel to use a value that is stored in the worksheet simply by clicking the cell that contains the value.

BE SURE TO display the worksheet you want to work with before carrying out these steps.

To enter a formula by typing values:

1   Click the cell in which you want the results of the formula to appear.

2   Type = (an equal sign), followed by the first value.

3   Type an arithmetic operator (+, -, *, or /), followed by another value.

4   Continue to build the formula as necessary—for example, =5+13-4*6+4/2.

   Tip   By default, Excel performs multiplication and division before addition and subtraction. To tell Excel to perform calculations in a different order, use parentheses—for example, =((5+13-4)*(6+4))/2.

5   Complete the entry.

   Excel performs the calculation and puts the result in the cell containing the formula.

To enter values in a formula by clicking cells:

1   Click the cell in which you want the results of the formula to appear.

2   Type = (an equal sign), and click the cell containing the first value.

Excel adds the cell reference to the formula—for example, =E7.

3   Type an arithmetic operator (+, -, *, or /), and click another cell.

4   Continue to build the formula as necessary—for example, =E7+E8-E9*E10+E11/E12.

5   Complete the entry to have Excel perform the calculation.

Practice Exercise

In this exercise, you will enter simple arithmetic formulas in a worksheet.

USE the *DoArithmetic* workbook in the *My Documents\Microsoft Press\MOS 2003 Study Guide\Excel* *E03C-2-3* practice file folder.

Open the *DoArithmetic* workbook. Click cell **G49**, type the formula **=(23+47)/2**, and then complete the entry. Click cell **F66**, and enter a formula that adds the values in cells **F63**, **F64**, and **F65**. Then close the *DoArithmetic* workbook without saving it.

Using a Function in a Formula

Excel has many powerful built-in functions that are a sort of shorthand for the various formulas used in mathematical, logical, statistical, financial, trigonometric, logarithmic, and other types of calculations. Its simplest function is SUM, which you use to total a set of values. Because the SUM function is used so often, it has its own button, called AutoSum, on the Standard toolbar. You can use the AutoSum button whenever you want a total to appear at the bottom of a column or to the right of a row of values.

If you want to total values that appear elsewhere in the worksheet, or if you want to use other functions in your formulas, you need to create the formula from scratch. You type an equal sign, followed by the function name and a set of values (or the addresses of cells where the values are stored) enclosed in parentheses—for example, =SUM(D3:D300). You can type the function name, or you can use the Insert Function button to help you select the correct function and set up the formula. The values in parentheses constitute the function's argument, which gives Excel the additional information it needs to perform the function. In this case, there is only one argument, but some functions require several.

BE SURE TO display a worksheet containing values on which you can perform calculations before carrying out these steps.

To total values by using the AutoSum button:

1   Click the first blank cell below a column of values or to the right of a row of values.

AutoSum

2   On the Standard toolbar, click the **AutoSum** button.

Excel looks above and then to the left of the active cell for an adjacent range of values to total. It then enters the appropriate SUM function in the cell and in the formula bar.

3   Complete the entry.

To enter a function from scratch:

1 Click the cell in which you want the results of the formula to appear.

2 Type = (an equal sign), followed by the function name and ((an open parenthesis)—for example, =SUM(.

> **Tip** If you don't type a function name in capital letters, Excel capitalizes it for you when you complete the entry. If Excel doesn't respond in this way, you have probably typed the name incorrectly.

3 Click the cell or select the range of cells containing the values you want to use as the formula's argument.

4 Type) (a close parenthesis), and complete the entry.

To enter a function by using the Insert Function button:

1 Click the cell in which you want the results of the formula to appear.

2 At the left end of the formula bar, click the **Insert Function** button.

Insert
Function

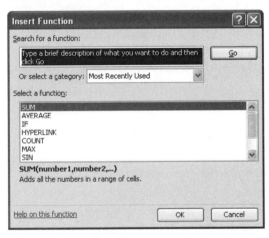

3 Do one of the following:

- In the **Search for a function** box, type a brief description of the function you are looking for, and click **Go**. The **Or select a category** box changes to **Recommended**, and the **Select a function** list box shows the functions that most closely match what you are looking for.

- Click the **Or select a category** down arrow, and click the function category you want.

4 In the **Select a function** list box, click the function you want.

The area below the list box displays the format, or syntax, of the function and describes its purpose.

5   Click **OK**.

Excel enters values for the function's first argument, and displays the Function Arguments dialog box so that you can confirm or change it.

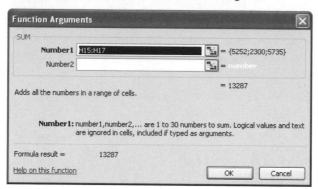

6   Do one of the following:

- To insert the formula with Excel's suggested argument, click **OK**.

- To change the argument, click the **Collapse** button at the right end of the argument box you want to change, click the correct cell or select the correct range in the worksheet, click the **Expand** button, and click **OK** to close the dialog box and complete the entry.

Practice Exercise

In this exercise, you will use three methods to enter three functions that perform calculations on the same set of values.

USE the *UseFunction* workbook in the *My Documents\Microsoft Press\MOS 2003 Study Guide\Excel \E03C-2-3* practice file folder.

Open the *UseFunction* workbook. In cell **D18**, use the **AutoSum** button to total the values in the **Amount of Sale** column. In cell **D19**, find the average sale amount by typing **=AVERAGE** and specifying **D2:D17** as the argument. In cell **D20**, use the **Insert Function** button to find the **MIN** function, and specify **D2:D17** as the argument. Then close the *UseFunction* workbook without saving it.

Using Cell and Range References in a Formula

The arguments in formulas usually consist of the addresses, or references, of cells or ranges. These cells and ranges can contain simple values, or they can contain formulas whose results can be used in other formulas.

By default, the references are relative, meaning that they refer to cells by their position in relation to the cell containing the formula. If you create the formula =SUM(D2:D14) in cell D15 and then copy the formula to cell F15, Excel changes the formula to =SUM(F2:F14) so that the argument still references the range in the same position relative to the cell containing the formula.

When you don't want arguments to change if you move or copy their formulas, you need to use absolute references, meaning that they refer to cells by their fixed position in the worksheet. To make a reference absolute, you add dollar signs before its column letter and row number. If you copy the formula =SUM($D$2:$D$14) from cell D15 to cell F15, Excel will not change the formula and the argument will still refer to D2:D14.

Tip References can also be partially relative and partially absolute. For example, $D2 has an absolute column reference and a relative row reference, and D$2 has a relative column reference and an absolute row reference.

BE SURE TO display a worksheet containing values on which you can perform calculations and at least one existing formula before carrying out these steps.

To use the results of one formula in another formula.

1   Click the cell in which you want the results of the formula to appear.
2   Build the formula as usual, clicking the cell whose formula results you want to use in the current formula.
3   Finish the formula by completing the entry.

To use the same formula elsewhere in the worksheet with a different set of values:

1   Right-click the cell containing the formula, and click **Copy** on the shortcut menu.
2   Right-click the cell in which you want to use the formula, and click **Paste** on the shortcut menu.

    Excel calculates the formula using values stored in the same relative position as the values used by the original formula.

To use the same formula elsewhere in the worksheet with the same set of values:

1   Click the cell containing the formula you want to use, and insert **$** (a dollar sign) to the left of each column letter and row number in the formula's argument.
2   Right-click the cell containing the formula, and click **Copy** on the shortcut menu.
3   Right-click the cell in which you want to use the formula, and click **Paste** on the shortcut menu.

    Excel calculates the formula using the same values used by the original formula.

Practice Exercise

In this exercise, you will copy and paste a formula that uses a relative reference and then copy and paste the same formula after making the reference absolute. You will also use the results of one formula in another.

USE the *UseReferences* workbook in the *My Documents\Microsoft Press\MOS 2003 Study Guide\Excel \E03C-2-3* practice file folder.

Open the *UseReferences* workbook. Copy the formula in cell **D23**, and paste it into cell **E23** to get the total of the values in column **E**. Copy the formula from cell **E23** into cell **B4**. Undo the action when the error message appears in the cell, and change the references in cell **E23** to make them absolute instead of relative. Then copy the formula in cell **E23** into cell **B4** again. In cell **B3**, enter the formula **=D23** to repeat the figure for total sales at the top of the worksheet. Then close the *UseReferences* workbook without saving it.

Use Statistical, Date and Time, Financial, and Logical Functions

E03C-2-4   The skills measured by this objective include the following:

- ■ Using statistical functions in formulas
- ■ Using date and time functions in formulas
- ■ Using financial functions in formulas
- ■ Using logical functions in formulas

Excel's functions can perform a wide variety of complex mathematical calculations. They include dozens of functions for statistical analysis, for performing calculations on dates and times, and for helping with financial planning and accounting. They also include logical functions, such as TRUE, FALSE, and IF.

Using Statistical Functions in Formulas

Excel includes dozens of functions for use in statistical analysis, some simple and some complex. You can access these functions through the Insert Function dialog box, which gives a brief description of each function when you select it.

BE SURE TO display a worksheet containing values on which you can perform statistical calculations before carrying out these steps.

To use a statistical function:

1   Click the cell in which you want the results of the formula to appear.

2   At the left end of the formula bar, click the **Insert Function** button.

fx

Insert
Function

3   In the Insert Function dialog box, click the **Or select a category** down arrow, and click **Statistical** in the list.

4   Scroll the list of functions in the **Select a function area**, click the function you want, and then click **OK**.

5   Enter the arguments in the Function Arguments dialog box.

The number of required arguments varies depending on the function you chose. You can click an argument's text box to read a tip about the argument.

6   Click **OK**.

Practice Exercise

In this exercise, you will search the statistical functions and use one of them in a worksheet.

USE the *CalculateStatistics* workbook in the *My Documents\Microsoft Press\MOS 2003 Study Guide\Excel \E03C-2-4* practice file folder.

Open the *CalculateStatistics* workbook. Click cell **D21**, and then use the Insert Function dialog box to find the **MAX** function. Adjust the argument so that it finds the maximum value in the range **D2:D17**. Then close the *CalculateStatistics* workbook without saving it.

Using Date and Time Functions in Formulas

To perform calculations with calendar dates or the time of day, you can use one of Excel's date and time functions. Excel can insert the current date or use values that represent dates and times to perform calculations such as determining the number of days between two different events. You can access these functions through the Insert Function dialog box, which gives a brief description of each function when you select it.

BE SURE TO display a worksheet containing dates or times before carrying out these steps.

To use a date and time function:

Insert
Function

1   Click the cell in which you want the results of the formula to appear.

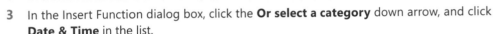

2   At the left end of the formula bar, click the **Insert Function** button.

3   In the Insert Function dialog box, click the **Or select a category** down arrow, and click **Date & Time** in the list.

4   Scroll the list of functions in the **Select a function area**, click the function you want, and then click **OK**.

5   Enter the arguments in the Function Arguments dialog box.

6   Click **OK**.

Practice Exercise

In this exercise, you will search for the date and time functions and use one of them in a worksheet.

USE the *CalculateDate* workbook in the *My Documents\Microsoft Press\MOS 2003 Study Guide \E03C-2-4* practice file folder.

Open the *CalculateDate* workbook. Click cell **B2**, and then use the Insert Function dialog box to find the **WEEKDAY** function. Use cell **A2** as the argument. Then use the fill handle to copy the formula to the other cells in the column. Close the *CalculateDate* workbook without saving it.

Using Financial Functions in Formulas

Excel's financial functions can help you calculate interest rates or payments, determine the future value of an investment, or look at depreciation. You can access these functions through the Insert Function dialog box, which gives a brief description of each function when you select it.

BE SURE TO display a worksheet containing values on which you can perform financial calculations before carrying out these steps.

To use a financial function:

Insert
Function

1   Click the cell in which you want the results of the formula to appear.

2   At the left end of the formula bar, click the **Insert Function** button.

3   In the Insert Function dialog box, click the **Or select a category** down arrow, and click **Financial** in the list.

4   Scroll the list of functions in the **Select a function area**, click the function you want, and then click **OK**.

5   Enter the arguments in the Function Arguments dialog box.

6   Click **OK**.

To calculate loan payments with the PMT function:

1   Click the cell in which you want the results of the formula to appear.

2   Click the **Insert Function** button.

Insert
Function

3   In the Insert Function dialog box, click **Financial** in the **Or select a category** list.

4   Click **PMT** in the **Select a function** list, and click **OK**.

5   In the **Rate** (for interest rate) box, type the necessary formula to specify the monthly interest rate—for example, B6/12 or 5%/12.

6   In the **Nper** (for number of periodic payments) box, type the total number of payments or click a cell containing the number of payments.

7   In the **Pv** (for present value of the amount borrowed, or the price) box, type the value or click a cell containing the price.

8   Click **OK** to close the dialog box.

Practice Exercise

In this exercise, you will use a financial function in a formula to calculate the monthly payment for a piece of equipment that you want to buy.

USE the *CalculateFinances* workbook in the *My Documents\Microsoft Press\MOS 2003 Study Guide\Excel \E03C-2-4* practice file folder.

Open the *CalculateFinances* workbook. Click cell **D6**, and use the Insert Function dialog box to find and insert the **PMT** function. Use the other values in column **D** as the arguments. Then close the *CalculateFinances* workbook without saving it.

Using Logical Functions in Formulas

You can use Excel's logical functions (TRUE, FALSE, AND, OR, IF, NOT) to determine whether one or more conditions are met and return a value such as True or a custom value.

BE SURE TO display a worksheet containing values on which you can perform calculations before carrying out these steps.

To use a logical function:

1   Click the cell in which you want the results of the formula to appear.

2   At the left end of the formula bar, click the **Insert Function** button.

Insert
Function

3   In the Insert Function dialog box, click the **Or select a category** down arrow, and click **Logical** in the list.

4   Scroll the list of functions in the **Select a function area**, click the function you want, and then click **OK**.

5   Enter the arguments in the Function Arguments dialog box, and then click **OK**.

Practice Exercise

In this exercise, you will use an IF function that determines the type of customer for each sale based on the invoice number.

USE the *CalculateLogic* workbook in the *My Documents\Microsoft Press\MOS 2003 Study Guide\Excel \E03C-2-4* practice file folder.

Open the *CalculateLogic* workbook. Click cell **C7**, and then enter the formula **=IF(RIGHT(B7)="R","Retail","Individual")**. This formula looks at the rightmost character of the entry in cell B7 and enters the value *Retail* if it is R and the value *Individual* if it is not R. Use the fill handle to copy the formula to the other cells in the column. Then close the *CalculateLogic* workbook without saving it.

Create, Modify, and Position Diagrams and Charts Based on Worksheet Data

E03C-2-5   The skills measured by this objective include the following:

- ■ Creating, modifying, and positioning diagrams
- ■ Creating, modifying, and positioning charts

Sometimes it's easiest to grasp concepts or data by glancing at a diagram or chart. When you want to present ideas and add visual interest, you can use Excel's diagrams to illustrate concepts, flow patterns, hierarchies, or relationships between entities. To have Excel convert worksheet data to a graphical format, you can use Excel's charting capabilities.

Creating, Modifying, and Positioning Diagrams

You can use six types of diagrams to illustrate your worksheets. The most common diagram is probably the organization chart, which shows the hierarchical relationship of departments or individuals in a company or organization. Other available formats include cycle, radial, pyramid, Venn, and target diagrams. Each diagram appears with its own toolbar, which gives you options for inserting and moving shapes and changing the diagram's layout.

BE SURE TO display the worksheet you want to work with and the Drawing toolbar before carrying out these steps.

To create an organization chart:

Insert
Diagram or
Organization
Chart

1   On the Drawing toolbar, click the **Insert Diagram or Organization Chart** button.

2 Click **OK**.

A default organization chart object is inserted into the worksheet, with the top chart box selected. The Organization Chart toolbar is also displayed.

3 Click a chart box, and type its text.

4 To delete any box you don't need, point to its border, and when the pointer changes to a double-sided arrow, right-click it, and click **Delete** on the shortcut menu.

To add co-worker, subordinate, or assistant boxes:

1 Click the chart box to which you want to assign a co-worker, subordinate, or assistant.

2 On the Organization Chart toolbar, click the **Insert Shape** down arrow, and click the appropriate button on the drop-down menu.

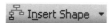

A new chart box is placed in the corresponding relationship to the selected chart box.

3 Click the new chart box, and type the text you want.

To change the style of an organization chart:

Autoformat

1 On the Organization Chart toolbar, click the **Autoformat** button.

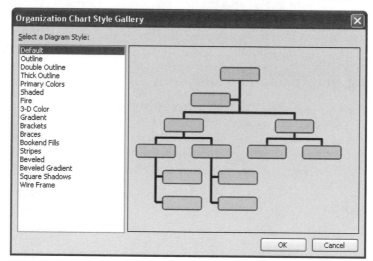

2 In the **Select a Diagram Style** list, click the diagram style you want.

3 Click **OK**.

The style of the organization chart changes to reflect your choice.

To format the text in chart boxes:

1   Click the chart box you want to format.

2   On the Organization Chart toolbar, click the **Select** down arrow, and click **Level**.

     All chart boxes at the same level are selected.

3   On the Formatting toolbar, click buttons to format the text of the chart boxes.

To change the layout of an organization chart:

1   On the Organization Chart toolbar, click the **Layout** button.

2   In the drop-down palette, click one of the available options.

To position and size an organization chart or diagram:

1   Move the chart by clicking it to select it, and dragging it by its frame to the new location.

2   Adjust the size of the chart by dragging one of its handles.

     To adjust the size proportionally, hold down the **SHIFT** key while dragging a corner handle.

Practice Exercise

In this exercise, you will create, modify, and position a diagram.

USE the *CreateDiagram* workbook in the *My Documents\Microsoft Press\MOS 2003 Study Guide\Excel \E03C-2-5* practice file folder.

Open the *CreateDiagram* workbook. Insert an organization chart. Then fill in the chart as follows: In the top box, type **Karen Berg**, press the **ENTER** key, and type **Owner**. In the lower-left box, type **Kim Akers** and **Head Buyer**. In the lower-middle box, type **David Ortiz** and **Assistant**. Type **Gardening Teachers** in the lower-right box, and then click away from the chart boxes but within the organization chart object. Add a subordinate **Office Staff** box to the lower-left box, a subordinate **Sales Staff** box to the lower-middle box, and a subordinate **Students** box to the lower-right box. Apply the **Brackets** style to the organization chart. Select all chart boxes at the same level as **Kim Akers**, and add the **Karen Berg** box to the selection. Then make the first two chart levels bold. Align the organization chart with the worksheet's header row, and stretch the organization chart's frame to the same height as the worksheet's data. Then close the *CreateDiagram* worksheet without saving it.

Creating, Modifying, and Positioning Charts

You can create charts in three ways: in the current worksheet, as a separate sheet in the current workbook, or in another workbook. When you create a chart, the Chart Wizard and the Microsoft Graph program actually do all the work.

After Graph plots the data in a selected range, you can drag the chart to a different location and adjust its size by dragging its handles. You can also format the chart in various ways. However, Excel maintains a link between the chart and its underlying data, so if you want to change the data, you make the changes in the worksheet. Then Graph redraws the graph to reflect the change.

When you don't need a graph any more, you can simply delete it.

BE SURE TO display a worksheet containing values with which you can create a chart before carrying out these steps.

To create a chart:

1   Select the range of cells you want to plot.

Chart Wizard

2   On the Standard toolbar, click the **Chart Wizard** button.

You can also click Chart on the Insert menu to display the Chart Wizard's first page.

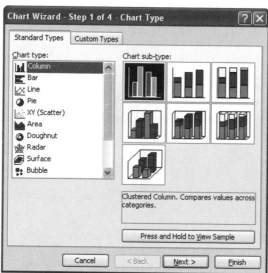

3   On either the **Standard Types** or **Custom Types** tabs, select the type of chart you want from the **Chart type** list.

4   If necessary, select the sub-type you want.

5   Click **Next**.

6   If necessary, change the data range, and then click **Next**.

7   Select one of the tabs, and make selections to customize the chart. To accept the default settings, click **Next**.

8   Do one of the following:

   ■   To display the chart in the current worksheet, select the **As object in** option.

   ■   To display the chart in a new worksheet, select the **As new sheet** option, and if you want, type a name for the new sheet in the adjacent text box.

9   Click **Finish** to plot the chart and display the Chart toolbar.

To move a chart:

1   Verify that the chart you want to move is selected. (It should be surrounded by handles.) If it isn't, click it once.

2   Move the pointer over the chart.

3   When a Chart Tips box that says *Chart Area* appears, drag the chart until it is positioned where you want.

To size a chart:

1   Verify that the chart you want to size is selected.

2   Point to a handle, and drag in the appropriate direction to increase or decrease the size of the frame.

    To change the height and width proportionally, hold down the **SHIFT** key and drag a corner handle diagonally inward or outward.

To update a chart's data:

1   Click a cell containing the chart's underlying data.

2   Change the data in the cell, and then complete the entry.

    Excel updates the chart.

To change the formatting of an existing chart:

1   Double-click the feature of the chart that you want to change.

2   In the Format dialog box, adjust settings as necessary, and then click **OK**.

To delete a chart:

1   Verify that the chart you want to delete is selected.

2   Press the **DELETE** key.

Practice Exercise

In this exercise, you will create a chart in the current worksheet and then change its size and position. You will also change the data used in the chart.

USE the *CreateChart* workbook in the *My Documents\Microsoft Press\MOS 2003 Study Guide\Excel \E03C-2-5* practice file folder.

Open the *CreateChart* workbook. Select the data in the range **A2:C5**, and use it to create a stacked area chart in the current worksheet, entering **Sales for 1st Quarter, 2004** as the chart title. Drag the chart to the right of the data in the worksheet, and size it so that it fits comfortably on the screen. Update the chart by entering the value **23545** in cell **D24**. Then close the *CreateChart* workbook without saving it.

E03C-2 Review

Number	Objective	Mastered
E03C-2-1	Filter lists using AutoFilter	
	Displaying rows with a specific entry in a specific column	❑
	Displaying rows that match certain criteria	❑
E03C-2-2	Sort lists	
	Sorting on one column	❑
	Sorting on two or three columns	❑
E03C-2-3	Insert and modify formulas	
	Doing simple arithmetic	❑
	Using a function in a formula	❑
	Using cell and range references in a formula	❑
E03C-2-4	Use statistical, date and time, financial, and logical functions	
	Using statistical functions in formulas	❑
	Using date and time functions in formulas	❑
	Using financial functions in formulas	❑
	Using logical functions in formulas	❑
E03C-2-5	Create, modify, and position diagrams and charts based on worksheet data	
	Creating, modifying, and positioning diagrams	❑
	Creating, modifying, and positioning charts	❑

E03C-3

Formatting Data and Content

The skills tested by this section of the Microsoft Office Specialist Excel 2003 Core Exam all relate to ways that you can format an Excel worksheet. Specifically, the following objectives are associated with this set of skills:

Number	Objective
E03C-3-1	Apply and modify cell formats
E03C-3-2	Apply and modify cell styles
E03C-3-3	Modify row and column formats
E03C-3-4	Format worksheets

 Important Before you can do the practice exercises associated with this skill set, you need to install the practice files from the book's companion CD to their default location. See "Installing the Practice Files" on page xxv for more information.

Apply and Modify Cell Formats

E03C-3-1   The skills measured by this objective include the following:

- Changing the look of cells and cell entries
- Changing cell alignment
- Applying an AutoFormat
- Changing the format of cell entries
- Copying formatting

One of Excel's strengths is the many ways you can change the formatting of cells and thus the look of worksheets. By changing fonts, adding color and background shading, changing the size and alignment of text, and adding background patterns and borders, your worksheets can run the gamut from restrained to extravagant.

Changing the Look of Cells and Cell Entries

When you want to make tables of data easier to read, you can use character formatting to distinguish different categories of information. This type of formatting changes the look of the worksheet's entries. You can also change the look of the cells themselves by adding borders and shading. You can apply this type of formatting to cells that already contain entries, or you can format empty cells so that future entries will look the way you want.

BE SURE TO display the worksheet you want to work with before carrying out these steps.

To format characters by using toolbar buttons:

1   Select the cell(s) that contain the text or numbers that you want to format.

2   On the Formatting toolbar, do any of the following:

   ■   To change the typeface, click the **Font** down arrow, and then click a different font.

   ■   To make the font larger or smaller, click the **Font Size** down arrow, and then click a different size.

Font Size

B

Bold

   ■   To make an entry bold, click the **Bold** button.

I

Italic

   ■   To italicize text or numbers, click the **Italic** button.

U

Underline

   ■   To underline and entry, click the **Underline** button.

A ▾

Font Color

   ■   To change the color of text or numbers, click the **Font Color** down arrow, and then click a color in the palette.

To format characters by using the Font dialog box:

1   Select the cell(s) you want to format.

2   On the **Format** menu, click **Cells**, and then click the **Font** tab in the Format Cells dialog box.

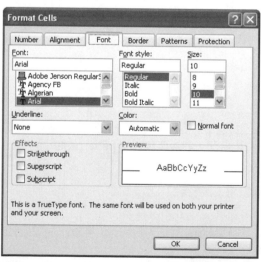

3   Make the changes you want to the font, font style, size, color, or other effects.

4   Click **OK**.

To quickly add borders:

1 Select the cell(s) you want to surround with a border.

Borders

2 On the Formatting toolbar, click the **Borders** down arrow to display a palette of options.

3 Do one of the following:

■ Click the button that adds the type of border you want.

■ Click **Draw Borders**, and use the mouse to designate which cells get borders.

To quickly shade a cell:

1 Select the cell(s) you want to shade.

Fill Color

2 On the Formatting toolbar, click the **Fill Color** down arrow to display a palette of colors.

3 Click the button that adds the color you want.

To add borders and shading by using the Format Cells dialog box:

1 Select the cell(s) you want to format.

2 On the **Format** menu, click **Cells**, and then click the **Border** tab.

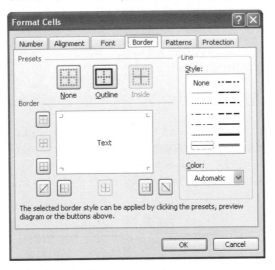

3 Make the selections you want.

4   Click the **Patterns** tab.

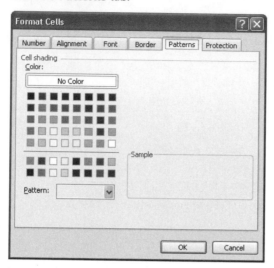

5   Make the selections you want.

6   Click **OK**.

To preformat cells:

1   Select the cells you want to preformat.

2   Specify the formatting you want.

Any entries you make in these cells will be formatted as specified.

Practice Exercise

In this exercise, you will change cell formatting.

USE the *ChangeLook* workbook in the *My Documents\Microsoft Press\MOS 2003 Study Guide\Excel\E03C-3-1* practice file folder.

Open the *ChangeLook* workbook. Click cell **A1**, make the text bold and italic, and change the size to 16 points. Shade cells **A1:C1** with yellow, and then add a border around cells **A8:E8**. Change the font in cells **A8:E8** to **Times New Roman**, and change the font color in those cells to **Brown**. Close the *ChangeLook* workbook without saving it.

Changing Cell Alignment

By default, Excel left-aligns text and right-aligns values horizontally, and bottom-aligns all entries vertically. You can override this default alignment for individual cells, entire columns, or entire rows.

BE SURE TO display the worksheet you want to work with before carrying out these steps.

To quickly change horizontal alignment:

1   Select the cell(s) for which you want to change the alignment.

280

2 On the Formatting toolbar, do one of the following:

Align Left

■ To align entries on the left, click the **Align Left** button.

Center

■ To center entries in their cells, click the **Center** button.

Align Right

■ To align entries on the right, click the **Align Right** button.

To change vertical alignment:

1 Select the cell(s) for which you want to change the alignment.

2 On the **Format** menu, click **Cells**, and then click the **Alignment** tab.

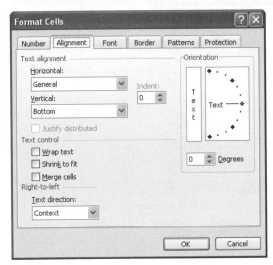

3 In the **Text alignment** area, change the setting in the **Vertical** box.

4 Click **OK**.

Practice Exercise

In this exercise, you will change horizontal and vertical alignment.

USE the *ChangeAlignment* workbook in the *My Documents\Microsoft Press\MOS 2003 Study Guide\Excel \E03C-3-1* practice file folder.

Open the *ChangeAlignment* workbook. Select column **A**, and left-align its entries. Change the alignment of cell **A1** to center. Select row **1**, and bottom-align its entries. Close the *ChangeAlignment* workbook without saving it.

Applying an AutoFormat

Excel's AutoFormats are a collection of professional designs that you can apply to a worksheet. The designs include formatting for numbers, borders, font, fill, and alignment. If a worksheet is set up with row and column headings and aggregate rows such as totals, using an AutoFormat is a quick and effortless way to give a worksheet a polished look.

BE SURE TO display the worksheet you want to work with before carrying out these steps.

To apply an AutoFormat:

1　Select the range of cells to which you want to apply an AutoFormat.

2　On the **Format** menu, click **AutoFormat**.

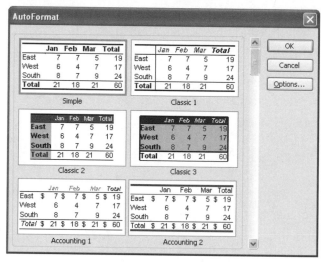

3　Click one of the AutoFormats, and click **OK**.

Tip　To apply only some of an AutoFormat's characteristics, click Options in the AutoFormat dialog box, and make sure that only the options you want (such as Alignment or Border) are selected.

To remove an AutoFormat:

1　Select a cell within the range to which the AutoFormat is applied.

2　On the **Format** menu, click **AutoFormat**.

3　Select the **None** option, and click **OK**.

Practice Exercise

In this exercise, you will apply and then remove an AutoFormat.

USE the *ApplyAutoFormat* workbook in the *My Documents\Microsoft Press\MOS 2003 Study Guide\Excel \E03C-3-1* practice file folder.

Open the *ApplyAutoFormat* workbook. Click any cell in the part of the worksheet that contains data, and apply the **Colorful 2** AutoFormat. Then remove the AutoFormat from the worksheet. Close the *ApplyAutoFormat* workbook without saving it.

Changing the Format of Cell Entries

You can assign a format to cell entries that indicates their data type. If you don't assign a specific format, Excel displays entries in its default General format. With this format, Excel assesses what you type and displays the entry the way it thinks it should be displayed. For example, when you enter a date, Excel displays it in a date format.

You can make some simple adjustments to the format of cell entries by clicking buttons on the Formatting toolbar, but for more comprehensive changes, you use the Number tab of the Format Cells dialog box.

BE SURE TO display the worksheet you want to work with before carrying out these steps.

To display values with commas:

Comma
Style

1   Select the appropriate cell(s).

2   On the Formatting toolbar, click the **Comma Style** button.

To change the number of decimal places:

1   Select the appropriate cell(s)

2   On the Formatting toolbar, do one of the following:

Decrease
Decimal

■   To decrease the number of decimal places (for example, in currency values), click the **Decrease Decimal** button.

Increase
Decimal

■   To increase the number of decimal places, click the **Increase Decimal** button.

To format values as currency:

1   Select the cell(s) you want to format.

2   On the Formatting toolbar, click the **Currency Style** button.

Currency
Style

To apply other formats:

1   Select the appropriate cell(s).

2   On the **Format** menu, click **Cells**, and then click the **Number** tab.

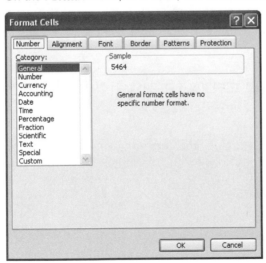

3   Click a category to see its corresponding options on the right.

4   Select the options you want, and click **OK**.

Practice Exercise

In this exercise, you will change the formatting of values, and then work with Date formatting.

USE the *ChangeFormat* workbook in the *My Documents\Microsoft Press\MOS 2003 Study Guide\Excel \E03C-3-1* practice file folder.

Open the *ChangeFormat* workbook. Select column **D**, and format it first with commas, and then as currency. Select column **A**, and then change the date formatting so that months and years are both written out in full. Close the *ChangeFormat* workbook without saving it.

Copying Formatting

You can save a lot of formatting time by copying combinations of character and cell formatting and number formats from one cell to other cells. For example, if you format headings to be bold and centered, you can apply those styles to any cells in the worksheet simply by copying them.

BE SURE TO display a worksheet containing formatting you want to copy before carrying out these steps.

To copy formatting from one cell to another cell:

Format
Painter

1   Click the cell or select the range that contains the formatting you want to copy.

2   On the Standard toolbar, click the **Format Painter** button.

3   Click the cell or select the range to which you want to copy the formatting.

To paint formatting into multiple cells or ranges:

Format
Painter

1   Click the cell or select the range that contains the formatting you want to copy.

2   On the Standard toolbar, double-click the **Format Painter** button.

3   Click each cell or select each range to which you want to copy the formatting.

4   Click the **Format Painter** button again to toggle it off.

Practice Exercise

In this exercise, you will copy formatting from one part of a worksheet to another.

USE the *CopyFormat* workbook in the *My Documents\Microsoft Press\MOS 2003 Study Guide\Excel\E03C-3-1* practice file folder.

Open the *CopyFormat* workbook. Copy the formatting in cells **B3:C3** to the headings in cells **A9:E9**. Close the *CopyFormat* workbook without saving it.

Apply and Modify Cell Styles

E03C-3-2   The skills measured by this objective include the following:

■   Apply a style
■   Modify a style

Styles are predetermined sets of formatting that you can apply to one or more cells in a worksheet. Unlike AutoFormats, which govern the appearance of an entire worksheet, you can use a style to apply a particular combination of formatting to a particular column, row, or cell—for example, to a row of column headings. You can apply one of Excel's existing styles or modify a style to suit your needs.

Apply a Style

Styles are tools you can use to format a worksheet quickly. You can use Excel's built-in styles to format cells in currency, comma, percent, or normal styles.

BE SURE TO display the worksheet you want to work with before carrying out these steps.

To apply an existing style:

1 Select the cell or a range you want to format.

2 On the **Format** menu, click **Style**.

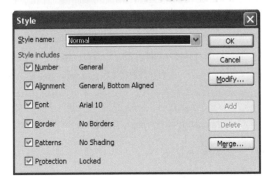

3 Click the **Style name** down arrow, and click the style you want in the drop-down list.

4 Click **OK**.

Practice Exercise

In this exercise, you will apply a style to a column of values in a worksheet.

USE the *ApplyStyle* workbook in the *My Documents\Microsoft Press\MOS 2003 Study Guide\Excel\E03C-3-2* practice file folder.

Open the *ApplyStyle* workbook. Select column **D**, and apply the **Currency [0]** style. Then apply the **Currency** style. Close the *ApplyStyle* workbook without saving it.

Modify a Style

You can easily modify Excel's built-in styles by adjusting the number, alignment, font, border, or pattern formatting. With a customized style at your disposal, you can quickly format data in worksheets to look the way you want. When you modify a style, the formatting of all the data to which that style has already been applied changes to reflect the new style definition.

BE SURE TO display a worksheet in which styles have been applied to cells before carrying out these steps.

To modify a style:

1 On the **Format** menu, click **Style**.

2 Click the **Style name** down arrow, and then click the style you want to modify in the drop-down list.

3   Click the **Modify** button, and in the Format Cells dialog box, make the necessary changes, and click **OK**.

4   Click **OK** in the Style dialog box to apply the modified style to the current selection.

Tip   You can create an entirely new style at any time. In the Style dialog box, enter a name in the "Style name" text box, and select the options you want from the "Style includes" list. Click the Modify button, specify the style's formatting in the Format Cells dialog box, and click OK. You can click OK in the Style dialog box to apply the new style to the current selection, or click Add to add the new style to the "Style name" list without applying it.

Practice Exercise

In this exercise, you will modify one of Excel's styles and apply the modified style to data in a worksheet.

USE the *ModifyStyle* workbook in the *My Documents\Microsoft Press\MOS 2003 Study Guide\Excel\E03C-3-2* practice file folder.

Open the *ModifyStyle* workbook. Select the range **D2:D17**, modify the **Currency** style to include a bright green background fill, and then apply the style to the range. Click a cell away from column **D**, and then modify the **Currency** style again, removing the green background and returning the setting to **No Color**. Close the *ModifyStyle* workbook without saving it.

Modify Row and Column Formats

E03C-3-3   The skills measured by this objective include the following:

- Adjusting column widths and row heights
- Hiding and revealing rows and columns
- Inserting and deleting rows and columns

In addition to changing the formatting of the data in a worksheet, you can also change its structure. You can change the width of columns and height of rows to accommodate long entries, and you can add, delete, and hide columns and rows.

Adjusting Column Widths and Row Heights

Most worksheets have entries of varying lengths. Both long entries and short entries look better if they fit snugly in their columns, so it is important to be able to adjust column widths quickly and easily. For some worksheets, you might also need to be able to adjust row heights.

Tip   By default, Excel does not "wrap" text entries in a cell. If a long text entry won't fit in its cell and you don't want to widen the column, you can wrap the text to more than one line, or if the text is a heading, you can rotate it. Either action increases the height of the row. On the Format menu, click Cells, and click the Alignment tab. Select the "Wrap text" check box to wrap the text, or change the settings in the Orientation area. To remove text rotation, set Degrees to 0.

BE SURE TO display the worksheet you want to work with before carrying out these steps.

To adjust the width of a column:

1 Select the column(s) whose width you want to adjust.

2 On the **Format** menu, click **Column** and then **Width**.

3 Enter the width you want in the **Column width** box, and click **OK**.

To adjust the width of a column to fit its longest entry:

- On the **Format** menu, click **Column** and then **AutoFit Selection**.
- Double-click the right border of the column's header.

To change the width of multiple columns:

1 Select the columns whose widths you want to adjust.

2 Point to the border between any two selected column headers, and drag to the left or right.

To change the standard column width:

1 On the **Format** menu, click **Column** and then **Standard Width**.

2 Type a new value in the **Standard column width** box, and click **OK**.

To adjust the height of a row:

1 Select the row(s) whose height you want to adjust.

2 On the **Format** menu, click **Row** and then **Height**.

3 Enter the width you want in the **Row height** box, and click **OK**.

To change the height of multiple rows:

1 Select the rows whose heights you want to adjust.

2 Point to the border between any two selected row headers, and drag up or down.

Practice Exercise

In this exercise, you will adjust row heights and column widths to fit data.

USE the *AdjustWidth* workbook in the *My Documents\Microsoft Press\MOS 2003 Study Guide\Excel\E03C-3-3* practice file folder.

Open the *AdjustWidth* workbook. Widen columns **A** through **D** to **10.71**, and double the height of row **1**. Then resize column **A** so that it fits its widest entry. Close the *AdjustWidth* workbook without saving it.

Hiding and Revealing Columns and Rows

If your worksheet includes rows or columns of information that you don't need to have in view, you can hide them and then reveal them again when you want to see them. Being able to hide columns and rows is also useful when you don't want everyone to be aware of confidential information in a worksheet. For example, if you need to print a worksheet that includes one column of proprietary data that you don't want circulated with the rest of the worksheet, you can hide just that column before printing.

BE SURE TO display the worksheet you want to work with before carrying out these steps.

To hide or reveal a column or row:

- Right-click the column or row header, and click **Hide** on the shortcut menu.
- Select the columns or rows that appear on either side of a hidden element, right-click the selection, and click **Unhide** on the shortcut menu.

Practice Exercise

In this exercise, you will hide and then reveal a column.

USE the *HideColumn* workbook in the *My Documents\Microsoft Press\MOS 2003 Study Guide\Excel\E03C-3-3* practice file folder.

Open the *HideColumn* workbook. Hide column **D**. Then bring it back into view by unhiding it. Close the *HideColumn* workbook without saving it.

Inserting and Deleting Columns and Rows

Inserting a new column or row into a worksheet is often easier than moving data to make room for new entries. To tell Excel where you want to make the insertion, you select the column to the right or the row below the desired location. To insert more than one column or row at a time, select the number of columns or rows you want to insert.

Deleting a column or row you no longer need is just as easy as inserting one. When you delete a column or row, you remove it from the worksheet completely, whereas deleting the entries leaves a blank column or row ready to receive new data.

BE SURE TO display the worksheet you want to work with before carrying out these steps.

To insert a column or row:

1 Right-click the column header to the right or the row header below where you want to make the insertion.

2 Click **Insert** on the shortcut menu.

To insert multiple columns or rows:

1 Select the number of columns or rows you want to insert by dragging through the column headers to the right or the row headers below where you want to make the insertion.

2 On the **Insert** menu, click **Columns** or **Rows**.

To delete a column or row:

1 Right-click the header of the column or row you want to delete.

2 Click **Delete** on the shortcut menu.

Practice Exercise

In this exercise, you will insert and delete columns and rows.

USE the *InsertColumn* workbook in the *My Documents\Microsoft Press\MOS 2003 Study Guide\Excel \E03C-3-3* practice file folder.

Open the *InsertColumn* workbook. Insert a column to the left of column **C**, and then delete it. Insert two rows above row **7**, and then delete them. Delete row **3**. Then close the *InsertColumn* workbook without saving it.

Format Worksheets

E03C-3-4   The skills measured by this objective include the following:

■ Changing a worksheet's name, tab, and background

■ Hiding and revealing a worksheet

When a workbook contains several worksheets, you might need to be able to readily distinguish one worksheet from another. You can modify a worksheet's tab color, sheet name, and background to make it stand out, and you can hide worksheets that provide supporting or confidential information that you don't want to be readily visible.

Changing a Worksheet's Name, Tab, and Background

The names Excel assigns to sheet tabs are functional but not very informative. You can easily change the sheet's name, and you can change its tab color to make it stand out. You can also place a graphic in the worksheet's background.

E03C-3: **Formatting Data and Content**

BE SURE TO display the worksheet you want to work with before carrying out these steps.

To rename a worksheet:

1 Double-click the sheet tab of the worksheet you want to rename.

Excel selects the text on the tab.

2 Type the new name, and press **ENTER**.

To change the color of a worksheet tab:

1 Right-click the sheet tab, and click **Tab Color** on the shortcut menu.

2 Click a color on the palette that appears, and click **OK**.

When the tab is active, the color you chose appears along the bottom of the tab. When the tab is not active, the entire tab appears in the color you chose.

To add an image to the background of a worksheet:

1 On the **Format** menu, click **Sheet** and then **Background**.

2 Navigate to the image you want to use as the background, and click it.

3 Click **Insert**.

To remove the background image, click Sheet and then Delete Background on the Format menu.

Practice Exercise

In this exercise, you will rename worksheet tabs and change their color. Then you will add and remove a background image.

USE the *NameWorksheet* workbook and the *WashoutLogo* graphic file in the *My Documents\Microsoft Press \MOS 2003 Study Guide\Excel\E03C-3-4* practice file folder.

Open the *NameWorksheet* workbook. Change **Sheet1**'s tab to green, and rename it **Quarter1**. Change **Sheet2**'s tab to yellow, and rename it **Quarter2**. Insert the *WashoutLogo* graphic file as the background of the **Quarter1** worksheet, and then delete the background. Close the *NameWorksheet* workbook without saving it.

Hiding and Revealing a Worksheet

Sometimes you might need to hide an entire worksheet from view instead of just a few rows or columns. When a worksheet is hidden, you cannot print it.

BE SURE TO display the worksheet you want to work with before carrying out these steps.

To hide or reveal a worksheet:

■ On the **Format** menu, click **Sheet** and then **Hide**.

■ On the **Format** menu, click **Sheet** and then **Unhide**. When the Unhide dialog box appears, click the sheet you want to reveal, and click **OK**.

Practice Exercise

In this exercise, you will hide and then unhide a worksheet.

USE the *HideWorksheet* workbook in the *My Documents\Microsoft Press\MOS 2003 Study Guide\Excel \E03C-3-4* practice file folder.

Open the *HideWorksheet* workbook. Hide the **Quarter2** sheet, and then reveal it again. Close the *HideWorksheet* workbook without saving it.

E03C-3 Review

Number	Objective	Mastered
E03C-3-1	Apply and modify cell formats	
	Changing the look of cells and cell entries	❑
	Changing cell alignment	❑
	Applying an AutoFormat	❑
	Changing the format of cell entries	❑
	Copying formatting	❑
E03C-3-2	Apply and modify cell styles	
	Apply a style	❑
	Modify a style	❑
E03C-3-3	Modify row and column formats	
	Adjusting column widths and row heights	❑
	Hiding and revealing rows and columns	❑
	Inserting and deleting rows and columns	❑
E03C-3-4	Format worksheets	
	Changing a worksheet's name, tab, and background	❑
	Hiding and revealing a worksheet	❑

E03C-4
Collaborating

The skills tested by this section of the Microsoft Office Specialist Excel 2003 Core Exam relate to the Excel comments feature, which makes it is easy to collaborate with other people on the creation and formatting of worksheets. Specifically, the following objective is associated with this set of skills:

Number	Objective
E03C-4-1	Insert, view, and edit comments

Important   Before you can do the practice exercises associated with this skill set, you need to install the practice files from the book's companion CD to their default location. See "Installing the Practice Files" on page xxv for more information.

Insert, View, and Edit Comments

E03C-4-1   The skills measured by this objective include the following:

- Attaching a comment to a worksheet cell
- Editing or deleting a comment

You might want to attach a comment to a cell for a variety of reasons—for example, to explain a formula or to remind yourself to check an assumption.

Attaching a Comment to a Worksheet Cell

Attaching a comment to a cell is an easy way to communicate with other people who might be using or evaluating your worksheets. Along with the text of the comment, Excel includes the user name of the person who inserted it. Excel flags the upper-right corner of commented cells with a small red triangle. You can specify that a comment is displayed all the time, or have it pop up only when you want to read it.

BE SURE TO display the worksheet you want to work with before carrying out these steps.

To attach a comment:

1   Click the cell or select the range to which you want to attach the comment.

2   On the **Insert** menu, click **Comment**.

3   Type the comment in the text box that appears.

4   Click anywhere outside the cell and text box to insert the comment.

   A red triangle appears in the upper-right corner of the cell to indicate the presence of a comment.

To display a comment:

- To display the comment box temporarily, point to the cell.

- To permanently display the comment box, right-click the cell, and click **Show/Hide Comments** on the shortcut menu.

- To hide a permanently displayed comment box, right-click the cell, and click **Hide Comment** on the shortcut menu.

- To position and size comment boxes so that they don't overlap, click them and drag their frames and sizing handles.

Practice Exercise

In this exercise, you will attach a few comments to cells, display them, and then move them so that they can be read easily.

USE the *AttachComment* workbook in the *My Documents\Microsoft Press\MOS 2003 Study Guide\Excel \E03C-4-1* practice file folder.

   Open the *AttachComment* workbook. Attach a comment to cell **C10** that reads **This product will be discontinued next season.** Attach a comment to cell **C11** that reads **Do we need to find a new vendor for this product? Discuss with Karen.** Set both comments so that they are permanently visible, and then arrange them so that they can both be read at the same time. Resize the comments so that they take up no more room than necessary to display their text. Then close the *AttachComment* workbook without saving it.

Editing or Deleting a Comment

   After a comment has been attached to a cell, you can go back and update the comment or delete it altogether.

BE SURE TO display the worksheet you want to work with before carrying out these steps.

   To edit a comment:

Edit
Comment

1   Click the cell containing the comment, and do one of the following:

- On the Reviewing toolbar, click the **Edit Comment** button.

- Right-click the cell, and click **Edit Comment** on the shortcut menu.

- On the **Insert** menu, click **Edit Comment**.

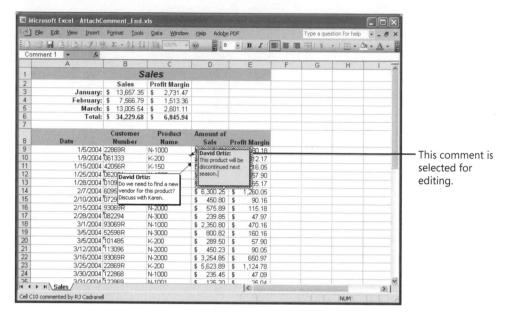

This comment is selected for editing.

2 Make your changes, and then click away from the comment box and the cell.

To delete a comment:

● Click the cell containing the comment, and do one of the following:

■ On the Reviewing toolbar, click the **Delete Comment** button.

■ Right-click the cell, and click **Delete Comment** on the shortcut menu.

■ On the **Edit** menu, click **Clear** and then **Comments**.

Delete
Comment

Practice Exercise

In this exercise, you will edit a comment.

USE the *EditComment* workbook in the *My Documents\Microsoft Press\MOS 2003 Study Guide\Excel \E03C-4-1* practice file folder.

Open the *EditComment* workbook. Hide both of the comments. Add the words **and Kim** to the end of the second sentence of the comment in cell **C11**, and then delete the words *for this product*. Delete the comment attached to cell **C10** entirely. Then close the *EditComment* workbook without saving it.

E03C-4 Review

Number	Objective	Mastered
E03C-4-1	Insert, view, and edit comments	
	Attaching a comment to a worksheet cell	❑
	Editing or deleting a comment	❑

E03C-5
Managing Workbooks

The skills tested by this section of the Microsoft Office Specialist Excel 2003 Core Exam all relate to tasks you might need to carry out with an Excel workbook. Specifically, the following objectives are associated with this set of skills:

Number	Objective
E03C-5-1	Create new workbooks from templates
E03C-5-2	Insert, delete, and move cells
E03C-5-3	Create and modify hyperlinks
E03C-5-4	Organize worksheets
E03C-5-5	Preview data in other views
E03C-5-6	Customize window layout
E03C-5-7	Set up pages for printing
E03C-5-8	Print data
E03C-5-9	Organize workbooks using file folders
E03C-5-10	Save data in appropriate formats for different uses

Important Before you can do the practice exercises associated with this skill set, you need to install the practice files from the book's companion CD to their default location. See "Installing the Practice Files" on page xxv for more information.

Create New Workbooks from Templates

E03C-5-1   The skills measured by this objective include the following:

- Creating a workbook based on a template

Instead of starting with blank worksheets in a new workbook, you can save time by creating the workbook based on a template. An Excel template already has some of the worksheet setup work done for you. Depending on the template, this can be anything from a few headings and formulas to a fully formatted worksheet complete with formulas, ready for you to plug in your numbers.

Creating a Workbook Based on a Template

To use a template, you simply open a copy of it and work with it as though it were any other Excel workbook. When you save the workbook, Excel treats it as a new file to which you have to assign a name. That way, the template itself remains unchanged and is available the next time you need it to start a different workbook. This system means you can use the same template to create an unlimited number of new workbooks.

BE SURE TO start Excel and display the New Workbook task pane before carrying out these steps.

To create a workbook based on a template:

1   In the New Workbook task pane, click the **On my computer** link, and when the Templates dialog box appears, click the **Spreadsheet Solutions** tab.

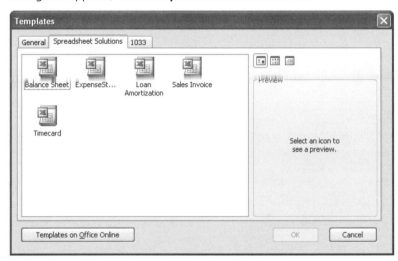

2   Double-click the icon for the template on which you want to base the new workbook.

3   Customize the new workbook with your own information.

4   Save and close the workbook.

Practice Exercise

In this exercise, you will create an invoice worksheet based on a template.

NO practice files are required for this exercise.

From the New Workbook task pane, display the Templates dialog box. Look through Excel's available templates, and create a workbook based on **Sales Invoice**. In the **Invoice No.** field, type **1231**. Type your own name, address, and phone number in the **Customer** area. Enter **2** in the **Qty** column, **Assorted Chrysanthemums** in the **Description** column, and **5.00** in the **Unit Price** column. Save the new workbook in the *My Documents\Microsoft Press\MOS 2003 Study Guide\Excel\E03C-5-1* practice file folder as **Invoice 1231**. Then close the workbook.

Insert, Delete, and Move Cells

E03C-5-2   The skills measured by this objective include the following:

   ■   Inserting and deleting cells
   ■   Copying and moving entries
   ■   Controlling how Excel pastes

While developing worksheets, you will often need to insert and delete cells, or copy and move cell entries. Knowing how to perform these tasks efficiently makes it easier to avoid unexpected results.

Inserting and Deleting Cells

Sometimes you need to insert only a few cells, and inserting an entire column or row would disrupt some of your entries. You can insert cells anywhere you need them. When you insert cells in the middle of a worksheet, Excel gives you the option of shifting the existing cells either down or to the right.

BE SURE TO display the worksheet you want to work with before carrying out these steps.

To insert cells:

1   Adjacent to the location where you want to insert cells, select the number of cells you want to insert.

2   On the **Insert** menu, click **Cells**.

3   Do one of the following:

■   To move adjacent cells to make room for the inserted cells, select either the **Shift cells right** or **Shift cells down** option.

■   To insert whole rows or columns, select either the **Entire row** or **Entire column** option.

4   Click **OK** to close the dialog box.

To delete cells:

1   Select the cells you want to delete.

2   On the **Edit** menu, click **Delete**.

3   Select either **Shift cells left** or **Shift cells up** to move adjacent cells to fill the gap created by the deleted cells.

4   Click **OK** to close the dialog box.

Practice Exercise

In this exercise, you will insert and delete cells.

USE the *InsertCells* workbook in the *My Documents\Microsoft Press\MOS 2003 Study Guide\Excel\E03C-5-2* practice file folder.

Open the *InsertCells* workbook. Select cells **D16:D17**, and insert two cells, shifting the existing cells down. Select cells **B16:D17**, and delete them, shifting the adjacent cells up. Then close the *InsertCells* workbook without saving it.

Copying and Moving Entries

You can copy or move an entry or group of entries anywhere within the same worksheet, to a different worksheet, or even between workbooks. Whether you want to copy or move entries, you can click buttons on the Standard toolbar or click the equivalent commands on the Edit menu.

When you need to copy or move several discrete entries, you don't have to handle them one at a time. The Office Clipboard can store up to 24 items, and they are all available for pasting at any time. To paste one of the stored items, you display the Clipboard task pane and choose the items you want to paste.

Tip The Office Clipboard works with all of the Microsoft Office System 2003 applications, so you can copy and move items among them.

BE SURE TO display the worksheet you want to work with before carrying out these steps.

To copy entries:

1   Select the cell or range that contains the entries you want to copy.

Copy

2   On the Standard toolbar, click the **Copy** button.

You can also click Copy on the Edit menu, or right-click the cell or range and click Copy on the shortcut menu.

3   Click the cell to which you want to copy the entries.

If you are copying a range, click the first cell of the range to which you want to copy the entries.

Paste

4   On the Standard toolbar, click the **Paste** button.

Until you perform another type of action, you can paste the same entry or entries repeatedly.

To move entries:

1   Select the cell or range that contains the entries you want to move.

Cut

2   On the Standard toolbar, click the **Cut** button.

You can also click Cut on the Edit menu, or right-click the cell or range and click Cut on the shortcut menu.

3   Click the cell to which you want to move the entries.

If you are moving a range, click the first cell of the range to which you want to move the entries.

Paste

4   On the Standard toolbar, click the **Paste** button.

To paste one or more entries from the Clipboard:

1   Select the cell or range that contains the entries you want to copy or move, and copy or cut them.

2   If the Clipboard task pane does not open, display it by clicking **Task Pane** on the **View** menu, clicking the **Other Task Panes** down arrow, and clicking **Clipboard**.

Tip   If you want the Clipboard task pane to appear whenever you cut or copy more than one item of information from Excel or any other Office program, click the task pane's Options button and click Show Office Clipboard Automatically.

3   In the Clipboard task pane, do one of the following:

■   To paste an item from the Clipboard, point to it, click its down arrow, and then click **Paste**.

■   To paste all the items on the Clipboard, click **Paste All**.

Practice Exercise

In this exercise, you will copy and paste entries, both with and without the help of the Clipboard task pane.

USE the *CopyEntries* workbook in the *My Documents\Microsoft Press\MOS 2003 Study Guide\Excel\E03C-5-2* practice file folder.

Open the *CopyEntries* workbook. Copy the entry in cell **B11**, and paste it into cell **B18**. Copy the entry in cell **C7**, and paste it into cell **C18**. Use the Clipboard task pane to paste **93069R** into cell **B19** and **K-150** into cell **C19**. Then close the *CopyEntries* workbook without saving it.

Controlling How Excel Pastes

For more control over how Excel pastes, you can use the Paste Special command. This command is available whether you are pasting Excel data or data from another program. The options available vary depending on what you plan to paste. If you are pasting Excel data, you have the option to include or exclude such things as formulas, values, comments, formatting, and borders.

BE SURE TO display the worksheet you want to work with before carrying out these steps.

To use the Paste Special command for Excel data:

1   Select the cell or range that contains the entries you want to copy or move, and copy or cut them.

2   Click the cell to which you want to copy the entries.

    If you are copying a range, click the first cell of the range to which you want to copy the entries.

3   On the **Edit** menu, click **Paste Special**.

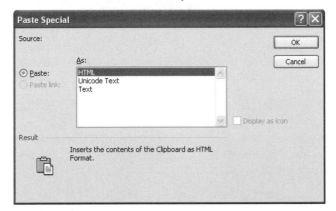

4   Select the options you want, and click **OK**.

    If you click "Paste link," double-clicking the pasted information will highlight the cell from which it was copied and display an absolute reference to that cell.

See Also   For information about absolute and relative references, refer to E03C-2-3, "Insert and Modify Formulas."

To use the Paste Special command with items from other programs:

1   Cut or copy the item that you want to paste.

2   Click the cell to which you want to copy the item.

3   On the **Edit** menu, click **Paste Special**.

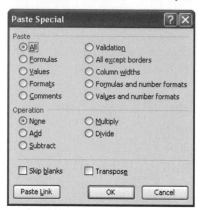

The options shown in this dialog box vary depending on what you are pasting. For example, a graphic's options will differ from the options for text.

4   Select the options you want, and click **OK**.

Practice Exercise

In this exercise, you will use Excel's Paste Special command to control what Excel pastes into cells.

USE the *ControlPasting* workbook in the *My Documents\Microsoft Press\MOS 2003 Study Guide\Excel \E03C-5-2* practice file folder.

Open the *ControlPasting* workbook. Copy the data in cell **D21**, and paste it into cell **B2**, making sure to include everything except the borders. Then close the *ControlPasting* workbook without saving it.

Create and Modify Hyperlinks

E03C-5-3   The skills measured by this objective include the following:

■ Inserting a hyperlink

■ Editing a hyperlink

Sometimes you might need to jump to another Excel workbook, another file or document, or a page on the Internet or a local intranet. You can insert a hyperlink into an Excel worksheet that you can use to move to any of these destinations with one click.

Inserting a Hyperlink

A hyperlink is text or a graphic that, when clicked, moves you to another location. In Excel, this location can be in any of the following:

■ Another place in the same worksheet

■ A different worksheet in the same workbook

- A different workbook or other type of file
- A Web page
- A message window containing a specific e-mail address

BE SURE TO display the worksheet you want to work with before carrying out these steps.

To insert a hyperlink:

1   Right-click the cell or object you want to use as the hyperlink, and click **Hyperlink** on the shortcut menu.

2   In the **Link to** area, click the type of hyperlink you want to create.

3   Select other options as necessary.

4   If you want to create a tip that will be displayed when the pointer is over the hyperlink, click the **ScreenTip** button, type the text you want in the **Set Hyperlink ScreenTip** text box, and click **OK**.

5   Click **OK** again to return to your worksheet.

Practice Exercise

In this exercise, you will insert a hyperlink to another worksheet, and then insert a hyperlink to a Web page.

USE the *InsertHyperlink* workbook in the *My Documents\Microsoft Press\MOS 2003 Study Guide\Excel \E03C-5-3* practice file folder.

Open the *InsertHyperlink* workbook. In cell **B8** of the **Quarter1** worksheet, insert a hyperlink to the **Sales Reps** worksheet. Test the hyperlink, and then click cell **C2** on the **Sales Reps** worksheet. Enter **Web site** in the cell, and then insert a hyperlink from that cell to The Garden Company's website at **www.thegardencompany.msn.com**. (This is a fictitious website, so you cannot test this link.) Close the *InsertHyperlink* workbook without saving it.

Editing a Hyperlink

You will need to edit a hyperlink if its destination moves or if you want it to point to a different location or file. If a hyperlink's destination is no longer available, you might need to remove the hyperlink altogether.

BE SURE TO display a worksheet containing a hyperlink before carrying out these steps.

To edit a hyperlink:

1   Right-click the hyperlink, and click **Edit Hyperlink** on the shortcut menu.
2   Make the necessary changes, and then click **OK**.

To remove a hyperlink:

● Right-click the hyperlink, and click **Remove Hyperlink** on the shortcut menu.

Practice Exercise

In this exercise, you will edit a worksheet's existing hyperlinks.

USE the *EditHyperlink* workbook in the *My Documents\Microsoft Press\MOS 2003 Study Guide\Excel \E03C-5-3* practice file folder.

Open the *EditHyperlink* workbook. Edit the hyperlink in cell **B8** of the **Quarter1** worksheet by adding a ScreenTip that says **Display list of sales reps**. Then edit the hyperlink in cell **C2** of the **Sales Reps** worksheet so that it points to **www.thegardencompany.msn.com /productindex**. Close the *EditHyperlink* workbook without saving it.

Organize Worksheets

E03C-5-4   The skills measured by this objective include the following:

■ Inserting and deleting worksheets
■ Moving a worksheet

When you create workbooks that contain multiple worksheets, you will often need to add new worksheets and delete ones you no longer use. You might also need to shuffle the positions of worksheets to make their tab order more logical.

Inserting and Deleting Worksheets

By default, each new workbook you create contains three sheets. Three might be more than you need, or it might not be enough. A workbook must have at least one worksheet, and it can have as many as 255.

See Also   For information about changing the default number of worksheets, refer to E03E-5-4, "Modify Excel Default Settings."

It's easy to delete worksheets, but you should be aware that Excel deletes them permanently—there is no Undo safety net. So before you delete a worksheet, you should always scrutinize it to confirm that you are deleting the correct one.

BE SURE TO display the worksheet you want to work with before carrying out these steps.

To insert a worksheet:

1   Activate the sheet to the left of which you want to insert a new sheet.

2   On the **Insert** menu, click **Worksheet**.

To delete a worksheet:

1   Click the tab of the worksheet you want to delete.

2   On the **Edit** menu, click **Delete Sheet**.

Practice Exercise

In this exercise, you will insert and delete worksheets in a workbook.

USE the *InsertWorksheet* workbook in the *My Documents\Microsoft Press\MOS 2003 Study Guide\Excel \E03C-5-4* practice file folder.

Open the *InsertWorksheet* workbook. Insert a new worksheet between the two existing worksheets, double-click its tab, and name the new worksheet **Product Key**. Insert a worksheet to the left of the **Sales Reps** worksheet, and name the new worksheet **Products**. Then delete the **Product Key** worksheet. Close the *InsertWorksheet* workbook without saving it.

Moving a Worksheet

You can effectively "move" a worksheet by cutting and pasting all its information into a different worksheet. However, you can also literally move worksheets to a different position in a workbook. You can also move a worksheet from one workbook to another.

BE SURE TO display the worksheet you want to work with before carrying out these steps.

To move a worksheet in the same workbook:

1   Point to the tab of the worksheet you want to move, and hold down the left mouse button.

2   Drag the sheet pointer to the right or left until it sits in the location you want.

As you drag, Excel indicates with an arrowhead where it will move the worksheet when you release the mouse button.

To move a worksheet to a different workbook:

1   Open both the workbook you are moving the worksheet from and the one you are moving it to.

2   On the **Window** menu, click **Arrange**.

3   Select the window arrangement option you want, and click **OK**.

4   Activate the worksheet you want to move by clicking its tab.

5   Drag the sheet pointer over the tabs of the sheets in the other workbook's window, releasing the mouse button when the pointer sits in the location you want.

See Also   For information about arranging windows, refer to E03C-5-6, "Customize Window Layout."

Practice Exercise

In this exercise, you will rearrange worksheets in a workbook.

USE the *MoveWorksheet* workbook in the *My Documents\Microsoft Press\MOS 2003 Study Guide\Excel \E03C-5-4* practice file folder.

Open the *MoveWorksheet* workbook. Move the **Sales Reps** worksheet so that it is between the other two worksheets. Then close the *MoveWorksheet* workbook without saving it.

Preview Data in Other Views

E03C-5-5   The skills measured by this objective include the following:

- Previewing a worksheet that will be printed
- Previewing a Web workbook.

Data that looks the way you want in Excel still might not be ready to distribute in print or Web formats. For example, the page breaks might not be where you expect them in print format. To check how your workbooks will appear in print or online, you can preview them in Excel.

Previewing a Worksheet That Will Be Printed

Usually you'll want to preview a worksheet before you print it to make sure that single-page worksheets fit neatly on the page and that multi-page worksheets break in logical places. If you are not satisfied with the way your worksheet will look when printed, you can change the page setup or insert custom page breaks.

See Also   For information about page setup and custom page breaks, refer to E03C-5-7, "Set Up Pages for Printing."

BE SURE TO display the worksheet you want to work with before carrying out these steps.

To preview a worksheet:

Print Preview

1   Activate the sheet you want to preview.

2   On the Standard toolbar, click the **Print Preview** button.

3   Do any of the following:

- To examine part of the page in more detail, move the mouse pointer over the page, where it changes to a small magnifying glass, and click. Click again to zoom out.
- If your worksheet has more than one page, click the **Next** button to move ahead one page and the **Previous** button to move back a page.
- To access the Page Setup dialog box, click the **Setup** button.
- To display guides that show the top, bottom, left, and right margins and markers that show the column widths, click the **Margins** button. Click and drag the guides or markers to alter margins or column widths.

4   On the Print Preview toolbar, click the **Close** button to turn off print preview, or click **Print** to print the workbook.

Practice Exercise

In this exercise, you will use Print Preview to examine how a worksheet will look when printed, and to change its margins.

USE the *PreviewWorksheet* workbook in the *My Documents\Microsoft Press\MOS 2003 Study Guide\Excel \E03C-5-5* practice file folder.

Open the *PreviewWorksheet* workbook. Switch to Print Preview, and then zoom in on the page. Zoom back out, and then move to the second page. Adjust the margins so that all of the data fits on one page, and then widen the two right columns to better fill the right side of the page. Close Print Preview, and then close the *PreviewWorksheet* workbook without saving it.

Previewing a Web Workbook

Before you save a workbook as a Web page, you will want to preview it to get an idea of how it will look when viewed in a Web browser. You can also test any hyperlinks, duplicating the experience of the people who will be viewing your worksheet over the Internet or an intranet. If anything is amiss, you can go back to Excel and correct it, and then preview again.

BE SURE TO display the worksheet you want to work with before carrying out these steps.

To preview a workbook as a Web page:

1   Display the worksheet you want to preview.

2   On the **File** menu, click **Web Page Preview**.

    Your Web browser starts, converts the workbook file temporarily to HTML format, and displays the workbook.

3   Scroll the worksheet to preview it, and click any links that you want to test.

4   For a multi-tabbed workbook, click the tabs at the bottom of the browser window to see each of the worksheets.

5   Click the **Close** button to return to Excel.

Practice Exercise

In this exercise, you will preview a worksheet as a Web page.

USE the *PreviewWeb* workbook in the *My Documents\Microsoft Press\MOS 2003 Study Guide\Excel \E03C-5-5* practice file folder.

Open the *PreviewWeb* workbook. Preview the active worksheet as a Web page, being sure to scroll the page to see all the data. Switch to the second sheet in the workbook, and then close the browser window. Close the *PreviewWeb* workbook without saving it.

Customize Window Layout

E03C-5-6   The skills measured by this objective include the following:

- Splitting a window
- Freezing a column or row
- Arranging windows
- Hiding and revealing workbooks

Excel offers a number of ways that you can control how worksheets and workbooks are displayed on your screen. For example, you can display different parts of a worksheet at the same time and scroll each part independently. You can also display more than one workbook and hide and reveal workbooks.

Splitting a Window

When you split a window, you insert a dividing bar, either vertically or horizontally, that in effect creates two window panes. You can then scroll each pane independently of the other, bringing two sections of the worksheet into view at the same time.

BE SURE TO display the worksheet you want to work with before carrying out these steps.

To split a window horizontally:

1   Click any cell in column **A** except **A1**.

2   On the **Window** menu, click **Split**.

3   Point to the horizontal bar that divides the window into two panes, and when the pointer changes to a double-headed arrow, drag the bar up or down to size the panes.

4   Use the vertical scroll bar of either pane to bring the rows you want into view.

To split a window vertically:

1   Click any cell in row **1** except **A1**.

2   On the **Window** menu, click **Split**.

3   Point to the vertical bar that divides the window into two panes, and when the pointer changes to a double-headed arrow, drag the bar to the left or right to size the panes.

4   Use the horizontal scroll bar to bring the columns you want into view.

To split a window horizontally and vertically:

1   Select a single cell that is not in column **A** or row **1**.

2   On the **Window** menu, click **Split**.

3   Adjust the sizes of the panes, and use the scroll bars to display the desired columns and rows.

To remove a dividing bar:

- Double-click the bar.
- On the **Window** menu, click **Remove Split**.
- Drag the dividing bar to the top or left edge of the worksheet.

Practice Exercise

In this exercise, you will split a window and examine how this changes your view of the data.

USE the *SplitWindow* workbook in the *My Documents\Microsoft Press\MOS 2003 Study Guide\Excel \E03C-5-6* practice file folder.

Open the *SplitWindow* workbook. Click cell **A8**, and split the window. Scroll down in the lower pane while keeping the summary in the top pane in view. Remove the split. Then close the *SplitWindow* workbook without saving it.

Freezing a Column or Row

As you scroll through a worksheet, column and row headings might scroll out of sight. You can freeze the column or row containing the headings to keep them in view. That way, if you have a complicated worksheet with many columns or rows, you can make sure you are looking at the correct data.

BE SURE TO display the worksheet you want to work with before carrying out these steps.

To freeze columns or rows:

1 Do one of the following:

- To freeze a row, select the row below it.

- To freeze a column, select the column to the right of it.

- To freeze both a row and a column, select a single cell below the row and to the right of the column.

2 On the **Window** menu, click **Freeze Panes**.

To unfreeze columns or rows:

- On the **Window** menu, click **Unfreeze Panes**.

Practice Exercise

In this exercise, you will freeze and unfreeze rows and columns.

USE the *FreezeRow* workbook in the *My Documents\Microsoft Press\MOS 2003 Study Guide\Excel \E03C-5-6* practice file folder.

Open the *FreezeRow* workbook. Freeze the top row so that it will stay in view while you scroll down the worksheet. Unfreeze the row, and then freeze both the first row and the first column. Unfreeze again, and then close the *FreezeRow* workbook without saving it.

Arranging Windows

Sometimes you might want to open two or more workbooks and compare them side by side. You can have Excel size the windows for multiple workbooks so that they fit beside each other or one below the other.

BE SURE TO open the workbooks you want to arrange and to close all other open programs and files before carrying out these steps.

To arrange the open windows:

1   On the **Window** menu, click **Arrange**.

2   Do one of the following:

■   To see the workbooks in separate windows in columns and rows on the screen, select the **Tiled** option.

■   To see the workbooks in separate windows arranged one below the other, select the **Horizontal** option.

■   To see the workbooks in separate windows arranged side by side, select the **Vertical** option.

■   To see the workbooks stacked on top of each other so that they overlap, select the **Cascade** option.

3   Click the workbook you want to work with, and use the scroll bars to bring into view the rows you want to see.

Practice Exercise

In this exercise, you will open two workbooks and arrange their windows so that you can see both at the same time.

USE the *ArrangeWindows* and *ArrangeWindows2* workbooks in the *My Documents\Microsoft Press \MOS 2003 Study Guide\Excel\E03C-5-6* practice file folder.

Open both the *ArrangeWindows* and *ArrangeWindows2* workbooks. First arrange the workbooks so that their windows are tiled, and then arrange them horizontally. Also try out the cascading and vertical arrangements. Then close the *ArrangeWindows* and *ArrangeWindows2* workbooks without saving them.

Hiding and Revealing Workbooks

When you have more than one workbook open, you can hide a workbook to keep it out of the way while you concentrate on others. You might also want to hide a workbook if you don't want prying eyes to see that you are working on it.

BE SURE TO open the workbook you want to work with before carrying out these steps.

To hide a workbook:

● On the **Window** menu, click **Hide**.

Tip If you close Excel while a workbook is hidden, the next time you open that workbook, it will still be hidden.

To display a hidden workbook:

1 On the **Window** menu, click **Unhide**.

2 Click the name of the workbook you want to display.

3 Click **OK**.

Practice Exercise

In this exercise, you will hide and then unhide a workbook.

USE the *HideWorkbook* workbook in the *My Documents\Microsoft Press\MOS 2003 Study Guide\Excel \E03C-5-6* practice file folder.

Open the *HideWorkbook* workbook, and hide it. Then unhide it, and close the workbook without saving it.

Set Up Pages for Printing

E03C-5-7   The skills measured by this objective include the following:

■ Specifying a print area
■ Controlling what appears on each page
■ Adding a header or footer

On the screen, a large Excel worksheet can extend column after column and row after row in both directions. However, if you are going to print a worksheet, you need to think about the limitations of a sheet of paper. If you want the data to be readable, you need to make sure it fits neatly and logically on as few pages as possible.

Specifying a Print Area

When printing a worksheet, you don't have to print all of it. You can designate a particular part of the worksheet to print. After you set a print area, printing is limited to the data in that area until you clear it to print the entire worksheet again.

Tip You don't have to set a print area if you want to print part of a worksheet only once. You can select the range of cells you want to print, display the Print dialog box, and select the Selection option.

BE SURE TO display the worksheet you want to work with before carrying out these steps.

To specify a print area:

1 Select the range of cells you want to print.

2 On the **File** menu, click **Print Area** and then **Set Print Area**.

Tip You can also set a print area on the Sheet tab of the Page Setup dialog box. Click the "Print area" box, click the Collapse button, select the range you want, click the Expand button, and click OK.

To clear the print area:

● On the **File** menu, click **Print Area** and then **Clear Print Area**.

Practice Exercise

In this exercise, you will set and clear a print area.

USE the *SetPrintArea* workbook in the *My Documents\Microsoft Press\MOS 2003 Study Guide\Excel \E03C-5-7* practice file folder.

Open the *SetPrintArea* workbook. Designate cells **A1:E6** as the print area. Then clear the print area, and close the *SetPrintArea* workbook without saving it.

Controlling What Appears on Each Page

To get data to fit the way you want it to on a printed page, you can rotate the worksheet so that it prints horizontally (Landscape) instead of vertically (Portrait), adjust the margins, or scale the worksheet so that it prints smaller or larger than it actually is. You can also manipulate the page breaks and specify that row and column headings should appear on all pages.

BE SURE TO display the worksheet you want to work with before carrying out these steps.

To change page orientation:

1 On the **File** menu, click **Page Setup**.

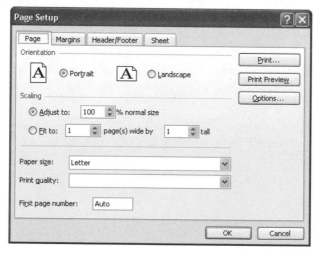

2   In the **Orientation** area, select either the **Portrait** (vertical) or **Landscape** (horizontal) option.

3   Click **OK**.

To scale the worksheet during printing:

1   On the **File** menu, click **Page Setup**.

2   In the **Scaling** area, designate a percentage in the **Adjust to** box, or enter numbers in the **Fit to** boxes to force the worksheet to expand or shrink to a designated number of pages.

3   Click **OK**.

To change the margins:

1   On the **File** menu, click **Page Setup**, and then click the **Margins** tab.

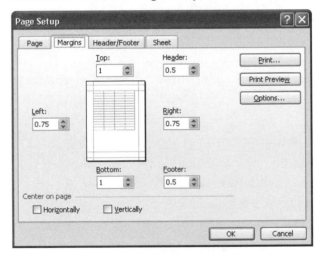

2   Change the **Top**, **Bottom**, **Left**, and **Right** options to the setting you want.

3   In the **Center on page** area, select the **Horizontally** and/or **Vertically** check boxes to center the worksheet on the page.

    The preview box in the center of the dialog box shows you the effects of your changes as you make them.

4   Click **OK**.

To repeat headings on multi-page worksheets:

1 On the **File** menu, click **Page Setup**, and then click the **Sheet** tab.

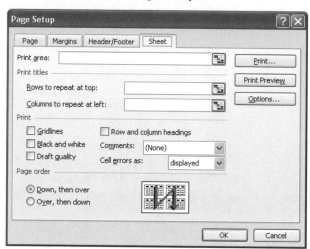

2 In the **Print titles** area, select the range(s) you want Excel to repeat at the top or left of the worksheet.

3 Click **OK**.

To change worksheet page breaks:

1 Click the cell below the row at which you want to break the page.

2 On the **Insert** menu, click **Page Break**.

Excel indicates the break with a dashed line.

To remove a manual page break:

1 Select the cell immediately below the page break.

2 On the **Insert** menu, click **Remove Page Break**.

To remove all page breaks in a worksheet:

1 Select the entire worksheet by clicking the intersection of the row and column headers in the upper-left corner of the worksheet.

2 On the **Insert** menu, click **Reset All Page Breaks**.

Practice Exercise

In this exercise, you will scale a worksheet for printing, adjust the margins, and change the page breaks.

USE the *ControlPages* workbook in the *My Documents\Microsoft Press\MOS 2003 Study Guide\Excel \E03C-5-7* practice file folder.

Open the *ControlPages* workbook. Display the Page Setup dialog box, and set the worksheet to print on one page. Then set the scaling back to **100%**. Set the top and bottom margins to **2** inches, and center the data vertically on the page. Set the top and bottom margins back to **1** inch, and center the data horizontally. Remove all the page breaks, and then insert a new page break following row **40**. Close the *ControlPages* workbook without saving it.

Adding a Header or Footer

If you want to number the pages of a worksheet, you can create a header or footer. You can also use a header or footer to display other information about a worksheet, such as its name or date of creation.

BE SURE TO display the worksheet you want to work with before carrying out these steps.

To add a header or footer:

1   On the **File** menu, click **Page Setup**, and click the **Header/Footer** tab.

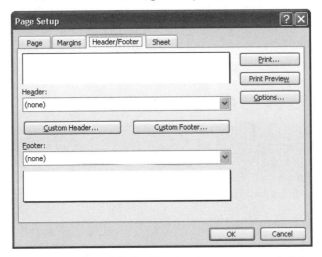

2   To add a header, click the **Header** down arrow, and click an item in the drop-down list.

3   To add a footer, click the **Footer** down arrow, and click an item in the drop-down list.

4   Click **OK**.

By default, Excel centers the specified text at the top and bottom of the page.

To create a custom header or footer:

1   On the **File** menu, click **Page Setup**, and click the **Header/Footer** tab.

2   Click either the **Custom Header** or **Custom Footer** button, and do any of the following:

- ■ Type the text you want in the appropriate area box.

- ■ Click a button to insert a code that tells Excel what to print in that location.

- ■ To add a picture, click the **Insert Picture** button, and select the picture you want. To format the picture, click the text box that contains the picture, and then click the **Format Picture** button.

- ■ To format the header or footer, select the text or code you want to format, and click the **Font** button (the capital A) to display the Font dialog box, where you can make your selections.

3   Click **OK**.

Practice Exercise

In this exercise, you will add a header and footer to a worksheet.

USE the *AddHeader* workbook in the *My Documents\Microsoft Press\MOS 2003 Study Guide\Excel \E03C-5-7* practice file folder.

Open the *AddHeader* workbook. Display the **Header/Footer** tab of the Page Setup dialog box, and add a header with a page number. Then create a custom footer by inserting the date and time in the left section, your name in the center section, and the file path in the right section. Close the *AddHeader* workbook without saving it.

Print Data

E03C-5-8   The skills measured by this objective include the following:

- ■ Printing selections, worksheets, and workbooks

After you have all the settings in the Page Setup dialog box the way you want them and have examined the result in Print Preview, it's time to send the file to the printer for printing. The Print dialog box controls the number of copies, the range of pages, the printer to use, and whether to print the entire workbook, certain sheets, or a particular selection.

Printing Selections, Worksheets, and Workbooks

When you are ready to print, you can click the Print button on the Standard toolbar to print one copy of the active worksheet on the default printer. If you want to print part of a worksheet or the entire workbook, or if you want to change any of the default print settings, you need to print from the Print dialog box instead.

BE SURE TO display the worksheet you want to work with before carrying out these steps.

To print one copy of a worksheet using the default settings:

- ● On the Standard toolbar, click the **Print** button.

Print

To print part of a worksheet or change other print settings:

1   If you want to print a range of cells, select that range.

2   On the **File** menu, click **Print**.

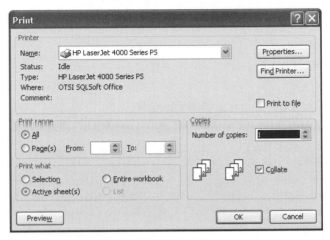

3   To change the default printer, click the **Name** down arrow in the **Printer** area, and select the printer you want.

4   To specify what you want to print, do one of the following:

   ■ To print a selected range, select the **Selection** option in the **Print what** area.

   ■ To print all the worksheets in a workbook, select the **Entire Workbook** option in the **Print what** area.

   ■ To print specific pages of a worksheet, select the **Pages** option in the **Print range** area, and then specify the pages you want to print in the **From** and **To** boxes.

5   In the **Copies** area, specify the number of copies you want to print.

6   Click **OK**.

Practice Exercise

In this exercise, you will open and print copies of a workbook.

USE the *PrintData* workbook in the *My Documents\Microsoft Press\MOS 2003 Study Guide\Excel\E03C-5-8* practice file folder.

Open the *PrintData* workbook. Select the range **A1:E6**, and then display the Print dialog box. Choose the printer you want to use, and then print two copies of the selected range. Print one copy of the second page. Then print one copy of the entire workbook. Close the *PrintData* workbook without saving it.

Organize Workbooks Using File Folders

E03C-5-9   The skills measured by this objective include the following:

- ■ Creating a folder in which to save a workbook
- ■ Renaming or deleting a workbook or folder

When you are working in Excel, you don't have to quit the program and use My Computer to create and manage the folders in which to store your files. You can perform most common organization tasks from within Excel.

Creating a Folder in Which to Store a Workbook

To save a new workbook in Excel, you click the Save button on the Standard toolbar or click the Save As command on the File menu. Either action displays the Save As dialog box, where you can name the file and indicate where you want to store it. To keep your workbooks organized and easily accessible, you can store related workbooks in a folder. You can create folders ahead of time in My Computer, or you can create them as you need them in the Save As dialog box.

Tip   You can also create and manage folders in the Open dialog box.

BE SURE TO open the workbook you want to work with before carrying out these steps.

To create a folder while saving a workbook:

1   On the **File** menu, click **Save As**.

The Save As dialog box appears.

Save

Tip   If this is the first time you saved the document, you can also click the Save button on the Standard toolbar to display this dialog box.

2   If you want to store the document in a subfolder of an existing folder, navigate to that folder and display its contents.

Create New
Folder

3   On the toolbar to the right of the **Save in** box, click the **Create New Folder** button.

4   Type a name for the folder, and click **OK**.

Excel creates the new folder and makes it the current folder.

5   Assign a file name to the workbook, and click **Save**.

Practice Exercise

In this exercise, you will create a new folder while saving a workbook.

USE the *CreateFolder* workbook in the *My Documents\Microsoft Press\MOS 2003 Study Guide\Excel \E03C-5-9* practice file folder.

Open the *CreateFolder* workbook, and then open the Save As dialog box. Navigate to the *My Documents\Microsoft Press\MOS 2003 Study Guide\Excel\E03C-5-9* practice file folder. Create a new folder, and name it **FirstFolder**. Name the workbook **FirstSave**, and save it in the new folder. Then close the *FirstSave* workbook.

Renaming or Deleting a Workbook or Folder

After creating a folder, you might decide that you want to change its name or that you no longer need it. Similarly, you might want to rename or delete a workbook. You can perform these organizational tasks from within Excel in either the Save As or Open dialog box.

BE SURE TO start Excel before carrying out these steps.

> **Tip** To rename the current workbook, you use the Save As command on the File menu. You cannot use the following steps to rename or delete the current workbook or the folder containing the current workbook.

To rename a workbook or folder:

1   On the **File** menu, click **Open**.

    The Open dialog box appears.

    > **Tip** You can also click the Open button on the Standard toolbar to display this dialog box.

Open

2   Navigate to the folder where the workbook or folder you want to rename is stored, and click it once.

Tools ▾

3   On the toolbar to the right of the **Look in** box, click the **Tools** button, and then click **Rename** on the drop-down menu.

    The workbook or folder is highlighted.

4   Enter a new name for the workbook or folder, and press **ENTER**.

To delete a workbook or folder:

1   On the **File** menu, click **Open**.

    The Open dialog box appears.

2   Navigate to the folder where the workbook or folder you want to delete is stored, and click it once.

Tools ▾

3   On the toolbar to the right of the **Look in** box, click the **Tools** button, and then click **Delete** on the drop-down menu.

4   Click **Yes** to confirm deletion.

    The workbook or folder is deleted.

Practice Exercise

In this exercise, you will rename a folder and delete the workbook it contains.

USE the *RenameFolder* folder and the *DeleteWorkbook* workbook in the *My Documents\Microsoft Press \MOS 2003 Study Guide\Excel\E03C-5-9* practice file folder.

> Display the Open dialog box, and navigate to the *My Documents\Microsoft Press \MOS 2003 Study Guide\Excel\E03C-5-9* practice file folder. In the list of workbooks and folders, change the name of **RenameFolder** to **SecondFolder**. Then double-click **SecondFolder** to display its contents, and delete **DeleteWorkbook**. Close the Open dialog box.

Save Data in Appropriate Formats for Different Uses

E03C-5-10   The skills measured by this objective include the following:

■ Saving a workbook for use in another program

■ Saving a selection, worksheet, or workbook as a Web page

Because you might want to create a workbook in Excel but be able to use it in another program, the Save As dialog box includes a "Save as type" setting that you use to easily change the workbook's file format.

Saving a Workbook for Use in Another Program

Being able to save a workbook in another file format is important if you share worksheets with people who use previous versions of Excel (such as Excel 97) or other programs (such as dBASE).

BE SURE TO open the workbook you want to work with before carrying out these steps.

> To save a workbook for use in another program:
>
> 1   On the **File** menu, click **Save As**.
>
>   The Save As dialog box appears.
>
> 2   In the **File name** box, type a new name for the workbook.
>
> 3   Click the **Save as type** down arrow, and click the file format you want to use.
>
> 4   Click **Save**.

Practice Exercise

In this exercise, you will save a workbook in comma-delimited (*.csv*) format, which can be read and interpreted by many spreadsheet and database programs.

USE the *SaveFormat* workbook in the *My Documents\Microsoft Press\MOS 2003 Study Guide\Excel \E03C-5-10* practice file folder.

> Open the *SaveFormat* workbook, and then in the *My Documents\Microsoft Press \MOS 2003 Study Guide\Excel\E03C-5-10* practice file folder, save the file as **SaveCSV** in **CSV (Comma delimited)** format, opting to omit any incompatible features. Then close the *SaveCSV* workbook.

Saving a Selection, Worksheet, or Workbook as a Web Page

You can save any part of an Excel workbook as a Web page so that it can be viewed in a Web browser such as Microsoft Internet Explorer. When you save Excel data as a Web page, it is saved with a coding system called HTML (HyperText Markup Language). You can bring a Web worksheet back into Excel for further editing at any time.

BE SURE TO open the workbook you want to work with before carrying out these steps.

To save a workbook or part of a workbook as a Web page:

1 If you want to save only part of a worksheet, select the range you want to save.

2 On the **File** menu, click **Save as Web Page**.

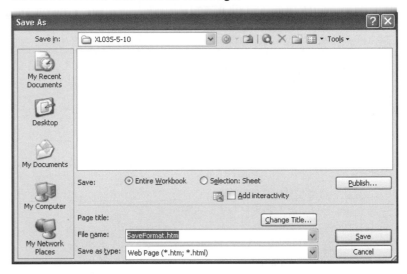

3 Do one of the following:

■ To save the entire workbook, select the **Entire Workbook** option.

■ To save the selected range, select the **Selection** option.

4 To change the title that will appear in the title bar of a Web browser when the page is viewed, click **Change Title**, type the title you want, and click **OK**.

5 If necessary, change the name in the **File name** box, and click **Save**.

The workbook is saved as a Web page with *.htm* as the file name extension.

Practice Exercise

In this exercise, you will save a workbook as a Web page with a new title.

USE the *SaveWeb* workbook in the *My Documents\Microsoft Press\MOS 2003 Study Guide\Excel\E03C-5-10* practice file folder.

Open the *SaveWeb* workbook. Save the entire workbook as a Web page, changing the page title to **Sales Figures** and the file name to **Sales**. Close your Web browser, and then close the *SaveWeb* workbook without saving it.

E03C-5 Review

Number	Objective	Mastered
E03C-5-1	Create new workbooks from templates	
	Creating a workbook based on a template	❏
E03C-5-2	Insert, delete and move cells	
	Inserting and deleting cells	❏
	Copying and moving entries	❏
	Controlling how Excel pastes	❏
E03C-5-3	Create and modify hyperlinks	
	Inserting a hyperlink	❏
	Editing a hyperlink	❏
E03C-5-4	Organize worksheets	
	Inserting and deleting worksheets	❏
	Moving a worksheet	❏
E03C-5-5	Preview data in other views	
	Previewing a worksheet that will be printed	❏
	Previewing a Web workbook	❏
E03C-5-6	Customize Window layout	
	Splitting a window	❏
	Freezing a column or row	❏
	Arranging windows	❏
	Hiding and revealing workbooks	❏
E03C-5-7	Set up pages for printing	
	Specifying a print area	❏
	Controlling what appears on each page	❏
	Adding a header or footer	❏
E03C-5-8	Print data	
	Printing selections, worksheets, and workbooks	❏
E03C-5-9	Organize workbooks using file folders	
	Creating a folder in which to save a workbook	❏
	Renaming or deleting a workbook or folder	❏
E03C-5-10	Save data in appropriate formats for different uses	
	Saving a workbook for use in another program	❏
	Saving a selection, worksheet, or workbook as a Web page	❏

Part IV
Microsoft Office Specialist
Excel 2003 Expert Exam

This part of the book covers the skills you need to have for certification as a Microsoft Office Specialist in Microsoft Office Excel 2003 at the expert level. Specifically, you will need to be able to complete tasks that require the following skills:

Number	Skill Set
E03E-1	Organizing and analyzing data
E03E-2	Formatting data and content
E03E-3	Collaborating
E03E-4	Managing data and workbooks
E03E-5	Customizing Excel

You can use these more advanced skills to create almost any workbook used in a business environment.

Knowledge You Need Before Studying for This Exam

Before you begin studying for this exam, you should have mastered all the skills required for Microsoft Office Specialist certification in Excel 2003 at the core level. You might want to review Part III, "Microsoft Office Specialist Excel 2003 Core Exam" on page 237.

E03E-1

Organizing and Analyzing Data

The skills tested by this section of the Microsoft Office Specialist Excel 2003 Expert Exam all relate to ways that you can extract information from the data in an Excel workbook. Specifically, the following objectives are associated with this set of skills:

Number	Objective
E03E-1-1	Use subtotals
E03E-1-2	Define and apply advanced filters
E03E-1-3	Group and outline data
E03E-1-4	Use data validation
E03E-1-5	Create and modify list ranges
E03E-1-6	Add, show, close, edit, merge, and summarize scenarios
E03E-1-7	Perform data analysis using automated tools
E03E-1-8	Create PivotTable and PivotChart reports
E03E-1-9	Use Lookup and Reference functions
E03E-1-10	Use Database functions
E03E-1-11	Trace formula precedents, dependents, and errors
E03E-1-12	Locate invalid data and formulas
E03E-1-13	Watch and evaluate formulas
E03E-1-14	Define, modify, and use named ranges
E03E-1-15	Structure workbooks using XML

 Important Before you can do the practice exercises associated with this skill set, you need to install the practice files from the book's companion CD to their default location. See "Installing the Practice Files" on page xxv for more information.

Use Subtotals

E03E-1-1   The skills measured by this objective include the following:

■   Calculating subtotals

If your worksheet includes a lot of data and you want to calculate subtotals, you don't have to create a formula for each calculation. You can have Excel calculate subtotals across an entire range.

Calculating Subtotals

Before you can calculate subtotals, you must first sort the data into discrete groups. For example, in a worksheet that shows sales figures for each day of the month, where the same product names appear multiple times, you can sort the data by product and then have Excel calculate subtotals for each group.

When you calculate subtotals, Excel assigns the rows used in each calculation to a group and outlines the worksheet based on the groupings. You can expand or contract the outline to hide or display the rows in each group.

See Also For information about outlines, refer to E03E-1-3, "Group and Outline Data."

BE SURE TO display the worksheet you want to work with and sort the data before carrying out these steps.

To calculate subtotals:

1 Select the range of data for which you want to calculate subtotals, including the column headings.

2 On the **Data** menu, click **Subtotals**.

The options in the "At each change in" and "Add subtotal to" boxes are the names of the column headings.

3 In the **At each change in** box, specify how you want the data grouped for calculating subtotals.

4 In the **Use function** box, specify the function to be used for calculating the subtotals.

5 In the **Add subtotal to** box, select one or more of the available options.

6 Select any other options you want, and then click **OK**.

After each change of data, Excel inserts a total row with data inserted into the columns you requested.

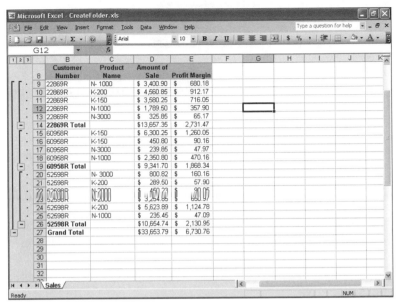

7   Use the buttons at the far left of the worksheet to expand and collapse the data to display only the grand total, only the grand total and subtotals, or all the data.

Practice Exercise

In this exercise, you will find subtotals for each product listed in a worksheet.

USE the *FindSubtotals* workbook in the *My Documents\Microsoft Press\MOS 2003 Study Guide\Excel \E03E-1-1* practice file folder.

Open the *FindSubtotals* workbook. Calculate subtotals for each product, adding the subtotals to both the **Amount of Sale** and **Profit Margin** columns. Then close the *FindSubtotals* workbook without saving it.

Define and Apply Advanced Filters

E03E-1-2   The skills measured by this objective include the following:

■   Creating a criteria range for advanced filtering

In addition to using AutoFilter to extract the information you want to work with from a long list of data in a worksheet, you can use the Advanced Filter command to hide the rows in a worksheet that do not meet the criteria you choose.

See Also   For information about AutoFilter, refer to E03C-2-1, "Filter Lists Using AutoFilter."

Creating a Criteria Range for Advanced Filtering

To use Excel's Advanced Filter feature, you create a criteria range above the data you want to filter. A criteria range is useful for extracting records based on calculated criteria, because you can use Excel's functions in the criteria formulas. Using these criteria, you can either filter the list in place, just like AutoFilter, or copy the filtered list to another location.

To create a criteria range above your data, you insert a minimum of three blank rows and use them as follows:

- You fill in the top row with the same column headings that the data range uses, spelling them exactly as they appear in the data range.

- In the row below these headings, you enter the criteria for filtering the data. The criteria can be entries or parts of entries; they can be simple greater than or less than statements; or they can be formulas, such as one that will filter out all values in a column that are above the average value. The criteria can also include wildcard characters, such as ? or *.

- You leave the bottom row blank so that it separates the criteria range from the data range.

If you want to see the rows whose entries in a particular column meet two criteria—for example, sales that are over $1,000 but under $10,000—you add two column headings to the first row and two criteria to the second row. You can repeat the headings in as many columns as you need, and you can enter as many rows of criteria as you need.

BE SURE TO display the worksheet you want to work with before carrying out these steps.

To create a criteria range and use advanced filtering:

1. Create a criteria range above the list.

2. In the first row, enter the appropriate column headings.

3. In the second row, enter the criteria you want Excel to use to filter the data.

   For example, you might want to see all the sales made on Fridays.

4. In any additional rows, enter the appropriate search criteria for other items you want to filter, making sure that you leave at least one blank row between the criteria range and the data range.

5. Click any cell in the data range, and on the **Data** menu, click **Filter** and then **Advanced Filter**.

6   In the **List range** box, enter the reference of the list range (including column headings).

7   In the **Criteria range** box, enter the reference of the criteria range (again including the column headings).

8   If you want to copy the filtered data to another location, select the **Copy to another location** option, and enter the location's reference in the **Copy to** box.

9   Click **OK**.

Excel extracts the requested information from the data range.

10   If you have filtered the data range itself, redisplay all the rows by clicking **Filter** and then **Show All** on the **Data** menu.

Practice Exercise

In this exercise, you will use Advanced Filtering to find all sales of two products that meet certain criteria.

USE the *AdvancedFilterData* workbook in the *My Documents\Microsoft Press\MOS 2003 Study Guide\Excel \E03E-1-2* practice file folder.

Open the *AdvancedFilterData* workbook. Create a criteria range above the data range. Enter filtering criteria to find all sales of the N-1000 product that are over $2,000 but under $3,000. Filter the data range in place (don't copy the results to a different location). Show all the data again, and then close the *AdvancedFilterData* workbook without saving it.

Group and Outline Data

E03E-1-3   The skills measured by this objective include the following:

■   Outlining a worksheet

If the data in your worksheet falls into obvious groups—for example, if your worksheet includes subtotals—you can use Excel's outline feature to hide the detail and show just the subtotals. You can then expand the outline and show the detailed information again. In other words, you can view as little or as much of the worksheet as you want.

Outlining a Worksheet

There are two ways to outline a worksheet: automatically and manually. To outline a worksheet automatically, your worksheet must include summary rows or columns that are adjacent to the detail data. These summary rows or columns must contain a summary formula that references cells within the range of the detail data. To outline a worksheet manually, you select the rows or columns that you want to make subordinate to summary rows and then tell Excel to group them together.

BE SURE TO display the worksheet you want to work with before carrying out these steps.

To outline a worksheet automatically:

1   Select all the cells containing data.

2   On the **Data** menu, click **Group and Outline** and then **Auto Outline**.

Excel searches for what it considers to be the rows or columns containing the summary formulas, and then uses this information to create row and column outline levels.

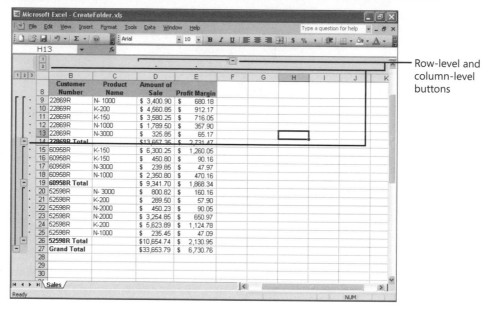

Row-level and column-level buttons

Tip By default, Excel expects to find summary rows below the detail data and summary columns to the right of detail data. To change this setting, click Group and Outline and then Settings on the Data menu. In the Settings dialog box, clear the check boxes in the Direction area.

3   Use the row-level buttons and column-level buttons in the upper-left corner of the window to expand and collapse the outline, as follows:

   ■ To collapse an outline level, click the buttons marked with minus signs above or to the left of the worksheet.

   Excel deduces that the row or column containing the summary formula is the "bottom line" of the collapsed section and displays only that row or column.

   ■ To expand collapsed levels, click the buttons marked with plus signs.

   ■ To show only the first level rows, click the **1** button, or click the **2** button to show both first and second level rows.

To outline a worksheet manually:

1   Select the detail columns or rows that you want to make subordinate (demote).

2   On the **Data** menu, click **Group and Outline** and then **Group**.

3   Continue grouping data until you have grouped all the data that you want to outline.

4   To collapse a subordinate group, click the buttons marked with minus signs above or to the left of the worksheet.

5 To expand collapsed levels, click the buttons marked with plus signs.

6 To show only the first level rows, click the **1** button, or click the **2** button to show both first and second level rows.

To leave outline mode:

● On the **Data** menu, click **Group and Outline** and then **Clear Outline**.

Practice Exercise

In this exercise, you will outline a worksheet manually and then outline another worksheet automatically.

USE the *OutlineData* workbook in the *My Documents\Microsoft Press\MOS 2003 Study Guide\Excel \E03E-1-3* practice file folder.

Open the *OutlineData* workbook. In the **Sales1** worksheet, select and group the four rows with details about sales of the K-150 product. Select and group the detail rows for each of the other four products. Collapse the details for sales of the K-150 and N-2000 products, and then collapse the outline so that it shows only first-level rows. Expand the outline to show all rows. Switch to the **Sales2** worksheet, and outline it automatically. Expand and collapse some levels, and then clear the outline. Close the *OutlineData* workbook without saving it.

Use Data Validation

E03E-1-4   The skills measured by this objective include the following:

■ Avoiding input errors

To restrict the data that can be entered into a cell or range, you can set up rules governing the input that Excel will accept. This reduces the chances for input errors.

Avoiding Input Errors

Excel's data validation criteria can restrict cell entries to whole numbers or decimals within a certain range, to dates or times within a certain range, or to text entries of a specified length. You can restrict entries even more tightly by adding a drop-down list to a cell and asking users to choose an entry from the items in the list. You can also switch the error message that appears when invalid data is entered from one that stops the data from being entered to one that simply issues a warning but still allows the invalid data.

BE SURE TO display the worksheet you want to work with before carrying out these steps.

To set data validation:

1 Select the range of cells to which you want to apply the validation limits.

2 On the **Data** menu, click **Validation**.

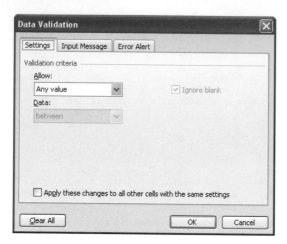

3   On the **Settings** tab , click the **Allow** down arrow, and specify the criteria for the selected range.

> **Tip**   On the Input Message tab, you can create a comment that will appear beside the validated cells, giving instructions about what should be entered. On the Error Alert tab, you can create a message that will appear when an entry deviates from the validation criteria you set. To stop invalid data from being entered, click the Style down arrow, and click Stop. To display a message that warns about but allows invalid data, click the Style down arrow, and click Warning.

4   Click **OK**.

To remove data validation:

1   Select the cell or range to which validation has been applied.

2   On the **Data** menu, click **Validation** and then **Clear All**.

Practice Exercise

In this exercise, you will set some validation rules for data entry, and then enter some data.

USE the *ValidateData* workbook in the *My Documents\Microsoft Press\MOS 2003 Study Guide\Excel \E03E-1-4* practice file folder.

Open the *ValidateData* workbook. Select column **A**, and set validation criteria to accept only whole numbers greater than 100. Do not display an input message, but include a **Stop** alert with the error message **Must be whole number greater than 100**. Then try to enter **27** in cell **A2**. When Excel will not accept the entry, change it to **101**, and press **TAB**. In cell **B2**, enter **April 2, 2004**, and in cell **C2**, enter **Analyst**. Click the down arrow that appears next to cell **D2**, and click **salaried** in the drop-down list. Then close the *ValidateData* workbook without saving it.

Create and Modify List Ranges

E03E-1-5   The skills measured by this objective include the following:

■ Creating and modifying a list

You can designate a portion of an Excel worksheet as a list—a discrete portion of a worksheet that can be filtered, sorted, printed, and even published to a SharePoint site separately from the rest of the worksheet. A worksheet can include multiple lists.

Creating and Modifying a List

When you designate a range of data as a list, Excel surrounds the list with a blue border to set it off from the rest of the worksheet. By default, AutoFilter down arrows appear adjacent to the headings so that you can easily filter the data in the list. Excel also adds an insert row, which you can use to insert new rows of data. Optionally, you can insert a total row in which to total the values in columns. Clicking a cell in the total row displays a down arrow that you can use to change the function used in the total-row calculation—for example, you can change the function so that it averages the values instead of totals them.

BE SURE TO display the worksheet you want to work with before carrying out these steps.

To create a list:

1   Select the range you want designated as a list.

2   On the **Data** menu, click **List** and then **Create List**.

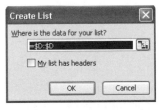

3   If the selected data has column headings, select the **My list has headers** check box.

4   Click **OK**.

The list is highlighted, and the List toolbar appears. (If you don't see the List toolbar, click Toolbars and then List on the View menu.)

Tip   You can modify a list in most of the same ways in which you modify any other range. You can format cells; filter and sort data; insert, delete, and hide rows or columns; and create charts based on the data in the list.

To resize the list:

● Do either of the following:

■ Drag the resize handle in the lower-left corner of the list.

■ On the **Data** menu, click **List** and then **Resize List**, and in the Resize List dialog box, select the new data range to apply to the list.

To insert a new row in the list:

- Do any of the following:

    - Right-click the list where you want to insert a new row, and click **Insert** on the shortcut menu.

    - On the **List** toolbar, click **Insert** and then **Row**.

    - In the last row (marked with a blue asterisk), type or paste data to add to the list.

To add a total row to a list:

1   Click anywhere in the list, and on the List toolbar, click the **Toggle Total Row** button.

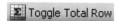

A total is calculated and inserted in a new row at the end of the list.

2   Click the down arrow for the new total, and click the function you want to apply.

To convert a list back into a ordinary range:

1   Click a cell in the list.

2   On the **Data** menu, click **List** and then **Convert to Range**.

3   Click **Yes** when asked to confirm the conversion.

Practice Exercise

In this exercise, you will convert a range of data into a list.

USE the *CreateList* workbook in the *My Documents\Microsoft Press\MOS 2003 Study Guide\Excel\E03E-1-5* practice file folder.

Open the *CreateList* workbook. Convert the range containing data, including the headings, into a list. Display the total row. Insert a new row with a date of **3/31/2004**, a customer number of **22869R**, a product name of **K-150**, and an amount of sale of **225.89**. Resize the list to include column **F**, and then convert the list back to a data range. Close the *CreateList* workbook without saving it.

Add, Show, Close, Edit, Merge, and Summarize Scenarios

E03E-1-6   The skills measured by this objective include the following:

- Creating and showing scenarios
- Merging scenarios
- Creating a scenario report

A scenario is a version of a worksheet that shows the results of various conditions or assumptions. By creating scenarios that reflect different circumstances, you can display different results and can assess the impact of changes.

Creating and Showing Scenarios

You use Excel's Scenario Manager to name each scenario, designate the cells that will change, and enter the changing values. Then you can easily compare the results of the changes.

BE SURE TO display the worksheet you want to work with before carrying out these steps.

To create multiple scenarios:

1 On the **Tools** menu, click **Scenarios**.

2 Click the **Add** button.

3 In the **Scenario name** box, type a name for the first scenario.

4 In the **Changing cells** box, designate which cells will change depending on the scenario. You can hold down the **CTRL** key and click up to 32 cells.

5 Click **OK** to display the Scenario Values dialog box.

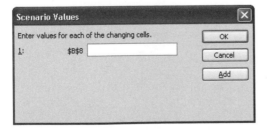

6   Click **Add** to keep the existing values in the changing cells and add a second scenario.

7   Type a name for the second scenario, and click **OK**.

8   Change the values to reflect the conditions of the second scenario.

9   Repeat steps 6 through 8 to add additional scenarios.

10   Click **OK**, and then click **Close** to close the Scenario Manager dialog box.

To show a scenario:

1   On the **Tools** menu, click **Scenarios**.

2   In the **Scenarios** list, click the scenario you want.

3   Click **Show**.

     The cells change based on the values you defined for the scenario you chose.

4   Continue selecting scenarios from the list and clicking **Show** until you have completed your analysis.

Practice Exercise

In this exercise, you will create and show two scenarios.

USE the *CreateScenario* workbook in the *My Documents\Microsoft Press\MOS 2003 Study Guide\Excel \E03E-1-6* practice file folder.

Open the *CreateScenario* workbook. Create a scenario called **Current Location** that uses the existing values, and designate cells **B3**, **B4**, and **B7** as the changing cells. Add a second scenario called **Uptown Location**, and enter these values for the changing cells: **37000** for **B3**, **7800** for **B4**, and **4500** for **B7**. Compare the two scenarios, switching back and forth between them two or three times. Then close the *CreateScenario* workbook without saving it.

Merging Scenarios

You can create a worksheet with a scenario and then send copies to colleagues so they can input their scenario values. When they return their copies, you can click the Merge button in the Scenario Manager dialog box, select their worksheets, and merge them into Scenario Manager. You can then view and edit their scenarios or use them in summary reports.

BE SURE TO display the workbook(s) containing the worksheets you want to work with before carrying out these steps.

To merge scenarios:

1   On the **Tools** menu, click **Scenarios** to display the Scenario Manager dialog box.

2   Click the **Merge** button.

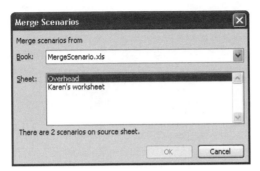

3 Select the workbooks and worksheets you want to merge, and click **OK**.

4 To view one of the merged scenarios, click **Show**.

Practice Exercise

In this exercise, you will merge a scenario from one worksheet with the scenarios from another worksheet.

USE the *MergeScenario* workbook in the *My Documents\Microsoft Press\MOS 2003 Study Guide\Excel \E03E-1-6* practice file folder.

Open the *MergeScenario* workbook. Make sure the **Overhead** worksheet is active, and then merge the scenario called **Downtown Location** from the **Karen** worksheet with the scenarios that are already in the **Overhead** worksheet. Then close the *MergeScenario* workbook without saving it.

Creating a Scenario Report

After you have finished building scenarios, you can use Scenario Manager to print a report. The Scenario Summary report displays the values of all the scenarios and their effects on the result cells.

BE SURE TO display a worksheet containing two or more scenarios before carrying out these steps.

To create a scenario report:

1 On the **Tools** menu, click **Scenarios** to display the Scenario Manager dialog box.

2 Click the **Summary** button.

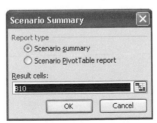

3 To print a pivot table instead of a scenario summary, select the **Scenario PivotTable report** option.

4 If you want, change the location of the result cell(s).

5   Click **OK**.

Scenario Manager creates a new sheet called Scenario Summary (or Scenario PivotTable) in the workbook and builds the report. The report appears in outline format so that you can easily hide or display rows and columns by clicking the plus or minus buttons to expand or collapse the outline.

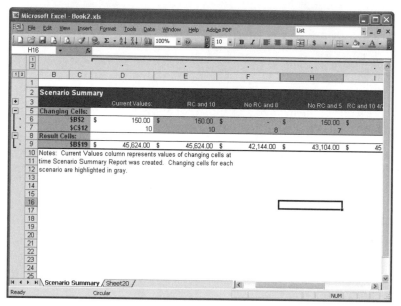

Practice Exercise

In this exercise, you will create a scenario report.

USE the *CreateScenarioReport* workbook in the *My Documents\Microsoft Press\MOS 2003 Study Guide\Excel \E03E-1-6* practice file folder.

Open the *CreateScenarioReport* workbook. Create a scenario summary report, and then create a PivotTable report. Then close the *CreateScenarioReport* workbook without saving it.

Perform Data Analysis Using Automated Tools

E03E-1-7   The skills measured by this objective include the following:

- ■ Using the Analysis ToolPak
- ■ Using Goal Seek
- ■ Using a data table
- ■ Using the Solver

Excel includes a group of tools for analyzing data while taking variables into account. These tools are the Analysis ToolPak, the target-hunting Goal Seek, the variable-swapping data table, and the value-adjusting Solver.

Tip These advanced analysis tools perform the complex types of calculations needed by professional analysts. This discussion merely scratches the surface of their capabilities. To find out more, search www.microsoft.com for more information.

Using the Analysis ToolPak

The Analysis ToolPak is one of the add-in programs that comes with Excel. It includes an array of tools and functions that you can use for financial, statistical, and engineering analysis.

BE SURE TO display the worksheet you want to work with before carrying out these steps.

To perform data analysis using the Analysis ToolPak:

1   On the **Tools** menu, click **Data Analysis**.

   Tip If you do not see the Data Analysis command on the Tools menu, click Add-Ins to display the Add-Ins dialog box. Select the Analysis ToolPak check box, and click OK to install the add-in.

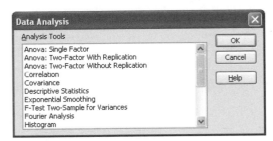

2   Click the analysis tool that you want to use, and then click **OK**.

   Each of the analysis tools has its own dialog box that you use to perform a specific type of analysis.

Practice Exercise

In this exercise, you will use the Rank and Percentile data analysis tool that is included in the Analysis ToolPak.

USE the *AnalyzeData* workbook in the *My Documents\Microsoft Press\MOS 2003 Study Guide\Excel \E03E-1-7* practice file folder.

   Open the *AnalyzeData* workbook. Display the Data Analysis dialog box, and in the list of analysis tools, click **Rank and Percentile**. Set the input range to **A2:B21**, grouped by columns, with labels in first row, and output to a new worksheet. Study the resulting data, and then close the *AnalyzeData* workbook without saving it.

Using Goal Seek

When you are missing a piece of information that you need to use an Excel function, you can use Goal Seek to find the missing argument. For example, you can calculate the maximum amount you can afford to pay for something without exceeding a specific monthly payment.

BE SURE TO display the worksheet you want to work with before carrying out these steps.

To find an unknown value by using Goal Seek:

1 Click the cell where the formula appears.

2 On the **Tools** menu, click **Goal Seek**.

Excel displays the Goal Seek dialog box with a reference to the selected cell in the "Set cell" box.

3 Type the desired value in the **To value** box to tell Excel the maximum value allowed in the cell.

4 In the **By changing cell** box, click the cell that contains the unknown value you want Excel to find.

5 Click **OK** to close the dialog box.

6 Click **OK** in the status box.

The Goal Seek Status dialog box displays the results of adjusting the values.

Practice Exercise

In this exercise, you will use Goal Seek to find the maximum price you can afford to pay for a piece of equipment that you are currently leasing for $2,200 a month, assuming that you can get a five-year loan at 8% interest.

USE the *SeekGoal* workbook in the *My Documents\Microsoft Press\MOS 2003 Study Guide\Excel\E03E-1-7* practice file folder.

Open the *SeekGoal* workbook. Click cell **B7**, which contains the formula for calculating the monthly payment on the loan by using the values in cells B4:B6. Open the Goal Seek dialog box, and indicate that Excel should vary the purchase price in cell **B4** in order to arrive at a maximum payment of **2200** in cell B7. After Excel calculates the maximum payment, close the *SeekGoal* workbook without saving it.

Using a Data Table

Sometimes you might have several different values that you want to plug into a formula. For example, you might want to see the effect of rising or falling interest rates on the payment for a loan with an adjustable interest rate. You could make separate calculations for several different interest rates, but Excel makes this sort of calculation easy with a tool called data tables.

To use a data table, you list the possible interest rates and then have Excel calculate the resulting payment for each one. You can use a data table to display the results of a formula with either one or two varying values.

BE SURE TO display the worksheet you want to work with before carrying out these steps.

To use a data table to see the effects of one variable value in a formula:

1 Set up a list of possible values for the argument that will vary in the formula.

   You can enter the values in a column or in a row.

2 Do either of the following:

   ■ If the values are in a column, click the cell that is in the row above the first value and one cell to the right of the column of values.

   ■ If the values are in a row, click the cell that is in the column to the left of the first value and one row below the row of values.

3 Type the formula you want Excel to calculate, using either a reference to the blank cell above the value column or a reference to the blank cell to the right of the value row as the argument that will vary.

   This blank cell is called the input cell. It can be any cell on the worksheet, but using this particular cell keeps the input cell in a predictable location. When Excel performs the calculation, it will act as though each varying value in turn occupies the input cell and will enter the results of the formula with that value in the column below or the row to the right of the formula.

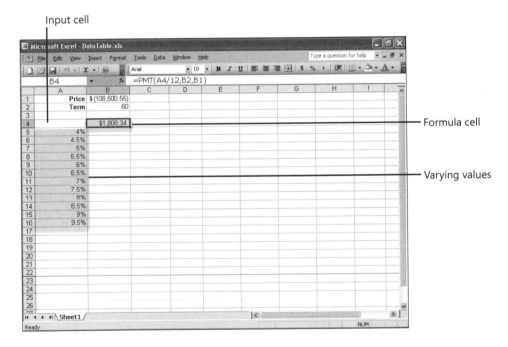

Input cell

Formula cell

Varying values

Tip In the formula shown here, the varying interest-rate values are divided by 12 to convert the annual rate to a monthly rate. Because the input cell (A4) is currently empty, the result shown is the monthly payment with an interest rate of 0%.

4 Select the range of cells that includes the formula and the varying values.

5   On the **Data** menu, click **Table**.

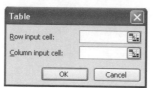

6   Do one of the following:

■   If the varying values are in a column, enter the reference to the input cell in the **Column input cell** box.

■   If the varying values are in a row, enter the reference to the input cell in the **Row input cell** box.

7   Click **OK** to close the dialog box.

Excel fills in the cells of the data table with the result of calculating the formula for each of the values in the list.

Tip   Each result is calculated by the formula {=TABLE(,*address of input cell*)}. The brackets show that Excel is using an array for the calculation. An array is a set of values used when calculating formulas that either take multiple values as one of their arguments or produce multiple values as their result.

To use a data table to see the effects of two variable values in a formula:

1   Set up two lists of possible values for two arguments that will vary in the formula, one running down a column and the other running across a row, with one blank cell at their intersection.

2   Enter the formula in the blank cell at the intersection of the column and row, using references to two empty cells as the input cells for the two arguments that will vary.

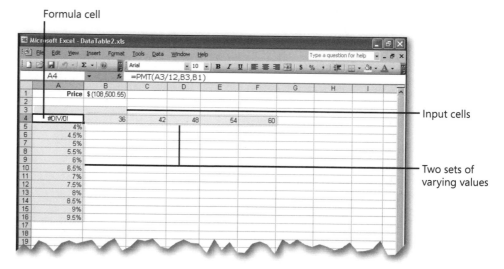

3   Select the range of cells that includes the formula and the varying values.

4 On the **Data** menu, click **Table**.

5 In the **Column input cell** box, enter a reference to the input cell for the varying values listed in the column.

6 In the **Row input cell** box, enter a reference to the input cell for the varying values listed in the row.

7 Click **OK** to close the dialog box.

Excel fills in the cells of the data table with the result of calculating the formula for each of the values in the two lists.

Practice Exercise

In this exercise, you will calculate the results of a formula by using a data table to display the effects of two variables.

USE the *UseDataTable* workbook in the *My Documents\Microsoft Press\MOS 2003 Study Guide\Excel \E03E-1-7* practice file folder.

Open the *UseDataTable* workbook. In cell **D9**, enter the following formula: **=PMT(B5/12,B6,B4)**. Then enter the following loan terms in cells **E9:H9**: **36, 48, 60, 72**. In cells **D10:D15**, enter the following interest rates: **6.0, 6.5, 7.0, 7.5, 8.0, 8.5**. Then use a data table to show the matrix that results when the formula is calculated using each of the two sets of variables. Then close the *UseDataTable* workbook without saving it.

Using Solver

You can use Solver in conjunction with a formula to find the most advantageous value for a target cell. To find this value, Solver manipulates adjustable values in one or more other cells that have some relation to the formula in the target cell. The formula doesn't have to reference the cells containing the adjustable values directly. It might reference cells that contain formulas that in turn reference the adjustable cells.

You can require Solver to work within one or more constraints. For example, if you want Solver to determine the optimal asset allocation for an investment portfolio, the adjustable cells would contain the percentages that each asset in the portfolio represents. The constraint would be that the total of the allocations must equal 100 percent. You can place constraints on the target cell, on the cells containing the adjustable values, or on other cells that have a relationship to the target cell.

BE SURE TO display the worksheet you want to work with before carrying out these steps.

To use Solver:

1 Click the target cell containing the formula for which you want to find the best value.

2 On the **Tools** menu, click **Solver**, and make sure the address of the target cell appears in the **Set Target Cell** box.

Tip If you do not see the Solver command on the Tools menu, click Add-Ins to display the Add-Ins dialog box. Select the Solver Add-in check box, and click OK to install it.

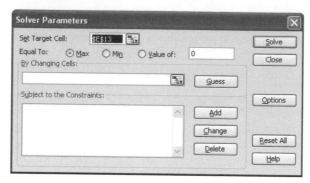

3   Do one of the following:

   ■   To find the highest value for the target cell, select the **Max** option.

   ■   To find the lowest value, select the **Min** option.

   ■   To find the variables that will produce a specific value, select the **Value of** option.

4   In the **By Changing Cells** box, enter the cells or ranges of the cells whose values can be adjusted.

5   If you want Solver to take any constraints into account, click **Add**.

6   To enter a cell reference in the **Cell Reference** box, click the cell or select the range whose values you want to constrain. Then change the operator in the middle box as necessary, and enter a value in the **Constraint** box by clicking a cell containing the constraining value or typing the value directly. Then click **Add**.

   For example, you might specify that the value of a particular cell cannot exceed $10,000.

7   Repeat this process for each additional constraint, clicking **OK** when you have finished.

   Back in the Solver Parameters dialog box, the constraints are now listed in the "Subject to the Constraints" box.

8   Click **Solve**.

   Solver examines the scenario and reports whether it was able to find a solution.

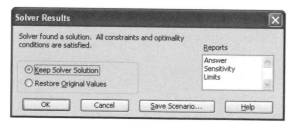

9 Do one of the following:

- To retain Solver's adjusted values, select the **Keep Solver Solution** option.
- To discard Solver's entries, select the **Restore Original Values** option.

10 Click **OK**.

Practice Exercise

In this exercise, you will use Solver to determine the total number of each of three possible gift basket configurations that can be assembled using available inventory, to maximize profits.

USE the *UseSolver* workbook in the *My Documents\Microsoft Press\MOS 2003 Study Guide\Excel\E03E-1-7* practice file folder.

Open the *UseSolver* workbook. Use Solver to determine how many of each gift basket to assemble to maximize profits. Use cell **D15** (the total profits) as the target cell, have Excel change cells **D3:F3** (the number of each basket to assemble), and add the constraint that cells **C5:C11** must be less than or equal to cells **B5:B11** (the number of pieces used must be less than or equal to the number in inventory). Add a second constraint that says cells **D3:F3** must be greater than or equal to zero. After solving, keep Solver's solution. Then close the *UseSolver* workbook without saving it.

Create PivotTable and PivotChart Reports

E03E-1-8   The skills measured by this objective include the following:

- Creating a PivotTable report
- Filtering and modifying a PivotTable report
- Plotting a PivotTable as a PivotChart

Another way of looking at a summary of the data in a worksheet is to create a PivotTable report. You can use this type of report to summarize any kind of data, including money, statistics, and measurements. You can also convert the PivotTable report into a PivotChart, which will retain any formatting you have done in the table.

Creating a PivotTable Report

You can use Excel's PivotTable and PivotChart Wizard to go through the steps of creating a PivotTable report with the type of summary calculation you specify. After you create a Pivot-Table, you can reformat it by "pivoting" rows and columns on the screen to display different views of the data.

Constructing a PivotTable is a two-step process:

- First you use the PivotTable and PivotChart Wizard to identify the data for which you want to create a PivotTable. The data must be organized in columns and rows, with headings at the top of each column. Each column of data will be identified as a field. The wizard then creates the table's foundation.

■ You finish the job by placing the fields in the table so that you can analyze the data. You put fields that contain identifying information in the page, column, and row areas of the table and fields that contain numeric data in the data area. Excel uses the specified type of calculation to summarize the data. (The default is to total each column and each row.)

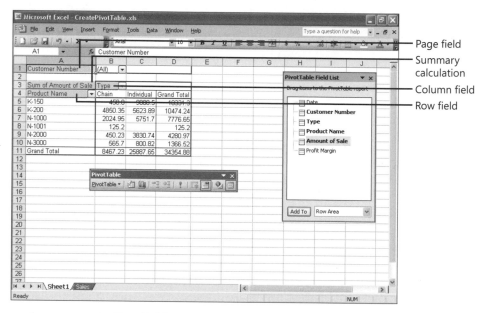

After you have created a PivotTable report, you can easily modify it if it doesn't show the correct results. You can remove fields and add new ones, and you can change the type of summary calculation used.

You can also zone in on particular items of information by filtering the report. At the right ends of the identifying fields in the PivotTable are down arrows that are similar in appearance and function to those that appear when you apply a filter to a worksheet. You can use them to display specific categories of data, hiding the other entries.

BE SURE TO display a worksheet containing data organized as a list with labeled columns before carrying out these steps.

To create a PivotTable report:

1   On the **Data** menu, click **PivotTable and PivotChart Report**.

The first page of the PivotTable and PivotChart Wizard asks you to identify the location of the data and the type of report you want to create.

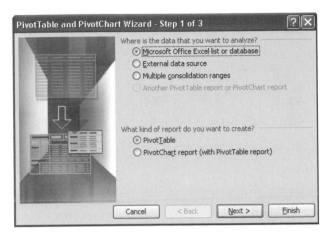

2   Do the following, and then click **Next**.

- Select the data option you want. You can use a single list that was created in Excel, a database that was created in a program like Access or SQL (Structured English Query Language), or multiple ranges.

- Select the **PivotTable** option to create just the table, or select the **PivotChart report** option to create both a chart and a table.

3   On the wizard's second page, select the range of data you want to use, and click **Next**.

Tip   If you know you will add data to the range for which you are constructing the PivotTable, assign a name to the range, and enter that name in the Range box on the wizard's second page.

4   Select an option to tell Excel where you want the PivotTable inserted, and click **Finish**.

Excel creates a PivotTable and displays the PivotTable Field List task pane and the PivotTable toolbar.

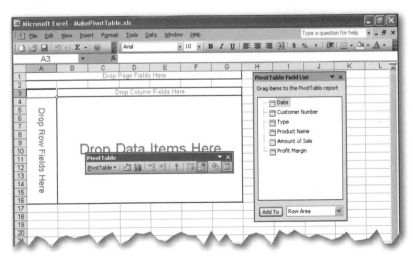

5 Drag fields containing identifying information from the **PivotTable Field List** to the row and column areas of the PivotTable.

6 Drag a field containing numeric data to the data area.

To modify a PivotTable report:

1 Select a field, and drag it outside of the PivotTable to remove it.

2 Drag a new field into the table to replace the old one.

To change the type of calculation:

1 Click the cell containing the calculation.

Field
Settings

2 On the PivotTable toolbar, click the **Field Settings** button.

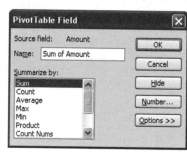

3 In the **Summarize by** list, select the function you want.

4 To format the values produced by the summary calculation, click the **Number** button to display the Format Cells dialog box.

5 Select the format you want, and click **OK**.

6 Click **OK** to close the PivotTable Field dialog box.

To edit the data and update a pivot table:

1 In the source worksheet, change the data as necessary.

2 Click any cell in the PivotTable.

Refresh Data

3 On the PivotTable toolbar, click the **Refresh Data** button.

You can also click Refresh Data on the Data menu.

To filter in a pivot table:

1 Click the down arrow for the identifying field that you want to filter.

A list of all the components of that field appears.

2 Depending on the way the components are listed, do one of the following:

■ Clear the check boxes of all the items you don't want to see, and click **OK**.

■ Click the item you do want to see, and click **OK**.

The field in the page area can be filtered to view either all components or only one component.

3   To redisplay all the information, click the down arrow, and do one of the following:

■   Select the **Show All** check box, and click **OK**.

■   Click **All**, and then click **OK**.

Practice Exercise

In this exercise, you will use an existing data sheet to create a PivotTable report. You will then update and modify the PivotTable.

USE the *CreatePivotTable* workbook in the *My Documents\Microsoft Press\MOS 2003 Study Guide\Excel \E03E-1-8* practice file folder.

Open the *CreatePivotTable* workbook. Create a PivotTable report using the data in the range **A1:F18**, and put the PivotTable report in a new worksheet. Drag the **Customer Number** field to the page area, the **Product Name** field to the row area, the **Type** field to the column area, and the **Amount of Sale** field to the data area. Then update the **Sales** worksheet by changing the entry in cell **E18** to **$500**. Switch back to the **PivotTable** worksheet, and refresh the data in the PivotTable. Filter the data in the PivotTable to show only the data for the **K-150** and **K-200** products. Then redisplay the data for all the products. Change the summary calculation so that it averages the sales amounts instead of totaling them. Then replace the **Amount of Sale** field in the data area with the **Profit Margin** field. Close the *CreatePivotTable* workbook without saving it.

Plotting a PivotTable as a PivotChart

You can easily get a visual representation of the data in a PivotTable by plotting the data as a PivotChart.

BE SURE TO display a worksheet containing a PivotTable before carrying out these steps.

To plot a PivotTable as a PivotChart:

Chart
Wizard

●   With the PivotTable displayed, click the **Chart Wizard** button on the PivotTable toolbar.

The wizard inserts a chart sheet in the workbook, plots the data in the PivotTable as a column chart, and displays the Chart toolbar.

To filter the display of the chart:

1   Click the down arrow at the right end of an axis-label or legend field button.

A list of all the components of that field appears.

2   Depending on the way the components are listed, do one of the following:

■   Clear the check boxes of all the items you don't want to see, and click **OK**.

■   Click the item you do want to see, and click **OK**.

3   To redisplay all the information, click the down arrow, and do one of the following:

■   Select the **Show All** check box, and click **OK**.

■   Click **All**, and then click **OK**.

To change the chart type:

Chart Type

- On the Chart toolbar, click the **Chart Type** down arrow, and click the option you want in the drop-down list.

- On the **Chart** menu, click **Chart Type**, and select the option you want.

Practice Exercise

In this exercise, you will plot a PivotTable as a PivotChart, and then modify the chart.

USE the *CreatePivotChart* workbook in the *My Documents\Microsoft Press\MOS 2003 Study Guide\Excel \E03E-1-8* practice file folder.

Open the *CreatePivotChart* workbook. Plot the PivotTable as a PivotChart. Then filter the chart based on the **Type** field so that only chain-store sales are visible. Change the chart type to a bar chart. Then close the *CreatePivotChart* workbook without saving it.

Use Lookup and Reference Functions

E03E-1-9   The skills measured by this objective include the following:

- Looking up information

You can use Excel's Lookup and Reference functions in formulas to look up information that already exists in the same worksheet or a different worksheet.

Looking Up Information

Among Excel's Lookup and Reference functions are ones that tell you how many columns, rows, or contiguous areas are in a particular range reference. Others return specific information such as a row number or a column letter. Of all the Lookup and Reference functions, you are most likely to use VLOOKUP, which you use to look up information stored in an existing worksheet so that you can use it elsewhere on the same worksheet or in a different one. VLOOKUP is designed for use with vertically oriented tables. The similar HLOOKUP function is also available for use with horizontally oriented tables.

Excel needs three pieces of information to carry out the VLOOKUP function:

- The entry you want it to look up
- The range of the lookup table
- The position in the table (expressed as a number) of the column from which the function should copy a corresponding value

For example, suppose you want to look up an employee's salary in a salary table. You supply the name of the employee, the range of the salary table, and the number of the column containing salary information. Excel searches down the leftmost column of the lookup table for the row that contains the employee's name. If Excel finds the name, it looks along that row to the specified column. The result of the VLOOKUP function is the value from the cell at the intersection of the row and column, which is the salary for that employee.

BE SURE TO display the worksheet you want to work with and to have data that you can use as a lookup table available before carrying out these steps.

To use one of Excel's Lookup and Reference functions:

Insert
Function

1 Click the cell in which you want to insert the function.

2 At the left end of the formula bar, click the **Insert Function** button.

3 In the Insert Function dialog box, click the **Or select a category** down arrow, and click **Lookup & Reference**.

4 In the **Select a function** list box, click a function, and click **OK**.

5 In the Function Arguments dialog box, specify all the required arguments for the function, and click **OK**.

See Also For information about entering formulas, refer to E03C-2-3, "Insert and Modify Formulas."

To look up information in a vertically oriented table:

1 Make sure that the data you want to use as a lookup table is sorted in ascending order.

2 In the worksheet, click the cell in which you want the results of the formula to appear.

Insert
Function

3 At the left end of the formula bar, click the **Insert Function** button.

4 In the Insert Function dialog box, click the **Or select a category** down arrow, and click **Lookup & Reference**.

5 In the **Select a function** list box, click **VLOOKUP**.

6 Click **OK** to close the Insert Function dialog box and display the Function Arguments dialog box.

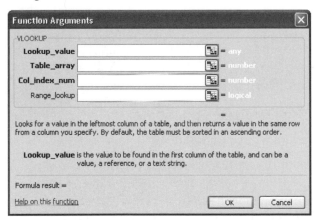

7 In the **Lookup_value** box, do one of the following:

- Type the value or text entry you want Excel to look up.

- Click the **Collapse** button, click a cell containing the item you want to look up, and then click the **Expand** button.

8 In the **Table_array** box, specify the range occupied by the lookup table.

9 In the **Col_index_num** box, type the number of the column where Excel will find the value you are looking for.

10 Click **OK**.

Tip By default, VLOOKUP searches for the closest match to the Lookup_value argument you specify. If you want the VLOOKUP function to look for an exact match, in the Function Arguments dialog box, enter =False in the Range_lookup box.

Practice Exercise

In this exercise, you will use the VLOOKUP function to retrieve information from one workbook and insert it into another.

USE the *LookUpInfo* and *Info* workbooks in the *My Documents\Microsoft Press\MOS 2003 Study Guide\Excel \E03E-1-9* practice file folder.

Open the *LookUpInfo* and *Info* workbooks. In cell **C10** of the *LookUpInfo* workbook, insert a VLOOKUP function. Designate cell **A10** as the lookup value. To designate the lookup table, switch to the *Info* workbook, and click the tab of the **Rates** worksheet to insert its name and location into the **Table_array** box. Then select all the data on the **Rates** worksheet to complete the reference. Finally, complete the function by designating **2** as the number of the column containing the information you are looking for. Back in the *LookUpInfo* workbook, copy the formula in cell **C10** to **C11:C14**. Then close the *LookUpInfo* and *Info* workbooks without saving them.

Use Database Functions

E03E-1-10   The skills measured by this objective include the following:

- Creating formulas that use Database functions

When working with list ranges, you can use special database functions, such as DSUM, DMIN, DMAX, and DAVERAGE. These database functions are similar to their standard equivalents (SUM, MIN, MAX, AVERAGE, and so on), except that you can instruct Excel to include in the calculation only the values that meet specific criteria.

Creating Formulas That Use Database Functions

Database functions require three arguments:

- The reference of the range that constitutes the list (or database).
- The column (or field) on which the calculation is to be performed, identified either by its heading in quotation marks (for example, "Cost"), by the cell reference of the heading, or by its position in the list expressed as a number.
- The reference of the range containing the conditions (or criteria) for the values to be used in the calculation. You set up the criteria range above or beside the range occupied by the list, with at least one row or column separating the criteria range from the list.

See Also For information about criteria ranges, refer to E03E-1-2, "Define and Apply Advanced Filters."

BE SURE TO display the worksheet you want to work with before carrying out these steps.

To use a database function:

1 Set up the criteria range with the conditions of the formula in blank rows above or beside the list range, leaving at least one blank row or column between the criteria range and the list.

2 Click the cell in which you want to enter the formula.

3 At the left end of the formula bar, click the **Insert Function** button.

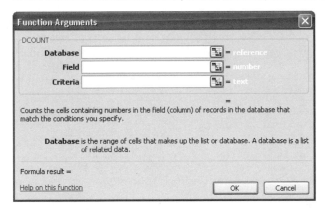

Insert
Function

4 In the Insert Function dialog box, click the **Or select a category** down arrow, and click **Database**.

5 In the **Select a function** list box, click a function, and click **OK**.

6 In the **Database** box, designate the range of the list or database.

7 In the **Field** box, enter the column to be used in the calculation.

8 In the **Criteria** box, designate the criteria range, including at least one column heading and the cell below it.

9 Click **OK**.

Excel checks the criteria range for the conditions under which it should perform the calculation, extracts any values that meet the conditions from the designated column in the designated database, and displays the results of the calculation for just those values in the cell containing the formula.

Practice Exercise

In this exercise, you will use the DMIN function to find the smallest sale with a profit margin over $100.

USE the *UseDatabaseFunction* workbook in the *My Documents\Microsoft Press\MOS 2003 Study Guide\Excel \E03E-1-10* practice file folder.

Open the *UseDatabaseFunction* workbook. In cells **G1:G2**, enter a criteria range that specifies records with a profit margin greater than $1,000. Then insert a DSUM Database function in cell **D19**. Designate **A1:E18** as the list range, the **Amount of Sale** column as the target of the calculation, and **G1:G2** as the criteria range. After Excel displays the results of the formula (the total sales of the two rows whose profit margins were over $1,000), close the *UseDatabaseFunction* workbook without saving it.

Trace Formula Precedents, Dependents, and Errors

E03E-1-11   The skills measured by this objective include the following:

■ Fixing errors

■ Auditing a worksheet

Despite your best intentions, sometimes you make errors when working with Excel's functions and formulas. If Excel can't calculate a result, it lets you know and tries to identify the error so that you can locate and resolve it. Reviewing a worksheet to rectify an error in a formula is called auditing.

Fixing Errors

Sometimes, instead of displaying the result of a formula in a cell, Excel displays an error code. Here is a list of the most common error codes and a brief explanation of what causes them.

Error	Explanation
#####	The column is too narrow to display the value, or you might have used a negative number for a date or time.
#DIV/0!	The result of the formula is undefined because you attempted to divide by zero.
#NAME?	The formula contains text that Excel does not recognize. You might have misspelled a name or function or used a name that does not exist. Or you might have forgotten to enclose text in quotation marks or include a colon in a range reference.
#NUM!	The formula contains an invalid numeric value. You might have entered an argument incorrectly in a function, or the result might be a number that is too large or too small for Excel to handle.
#REF!	The formula uses a cell reference that is invalid. You might have deleted a cell used by the formula.
#VALUE!	The wrong type of argument is used in the formula. You might have entered text instead of a logical value or a number, or you might have entered a range where a single value is required.

When you select the cell containing the error message, an Error button appears. If you can't remember what the error message means, point to the button to see a ScreenTip. The fastest way to get help is to click the Error button and then click an item on the drop-down menu that appears.

BE SURE TO display the worksheet you want to work with before carrying out these steps.

To get help with fixing an error:

1   Click the cell containing the error message, and when the **Error** button appears, click it.

2   On the drop-down menu, do one of the following:

■ To open Microsoft Excel Help's topic for this error message, click **Help on this error**.

■ To break the formula into steps and get help evaluating it, click **Show Calculation Steps**.

■ If you can see what's wrong with the formula and don't need any help from Excel, click **Edit in Formula Bar**, and make your changes there.

■ To open the Formula Auditing toolbar, click **Show Formula Auditing Toolbar**.

3 Proceed with correcting the formula.

Practice Exercise

In this exercise, you will fix some common errors in formulas.

USE the *FixError* workbook in the *My Documents\Microsoft Press\MOS 2003 Study Guide\Excel\E03E-1-11* practice file folder.

Open the *FixError* workbook. Scan the worksheet for error messages, and investigate and correct the errors. Then close the *FixError* workbook without saving it.

Auditing a Worksheet

As you gain experience and start to create more complex formulas, the likelihood that you will introduce errors increases. Excel includes auditing tools that you can use to locate errors in a formula by tracing its dependents and precedents. A dependent is a cell with a formula that references (that is, it *depends* on) at least one other cell. The cells the formula depends on are known as its *precedents*. To access the auditing tools, click Formula Auditing on the Tools menu. You can then fix the errors using standard editing techniques. To quickly assess errors, you can have Excel draw blue tracer arrows connecting a cell to its precedents or dependents.

Tip You can also look at formulas and their precedents in Formula Auditing Mode. If you click a cell containing a formula while Formula Auditing Mode is active, Excel assigns each argument in the formula a different color and puts a border of the same color around any cells or ranges that are precedents for the formula.

BE SURE TO display the worksheet you want to work with before carrying out these steps.

To trace an error:

1 Click the cell with the error message, and on the **Tools** menu, click **Formula Auditing** and then **Trace Error**.

Excel connects the formula to its precedents with blue tracer arrows.

2 If you need to look further, continue clicking **Trace Error** to trace precedents of precedents.

3 On the **Data** menu, click **Formula Auditing** and then **Remove All Arrows** to turn off the arrows.

To trace precedents or dependents:

1 Click the cell whose precedents or dependents you want to trace.

2 On the **Tools** menu, click **Formula Auditing** and then either **Trace Dependents** or **Trace Precedents**.

Excel connects the cell to its precedents or dependents with blue tracer arrows.

3   If you need to look further, continue clicking either **Trace Dependents** or **Trace Precedents** to find precedents of precedents or dependents of dependents.

4   On the **Data** menu, click **Formula Auditing** and then **Remove All Arrows** to turn off the arrows.

Tip   If you create a circular reference—one in which the results of the formula change the results of one of the formula's precedents, in a never ending circle—you can can use the buttons on the Circular Reference toolbar to track down its components. The relationships are indicated in the worksheet by tracer arrows.

Practice Exercise

In this exercise, you will trace dependents and precedents, and then remove tracer arrows.

USE the *TraceError* workbook in the *My Documents\Microsoft Press\MOS 2003 Study Guide\Excel \E03E-1-11* practice file folder.

Open the *TraceError* workbook. Click cell **D15**, and trace its precedents back as many levels as possible. Remove the precedent arrows. Then click cell **E11**, and trace its dependents as far forward as possible. Click cell **C6**, and trace its precedents as far back as possible. Remove all the arrows. Then close the *TraceError* workbook without saving it.

Locate Invalid Data and Formulas

E03E-1-12   The skills measured by this objective include the following:

- Using Error Checking
- Circling invalid data

Excel includes two tools that can sweep through an entire worksheet and find problems. You can use the Error Checking feature to locate and work through any formulas with errors. You can also have Excel circle all the cells that contain entries in violation of data validation rules.

Using Error Checking

If you revamp a large and complicated worksheet, you run the risk of introducing errors in some of its formulas. It's not practical to visually scan a large worksheet's thousands of entries looking for cells with error messages. Instead, you can use Excel's Error Checking feature, which can almost instantly locate errors in even the largest worksheet. In the Error Checking dialog box, you have the option of evaluating the formula, editing it, or ignoring it. You can also readily access Microsoft Excel Help from this dialog box.

BE SURE TO display the worksheet you want to work with before carrying out these steps.

To use Error Checking:

1   On the **Tools** menu, click **Error Checking**.

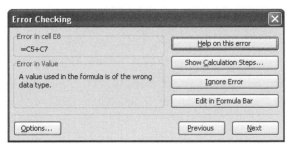

2 Use the tools in the dialog box to help resolve the error.

3 Click **Next** to move to the next error.

4 Continue resolving errors until Excel tells you that the error check is complete.

5 Click **OK** to close the message box.

Practice Exercise

In this exercise, you will use error checking to find and correct errors in a worksheet.

USE the *CheckError* workbook in the *My Documents\Microsoft Press\MOS 2003 Study Guide\Excel \E03E-1-12* practice file folder.

Open the *CheckError* workbook. Use Excel's Error Checking feature to find and correct errors in the worksheet's formulas. Then close the *CheckError* workbook without saving it.

Circling Invalid Data

Even though you can create a validation rule to ensure that the correct type of data is entered in a cell or range of cells, there are still two ways that those cells might contain data that breaks the rule:

- If you apply a validation rule to a range that already has data entered in it, Excel will alert you only if you enter new data in violation of the rule, not if the existing data violates the rule.

- Your validation rule might have an error alert set simply to warn about invalid data but not to stop it from being entered.

To check whether the data in a worksheet is valid, you can tell Excel to mark all the invalid data by placing red circles around it. You can then scroll through the workbook, resolving any data problems identified by red circles.

BE SURE TO display the worksheet you want to work with and to display the Formula Auditing toolbar before carrying out these steps.

To circle invalid data:

Circle Invalid Data

1 On the Formula Auditing toolbar, click the **Circle Invalid Data** button.

Excel places red circles around any cells with invalid data.

2 Correct the invalid entries one at a time to remove the red circles.

Clear
Validation
Circles

3   If you want to retain some invalid entries, click the **Clear Validation Circles** button to remove their circles.

Practice Exercise

In this exercise, you will have Excel circle invalid data.

USE the *CircleData* workbook in the *My Documents\Microsoft Press\MOS 2003 Study Guide\Excel \E03E-1-12* practice file folder.

Open the *CircleData* workbook. Have Excel circle any invalid data. Change the incorrect employee number to **101**, and then change the incorrect year to **2004**. Clear any remaining invalid-data circles. Then close the *CircleData* workbook without saving it.

Watch and Evaluate Formulas

E03E-1-13   The skills measured by this objective include the following:

- Watching a cell
- Evaluating a formula

Excel includes two other tools that help you keep a close eye on your data. You can use the Watch Window to watch the value in a cell no matter where in the worksheet or workbook you might be. You can use the Evaluate Formula dialog box to evaluate formulas one step at a time.

Watching a Cell

If you need to keep an eye on the values in one or more cells no matter where you are in a worksheet (or even if you are working in a different workbook altogether), you can add them to Excel's Watch Window. The Watch Window keeps you apprised of the value in the watched cell. If it contains a formula, the formula also appears in the Watch Window. When the value in the cell changes, it changes in the Watch Window. You can dock the Watch Window like a toolbar, or have it floating over the active worksheet. As long as the workbook is open, cells remain listed in the Watch Window until you delete them, even if you close and then reopen the Watch Window. If you save the workbook while cells are displayed in the Watch Window, they will still be there the next time you open the workbook.

BE SURE TO display the worksheet you want to work with before carrying out these steps.

To open the Watch Window and add a cell to it:

1   On the **Tools** menu, click **Formula Auditing** and then **Show Watch Window**.

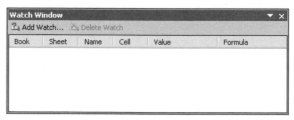

2   In the Watch Window, click **Add Watch**, click the cell you want to watch, and then click **Add**.

If you select a range of cells, Excel lists those cells individually in the Watch Window.

Practice Exercise

In this exercise, you will add and delete cells from the Watch Window.

USE the *WatchCell* workbook in the *My Documents\Microsoft Press\MOS 2003 Study Guide\Excel \E03E-1-13* practice file folder.

Open the *WatchCell* workbook. Add cell **D15** to the Watch Window. Update the value in the Watch Window by changing the value in cell **F3** to **50**. Delete the cell from the Watch Window, and then close the *WatchCell* workbook without saving it.

Evaluating a Formula

If a formula is not producing the results you expect, you can use the Evaluate Formula dialog box to step through the formula to determine where a problem might be. The formula appears in the dialog box's Evaluation area. With each click of the Evaluate button, Excel replaces cell references in the formula with their values, combines the values, and finally shows just the formula's result, with the option to restart the evaluation. Clicking the Step In button when a cell reference is active (underlined) in the Evaluation window opens a separate Evaluation window that displays the cell's value. Clicking Step Out closes the second window and resumes the evaluation.

BE SURE TO display the worksheet and click the cell containing the formula you want to work with before carrying out these steps.

To evaluate a formula:

1   Click the cell containing the formula you want to evaluate.

2   On the **Tools** menu, click **Formula Auditing** and then **Evaluate Formula**.

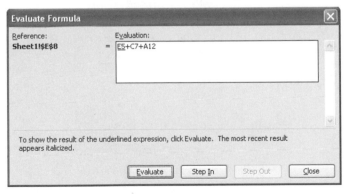

3   Click the **Evaluate** button as many times as necessary to evaluate the formula.

4   Click **Close** to close the Evaluate Formula dialog box.

Practice Exercise

In this exercise, you will evaluate a formula.

USE the *EvaluateFormula* workbook in the *My Documents\Microsoft Press\MOS 2003 Study Guide\Excel \E03E-1-13* practice file folder.

Open the *EvaluateFormula* workbook. Use the Evaluate Formula dialog box to evaluate the two formulas that contain errors. Then close the *EvaluateFormula* workbook without saving it.

Define, Modify, and Use Named Ranges

E03E-1-14 The skills measured by this objective include the following:

■ Naming a cell or range

■ Using a name in a formula

It is often easier to refer to a cell or range by a name instead of by its address. For example, if cell E17 contains a formula that calculates the total cost of a product, you could name the cell "Cost" and then use that name elsewhere on the worksheet instead of the cell's reference.

Naming a Cell or Range

Many of the calculations performed in a worksheet might use the results of the same formula. Instead of repeating that formula wherever it is needed, you can insert the formula once and then reference its results in all the other calculations. For example, you might set up a formula in cell B5 of a worksheet to total the manufacturing costs of a product. You might then reference cell B5 in other formulas that include the product's total manufacturing costs as one of their arguments.

However, worksheets are rarely static. If you move a value or formula that is referenced in other formulas, those formulas will return errors. To avoid this problem, you can assign the contents of a cell or range a name and use that name in the formulas instead of the cell or range reference. Then the formulas' arguments will always be correct no matter where in the worksheet you move the named contents. For example, if you assign the name Costs to the formula in cell B5 and then use that name in other formulas, you can move the formula named Costs anywhere you want without disrupting the formulas that include Costs as one of their arguments.

The following rules apply when you name cells or ranges:

■ Although you can use a number within a name, you must start the name with a letter, an underscore, or a backslash.

■ Spaces are not allowed in cell and range names, so you can either leave them out or use underscore characters to represent spaces. (For example, you cannot use 2002 as a name, but you can use Totals_2002 or Totals2002.)

After you have named a cell or range, you can jump quickly to it by pressing the F5 key, or by clicking the name in the Go To dialog box and clicking OK.

BE SURE TO display the worksheet you want to work with before carrying out these steps.

To name a cell or range:

1   Select the cell or range of cells you want to name.

2   On the **Insert** menu, click **Name** and then **Define**.

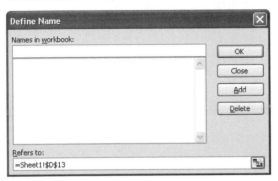

Excel looks above and to the left of the selected cell or range for a text entry that will serve as a name.

3   If necessary, replace the name in the **Names in workbook** box with the name you want.

4   Click **OK**.

Tip   You can also click the Name box at the left end of the formula bar, type a name, and press ENTER.

Practice Exercise

In this exercise, you will name a cell and name a range.

USE the *NameCell* workbook in the *My Documents\Microsoft Press\MOS 2003 Study Guide\Excel\E03E-1-14* practice file folder.

Open the *NameCell* workbook. Click cell **D19**, and name it **Total**. Then select the range **D2:D18**, and name it **Amount**. Close the *NameCell* workbook without saving it.

Using a Name in a Formula

Using names in formulas makes your worksheets much more flexible than using cell references. If the information referenced in a formula moves as a result of changes you make to a worksheet, Excel adjusts the definition of the name so that the formula continues to access the correct information.

BE SURE TO display a worksheet in which you have defined the names you want to use before carrying out these steps.

To create a formula that includes a named cell or range:

1   Click the cell in which you want to insert a formula.

2   Construct the formula in the usual way, until you want to include the name of a cell or range as an argument.

3   On the **Insert** menu, click **Name** and then **Paste**.

4   Select the name you want, and click **OK**.

5   Finish constructing the formula.

To replace a cell or range reference in an existing formula with a name:

1   Click the cell that contains the formula you want to update.

2   In the formula bar, select the cell or range reference by dragging through it.

3   On the **Insert** menu, click **Name** and then **Paste**.

4   Select the appropriate name, and click **OK**.

5   Complete the entry (the result should not change).

Practice Exercise

In this exercise, you will use cell and range names in a couple of formulas.

USE the *UseName* workbook in the *My Documents\Microsoft Press\MOS 2003 Study Guide\Excel\E03E-1-14* practice file folder.

Open the *UseName* workbook. Replace the formula in cell **D23** with **=SUM(Amount)**. Replace the formula in cell **B2** with **=Total**. Then close the *UseName* workbook without saving it.

Structure Workbooks Using XML

E03E-1-15   The skills measured by this objective include the following:

■   Adding and deleting a data map

■   Setting up an XML worksheet and entering data

In a large organization, data is often created in a variety of programs to handle such tasks as order processing and inventory management. It is important to be able to move information from the program that created it to the program best equipped to perform a specific task. To make Excel data portable, you can structure it in Extensible Markup Language (XML).

Adding and Deleting a Data Map

To save an Excel worksheet in XML format, you need to apply a data map to it. This data map is based on an XML schema, which describes the structure allowed in the worksheet, including the names of structural elements and what elements can contain what other elements. For example, a class catalog might consist of classes, each of which can contain only one title, instructor, date, time, description, cost, and classroom.

Generally, companies employ a specialist with in-depth knowledge of XML to create custom schemas, but after a schema is created, anyone can attach it to an Excel worksheet as a data map and use it to structure the worksheet's data.

BE SURE TO open the workbook to which you want to attach a data map and to have an XML schema available before carrying out these steps.

To add a data map to a worksheet:

1   On the **Data** menu, click **XML** and then **XML Source**.

    The XML Source task pane appears.

2   At the bottom of the task pane, click **XML Maps**.

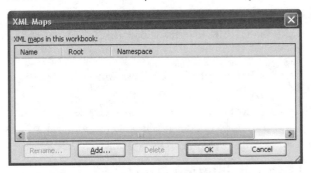

3   Click **Add** to open the XML Source dialog box.

4   Navigate to the folder where the schema on which you want to base this data map is stored, and click **Open**.

    The schema is added to the XML Maps dialog box with _Map appended to its name.

5   Click **OK**.

    The mapped structure from the schema appears in the XML Source task pane.

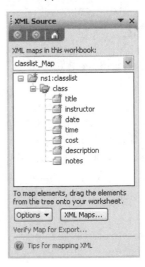

Tip   Required elements have a red star on their icons in the XML Source task pane.

To delete a data map:

1   On the **Data** menu, click **XML** and then **XML Source**.

    The XML Source task pane appears.

2   At the bottom of the task pane, click **XML Maps**.

3   In the XML Maps dialog box, click the map you want to delete, and then click **Delete**.

4   When a message warns that you will no longer be able to import or export XML data using this map, click **OK** to confirm the deletion.

    Tip   You can also rename a selected data map in the XML Maps dialog box.

Practice Exercise

In this exercise, you will add an XML schema to a workbook and make it available as a data map.

USE the *GardenClassSchema* file in the *My Documents\Microsoft Press\MOS 2003 Study Guide\Excel \E03E-1-15* practice file folder.

Start Excel, and with a blank worksheet open, display the XML Source task pane. Open the XML Maps dialog box, and add *GardenClassSchema* as a data map. Then close the blank workbook without saving it.

Setting Up an XML Worksheet and Entering Data

After you have added a data map to a worksheet, you can apply the mapped structure to the cells in the worksheet. You apply the structure by dragging elements from the XML Source task pane to the appropriate worksheet cells. Depending on the type of schema you are working with, an icon might appear next to the cell so that you can chose whether and where you want the element's label to appear. After you have dragged an element onto the worksheet, its name appears in bold in the XML Source task pane. If you use an element and then decide you don't want it in the worksheet, you can easily remove it.

You can apply structure to blank cells or to cells that already contain data. If you apply the structure to existing data that does not comply with the format specified by the schema, you can choose to retain the data's formatting or to change it to match the schema's type definition.

When you have set up the XML structure in the worksheet, you can determine how data is entered by setting options in the XML Source task pane and the XML Map Properties dialog box. You are then ready to enter data, either by importing an XML file in which the data has the same structure as that of the worksheet, or by typing the data directly in the worksheet.

After you have entered data, you can edit it by using standard editing techniques. You can change and replace the data in cells, and insert or delete rows and columns.

When you are satisfied with the worksheet, you can save it in XML Spreadsheet format to preserve its structure. When you save an XML worksheet, the structure is not validated to ensure that it complies with the rules established by the attached schema. You can also export the structured data as a file that can be used in other programs. When you export a data file, the structure of the data is validated.

See Also   For information about exporting an XML data file, refer to E03E-4-2, "Export Data from Excel."

BE SURE TO display a worksheet to which you have added a data map and to open the XML Source task pane before carrying out these steps.

To structure a worksheet before entering data:

1   In the XML Source task pane, point to the element you want to apply, and drag it to the heading of the column containing that element's data.

2   If a **Header Options** button appears beside the element, click it, and specify where to put the XML heading for the element.

The element's heading appears in bold in both the worksheet and the XML Source task pane. In the worksheet, the heading has a down arrow that you can use to filter the data that will be entered in the column below. A blue border surrounds the heading and the cell below, which contains an asterisk to indicate where you should enter data.

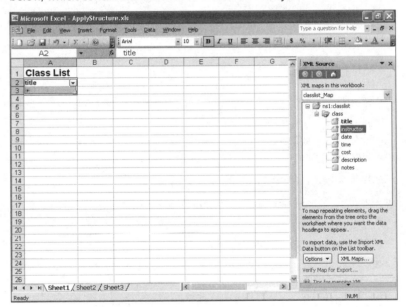

3   Continue dragging elements to adjacent cells in the worksheet until you have set up a structured area with all the elements in place.

Tip   If you want to add all the elements in a data map to an worksheet, you can simply drag the top-level element to the first cell in the structured area.

To structure a worksheet containing existing data:

1   In the XML Source task pane, point to the element you want to apply, and drag it to the corresponding cell in the worksheet.

2 If a **Header Options** button appears beside the element, click it, and click **My Data Already Has a Heading**.

The element's heading appears in bold in the XML Source task pane. In the worksheet, the column heading has a down arrow that you can use to filter the data in the column below. A blue border surrounds the heading and the data in the cells below, including a cell containing an asterisk, which is where you should enter any additional data.

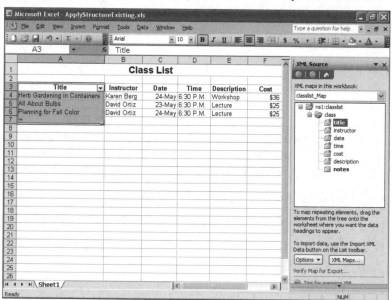

3 Continue dragging elements to headings in the worksheet until you have structured all the existing data.

To set XML options and properties:

1 In the XML Source task pane, click the **Options** button.

2 Select or clear the options on the menu to do any of the following:

- Preview your data in the task pane.

- Hide the help messages that appear in the task pane to guide you.

- Extend the blue border that designates structured data to include any adjacent elements that you apply to cells in the worksheet.

- Tell Excel that your data already has headings.

- Tell Excel not to put blue borders around structured data unless it is active.

3 With an area of structured data active, click the **XML Map Properties** button on the List toolbar.

XML Map
Properties

4   Do any of the following:

■ To ensure that the structure of the worksheet complies with the specifications of the attached data map, select the **Validate data against schema for import and export** check box in the **XML schema validation** area.

■ Select or clear the check boxes in the **Data formatting and layout** area to determine how the data you import or enter will appear in the worksheet.

■ To control whether new data is added to or overwrites existing data, select an option in the **When refreshing or importing data** area.

5   Click **OK** to close the XML Map Properties dialog box.

To import an XML data file into a structured worksheet:

1   Click the cell in the first column of the blank row of the structured area—the cell containing the asterisk.

2   On the List toolbar, click the **Import XML Data** button.

3   Navigate to the folder containing the file you want to import.

Import XML
Data

4   Click the file, and then click **Import**.

Depending on whether the you chose to add new data or overwrite existing data in the XML Map Properties dialog box, the data is appended to or replaces any existing structured data.

To enter data directly into a structured worksheet:

1   Click the cell in the first column of the blank row of the structured area—the cell containing the asterisk.

2   Type entries in the cells of the structured area, just as you would type them in an unstructured worksheet.

To save a structured worksheet as XML:

1   On the **File** menu, click **Save As**.

2   In the Save As dialog box, click the **Save as type** down arrow, and click **XML Spreadsheet** in the drop-down list.

3   Click **Save** to save the worksheet as an XML spreadsheet.

367

Practice Exercise

In this exercise, you will structure a worksheet, import structured data, type new data, and save the workbook in XML Spreadsheet format.

USE the *ApplyStructure* workbook and the *May* XML data file in the *My Documents\Microsoft Press\MOS 2003 Study Guide\Excel\E03E-1-15* practice file folder.

Open the *ApplyStructure* workbook. Drag the **title** element to cell **A3** and the **instructor** element to cell **B3**. Then in turn drag **date**, **time**, **cost**, and **description** to adjacent cells in the same row. (Don't add the optional "notes" element.) Then click the asterisk cell, and import the *May.xml* data file from the *My Documents\Microsoft Press\MOS 2003 Study Guide\Excel\E03E-1-15* practice file folder. Click the asterisk cell, and add another class called **Selecting Roses**, with **Karen Berg** as the instructor and **Workshop** as the description. Save the *ApplyStructure* workbook as an XML workbook called **MayClassList** in the *My Documents\Microsoft Press\MOS 2003 Study Guide\Excel\E03E-1-15* practice file folder. Then close the *MayClassList* workbook without saving it.

E03E-1 Review

Number	Objective	Mastered
E03E-1-1	Use subtotals	
	Calculating subtotals	❏
E03E-1-2	Define and apply advanced filters	
	Creating a criteria range for advanced filtering	❏
E03E-1-3	Group and outline data	
	Outlining a worksheet	❏
E03E-1-4	Use data validation	
	Avoiding input errors	❏
E03E-1-5	Create and modify list ranges	
	Creating and modifying a list	❏
E03E-1-6	Add, show, close, edit, merge and summarize scenarios	
	Creating and showing scenarios	❏
	Merging scenarios	❏
	Creating a scenario report	❏
E03E-1-7	Perform data analysis using automated tools	
	Using the Analysis ToolPak	❏
	Using Goal Seek	❏
	Using a data table	❏
	Using Solver	❏

Number	Objective	Mastered
E03E-1-8	Create PivotTable and PivotChart reports	
	Creating a PivotTable report	❏
	Filtering and modifying a PivotTable report	❏
	Plotting a PivotTable as a PivotChart	❏
E03E-1-9	Use Lookup and Reference functions	
	Looking up information	❏
E03E-1-10	Use Database functions	
	Creating formulas that use Database functions	❏
E03E-1-11	Trace formula precedents, dependents and errors	
	Fixing errors	❏
	Auditing a worksheet	❏
E03E-1-12	Locate invalid data and formulas	
	Using Error Checking	❏
	Circling invalid data	❏
E03E-1-13	Watch and evaluate formulas	
	Watching a cell	❏
	Evaluating a formula	❏
E03E-1-14	Define, modify and use named ranges	
	Naming a cell or range	❏
	Using a name in a formula	❏
E03E-1-15	Structure workbooks using XML	
	Adding and deleting a data map	❏
	Setting up an XML worksheet and entering data	❏

E03E-2
Formatting Data and Content

The skills tested by this section of the Microsoft Office Specialist Excel 2003 Expert Exam all relate to advanced ways that you can format content in an Excel workbook. Specifically, the following objectives are associated with this set of skills:

Number	Objective
E03E-2-1	Create and modify custom data formats
E03E-2-2	Use conditional formatting
E03E-2-3	Format and resize graphics
E03E-2-4	Format charts and diagrams

 Important   Before you can do the practice exercises associated with this skill set, you need to install the practice files from the book's companion CD to their default location. See "Installing the Practice Files" on page xxv for more information.

Create and Modify Custom Data Formats

E03E-2-1   The skills measured by this objective include the following:

- Creating a custom number format

Like many other aspects of Excel, the data formats applied to entries in cells can also be customized.

Creating a Custom Number Format

If none of the formats on the Number tab of the Format Cells dialog box meet your needs, you can create a custom number format. You simply select the cells you want to format, apply a format that is close to what you want, and then modify the format until it is exactly what you want.

After you create a custom number format, you can easily apply it to other values in the usual way.

BE SURE TO display the worksheet you want to work with before carrying out these steps.

To create a custom number format:

1   Select the cell or range for which you want to create the format.

2   On the **Format** menu, click **Cells**, and then click the **Number** tab.

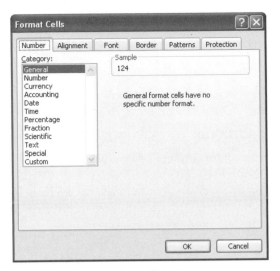

3   In the **Category** list box, click **Custom**.

4   In the **Type** list box, click the format you want to use as a starting point.

5   Modify this format by clicking the **Type** box and entering the formatting codes that you
    want to apply.

    For a complete list of Excel's formatting codes, search the Help file for *Number format codes*.

6   Click **OK** to apply the new format to the current selection.

To apply a custom format you have already created:

1   Select the cell or range you want to format.

2   On the **Format** menu, click **Cells**, and then click the **Number** tab.

3   In the **Category** list box, click **Custom**, and then in the **Type** list box, click the custom format.

4   Click **OK**.

Practice Exercise

In this exercise, you will create and apply a custom number format.

USE the *CreateFormat* workbook in the *My Documents\Microsoft Press\MOS 2003 Study Guide\Excel
\E03E-2-1* practice file folder.

Open the *CreateFormat* workbook. Create a new custom date format that will display the
first date in column **A** as *2004 January 05*. Apply the custom format to all the dates in column
A. Then close the *CreateFormat* workbook without saving it.

Use Conditional Formatting

E03E-2-2   The skills measured by this objective include the following:

■ Monitoring a worksheet with conditional formatting

Not all of Excel's formatting remains static until you change it. You can set formatting so that it responds to changing values in a worksheet.

Monitoring a Worksheet with Conditional Formatting

To monitor a worksheet, you can set up conditional formatting criteria to draw attention to cells. For example, you can specify that a cell's value should be displayed in magenta if it is over 200,000. When it is no longer necessary to monitor the worksheet for that condition, you can delete the conditional formatting. You can apply up to three conditional formats to one cell. For example, a cell's background can be green if the value is under 1000, turn yellow if between 1000 and 5000, and turn red if over 5000.

BE SURE TO display the worksheet you want to work with before carrying out these steps.

To use conditional formatting:

1   Click the cell whose condition you want to monitor.

2   On the **Format** menu, click **Conditional Formatting**.

3   Set the conditions that must be met.

For example, you might want conditional formatting to be activated if the cell value is less than or equal to 4000.

4   Click **Format**.

The Format Cells dialog box appears.

5   Specify the formatting to be used if the value meets the conditional formatting criteria.

6   Click **OK** to close the Format Cells dialog box, and click **OK** again to close the Conditional Formatting dialog box.

To delete conditional formatting:

1   Click the formatted cell(s).

2   On the **Format** menu, click **Conditional Formatting**.

3   Click **Delete**, select the check box(es) for the condition(s) you want to delete, and click **OK**.

4   Click **OK** to close the Conditional Formatting dialog box.

Practice Exercise

In this exercise, you will apply conditional formatting to a cell.

USE the *FormatCondition* workbook in the *My Documents\Microsoft Press\MOS 2003 Study Guide\Excel \E03E-2-2* practice file folder.

Open the *FormatCondition* workbook. Click cell **D19**, and add conditional formatting so that the style will be bold and italic and the background will change to light yellow if the value displayed is greater than or equal to 35000. Change the value in cell **D8** to **1200**, and observe the effect on the cell with conditional formatting. Then remove the conditional formatting from the cell, and close the *FormatCondition* workbook without saving it.

Format and Resize Graphics

E03E-2-3   The skills measured by this objective include the following:

- Controlling the contrast and brightness of a graphic
- Sizing, scaling, cropping, and rotating a graphic

When you insert a graphic into a worksheet, you might want to adjust its colors, its size, or its orientation. For precise control over size and other graphic attributes, you need to be familiar with the advanced options in the Format Picture dialog box.

Controlling the Contrast and Brightness of a Graphic

Sometimes the colors in a graphic might be too bright or too muted for your worksheet. Although you cannot make radical color changes to most types of graphics from within Excel, you can manipulate their contrast and brightness by using buttons on the Picture toolbar.

BE SURE TO display a worksheet containing a graphic before carrying out these steps.

To control contrast and brightness:

Color

1   On the Picture toolbar, click the **Color** button, and then click **Washout**.

The picture's colors decrease in intensity.

2   To control the brightness of the graphic, do one of the following:

Less
Brightness

- To decrease the brightness, click the **Less Brightness** button on the Picture toolbar.

More
Brightness

- To increase the brightness, click the **More Brightness** button.

Tip   Clicking Reset Picture restores the graphic to its original format. Any manual changes you made will be lost.

3   To control the contrast of the graphic, do one of the following:

Less Contrast

- To decrease the contrast, click the **Less Contrast** button on the Picture toolbar.

More
Contrast

- To increase the contrast, click the **More Contrast** button.

373

Practice Exercise

In this exercise, you will experiment with the colors in a logo.

USE the *ColorGraphic* workbook in the *My Documents\Microsoft Press\MOS 2003 Study Guide\Excel \E03E-2-3* practice file folder.

Open the *ColorGraphic* workbook. Click The Garden Company logo to select it, and make sure the Picture toolbar is displayed. Use the **Color** button to create a washout effect, and then reduce the logo's brightness and increase its contrast. Close the *ColorGraphic* workbook without saving it.

Sizing, Scaling, Cropping, and Rotating a Graphic

After you insert a graphic into a worksheet, you can click it to select it and then open the Format Picture dialog box, where you can make the following changes:

- You can control whether the width and height of the graphic can be changed independently; in other words, whether the graphic can be distorted or whether its aspect ratio must be maintained.

- You can change the scale of the graphic to increase or decrease its size in proportion to its original size.

- You can crop away parts of a graphic that you don't need.

- You can reset the graphic back to its original size and uncropped state.

BE SURE TO display a worksheet containing a graphic before carrying out these steps.

To change the height and width of a graphic independently:

1 If the graphic is not selected, click it.

2 Right-click the graphic, click **Format Picture** on the shortcut menu, and then click the **Size** tab.

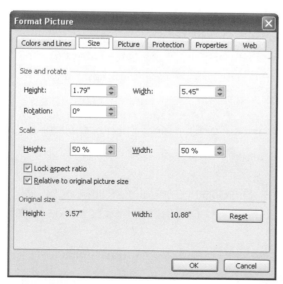

3 Clear the **Lock aspect ratio** check box, and then change either the **Height** or the **Width** settings.

4 Click **OK**.

The picture is resized, distorting the original aspect ratio.

To scale a graphic:

1 If the graphic is not selected, click it.

2 Right-click the graphic, click **Format Picture** on the shortcut menu, and then click the **Size** tab.

3 Make sure the **Lock aspect ratio** check box is selected, and then in the **Scale** area, change the **Height** or **Width** setting by entering a new percentage.

4 Click **OK**.

The picture is scaled to the percentage you specified, maintaining the original aspect ratio.

To crop a graphic visually:

1 If the graphic is not selected, click it.

2 If the Picture toolbar is not visible, right-click the graphic, and on the shortcut menu, click **Show Picture Toolbar**.

3 On the Picture toolbar, click the **Crop** button.

Crop

4 Point to the handle on the side from which you want to crop away part of the graphic, and drag inward until you have hidden the desired amount of the image.

5 On the Picture toolbar, click the **Crop** button again to turn off the cropping tool.

To crop a graphic precisely:

1 If the graphic is not selected, click it.

2 Right-click the graphic, and click **Format Picture** on the shortcut menu, and then click the **Picture** tab.

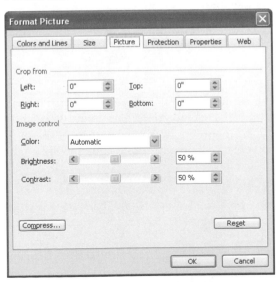

375

3   In the **Crop from** area, change the contents of the **Top**, **Bottom**, **Left**, or **Right** box to crop a precise amount away from the specified side of the graphic.

4   Click **OK**.

To rotate a graphic:

1   Right-click the graphic, click **Format Picture** on the shortcut menu, and then click the **Size** tab.

2   In the **Rotation** box, use the arrows to select the desired degree of rotation, and click **OK**.
    The graphic is rotated to the degree you selected.

    Tip   To rotate a graphic in 90-degree increments, you can use the Rotate button on the Picture toolbar.

Practice Exercise

In this exercise, you will scale a graphic, crop away parts of it, and rotate it to create the effect you want.

USE the *ScaleGraphic* workbook in the *My Documents\Microsoft Press\MOS 2003 Study Guide\Excel\E03E-2-3* practice file folder.

Open the *ScaleGraphic* workbook. Display the Format Picture dialog box, and scale the graphic to approximately 125% percent. Then crop the bottom leaf away from the graphic, and use the **Rotate** button to rotate the graphic until the stem of the leaf is pointing toward the bottom of the picture. Display the **Size** tab of the Format Picture dialog box, and refine the degree of rotation to **185**. Then close the *ScaleGraphic* workbook without saving it.

Format Charts and Diagrams

E03E-2-4   The skills measured by this objective include the following:

■ Formatting a chart
■ Formatting an organization chart

You can format charts much as you can most other items in Excel. You can change the chart type, as well as its fonts, colors, and styles.

Formatting a Chart

By default, Microsoft Graph plots worksheet data as a two-dimensional column chart. You can change the chart type to any of 14 standard formats, many with both two-dimensional and three-dimensional variations. If none of the standard types meets your needs, Graph also includes several less-common custom types, including combination charts that plot one type on top of another as an "overlay."

Tip   If you frequently use a type other than a two-dimensional column chart, you can change Graph's default type. On the Chart menu, click Chart Type. Then click one of the options in the "Chart type" box, and click "Set as default chart."

In addition to changing the chart type, you can change the formatting of the chart's component objects. To format an object, you first select it, either by clicking the object itself or by clicking its name in the Chart Objects box on Graph's Standard toolbar. You then use various formatting techniques, depending on whether the object is a required chart component, such as the chart area and axes, or an optional component, such as the gridlines, titles, and legend.

BE SURE TO display a worksheet containing a chart before carrying out these steps.

To change the chart type:

1 Click the chart to activate Microsoft Graph.

The chart and datasheet appear along with Graph's toolbars and menus.

Chart Type

2 On the Chart toolbar, click the **Chart Type** down arrow.

The palette of chart types appears.

3 Click the button for the type of chart you want.

The chart is redrawn in the selected format, and the image on the Chart Type button changes to reflect the type of the chart you selected.

To use custom chart types:

1 Click the chart to activate Microsoft Graph.

2 On the **Chart** menu, click **Chart Type**, and then click the **Custom Types** tab.

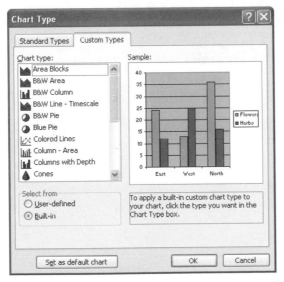

3   Scroll through the **Chart type** list, selecting any options that catch your eye and noting their effect in the **Sample** box on the right.

4   Click the chart type you want, and click **OK**.

To turn optional chart objects on or off:

1   Click the chart to open it in Graph.

2   On the **Chart** menu, click **Chart Options**.

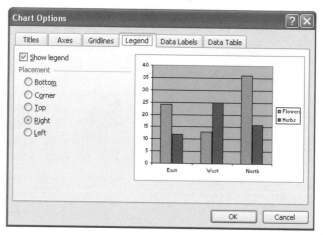

3   Do any of the following:

■   To add a title, click in the **Chart title** box on the **Titles** tab, and type the text you want.

Tip   After you close the Chart Options dialog box, you can add a second line of text to the title by clicking at the end of the title, pressing ENTER, and typing the text you want.

■   To attach text to the axes, click in the appropriate axes text boxes on the **Titles** tab, and type the text.

■   To add gridlines, click the **Gridlines** tab, and in the **Category (X) axis, Series (Y) axis, and Value (Z) axis** areas, select the gridline options you want.

Tip   The x-axis shows the information categories, for example, sales and expenses; the y-axis shows the data points (plotted values).

■   To turn off or reposition the legend, make your selections on the **Legend** tab.

■   To turn on data labels or display a data table, make your selections on the **Data Labels** or **Data Table** tab.

4   Click **OK**.

To reposition or size a chart object:

1   Click the chart to open it in Graph, and click the part of the chart you want to reposition.

Tip   If you have trouble selecting the object you want, click the Chart Objects down arrow on the Chart toolbar, and in the drop-down list, click the object you want to format.

2   Do any of the following:

- To move the selected object, drag it within the chart area.
- To size the selected object, drag its sizing handles.

To format the chart's objects:

1   Click the chart to open it in Graph, and select the part of the chart you want to format.

2   Do any of the following:

- To format an axis label, right-click the axis, and click **Format Axis** on the shortcut menu. On the **Number** tab, select the category you want from the **Category** list, and make any necessary changes to the options. On the **Scale** tab, select options or enter numbers if you want to change the scale of the display units. Then click **OK**.
- To format the legend, right-click it, and click **Format Legend** on the shortcut menu. Display the appropriate tab, select the options you want, and click **OK**.
- To format the chart's border, right-click the chart area, and click **Format Chart Area** on the shortcut menu. In the **Border** area of the **Patterns** tab, click the **Weight** down arrow, and click the item you want in the drop-down list. Use the **Style** and **Color** drop-down lists to change the style and color of the border. To add a shadow or round corners, select the appropriate check boxes, and then click **OK**.
- To format data markers, right-click any marker, and click **Format Data Series** on the shortcut menu. Display the appropriate tab, make the changes you want, and click **OK**.

To add a note to a chart:

1   With the graph selected, check that no specific graph element is selected.
2   Click in the formula bar, type the note, and press **ENTER**.
    Excel displays a text box containing the note in the middle of the graph.
3   Use the frame and handles surrounding the text box to reposition and size the note.
4   To format the text box, right-click the box, and then click **Format Text Box** on the shortcut menu.
5   In the Format Text Box dialog box, make the selections you want, and click **OK**.

379

Practice Exercise

In this exercise, you will modify the appearance of a chart by changing the chart type. You'll then change the size of the chart area and the color of the plot area, modify the legend, and put a border around the chart.

USE the *FormatChart* workbook in the *My Documents\Microsoft Press\MOS 2003 Study Guide\Excel\E03E-2-4* practice file folder.

Open the *FormatChart* workbook, and change the chart type to a line chart. Drag the chart area's handles so that its right frame roughly aligns with column **J** and its bottom frame roughly aligns with row **25**. Select the plot area—the gray area of the chart—and use the **Fill Color** button on the Formatting toolbar to change the background of the chart to light green. Remove the horizontal gridlines from the chart. Then give the chart the title **Customer Transactions**, move the legend to the bottom of the chart area, and reposition the plot area so it sits above the legend. Change the font size of the legend to **10** points. Put a border around the entire chart area, and make any other formatting adjustments you want. Then click outside the chart to deselect it, and after admiring your handiwork, close the *FormatChart* workbook without saving it.

Formatting an Organization Chart

Excel's default organization chart is perfectly functional as it is, but you can change its look very quickly by applying an autoformat to it or by formatting its text, boxes, and lines.

BE SURE TO display a worksheet containing an organization chart before carrying out these steps.

To quickly format an organization chart:

1   Click the organization chart to select it.

Autoformat

2   On the Organization Chart toolbar, click the **Autoformat** button.

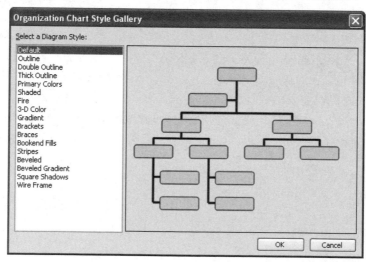

3 In the **Select a Diagram Style** list, click the style you want, and then click **OK**.

The selected style is applied to your organization chart.

To modify the lines of an organization chart:

1 On the Organization Chart toolbar, click the **Select** down arrow, and then click **All Connecting Lines** on the drop-down menu.

All connecting lines in the organization chart are selected.

2 On the **Format** menu, click **AutoShape**.

3 In the **Line** area, click the **Color** down arrow, and click the color you want in the palette that appears.

4 In the **Arrows** area, click the **Begin style** or **End style** down arrow, click the style you want, and then click **OK**.

5 Click the blank area to the right of the organization chart to deselect it.

Practice Exercise

In this exercise, you will change the formatting of an organization chart.

USE the *FormatOrgChart* workbook in the *My Documents\Microsoft Press\MOS 2003 Study Guide\Excel \E03E-2-4* practice file folder.

Open the *FormatOrgChart* workbook. Change the style of the organization chart to **Beveled**, and then change the style back to **Default**. Select all the connecting lines, display the Format AutoShape dialog box, and change the color of the lines to red. Then attach arrows to the lines. Deselect the organization chart, and then close the *FormatOrgChart* workbook without saving it.

E03E-2 Review

Number	Objective	Mastered
E03E-2-1	Create and modify custom data formats	
	Creating a custom number format	❑
E03E-2-2	Use conditional formatting	
	Monitoring a worksheet with conditional formatting	❑
E03E-2-3	Format and resize graphics	
	Controlling the contrast and brightness of a graphic	❑
	Sizing, scaling, cropping, and rotating a graphic	❑
E03E-2-4	Format charts and diagrams	
	Formatting a chart	❑
	Formatting an organization chart	❑

E03E-3
Collaborating

The skills tested by this section of the Microsoft Office Specialist Excel 2003 Expert Exam all relate to the Excel features that make it is easy to collaborate with other people on the creation and formatting of worksheets. Specifically, the following objectives are associated with this set of skills:

Number	Objective
E03E-3-1	Protect cells, worksheets, and workbooks
E03E-3-2	Apply workbook security settings
E03E-3-3	Share workbooks
E03E-3-4	Merge workbooks
E03E-3-5	Track, accept, and reject changes to workbooks

Important   Before you can do the practice exercises associated with this skill set, you need to install the practice files from the book's companion CD to their default location. See "Installing the Practice Files" on page xxv for more information.

Protect Cells, Worksheets, and Workbooks

E03E-3-1   The skills measured by this objective include the following:

- Preventing changes to cells, worksheets, and workbooks

Sometimes you will want people to be able to open a workbook but not make changes to it. Or you might want to allow changes to some parts but not others. In Excel you can restrict the editing of a specific cell, range, worksheet, or entire workbook.

Preventing Changes to Cells, Worksheets, and Workbooks

There are three ways to protect a worksheet or a cell or range within a worksheet:

- You can assign a password to a named cell or range. No one will be able to make changes to the cell or range unless they know the password.
- You can lock a cell or range and then turn on worksheet protection.
- You can prevent certain types of changes to a worksheet and allow others.

See Also   For information about preventing changes to entire workbooks, refer to E03E-3-2, "Apply Workbook Security Settings."

BE SURE TO open the workbook you want to work with before carrying out these steps.

To password protect a cell or range:

1   Select the cell or range you want to protect.

2   On the **Tools** menu, click **Protection** and then **Allow Users to Edit Ranges**.

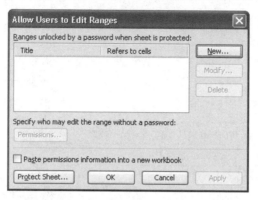

3   Click the **New** button.

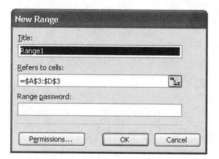

4   In the **Title** box, type a name for the range.

5   In the **Range password** box, type a password.

6   Click **OK**.

7   In the Confirm Password dialog box, retype the password, and click **OK**.

8   Click **OK** again to close the Allow Users to Edit Ranges dialog box.

To lock a cell or range:

1   Select the cell or range you want to lock.

2   Right-click the selection, click **Format Cells** on the shortcut menu, and then click the **Protection** tab.

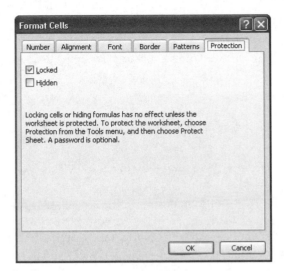

3   Select the **Locked** check box, and click **OK**.

>   **Tip**   You can also select the Hidden check box if you want to hide the formulas in the cells.

4   On the **Tools** menu, click **Protection** and then **Protect Sheet**.

5   Select the **Protect worksheet and contents of locked cells** check box.

6   Click **OK**.

To prevent changes to an entire worksheet:

1   On the **Tools** menu, click **Protection** and then **Protect Sheet**.

2   To allow a specific type of change to be made to the worksheet without entering the password, select the check box for that element.

3 In the **Password to unprotect sheet** box, type a password, and then click **OK**.

4 The Confirm Password dialog box, type the password again, and click **OK**.

People who don't know the password will be able to make only the unrestricted changes to the worksheet.

Practice Exercise

In this exercise, you will assign a password to a range of cells, hide a formula, and then protect an entire worksheet.

USE the *ProtectCells* workbook in the *My Documents\Microsoft Press\MOS 2003 Study Guide\Excel\E03E-3-1* practice file folder.

Open the *ProtectCells* workbook. Select **A2:B27**, and in the New Range dialog box, give the range the title **Customer Number and Product** and assign a range password. Hide the formula in **D6**, and then assign a password to protect the worksheet. Unprotect the worksheet, and delete the **Customer Number and Product** range so that **A2:B27** is no longer locked. Protect the entire worksheet again, and then try to change the contents of any cell. Unprotect the worksheet, and then close the *ProtectCells* workbook without saving it.

Apply Workbook Security Settings

E03E-3-2   The skills measured by this objective include the following:

- ■ Authenticating a workbook with a digital signature
- ■ Using a digital signature to authenticate a workbook
- ■ Setting a password
- ■ Adjusting macro settings

It's important to know how to protect your workbooks from unwanted changes, and there are several ways to do that, including through the use of passwords and digital signatures. But in today's environment, you also need to know how to carry protection one step further by adjusting your macro settings to avoid getting hit by viruses, each of which has the potential to destroy your files.

Authenticating a Workbook with a Digital Signature

Because of the proliferation of viruses and the ability to hide the true origins of a workbook, it is sometimes necessary to be able to guarantee a workbook's source. When you create a workbook that will be circulated to other people via e-mail or the Web, you might want to consider attaching a digital signature, which is an electronic stamp of authentication. Certified digital signatures can be obtained from companies such as VeriSign. The digital signature confirms the origin of the workbook and guarantees that no one has tampered with the workbook since it was signed.

BE SURE TO open the workbook you want to work with and have a digital signature available before carrying out these steps.

To attach a digital signature to a workbook:

1 On the **Tools** menu, click **Options**, and then click the **Security** tab.

2 Click **Digital Signatures**.

3 In the Digital Signature dialog box, click **Add**.

4 In the Select Certificate dialog box, click a certificate in the list, and click **OK**.

5 Click **OK** twice to close the Digital Signature and Options dialog boxes.

The word *(Signed)* now appears in Excel's title bar.

6 On the Standard toolbar, click the **Save** button to save the workbook.

To view the digital signatures attached to a signed workbook:

1 On the **Tools** menu, click **Options**, and then click the **Security** tab.

2 Click **Digital Signatures**.

3 In the Digital Signature dialog box, check the list of signers and see who issued their digital IDs.

4 Click **OK** twice to close the Digital Signature and Options dialog boxes.

Practice Exercise

Because you need an authentic digital signature to be able to carry out this task, there is no practice exercise for this topic.

Setting a Password

If you want only certain people to be able to open a workbook, you can assign a password to it. To open the workbook, each user must enter the password exactly as it was set, including spaces, symbols, and uppercase and lowercase characters.

Tip If you want other people to be able to read or copy the workbook but not change it, you can make it read-only. You can also set the "Read-only recommended" option.

BE SURE TO open the workbook you want to work with before carrying out these steps.

To set a password for a workbook:

1 On the **File** menu, click **Save As**.

The Save As dialog box appears.

Tools ▾ 2 On the toolbar, click the **Tools** button, and then click **General Options**.

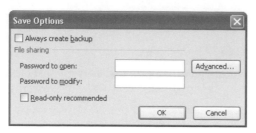

3   Do one of the following:

■   If you want only authorized people to be able to open the workbook, type a password in the **Password to open** box.

■   If you want only authorized people to be able to change the workbook, type a password in the **Password to modify** box. (Unauthorized people will still be able to open a read-only copy of the workbook.)

Tip   Don't use common words or phrases as passwords, and don't use the same password for multiple workbooks.

4   Click **OK** to close the Save Options dialog box.

The Confirm Password dialog box appears.

5   Type the password(s) again, and click **OK**.

6   In the Save As dialog box, click **Save**.

To remove a workbook's password:

1   On the **File** menu, click **Save As**.

The Save As dialog box appears.

2   On the toolbar, click the **Tools** button, and then click **General Options**.

3   In the Save Options dialog box, select the contents of the **Password to open** or **Password to modify** box, press DELETE, and then click **OK**.

The workbook's password protection is removed.

4   In the Save As dialog box, click **Save**.

Practice Exercise

In this exercise, you will set a password for a workbook, and then you'll remove the protection.

USE the *SetPassword* workbook in the *My Documents\Microsoft Press\MOS 2003 Study Guide\Excel\E03E-3-2* practice file folder.

Open the *SetPassword* workbook. In the Save Options dialog box, set a password that must be entered to open the workbook. Redisplay the Save Options dialog box, and delete the contents of the **Password to open** box. Save the *SetPassword* workbook, and then close it.

Adjusting Macro Settings

To avoid the risk of virus infection from contaminated Excel files, your computer's macro security level might be set to High. This setting prevents you from running macros that do not have digital signatures that guarantee that they were issued by a trusted source. (If you select the even more rigorous Very High setting, you can open workbooks that contain macros only if they are stored in specific locations.)

To run the macros in a workbook, you might need to set your security level to Medium. With this setting, you will be prompted to enable the workbook's macros whenever you open it.

Tip Don't be tempted to set security to Low to avoid this prompt. The pain that a virus can inflict is simply not worth saving that extra click.

BE SURE TO start Excel and have a workbook containing a macro available before carrying out these steps.

To adjust your computer's macro security level:

1   On the **Tools** menu, click **Macro** and then **Security**.

2   On the **Security Level** tab, click **Medium**, and click **OK**.

3   Open the workbook containing macros, and when the Security Warning dialog box appears, click **Enable Macros**.

Practice Exercise

In this exercise, you will change your macro security settings.

USE the *ChangeSettings* workbook in the *My Documents\Microsoft Press\MOS 2003 Study Guide\Excel \E03E-3-2* practice file folder.

With Excel running, make sure your macro security setting is set to **High**. Then open the *ChangeSettings* workbook. When a message appears saying that macros are disabled because your security setting is too high, change your macro security setting to **Medium**, and close the workbook. Then open the workbook again. When prompted, choose to disable macros. Change your macro security setting back to **High**, and close the *ChangeSettings* workbook without saving it.

Share Workbooks

E03E-3-3   The skills measured by this objective include the following:

■ Creating a shared workbook

■ Using a shared workbook

If a workbook needs input from several people but you don't have time for each person to look at it independently, you can share it over a network so everyone can work on it at the same time.

Creating a Shared Workbook

If you work on a network and you want others to be able to access and make changes to a workbook that you created, you can share the workbook. After a workbook is shared, more than one person can edit it simultaneously.

You can control whether and for how long Excel keeps a record of changes to the workbook. By default, Excel keeps this history for 30 days. You can also control how Excel resolves conflicts between changes made by different people. If you want to know exactly what changes other people make to the workbook, you can require that all changes be made using tracked changes, which you can then review and accept or reject.

See Also   For information about tracked changes, refer to E03E-3-5, "Track, Accept, and Reject Changes to Workbooks."

BE SURE TO open the workbook you want to work with before carrying out these steps.

To create a shared workbook:

1   On the **Tools** menu, click **Share Workbook**.

2 On the **Editing** tab, select the **Allow changes by more than one user at the same time** check box.

3 On the **Advanced** tab, do any of the following:

   ■ Make any necessary adjustments to whether and for how long Excel keeps a record of changes to the shared workbook.

   ■ Set how often the shared workbook should be saved.

   ■ Specify how conflicting changes should be applied.

4 Click **OK**.

To require that edits to a shared workbook must be made in tracked changes:

1 On the **Tools** menu, click **Protection** and then **Protect Shared Workbook**.

2 Select the **Sharing with track changes** check box, and click **OK**.

Practice Exercise

In this exercise, you will share a workbook so that multiple users can make changes to it and their changes will be tracked.

USE the *ShareWorkbook* workbook in the *My Documents\Microsoft Press\MOS 2003 Study Guide\Excel \E03E-3-3* practice file folder.

Open the *ShareWorkbook* workbook. Share the workbook, allowing multiple users to make editing changes to it. Keep a change history of **45** days, and automatically save all changes every **45** minutes. Protect the shared workbook so that sharing with track changes is required. Then close the *ShareWorkbook* workbook without saving it.

Using a Shared Workbook

You can open and modify a shared workbook the same way you would any other workbook. If tracked changes are required, all your edits are tracked. When you save your changes, you can resolve any conflicts with changes made at the same time by other people. You can also check the history of all changes made to the worksheet.

BE SURE TO open a shared workbook before carrying out these steps.

To make changes to a shared workbook:

1 Make the necessary changes to the workbook in the usual ways.

Tip You can check who else is making changes to the workbook on the Editing tab of the Share Workbook dialog box.

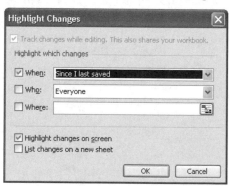

Save

2 On the Standard toolbar, click the **Save** button.

If any of the changes you made conflict with the changes made by another user, the Resolve Conflicts dialog box appears.

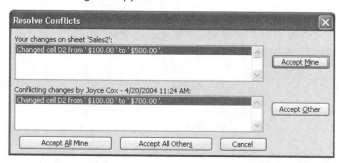

3 Do one of the following:

- To keep your change and move to the next conflict, click **Accept Mine**.
- To keep the other person's change and move to the next conflict, click **Accept Other**.
- To keep all your changes, click **Accept All Mine**.
- To keep all the other person's changes, click **Accept All Others**.

4 Close the Resolve Conflicts dialog box.

To see the history of changes to a shared workbook:

1 On the **Tools** menu, click **Track Changes** and then **Highlight Changes**.

2   Click the **When** down arrow, and click **All** in the drop-down list.

3   If necessary, clear the **Who** and **Where** check boxes.

4   At the bottom of the dialog box, select the **List changes on a new sheet** check box.

5   Click **OK**.

6   Back in the workbook, click the **History** tab to view the changes made to the worksheet.

Practice Exercise

In this exercise, you will open a shared workbook and view its change history.

USE the *UseSharedWorkbook* workbook in the *My Documents\Microsoft Press\MOS 2003 Study Guide\Excel \E03E-3-3* practice file folder.

Open the *UseSharedWorkbook* workbook. In the Highlight Changes dialog box, select the options to view all changes made by everyone. You want to see only the changes, so specify that the changes should be listed on a separate sheet. After viewing the changes, close the *UseSharedWorkbook* workbook without saving it.

Merge Workbooks

E03E-3-4   The skills measured by this objective include the following:

■ Comparing and merging workbooks

If you send a workbook for review, you need a way to examine all the suggested changes in all the versions of the workbook that are returned to you. This task can be cumbersome, especially if you have asked several people to review the workbook. Excel's Compare and Merge Workbooks command simplifies the process.

Comparing and Merging Workbooks

Sometimes you might want to compare several versions of the same workbook. For example, if you sent a workbook out for review by colleagues, you might want to compare their edited versions with the original workbook. Or you might want to compare an earlier version of a workbook with the current version.

If you turned on tracked changes (which automatically shares the workbook) before you sent the workbook out for review, and if the reviewers saved the file with a different file name, you can have Excel merge the workbooks into one workbook and show the differences as tracked changes that appear in comments. The changes from each successive merged version override the changes of the previous version.

See Also   For information about tracked changes, refer to E03E-3-5, "Track, Accept, and Reject Changes to Workbooks."

BE SURE TO open the workbook you want to work with and to have at least one other version of the workbook available before carrying out these steps.

To compare and merge workbooks:

1   On the **Tools** menu, click **Compare and Merge Documents**.

2   Navigate to the folder where the file you want to compare and merge with the original workbook is stored.

3   Click the workbook, or select multiple workbooks, and click **OK**.

The changes from the selected workbook are transferred to the open workbook, and changed cells are flagged with a blue triangle in the upper-left corner.

To view the changes in a merged workbook:

● Point to a cell flagged with a blue triangle to display a comment that tells you who made what change.

Practice Exercise

In this exercise, you will merge a workbook with two other versions of it.

USE the *CompareMerge, Merge1,* and *Merge2* workbooks in the *My Documents\Microsoft Press \MOS 2003 Study Guide\Excel\E03E-3-4* practice file folder.

Open the *CompareMerge* workbook. Display the Select Files to Merge Into Current Workbook dialog box, navigate to the *My Documents\Microsoft Press\MOS 2003 Study Guide\Excel \E03E-3-4* practice file folder, and merge the *Merge1* workbook into the open workbook. Repeat this process with the *Merge2* workbook. Set the option to highlight all changes, and scroll down the worksheet to see the changes. Then close the *CompareMerge* workbook without saving it.

Track, Accept, and Reject Changes to Workbooks

E03E-3-5   The skills measured by this objective include the following:

■   Tracking changes to a workbook

■   Accepting and rejecting changes

When you create a workbook, you will probably not want other people to change it without your knowledge. Maintaining content control is particularly important with financial workbooks, where changes can produce misleading information.

Tracking Changes to a Workbook

When two or more people collaborate on a workbook, one person usually creates and "owns" the workbook and the others review it, suggesting changes to make it more accurate, logical, or readable. If you are the owner of a workbook, you can turn on the Track Changes feature so that the revisions are recorded without the original data being lost. The workbook shows the change but stores the old data and information about who made the change and when for a specified period of time. You can view this information in a comment attached to the changed cell or in a History worksheet.

Tip   Excel tracks data changes but not formatting changes.

BE SURE TO open the workbook you want to work with before carrying out these steps.

To track changes:

1   On the **Tools** menu, click **Track Changes** and then **Highlight Changes**.

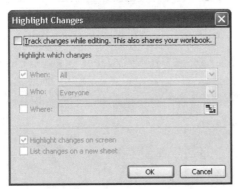

2   Select the **Track changes while editing** check box.

3   Do any of the following:

- ■ To refine which changes will be tracked, make changes to the **When**, **Who**, and **Where** settings.

- ■ To turn off tracking in the cells of the worksheet, clear the **Highlight changes on screen** check box.

- ■ To show the changes in a separate History worksheet, select the **List changes on a new sheet** check box.

4   Click **OK**.

The workbook can now be edited in the usual way.

Practice Exercise

In this exercise, you will turn on tracked changes and make changes to the workbook.

USE the *TrackChanges* workbook in the *My Documents\Microsoft Press\MOS 2003 Study Guide\Excel \E03E-3-5* practice file folder.

Open the *TrackChanges* workbook. In the Highlight Changes dialog box, select the option that will highlight all changes made while editing. Make sure you can view changes made by everyone. Then make a few changes to the worksheet. Close the *TrackChanges* workbook without saving it.

Accepting and Rejecting Changes

When a workbook contains tracked changes, you can review and accept or reject the changes made by a specific reviewer or all reviewers. You can also review only changes made since your last review or since a certain date, and you can review changes made to specific parts of the worksheet.

Whether you accept or reject a change is recorded in the change history. By default, items in the change history are maintained for 30 days from the date the information was recorded.

See Also   For information about changing how long history is maintained, refer to E03C-3-3, "Share Workbooks."

BE SURE TO display a worksheet containing tracked changes before carrying out these steps.

To accept or reject changes:

1   On the **Tools** menu, click **Track Changes** and then **Accept or Reject Changes**.

2   If necessary, make changes to the **When**, **Who**, and **Where** settings, and click **OK**.

Tip   You cannot skip a change after you have started the process of accepting or rejecting them, and controlling these options carefully is the only way to handle some changes but not others in a single process.

The Accept or Reject Changes dialog box appears with information about the first change in the worksheet.

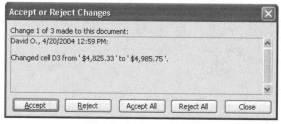

3   Do one of the following:
- To accept the change, click **Accept**.
- To reject the change, click **Reject**.
- To accept all the changes in the workbook, click **Accept All**.
- To reject all the changes, click **Reject All**.

4   When you have finished handling all the changes, click **Close** to close the dialog box.

Practice Exercise

In this exercise, you will select and accept changes made by one user.

USE the *AcceptChanges* workbook in the *My Documents\Microsoft Press\MOS 2003 Study Guide\Excel \E03E-3-5* practice file folder.

Open the *AcceptChanges* workbook. Select changes made only by David O. Reject the first change, and accept the rest of the changes. Then close the *AcceptChanges* workbook without saving it.

E03E-3 Review

Number	Objective	Mastered
E03E-3-1	Protect cells, worksheets, and workbooks	
	Preventing changes to cells, worksheets, and workbooks	❏
E03E-3-2	Apply workbook security settings	
	Authenticating a workbook with a digital signature	❏
	Using a digital signature to authenticate a workbook	❏
	Setting a password	❏
	Adjusting macro settings	❏
E03E-3-3	Share workbooks	
	Creating a shared workbook	❏
	Using a shared workbook	❏
E03E-3-4	Merge workbooks	
	Comparing and merging workbooks	❏
E03E-3-5	Track, accept, and reject changes to workbooks	
	Tracking changes to a workbook	❏
	Accepting and rejecting changes	❏

E03E-4

Managing Data and Workbooks

The skills tested by this section of the Microsoft Office Specialist Excel 2003 Expert Exam all relate to advanced tasks you might need to carry out with an Excel workbook. Specifically, the following objectives are associated with this set of skills:

Number	Objective
E03E-4-1	Import data to Excel
E03E-4-2	Export data from Excel
E03E-4-3	Publish and edit Web worksheets and workbooks
E03E-4-4	Create and edit templates
E03E-4-5	Consolidate data
E03E-4-6	Define and modify workbook properties

Important   Before you can do the practice exercises associated with this skill set, you need to install the practice files from the book's companion CD to their default location. See "Installing the Practice Files" on page xxv for more information.

Import Data to Excel

E03E-4-1   The skills measured by this objective include the following:

- Importing data from an external data source
- Importing data from a Web page

When the information you want to use in Excel already exists somewhere else, you don't have to retype the data. Instead, you can import it.

Importing Data from an External Data Source

If the data you want to use is contained in a file created in another program, sometimes you can simply open the file in Excel by setting the "Files of type" setting to the format of the file you want to open, navigating to the correct folder, and double-clicking the file.

If the source data is updated frequently and you want a worksheet to always reflect the most recent version, you might want to create an external data range. The data in this range is pulled from the source file every time you open the workbook and can be dynamically updated while you are working with the workbook.

BE SURE TO open the workbook you want to work with before carrying out these steps.

To open a file created in another program:

Open

1 On the Standard toolbar, click the **Open** button.

2 In the Open dialog box, click the **Files of type** down arrow, and click the type of file you want to open, or click **All Files** in the drop-down list.

3 Navigate to the folder containing the file you want to open, and double-click the file.

Depending on what type of file you are trying to open, you might need to give some additional instructions in another dialog box. You will probably need to make some adjustments or formatting changes to make the data fit within the worksheet.

To create an external data source:

1 On the **Data** menu, click **Import External Data** and then **Import Data**.

2 In the Select Data Source dialog box, click **New Source**.

The first page of the Data Connection Wizard appears.

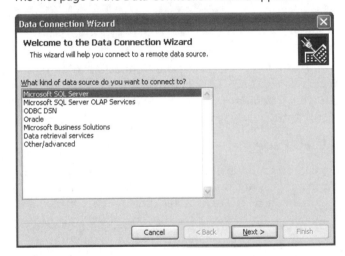

3 Click the type of data source you want to connect to, and click **Next**.

For example, to connect to an Access database, click OBDC DSN.

4 Identify the data source you want in the wizard's remaining pages, and click **Finish**.

5 Back in the Select Data Source dialog box, click **Open**.

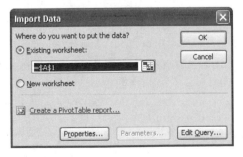

399

6   Do one of the following:

- To set up the external data range on the open worksheet, click **Existing worksheet**, and then click the upper-left cell of the range.

- To set up the external data range in the upper-left corner of a new worksheet, click **New worksheet**.

7   Click **OK**.

Excel imports the data into the range you specified, and displays the External Data toolbar, which contains buttons you can use to work with the external data.

Tip   The data source is added to the list of available sources in the Select Data Source dialog box so that you can pull information from this source into other worksheets without having to run the Data Connection Wizard again.

Practice Exercise

In this exercise, you will set up an external data range that imports information from a table in an Access database.

USE the *ImportData* workbook and the *DataSource* database in the *My Documents\Microsoft Press \MOS 2003 Study Guide\Excel\E03E-4-1* practice file folder.

Open the *ImportData* workbook. Using the Data Connection Wizard, navigate to *My Documents\Microsoft Press\MOS 2003 Study Guide\Excel\E03E-4-1*, and import the **Employee** table from the **DataSource** database into the open workbook. Then close the *ImportData* workbook without saving it.

Importing Data from a Web Page

If the source of the data you want to use in a worksheet is a Web page on the Internet or an intranet, you can import it as static or refreshable data by using the Past Options command. You can also simply open an HTML or XML file directly in Excel.

BE SURE TO display the worksheet you want to work with before carrying out these steps.

To import data from a Web page:

1   Open your Web browser, and browse to the Web page containing the data you want to import.

2   Select the data, and on the **Edit** menu, click **Copy**.

3   Click the cell in the upper-left corner of the range where you want to past the data, and on the **Edit** menu, click **Paste**.

Excel pastes in the data and displays a Paste Options button in the lower-right corner of the data range.

4   Click the **Paste Options** button, and then click **Create Refreshable Web Query** on the button's menu.

The New Web Query dialog box appears, showing the Web page with a yellow arrow button beside each page element that you can import.

5   Scroll the New Web Query dialog box until you can see the data you want to import, and click the yellow arrow button adjacent to the data.

6   Click **Import**.

The dialog box closes, and after a few seconds, the data in the worksheet is refreshed. It is now dynamically linked to the data on the source Web page, and you can perform calculations on the data as you would on any other values.

Practice Exercise

In this exercise, you will create a link to data in a Web page.

USE the *ImportWeb* workbook in the *My Documents\Microsoft Press\MOS 2003 Study Guide\Excel\E03E-4-1* practice file folder.

Open the *ImportWeb* workbook. Start your browser, and go to *http://moneycentral.msn.com*. Under **Investing**, click **Stocks**, and under **Find Stocks**, click **Top-Rated Stocks**. Then under **Overall Rating**, click **Top Rated 50**. Copy the first line in the table, activate the *ImportWeb* workbook, and with cell **A1** selected, paste the line into the worksheet. Create a refreshable Web query. In the New Web Query dialog box, click the yellow arrow button adjacent to the top 50 table, and then click **Import**. After the data in the worksheet is refreshed to show the complete table, close the *ImportWeb* workbook without saving it.

Export Data from Excel

E03E-4-2   The skills measured by this objective include the following:

■   Exporting an XML data file

If you create a large worksheet and then decide you want to manipulate it with more powerful database tools than those provided by Excel, you can import the worksheet's data into an Access database. You can also structure the data in XML format and export it as an XML data file that can be used in a broader range of programs.

Exporting an XML Data File

After you have mapped the contents of a worksheet using an XML data map, you can either save it in XML Spreadsheet format or save or export it as an XML data file. The advantage of doing the latter is that other people can more easily manipulate the data in other programs to meet their needs.

See Also   For information about applying data maps and saving workbooks in XML Spreadsheet format, refer to E03E-1-16, "Structure Workbooks Using XML."

BE SURE TO display a worksheet to which you have applied a data map before carrying out these steps.

To save an XML data file:

1   On the **File** menu, click **Save As**.

2   In the Save As dialog box, navigate to the folder where you want to save the file.

3   In the **File name** box, type a name for the XML data file.

4   Click the **Save as type** down arrow, and click **XML Data** in the drop-down list.

5   Click **Save**, and then click **Continue** to acknowledge that some features might be lost when saving the file in the XML Data format.

    If more than one XML map is applied to the workbook, the Export XML dialog box appears.

6   Click the XML map you want to use, and click **OK**.

To export an XML data file:

1   On the **Data** menu, click **XML** and then **Export**.

    If more than one XML map is applied to the workbook, the Export XML dialog box appears.

2   Click the XML map you want to use, and click **OK**.

3   In the Export XML dialog box, navigate to the folder where you want to save the file.

4   In the **File name** box, type a name for the XML data file.

5   Click **Export**.

Practice Exercise

In this exercise, you will export a worksheet's information as an XML data file.

USE the *ExportXML* workbook in the *My Documents\Microsoft Press\MOS 2003 Study Guide\Excel\E03E-4-2* practice file folder.

Open the *ExportXML* workbook. Open the Export XML dialog box, and navigate to the *My Documents\Microsoft Press\MOS 2003 Study Guide\Excel\E03E-4-2* practice file folder. Assign **NewXML** as the name of the XML data file, and export the file. Close the *ExportXML* workbook without saving it.

Publish and Edit Web Worksheets and Workbooks

E03E-4-3   The skills measured by this objective include the following:

■   Publishing a worksheet as a Web page

If your organization uses an intranet or a website to distribute information, you might want to take advantage of Excel's Web publishing capabilities, which you can use to save an Excel worksheet as a Web page on a server.

Publishing a Worksheet as a Web Page

Excel workbooks can be published as Web pages only in noninteractive format. However, worksheets or parts of worksheets can be published in interactive format. Visitors can view a noninteractive workbook over the Internet or an intranet but cannot change it. With an interactive worksheet, users can enter, format, calculate, analyze, sort, and filter data.

BE SURE TO display the worksheet you want to work with before carrying out these steps.

To publish a worksheet as a Web page:

1   If you want to publish only part of a worksheet as a Web page, select the range you want to publish.

2   On the **File** menu, click **Save as Web Page**.

3   Do one of the following:

■   To publish the entire workbook, select the **Entire Workbook** option.

■   To publish the worksheet or selected range, select the **Selection** option.

4   If necessary, change the name in the **File name** box.

5   Click the **Publish** button.

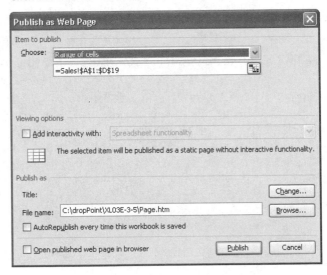

6   Do any of the following:

- ■ To allow people who are viewing the Web page to be able to change its values and formulas, select the **Add interactivity with** check box, and if necessary, change the functionality setting in the adjacent box.

- ■ To change the title, click the **Change** button to the right of **Title** in the **Publish as** area. Then type the title you want, and click **OK**.

- ■ To publish a new version of the Web page whenever a change is made to the workbook and saved, select the **AutoRepublish every time this workbook is saved** check box.

- ■ To open the file in your Web browser, select the **Open published web page in browser** check box.

7   If the path in the **File name** box does not reflect the folder where the Web page must be stored to be available to other people, click the **Browse** button, navigate to the folder, and click **OK**.

8   Click **Publish**.

To use an interactive Web worksheet:

1   Display the Web page in your browser.

2   Do any of the following:

- ■ Change any cell entry and/or add new entries, including formulas.

- ■ Sort entries in ascending or descending order.

- ■ Filter column entries.

- ■ Change the formatting of the worksheet.

3   Close your Web browser.

Practice Exercise

In this exercise, you will save a workbook as a Web page with interactivity and a new title.

USE the *SaveWeb* workbook in the *My Documents\Microsoft Press\MOS 2003 Study Guide\Excel\E03E-4-3* practice file folder.

Open the *SaveWeb* workbook. Publish the current worksheet as a Web page, adding interactivity with spreadsheet functionality, specifying that the published page will be opened in a Web browser, and changing the page title to **Sales Figures** and the file name to **Sales**. Click the **Browse** button, and for practice, change the path to point to the *My Documents \Microsoft Press\MOS 2003 Study Guide\Excel\E03E-4-3* practice file folder. Click **Publish**, and when the Web page opens in your browser, test the worksheet's interactivity by experimenting with the buttons in the toolbar above the data. When you have finished, close your Web browser, and then close the *SaveWeb* workbook without saving it.

Create and Edit Templates

E03E-4-4   The skills measured by this objective include the following:

- ■ Saving and using a custom workbook template
- ■ Editing a workbook template

When you have spent some time creating a workbook, you can always save it with a different name and plug in new values to create a different workbook. However, an even easier way to reuse workbooks is to create a template.

Saving and Using a Custom Workbook Template

You can save any workbook as a template—a pattern that includes the structure, formatting, and other constant elements to be included in a particular type of workbook. If you want your templates to be available in the Templates dialog box that appears when you click "On my computer" in the New Workbook task pane, you need to save them in the default folder.

See Also   For information about changing the default template location, refer to E03E-5-4, "Modify Excel Default Settings."

After you have saved a custom template, you can use it as the basis for new workbooks in the same way you would a built-in template.

BE SURE TO open the workbook you want to save as a template before carrying out these steps.

To save a template:

1   Remove any information that is specific to this workbook and not applicable to other workbooks you might create based on this template.

2   On the **File** menu, click **Save As**.

3   In the Save As dialog box, click **Save as type** down arrow, and click **Template** in the drop-down list.

4   In the **File Name** box, type the name you want for the template.

5   Click **Save**.

To create a workbook based on a template:

1   On the **File** menu, click **New**.

2   In the New Workbook task pane, click the **On my computer** link.

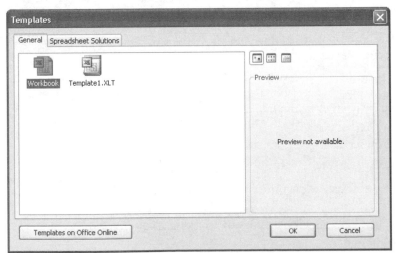

3 On the **General** tab, double-click the icon for the template on which you want to base the workbook.

Excel opens a new workbook that has all the content and formatting of the template. You can then save the workbook with its own file name.

Practice Exercise

In this exercise, you will save a workbook as a template in the default template location. You will then create a new workbook based on the template.

USE the *SaveTemplate* workbook in the *My Documents\Microsoft Press\MOS 2003 Study Guide\Excel \E03E-4-4* practice file folder.

Open the *SaveTemplate* workbook. Save the file on your computer as a template named **Sales** in the default *Templates* folder, and then close the template (don't quit Excel). Open a new workbook based on the **Sales** template. Close the new workbook without saving it.

Editing a Workbook Template

After you create a workbook template, it isn't cast in stone. You can change its content and formatting at any time and then save your changes so that they become part of the template.

BE SURE TO open a workbook based on the template you want to edit before carrying out these steps.

To edit a template:

1 Make the necessary changes to the active workbook.

2 On the **File** menu, click **Save As**.

3 In the Save As dialog box, click **Save as type** down arrow, and click **Template** in the drop-down list.

4 With the name of the existing template in the **File Name** box, click **Save**.

5 Click **Yes** when asked if you want to replace the existing file.

Practice Exercise

In this exercise, you will open a template and make changes to it.

USE the *EditTemplate* workbook template in the *My Documents\Microsoft Press\MOS 2003 Study Guide \Excel\E03E-4-4* practice file folder.

Open the *EditTemplate* workbook template (not a new workbook based on the template). On all four worksheets, change the fill color of cells **A5:B5** to light green, and the text in cell **A2** to red. Then close the *EditTemplate* workbook template without saving it.

Consolidate Data

E03E-4-5 The skills measured by this objective include the following:

■ Consolidating data from two or more worksheets

Often you will want to summarize the data in a worksheet in some way—for example, by totaling sets of entries. One way to create a summary is by using a technique called consolidation.

Consolidating Data from Two or More Worksheets

If you accumulate similar types of data in similar formats in several different worksheets, you can perform calculations across all the worksheets and put the results of the calculations in yet another worksheet, with links to the source data. Then if any of the source data changes, the summary changes too.

To consolidate data from more than one worksheet, the data in each of the source worksheets must be arranged in the same way. For example, if a workbook has four worksheets that record the sales per quarter for each of several products, the products must all appear in the same order starting in the same row of the same column on each worksheet.

Tip Because of these rigorous organizational requirements, it is a good idea to use a template when setting up worksheets that will be consolidated.

BE SURE TO open a workbook containing multiple similar worksheets before carrying out these steps.

To consolidate data from multiple worksheets:

1   Display the worksheet in which you want to summarize the data in the other worksheets, and set that worksheet up exactly the same way as the others.

2   Select the cell where you want the consolidated data to start.

3   On the **Data** menu, click **Consolidate**.

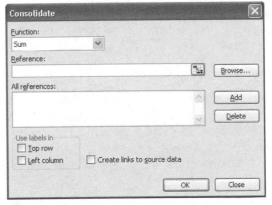

4   Click the **Function** down arrow, and click the function you want Excel to use for the summary calculation.

5   Click the **Collapse** button at the right end of the **Reference** box, click the first source worksheet, and click the cell or drag through the range you want to summarize.

6   Click the **Expand** button at the right end of the floating **Reference** box, and in the Consolidate dialog box, click **Add**.

An absolute reference to the worksheet and range you selected appears in the "All references" list box.

7   Repeat steps 5 and 6 for all the worksheets you want to include in the consolidation.

8   To maintain a link between the summary calculation and the source data, select the **Create links to source data** check box.

9 Click **OK** to close the dialog box and consolidate the data.

The results appear in outline format on the summary worksheet.

See Also For information about working with outlined data, refer to E03E-1-3, "Group and Outline Data."

Practice Exercise

In this exercise, you will export a worksheet's information as an XML data file.

USE the *ConsolidateData* workbook in the *My Documents\Microsoft Press\MOS 2003 Study Guide\Excel \E03E-4-5* practice file folder.

Open the *ConsolidateData* workbook. Activate the **Total** worksheet, click cell **B6**, and display the Consolidate dialog box. Select the **Sum** function, and specify that you want to consolidate the data in **B6:B14** on all four quarter worksheets. Create a link to the source data. After Excel calculates totals for all the products for the entire year, change the value in cell **B6** on the **1st Qtr** worksheet to **$100,331.30**. After observing the effect on the cell **B6** in the **Total** worksheet, close the *ConsolidateData* workbook without saving it.

Define and Modify Workbook Properties

E03E-4-6   The skills measured by this objective include the following:

■ Viewing and changing workbook properties

Excel stores information about each document as a set of properties. You can view all of this information, and you can change some of it.

Viewing and Changing Workbook Properties

You can view summary information about any workbook by displaying its Properties dialog box. Of the five tabs in this dialog box, you are likely to use the Summary tab most frequently. This tab displays information you can enter and change to identify the workbook in any way that is meaningful to you. For example, you can enter a title, subject, and author, as well as the category the workbook has been assigned to and any relevant keywords or comments.

You don't have to open a workbook and display its Properties dialog box to see its description. The author, title, subject, first few characters of any comment entered on the Summary tab of the Properties dialog box is displayed in a ScreenTip when you point to the workbook in My Computer or Windows Explorer. (The file type, the date the file was last modified, and its size are also displayed.) If you have many workbooks stored on your computer, this information can help you find the one you need.

BE SURE TO open the workbook you want to work with before carrying out these steps.

To review and change summary information:

1 On the **File** menu, click **Properties**.

The General tab of the Properties dialog box appears. This tab displays information generated by Excel, such as the workbook's file name, location, and size; and the dates of creation, modification, and last access. You cannot change this information.

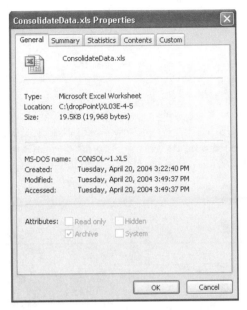

2 Click the **Summary** tab.

The Summary tab of the Properties dialog box displays information you can change.

3 Make any necessary adjustments to the title, subject, author, or comments.

4 Click **OK** to close the Properties dialog box.

See Also For information about assigning categories, keywords, and a hyperlink base, refer to W03E-4-6, "Customize Document Properties."

Practice Exercise

In this exercise, you will open a workbook's Properties dialog box and review and change some of its summary information.

USE the *ReviewSummary* workbook in the *My Documents\Microsoft Press\MOS 2003 Study Guide\Excel \E03E-4-6* practice file folder.

Open the *ReviewSummary* workbook, and then open its Properties dialog box. Read the information on the **General** tab, and then click the **Summary** tab. In the **Subject** box, type **Average Profit Margin**, and in the **Comments** box, type **Average profit margin for all products**. Close the Properties dialog box, and then close the *ReviewSummary* workbook without saving it.

E03E-4 Review

Number	Objective	Mastered
E03E-4-1	Import data to Excel	
	Importing data from an external data source	❏
	Importing data from a Web page	❏
E03E-4-2	Export data from Excel	
	Exporting an XML data file	❏
E03E-4-3	Publish and edit Web worksheets and workbooks	
	Publishing a worksheet as a Web page	❏
E03E-4-4	Create and edit templates	
	Saving and using a custom workbook template	❏
	Editing a workbook template	❏
E03E-4-5	Consolidate data	
	Consolidating data from two or more worksheets	❏
E03E-4-6	Define and modify workbook properties	
	Viewing and changing workbook properties	❏

E03E-5

Customizing Excel

The skills tested by this section of the Microsoft Office Specialist Excel 2003 Expert Exam all relate to ways that you can tailor Excel to make your working environment efficient and productive. Specifically, the following objectives are associated with this set of skills:

Number	Objective
E03E-5-1	Customize toolbars and menus
E03E-5-2	Create, edit, and run macros
E03E-5-3	Modify Excel default settings

 Important   Before you can do the practice exercises associated with this skill set, you need to install the practice files from the book's companion CD to their default location. See "Installing the Practice Files" on page xxv for more information.

Customize Toolbars and Menus

E03E-5-1   The skills measured by this objective include the following:

- Customizing a toolbar
- Creating a custom menu

You might find that you use some toolbar buttons and menu commands frequently, and others almost never. Or you might need to create a custom toolbar or menu for a specific task. You can customize Excel's menus and toolbars to better suit the way you work.

Customizing a Toolbar

By default, the Standard and Formatting toolbars appear on one row at the top of the screen. When they occupy just one row, Excel arranges the toolbars to show only the buttons you use most often. To see all buttons on a toolbar, you can click the Toolbar Options button at the right end of a toolbar.

Tip   To switch between displaying toolbars on one row and two rows, click the Toolbar Options button, and then click "Show Buttons on One Row" or "Show Buttons on Two Rows."

You can customize toolbars by adding, removing, and arranging buttons. You can also use the Customize dialog box to create a custom toolbar that displays the buttons you use most frequently. By using a custom toolbar, you can avoid having to jump between multiple menus or toolbars to complete your work.

BE SURE TO start Excel before carrying out these steps.

To display the Standard and Formatting toolbars on two rows:

Toolbar
Options

1 Click the **Toolbar Options** button of either toolbar.

2 Click **Show Buttons on Two Rows**.

3 To return to one row, repeat steps 1 and 2, clicking **Show Buttons on One Row**.

To display or hide toolbar buttons:

Toolbar
Options

1 Display the toolbar you want to customize.

2 At the right end of the toolbar, click the **Toolbar Options** button.

3 Click **Add or Remove Buttons**, and then click the toolbar's name.

Excel displays a submenu of all the buttons assigned to that toolbar. (The checked buttons are currently displayed on the toolbar.)

4 Do one of the following:

- Select the check boxes of any buttons you want to display.

- Clear the check boxes of any buttons you want to hide.

5 Click away from the submenu.

The menu closes, and the toolbar is updated to reflect your changes.

To reset toolbar buttons:

Toolbar
Options

1 At the right end of the toolbar, click the **Toolbar Options** button.

2 Click **Add or Remove Buttons**, and then click the toolbar's name.

3 On the submenu, click **Reset Toolbar**.

The toolbar is restored to its default settings.

To create a custom toolbar:

1 Right-click any toolbar, click **Customize** on the shortcut menu, and click the **Toolbars** tab.

2 Click **New**.

New Toolbar
Toolbar name:
Custom 1
OK   Cancel

3 In the **Toolbar name** box, type a unique name for this toolbar, and then click **OK**.

A small, empty, floating toolbar appears next to the Customize dialog box.

4 In the Customize dialog box, click the **Commands** tab.

5 In the **Commands** list, click the command you want, and drag it to the new toolbar.

Tip You can also use this technique to add buttons to Excel's built-in toolbars.

6   Continue adding command buttons to the new toolbar.

7   Click **Close** to close the Customize dialog box.

To delete a custom toolbar:

1   Right-click any toolbar, and click **Customize** on the shortcut menu to open the Customize dialog box, and then click the **Toolbars** tab.

2   Scroll down the **Toolbars** list, click the toolbar you want to delete, and click **Delete**.

3   Click **OK** to confirm the deletion, and then click **Close** to close the Customize dialog box.

Practice Exercise

In this exercise, you will display and hide buttons on the Standard toolbar, and then restore the Standard toolbar to its default settings. You will also create a custom toolbar, use its buttons to format a worksheet, and then delete it.

USE the *CustomizeToolbar* workbook in the *My Documents\Microsoft Press\MOS 2003 Study Guide\Excel \E03E-5-1* practice file folder.

Open the *CustomizeToolbar* workbook. Use the Standard toolbar's **Toolbar Options** button to hide the **Chart Wizard**, **Drawing**, and **Autosum** buttons. Then display the **PivotTable and PicotChart Report** button. Restore the Standard toolbar to its default settings, and then display the **Toolbars** tab of the Customize dialog box. Create a new toolbar called **CustomToolbar**. Then add the **Font Color**, **Font Size**, and **Borders** buttons from the **Commands** list for the **Format** category to the CustomToolbar toolbar. In the worksheet, select the **Lease vs. Purchase** heading, and use the **Borders** button to add a thick box border around it. Display the **Toolbars** tab of the Customize dialog box, delete the **CustomToolbar** toolbar, and confirm the deletion. Close the *CustomizeToolbar* workbook without saving it.

Creating a Custom Menu

If you want to control which commands appear on which menus, you can customize any menu. You can remove commands you never use and add commands you use often. For specialized tasks, you can even create new menus that can be attached to a template or a specific workbook. For example, you might want to create a menu for a particular project and then delete it when you are finished.

BE SURE TO start Excel before carrying out these steps.

To create a custom menu:

1   On the **Tools** menu, click **Customize**, and then click the **Commands** tab if it's not already active.

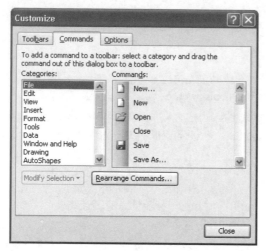

2　Scroll down to the end of the **Categories** list, and click **New Menu**.

The New Menu appears in the Commands list.

3　Drag **New Menu** from the **Commands** list to the desired position on the menu bar.

Tip　If you later want to change the position of a menu, you can hold down the ALT key while you drag the menu to a new location.

4　On the menu bar, right-click **New Menu**, and then in the **Name** box on the shortcut menu, select the words **New Menu**, type a more specific name, and press **ENTER**.

5　In the **Categories** list of the Customize dialog box, click the name of the menu whose commands you want to add to the new menu.

6　In the **Commands** list, click the command you want.

7　Drag the command up to the menu bar and over the new menu, and when an empty menu appears, drag the command onto the menu, and release the mouse button.

The command appears on the menu.

Tip　You can also use this technique to add commands to Excel's built-in menus.

8　Continue adding commands to the new menu.

9　Click **Close** to close the Customize dialog box.

To delete a custom menu:

1　Right-click any toolbar, and click **Customize** on the shortcut menu.

2　On Excel's menu bar, right-click the custom menu, and then click **Delete** on the shortcut menu.

Tip　You can also hold down the ALT key and drag the custom menu into the worksheet window.

3　Click **Close** to close the Customize dialog box.

To reset the menus:

1   On the **Tools** menu, click **Customize**, and then click the **Options** tab if it's not already active.

2   Click **Reset menu and toolbar usage data**, and then click **Yes**.

Excel resets your menus and toolbars to their default settings so that they appear the way they did when you first started the program.

3   Click **Close** to close the Customize dialog box.

Practice Exercise

In this exercise, you will add and delete commands on Excel's menus, create and delete a custom menu, and then restore the original menu settings.

USE the *CustomizeMenu* workbook in the *My Documents\Microsoft Press\MOS 2003 Study Guide\Excel \E03E-5-1* practice file folder.

Open the *CustomizeMenu* workbook. Display the **Commands** tab of the Customize dialog box, and then in the **Categories** list, click **Charting**. Drag **Column Chart** to the **Format** menu, position the command below *Style* at the bottom of the menu, and then click the menu's name to close it. Create a new menu, drag it to the right of the **Help** menu on the menu bar, and name it **CustomMenu**. In the Customize dialog box, display the **Format** commands, and drag **Distributed Align** onto the empty **CustomMenu** menu. Then drag **Vertically Distribute** onto the menu, positioning it below the *Distributed Align* command. Close the Customize dialog box. In the worksheet, click cell **A3**, and on the **CustomMenu** menu, click **Distributed Align** to distribute *Current lease per month* across the cell. Display the Customize dialog box, right-click the **CustomMenu** menu on the menu bar, and click **Delete** on the shortcut menu. Then reset the menus to their default settings, remove **Column Chart** from the **Format** menu, and close the *CustomizeMenu* workbook without saving it.

Create, Edit, and Run Macros

E03E-5-2   The skills measured by this objective include the following:

■ Creating, running, and deleting a macro

■ Editing a macro

To make repetitive tasks quick and easy, you can create a macro to perform a series of steps with a single click. You can also modify the macro as your needs change and delete the macro when you are finished with it.

Creating, Running, and Deleting a Macro

A macro is a series of commands (keystrokes and instructions) that you can repeat with a single command. You can use macros to automate many tasks in Excel, such as performing calculations, formatting text, and sorting and consolidating data. If you are familiar with Visual Basic for Applications, you can create a macro from scratch in the Visual Basic Editor, but you can also record a set of steps as a macro.

Macros are not separate files. They are attached to a particular workbook. However, if you associate a macro with the Personal Macro Workbook, they will be available whenever you use Excel. When you no longer need a macro, you can easily delete it.

Tip Macros can contain viruses—destructive computer programs that can destroy information on your computer. If you frequently run macros created by other people, you should purchase and install anti-virus software.

BE SURE TO display the worksheet from which you want to be able access the macro before carrying out these steps.

To record a macro:

1   Get ready to record the macro steps.

   For example, if you are going to insert an object, position the insertion point. Or if you are going to work with a text selection, select the text.

2   On the **Tools** menu, click **Macro** and then **Record New Macro**.

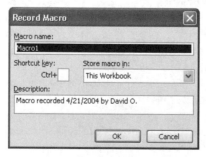

3   In the **Macro name** box, type a unique name for this macro.

4   If you want to be able to run the macro by pressing a key combination, enter an uppercase or lowercase letter in the **Shortcut key** box.

Tip   If you choose a key combination that is used for carrying out a command, the combination will run the macro instead.

5   If you want to store the macro with a workbook other than the open one, click the **Store macro in** down arrow, and make your selection.

6   Click **OK**.

Excel closes the dialog box and displays the Stop Recording toolbar, which has buttons that you can click to stop or pause the recording.

Relative
Reference

7   To be able to run the macro anywhere in a worksheet, click the **Relative Reference** button on the Stop Recording toolbar.

8   In the worksheet, perform the steps of the task for which you are recording the macro.

9   On the Stop Recording toolbar, click the **Stop Recording** button.

Stop
Recording

The macro stops recording, and the Stop Recording toolbar closes.

To run a macro:

●   Do one of the following:

■   Press the macro's keyboard shortcut.

■   On the **Tools** menu, click **Macro** and then **Macros** to display the Macro dialog box. Then in the list of macros, click the macro you want, and click **Run**.

If you cannot run a macro, your security level is probably set too high.

See Also   For information about changing the security level, refer to E03E-3-2, "Apply Workbook Security Settings."

To delete a macro:

1   On the **Tools** menu, click **Macro** and then **Macros.**

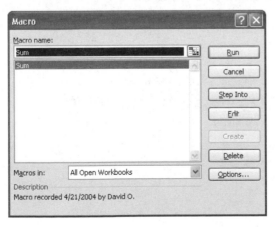

> **2** In the list of macros, click the macro you want to delete.
>
> **3** Click **Delete**, and when prompted to confirm that you want to delete the macro, click **Yes**.
>
> **4** Click **Close** to close the Macros dialog box.

Practice Exercise

In this exercise, you will create a macro that formats the basic elements of a letter, and then you'll run the macro.

USE the *RecordMacro* workbook in the *My Documents\Microsoft Press\MOS 2003 Study Guide\Excel \E03E-5-2* practice file folder.

> Open the *RecordMacro* workbook, and click cell **E19**. Display the Record Macro dialog box, name the new macro **Sum**, assign **CTRL+S** as the shortcut key, and store the macro in this workbook. Set the macro to record relative references. Then use the **AutoSum** button to total the amounts in the **Profit Margin** column. Stop recording the macro. Click cell **D19**, and use the macro's shortcut key to total the amounts in the **Amount of Sale** column. Delete the formulas inserted by the macro in **D19** and **E19**. Click **E19**, and record a new macro that uses relative references and calculates the average of the amounts in the **Profit Margin** column. Then run the macro in cell **D19** to calculate the average of the amounts in the **Amount of Sale** column. Close the *RecordMacro* workbook without saving it.

Editing a Macro

Sometimes a macro does not work as you expect, and you need to modify it. You can record the macro again to correct the problem. However, because macros are instructions written in Microsoft Visual Basic for Applications (VBA), you can edit the macro in the Visual Basic Editor.

Excel macros are stored in modules within a Visual Basic macro project that is stored in a workbook or template. To edit a macro, you display the Visual Basic Editor program window, click the module you want to work on, and make changes.

BE SURE TO display a worksheet from which you can access the macro you want to edit before carrying out these steps.

To edit a macro:

> **1** On the **Tools** menu, click **Macro** and then **Macros**.
>
> **2** In the list of macros, click the macro you want, and click **Edit**.
>
> The macro's instructions are displayed in the Visual Basic Editor code window.

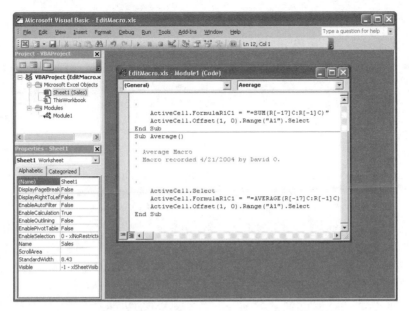

3 Scroll the window to find the section of code you want to edit.

4 Make the necessary changes.

> **Tip** As you type, the Visual Basic Editor displays a menu of possible commands. You can click a command on the menu instead of typing the entire command. For information about inserting and editing macro commands in the Visual Basic Editor or about creating macros that perform tasks that cannot be recorded, use the Help menu in the Visual Basic Editor window.

5 On the **File** menu, click **Close and Return to Microsoft Excel**.

The Visual Basic Editor closes, and the macro is saved with the change.

Practice Exercise

In this exercise, you will edit an existing macro to add character formatting.

USE the *ModifyMacro* workbook in the *My Documents\Microsoft Press\MOS 2003 Study Guide\Excel \E03E-5-2* practice file folder.

> With macro security set to **Medium**, open the *ModifyMacro* workbook, and click **Enable Macros** to display the workbook. Display the Macros dialog box, and open the *Headings* macro in the Visual Basic Editor code window. At the bottom of the ModifyMacro - Module 2 (Code) window, change the **ColorIndex** to **45**. Close the Visual Basic Editor, and when you return to Excel, click cell **A1**. Run the **Headings** macro, and then close the *ModifyMacro* workbook without saving it.

Modify Excel Default Settings

E03E-5-3   The skills measured by this objective include the following:

■ Changing the default number of worksheets, font settings, and file locations

Excel specifies certain default settings, but you can change many of these settings, including the default font settings, the default number of worksheets in a new workbook, and the default location where files are saved.

Changing the Default Number of Worksheets, Font Settings, and File Locations

When you open a new blank workbook, it contains three worksheets titled Sheet1, Sheet2, and Sheet3. If your workbooks usually contain one worksheet or five worksheets, you can change the default number so that you do not have to continually add or delete sheets.

If you make entries in a new workbook without formatting them, Excel makes the entries 10-point Arial. You might prefer to create most of your workbooks in a different font or size. Instead of manually adjusting settings in every workbook you create, you can simply change the default font and size to the setting you prefer.

By default, Excel saves workbooks in the *C:\Documents and Settings\[YourName]\My Documents* folder. If you keep workbooks in a different folder, you can easily change this location so that you don't have to navigate in the Save As dialog box every time you save a new workbook.

BE SURE TO open a workbook before carrying out these steps.

Tip   Before you modify any default setting, it is a good idea to make note of the original setting in case you want to restore it later.

To change Excel's default settings:

1   On the **Tools** menu, click **Options**, and then click the **General** tab.

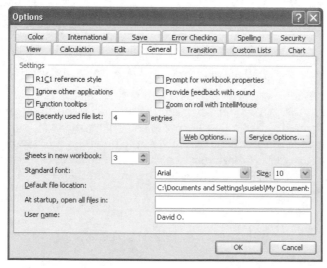

2   Do any of the following:

- Change the **Sheets in new workbook** setting to the number of sheets you want.
- Change the **Standard font** settings to the font and size you want.
- Change the **Default file location** setting to the folder you want to appear by default in the Save As dialog box.

3   Click **OK**.

4   When Excel tells you that you will need to quit and restart Excel for the new settings to take effect, click **OK**.

5   Quit Excel, restart the program, and test your new defaults with the new workbook.

Tip   In the "At startup, open all files in" box on the General tab of the Options dialog box, you can specify a folder. When you start Excel, the program automatically opens any files stored in this folder.

Practice Exercise

In this exercise, you will modify the default number of worksheets, the default font and size, and the default storage location for new Excel workbooks.

USE the *SetDefaults* workbook in the *My Documents\Microsoft Press\MOS 2003 Study Guide\Excel\E03E-5-3* practice file folder.

Open the *SetDefaults* workbook, and display the **General** tab of the Options dialog box. Change the number of sheets in a new workbook to **1**, and change the standard font to **Verdana** and **11**. Then click the **Default file location** box, press the **END** key, and append **\Microsoft Press\MOS 2003 Study Guide\Excel\E03E-5-3** to the existing entry. Instead of clicking OK to implement the new settings, click **Cancel** to leave the current settings intact. Then close the *SetDefaults* workbook without saving it.

E03E-5 Review

Number	Objective	Mastered
E03E-5-1	Customize toolbars and menus	
	Customizing a toolbar	❏
	Creating a custom menu	❏
E03E-5-2	Create, edit, and run macros	
	Creating, running, and deleting a macro	❏
	Editing a macro	❏
E03E-5-3	Modify Excel default settings	
	Changing the default number of worksheets, font settings, and file locations	❏

Part V

Microsoft Office Specialist PowerPoint 2003 Exam

This part of the book covers the skills you need to have for certification as a Microsoft Office Specialist in Microsoft Office PowerPoint 2003. Specifically, you will need to be able to complete tasks that require the following skills:

Number	Skill Set
P03C-1	Creating content
P03C-2	Formatting content
P03C-3	Collaborating
P03C-4	Managing and delivering presentations

You can use these basic skills to create the presentations most commonly used in a business environment.

Knowledge You Need Before Studying for This Exam

We assume that you have been working with PowerPoint for a while and that you know how to carry out fundamental tasks that are not specifically mentioned in the Microsoft Office Specialist objectives for PowerPoint 2003. Before you begin studying for this exam, you might want to scan this section to make sure you are familiar with this information.

Understanding PowerPoint's Normal View

You will do most of the content development work for your presentations in Normal view. In this view, the program window is divided into three panes.

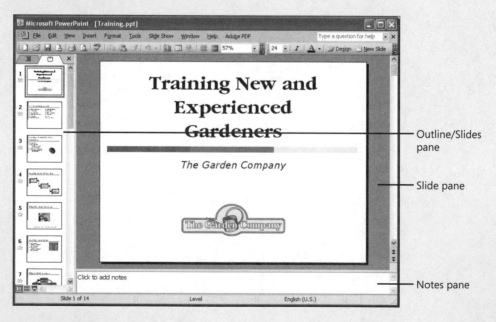

You perform different tasks in different panes, so make sure you are familiar with them before proceeding.

See Also   For information about other PowerPoint views, refer to P03C-4-1, "Organize a Presentation."

Selecting in PowerPoint

Before you can edit or format existing text, you have to select it. Selected text appears highlighted on the screen. You can select specific items as follows:

- To select a word, double-click it. The word and the space following it are selected. Punctuation following a word is not selected.
- To select all the text on a slide, click its slide icon on the Outline tab of the Outline/Slides pane.
- To select a bullet point, click its bullet on either the Outline tab of the Outline/Slides pane or in the Slide pane.

You can select adjacent words, lines, or paragraphs by dragging through them. Or you can position the insertion point at the beginning of the text you want to select, and hold down the SHIFT key. Then either press an arrow key to select the characters one at a time or click at the end of the text that you want to select to select a whole word or section.

In the Slide pane, the text is displayed in a text object. (An object is a discrete element of a slide that can be positioned and sized independently of other objects.) Before you can manipulate a text object, you first need to select it in one of two ways:

- Clicking anywhere in a text object displays a slanted-line selection box around the object. You can then add new text, or delete or edit existing text.

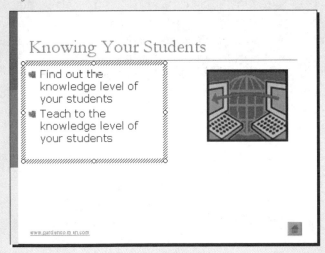

■ Clicking the edge of a slanted-line selection box selects the entire object and displays a dotted selection box around the object. You can then manipulate the object as a unit—for example, you can move the text object or delete it.

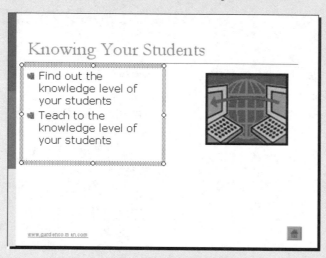

To deselect a text object, you click a blank area of the slide.

Moving Around a Presentation

When developing a presentation in Normal view, you can move around in several ways:

■ On the Outline tab of the Outline/Slides pane, you can click a slide icon to display that slide in the Slides pane.

■ On the Slides tab of the Outline/Slides pane, you can click any slide to display it in the Slides pane.

■ At the bottom of the vertical scroll bar to the right of the Slide pane, you can click the Previous Slide or Next Slide buttons to move backward or forward one slide at a time. (Clicking the up or down scroll arrow has the same effect).

■ You can drag the scroll box on the vertical scroll bar to move to a different slide in a presentation. As you drag, a ScreenTip tells you which slide will be displayed if you release the mouse button.

P03C-1

Creating Content

The skills tested by this section of the Microsoft Office Specialist PowerPoint 2003 Exam all relate to the creating of presentations and their contents. Specifically, the following objectives are associated with this set of skills:

Number	Objective
P03C-1-1	Create new presentations from templates
P03C-1-2	Insert and edit text-based content
P03C-1-3	Insert tables, charts, and diagrams
P03C-1-4	Insert pictures, shapes, and graphics
P03C-1-5	Insert objects

 Important Before you can do the practice exercises associated with this skill set, you need to install the practice files from the book's companion CD to their default location. See "Installing the Practice Files" on page xxv for more information.

Create New Presentations from Templates

P03C-1-1   The skills measured by this objective include the following:

- Creating a presentation by using the AutoContent Wizard
- Creating a presentation by using a design template

You create new presentations by using the New Presentation task pane, where you can choose from five different methods: creating a blank presentation, using one of Power-Point's built-in design templates, using the AutoContent Wizard, using an existing presentation, and creating an electronic photo album.

Creating a Presentation by Using the AutoContent Wizard

When you want to create a new presentation, the AutoContent Wizard can save time by helping you organize and write the presentation's text. The wizard steps you through the process, prompting you for information. The result is a presentation with placeholders for the points you might want to cover in that type of presentation. You can then modify the presentation.

BE SURE TO start PowerPoint and display the New Presentation task pane before carrying out these steps.

To create a presentation by using a wizard:

1   In the New Presentation task pane, click **From AutoContent Wizard**.

The AutoContent Wizard displays its Start page. On the left side of the page is a "roadmap" of the pages with the active page indicated by a green box.

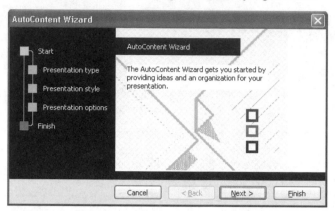

2 Read the introduction, and click **Next**.

To help you identify presentation types quickly, the wizard organizes presentations by category.

3 Click the button for the presentation type you want.

Presentations in that category appear in the list on the right side of the page.

4 Click the specific type of presentation you want, and click **Next**.

The wizard prompts you to specify how you will display the presentation.

5 Select the option for the type of presentation display you want, and click **Next**.

The wizard prompts you to enter information for the title slide and for footer information to be included on each slide.

See Also For information about footers, refer to P03C-2-7, "Work with Masters."

6 Click the **Presentation title** text box, type the title of the presentation, and press the **TAB** key to move the insertion point to the **Footer** box.

7 In the **Footer** box, type the information you want to appear at the bottom of each slide.

8 Depending on whether you want to display the date and slide number on each slide, select or clear the **Date last updated** and **Slide number** check boxes.

9 Click **Finish**.

The PowerPoint presentation window appears in Normal view with content inserted by the wizard in outline form in the Outline/Slides pane and the title slide in the Slide pane. The name on the title slide is the name of the registered PowerPoint user.

10 Save the presentation.

See Also For information about saving presentations, refer to P03C-4-6, "Save and Publish Presentations."

Practice Exercise

In this exercise, you will create a presentation by using the AutoContent Wizard.

NO practice file is required for this exercise.

Display the New Presentation task pane, and click **From AutoContent wizard**. Read the introduction, and then click **Next**. Work your way through the wizard's pages, selecting the **Sales/Marketing** category, the **Product/Services Overview** presentation, and the **On-screen presentation** option. Enter Training Classes as the presentation's title and **The Garden Company** as the footer. Hide the date but display the slide number on each slide. Click **Finish,** and save the presentation as **CreateAutoContent** in the *My Documents \Microsoft Press\MOS 2003 Study Guide\PowerPoint\P03C-1-1* folder. Then close the *CreateAutoContent* presentation.

Creating a Presentation by Using a Design Template

When you don't need help with the content of a presentation but do need help with its design, you can start a new presentation, without any sample text, based on a design template. A design template is a blank presentation with a professionally designed format and color scheme to which you can add slides with the layout you want, such as a slide with a graph. You then type text and add any other desired elements.

BE SURE TO start PowerPoint and display the New Presentation task pane before carrying out these steps.

To create a presentation by using a template:

1   In the New Presentation task pane, click **From design template**.

A blank presentation opens, and the Slide Design task pane appears, showing thumbnails of a variety of design templates.

Tip   PowerPoint can display design thumbnails in two sizes. To change the size of the thumbnails, point to any thumbnail, click its down arrow, and on the drop-down menu that appears, click Show Large Previews to toggle large thumbnails on or off.

2   In the Slide Design task pane, click the design you want to apply to the new slide.

A title slide with the chosen design appears in the Slide pane.

3   At the right end of the task pane's title bar, click the **Other Task Panes** down arrow, and then click **Slide Layout**.

The Slide Layout task pane appears, with thumbnails of layouts you can apply to the slide.

4   In the **Text Layouts** area, click the thumbnail of the layout you want to apply.

PowerPoint applies the layout to the selected slide.

5   On the Formatting toolbar, click the **New Slide** button, and then in the **Text Layouts** area of the Slide Layout task pane, click a the layout you want for this slide.

6   Continue adding the slides you need to the presentation.

7   Save the presentation.

See Also   For information about saving presentations, refer to P03C-4-6, "Save and Publish Presentations."

Practice Exercise

In this exercise, you will create a presentation by using a design template.

NO practice file is required for this exercise.

Display the New Presentation task pane, and click **From design template**. If the Slide Design task pane displays small thumbnails, switch to large thumbnails to make it easier to see the designs. Scroll down the Slide Design task pane until you see the Maple design, and display a title slide with the Maple design in the Slide pane. Display the Slide Layout task pane, and change the slide to the **Title Only** layout. Add a new slide to the presentation, and change the slide to the **Title and Content** layout. Save the presentation in the *My Documents \Microsoft Press\MOS 2003 Study Guide\PowerPoint\P03C-1-1* folder with the name **CreateDesignTemplate**. Then close the *CreateDesignTemplate* presentation.

Insert and Edit Text-Based Content

P03C-1-2   The skills measured by this objective include the following:

- Adding and editing text
- Changing the hierarchical level of text
- Importing text from other sources
- Checking spelling and style
- Using the Thesaurus to find the best word

PowerPoint offers a variety of ways for you to insert text in slides. You can add titles, subtitles, and bulleted lists to existing text placeholders or import text from other sources, such as Microsoft Word. When you finish adding your text, you can edit it, check its spelling, or get suggestions on word usage.

Adding and Editing Text

A typical slide contains a title and a list of items, called bullet points. Items called subpoints might be indented below the bullet points. You can add and edit all these types of text either in the Slide pane or on the Outline tab of the Outline/Slides pane. As you type, the text appears in both places.

To edit existing text, you select the text you want to work with and then use standard editing techniques. For example, to delete text, you select it and press either the DELETE key or the BACKSPACE key. To replace text, you select it and type the new text.

See Also   For information about selecting text and objects on PowerPoint slides, refer to "Knowledge You Need Before Studying for This Exam" on page 424.

BE SURE TO open the presentation you want to work with in Normal view before carrying out these steps.

To add a title and subtitle to a new title slide in the Slide pane:

1   Click the **Click to add title** text placeholder.

A selection box surrounds the placeholder, and a blinking insertion point appears in the box.

2   Type the title you want.

The title also appears on the Outline tab of the Outline/Slides pane.

3   Click the **Click to add subtitle** text placeholder.

The title text object is deselected, and the subtitle object is selected.

4   Type the subtitle text you want.

To add a title to a new slide on the Outline tab:

1   Click to the right of the icon for the slide to which you want to add a title.

The slide icon is selected in the outline, and the blinking insertion point indicates where the text you type will appear.

2   Type the text you want.

The text appears both on the Outline tab and as the title of the slide in the Slide pane.

See Also   You cannot add text other than titles on the Outline tab without knowing how to change the hierarchical level of the text. Refer to the next section, "Changing the Hierarchical Level of Text."

To add text to a new bullet point slide in the Slide pane:

1   Click the **Click to add title** text placeholder.

A selection box surrounds the placeholder, and a blinking insertion point appears in the box.

2   Type the title you want.

Tip   If the slide is empty, you can also simply start typing. When you start typing without first selecting a placeholder, PowerPoint enters the text into the title text object.

The text appears both in the Slide pane and on the Outline tab.

3   Click the bullet point text object, type the text you want, and press **ENTER**.

PowerPoint adds a new bullet point at the same level. (Its bullet will change color when you add text.)

4   Type any additional bullet points you want, pressing **ENTER** after all but the last one.

To select and replace a title or part of a bullet point:

1   Either in the Slide pane or on the **Outline** tab, drag across the text you want to replace.

2   Type the new text.

What you type replaces the selection.

Tip   If you make a mistake while typing, press BACKSPACE to delete the error and then type the correction.

To select and replace an entire bullet point:

1   Click anywhere in the bulleted list, point to the bullet, and when the pointer changes to a four-headed arrow, click once to select the entire bullet point.

2   Type the new bullet point text.

To break one bullet point into two:

1 Click the bullet point where you want to break it apart.

2 Press the **ENTER** key.

PowerPoint breaks the bullet point at the insertion point, preceding the second part with a new bullet.

3 Edit the two parts as necessary to correct capitalization and punctuation.

To delete a bullet point:

1 Click a bullet to select the text of the bullet point.

2 Press the **DELETE** key.

Practice Exercises

In this exercise, you will add text to slides.

USE the *EnterText* and *EditText* presentations in the *My Documents\Microsoft Press\MOS 2003 Study Guide \PowerPoint\P03C-1-2* practice file folder.

Open the *EnterText* presentation. In the Slide pane, enter **How to Transplant a Tree** as the slide's title. Then enter **Karen Berg** as the subtitle, press **ENTER**, and type **The Garden Company**. Add a new slide, and without clicking anywhere, type **Overview**. On the **Outline** tab, click to the right of Slide 2's title, press **ENTER** to add a new slide, and type **First Steps**. In the Slide pane, click the bullet on Slide 3, type **Choose the right time to transplant**, and press **ENTER**. Type **Prepare the soil**, and press **ENTER**. Type **Prepare the roots**, and press **ENTER**. Then close the *EnterText* presentation without saving it.

Open the *EditText* presentation. On the **Outline** tab, click Slide 4's icon to select the slide, and press the **DELETE** key. Then, working either in the Slide pane or on the **Outline** tab, select the title of Slide 2, and replace it with **Customer Training Classes**. Select the first bullet point on Slide 2, and type **Create gardening classes for customers to instill confidence in their ability to perform projects on their own and promote products to help the customer get the job done right** (no period). Click the second bullet on Slide 2, and type **Create training classes for instructors who will teach the gardening classes** (again, no period). In the first bullet point on Slide 2, click to the right of the word *customers*, and press **ENTER** to break the bullet point into two. Then delete *to*, and change *instill* to **Instill**. Click at the right end of the word *own*, press **ENTER**, delete *and*, and change *promote* to **Promote**. Add **Class** to the beginning of Slide 3's title. Replace the text of the first bullet point with **Hands-on training** (no period). Click the second bullet, type **Step-by-step instruction**, and then press **ENTER** to create a new bullet. Type **Full-color handouts**. Select the text of the next bullet point, and delete it. Delete the last bullet point, and then press **BACKSPACE** twice to remove the gray bullet. Close the *EditText* presentation without saving it.

Changing the Hierarchical Level of Text

The hierarchical level of the text on a slide is easy to see on the Outline tab, where bullet points are indented below titles and subpoints are indented below bullet points. If you want to change the hierarchical level of text, you do so by increasing (demoting) or decreasing (promoting) its indent level. Demoting a slide title makes it a bullet point on the previous slide, and demoting a bullet point makes it a subpoint. Promoting a bullet point makes it a slide title, and promoting a subpoint makes it a bullet point.

BE SURE TO open the presentation you want to work with in Normal view and display the Outlining toolbar before carrying out these steps.

To promote or demote text by clicking toolbar buttons as you enter the text:

1 On the **Outline** tab of the Outline/Slides pane, click to the right of the icon for the slide to which you want to add text.

The slide icon is selected in the outline and the blinking insertion point indicates where the text you type will appear.

2 Type the title you want, press **ENTER**, and then press **TAB**.

PowerPoint adds another slide.

Demote

3 On the Outlining toolbar, click the **Demote** button.

The slide changes to a bullet point.

4 Type the first bullet point, and press **ENTER**.

PowerPoint adds a second bullet point at the same level.

5 On the Outlining toolbar, click the **Demote** button.

The bullet point changes to a subpoint.

6 Type the text you want, and press **ENTER**.

PowerPoint adds a new subpoint at the same level.

Promote

7 On the Outlining toolbar, click the **Promote** button.

PowerPoint changes the subpoint to a bullet point.

8 Type the text you want, and press **ENTER**.

9 On the Outlining toolbar, click the **Promote** button again.

PowerPoint changes the bullet point to the title of a new slide.

10 Type any additional titles, bullet points, or subpoints, pressing **ENTER** and clicking the **Demote** or **Promote** button as necessary to create the levels you want.

To promote or demote text by pressing keys as you enter the text:

1 Do one of the following:

■ In the Slide pane, click the bullet point text object, type the text you want, and press **ENTER**.

■ On the **Outline** tab, click to the right of a bullet point, press **ENTER**, type a bullet point, and press **ENTER** again.

PowerPoint adds a new bullet point at the same level.

433

2　Press the **TAB** key.

The bullet point changes to a subpoint.

3　Type the text you want, and press **ENTER**.

PowerPoint adds a new subpoint at the same level.

4　Press **SHIFT+TAB**.

PowerPoint changes the subpoint to a bullet point.

5　Type the text you want, and press **ENTER**.

6　Press **SHIFT+TAB** again.

PowerPoint changes the bullet point to the title of a new slide.

Tip　Instead of pressing ENTER and then pressing SHIFT+TAB, you can press CTRL+ENTER to create a new slide instead of another bullet.

7　Type any additional titles, bullet points, or subpoints, pressing **ENTER**, **TAB**, and **SHIFT+TAB** as necessary to create the levels you want.

To promote and demote existing text:

1　Click anywhere in the text that you want to demote or promote.

2　To demote the text, click the **Demote** button on the Outlining toolbar, or press **TAB**.

Demote

3　To promote the text, click the **Promote** button on the Outlining toolbar, or press **SHIFT+TAB**.

Promote

Practice Exercise

In this exercise, you will adjust the hierarchical level of text by pressing keys as you enter the text.

USE the *ChangeLevel* presentation in the *My Documents\Microsoft Press\MOS 2003 Study Guide \PowerPoint\P03C-1-2* practice file folder.

Open the *ChangeLevel* presentation, and move to Slide 2. On the **Outline** tab, click to the right of *Prepare the roots*, and press **ENTER**. Type **Transporting the Tree**, and press **SHIFT+TAB** to turn the bullet point into a new slide. Type **Be gentle** as the first bullet for Slide 3, and then press **ENTER**. Type **Go slowly**, press **ENTER**, and then type **Take extra care**. Press **CTRL+ENTER** to create a new slide instead of another bullet. Type **Summary**. Type **Create a plan** as the first bullet, and press **ENTER**. Type **Take your time**, and press **ENTER**. Type **Enjoy the results**. Then close the *ChangeLevel* presentation without saving it.

Importing Text from Other Sources

You can insert text from another program into a PowerPoint presentation. The text can be in Microsoft Word format (*.doc*), RTF (Rich Text Format—*.rtf*), or plain text (*.txt*). You can also insert a Web document in HTML (Hypertext Markup Language—*.htm* or *.html*) into a presentation. When you import a Word or RTF document, PowerPoint creates an outline of slide titles and bullet points based on heading styles in the inserted document. When you insert a plain text document, paragraphs not preceded by tabs become slide titles, and paragraphs preceded by tabs become bullet points. When you insert an HTML document, it appears in a text box on the slide.

You can also start a new presentation from a Word outline by simply opening the outline in PowerPoint.

BE SURE TO open the presentation you want to work with in Normal view before carrying out these steps.

To insert a Word outline in a presentation:

1   On the **Outline** tab, click the slide or bullet point before which you want to insert the outline.

2   On the **Insert** menu, click **Slides from Outline** (not Slides from Files).

3   Navigate to the folder that contains the Microsoft Word document you want to insert, click the name of the file, and then click **Insert**.

PowerPoint inserts the Word outline into the presentation.

Tip   If a message tells you that you need to install a converter, insert the Microsoft Office 2003 installation CD-ROM, and click OK.

To open a Word outline in PowerPoint:

Open

1   On the Standard toolbar, click the **Open** button.

2   Move to the folder containing the Word outline you want to open.

3   Click the **Files of type** down arrow, and click **All Files**.

4   Double-click the outline file you want to use.

PowerPoint opens a new presentation with the outline's main headings as slide titles, secondary headings as bullet points, and so on.

Practice Exercise

In this exercise, you will import text from a Microsoft Word outline.

USE the *InsertOutline* presentation and the *Outline* file in the *My Documents\Microsoft Press\MOS 2003 Study Guide\PowerPoint\P03C-1-2* practice file folder.

Open the *InsertOutline* presentation. On the **Outline** tab, click to the right of the *Full color handouts* bullet point on Slide 3. Display the Insert Outline dialog box, navigate to the *My Documents\Microsoft Press\MOS 2003 Study Guide\PowerPoint\P03C-1-2* practice file folder, and insert the *Outline* file. Deselect the text, and scroll down to see Slides 4 through 7. Close the *InsertOutline* presentation without saving it.

Checking Spelling and Style

By default, PowerPoint's spelling checker checks the spelling of the entire presentation against its built-in dictionary and marks words that are not in its dictionary with a wavy red underline. You can use two different methods to ensure that the words in your presentations are spelled correctly:

- When you see a wavy red line under a word, you can right-click the word and choose the correct spelling from the shortcut menu, or tell PowerPoint to ignore the word.

- You can tell PowerPoint to check the entire presentation. PowerPoint displays a dialog box if it encounters a word that is not in its dictionary, and you can then decide how to deal with the word.

You can also have PowerPoint check for violations of style rules, such as the number of fonts or bullet points allowed on a slide, the capitalization or punctuation, or the font sizes that can be used.

BE SURE TO open the presentation you want to work with in Normal view before carrying out these steps.

To correct a word that PowerPoint flags as misspelled:

1   Right-click any word with a wavy red underline.

2   In the drop-down list, click the correct spelling of the word.

To check the spelling of an entire presentation:

Spelling

1   Display Slide 1, and on the Standard toolbar, click the **Spelling** button.

PowerPoint begins checking the spelling in the presentation, displaying the Spelling dialog box with suggested alternatives if it encounters a word that is not in its dictionaries.

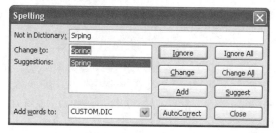

2   Do one of the following:

- If the word is misspelled, click one of PowerPoint's suggested alternatives, or type the correct spelling, and click **Change** or **Change All**.

- If the word is correct and you use it often, click **Add** to add the word to the supplemental dictionary.

- If the word is correct and you don't use it often, click **Ignore** or **Ignore All** to take no action.

3   When PowerPoint finishes the spelling check, click **OK**.

To check the style of a presentation:

1   On the **Tools** menu, click **Options**, and then click the **Spelling and Style** tab.

2   Select the **Check style** check box, click **Enable Assistant** if asked to enable the Office Assistant, and then click **Style Options** to display the Style Options dialog box.

3   On the **Case and End Punctuation** tab, enter your preferences for capitalization and punctuation at the end of titles and paragraphs.

4   On the **Visual Clarity** tab, set limits for the number and size of fonts, the maximum number of bullets, and the maximum number of lines for titles and bullets.

5   Close the Style Options dialog box, and then close the Options dialog box by clicking **OK**.

6   To check a slide's style, click its text or select an object. If the slide does not follow the style rules, a yellow light bulb appears on the slide's left side. Double-click it to have the Office Assistant give you the option to change the text on the slide, ignore the style rule for this presentation, or change the style checking options for all presentations.

7   Continue double-clicking yellow light bulbs until you have finished checking the slide's style.

Practice Exercise

In these exercises, you will check a presentation's spelling.

USE the *CheckSpelling* presentation in the *My Documents\Microsoft Press\MOS 2003 Study Guide\PowerPoint \P03C-1-2* practice file folder.

Open the *CheckSpelling* presentation. Move to Slide 2, and right-click the word **arrangement**. Click **arrangement** in the list to replace the misspelled word. Move to Slide 1, and start the spelling checker. Click **Change** to correct the word *Maintanance*, and then click **Change** again to correct the word *Bouquays*. Add *TGCGardenersOnly* to the dictionary. On the **Tools** menu, click **Options**, and then click the **Spelling and Style** tab. Change the style options so

437

that PowerPoint will check for inconsistent punctuation in the presentation, and then display all the slides in turn, clicking each one. If a yellow light bulb appears on a slide, click it for a suggestion from the Office Assistant about consistent style, accepting or rejecting the suggestions as appropriate. Close the *CheckSpelling* presentation without saving it, and turn off the **Check style** option.

Using the Thesaurus to Find the Best Word

Language is often contextual—the language you use in a presentation to club members is different from the language you use in a business presentation. To make sure you are using words that best convey your meaning, you can use PowerPoint's Thesaurus to look up alternative words, or synonyms, for a selected word. To use the Thesaurus, you select the word you want to look up, and on the Tools menu, click Thesaurus. The Research task pane appears, displaying a list of synonyms with equivalent meanings.

BE SURE TO open the presentation you want to work with in Normal view before carrying out these steps.

To find and substitute a synonym:

1 Double-click a word for which you want to view synonyms.

2 On the **Tools** menu, click **Thesaurus**.

The Research task pane appears, listing synonyms for the word.

3 If you find a synonym that you want to use, point to it, click the down arrow that appears to its right, and on the drop-down menu, click **Insert**.

4 If you want to look up a word that appears on the menu, click or double-click it.

Practice Exercise

In this exercise, you will find a synonym for a word in a presentation by using the Thesaurus.

USE the *FindWord* presentation in the *My Documents\Microsoft Press\MOS 2003 Study Guide\PowerPoint \P03C-1-2* practice file folder.

Open the *FindWord* presentation. Move to **Slide 2**, and double-click the word **Comfortable** in the title. Use the Thesaurus to find and substitute the word *Relaxed*. Close the *FindWord* presentation without saving it.

Insert Tables, Charts, and Diagrams

P03C-1-3   The skills measured by this objective include the following:

■ Creating tables

■ Creating charts

■ Creating diagrams

PowerPoint includes several ways to present data in organized formats. You can use tables to display general data in a structured format, charts to display visual representations numerical data, and diagrams to show the hierarchical structure of a company or other organization. To insert a table, chart, or diagram, first add a slide that includes a content layout. Then click the icon for the content you want to add. After the object is in place, you can customize and format it to display the data exactly the way you want it to appear.

Creating Tables

To present a lot of data in an organized and readable format, a table is often best. After adding a slide with a content layout, click the layout's Insert Table icon, specify the number of columns and rows, and then enter data in the table's cells, using the TAB key to move the insertion point from cell to cell.

You can easily change the structure of an existing table. You can add columns or rows to accommodate new data, and you can delete columns or rows you don't need. You can also merge (combine) cells to create one cell that spans two or more columns or rows, and you can split a single cell into two or more cells. Using the buttons on the Formatting toolbar or the specialized Tables and Borders toolbar, you can add color and borders and change text alignment in a table.

Tip To work with tables, you need to know how to make selections. To select a cell, drag through its text. To select a column or row, click anywhere in it, and then on the Tables and Borders toolbar, click the Table button and then click Select Column or Select Row. To select an entire table, click anywhere in it, and press CTRL+A.

BE SURE TO open a presentation containing a slide with a content layout in Normal view before carrying out these steps.

To insert a table:

Insert Table

1   In the Slide pane, click the **Insert Table** icon to display the Insert Table dialog box.

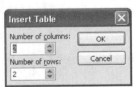

2   Enter the number of columns and rows you want in your table, and click **OK**.

A blank table with the structure you specified appears, and the Tables and Borders toolbar is displayed.

To fill in a table:

1   Check that the insertion point is blinking in the upper-left cell of the table. Then type the text you want, pressing the **TAB** key to move from cell to cell.

2   Press **TAB** in the lower-right cell to add a new row to the table.

3   Press the **ENTER** key to create a new paragraph within the same cell.

To insert rows or columns:

Tables and Borders

1   On the Standard toolbar, click the **Tables and Borders** button to display the Tables and Borders toolbar.

2   Click a cell adjacent to where you want to insert the column or row.

Table ▾

3   On the Tables and Borders toolbar, click the **Table** button.

A drop-down menu of options appears.

4   Click **Insert Columns to the Right**, **Insert Columns to the Left**, **Insert Rows Above**, or **Insert Rows Below**.

To delete rows and columns:

1   Display the Tables and Borders toolbar, and then click a cell in the column or row you want to delete.

Table ▾

2   On the Tables and Borders toolbar, click the **Table** button, and then click **Delete Rows** or **Delete Columns**.

To change the character formatting of table text:

1   Select the cell or cells you want to format.

2   On the Formatting toolbar, click the appropriate button to make the text bold, italic, or underlined.

To change the vertical alignment of table text:

1   Select the cell or cells you want to format.

2   On the Tables and Borders toolbar, do one of the following:

Align Top

■ To position the text at the top of the cell, click the **Align Top** button.

Center Vertically

■ To position the text in the center of the cell, click the **Center Vertically** button.

Align Bottom

■ To position the text at the bottom of the cell, click the **Align Bottom** button.

Tip   For more options, click Table on the Format menu to open the Format Table dialog box. Then on the Text Box tab, click the "Text alignment" down arrow, and click an item in the drop-down list.

To change the background color of a cell:

1   Select the cell or cells you want to format, and display the Tables and Borders toolbar.

Fill Color

2   On the Tables and Borders toolbar, click the **Fill Color** down arrow.

A drop-down palette of colors appears.

3   Click the color you want to apply to the cell.

The cell is filled with the color you selected.

To split and merge table cells by drawing lines:

Draw Table

1 Display the Tables and Borders toolbar, and click the **Draw Table** button.

2 Draw a horizontal or vertical line in the location where you want to split a cell.

A dotted line appears as you draw the line. When you release the mouse button, the cell is split into two cells.

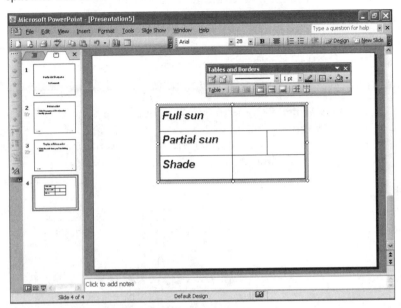

The Draw Table tool remains active until you click another tool, or until you click the Draw Table button to turn off the tool.

Eraser

3 On the Tables and Borders toolbar, click the **Eraser** button.

4 Click a line that divides two cells.

The two cells merge into one cell.

5 On the Tables and Borders toolbar, click the **Eraser** button to turn off the tool.

To merge and split table cells by clicking buttons:

Merge Cells

1 Display the Tables and Borders toolbar, and select the cells you want to merge.

2 On the Tables and Borders toolbar, click the **Merge Cells** button.

The selected cells become one cell.

Split Cell

3 With a cell selected, click the **Split Cell** button on the Tables and Borders toolbar.

The cell is split into two cells.

441

Practice Exercise

In this exercise, you will create and format a table.

USE the *InsertTable* presentation in the *My Documents\Microsoft Press\MOS 2003 Study Guide\PowerPoint \P03C-1-3* practice file folder.

Open the *InsertTable* presentation. Move to Slide 9, and insert a table with the number of columns set to **2** and the number of rows set to **4**. Check that the insertion point is blinking in the upper-left cell of the table. Then type **Class**, press **TAB**, type **Classroom**, and press **TAB** again. In the second row, type **Trees and Shrubs**, press **ENTER**, type **Lawn Care**, press **TAB**, type **Rear Patio**, and press **TAB** again. Enter **Flowers** and **Room 1** in the third row, and **Indoor Plants** and **Greenhouse** in the fourth row. Select the *Class* and *Classroom* cells, and make them bold. Center the text in the cells horizontally and vertically. Change the fill color to red. Use the **Draw Table** button to draw a horizontal line between *Trees and Shrubs* and *Lawn Care*. Draw a vertical line in the middle of the cell that contains *Room 1*, and then use the **Eraser** tool to merge the cells back together. Turn off the **Eraser** tool. Then close the *InsertTable* presentation without saving it.

Creating Charts

To display numeric data visually, you can use Microsoft Graph, a program that works with PowerPoint to insert a chart as an object into a slide. In Graph, data is displayed in a datasheet and plotted in the chart.

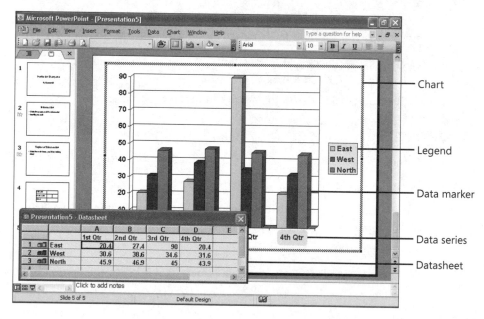

The datasheet is made up of elements that help enter and organize data, as follows:

- Rows and columns of cells hold values, or data points, that make up a data series.
- The first row and column of the datasheet hold the names of the data series. These are the equivalent of column and row headings in a table or Excel worksheet.
- Down the left side and across the top of the datasheet are gray control boxes that you use to work with rows or columns of data..

To enter data into the datasheet, you can type it, or you can import it or copy and paste it from another program.

The chart is made up of elements that help display the data from the datasheet, as follows:

- Each data point in each data series is represented graphically in the chart by a data marker.
- The data is plotted against an x-axis (also called the category axis) and a y-axis (also called the value axis). Three-dimensional charts also have a z-axis.
- A legend includes a key for identifying the data series.

Graph comes with 14 types of charts, each with two-dimensional and three-dimensional variations. After you select a chart type, you can format the chart to get the results that you want.

BE SURE TO open a presentation containing a slide with a content layout in Normal view before carrying out these steps.

To create a chart:

Insert Chart

1. In the Slide pane, click the **Insert Chart** icon.

    Microsoft Graph starts, and its menus and Standard and Formatting toolbars replace Power-Point's. The datasheet and chart appear with default data that you can replace with your own data.

2. Click a cell in the datasheet, type its entry, and press the **TAB** key to move to the next active cell.

3. Continue inserting entries until you have typed all the values you want Graph to plot as a chart.

    As you type, Graph plots the data.

To work with the datasheet:

Close

- To hide the datasheet, click its **Close** button.
- To move the datasheet, drag it by its title bar.

View
Datasheet

- To display the datasheet, click the **View Datasheet** button on Graph's Standard toolbar.
- To change the size of the datasheet, drag the lower-right corner of its window.

To import data into a chart:

1   In the datasheet, click the cell you want to use as the starting point for importing data.

Import File

2   On Graph's Standard toolbar, click the **Import File** button.

3   Navigate to the location of the file you want to import, click its name, and then click **Open**.

4   Click **OK** to overwrite the current data in the datasheet.

To change the chart type:

1   On the **Chart** menu, click **Chart Type**.

The Chart Type dialog box appears.

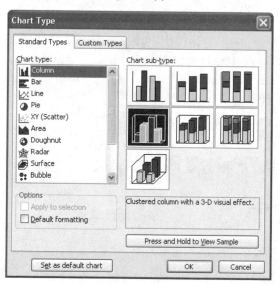

2 If you don't see the type of chart you want on the **Standard Types** tab, click the **Custom Types** tab to display more complex chart types.

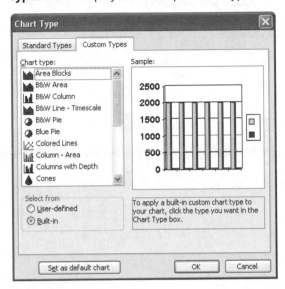

3 On either the **Standard Types** or the **Custom Types** tab, click the type of chart you want in the **Chart type** list.

4 If you used the **Standard Types** tab, click a variation in the **Chart sub-type** area.

5 Click **OK**.

The chart changes to the chart type you selected.

Tip   You can also click the Chart Type down arrow on Graph's Standard toolbar, and then click the chart type in the drop-down palette.

Chart Type

To change a chart's font size:

1 Click the chart area to select the entire chart.

When the chart area is selected, *Chart Area* appears in the Chart Objects box on Graph's Standard toolbar. You can also select the chart area by clicking it in the Chart Objects drop-down list.

Font Size

2 On Graph's Formatting toolbar, click the **Font Size** down arrow, and then click the font size you want.

The font size used for the legend and the x-axis and y-axis data labels changes to the size you selected.

To format chart gridlines:

1 On the **Chart** menu, click **Chart Options**, and then click the **Gridlines** tab.

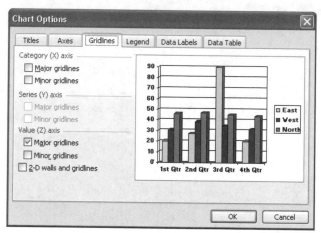

2 Select the gridline options you want to apply.

3 Click **OK**.

To rotate the labels on a chart's axes:

1 In the chart, click the axis whose labels you want to rotate.

Black handles appear at the ends of the axis.

Angle
Counter-
clockwise

2 On Graph's Formatting toolbar, click the **Angle Counterclockwise** button.

The angle of the axis text changes to 45 degrees.

Practice Exercise

In this exercise, you will create and format a chart.

USE the *InsertChart* presentation and the *Sales* file in the *My Documents\Microsoft Press\MOS 2003 Study Guide\PowerPoint\P03C-1-3* practice file folder.

Open the *InsertChart* presentation, and display Slide 11. Start Microsoft Graph, and in the datasheet, designate the blank cell above *East* and to the left of *1st Quarter* as the cell Graph will use as the starting point for importing data. Then import the *Sales* file stored in the *My Documents\Microsoft Press\MOS 2003 Study Guide\PowerPoint\P03C-1-3* practice file folder, overwriting the current data in the datasheet. Type **40000** in cell **A4** and **46000** in cell **B4**. Close the datasheet, and then change the chart type to **3-D Bar Chart**. Change the chart type again, this time to **Columns with Depth**, and then change the font size to **18**. Display the **Gridlines** tab of the Chart Options dialog box, and set the z-axis to show major gridlines. Then in the chart, change the angle of the x-axis labels to 45 degrees. Click away from the chart to deselect the chart object and quit Graph. Close the *InsertChart* presentation without saving it.

Creating Diagrams

You can use PowerPoint's diagramming tool to create a variety of diagrams, including organization charts. An organization chart uses boxes to show the relationships among the elements of an organization—for example, the relationship between a manager and her subordinates, or between a parent company and its subsidiaries.

Tip You can also create Venn, cycle, pyramid, target, and radial diagrams.

After you create the organization chart, you can add new boxes for co-workers, subordinates, or assistants, delete boxes, and you can rearrange boxes. You can also change the entire chart's style or format boxes and connecting lines individually.

BE SURE TO open a presentation containing a slide with a content layout in Normal view before carrying out these steps.

To create an organization chart:

Insert Diagram or Organization Chart

1 In the Slide pane, click the **Insert Diagram or Organization Chart** icon.

2 With the **Organization Chart** option selected, click **OK**.

A default organization chart object is inserted into the slide, with the top chart box selected. The Organization Chart toolbar is also displayed.

3 Click a chart box, and type the text you want.

4 Continue filling in as many of the default chart boxes as you need.

5 To delete a box you don't need, right-click it, and click **Delete** on the shortcut menu.

To add co-worker, subordinate, or assistant boxes:

1 Click the chart box to which you want to assign a co-worker, subordinate, or assistant.

2 On the Organization Chart toolbar, click the **Insert Shape** down arrow, and click the appropriate button on the drop-down menu.

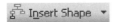

A new chart box is placed in the corresponding relationship to the selected chart box.

3 Click the new chart box, and type the text you want.

447

To change the style of an organization chart:

Autoformat

1   On the Organization Chart toolbar, click the **Autoformat** button.

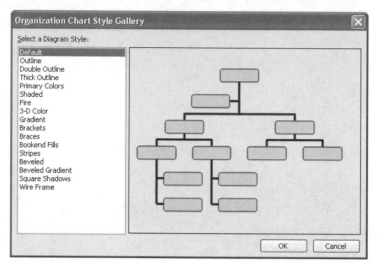

2   In the **Select a Diagram Style** list, click the diagram style you want.

3   Click **OK**.

The style of the organization chart changes.

To format the text in chart boxes:

1   Click the chart box you want to format.

Select

2   On the Organization Chart toolbar, click the **Select** down arrow, and click **Level** on the drop-down menu.

All chart boxes at the same level are selected.

3   On the Formatting toolbar, click buttons to format the text of the chart boxes.

To resize or reposition an organization chart:

Fit Text

1   On the Organization Chart toolbar, click the **Fit Text** button.

The text in the organization chart increases in size to fill the boxes.

2   Drag a corner handle to increase or decrease the organization chart's frame to the desired width or length.

3   Point to the object's frame (not a handle), and when the pointer changes to a four-headed arrow, drag it to the desired location on the slide.

To change the layout of an organization chart:

1   On the Organization Chart toolbar, click the **Layout** button.

2   On the drop-down menu, click one of the available options.

Practice Exercise

In this exercise, you will create and format a diagram.

USE the *InsertOrg* presentation in the *My Documents\Microsoft Press\MOS 2003 Study Guide\PowerPoint \P03C-1-3* practice file folder.

Open the *InsertOrg* presentation. Move to Slide 12, and double-click the **Insert Diagram or Organization Chart** icon. Click **OK** to create an organization chart. Then fill in the chart as follows: Type **Karen Berg** in the top box, press the **ENTER** key, and type **Owner**. Type **Kim Akers** in the lower-left chart box, press **ENTER**, and type **Head Buyer**. Type **David Ortiz** in the lower-middle chart box, press **ENTER**, and type **Assistant**. Type **Gardening Teachers** in the lower-right chart box, and then click away from the chart boxes but within the organization chart object. Add a subordinate **Office Staff** box to the lower-left chart box, add a subordinate **Sales Staff** box to the lower-middle chart box, and add a subordinate **Students** box to the lower-right chart box. Apply the **Brackets** style to the organization chart. Select all chart boxes at the same level as Kim Akers, hold down the **SHIFT** key, and add the *Karen Berg* box to the selection. Then make the first two chart levels bold. Fit the organization chart to its contents. Then align the object with the line under the title, and stretch the organization chart's frame to the same width as the line. Close the *InsertOrg* presentation without saving it.

Insert Pictures, Shapes, and Graphics

P03C-1-4   The skills measured by this objective include the following:

■ Adding clip art
■ Adding pictures
■ Adding shapes
■ Adding WordArt

Pictures, shapes, and other graphics can create more interesting and visually appealing presentations. You can add several types of graphics to your slides, including clip art; pictures or photographs that have been saved as graphics files; shapes such as rectangles, arrows, or starbursts; and fancy, stylized text.

Adding Clip Art

PowerPoint includes hundreds of professionally designed pieces of clip art. To add a slide with a clip art image to a presentation, you add a slide with a content layout, and click its Insert Clip Art icon, or you can add the image from the Clip Art task pane. If you can't find the image you want, you can search for additional images in Microsoft Office Online, a clip art gallery that Microsoft maintains on its website.

BE SURE TO open a presentation containing a slide with a content layout in Normal view before carrying out these steps.

To insert clip art:

Insert Clip
Art

1   In the Slide pane, click the **Insert Clip Art** icon.

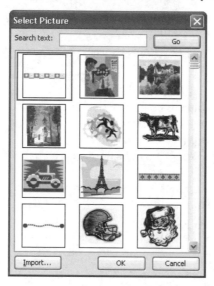

2   Scroll through the clip art images until you find one you like, and click the image.

3   Click **OK** to insert the image.

To search for a piece of clip art by keyword and then insert it:

1   On the **Insert** menu, click **Picture** and then **Clip Art**.

The Clip Art task pane opens.

2   In the **Search for** box at the top of the task pane, type a keyword that identifies the type of clip art you are looking for, and click **Go**.

All the available clip art associated with that keyword is displayed. If you are connected to the Internet, clip art that is available from Office Online is displayed along with the clip art installed on your hard disk.

3   Click the clip art image you want to insert.

Practice Exercise

In this exercise, you will add a clip art image to a slide.

USE the *InsertClipArt* presentation in the *My Documents\Microsoft Press\MOS 2003 Study Guide\PowerPoint \P03C-1-4* practice file folder.

Open the *InsertClipArt* presentation. Move to Slide 2, click a blank area of the content place-holder, and display the Clip Art task pane. Search for clip art with the keyword **leaves**, and then insert the stylized image of the two leaves. Deselect the image, and close the Clip Art task pane. Move to Slide 3, and click the **Insert Clip Art** icon in the content placeholder.

Insert the stylized drawing of a cornucopia, and then drag the clip art image to the lower-right corner of the slide. Close the *InsertClipArt* presentation without saving it.

Adding Pictures

You can add pictures created in other programs and saved as files, scanned pictures, or digital photographs to a slide. After you insert any picture, you can modify it by using the buttons on the Picture toolbar.

BE SURE TO open a presentation containing a slide with a content layout in Normal view before carrying out these steps.

To insert a picture from a file by using the Insert Picture icon:

Insert
Picture

1   In the Slide pane, click the **Insert Picture** icon.

2   Navigate to the folder that contains the picture you want to insert, and click it.

3   Click **Insert**.

The picture is added to the slide, and the Picture toolbar appears.

To insert a picture from a file by using the Picture command:

1   In the Slide pane, click a blank area of the slide, and on the **Insert** menu, click **Picture** and then **From File**.

The Insert Picture dialog box appears.

2   Navigate to the location where your picture is stored, and click it.

3   Click **Insert**.

The picture is added to the slide, and the Picture toolbar appears.

To create a new photo album:

1   In the Slide pane, click a blank area of the slide, and on the **Insert** menu, click **Picture** and then **New Photo Album**.

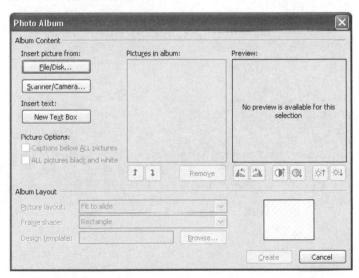

2   Click **File/Disk**.

The Insert New Pictures dialog box appears.

3   Navigate to the location where your picture files are stored, and click the pictures you want to add, holding down the **SHIFT** key to select multiple pictures.

4   Click **Insert**.

The selected pictures are now listed in the "Pictures in album" list.

5   In the **Album Layout** area, click the **Picture layout** down arrow, and then click the layout you want.

6   Click the **Frame shape** down arrow, and then click the frame shape you want.

7   To rearrange the pictures in the album, click a picture you want to move in the **Pictures in album** box, and then click the **Move Down** or **Move Up** button until the selected picture is where you want it.

8   Click **Create**.

The Photo Album dialog box closes, and a new PowerPoint presentation called *Photo Album* opens with the layout you chose.

Practice Exercise

In this exercise, you will first add pictures to slides and then insert and format a photo album.

USE the *InsertPic* presentation and the files for *Picture01* through *Picture12* in the *My Documents\Microsoft Press\MOS 2003 Study Guide\PowerPoint\P03C-1-4* practice file folder.

Open the *InsertPic* presentation. Using the content placeholder on Slide 4, insert *Picture01*, *Picture02*, *Picture03*, and *Picture04* from the *My Documents\Microsoft Press\MOS 2003 Study Guide\PowerPoint\P03C-1-4* practice file folder. Then create a new photo album presentation containing *Picture05* through *Picture12*. Change the album's layout to **4 pictures with title**, and set the frame shape to **Oval**. In the **Pictures in album** box, move **Picture12** to the bottom of the list. Save the presentation with these specifications, and then close the photo album (don't close PowerPoint). When you return to the *InsertPic* presentation, close it without saving it.

Adding Shapes

To create almost any shape in PowerPoint, you select a drawing tool or an AutoShape from the Drawing toolbar and then drag in the location where you want the shape to appear. The exception is free-form shapes, which are made up of multiple lines and curves.

After you draw a shape, it is surrounded by a set of handles. You use the white sizing handles to change the size of a shape, the yellow diamond-shaped adjustment handle to alter the appearance of a shape without changing its size, and the green rotating handle to adjust the angle of rotation of a shape.

You can copy or cut a selected shape or multiple shapes to the Office Clipboard and then paste the shapes in other parts of the presentation. When you copy multiple shapes, the Clipboard task pane displays all the items, and you can then paste them elsewhere in the same presentation, in another presentation, or in any Office program, either individually or all at once.

BE SURE TO open the presentation you want to work with in Normal view and display the Drawing toolbar before carrying out these steps.

To add a shape:

1   On the Drawing toolbar, click **AutoShapes**, and then click the type of shape you want to add.

A palette of options appears.

2   Click the specific shape you want.

In the presentation window, the pointer changes to a crosshair.

3   On the slide, point to where you want to draw the shape, and then drag until the shape is the desired size.

Tip   If you click AutoShapes and then More AutoShapes on the Drawing toolbar, Power-Point opens the Clip Art task pane with clip art shapes displayed. You can then click a shape to add it to the current slide.

To copy an existing shape:

1   Click the shape you want to copy.

Copy

2   On the Standard toolbar, click the **Copy** button.

A copy of the shape is stored on the Office Clipboard.

Paste

3   On the Standard toolbar, click the **Paste** button.

A copy of the shape is pasted on top of the original shape.

4   Drag the copy of the shape to the desired location.

Tip   To move a shape horizontally or vertically in a straight line, hold down the SHIFT key while you drag the shape.

Practice Exercise

In this exercise, you will add shapes to slides.

USE the *DrawShape* presentation in the *My Documents\Microsoft Press\MOS 2003 Study Guide\PowerPoint \P03C-1-4* practice file folder.

Open the *DrawShape* presentation. Move to Slide 8, and on the left side of the slide, draw a right arrow about 1 inch long, with its point aligned with the capital letter *A*. Copy the arrow, and drag the copy about half an inch to the right of the original arrow, aligning the two shapes. Create another copy of the arrow about half an inch to the right of the second one. Select and copy all three arrows, paste them from the Clipboard task pane back onto the slide, and then close the task pane. Drag the copied set of arrows down and to the right. Close the *DrawShape* presentation without saving it.

Adding WordArt

You can enhance your presentations visually by using WordArt to create fancy stylized text that goes beyond the kinds of effects you can achieve with combinations of font, font size, and font styles. In effect, WordArt turns words into a picture. You can use WordArt to emphasize short phrases, such as *Our Customers Come First*, or a single word, such as *Welcome*.

You don't have to be an artist to create stylized text. WordArt includes a gallery of choices that you can manually stretch horizontally, vertically, or diagonally. You can also change the character spacing and rotate the text to reshape it. You can edit the text in other ways in the Edit WordArt Text dialog box.

BE SURE TO open the presentation you want to work with in Normal view and display the Drawing toolbar before carrying out these steps.

To insert WordArt:

Insert
WordArt

1 On the Drawing toolbar, click the **Insert WordArt** button.

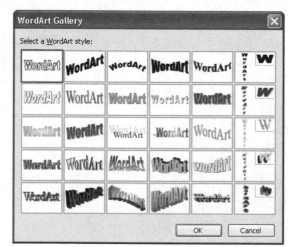

2 Click the WordArt style you want to use.

3 Click **OK**.

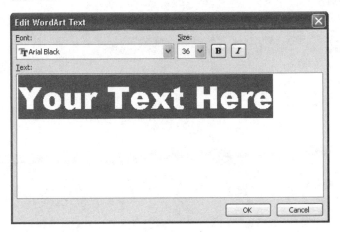

4 In the **Text** box, type the text you want WordArt to display.

5 Change the **Font** and **Size** settings as necessary.

6 Click **OK**.

To change the shape of an existing WordArt object:

1 Select the WordArt object.

2 On the WordArt toolbar, click the **WordArt Shape** button.
   A palette of shapes appears.

WordArt
Shape

3 Click the shape you want.

To change the design of an existing WordArt object:

1 Select the WordArt object.

2 On the WordArt toolbar, click the **WordArt Gallery** button.
   The WordArt Gallery dialog box appears.

WordArt
Gallery

3 Click the design you want.

To change WordArt character spacing:

1 Select the WordArt object.

2 On the WordArt toolbar, click the **WordArt Character Spacing** button.

WordArt
Character
Spacing

3 On the drop-down menu, click the setting you want.
   The width of the WordArt object increases or decreases.

To change WordArt size and position:

1   Select the WordArt object.

Format
WordArt

2   On the WordArt toolbar, click the **Format WordArt** button, and then click the **Size** tab.

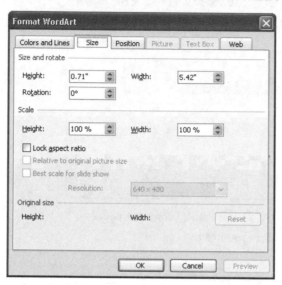

3   In the **Size and rotate** area, change the **Height**, **Width**, and **Rotation** settings so that the WordArt appears the way you want it.

4   Click the **Position** tab.

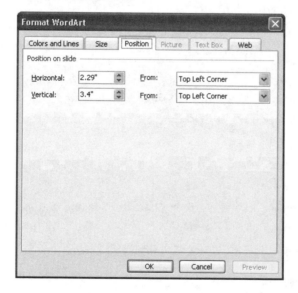

5 Change the **Horizontal** and **Vertical** settings to specify the position you want.

6 Click **OK**.

Tip You can also drag the object to the correct position and size it manually by dragging its handles.

To add a shadow to a WordArt object:

1 Select the WordArt object.

2 On the Drawing toolbar, click the **Shadow Style** button.

A palette of shadow options appears.

Shadow
Style

3 Click the shadow style you want.

4 Click the **Shadow Style** button again, and then click **Shadow Settings**.

The Shadow Settings toolbar appears.

5 On the Shadow Settings toolbar, click the appropriate button to increase the depth of the shadow by nudging it up, down, to the left, or to the right.

Practice Exercise

In this exercise, you will add WordArt to a slide.

USE the *InsertWordArt* presentation in the *My Documents\Microsoft Press\MOS 2003 Study Guide\PowerPoint \P03C-1-4* practice file folder.

Open the *InsertWordArt* presentation, and make sure the Drawing toolbar is displayed. Insert a WordArt object that has the style in the third column of the fourth row of the Word-Art palette. When the Edit WordArt Text dialog box appears, type **In the Herb Garden** in the **Text** box. Change the size to **60**, and then click **OK**. Change the WordArt object's shape to **Triangle Up** and its character spacing to **Very Loose**. Then change its height to approximately 2 inches and its vertical position to 0.5 inches. Assign **Shadow Style 18** to the object, and nudge the shadow to the left several times. Click a blank area of the slide to admire the results, and then close the *InsertWordArt* presentation without saving it.

Insert Objects

P03C-1-5   The skills measured by this objective include the following:

■ Inserting a Word table
■ Inserting an Excel worksheet
■ Inserting a media clip

You can easily insert objects created in other programs in your PowerPoint presentations, such as a Word table, an Excel chart, a movie, or a sound file.

Inserting a Word Table

If you have already created a table in Word, you can insert that table into a PowerPoint slide as an embedded object instead of retyping it. For best results, the Word document containing the table should contain no other text.

BE SURE TO open the presentation you want to work with in Normal view before carrying out these steps.

To insert a table from Word:

1   On the **Insert** menu, click **Object**.

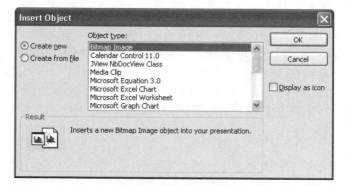

2   Click **Create from file**, and then click **Browse**.

3   In the Browse dialog box, navigate to the storage location of the Word document containing the table, double-click the file name, and click **OK**.

The table is embedded in the slide as an object.

4   Double-click the table object.

5   Drag the object's handles to size its frame to fit snugly around the table, and then click outside the object to return to PowerPoint.

You can now move and size the object in PowerPoint to make sure it is readable and attractive.

Tip   Double-clicking the embedded table object opens it for editing in Word, and Word's menus and toolbars replace PowerPoint's. You can then use Word to format and otherwise manipulate the table.

Practice Exercise

In this exercise, you will insert and format a Word table.

USE the *InsertWordTable* presentation and *WordTable* file in the *My Documents\Microsoft Press\MOS 2003 Study Guide\PowerPoint\P03C-1-5* practice file folder.

Open the *InsertWordTable* presentation. Move to Slide 9, and embed the *WordTable* file from the practice file folder. Double-click the table to activate Word's menus and toolbars, and then change the size of the font in the bottom three rows to **22 points**. Close the *InsertWord-Table* presentation without saving it.

Inserting an Excel Worksheet

PowerPoint's table capabilities are perfectly adequate for the display of simple information that is unlikely to change during the useful life of the presentation. However, if your data involves calculations or is likely to require updating, you will probably want to maintain the information in an Excel worksheet. You can then embed the worksheet in a slide as an object, or you can link the slide to the worksheet so that you won't have to worry about keeping the data up to date in more than one place. An embedded object maintains a direct connection to its original program, and you double-click it to edit it in the program in which it was originally created from within PowerPoint. A linked object is a representation on a slide of information that is still stored in an original document, and you edit the original document to update the linked object.

BE SURE TO open the presentation you want to work with in Normal view before carrying out these steps.

To insert an embedded Excel worksheet:

1   On the **Insert** menu, click **Object**.

The Insert Object dialog box appears.

2   Select the **Create from file** option, and then click **Browse**.

3   In the Browse dialog box, navigate to the location where the worksheet you want to insert is saved, double-click the file name, and click **OK**.

The worksheet is embedded in the presentation slide.

To insert a linked Excel worksheet:

1   On the **Insert** menu, click **Object**.

The Insert Object dialog box appears.

2   Select the **Create from file** option, and then click **Browse**.

3   In the Browse dialog box, navigate to the location where the worksheet you want to insert is saved, and double-click the file name in the list box.

4   In the Insert Object dialog box, select the **Link** check box, and click **OK**.

The worksheet is inserted in the presentation slide with a link to its source document.

To edit or format an embedded Excel worksheet:

1   Right-click the embedded worksheet, and on the shortcut menu, click **Worksheet Object** and then **Edit**.

The Excel workbook opens in the window, where Excel's menus and Standard and Formatting toolbars replace PowerPoint's.

2   Click the cell you want to edit or format, and make your changes.

3   Click a blank area of the slide.

Excel closes, PowerPoint's menus and toolbars are restored, and the embedded object is updated on the slide.

Practice Exercise

In this exercise, you will insert and format an embedded Excel worksheet.

USE the *InsertWorksheet* presentation and *Worksheet* file in the *My Documents\Microsoft Press\MOS 2003 Study Guide\PowerPoint\P03C-1-5* practice file folder.

Open the *InsertWorksheet* presentation. Move to Slide 8, and embed the *Worksheet* file from the practice file folder. Right-click the worksheet, and on the shortcut menu, click **Worksheet Object** and then **Edit**. Make the contents of cell **A1** bold, and change the contents of cell **B8** to **50**. Close the *InsertWorksheet* file without saving it.

Inserting a Media Clip

Including objects like sound clips and movies in a presentation can make it more interesting and help to hold the attention of an audience. Sounds can be one of PowerPoint's sound effects (which include applause, a cash register, and a drum roll), music or another audio file, or a narration that you record yourself. Movies can be digital videos produced with digitized video equipment, or they can be animated pictures, also known as animated GIFs, such as cartoons. (GIF stands for Graphics Interchange Format.)

Tip   Most of the movies in the Clip Organizer are actually animated GIF files. Like movies, animated GIFs add interest to your presentation. However, you can edit them by using the same simple techniques you use to edit pictures.

BE SURE TO open the presentation you want to work with in Normal view before carrying out these steps.

To insert a sound from the Clip Art task pane:

1   On the **Insert** menu, click **Movies and Sounds** and then **Sound from Clip Organizer**.
The Clip Art task pane appears.

2   In the Clip Art task pane, click the sound you want to insert.

3   Click the desired option for playing the sound automatically or only when clicked.

Tip   To hear the sound, you need a sound card and speakers installed on your computer and on the computer from which you will deliver the slide show.

To insert a sound by using a content layout:

Insert Media
Clip

1   In the Slide pane, click the **Insert Media Clip** icon.

    The Media Clip dialog box appears.

2   In the Media Clip dialog box, click the sound you want to insert, and click **OK**.

3   Click the desired option for playing the sound automatically or only when clicked.

To move a sound icon:

1   Click the sound icon (not one of its handles) to select it.

2   Drag the icon to the desired location.

To change a sound's action settings so that it plays when you point to it:

1   Click the sound icon to select the object.

2   On the **Slide Show** menu, click **Action Settings**.

3   When the Action Settings dialog box appears, click the **Mouse Over** tab.

4   Select the **Object action** option.

    The Play option appears in the box below.

5   Click **OK**.

    When running the slide show, you can now move the mouse pointer over the sound icon to play the sound.

To insert a movie clip by using a content layout:

Insert Media
Clip

1 In the Slide pane, click the **Insert Media Clip** icon.

If you are connected to the Internet, you will have more movie clips to choose from.

2 Click the movie clip you want to insert, and click **OK**.

The movie clip is inserted as an object in the middle of the content placeholder, and the Picture toolbar appears.

3 Adjust the size and position of the movie clip until it appears the way you want it.

Tip When you insert an object such as a movie, PowerPoint adjusts the layout of the slide to accommodate the type of object. You can control these automatic adjustments by clicking the Automatic Layout Options button that appears below the lower-right corner of the object.

Automatic
Layout
Options

To insert a movie from a file:

1 On the **Insert** menu, click **Movies and Sound** and then **Movie from File**.

2 Navigate to the folder that contains the movie file, and then double-click the file name.

3 Click the appropriate option to indicate how you want the movie to start.

The movie clip is inserted as an object.

To play a movie:

Slide Show

1 In the lower-left corner of the window, click the **Slide Show** button.

2 If the movie doesn't play automatically, double-click the movie object.

3 To pause the movie, click the movie object.

4 Click the movie object again to play the rest of the movie.

5 Press the **ESC** key to end the slide show.

To play a movie in a continuous loop:

1   Right-click the movie object, and on the shortcut menu, click **Edit Movie Object**.

The Movie Options dialog box appears, displaying the total playing time and file name of the movie.

2   In the **Play options** area, select the **Loop until stopped** check box.

3   Click **OK** to close the Movie Options dialog box.

Now when you play the movie, it will play repeatedly until you stop it.

Practice Exercise

In this exercise, you will insert sounds and a movie into a presentation. You will need a sound card and speakers installed on your computer for this exercise. (If you do not have this hardware, you can still follow the steps but you won't be able to hear the sound.)

USE the *InsertMedia* presentation and *InsertMovie* file in the *My Documents\Microsoft Press\MOS 2003 Study Guide\PowerPoint\P03C-1-5* practice file folder.

Open the *InsertMedia* presentation. On Slide 7, insert the **Chime** or other musical sound. Run the slide show, stopping it after you hear the sound. Move to Slide 3, and insert the **Claps Cheers** sound. Set the sound to play automatically. Drag the sound icon to the lower-right corner of the slide, and then play the sound. Move to Slide 6, and in the content place-holder, click the **Insert Media Clip** icon. Insert the **communication, computers** movie clip (the two computers with the globe behind them). Adjust the size and position of the movie clip until it is about the same height as the two adjacent bullet points and closer to the right margin of the slide. Move to Slide 5, and insert the *InsertMovie* file from the practice file folder. When a message asks how you want the movie to start, click **When Clicked**. Run the slide show and play the movies, pausing and then restarting them at least once. End the slide show, and then close the *InsertMedia* presentation without saving it.

P03C-1 Review

Number	Objective	Mastered
P03C-1-1	Create new presentations from templates	
	Creating a presentation by using the AutoContent Wizard	❏
	Creating a presentation by using a design template	❏
P03C-1-2	Insert and edit text-based content	
	Adding and editing text	❏
	Changing the hierarchical level of text	❏
	Importing text from other sources	❏
	Checking spelling and style	❏
	Using the Thesaurus to find the best word	❏
P03C-1-3	Insert tables, charts and diagrams	
	Creating tables	❏
	Creating charts	❏
	Creating diagrams	❏
P03C-1-4	Insert pictures, shapes and graphics	
	Adding clip art	❏
	Adding pictures	❏
	Adding shapes	❏
	Adding WordArt	❏
P03C-1-5	Insert objects	
	Inserting a Word table	❏
	Inserting an Excel worksheet	❏
	Inserting a media clip	❏

P03C-2
Formatting Content

The skills tested by this section of the Microsoft Office Specialist PowerPoint 2003 Exam all relate to formatting of presentation content. Specifically, the following objectives are associated with this set of skills:

Number	Objective
P03C-2-1	Format text-based content
P03C-2-2	Format pictures, shapes, and graphics
P03C-2-3	Format slides
P03C-2-4	Apply animation schemes
P03C-2-5	Apply slide transitions
P03C-2-6	Customize slide templates
P03C-2-7	Work with masters

 Important Before you can do the practice exercises associated with this skill set, you need to install the practice files from the book's companion CD to their default location. See "Installing the Practice Files" on page xxv for more information.

Format Text-based Content

P03C-2-1   The skills measured by this objective include the following:

- Changing the font, size, and font style of text
- Modifying text colors
- Changing text alignment
- Finding and replacing fonts

After you've added text to your presentations, you can format it so that it conveys information in an attractive and streamlined way.

Changing the Font, Size, and Font Style of Text

You can change the look of text by selecting it and changing its font, size, and font style (bold, italic, and so on). You can change these attributes individually by using buttons on the Formatting toolbar, or you can apply combinations of formatting to the selected text in the Font dialog box.

After you change the size of the text, you can adjust the size of its object to fit snugly around the text, either manually or by using the "Resize AutoShape to fit text" option.

BE SURE TO open the presentation you want to work with in Normal view before carrying out these steps.

To change the font:

1   Select the text whose font you want to change.

2   On the Formatting toolbar, click the **Font** down arrow, and click the name of the font you want to apply.

In the Slide pane, the title's font changes to the selected font, but in the Outline/Slides pane, the font is unchanged.

To change the font size:

1   Select the text whose size you want to change.

Font Size

2   On the Formatting toolbar, click the **Font Size** down arrow, and click the desired size in the drop-down list.

Tip   If the size you want is not available in the drop-down list, you can click the Font Size box and then type the size directly.

3   On the Formatting toolbar, do one of the following:

Increase
Font Size

  ■   To change to the next highest size, click the **Increase Font Size** button.

Decrease
Font Size

  ■   To change to the next lowest size, click the **Decrease Font Size** button.

Size changes are implemented only in the Slide pane.

To change the font style:

1   Select the text whose font style you want to change.

2   On the Formatting toolbar, do one of the following:

Bold

  ■   To make the selected text bold, click the **Bold** button.

Italic

  ■   To make the selected text italic, click the **Italic** button.

Underline

  ■   To underline the selected text, click the **Underline** button.

To change the formatting of text by using the Font dialog box:

1   Select the text you want to format.

2   On the **Format** menu, click **Font**.

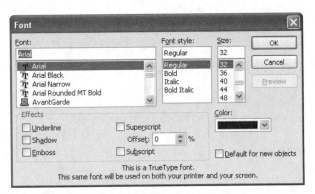

3   Change the font, font style, or size, and make any other necessary changes.

4   Click **OK**.

To change the size of an object to fit its text:

1   After all text formatting is complete, select the object you want to resize.

2   On the **Format** menu, click **Placeholder**.

> **Tip**   The name of this Format-menu command changes depending on the type of object selected.

3   Click the **Text Box** tab, select the **Resize AutoShape to fit text** check box, and click **OK**.

The object is adjusted to fit the size of the text.

Practice Exercise

In this exercise, you will change the font, style, size, and color of text in an outline.

USE the *FormatText* presentation in the *My Documents\Microsoft Press\MOS 2003 Study Guide\PowerPoint \P03C-2-1* practice file folder.

Open the *FormatText* presentation. Select Slide 1's title on the **Outline** tab of the Outline/ Slides pane. Make the title text bold. Select **The Garden Company**, italicize it, and then change the font size to **36**. Select the entire title, and increase its font size to **48** points. Change its font to **Times New Roman**. Select Slide 1's subtitle, and change its font to **Times New Roman**. Deselect the text in the outline to see the results, and then close the *FormatText* presentation without saving it.

Modifying Text Colors

Another easy way to change the look of a presentation is to change the text colors. The colors are controlled by a color scheme—a set of eight harmonious colors, each of which is assigned to a specific type of text. You can apply a different color from the scheme to selected text by using the Font Color button on the Formatting toolbar. However, the most dramatic way of changing colors is to change the presentation's color scheme, which instantly applies eight new colors to all the slides in the presentation.

If none of PowerPoint's built-in color schemes meets your needs, you can modify a color scheme to create a new one. You can select colors for the scheme from a standard color palette or specify colors based on RGB (red, green, and blue) values.

Tip Because a large percentage of the visible spectrum can be represented by mixing red, green, and blue, specifying RGB values is an easy way of identifying a specific shade of a specific color.

If you want to draw attention to a particular piece of text, you can select it and change it to a non–color-scheme color. The color you choose is then added to the Font Color button's drop-down palette so that you can easily use that color for other text in the presentation.

BE SURE TO open the presentation you want to work with in Normal view before carrying out these steps.

To change selected text to a different color in the current color scheme:

1   Select the text whose color you want to change.

Font Color

2   On the Formatting toolbar, click the **Font Color** down arrow.

A color palette appears, showing the eight colors of the current color scheme.

3   Click the desired color box in the color palette.

PowerPoint changes the color of the selected text.

To switch the color scheme:

Slide Design

1   On the Formatting toolbar, click the **Slide Design** button to open the Slide Design task pane.

2   In the Slide Design task pane, click **Color Schemes**.

    The available color schemes appear in the task pane.

3   Click the scheme to you want to apply.

To create a custom color scheme:

Slide Design

1   On the Formatting toolbar, click the **Slide Design** button to open the Slide Design task pane.

2   In the Slide Design task pane, click **Color Schemes**.

3   At the bottom of the Slide Design task pane, click **Edit Color Schemes**.

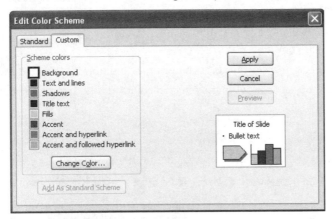

4   In the **Scheme colors** area, click the type of text you want to modify.

5   Click **Change Color**.

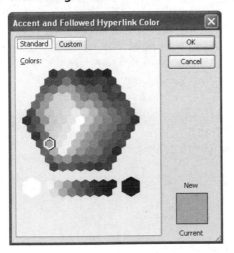

6 In the six-sided color palette, click the color you want.

The New color and the Current color appear in the lower-right corner of the Color dialog box.

7 Click **OK**.

8 Click **Add As Standard Scheme** to create a new color scheme.

9 Click **Apply**.

The custom color scheme appears in the Slide Design task pane, and PowerPoint applies it to all the slides.

To change all the text in an object to a new color:

1 Select the object whose text color you want to change.

Font Color

2 If necessary, display the Drawing toolbar, and then click the **Font Color** down arrow.

A color palette appears.

3 On the color palette, click **More Colors**.

The Colors dialog box appears.

4 In the color spectrum, click the color you want for the object's text, and then click **OK**.

The text in the object changes to the selected color, and the color is added to the Font Color button's palette.

Practice Exercise

In this exercise, you will create and apply a custom color scheme.

USE the *CreateScheme* presentation in the *My Documents\Microsoft Press\MOS 2003 Study Guide\PowerPoint \P03C-2-1* practice file folder.

Open the *CreateScheme* presentation. Move to Slide 8, and open the Slide Design task pane. In the Slide Design task pane, click **Color Schemes**, and then click **Edit Color Schemes**. Change the color of the **Text and lines** color box to dark orange (RGB values of **25**, **102**, and **0**). Change the **Title text** color to dark green (RGB values of **0**, **128**, and **0**). Change the remaining colors, picking shades of orange or red for **Accent** and **Accent and hyperlink**, and shades of green for **Fills** and **Accent and followed hyperlink**. When you have finished, click **Add As Standard Scheme** to create a new color scheme, and click **Apply**. Close the Slide Design task pane, and then close the *CreateScheme* presentation without saving it.

Changing Text Alignment

To control the way text is aligned within an object, you can select the object and click one of the alignment buttons on the Formatting toolbar.

BE SURE TO open the presentation you want to work with in Normal view before carrying out these steps.

To change the alignment of text:

1   Click the text you want to align.

2   On the Formatting toolbar, do one of the following:

Center

■ To center the text between the borders of the object that contains it, click the **Center** button.

Align Right

■ To align all the text at the right border, with a ragged left edge, click the **Align Right** button.

Align Left

■ To align all the text at the left border, with a ragged right edge, click the **Align Left** button.

Practice Exercise

In this exercise, you will change alignment.

USE the *AlignText* presentation in the *My Documents\Microsoft Press\MOS 2003 Study Guide\PowerPoint \P03C-2-1* practice file folder.

Open the *AlignText* presentation. Move to Slide 8. Click the text in the word processing box at the bottom of the slide, and center it. Close the *AlignText* presentation without saving it.

Finding and Replacing Fonts

With the Replace Fonts command, you can replace every instance of one font with another.

BE SURE TO open the presentation you want to work with in Normal view before carrying out these steps.

To find and replace a specific font:

1   On the **Format** menu, click **Replace Fonts**.

2   Click the **Replace** down arrow, and click the font you want to replace in the drop-down list.

3   Click the **With** down arrow, scroll down the drop-down list, and click the new font.

4   Click **Replace**.

Throughout the presentation, the text changes from the original font to the new font you selected.

5   Click **Close** to close the Replace Font dialog box.

Practice Exercise

In this exercise, you will change the Arial font to Impact throughout a document.

USE the *ReplaceFont* presentation in the *My Documents\Microsoft Press\MOS 2003 Study Guide\PowerPoint \P03C-2-1* practice file folder.

Open the *ReplaceFont* presentation. Display the Replace Fonts dialog box, specify **Arial** as the font you want to replace and **Impact** as the font you want to use instead. Click **Replace** to change all text formatted with the Arial font to the Impact font. Close the Replace Font dialog box, and review the slides, noticing that the note at the bottom of Slide 8 is now displayed in the Impact font. Close the *ReplaceFont* presentation without saving it.

Format Pictures, Shapes, and Graphics

P03C-2-2   The skills measured by this objective include the following:

- Sizing and cropping graphics
- Adjusting the color of graphics
- Aligning, connecting, and rotating graphics
- Adding effects to graphics

PowerPoint makes it easy to format all types of graphics, including pictures, shapes, and clip art, so that they fit the design and content of your presentations.

Sizing and Cropping Graphics

You can size a graphic by selecting it and dragging its sizing handles. You can also display the Size tab of the Format Picture dialog box, where you can enter specific dimensions for the height and width, or you can scale the graphic as a percentage of its current size or of its original size. You can specify that the height and width must be scaled proportionally, and you can optimize the size for a slide show.

If you need only part of a graphic, you can crop away the parts you don't want so that they do not show on the slide. The graphic is not altered—parts of it are simply hidden.

If you change the size of a graphic and then want to restore the original size, you can set the scale back to 100% or click Reset in the Format Picture dialog box.

BE SURE TO open the presentation you want to work with in Normal view before carrying out these steps.

To size a graphic by dragging its handles:

1   Select the graphic you want to resize.
2   Drag one of the handles to resize the graphic.

To size a graphic by using the Format Picture dialog box:

1   Double-click the graphic, and when the Format Picture dialog box appears, click the **Size** tab.

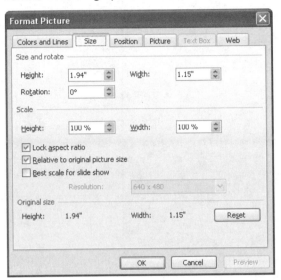

2   If you want to be able to distort the graphic by setting both the height and width, clear the **Lock aspect ratio** check box.

When this check box is selected, changing the setting in either the Height or Width box changes the other setting proportionally.

3   Do one of the following:

- In the **Size** area, replace the number in the **Height** or **Width** box with the size you want.
- In the **Scale** area, select the number in the **Height** or **Width** box, and type the percentage you want.

4   Click **Preview** to view the image without closing the dialog box.

5   Click **OK** to close the Format Picture dialog box.

To crop a graphic:

1   Select the graphic you want to crop.

Crop

2   On the Picture toolbar, click the **Crop** button.

The cropping handles appear around the selected graphic, and over the slide, the pointer changes to the cropping tool.

3   Drag the handles with the cropping tool to crop the graphic to the size you want.

4   Click a blank area of the slide to turn off the cropping tool.

To crop a graphic by using the Format Picture dialog box:

1 Double-click the graphic, and when the Format Picture dialog box appears, click the **Picture** tab.

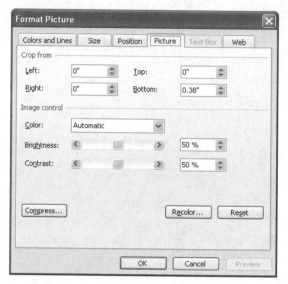

2 Enter measurements in the **Left**, **Right**, **Top**, or **Bottom** boxes to specify how much to crop from each side of the image.

3 Click **OK**.

Practice Exercise

In this exercise, you will size and crop two graphics.

USE the *SizeGraphic* presentation in the *My Documents\Microsoft Press\MOS 2003 Study Guide\PowerPoint \P03C-2-2* practice file folder.

Open the *SizeGraphic* presentation. Move to Slide 5, select the top picture, and drag the lower-right corner handle down until the picture covers about a third of the picture below it. Crop the bottom of the picture to align with the word *expensive* in the adjacent text. Turn off the cropping tool, and then click the bottom picture. Resize the picture to be the same width as the one above it. Crop the bottom picture from both the top and bottom so that it is about the same size as the one above it, with the bowling ball and the gazing globe in about the same position in each picture. Move the bottom picture upward, aligning its bottom edge with the last line of the second bullet point. Turn off the cropping tool, and deselect the picture. Close the *SizeGraphic* presentation without saving it.

Adjusting the Color of Graphics

After you have added a graphic to a slide, you can use buttons on the Picture toolbar to enhance the graphic's color, brightness, and contrast. You can also change the color of the graphic's background and border on the Colors and Lines tab of the Format Picture dialog box. On the Picture tab, you can specify whether the image should be colored (Automatic), gray, or black and white, and you can control its brightness and contrast.

You can change the colors used in some clip art images to create a different look or to match the current color scheme. Clicking the Recolor Picture button on the Picture toolbar displays a dialog box where you can change any of the image's existing colors.

At any time, you can click the Reset Picture button on the Picture toolbar to revert to the graphic's original color settings.

BE SURE TO open the presentation you want to work with in Normal view and display the Picture and Drawing toolbars before carrying out these steps.

To change a graphic to grayscale:

1   Select the graphic you want to convert to grayscale.

Color

2   On the Picture toolbar, click the **Color** button, and then click **Grayscale**.

The graphic is displayed in shades of gray.

To change the brightness and contrast of a graphic:

1   Select the graphic you want to recolor.

2   On the Picture toolbar, do any of the following:

More
Brightness

■   To increase the brightness, click the **More Brightness** button.

Less
Brightness

■   To decrease the brightness, click the **Less Brightness** button.

More
Contrast

■   To increase the contrast, click the **More Contrast** button.

Less
Contrast

■   To decrease the contract, click the **Less Contrast** button.

To change the color of a clip art image:

1   Select the clip art you want to recolor.

2   On the Picture toolbar, click the **Recolor Picture** button.

Recolor
Picture

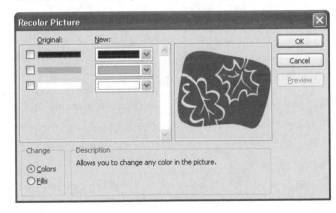

3 Select the **Fills** option to display the fill colors of the image.

4 In the **New** area, click the down arrow to the right of the color you want to change, and click the color box for the new color you want.

The color swatch changes to the selected color, and the preview box on the right shows that all parts of the image that had been the previous color are now the color you selected.

5 Click **OK**.

To change the color of a shape:

1 Select the shape whose color you want to change.

2 On the Drawing toolbar, do the following:

Line Color

■ To change the line color, click the **Line Color** button, and in the color palette, click the color you want.

Fill Color

■ To change the fill color, click the **Fill Color** button, and click the color you want.

The new line or fill color is applied to the shape.

Practice Exercise

In this exercise, you will modify the color of two pictures.

USE the *ColorGraphic* presentation in the *My Documents\Microsoft Press\MOS 2003 Study Guide\PowerPoint \P03C-2-2* practice file folder.

Open the *ColorGraphic* presentation. Move to Slide 5, select both pictures, and change them to grayscale. Increase the brightness twice, and then decrease the contrast twice. Change the color to **Automatic**. Close the *ColorGraphic* presentation without saving it.

Aligning, Connecting, and Rotating Graphics

You can fine-tune the alignment of graphics on slides in two ways:

■ By aligning them relative to each other

■ By aligning them relative to a fixed grid or adjustable horizontal and vertical guidelines

You can connect graphics with lines. When you select a connected graphic, small blue handles, called connection points, appear. You can drag one connection point to another to change the line, or you can drag an adjustment handle to change the line's shape.

You can rotate or flip a graphic by selecting it, clicking the Draw button on the Drawing toolbar, pointing to Rotate or Flip, and then clicking the desired option.

BE SURE TO open the presentation you want to work with in Normal view and display the Drawing toolbar before carrying out these steps.

To align graphics:

1 Select the graphics you want to align.

2 On the Drawing toolbar, click the **Draw** button, click **Align or Distribute**, and then click the appropriate option.

To align graphics with grids or guidelines:

1   Select the graphics you want to align.

2   On the **View** menu, click **Grid and Guides**.

3   Select both the **Display grid on screen** and **Display drawing guides on screen** check boxes.

4   Click **OK**.

    A dotted-line grid appears across the slide, and two heavier dotted drawing guides intersect in the center of the slide.

5   Point to the horizontal or vertical guide, and drag it to the desired location.

    As you drag, a guide indicator shows in inches how far you are from the center of the slide.

    Tip   If the guide indicator skips numbers as you drag the guides, the "Snap objects to grid" check box is selected in the Grid and Guides dialog box.

6   Point to the guide again, hold down the **CTRL** key, and drag a copy of the guide to the desired location.

7   Point to the dotted selection box around the graphics, hold down the **SHIFT** key, and drag the graphics to align with a guide or gridline.

    Holding down the **SHIFT** key while you drag makes it easier to drag horizontally without nudging the selected shapes up or down.

8   Press **ALT+F9** to turn off the guides, and press **SHIFT+F9** to turn off the grid.

To connect graphics:

1   On the Drawing toolbar, click **AutoShapes**, point to **Connectors**, and then on the drop-down menu, click the connector you want.

2   Point to one of the graphics you want to connect.

    Blue connection points appear, and the pointer changes to a small box, called the connection pointer.

3   Click one of the connection points, and drag to the second graphic you want to connect.

4　When connection points appear on the second shape, click one.

Red handles appear at each end of the line, indicating that the graphics are connected. A yellow, diamond-shaped adjustment handle might appear in the middle of the connection line, indicating that you can adjust the line's shape.

Undo

Tip　If square green handles appear at the ends of the line, the shapes are not connected. Click the Undo button to remove the line, and try drawing the connection line again.

To rotate or flip a graphic:

1　Select the graphic you want to rotate.

Draw ▾

2　On the Drawing toolbar, click the **Draw** button, click **Rotate or Flip** and then the appropriate option to rotate or flip the graphic the way you want.

Practice Exercise

In this exercise, you will align and connect shapes.

USE the *AlignShape* presentation in the *My Documents\Microsoft Press\MOS 2003 Study Guide\PowerPoint \P03C-2-2* practice file folder.

Open the *AlignShape* presentation. Make sure the Drawing toolbar is displayed. Move to Slide 4, select all three rectangles, and center them. Display the grid and drawing guides. Drag the selected shapes to the left until their left edges touch the leftmost gridline in the white area of the slide. Align the vertical guide with the *P* in *Preparing*. Drag the selected shapes to the right until their left edges touch the vertical guide. Drag the horizontal guide downward until it is aligned with the bottom of the *Research your topic* shape. Drag a copy of the guide downward until it is aligned with the bottom of the *Gather your supplies* shape. Click the middle shape, and click the slanted-line selection box to select the object. Drag the object's dotted selection box to the middle of the slide. Drag the bottom shape to the right side of the slide. Turn off the guides and grid. Add an elbow double-arrow connector between the top shape and the middle shape, and then add one between the middle shape and the bottom shape. Close the *AlignShape* presentation without saving it.

Adding Effects to Shapes

You can make dramatic changes to the look of a shape by adding effects to it. Effects include background textures, patterns, or pictures; shadows; and three-dimensional effects.

BE SURE TO open the presentation you want to work with in Normal view and display the Drawing toolbar before carrying out these steps.

To add a fill effect to a shape:

1　Select the shape to which you want to add a fill effect.

Fill Color

2　On the Drawing toolbar, click the **Fill Color** down arrow, and click **Fill Effects**.

3　Click the **Texture** tab, click the textured fill you want, and click **OK**.

The shape is filled with the new texture.

Tip　You can add a background pattern or picture from the Pattern or Picture tab.

To add a shadow to a shape:

Shadow
Style

1   Select the shape to which you want to add a shadow.

2   On the Drawing toolbar, click the **Shadow Style** button, and then click the shadow style you want.

3   On the Drawing toolbar, click the **Shadow Style** button, and then click **Shadow Settings**.

The Shadow Settings toolbar appears.

4   On the Shadow Settings toolbar, click the appropriate button to nudge the shadow up, down, left, or right.

The shadow moves slightly with each click.

Shadow
Color

5   On the Shadow Settings toolbar, click the **Shadow Color** down arrow, and then click the color you want.

Shadow
On/Off

6   To remove a shadow from a shape, click the **Shadow On/Off** button on the Shadow Settings toolbar.

The shadow is removed from the shape.

To add a 3-D effect to a shape:

1   Select the shape to which you want to apply a 3-D effect.

2   On the Drawing toolbar, click the **3-D Style** button, and then click the 3-D style you want.

3-D Style

Practice Exercise

In this exercise, you will add effects to a shape.

USE the *ChangeShape* presentation in the *My Documents\Microsoft Press\MOS 2003 Study Guide\PowerPoint \P03C-2-2* practice file folder.

Open the *ChangeShape* presentation. Make sure the Drawing toolbar is displayed. On Slide 8, type **Trees/shrubs** in the upper-left shape, type **Lawn care** in the upper-middle shape, and type **Flowers** in the upper-right shape. In the lower-left shape, type **Indoor plants**; in the lower-middle shape, type **Transplanting**; and in the lower-right shape, type **Landscaping.** Move to Slide 10, select the sun and the lightning bolt shapes, and add the **Water Droplets** textured fill to them. Apply **Shadow Style 6** to the shapes, and then nudge the shadows downward. Change the shadow color to orange, and then close the Shadow Settings toolbar. Change the color of the text in the sun's oval to **Blue**, and then change the font to **Comic Sans MS**. Close the *ChangeShape* presentation without saving it.

Format Slides

P03C-2-3   The skills measured by this objective include the following:

- Coloring and shading a slide background
- Modifying the slide layout
- Using a design template to make a presentation look consistent
- Setting the slide size and orientation

You can give a slide a more interesting appearance by customizing its background or changing its layout and page setup. You can achieve a consistent look for your presentations by using design templates.

Coloring and Shading a Slide Background

In PowerPoint, you can customize the background of a slide by adding a solid color, one or two colors that gradually shade from light to dark, a texture or pattern, or a picture.

BE SURE TO open the presentation you want to work with in Normal view before carrying out these steps.

To add a solid color to the background:

1 On the **Format** menu, click **Background**.

2 Below the preview in the **Background fill** box, click the down arrow to the right of the text box.

3 Click **More Colors** in the drop-down palette.

4 Select a color on either the **Standard** or **Custom** tabs of the Color dialog box, and click **OK**.

5 To use the color as the background of the current slide, click **Apply**, or to use it for all slides, click **Apply to All**.

To add a shaded background:

1 On the **Format** menu, click **Background**.

2 Below the preview in the **Background fill** box, click the down arrow to the right of the text box, and then click **Fill Effects**.

3   In the **Colors** area, do one of the following:

   ■   Select the **One color** option, click the **Color 1** down arrow, and click the color you want in the drop-down palette. Then in the box below, drag the slide control to the desired position to make the gradient darker or lighter.

   ■   Select the **Two colors** option, click the **Color 1** down arrow, and click the color you want in the drop-down palette. Then click the **Color 2** down arrow, and click the second color in the drop-down palette.

   ■   Select the **Preset** option to access a series of professionally designed color gradients of various angles and directions.

4   In the **Shading styles** area, select the direction you want the shading to run.

   The boxes in the Variants area change to the style you selected.

5   In the **Variants** area, click the box that displays the variant you want.

   The Sample box displays a preview of your selection.

6   Click **OK**.

7   To use the shade as the background of the current slide, click **Apply**, or to use it for all slides, click **Apply to All**.

To add a textured background to a slide:

1   On the **Format** menu, click **Background**.

2   Below the preview in the **Background fill** box, click the down arrow to the right of the text box, click **Fill Effects**, and then click the **Texture** tab.

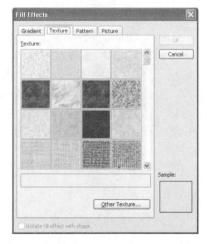

3   Double-click the textured fill you want.

4   To use the texture as the background of the current slide, click **Apply**, or to use it for all slides, click **Apply to All**.

To add a picture to a slide's background:

1   On the **Format** menu, click **Background**.

2   Below the preview in the **Background fill** box, click the down arrow to the right of the text box, click **Fill Effects**, and then click the **Picture** tab.

3   Click **Select Picture**, navigate to the folder that contains the picture you want to use, double-click the file name, and then click **OK**.

4   To use the picture as the background of the current slide, click **Apply**, or to use the picture for all slides, click **Apply to All**.

Practice Exercise

In this exercise, you will customize all the slide backgrounds in a presentation.

USE the *AddBackground* presentation in the *My Documents\Microsoft Press\MOS 2003 Study Guide \PowerPoint\P03C-2-3* practice file folder.

Open the *AddBackground* presentation. On Slide 7, apply a light green color with a vertical shading style to the slide background. Move to Slide 1, and apply the papyrus textured fill to the slide background. Then apply a solid white background to all the slides in the presentation. Close the *AddBackground* presentation without saving it.

Modifying the Slide Layout

If you want to rearrange the elements on a slide or change which elements are included, you need to modify the slide's layout. You can change the layout of an existing slide by selecting the slide and clicking a different layout thumbnail in the Slide Layout task pane. If you make changes to the layout of a slide—such as sizing or moving a placeholder—but then decide you would rather use the original layout, you can reapply the layout without losing text you have already entered by clicking a command in the layout thumbnail's drop-down list.

When you manually alter the layout or the types of items on a slide, PowerPoint uses an automatic layout behavior to apply a slide layout that matches your changes.

BE SURE TO open the presentation you want to work with in Normal view before carrying out these steps.

To switch to a different slide layout:

1   On the **Format** menu, click **Slide Layout**.
2   In the Slide Layout task pane, click the thumbnail of the slide layout you want.
3   Close the Slide Layout task pane.

To modify a slide layout:

1   Drag text objects and other elements to new locations on the slide.
2   Change the size of objects by dragging their sizing handles.
3   Add and delete elements to get the effect you want.

To reapply a slide's original layout:

1   On the **Format** menu, click **Slide Layout**.
2   In the Slide Layout task pane, point to the current thumbnail, and click the down arrow that appears to its right.
3   On the drop-down menu, click **Reapply Layout**.

    PowerPoint restores the objects on the slide to their original sizes and positions.

Practice Exercise

In this exercise, you will modify the layout of a slide.

USE the *ChangeLayout* presentation in the *My Documents\Microsoft Press\MOS 2003 Study Guide\PowerPoint \P03C-2-3* practice file folder.

Open the *ChangeLayout* presentation. On Slide 4, drag the bulleted list object to the bottom of the slide. Open the Slide Layout task pane, and reapply the slide's original layout. Then change the layout of the slide to the Title, Text, and Content slide layout. Close the Slide Layout task pane, and close the *ChangeLayout* presentation without saving it.

Using a Design Template to Make a Presentation Look Consistent

When you apply a template to a presentation, PowerPoint copies the information from the masters in the template to the corresponding masters in the presentation. All slides in a presentation then acquire the look of the template. You can use one of the many templates that come with PowerPoint, or you can create your own from existing presentations.

BE SURE TO open the presentation you want to work with in Normal view before carrying out these steps.

To apply a different template:

Slide Design

1   On the Formatting toolbar, click the **Slide Design** button.

    The Slide Design task pane appears.

2   With **Design Templates** active in the Slide Design task pane, click **Browse** at the bottom of the pane.

3 Navigate to the folder where the design template you want to apply is stored, and click its name.

A preview of the template's design is shown in the box on the right.

4 Click **Apply**.

PowerPoint applies the information from the design template to the masters in the presentation.

Practice Exercise

In this exercise, you will apply a design template to an existing presentation.

USE the *AddTemplate* presentation and *ApplyTemplate* template in the *My Documents\Microsoft Press \MOS 2003 Study Guide\PowerPoint\P03C-2-3* practice file folder.

Open the *AddTemplate* presentation, and then open the Slide Design task pane. Apply the *ApplyTemplate* design template to the presentation. Then close the Slide Design task pane, and close the *AddTemplate* presentation without saving it.

Setting the Slide Size and Orientation

PowerPoint opens a new presentation with these default slide settings: on-screen slide show, landscape orientation (10 x 7.5 inches), and slides starting at number one. By default, notes, handouts, and outlines are printed in portrait orientation (7.5 x 10 inches). You can use the Page Setup dialog box to change these settings.

BE SURE TO open the presentation you want to work with in Normal view before carrying out these steps.

To change slide size and orientation:

1 On the **File** menu, click **Page Setup**.

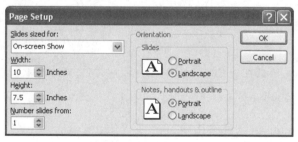

2 Click the **Slides sized for** down arrow, and then click the size you want. You can also use the **Width** and **Height** text boxes to set a custom size.

3 In the **Orientation** area, select the **Landscape** or **Portrait** options to change the orientation of slides, notes, and handouts.

4 Change the setting in the **Number slides from** box to start the presentation at slide number 2 or higher.

5 Click **OK**.

Practice Exercise

In this exercise, you will change the size of the slides, the orientation of notes and handouts, and the numbering of the slides.

USE the *ChangeSize* presentation in the *My Documents\Microsoft Press\MOS 2003 Study Guide\PowerPoint \P03C-2-3* practice file folder.

Open the *ChangeSize* presentation. Display the Page Setup dialog box, size the slides as **35mm Slides**, and then change the orientation of the notes, handout, and outline to **Landscape**. Number the slides starting from **10**. Then close the *ChangeSize* presentation without saving it.

Apply Animation Schemes

P03C-2-4   The skills measured by this objective include the following:

- Animating slides

You can animate text and graphics to make your presentations more eye-catching. PowerPoint includes many ready-made animation effects that you can apply to a slide, a group of slides, or an entire presentation.

Animating Slides

It's easy to add ready-made animation effects to a presentation. Common types of animation include the following:

- Text that appears on the screen one paragraph, word, or letter at a time
- Bullet points that appear one at a time
- Shapes that move
- Charts that appear one data series at a time

The easiest way to apply animation effects to a slide show is to use Animation Schemes in the Slide Design task pane, which provides one-click access to professionally designed animations. Most of these animations have associated sound effects. To preview each animation scheme, you can cycle through the various options until you find the animation that you want.

BE SURE TO open the presentation you want to work with in Slide Sorter view before carrying out these steps.

To apply an animation effect:

1   Click the slide or select the slides you want to work with.

2   On the **Slide Show** menu, click **Animation Schemes**.

The Slide Design task pane appears, displaying a selection of animation schemes.

3   In the **Apply to selected slides** area of the Slide Design task pane, click the animation effect you want.

PowerPoint applies the animation effect to the selected slides. An animation symbol appears to the left of the icon for each animated slide.

To apply an animation effect to an entire presentation:

1   On the **Slide Show** menu, click **Animation Schemes**.

    The Slide Design task pane appears.

2   In the **Apply to selected slides** area of the Slide Design task pane, click the animation effect you want.

3   Click the **Apply to All Slides** button.

    The effect is applied to all slides in the presentation.

To apply a custom animation effect to a slide:

1   Display the slide, and on the **Slide Show** menu, click **Custom Animation**.

2   Select an object on the slide.

3   In the Custom Animation task pane, click **Add Effect**, point to the type of effect you want, and then click a specific effect.

    The animation effect is demonstrated on the slide.

Practice Exercise

In this exercise, you will apply different animation effects to different slides.

USE the *AnimateSlide* presentation in the *My Documents\Microsoft Press\MOS 2003 Study Guide\PowerPoint \P03C-2-4* practice file folder.

Open the *AnimateSlide* presentation. Display Slide 3 in Slide Sorter view. Open the Slide Design task pane, and apply the **Fade in all** animation effect. Select Slides 2, 5, and 6, and apply the **Faded wipe** animation effect to them. Close the *AnimateSlide* presentation without saving it.

Apply Slide Transitions

P03C-2-5   The skills measured by this objective include the following:

■   Applying transition effects

You can add transition effects to your presentations to change the way a slide appears when replacing the previous slide. After you've added a transition effect, you can then customize its settings.

Applying Transition Effects

A slide transition is the visual effect of a slide as it moves on and off the screen during a slide show. Transitions include effects such as sliding into view from one of several directions, dissolving in from the outer edges or the center, and opening like a vertical blind.

Tip   If you apply both a transition effect and an animation effect to a slide, the transition effect occurs first.

Each slide can have only one transition. You can apply a transition to one slide at a time or to a group of slides by using the Slide Transition task pane.

BE SURE TO open the presentation you want to work with in Slide Sorter view before carrying out these steps.

To apply a transition effect:

1   Click the slide or select the slides to which you want to apply the transition.

  Tip   You can press CTRL+A to select all the slides in a presentation.

2   On the **Slide Show** menu, click **Slide Transition**.

  The Slide Transition task pane appears displaying the slide transition options currently applied to the selected slide.

3   In the **Apply to selected slides** area of the Slide Transition pane, scroll down the list, and click the transition effect you want to apply.

  PowerPoint demonstrates the transition effect on the slide miniature for the selected slide.

To customize a transition effect:

1   Open the Slide Transition task pane.

2   In the **Modify transition** area, click the **Speed** down arrow, and click the speed you want.

3   In the **Modify transition** area, click the **Sound** down arrow, and click the sound you want.

4   In the **Advance slide** area, select the **On mouse click** check box to advance the slide manually, or select the **Automatically after** check box and enter a time.

  If you select both check boxes, you can advance to the next slide with a mouse click before the full time has advanced.

Practice Exercise

In this exercise, you will apply a transition to a single slide, apply the same transition to multiple slides, and then set the transition speed.

USE the *AddTransition* presentation in the *My Documents\Microsoft Press\MOS 2003 Study Guide\PowerPoint \P03C-2-5* practice file folder.

Open the *AddTransition* presentation. Switch to Slide Sorter view, and open the Slide Transition task pane. Apply the **Dissolve** effect to Slide 1. Select all the slides except Slide 1, and apply the **Random Bars Horizontal** transition effect. Then change the speed of the **Random Bars Horizontal** transition effect to **Medium**. Close the *AddTransition* presentation without saving it.

Customize Slide Templates

P03C-2-6   The skills measured by this objective include the following:

  ■   Saving a presentation as a template

Instead of creating a new design template from scratch, you can modify a presentation based on one of PowerPoint's templates and then save it as a new design template that you can use for future presentations.

Saving a Presentation as a Template

If you create a presentation by using the AutoContent Wizard or a design template and then spend a lot of time customizing it to meet your needs, you might want to save the presentation as a new design template. That way, you won't have to repeat your work for any similar presentations that you create in the future.

Design templates have to be stored in the default Templates folder in order for them to appear automatically in the Slide Design task pane. If you store a template somewhere else, you can click Browse at the bottom of the pane, navigate to the folder where the template is stored, and double-click the template apply it to a presentation.

BE SURE TO open the presentation you want to work with before carrying out these steps.

To save a presentation as a template:

1 Edit and format the presentation so that it includes all the features you want to be part of the template.
2 On the **File** menu, click **Save As**.
3 In the Save As dialog box, type the name of the new template in the **File name** box.
4 Click the **Save as type** down arrow, and click **Design Template** in the drop-down list.
   PowerPoint displays the default Templates folder.
5 Click **Save**.

See Also   For information about creating a new presentation based on a template, refer to P03C-1-1, "Create New Presentations from Templates."

Practice Exercise

In this exercise, you will save a presentation as a design template.

USE the *SaveTemplate* presentation in the *My Documents\Microsoft Press\MOS 2003 Study Guide\PowerPoint \P03C-2-6* practice file folder.

Open the *SaveTemplate* presentation. Save the file as a design template in the *My Documents \Microsoft Press\MOS 2003 Study Guide\PowerPoint\P03C-2-6* practice file folder with the name **DesignTemplate**. Then close *SaveTemplate* without saving it.

Work with Masters

P03C-2-7   The skills measured by this objective include the following:

- Changing a presentation's masters
- Adding, deleting, and modifying placeholders
- Inserting content in headers and footers

The underlying structure of title slides, slides, handouts, and notes pages is controlled by a set of masters. Anything that appears on a master will appear on every corresponding slide or other element of the presentation.

Changing a Presentation's Masters

By default, PowerPoint presentations have four masters:

- The Slide Master controls the look of all the slides in the presentation.
- The Title Master controls the look of title slides.
- The Handout Master controls the look of student handouts.
- The Notes Pages Master controls the look of speaker notes.

Of these, the Slide Master and Title Master are the most important, and together they comprise the slide-title master pair.

Masters contain text placeholders for title text, paragraph text or bullet points, date and time, footer information, and slide numbers. (They might also contain placeholders for graphics.) These text placeholders control the text formatting throughout a presentation.

You make changes to the masters in Slide Master view. If you need more than one basic slide or title design for a presentation, or if you want to apply more than one template to a presentation, you can add an additional Slide Master or Title Master by using buttons on the Master toolbar, which appears when you switch to Slide Master view.

BE SURE TO open the presentation you want to work with in Normal view before carrying out these steps.

To display a presentation's masters:

1   On the **View** menu, click **Master** and then **Slide Master**.

The pane on the left shows slide miniatures of the Slide Master and Title Master, with Slide 2—the Title Master—selected. The Title Master appears in the Slide pane to the right, and the Slide Master View toolbar is displayed.

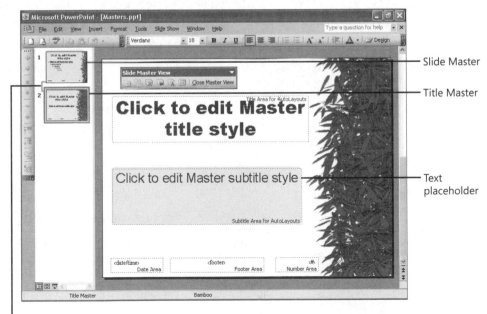

The two slides are connected to show that they are a slide-title master pair.

2   In the left pane, click Slide 1.

The Slide Master slide is displayed in the pane on the right.

To insert new masters:

Insert New
Slide Master

1   Switch to Slide Master view, and on the Slide Master View toolbar, click the **Insert New Slide Master** button.

In the left pane, a new Slide 3 with a generic slide design appears below Slide 2.

Insert New
Title Master

2   On the Slide Master View toolbar, click the **Insert New Title Master** button.

Slide 4 appears below Slide 3, with a generic title slide design. The two new masters are connected to show that they are a slide-title master pair. They both have gray thumbtacks to tell PowerPoint to preserve them even though they are not currently used in the presentation.

To apply a design template to masters:

1   Switch to Slide Master view, and click the Slide Master to which you want to apply the template.

Slide Design

2   On the Formatting toolbar, click the **Slide Design** button.

The Slide Design task pane appears with the Design Templates option active.

3   At the bottom of the Slide Design task pane, click **Browse**.

4   Navigate to the location where the template is stored, and double-click it.

The design template is applied to the slide-title master pair.

To modify the Handout and Notes masters:

1   On the **View** menu, click **Master** and then **Handout Master**.

The Handout Master appears, and the Handout Master View toolbar is displayed.

2   On the Handout Master View toolbar, click the button for the positioning style you want.

The master changes to show the selected layout.

Tip   Using the Handout Master View toolbar, you can show the positioning of one, two, three, four, six, or nine slides per page.

3   On the **View** menu, click **Master** and then **Notes Master**.

The Notes Master appears, showing the positions of the slide image and speaker notes on the notes pages. The Notes Master View toolbar is displayed.

4   On the Notes Master View toolbar, click buttons to make any adjustments you want.

Practice Exercise

In this exercise, you will create and manage multiple masters.

USE the *ChangeMaster* presentation and the *Bamboo* template in the *My Documents\Microsoft Press \MOS 2003 Study Guide\PowerPoint\P03C-2-7* practice file folder.

Open the *ChangeMaster* presentation. Display Slide Master view, and in the left pane, click Slide 1. Insert a new slide master, and then insert a new title master. Apply the **Bamboo** design template to the new slide-title master pair. Display the Handout Master, and change it to show three handouts per page. Close Master view, move to Slide 7, and apply the **Bamboo** design template to this slide. Close the Slide Design task pane, and then close the *ChangeMaster* presentation without saving it.

Adding, Deleting, and Modifying Placeholders

Adding and formatting placeholders in Slide Master view makes text objects consistent across all slides in a presentation. The master placeholders determine the style and position of those text objects—the title, bulleted text, date and time, slide number, and footer. You can format the master placeholders to look any way you want.

In addition to formatting the text, you can customize the bullets for individual bullet points or for all the bullet points in an object. You can change a bullet's font, style, and color, and you can replace it with picture or a number. You can also control the distance between a bullet and its text in much the same way you control indents in Word, by moving indent markers on a ruler.

BE SURE TO open the presentation you want to work with in Slide Master view before carrying out these steps.

To add a placeholder:

1   Display the Slide Master.

2   On the **Format** menu, click **Master Layout**.

3   Select the appropriate placeholder check box, and click **OK**.

The placeholder now appears on all slides in the presentation.

To delete a placeholder:

1   Select the placeholder object you want to delete.

2   Press **DELETE**.

To format placeholder text:

1   Select the text you want to modify.

2   On the Formatting toolbar, click the appropriate button to apply the formatting you want.

3   Click a blank area outside the text placeholder to deselect it.

To format bullet points in text placeholders:

1   Click anywhere in the text next to the bullet you want to modify.

The bullet point in the text placeholder is selected.

491

2 On the **Format** menu, click **Bullets and Numbering**.

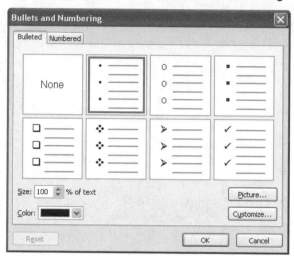

3 Change the size of the bullet by clicking the **Size** up or down arrow.

4 Click the **Color** down arrow, and click the color you want in the drop-down list.

To change the indentation of bullet points:

1 Select the text whose indentation you want to change.

2 On the **View** menu, click **Ruler**.

Horizontal and vertical rulers appear along the top and left edges of the Slide pane.
On the horizontal ruler are five sets of indent markers—one for each level in the bulleted list.

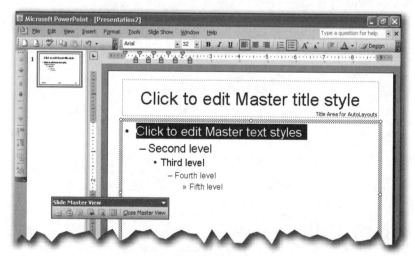

Left Indent marker

3 To change the left indent, drag the **Left Indent** marker to the desired location.

The First Line Indent marker and the Hanging Indent marker move with the Left Indent marker, maintaining the distance of the bullet from the bullet point.

▼
First Line
Indent
marker

4   To change the first line indent, drag the **First Line Indent** marker to the desired location on the ruler.

△
Hanging
Indent
marker

5   To change the hanging indent, drag the **Hanging Indent** marker to the desired location.

6   On the **View** menu, click **Ruler** to turn off the rulers.

Practice Exercise

In this exercise, you will modify and delete placeholders.

USE the *FormatMaster* presentation in the *My Documents\Microsoft Press\MOS 2003 Study Guide\PowerPoint \P03C-2-7* practice file folder.

Open the *FormatMaster* presentation. Switch to Slide Master view, and make sure Slide 1 is displayed. Change the font size of the **Number Area** placeholder to **18**, and change the font style of the *Second level* text to italic. In the same placeholder, increase the size of the first-level bullet point to **40**. Display the rulers, select the *Fifth level* text, and drag the fifth-level **Left Indent** marker (the square) to the right to the 4-inch mark on the ruler. Drag the fifth-level **First Line Indent** marker (the down-pointing triangle) to the 3-inch mark on the ruler. Drag the fifth-level **Hanging Indent** marker (the up-pointing triangle) to the 3-inch mark on the ruler. Then hide the rulers. Delete the **Number Area** placeholder, and then close Slide Master view. Close the *FormatMaster* presentation without saving it.

Inserting Content in Headers and Footers

Headers and footers contain information about the presentation, like the author or company name, the date and time, and the slide number. If you add a header and a footer to the Slide Master, it appears on every slide. You can also add different headers and footer to notes pages and handouts.

BE SURE TO open the presentation you want to work with in Normal view before carrying out these steps.

To add footers to slides:

1   On the **View** menu, click **Header and Footer**.

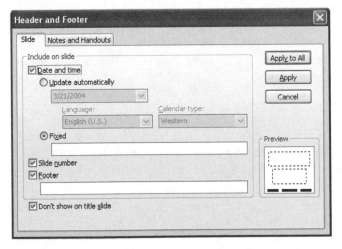

2 Select the **Footer** check box, and in the box below it, type the footer text you want.

In the Preview box, a black rectangle highlights the placement of the footer on the slides.

3 Click **Apply to All**.

To add headers and footers to notes and handouts:

1 On the **View** menu, click **Header and Footer**, and then click the **Notes and Handouts** tab.

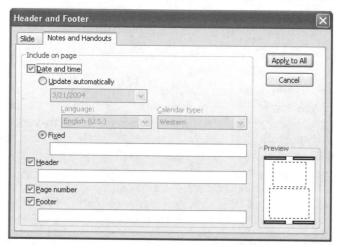

2 Select the **Header** check box, and type the header you want.

3 Select the **Footer** check box, and type the footer you want.

4 Click **Apply to All**.

To remove information from headers and footers:

1 On the **View** menu, click **Header and Footer**.

2 Do one of the following:

- To eliminate an item from all slides, clear that item's check box in the **Include on slide** area, and click **Apply to All**.

- To eliminate items from only one slide, select that slide, clear the check boxes of the items you want to remove, and click **Apply**.

- To remove all items from the title slide, select the **Don't show on title slide** check box, and click **Apply**.

Practice Exercise

In this exercise, you will add a footer to all slides except the title slide.

USE the *AddFooter* presentation in the *My Documents\Microsoft Press\MOS 2003 Study Guide\PowerPoint \P03C-2-7* practice file folder.

Open the *AddFooter* presentation. Open the Header and Footer dialog box, and then select the options to include an automatically updated date and time, a slide number, and a footer reading **The Garden Company**. Make sure these items will appear on all slides except the title slide. Then close the *AddFooter* presentation without saving it.

P03C-2 Review

Number	Objective	Mastered
P03C-2-1	Format text-based content	
	Changing the font, size, and font style of text	❏
	Modifying text colors	❏
	Changing text alignment	❏
	Finding and replacing fonts	❏
P03C-2-2	Format pictures, shapes and graphics	
	Sizing and cropping graphics	❏
	Adjusting the color of graphics	❏
	Aligning, connecting, and rotating graphics	❏
	Adding effects to graphics	❏
P03C-2-3	Format slides	
	Coloring and shading a slide background	❏
	Modifying the slide layout	❏
	Using a design template to make a presentation look consistent	❏
	Setting the slide size and orientation	❏
P03C-2-4	Apply animation schemes	
	Animating slides	❏
P03C-2-5	Apply slide transitions	
	Applying transition effects	❏
P03C-2-6	Customize slide templates	
	Saving a presentation as a template	❏
P03C-2-7	Work with masters	
	Changing a presentation's masters	❏
	Adding, deleting, and modifying placeholders	❏
	Inserting content in headers and footers	❏

P03C-3
Collaborating

The skills tested by this section of the Microsoft Office Specialist PowerPoint 2003 Exam all relate to the PowerPoint features that make it is easy to collaborate with other people on the creation and formatting of presentations. Specifically, the following objectives are associated with this set of skills:

Number	Objective
P03C-3-1	Track, accept, and reject changes in a presentation
P03C-3-2	Add, edit, and delete comments in a presentation
P03C-3-3	Compare and merge presentations

Important Before you can do the practice exercises associated with this skill set, you need to install the practice files from the book's companion CD to their default location. See "Installing the Practice Files" on page xxv for more information.

Track, Accept, and Reject Changes in a Presentation

P03C-3-1   The skills measured by this objective include the following:

- Viewing tracked changes
- Accepting and rejecting changes

In PowerPoint, you cannot turn on tracked changes for a presentation as you can for a document in Word. Tracked changes are applied only when two or more versions of a presentation are merged. You can then review the changes and accept or reject them.

Viewing Tracked Changes

When you merge presentations, PowerPoint shows the differences between the original and the reviewed versions with change markers. These markers show the details of the changes without obscuring the presentation or affecting its layout.

See Also For information about merging presentations, refer to P03C-3-3, "Compare and Merge Presentations."

You can use the Revisions task pane to see the details of the changes. You can see a list of the changes made to the current slide by all reviewers or a selected reviewer on the List tab, or see a graphical representation of the changes on the Gallery tab.

BE SURE TO open a presentation containing comments and tracked changes in Normal view before carrying out these steps.

To browse through changes:

1   On the **View** menu, click **Toolbars** and then **Revisions**.

The Revisions task pane appears, showing the comments and changes made to the first slide in the presentation. The comments and changes from each reviewer appear in a different color.

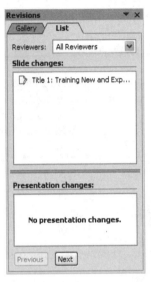

2   At the bottom of the Revisions task pane, click **Next**.

PowerPoint moves to the next comment or change in the presentation.

3   On the Reviewing toolbar, do one of the following:

Next Item

■   To move to the next change or comment in the presentation, click the **Next Item** button.

Previous Item

■   To move back to the previous change or comment, click the **Previous Item** button.

To display changes made by a specific reviewer or reviewers:

Reviewers...

1   On the Reviewing toolbar, click the **Reviewers** button.

2   Do any of the following:

■   Select the check boxes of reviewers whose changes you want to display.

■   Clear the check boxes for reviewers whose changes you want to hide.

■   Select or clear the **All Reviewers** check box to display or hide changes from all reviewers.

Practice Exercise

In this exercise, you view the tracked changes in a presentation.

USE the *ViewChanges* presentations in the *My Documents\Microsoft Press\MOS 2003 Study Guide\PowerPoint* *\P03C-3-1* practice file folder.

Open the *ViewChanges* presentation. Hide the changes made by Kim Akers, look at the change suggested for Slide 1, and then view the next change to the presentation. Redisplay all changes, including those by Kim Akers, and then click **Previous** to see the changes she suggested for Slide 2. Scroll through all changes to the slides by using the **Next** button. Then close the *ViewChanges* presentation without saving it.

Accepting and Rejecting Changes

When working with a presentation containing tracked changes, you can accept or reject one marker at a time, all markers on a slide, or all markers in a presentation. When you accept a change, PowerPoint incorporates it into the slide. When you reject a change, PowerPoint restores the original slide. You can also delete all markup in a slide or presentation.

BE SURE TO open a presentation containing comments and tracked changes in Normal view before carrying out these steps.

To preview the effect of accepting a change:

1   On the **View** menu, click **Toolbars** and then **Revisions** to open the Revisions task pane.

2   In the Revisions task pane, click the **Gallery** tab.

    This tab shows you what the current slide will look like if you accept all changes.

To apply or reject a change:

1   On the slide, click the change marker of the change you want to accept.

    A ScreenTip displays the content of the change.

2   On the Reviewing toolbar, do one of the following:

Apply

■ To accept the change, click the **Apply** button.

Unapply

■ To reject the change, click the **Unapply** button.

To apply or reject all changes:

Apply

1   On the Reviewing toolbar, click the **Apply** down arrow, and do one of the following:

■ To apply all changes on the current slide, click **Apply All Changes to the Current Slide**.

■ To apply all changes in the presentation, click **Apply All Changes to the Presentation**.

Unapply

2   On the Reviewing toolbar, click the **Unapply** down arrow, and do one of the following:

■ To reject all changes on the current slide, click **Unapply All Changes to the Current Slide.**

■ To reject all changes in the presentation, click **Unapply All Changes to the Presentation.**

To delete all markup:

1   Move to the slide containing the markup you want to delete.

Delete
Comment

2   On the Reviewing toolbar, click the **Delete Comment** down arrow, and do one of the following:

■ To delete all markup on the current slide, click **Delete All Markup on the Current Slide**.

■ To delete all markup in the presentation, click **Delete All Markup in this Presentation,** and then click **Yes**.

Practice Exercise

In this exercise, you will accept and reject changes in a presentation.

USE the *AcceptChanges* presentations in the *My Documents\Microsoft Press\MOS 2003 Study Guide \PowerPoint\P03C-3-1* practice file folder.

Open the *AcceptChanges* presentation. Click the change at the top of the **Slides** tab in the Outline/Slides pane, and accept the change. Then delete all the markup on Slide 1. Move to Slide 2, apply all its changes, and then delete all the remaining markup on the slide. Move to the next change in the presentation. Review the comment and the changes, accept them, and delete the markers. Move to the next change, and apply all the changes to the slide. Delete all the markers from Slide 4. Hide all changes made by Kim Akers, and move to the next change—a comment from Karen Berg. Review the comment, and then delete the slide. Redisplay the changes made by Kim Akers, and move to Slide 1. Then move to the next change. Switch to the **Gallery** tab of the Revisions task pane, review all the remaining changes, and then apply all the changes to the presentation. Delete all remaining markup in the presentation, and then close the *AcceptChanges* presentation without saving it.

Add, Edit, and Delete Comments in a Presentation

P03C-3-2   The skills measured by this objective include the following:

■ Adding comments

■ Working with comments

At any time while you are working on a presentation, you can add, edit, and delete comments. Comments are used for such tasks as providing explanations, questioning assumptions, or flagging missing information.

Adding Comments

You or your reviewers can insert comments without disrupting the text and layout of the slides by using the Comment command on the Insert menu.

BE SURE TO open the presentation you want to work with in Normal view before carrying out these steps.

To add a comment:

1   Display the slide to which you want to add a comment.

2   Do one of the following:

   ■ On the **Insert** menu, click **Comment**.

   ■ On the Reviewing toolbar, click the **Insert Comment** button.

Insert
Comment

A comment box appears with your name, today's date, and a blinking insertion point.

3   In the comment box, type the text of the comment.

4   Click anywhere outside the comment box.

The comment box closes, and a small box with your initials and the number 1 appears in the upper-left corner of the slide.

Practice Exercise

In this exercise, you will add comments to a presentation.

USE the *AddComments* presentation in the *My Documents\Microsoft Press\MOS 2003 Study Guide\PowerPoint \P03C-3-2* practice file folder.

Open the *AddComments* presentation. On Slide 1, insert a comment with the text **Does this cover everything?**, and then close the comment box. Move to Slide 3, select the first square object, insert a comment with the text **Any ideas for improving this slide?**, and then close the comment box. Move to Slide 10, insert a comment with the text **Ask Kim to prepare a report on potential class sizes and class costs**, and then close the comment box. Then close the *AddComments* presentation without saving it.

Working with Comments

You can edit, delete, show, or hide the comments in a presentation. You can also use the Revisions task pane to view the comments on the current slide.

BE SURE TO open a presentation containing comments in Normal view before carrying out these steps.

To edit a comment's text:

1   Double-click the comment box to open it.

2   Edit the text of the comment as usual, and then click outside the comment box to close it.

To change the name of the person making the comments:

1   On the **Tools** menu, click **Options**, and then click the **General** tab.

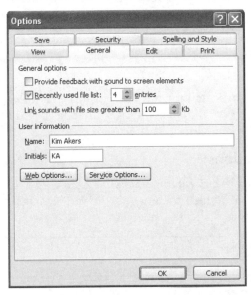

2   In the **User information** area, change the entries in the **Name** and **Initials** boxes.

3   Click **OK**.

To hide and display comments:

1   On the **View** menu, click **Toolbars** and then **Reviewing** to display the Reviewing toolbar.

Show/Hide
Markup

2   On the Reviewing toolbar, click the **Show/Hide Markup** button to toggle it off.
    The comment boxes disappear.

3   On the Reviewing toolbar, click the **Show/Hide Markup** button again to toggle it on.
    The comment boxes reappear.

To delete a comment:

● Do one of the following:

■   Right-click the comment box, and click **Delete Comment** on the shortcut menu.

Delete
Comment

■   On the Reviewing toolbar, click the **Delete Comment** button.

The comment is deleted from the slide and also from the Revisions task pane.

Practice Exercise

In this exercise, you will add, edit, and delete comments in a presentation.

USE the *EditComments* presentation in the *My Documents\Microsoft Press\MOS 2003 Study Guide \PowerPoint\P03C-3-2* practice file folder.

Open the *EditComments* presentation. Make sure the **Markup** button is active. Delete the comment on Slide 1. Move to Slide 3, and add **What about boxes with lighter backgrounds?** to the comment. Then close the *EditComments* presentation without saving it.

Compare and Merge Presentations

P03C-3-3   The skills measured by this objective include the following:

■ Comparing and merging presentations

When you compare and merge presentations, any edits made by reviewers show up as tracked changes. You can then accept the changes you want to keep and reject those you want to disregard.

Comparing and Merging Presentations

When one or more people review a presentation and send back their edited versions, you can merge those versions into the original presentation. PowerPoint then tracks all the changes so that you can easily review them in one place.

See Also   For information about accepting and rejecting tracked changes, refer to P03C-3-1, "Track, Accept, and Reject Changes."

BE SURE TO open the original version of the presentation you sent out for review before carrying out these steps.

To compare and merge presentations:

1   On the **Tools** menu, click **Compare and Merge Presentations**.
2   Navigate to the location where the first version you want to merge is stored, and click its file.
3   Click **Merge**.
4   Click **Continue**.

The Revisions task pane appears, showing the comments and changes made to the first slide in the presentation.

5   Repeat steps 1 through 4 to merge any additional versions of the presentation.

The comments and changes from each reviewer appear in a different color with their initials.

Practice Exercise

In this exercise, you will merge two reviewed versions of a presentation into the original, and then review the merged presentation.

USE the *CompareMerge*, *CompareMerge_KA*, and *CompareMerge_KB* presentations in the *My Documents \Microsoft Press\MOS 2003 Study Guide\PowerPoint\P03C-3-3* practice file folder.

Open the *CompareMerge* presentation. On the **Tools** menu, click **Compare and Merge Presentations**. Navigate to the *My Documents\Microsoft Press\MOS 2003 Study Guide \PowerPoint\P03C-3-3* folder, and select the *CompareMerge_KA* and *CompareMerge_KB* files. Merge the files, and then click **Continue**. Review the merged presentation, and then close the *CompareMerge* presentation without saving it.

P03C-3 Review

Number	Objective	Mastered
P03C-3-1	Track, accept, and reject changes in a presentation	
	Viewing tracked changes	❏
	Accepting and rejecting changes	❏
P03C-3-2	Add, edit, and delete comments in a presentation	
	Adding comments	❏
	Working with comments	❏
P03C-3-3	Compare and merge presentations	
	Comparing and merging presentations	❏

P03C-4

Managing and Delivering Presentations

The skills tested by this section of the Microsoft Office Specialist PowerPoint 2003 Exam all relate to the management and delivery of presentations. Specifically, the following objectives are associated with this set of skills:

Number	Objective
P03C-4-1	Organize a presentation
P03C-4-2	Set up slide shows for delivery
P03C-4-3	Rehearse timing
P03C-4-4	Deliver presentations
P03C-4-5	Prepare presentations for remote delivery
P03C-4-6	Save and publish presentations
P03C-4-7	Print slides, outlines, handouts, and speaker notes
P03C-4-8	Export a presentation to another Microsoft Office program

Important   Before you can do the practice exercises associated with this skill set, you need to install the practice files from the book's companion CD to their default location. See "Installing the Practice Files" on page xxv for more information.

Organize a Presentation

P03C-4-1   The skills measured by this objective include the following:

- Working with different views
- Organizing and deleting slides
- Adding and viewing notes
- Adding hyperlinks

In PowerPoint, you carry out different organizational tasks in different views, and you need to know which view to use when.

Working with Different Views

PowerPoint has four views to help you create, organize, and deliver presentations:

Normal
View

- In Normal view, you can work with a presentation in three ways: as a text outline or set of slide thumbnails in the Outline/Slides pane, as a slide in the Slide pane, and as speaker notes in the Notes pane.

Slide Sorter
View

- In Slide Sorter view, you can preview an entire presentation as thumbnails and easily delete and rearrange slides. You can perform other tasks by using buttons on the Slide Sorter toolbar.

- In Notes Page view, you can create notes that are too complex to be handled by Normal view's Notes pane. (There is no button for this view.)

Slide Show
View

- In Slide Show view, you can display slides as an electronic presentation, with the slides filling the entire screen.

- In Master view, you can make changes that affect all the slides in the presentation. (There is no button for this view.)

See Also   For information about Master view, refer to P03C-2-7, "Work with Masters."

To see more or less of the text on the screen, you can expand or reduce the zoom percentage of the presentation. Changing the zoom percentage affects only the view on your screen; it doesn't affect the size of the text in your presentation.

BE SURE TO open the presentation you want to work with before carrying out these steps.

To switch views:

- Do one of the following:
    - On the **View** menu, click the command for the view you want.
    - In the lower-left corner of the presentation window, click one of the view buttons.

To zoom to various percentages:

Zoom

1   On the Standard toolbar, click the **Zoom** down arrow, and click the zoom percentage you want.

2   On the Standard toolbar, click the **Zoom** box (not the down arrow) to select the current zoom percentage.

3   Type the zoom percentage you want, and press the **ENTER** key.

4   On the Standard toolbar, click the **Zoom** down arrow, and click **Fit**.

The entire page appears in the window.

Practice Exercise

In this exercise, you will switch among views and then set the zoom percentage.

USE the *ViewPresentation* presentation in the *My Documents\Microsoft Press\MOS 2003 Study Guide \PowerPoint\P03C-4-1 practice file folder*.

Open the *ViewPresentaton* presentation. In the Outline/Slides pane, make sure the Outline tab is active, and then click the slide icon adjacent to the *Features and Benefits* heading. In the Outline/Slides pane, click the **Slides** tab. Drag the scroll box to the top of the scroll bar, and select the first slide. Switch to Slide Sorter view, and then switch to Notes Page view. Then display the presentation in Normal view, with Slide 1 active. Change the zoom percentage to **50%**. Then close the *ViewPresentation* presentation without saving it.

Organizing and Deleting Slides

You might need to change the order of your slides to make them communicate your message most effectively. Rearranging a presentation is best done in Slide Sorter view, where you can drag slides from one location to another. In this view, you can also easily delete slides as necessary.

BE SURE TO open the presentation you want to work with in Slide Sorter view before carrying out these steps.

To move a slide:

1   Click the thumbnail of the slide you want to move.

2   Point to the thumbnail, and drag it to its new location.

    When you release the mouse button, the slide moves to its new position, and PowerPoint repositions and renumbers the other slides in the presentation.

To move a slide from another open presentation:

1   Open the presentation from which you want to move the slide.

2   On the **Window** menu, click **Arrange All**.

3   Drag the slide from one presentation window to the other.

To delete a slide:

1   Click the thumbnail of the slide you want to delete.

2   Do one of the following:

    ◼ Press the **DELETE** key.

    ◼ On the **Edit** menu, click **Delete Slide**.

    ◼ Right-click the slide, and click **Delete Slide** on the shortcut menu.

    The entire slide is deleted, and PowerPoint renumbers the slides sequentially.

To hide slide formatting in Slide Sorter view:

1   Hold down the **ALT** key.

2   Point to any slide, and hold down the mouse button.

    The slide's formatting disappears so that the title is easier to read.

Practice Exercise

In this exercise, you will rearrange the slides of a presentation into a more logical order, and you will delete an extraneous slide.

USE the *OrganizeSlides* presentation in the *My Documents\Microsoft Press\MOS 2003 Study Guide \PowerPoint\P03C-4-1 practice file folder.*

Open the *OrganizeSlides* presentation. Reposition Slide 3 so it is the last slide in the presentation. Delete Slide 4. Then close the *OrganizeSlides* presentation without saving it.

Adding and Viewing Notes

Each slide in a PowerPoint presentation has a corresponding notes page. As you create each slide, you can enter text notes that relate to the slide's content in the Notes pane in Normal view. However, if you want to include something other than text, you must switch to Notes Page view. You also switch to Notes Page view if you want to review the notes for all the slides. No matter which view you use to create notes, you can print them with thumbnails of the slides as handouts or as speaker notes.

See Also   For information about printing notes, refer to P03C-4-7, "Print Slides, Outlines, Handouts, and Speaker Notes."

BE SURE TO open the presentation you want to work with in Normal view before carrying out these steps.

To add notes to a slide:

1   In a slide's Notes pane, click the **Click to add notes** text placeholder.

The notes placeholder text disappears, and a blinking insertion point appears.

2   Type the note.

To add notes in Notes Page view:

1   On the **View** menu, click **Notes Page**.

The current slide appears with a slide thumbnail and its notes displayed.

2   Click the **Click to add text** placeholder.

3   Type the note.

To add a graphic to a note:

1   On the **View** menu, click **Notes Page**.

2   Click in the Notes pane, click **Picture** on the **Insert** menu, and then click the appropriate subcommand to insert the type of graphic you want.

Tip   You can also insert objects or use the AutoShapes button on the Drawing toolbar to draw shapes.

Practice Exercise

In this exercise, you will add notes to a slide, including inserting a set of graphics on a notes page.

USE the *AddNote* presentation and *OtherLogos* graphics file in the *My Documents\Microsoft Press\MOS 2003 Study Guide\PowerPoint\P03C-4-1 practice file folder*.

Open the *AddNote* presentation in Normal view, and type the following note: **We had these other color options for our logo, but in the end, we preferred this one because the colors are more appropriate for our company.** Switch to Notes Page view, and insert the *OtherLogos* graphics file. Move the graphic down so that it does not obscure the text, and then close the *AddNote* presentation without saving it.

Adding Hyperlinks

If you want to refer to information located outside your presentation, you can attach hyperlinks to text or objects. When clicked, hyperlinks jump to another slide in the same presentation, to a slide in a different presentation, to a file on your computer or your company's network or intranet, to a Web address, or to a message window for a specific e-mail address.

BE SURE TO open the presentation you want to work with in Normal view before carrying out these steps.

To insert a hyperlink:

1   Display the desired slide, and select the object or text to which you want to attach the hyperlink.

2   On the **Slide Show** menu, click **Action Settings**.

3   Select the **Hyperlink to** option, click the **Hyperlink to** down arrow, and do one of the following:

■ To add a hyperlink to another slide, click **Slide**, and then in the **Slide title** list, click the slide you want to link to.

■ To add a hyperlink to a file, click **Other File**, navigate to the file you want to link to, and double-click the file name.

■ To add a hyperlink to a Web site, click **URL**, and type the URL you want to link to.

4   Click **OK** to close the Action Settings dialog box, and then click a blank area of the slide.

The text is underlined and takes on the accent and hyperlink color in the slide color scheme.

To create a hyperlink by using the Insert Hyperlink dialog box:

1   Display the desired slide, and select the object or text to which you want to attach the hyperlink.

Insert
Hyperlink

2   On the Standard toolbar, click the **Insert Hyperlink** button.

3   Do one of the following:

■ To add a hyperlink to another slide, click the **Place in This Document** button, and then click the slide you want to link to.

■ To add a hyperlink to a file, click the **Existing File or Web Page** button, navigate to the file you want to link to, and then double-click the name of the file.

■ To add a hyperlink to a Web site, click the **Existing File or Web Page** button, and in the **Address** box, type the URL you want to link to.

■ To add a hyperlink that displays a message box containing an e-mail address, click the **E-mail Address** button, enter an e-mail address in the **E-mail address** box, and enter a subject in the **Subject** box.

4   Click **OK**.

Practice Exercise

In this exercise, you will add a hyperlink from one slide to another, a hyperlink to another file, and a hyperlink to a fictitious website.

USE the *CreateLink* presentation and *GardenBudget* workbook in the *My Documents\Microsoft Press\MOS 2003 Study Guide\PowerPoint\P03C-4-1 practice file folder*.

Open the *CreateLink* presentation. Move to Slide 3, select *Gather your supplies* in the middle text box, and add a hyperlink to Slide 5. Display Slide 3 in Slide Show view, and then click until the boxes and connectors are displayed. Display the pointer, click the *Gather your supplies* hyperlink, and then end the slide show. Move to Slide 7, select the chart object, and add a hyperlink to the *GardenBudget* workbook in the *My Documents\Microsoft Press\MOS 2003 Study Guide\PowerPoint\P03C-4-1 practice file folder*. Run the slide show, and when the chart appears on Slide 7, click it. Close the Excel workbook without saving your changes, and end the slide show. Display the slide master, select **www.gardenco.msn.com**, and insert a hyperlink to **http://www.gardenco.msn.com**. Close Master view, and run the slide show, noticing that the hyperlink appears on every slide. Then close the *CreateLink* presentation without saving it.

Set Up Slide Shows for Delivery

P03C-4-2   The skills measured by this objective include the following:

■ Creating a custom slide show
■ Working with action buttons
■ Working with hidden slides

PowerPoint has several features that can help you set up a slide show for delivery. You can customize slide shows for different audiences, add action buttons to more easily navigate through a presentation, and hide any slides you might not want to display during every slide show.

Creating a Custom Slide Show

If you plan to present variations of the same slide show to different audiences, you don't have to create a separate presentation for each audience. Instead, you can select slides from the presentation that are appropriate for a particular audience and group them as a custom show. You can then run the custom show using just those slides.

BE SURE TO open the presentation you want to work with in Normal view before carrying out these steps.

To create a custom show:

1   On the **Slide Show** menu, click **Custom Shows**.

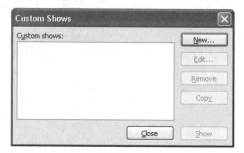

2   Click **New**.

The Define Custom Show dialog box appears, with a default name selected in the "Slide show name" box.

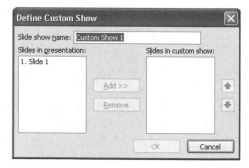

3 In the **Slide show name** box, type a name for the new custom show.

4 In the **Slides in presentation** box, click the first slide you want to add to the custom show, and then click **Add**.

The slide appears as Slide 1 in the "Slides in custom show" box on the right.

5 Continue adding slides to the custom show.

The slides appear in sequential order in the "Slides in custom show" box.

6 Click **OK**.

7 In the Custom Shows dialog box, click **Show** to start the custom slide show.

8 Click through all the slides, including the blank one at the end of the show.

To add, delete, or move slides in a custom show:

1 On the **Slide Show** menu, click **Custom Shows**.

2 In the **Custom shows** list, click the show you want to work with, and click **Edit**.

The Define Custom Show dialog box appears.

3 To add a slide, click the slide in the **Slides in presentation** list, and click **Add**.

4 To delete a slide, click the slide in the **Slides in custom show** box, and click **Remove**.

PowerPoint removes the slide from the custom show, but not from the main presentation.

5 To change the order in which a slide appears, click the slide in the **Slides in custom show** box, and click the up or down arrow until the slide is in the location you want.

Practice Exercise

In this exercise, you will create and edit a custom slide show.

USE the *CustomShow* presentation in the *My Documents\Microsoft Press\MOS 2003 Study Guide\PowerPoint \P03C-4-2* practice file folder.

Open the *CustomShow* presentation. Create a new custom slide show with the name **Contractors**, containing Slides 9, 2 through 4, 6 through 8, and 12 through 14. Run the custom show, and click through all the slides, including the blank one at the end. Then remove Slide 8 from the custom show, and run through it again. Close the *CustomShow* presentation without saving it.

Working with Action Buttons

You can add action buttons to a presentation to more easily navigate among slides when delivering a slide show to an audience. PowerPoint's predefined action buttons include the Home, Help, Information, Back, Next, Beginning, End, and Return buttons.

BE SURE TO open the presentation you want to work with before carrying out these steps.

To add a predefined action button:

1 Display the slide to which you want to add an action button.

2 On the **Slide Show** menu, click **Action Buttons**.

A button palette appears.

3 Click the type of action button you want to add, and drag the cross-hair pointer across the slide.

When you release the mouse button, the Action Settings dialog box appears with the "Hyperlink to" option selected and an option in the box below that corresponds to the action button you chose. At the bottom of the dialog box, the "Highlight click" check box is selected, but dimmed to indicate that you cannot change this setting.

4 To play a sound when the action button is clicked, select the **Play sound** check box, click the down arrow of the box below, and click the sound you want in the list.

5 Click **OK**.

6 Use the button's sizing handles to adjust its size, and then drag it to the location you want on the slide.

To add an action button to a custom hyperlink:

1   Display the slide to which you want to add a hyperlinked action button.

2   On the **Slide Show** menu, click **Action Buttons**.

3   Click **Custom** in the button palette, and drag the cross-hair pointer across the slide in the desired location.

4   In the Action Settings dialog box, click the **Hyperlink to** option, click its down arrow, and then click the type of hyperlink you want to create.

5   Select the target location as appropriate, and then click **OK**.

To add text to an action button:

1   Right-click the action button, and click **Add Text** on the shortcut menu.

2   Type the text you want.

3   Right-click the action button again, and click **Font** on the shortcut menu.

4   Specify the font, size, style, and color you want.

5   Click **OK**.

To format an action button with a background color and border:

1   Right-click the action button, click **Format AutoShape** on the shortcut menu, and then click the **Colors and Lines** tab.

2   In the **Line** area, click the **Color** down arrow, and click a border color.

3   Specify the dash and weight settings you want.

4   In the **Fill** area, click the button color you want.

5   Click **OK**.

Practice Exercise

In this exercise, you will add and modify an action button.

USE the *AddButton* presentation in the *My Documents\Microsoft Press\MOS 2003 Study Guide\PowerPoint \P03C-3-2* practice file folder.

Open the *AddButton* presentation, and move to Slide 11. Insert a Home action button on the right side of the slide. Use the action button's sizing handles to make it smaller, and then move it to the lower-left corner of the slide. Switch to Slide Show view with Slide 11 displayed, click the slide's action button to jump to the title slide, and then end the slide show. Close the *AddButton* presentation without saving it.

Working with Hidden Slides

You can hide a slide so that you can skip over it if its information is not useful to a particular audience. If you decide to display the slide while you are delivering a slide show, you can use the Go to Slide command. Alternatively, you can insert an action button on a visible slide that you can click to jump to the hidden slide.

BE SURE TO open the presentation you want to work with in Normal view before carrying out these steps.

To hide a slide:

● On the **Slides** tab of the Outline/Slides pane, right-click the slide you want to hide, and click **Hide Slide** on the shortcut menu.

PowerPoint puts a shadow box around and a diagonal line through the slide number to indicate that the slide is hidden.

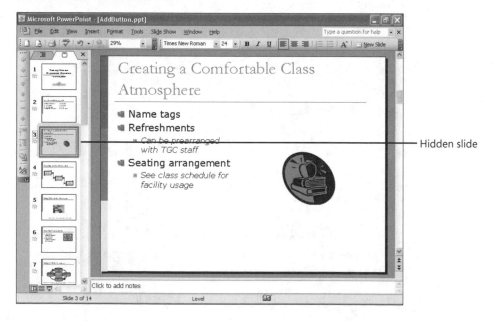

Hidden slide

Hide Slide

Tip In Slide Sorter view, you can select a slide and then click the Hide Slide button on the Slide Sorter toolbar.

To view a hidden slide:

1 Switch to Slide Show view.

2 Right-click anywhere on the screen, click **Go to Slide**, and then click the slide you want to display.

The hidden slide appears in Slide Show view.

Tip You can also link an action button to a hidden slide so that you can display the slide by clicking the button.

To unhide a slide:

● On the **Slides** tab of the Outline/Slides pane, right-click the hidden slide, and click **Hide Slide** on the shortcut menu.

Practice Exercise

In this exercise, you will hide a slide, display it during a slide show, and then create an action button that jumps to the hidden slide.

USE the *HideSlide* presentation in the *My Documents\Microsoft Press\MOS 2003 Study Guide\PowerPoint \P03C-4-2* practice file folder.

Open the *HideSlide* presentation, and then hide Slide 3. Run the slide show, and when all eight bullet points on Slide 2 are visible, skip over the hidden slide to Slide 4. Then exit the show. Run the show once more, and this time, when you finish displaying Slide 2, display the hidden Slide 3. Close the *HideSlide* presentation without saving it.

Rehearse Timing

P03C-4-3   The skills measured by this objective include the following:

■ Setting slide timings
■ Rehearsing a presentation

When you deliver a slide show, you can manually move from slide to slide, or you can have PowerPoint advance through the slides, displaying each slide for the time you specify. You can apply a timing to the slides, or you can rehearse the slide show and have PowerPoint set the timings to the amount of time you spend talking about each slide.

Setting Slide Timings

The length of time a slide appears on the screen is controlled by its slide timing. You can apply a timing to a single slide, a group of slides, or an entire presentation.

BE SURE TO open the presentation you want to work with in Slide Sorter view before carrying out these steps.

To set a timing for a single slide or group of slides:

1   Click the slide to which you want to add a timing.

2   On the Slide Sorter toolbar, click the **Slide Transition** button to open the Slide Transition task pane.

3   In the **Advance slide** area, select the **Automatically after** check box, and then click the up arrow until you reach the desired interval.

> **Tip**   If you select both check boxes in the "Advance slide" area, the slide will advance either after the specified time or when you click the mouse button.

4   The slide timing appears below the lower-left corner of the slide thumbnail.

To set a timing for all slides:

1   Click any slide in the presentation.

2   On the Slide Sorter toolbar, click the **Slide Transition** button to open the Slide Transition task pane.

3   In the **Advance slide** area, select the **Automatically after** check box, and then click the up arrow until you reach the desired interval.

4   At the bottom of the Slide Transition task pane, click the **Apply to All Slides** button.

PowerPoint applies the setting in the Slide Transition task pane to all the slides.

Practice Exercise

In this exercise, you will set timings for different slides in a presentation.

USE the *AddTimings* presentation in the *My Documents\Microsoft Press\MOS 2003 Study Guide\PowerPoint \P03C-4-3* practice file folder.

Open the *AddTimings* presentation. Display Slide 3 in Slide Sorter view, and set the slide to advance automatically after 2 seconds. Then set Slides 1 and 2 to advance after 5 seconds. Run the slide show, and then click Slide 3 and apply its setting to all the slides. Run the slide show again, and then close the *AddTimings* presentation without saving it.

Rehearsing a Presentation

If you are unsure how much time to allow for the slide timings of a presentation, you can rehearse the slide show while PowerPoint automatically tracks and sets the timing for you. The timings then reflect the amount of time you spend on each slide during the rehearsal. This technique is used when you want to spend more time talking about some slides than others, so you can pace your presentation.

BE SURE TO open the presentation you want to work with in Slide Sorter view before carrying out these steps.

To rehearse a presentation:

Rehearse
Timings

1 On the Slide Sorter toolbar, click the **Rehearse Timings** button.

PowerPoint switches to Slide Show view, starts the show, and displays the Rehearsal toolbar. A Slide Time counter is recording the length of time the first slide remains on the screen.

Next

2 Wait about 10 seconds, and then click the **Next** button.

3 Work your way slowly through the slide show, clicking **Next** to display each bullet point on each slide and then move to the next slide.

Repeat

4 If you want to repeat the rehearsal for a particular slide, click the **Repeat** button on the Rehearsal toolbar to reset the **Slide Time** setting for that slide to 0.00.00.

Close

5 If you want to start the entire rehearsal over again, click the Rehearsal toolbar's **Close** button, and when a message asks whether you want to keep the existing timings, click **No**.

6 At the end of the slide show, click **Yes**.

You return to Slide Sorter view, where the recorded timings have been added below each slide. The timing for the active slide, Slide 1, appears in the "Automatically after" box in the "Advance slide" area of the Slide Transition task pane, and you can manually adjust the timing if you want.

Practice Exercise

In this exercise, you will rehearse a slide show and allow PowerPoint to add slide timings based on the time you spend on each slide.

USE the *RehearseShow* presentation in the *My Documents\Microsoft Press\MOS 2003 Study Guide\PowerPoint \P03C-4-3* practice file folder.

Open the *RehearseShow* presentation. Use the Rehearse Timings feature to run through the entire slide show and record timings for each slide. At the end of the rehearsal, click **Yes** to keep the new slide timings. Then close the *RehearseShow* presentation without saving it.

Deliver Presentations

P03C-4-4   The skills measured by this objective include the following:

- Delivering a slide show
- Using on-screen tools for emphasis

You deliver a presentation by running it in Slide Show view. PowerPoint includes tools that you can use during the presentation to switch manually between slides or to emphasize certain points.

Delivering a Slide Show

The simplest way to advance from one slide to the next in Slide Show view is to click the mouse button. However, PowerPoint 2003 includes a popup toolbar that appears when you move the mouse pointer while in Slide Show view, which you use to move around in other ways.

If you are in the middle of a slide show and can't remember how to move to a particular slide, you can click the Navigation button on the popup toolbar and then click Help. Power-Point displays a long list of keyboard shortcuts for carrying out slide show tasks.

BE SURE TO open the presentation you want to work with in Slide Show view before carrying out these steps.

To run a slide show:

1   If the title slide has animated components, click the mouse button as many times as necessary to build the title slide.

2   To move to the next slide, do one of the following:
- Press **ENTER** or **SPACE**.
- On the popup toolbar, click the **Next** button.
- Click anywhere on the screen.
- Right-click anywhere on the slide, and on the shortcut menu, click **Next**.

3   To move to the previous slide, do one of the following:

- Press the **BACKSPACE** key.

- On the popup toolbar, click the **Previous** button.

- Right-click anywhere on the slide, and on the shortcut menu, click **Previous**.

4   To move to a specific slide, do one of the following:

- Type the slide number, and then press the **ENTER** key.

- Right-click anywhere on the slide, and on the shortcut menu, click **Go to Slide**, and then click the slide you want.

5   When you reach the blank slide at the end of the slide show, either leave it displayed while you wind up your presentation or press the **ESC** key to exit Slide Show view.

Practice Exercise

In this exercise, you will practice delivering a presentation by navigating among its slides.

USE the *DeliverShow* presentation in the *My Documents\Microsoft Press\MOS 2003 Study Guide\PowerPoint \P03C-4-4* practice file folder.

Open the *DeliverShow* presentation. Display Slide 1 in Slide Show view, and then use any method to advance to the next slide. Display the previous slide, and then display the next slide again. Click until the first bullet point on Slide 2 is displayed, and then jump directly back to the previous slide. Move to Slide 9, and click until the budget chart is displayed on the slide. End the slide show, and close the *DeliverShow* presentation without saving it.

Using Tools for Emphasis

During a slide show, you can display an arrow pointer so that you can draw the attention of your audience to particular parts of a slide. You can also annotate slides by using the pen tool to draw freehand lines and shapes in various ink colors, and you can use the highlighter tool to emphasize areas of the slide with splashes of color.

BE SURE TO open the presentation you want to work with in Slide Show view before carrying out these steps.

To display the arrow pointer:

1   Move the mouse.

The arrow pointer appears.

2   Point to the object on the slide to which you want to draw attention.

To use the pen tool:

1   Right-click anywhere on the screen, click **Pointer Options** on the shortcut menu, and then click either **Ballpoint Pen** or **Felt Tip Pen**.

The pointer now resembles the tip of the type of pen you chose.

2   Draw on the slide.

3   When you have finished marking up the slide, press the **ESC** key to switch to the arrow pointer.

Tip   When the pen tool is active in Slide Show view, clicking the mouse button does not advance the slide show to the next slide. You need to switch back to the arrow pointer to advance the slide using the mouse.

To change the color of the pen tool:

1   Right-click anywhere on the screen, click **Pointer Options** on the shortcut menu, and then click **Ink Color**.

A color palette appears.

2   On the **Ink Color** palette, click any color box.

The pointer changes to a pen in the color you chose.

3   Draw on the slide.

4   When you have finished marking up the slide, press the **ESC** key to switch to the arrow pointer.

To use the highlighter:

1   Right-click anywhere on the screen, click **Pointer Options** on the shortcut menu, and then click **Highlighter**.

2   Drag through the area you want to highlight.

3   When you have finished highlighting areas of the slide, press the **ESC** key to switch to the arrow pointer.

To erase the markup on a slide:

1   Right-click anywhere on the screen, and click **Pointer Options** on the shortcut menu.

2   Do one of the following:

■   To erase part of the markup on a slide, click **Eraser**, and then click the line you want to remove with the upper tip of the eraser tool.

■   To erase all the markup, click **Erase All Ink on Slide**.

3   Press the **ESC** key to switch to the arrow pointer.

Practice Exercise

In this exercise, you will use the pen tool while you run a slide show.

USE the *UsePen* presentation in the *My Documents\Microsoft Press\MOS 2003 Study Guide\PowerPoint \P03C-4-4* practice file folder.

Open the *UsePen* presentation, and switch to Slide Show view. Move to Slide 8, and activate the felt tip pen tool. Draw a line under the word *Key* in the slide's title, and then erase the line. Move to Slide 9 and display its chart. Change the ink color to green, and then draw circles around *$500* and *Fall/Winter* in the chart's title. Switch back to the arrow pointer, and advance to the next slide. Stop the slide show, discard your annotations, and close the *UsePen* presentation without saving it.

520

Prepare Presentations for Remote Delivery

P03C-4-5   The skills measured by this objective include the following:

■ Packaging a presentation for CD storage

When you need to transport a presentation for delivery in a remote location, you can use PowerPoint's Package for CD feature, which helps ensure that you have everything you need to successfully run the slide show.

Packaging a Presentation for CD Storage

A presentation can consist of many components. The Package for CD feature gathers all the components and compresses and saves them to a CD, floppy disk, or other type of removable media, or to a hard disk. Linked files are included in the presentation package by default. TrueType fonts are stored with the presentation if you select the Embed TrueType Fonts option. You also have the option of including the Microsoft Office PowerPoint Viewer, which can be used to deliver a presentation on a computer that doesn't have PowerPoint installed.

BE SURE TO open the presentation you want to package before carrying out these steps.

To package a presentation for CD:

1   On the **File** menu, click **Package for CD**.

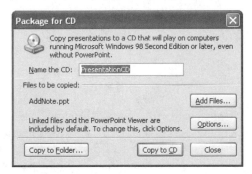

2   In the **Name the CD** box, type a name for the CD.

3   If you want to include embedded fonts in the package, click **Options**, select the **Embedded TrueType fonts** check box, and click **OK**.

4   If you don't want to include PowerPoint Viewer in the package, click **Options**, clear the **PowerPoint Viewer** check box, and click **OK**.

5   To specify whether the presentation will play automatically when the CD is inserted, click **Options**, and make a selection from the **Select how presentations will play in the viewer** drop-down list.

6   Do one of the following:

■ To copy the package to a CD, insert a blank CD in your CD-ROM burner, and click **Copy to CD**.

■ To copy the package to another location, click **Copy to Folder**, click **Browse**, navigate to the location to which you want to copy the package, and click **Select**. Then click **OK** to close the Copy to Folder dialog box.

PowerPoint displays a message box that reports its progress as it creates the presentation package.

To unpack and deliver the presentation in PowerPoint:

1   Insert the CD containing the presentation in the CD-ROM drive of the computer on which you will be delivering the presentation.

2   Navigate to the folder on the CD where the presentation is stored, and double-click the presentation.

To deliver the presentation in PowerPoint Viewer:

1   Insert the CD containing the presentation in the CD-ROM drive of the computer on which you will be delivering the presentation.

2   If PowerPoint Viewer does not launch automatically and begin running the slide show, navigate to the folder on the CD where the presentation is stored, and double-click the **pptview** file to open PowerPoint Viewer.

3   In the Microsoft Office PowerPoint Viewer dialog box, click the presentation, and then click **Open** to run the presentation.

Practice Exercise

In this exercise, you will package a presentation, including the embedded TrueType fonts, and view it in PowerPoint Viewer.

USE the *PackagePresentation* presentation in the *My Documents\Microsoft Press\MOS 2003 Study Guide \PowerPoint\P03C-4-5* practice file folder.

Open the *PackagePresentation* presentation. Create a presentation package that includes embedded TrueType fonts, and call it **TeachersShow**. Copy the presentation to a CD, or if a CD-Burner is not available, store the package in the *My Documents\Microsoft Press\MOS 2003 Study Guide\PowerPoint\P03C-4-5 practice file* folder. Close the presentation, and quit PowerPoint. Open the My Documents folder, and navigate to the package on the CD or in the *Microsoft Press\MOS 2003 Study Guide\PowerPoint\P03C-4-5* folder on your hard disk. Open and view the *TeachersShow* slide show with PowerPoint Viewer. Then close the presentation without saving it.

Save and Publish Presentations

P03C-4-6   The skills measured by this objective include the following:

■   Saving an entire presentation or a single slide

■   Saving and publishing a presentation as a Web page

You can save a PowerPoint presentation as overheads, slides, or an electronic slide show, or for publication on the Web as a Web page.

Saving an Entire Presentation or a Single Slide

Whether you want to save an entire presentation or a single slide, the process is basically the same. You display the Save As dialog box, assign the presentation or slide a name, and choose a location in which to store it on your computer's hard disk. The location can be an existing folder, or you can create a new folder as part of the save process.

The difference between saving a presentation and saving a slide is that slides are saved as graphic files. After choosing a graphic format in the "Save as type" drop-down list, you can specify whether to save only the displayed slide or all the slides in the presentation in the graphic file.

BE SURE TO open the presentation you want to save before carrying out these steps.

To save a presentation for the first time:

1   Do one of the following:

   Save

- On the Standard toolbar, click the **Save** button.

- On the **File** menu, click **Save** or **Save As**.

   The Save As dialog box appears, displaying the contents of the folder you last used in the Save As or Open dialog box.

2   In the **File name** box, type the name you want.

3   Do one of the following:

- Navigate to the folder in which you want to save the presentation.

   Create New
   Folder

- Navigate to the folder in which you want to create a subfolder for the presentation, click the **Create New Folder** button, type a name for the new folder, and click **OK**.

4   Click **Save**.

   PowerPoint saves the presentation with the name and in the location you specified.

To save a slide as a graphic file:

1   Display the slide you want to save.

2   On the **File** menu, click **Save As** to open the Save As dialog box.

3   In the **File name** box, type a name for the slide.

4   Navigate to the folder in which you want to save the slide, or create a new folder.

5   Click the **Save as type** down arrow, and then click the graphic format you want.

6   Click **Save**.

7   When a message asks whether you want to save the displayed slide or the entire presentation, click **Current Slide Only**.

Practice Exercise

In this exercise, you will save a presentation with a new name in a new folder, and then save a slide as a graphic.

USE the *SavePresentation* presentation in the *My Documents\Microsoft Press\MOS 2003 Study Guide \PowerPoint\P03C-4-6* practice file folder

Open the *SavePresentation* presentation, and save it as **NewPresentation** in a new subfolder of *My Documents\Microsoft Press\MOS 2003 Study Guide\PowerPoint\P03C-4-6* called **MyPresentation**. Then save only the title slide of the active presentation as **Title** in JPEG format. Close the *NewPresentation* presentation without saving it.

Saving and Publishing a Presentation as a Web Page

With PowerPoint, you can easily save a presentation as a Web page in HTML (Hypertext Markup Language) format. By default, PowerPoint saves all the components of the presentation, such as graphics, in a single file with the extension *.mht*. You can also save the presentation as a primary file with the extension *.htm* and a folder with the same name that contains all the components as separate files.

Tip If you move the Web presentation to another location, you must also move this folder; otherwise your Web browser won't be able to display the presentation.

In addition to saving a presentation as a Web page, you can publish it to a Web server so that it can be viewed by a broader audience. You can publish the entire presentation or only specified slides, optimize the presentation for display in specific Web browsers, and set options that control the Web page in various ways.

Before you save a presentation as a Web page, you should preview the presentation to see what it will look like when it's displayed in a Web browser. You can then make adjustments to your presentation in PowerPoint before converting it to Web format.

BE SURE TO open the presentation you want to save as a Web page before carrying out these steps.

Tip If Internet Explorer is not your default Web browser, follow the necessary prompts to proceed in your browser.

To preview a presentation as a Web page:

1   On the **File** menu, click **Web Page Preview**.

The message *Preparing for Web Page Preview* appears on the status bar, along with a status indicator, and then your Web browser opens, displaying the presentation as a Web page. The title bar displays the name assigned to the presentation in the Properties dialog box, and a navigation frame on the left side of the window lists all the slide titles. You can use the navigation frame to move from one slide to the next.

2   On the **File** menu, click **Close**.

Your browser closes, and you return to PowerPoint.

To set options for all Web pages:

1   On the **Tools** menu, click **Options**, and then click the **General** tab if it is not already active.

    Tip   Before saving a Web presentation, you might want to save the presentation's graphics in PNG (Portable Networks Graphics) format, which produces smaller files that can be down-loaded faster than those of other graphics formats. Then select the "Allow PNG as a graphics format" check box in the Web Options dialog box. PNG is recommended for Internet Explorer 5.0 or later, but not all other browsers support it.

2   Click **Web Options**, and then click the **Browsers** tab.

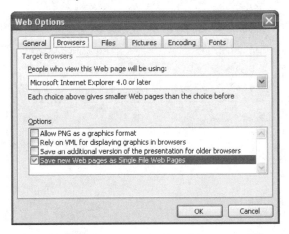

3   Click the **People who view this Web page will be using** down arrow, and click the browser most of your viewers will use.

4   Click the **General** tab.

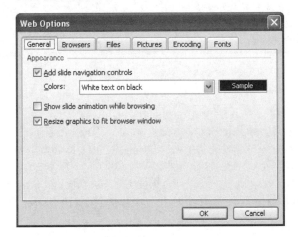

5 Do any of the following:

- ■ To have navigation controls appear on your Web pages, select the **Add slide naviga-tion controls** check box. Then click the **Colors** down arrow, and click the color option you want.

- ■ To have animation appear on your Web pages, select the **Show slide animation while browsing** check box.

6 Click **OK** to close the Web Options dialog box, and click **OK** again to close the Options dialog box.

To save a presentation as a Web page:

1 On the **File** menu, click **Save as Web Page**.

The Save As dialog box appears with *Single File Web Page* specified in the "Save as type" box at the bottom of the dialog box.

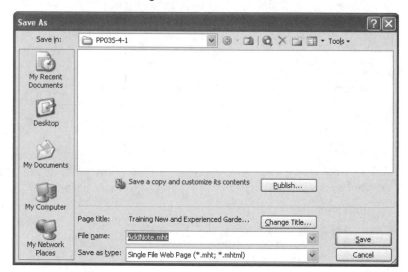

2 In the **File name** box, type the name you want.

3 Navigate to the folder in which you want to save the Web page.

4 Do any of the following:

- ■ To save the Web page components in a separate folder rather than embedding every-thing necessary to view the Web page in a single file, click the **Save as type** down arrow, and click **Web Page** in the drop-down list.

- ■ To have a descriptive title appear in the Web browser title bar rather than the name of the file, click **Change Title**, type the title you want, and click **OK**.

5 Click **Save**.

PowerPoint saves the presentation as a Web page.

To publish a presentation as a Web page:

1 On the **File** menu, click **Save as Web Page**.

2 In the **File name** box, type the name you want.

3 Navigate to the folder in which you want to save the Web page.

4 To save the Web page components in a separate folder rather than embedding everything necessary to view the Web page in a single file, click the **Save as type** down arrow, and click **Web Page** in the drop-down list.

5 Click **Publish**.

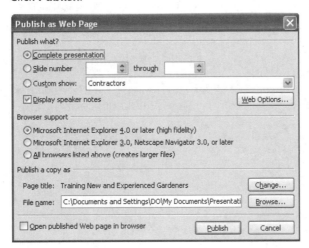

6 Do one of the following:

■ To publish the entire presentation, select the **Complete presentation** option.

■ To publish a selected range of slides, select the **Slide number** option and then enter the range of slides you want to publish.

■ To publish a custom slide show, select the **Custom show** option.

7 If necessary, change the browser compatibility setting in the **Browser support** area.

8 Click **Web Options**, make any other necessary changes, and click **OK**.

9 In the **Publish a copy as** area, set the page title and the location in which the Web page will be published.

10 Click **Publish**.

PowerPoint saves the presentation (or the specified slides) as a Web page in the specified location.

Practice Exercise

In this exercise, you will preview a presentation, set Web options, and publish four slides as a Web page.

USE the *CreateWeb* presentation in the *My Documents\Microsoft Press\MOS 2003 Study Guide\PowerPoint \P03C-4-6* practice file folder.

Open the *CreateWeb* presentation. Preview the presentation as a Web page. Display Slide 9, use the slide's **Home** button to redisplay Slide 1, and then close the browser. Set your Web options to allow PNG as a graphics format, display slide navigation controls, display presentation colors, and show slide animation while browsing. Then publish the first four slides of the presentation as a **Single File Web Page** with the name **WebPage**. Change the page title to **Teacher Training**, and specify *My Documents\Microsoft Press\MOS 2003 Study Guide \PowerPoint\P03C-4-6* as the storage location. Close the presentation, and then open **My Documents**. Navigate to the *My Documents\Microsoft Press\MOS 2003 Study Guide \PowerPoint\P03C-4-6* practice file folder, and double-click **WebPage.mht**. Display Slide 4, use the slide's **Home** button to redisplay Slide 1, and then close the browser.

Print Slides, Outlines, Handouts, and Speaker Notes

P03C-4-7   The skills measured by this objective include the following:

■ Previewing a presentation

■ Printing a presentation

When you want a hard copy of your presentation, PowerPoint gives you several options for printing it. You can change the page setup, print an outline, and print handouts or speaker notes.

Previewing a Presentation

You can use Print Preview to see how your presentation will look before you print it. While in Print Preview, you have the option of switching between various views so that you can examine notes, slides, outlines, and handouts. You can also switch between landscape and portrait orientation.

If you are using a black and white printer to print a presentation that you have created in color, you need to verify that the printed presentation will be legible. You can preview color slides in pure black and white or grayscale (shades of gray) to see how they will look when you print them.

BE SURE TO open the presentation you want to preview before carrying out these steps.

To preview a presentation:

Print Preview

1 On the Standard toolbar, click the **Print Preview** button.

The screen switches to print preview and displays the first slide as it will be printed with the current settings.

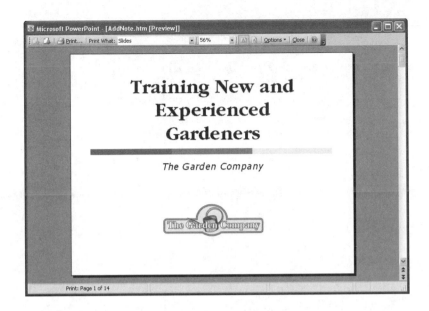

Tip If your default printer is not a color printer, the slide is shown in grayscale.

2 To navigate through the presentation, use buttons on the Print Preview toolbar to do the following:

Next Page

■ To move to the next page, click the **Next Page** button.

Previous Page

■ To move to the previous page, click the **Previous Page** button.

3 To preview handouts or notes pages, click the **Print What** down arrow on the Print Preview toolbar, and click the option you want.

4 To zoom in and out, move the pointer (which changes to a magnifying glass with a plus sign) over the slide, and click to zoom in. Then click again to zoom out.

Tip You can also change the percentage in the Zoom box on the Print Preview toolbar.

5 To change the orientation of handouts or notes pages, do the following:

Landscape

■ For horizontal orientation, click the **Landscape** button.

Portrait

■ For vertical orientation, click the **Portrait** button.

6 To preview the presentation in grayscale or black and white, click **Options** on the Print Preview toolbar, click **Color/Grayscale**, and then click the option you want.

Close

7 On the Print Preview toolbar, click the **Close Preview** button.

To view the presentation in grayscale or black and white without switching to Print Preview:

Color/
Grayscale

1 On the Standard toolbar, click the **Color/Grayscale** button, and then click **Grayscale**.

The slide switches from color to grayscale, and the Grayscale View toolbar appears. The slide thumbnails on the Slides tab of the Outline/Slides pane are still displayed in color, making it easier to compare the active slide in color and in grayscale.

2 To adjust the shades of black, white, and gray, click the **Setting** button on the Grayscale View toolbar, and click the option you want.

The slide changes to reflect your choice.

3 On the Grayscale View toolbar, click the **Close Grayscale View** button.

Close Grayscale View

The slide switches back to color.

Practice Exercise

In this exercise, you will preview a presentation before printing it.

USE the *PreviewPresentation* presentation in the *My Documents\Microsoft Press\MOS 2003 Study Guide \PowerPoint\P03C-4-7* practice file folder.

Open the *PreviewPresentation* presentation. Switch to Print Preview, and display handouts formatted with two slides per page and landscape orientation. Move to the next page, and use one method to zoom in on the page and another method to zoom back out. Display the slides again, preview the presentation in grayscale, and then close Print Preview. Switch the display to grayscale, and then switch to Slide Sorter view. Display Slide 1 in Normal view, and change the grayscale setting to black with grayscale fill. Switch back to color, and then close the *PreviewPresentation* presentation without saving it.

Printing a Presentation

Before you print a presentation, you might want to review the settings in the Page Setup dialog box. By default, PowerPoint sets up a new presentation as an on-screen slide show in landscape orientation (10 x 7.5 inches), with slides numbered starting at 1. Notes, handouts, and outlines are in portrait orientation (7.5 x 10 inches). You can use the Page Setup dialog box to modify these default settings.

After you have specified the size and orientation, PowerPoint prints slides and supplemental materials based on the default settings in the Print dialog box. You can display this dialog box and modify these settings at any time.

BE SURE TO open the presentation you want to print before carrying out these steps.

To change the default page setup settings:

1 On the **File** menu, click **Page Setup**.

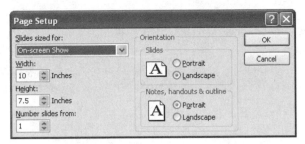

2   Click the **Slides sized for** down arrow, and click the setting you want in the drop-down list.

3   Make any additional changes you want to the size, orientation, or numbering, and click **OK**.

To print all the slides in a presentation with the default settings:

Print

● On the Standard toolbar, click the **Print** button.

PowerPoint prints one copy of each slide on your default printer.

To change the default print settings and then print:

1   On the **File** menu, click **Print**.

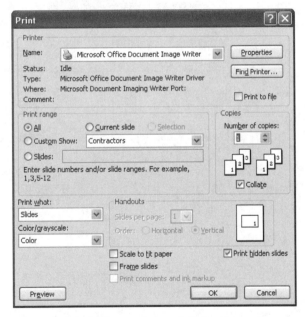

2   To switch to a different printer, click the **Name** down arrow in the **Printer** area, and click one of the printers in the list.

3   To customize the printer's settings for this particular print operation, click **Properties**, make any necessary changes in the Properties dialog box, and click **OK**.

4 In the **Print range** area of the Print dialog box, specify which slides you want to print.

5 In the **Copies** area, specify how many copies of each slide you want to print.

6 Click the **Print what** down arrow, and click the option you want.

If you choose to print handouts, PowerPoint activates the Handouts area and selects the "Frame slides" check box. You can then click the "Slides per page" down arrow, and click the number you want.

Tip You can print audience handouts in six formats: one, two, three, four, six, or nine slides per page.

7 To print in a color other than the default, click the **Color/grayscale** down arrow, and click the option you want.

8 Click **OK**.

PowerPoint prints according to your specifications.

Practice Exercise

In this exercise, you will print slides, handouts, and speaker notes.

USE the *PrintFile* presentation in the *My Documents\Microsoft Press\MOS 2003 Study Guide\PowerPoint \P03C-4-7* practice file folder.

Open the *PrintFile* presentation. Display the Page Setup dialog box and size the slides for **Letter Paper**. Then set the handouts to print horizontally on the page. Display the Print dialog box, and print the current slide in grayscale. Then print a complete set of handouts with two slides per page and the notes pages for Slides 1, 2, and 4. Close the *PrintFile* presentation without saving it.

Export a Presentation to Another Microsoft Office Program

P03C-4-8 The skills measured by this objective include the following:

- Sending a presentation to Microsoft Word

You can export a presentation outline or speaker notes directly from PowerPoint into a Microsoft Word document. If you want to use the text of the presentation in a different program, you can save it in Rich Text Format (RTF).

Sending a Presentation to Microsoft Word

When you export a presentation to Word, PowerPoint starts Word and copies the presentation's outline or notes pages to a blank document. (Obviously, you must have Word installed on your computer to be able to do this.) You can then save the document in the usual way.

BE SURE TO open the presentation you want to export before carrying out these steps.

To export a presentation to Microsoft Word:

1   On the **File** menu, click **Send To** and then **Microsoft Office Word**.

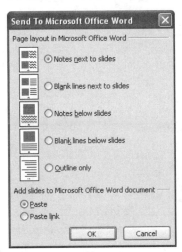

2   Select the page layout option you want, and click **OK**.

PowerPoint starts Word and inserts the presentation with the layout you chose into a blank Word document.

3   On Word's **File** menu, click **Save As**.

The Save As dialog box appears.

4   In the **File name** box, type the name you want.

5   Navigate to the folder where you want to store the presentation, and click **Save**.

Word saves the presentation in the designated folder.

6   On Word's **File** menu, click **Exit**.

Practice Exercise

In this exercise, you will send a presentation outline to Word.

USE the *SendOutline* presentation in the *My Documents\Microsoft Press\MOS 2003 Study Guide\PowerPoint \P03C-4-8* practice file folder.

Open the *SendOutline* presentation. Send the presentation outline to Word, and save the new document as **PPTOutline** in the *My Documents\Microsoft Press\MOS 2003 Study Guide \PowerPoint\P03C-4-8* folder. Close Word, and then close the *SendOutline* presentation without saving it.

P03C-4 Review

Number	Objective	Mastered
P03C-4-1	Organize a presentation	
	Working with different views	❏
	Organizing and deleting slides	❏
	Adding and viewing notes	❏
	Adding hyperlinks	❏
P03C-4-2	Set up slide shows for delivery	
	Creating a custom slide show	❏
	Working with action buttons	❏
	Working with hidden slides	❏
P03C-4-3	Rehearse timing	
	Setting slide timings	❏
	Rehearsing a presentation	❏
P03C-4-4	Deliver presentations	
	Delivering a slide show	❏
	Using on-screen tools for emphasis	❏
P03C-4-5	Prepare presentations for remote delivery	
	Packaging a presentation for CD storage	❏
P03C-4-6	Save and publish presentations	
	Saving an entire presentation or a single slide	❏
	Saving and publishing a presentation as a Web page	❏
P03C-4-7	Print slides, outlines, handouts, and speaker notes	
	Previewing a presentation	❏
	Printing a presentation	❏
P03C-4-8	Export a presentation to another Microsoft Office program	
	Sending a presentation to Microsoft Word	❏

Part VI

Microsoft Office Specialist
Access 2003 Exam

This part of the book covers the skills you need to have for certification as a Microsoft Office Specialist in Microsoft Office Access 2003. Specifically, you will need to be able to complete tasks that require the following skills:

Number	Skill Set
A03C-1	Structuring databases
A03C-2	Entering data
A03C-3	Organizing data
A03C-4	Managing databases

You can use these basic skills to create the databases most commonly used in a business environment.

Knowledge You Need Before Studying for This Exam

We assume that you have been working with Access for a while and that you know how to carry out fundamental tasks that are not specifically mentioned in the Microsoft Office Specialist objectives for Access 2003. Before you begin studying for this exam, you might want to scan this section to make sure you are familiar with this information.

Understanding Databases and Database Objects

In many computer applications, each document or object you work with is a separate file. An Access database, by contrast, is a single *.mdb* file that can store many different database objects. Each time you want to work with the database, you open the same file.

An Access database can include the following object types:

Object	Use to
Table	Store and view data
Query	Organize, combine, and filter data
Form	View and edit data in a custom format
Report	Print data in a custom format
Page	Display data in a Web page
Macro	Perform a series of actions automatically
Module	Run Visual Basic code

BE SURE TO start Access before carrying out these steps.

To open a database:

 Open

1 Click the **Open** button on the toolbar.

2 Navigate to the folder where the database you want to open is stored, click the database file, and click **Open**.

3 If Access displays a security warning, click **Open**.

See Also For information about this security warning, refer to "Understanding the Security Warning" later in this section.

Access displays the Database window, an Explorer-like window where all the objects for the database are shown. The Database window organizes objects into their seven types; you can click a type on the Objects bar to view a list of the corresponding objects. By clicking View buttons, you can select any of the following views: Large Icons, Small Icons, List, or Details.

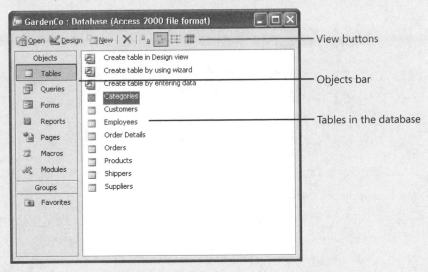

To open a database object:

1 On the **Objects** bar, click the type of object you want to open.

2 Do one of the following:

■ Click the object, and click **Open**.

■ To create a new object of that type, click **New**.

To rename a database object:

1 Click the object you want to rename.

2 On the **Edit** menu, click **Rename**.

3 Type a new name, and press **ENTER**.

To delete a database object:

Delete

1 Click the object you want to delete.

2 On the Database window's toolbar, click the **Delete** button.

3 Click **OK** when Access asks you to confirm the deletion.

To close a database:

● Close the Database window.

Understanding the Security Warning

Access databases can run Visual Basic program code, which could be used by a malicious person to harm your computer. When you open any Access database—including the practice files for this book—you'll see the following safety warning:

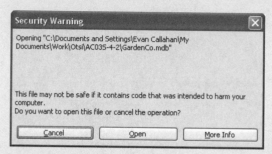

If you know the database is from a safe source, you can click Open without concern. If you click Cancel, Access doesn't open the database.

This warning can become tiresome. If you want to prevent the warning from appearing when you open a database, you can disable it. If you do, be sure never to accept an Access database from an untrustworthy source.

BE SURE TO start Access before carrying out these steps.

To disable the Access security warning:

1 On the **Tools** menu, click **Macro** and then **Security**.

2 On the **Security** tab, select the **Low** option, and click **OK**.

3 If Access asks whether you want to allow unsafe expressions, click **No**.

Saving in Access

Access saves changes to a database differently depending on whether they are changes to database objects or changes to data.

If you make changes to the design or layout of objects in a database, Access does not save them unless you specifically instruct it to. When you close an object to which you've made changes, Access asks whether you want to save it. When you make changes to data in tables, queries, or forms, Access saves them automatically as soon as you move to another record (or close the form or datasheet). You don't need to explicitly save changes to data.

BE SURE TO open the database you want to work with before carrying out these steps.

To save design and layout changes:

Save

● Click the **Save** button.

To save changes to data:

● Move to another record in the form or datasheet.

● To save without moving away from the record, click **Save Record** on the **Records** menu, or press **SHIFT+ENTER**.

A03C-1

Structuring Databases

The skills tested by this section of the Microsoft Office Specialist Access 2003 Exam all relate to creating and structuring an Access database. Specifically, the following objectives are associated with this set of skills:

Number	Objective
A03C-1-1	Create Access databases
A03C-1-2	Create and modify tables
A03C-1-3	Define and create field types
A03C-1-4	Modify field properties
A03C-1-5	Create and modify one-to-many relationships
A03C-1-6	Enforce referential integrity
A03C-1-7	Create and modify queries
A03C-1-8	Create forms
A03C-1-9	Add and modify form controls and properties
A03C-1-10	Create reports
A03C-1-11	Add and modify report control properties
A03C-1-12	Create a data access page

 Important Before you can do the practice exercises associated with this skill set, you need to install the practice files from the book's companion CD to their default location. See "Installing the Practice Files" on page xxv for more information.

Create Access Databases

A03C-1-1   The skills measured by this objective include the following:

- Creating a database by using the Database Wizard
- Creating a blank database

When you start using Microsoft Office Access 2003, the first thing you do is create a database. An Access database is a single file in which you store and organize your data.

Creating a Database by Using the Database Wizard

Creating a database structure from scratch can be a lot of work, but you can use the Database Wizard to create a complete database very quickly. The Database Wizard uses predefined templates to create sophisticated database applications. Access includes templates for creating contact management, expenses, order entry databases, and other business tasks.

539

BE SURE TO start Microsoft Access before carrying out these steps.

To create a database by using the Database Wizard:

New

1   If the New File task pane is not displayed, open it by clicking the **New** button on the Database toolbar.

2   In the **Templates** area of the task pane, click **On my computer**, and then click the **Databases** tab to display the available templates.

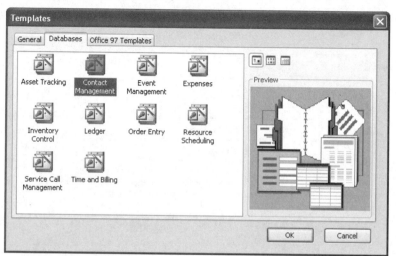

3   Double-click the template you want to use.

The File New Database dialog box appears.

4   Specify a folder and file name for the database, and click **Create**.

The first page of the Database Wizard appears, specifying the type of information that will be stored in this database.

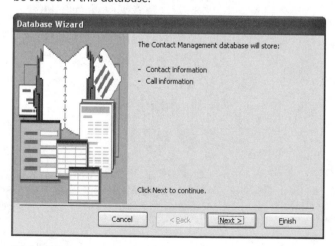

5   Click **Next**.

6   Follow the instructions on the remaining pages of the wizard, and click **Finish**.

The process of creating a database can take from several seconds to several minutes. The wizard creates the entire database application—including tables, queries, forms, reports, and modules—and then opens the newly created database and displays its Main Switchboard form.

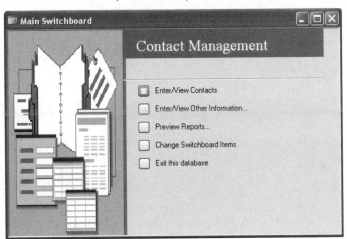

Practice Exercise

In this exercise, you will use the Database Wizard to create a database.

NO practice file is required for this exercise.

Open the New File task pane, and display the available templates. Create a new database based on the **Contact Management** template, save it in the *My Documents\Microsoft Press \MOS 2003 Study Guide\Access\A03C-1-1* practice file folder, and name it **Contacts**. Click **Next** to move through the wizard's pages, and then click **Finish**. In the *Contacts* database, display the **Contacts** form, click the **2** button to see the second page, and then close the form. In the Database window, click each object type on the **Objects** bar to see the different objects created by the Database Wizard. Then close the *Contacts* database.

Creating a Blank Database

In some cases, the Database Wizard won't be able to create the database you need. Instead, you will create a blank database and fill it with your own database structure.

BE SURE TO start Microsoft Access before carrying out these steps.

To create a blank database:

New

1   If the New File task pane is not displayed, open it by clicking the **New** button on the Database toolbar.

2   In the **New** area of the task pane, click **Blank database**.

The File New Database dialog box appears.

3   Specify a folder and file name for your database, and then click **Create**.

Access creates the database file and displays a blank Database window, ready for you to add tables and other objects.

Practice Exercise

In this exercise, you will create a blank database.

NO practice file is required for this exercise.

In the New File task pane, click **Blank database**. Create the new database in the *My Documents \Microsoft Press\MOS 2003 Study Guide\Access\A03C-1-1* practice file folder with the name **GardenCo**. Close the *GardenCo* database.

Create and Modify Tables

A03C-1-2   The skills measured by this objective include the following:

- Creating a table by using the Table Wizard
- Creating a table by entering data
- Creating and modifying a table in Design view

Unless the Database Wizard creates the tables you need, your first step in structuring a database is to create tables to store information. Tables are the core database objects, and they consist of fields (columns of information of the same kind, such as first names) and records (rows of information of various kinds about a single entity, such as a customer). An Access database can contain thousands of tables, and the number of records each table can contain is limited more by the space available on your hard disk than anything else.

See Also   For information about importing or linking a table to a database, refer to A03C-2-3, "Import Data to Access."

Creating a Table by Using the Table Wizard

Creating a table in Access involves many details, including specifying the table's fields, choosing their data types, and setting properties to determine their appearance and behavior. Fortunately, the Table Wizard can do most of this work for you.

BE SURE TO open the database you want to work with before carrying out these steps.

To create a table by using the Table Wizard:

1   On the **Object** bar of the Database window, click **Tables**.

2   Click the Database window's **New** button.

The New Table dialog box shows all the ways you can add a new table to a database.

3   Double-click **Table Wizard**.

The wizard's first page appears. You can display a list of either business tables or personal tables. Although these categories are generally oriented toward business or personal use, depending on the nature of your business or preferences, you might find the sample table you want in either list.

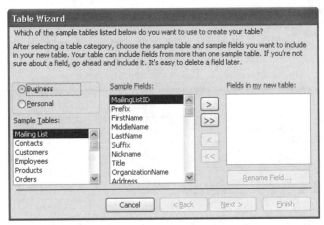

4   Select the **Business** or **Personal** option, and then click the table you want in the **Sample Tables** list.

When you click an item in the Sample Tables list, the Sample Fields list displays all the fields available for that table. (If you need more fields, you can add them after creating the table.)

5   Do one of the following:

- Click an item in the **Sample Fields** list, and then click the **>** button to move the selected field to the **Fields in my new table** list.

- Click the **>>** button to move all sample fields to the **Fields in my new table** list.

Tip   The < and << buttons remove one or all fields from your new table list.

6   If you want to rename a field in the **Fields in my new table** list, click the field, click the **Rename Field** button, type the new name in the Rename field dialog box, and click **OK**.

7   Click **Next** to move to the next page.

On the next page of the wizard, you name the new table and specify whether the wizard should set a primary key. A primary key consists of one or more fields that differentiate one record from another. By default, the wizard specifies a primary key field with the AutoNumber data type, so that Access will enter a consecutive ID number for each record in the table.

8   Complete the wizard by clicking **Next** to move from page to page, and then click **Finish** to create the new table.

The table opens in Datasheet view.

9   Enter data into the table's datasheet.

See Also   For information about entering data, refer to A03C-2-1, "Enter, Edit, and Delete Records."

10   Close the datasheet, clicking **Yes** if prompted to save changes to the table's layout.

Practice Exercise

In this exercise, you will use the Table Wizard to create two new tables.

USE the *CreateTables* database in the *My Documents\Microsoft Press\MOS 2003 Study Guide\Access \A03C-1-2* practice file folder.

Open the *CreateTables* database, and acknowledge the safety warning, if necessary. Use the Table Wizard to create a new table, selecting **Customers** from the **Business** list and including all the available fields. Accept *Customers* as the table name, and indicate that you will set the primary key using your own numbers or letters. Click **Finish** to create and open the **Customers** table, and then close the table. Use the Table Wizard again, this time selecting **Employees** from the **Business** list and including only the following fields:

EmployeeID	FirstName	LastName	Title
Address	City	StateOrProvince	PostalCode
HomePhone	Birthdate	DateHired	Photograph
Notes			

Rename the **StateOrProvince** field as State, and then click the **Next** button twice to accept the default table name and allow Access to create a primary key. Click **Finish**, and close the **Employees** table. Then close the *CreateTables* database.

Creating a Table by Entering Data

Although the Table Wizard can help you create most types of tables, you'll probably need to create some tables from scratch. For a simple table, the easiest method is to enter data and field names directly into a blank datasheet. When you close the datasheet, Access creates the new table, setting field data types based on the data you entered.

See Also   For information about entering data, refer to A03C-2-1, "Enter, Edit, and Delete Records."

BE SURE TO open the database you want to work with before carrying out these steps.

To create a table by entering data:

1   On the **Object** bar of the Database window, click **Tables**.

2   Double-click **Create table by entering data**.

A blank datasheet appears, with column selectors labeled Field1, Field2, and so on.

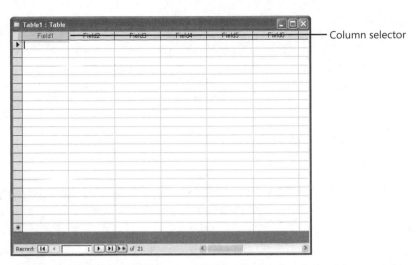

Column selector

3 To provide descriptive field names, double-click each column selector and type a name.

4 Enter data into the datasheet.

Save

5 On the Table Datasheet toolbar, click the **Save** button, type a name for the new table, and click **OK**.

6 When Access asks if you want to create a primary key, click **Yes** (unless you plan to add your own primary key later).

Access creates the new table and displays its datasheet. For each column of data you entered, Access adds a field to the table, gives it the name you specified, and selects an appropriate data type, such as Text, Number, or Date. The first field, called ID, is the primary key field created by Access. It has been assigned the AutoNumber data type, so Access enters a new number for each record.

See Also For information about data types, refer to A03C-1-3, "Define and Create Field Types."

---

7 If you want, enter more data, and then close the datasheet.

Practice Exercise

In this exercise, you will create a new table by entering data in a datasheet.

USE the *EnterData* database in the *My Documents\Microsoft Press\MOS 2003 Study Guide\Access\A03C-1-2* practice file folder.

Open the *EnterData* database, and acknowledge the safety warning, if necessary. With **Tables** active on the **Object** bar in the Database window, double-click **Create table by entering data**. Change **Field1** to **SupplierName**, **Field2** to **ContactName**, and **Field3** to **Phone**. In the first row, type **The Herb House, Douglas Groncki**, and **(805) 555-0128**. Save the table as **Suppliers**, allowing Access to create the primary key. Close the datasheet and the *EnterData* database.

Creating and Modifying a Table in Design View

In Access, you can view tables in two ways:

- In Datasheet view, you can view and enter data.
- In Design view, you can specify the structure of the table.

You don't have to use Design view to create tables, but it does provide the most control. In fact, even if you create tables by using the Table Wizard, you'll probably use Design view at some point to specify properties or make changes to table structure.

The Design view window is divided into two parts:

- The upper portion lists the fields in the table along with their data types. The data type determines the type of information you can store in the field.
- The lower portion lists the properties of the field that is active in the top portion. A small pane on the right provides a description of each property.

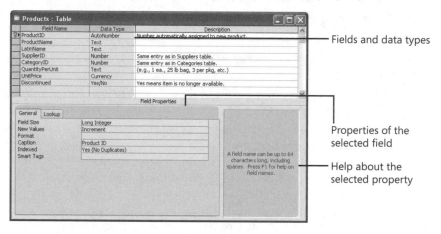

See Also   For information about data types, refer to A03C-1-3, "Define and Create Field Types."

BE SURE TO open the database you want to work with before carrying out these steps.

To create a new table:

1   On the **Object** bar of the Database window, click **Tables**.

2   Double-click **Create table in Design view**.

3   Do the following:

- In the **Field Name** column, type a name for the first field in the table.
- In the **Data Type** column, click the down arrow, and select the type of data you want to store, such as Text, Number, or Date/Time.
- If you want, enter descriptive text in the **Description** column.

Tip   When choosing names for fields, be as clear and consistent as possible to avoid confusion when entering data. Field names can include spaces, but they are then more difficult to use in queries and modules, so it is best not to use spaces.

4   Repeat step 3 for each field in the table.

Save

5   Click the **Save** button on the Table Design toolbar, type a name for the new table, and click **OK**.

6   When Access asks if you want to create a primary key, click **Yes** (unless you plan to add your own primary key later).

View

7   If you are ready to enter data, click the **View** button to move to Datasheet view; otherwise close the table.

To change the field structure of an existing table:

1   On the **Object** bar of the Database window, click **Tables**.

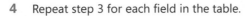
Design

2   Click the table you want to open, and on the Database window's toolbar, click the **Design** button.

3   To rearrange or change fields to create the field structure you want, do the following:

■ To make room for a new field above the active field, click the **Insert Rows** button on the Table Design toolbar.

Insert Rows

■ To remove a field (and any data it contains), click the field, and click the **Delete Rows** button on the Table Design toolbar.

Delete Rows

■ To rename a field, double-click the name in the **Field Name** column, type the new name, and press **ENTER**.

■ To move a field, click its row selector (the gray box on the left), and drag it to the new location.

Save

4   On the Table Design toolbar, click the **Save** button.

Access saves the new table structure.

View

5   If you are ready to enter data, click the **View** button to move to Datasheet view; otherwise close the table.

Practice Exercise

In this exercise, you will create a table, view its datasheet, and then modify its field structure.

USE the *ModifyFields* database in the *My Documents\Microsoft Press\MOS 2003 Study Guide\Access \A03C-1-2* practice file folder.

Open the *ModifyFields* database, and acknowledge the safety warning, if necessary. Create a table in Design view with the following fields:

Field Name	Data Type	Description
ProductID	AutoNumber	Number automatically assigned to new product
ProductName	Text	
QuantityPerUnit	Text	For example, "25 per box"
UnitPrice	Currency	

Save the table as **Products**, create a primary key, and switch to the datasheet. Then switch back to Design view, add a field called **LastOrdered** just above the **QuantityPerUnit** field, and give the new field a data type of **Date/Time**. Drag **UnitPrice** above **QuantityPerUnit**. Save and close the **Products** table, and then close the *ModifyFields* database.

Define and Create Field Types

A03C-1-3   The skills measured by this objective include the following:

- Setting the data type and size of a field
- Creating a primary key field
- Creating a lookup field

One of the strengths of Access is that it can help you keep data consistent. In a spreadsheet or word-processing document, people can enter almost any information in a cell or field. In an Access table, by contrast, you can be sure that a Number field always contains a number and a Date field always contains a date, because Access won't have it any other way. Access can also help you make sure that each value in a field is unique in the table—for example, to prevent the entry of the same serial number twice—or that values always come from a specific list. You can place a restriction on data entry, which ensures that the data is uniform and consistent.

Setting the Data Type and Size of a Field

Every field in a table has a data type, whether you created it manually, by using a wizard, or by importing data. To ensure that data entry is consistent and that sorting and calculations work properly, it is important that each field has the proper data type. For example, you can't perform mathematical calculations on numbers stored in a Text field; they must be stored in a Number or Currency field. Similarly, if you want to sort a list of dates chronologically, the field that stores them must have the Date/Time data type.

This table lists the Access data types and when you should use them:

Data Type	Use for
Text	Text or both text and numbers, such as addresses, or for numbers that do not require calculations, such as phone numbers (stores up to 255 characters)
Memo	Long text
Number	Numbers other than currency
Date/Time	Dates and times
Currency	Currency
AutoNumber	Unique ID value
Yes/No	Data that can be only one of two possible values, such as Yes or No
OLE Object	OLE objects, such as pictures, Microsoft Excel spreadsheets, or Word documents
Hyperlink	Hyperlinks, including file paths as well as Web links

The Field Size property also determines the data you can store in a field. You can set the Field Size property for the Text, Number, and AutoNumber data types. Text fields can be set to any number from 0 to 255. Number fields can be set to any of the following values:

Field Size	Stores Numbers
Byte	From 0 to 255 (no fractions).
Integer	From –32,768 to 32,767 (no fractions).
Long Integer	From –2,147,483,648 to 2,147,483,647 (no fractions). This is the default size.
Single	From –3.402823E38 to –1.401298E–45 for negative values and from 1.401298E–45 to 3.402823E38 for positive values.
Double	From –1.79769313486231E308 to –4.94065645841247E–324 for negative values and from 1.79769313486231E308 to 4.94065645841247E–324 for positive values.
Decimal	As large as $-10^{28} -1$ through $10^{28} -1$, depending on the setting of the Precision property. (To allow fractions, set the Scale property.)

By setting the Field Size property to a value that allows the largest valid entry, you prevent the user from entering certain types of invalid information. If you try to type more characters in a Text field than the number allowed by the Field Size setting, Access refuses to accept the entry. Likewise, a value that is below or above the limits of a Number field is rejected. For numbers, another benefit of using the smallest appropriate Field Size setting is that the database is more efficient.

To check the data types and sizes of the fields in a database, open each table in Design view. It is best to make changes before entering data, but you can also change data types in a table that already contains records. When you change the data type of a field, Access converts existing data and lets you know if there are any problems.

Tip Before changing data types or field sizes in tables containing data, it is a good idea to back up the database in case the conversion causes data to be lost.

BE SURE TO open the database containing the tables you want to work with before carrying out these steps.

To set data types and sizes:

1 On the **Object** bar of the Database window, click **Tables**.

2 Click the table you want to open, and on the Database window's toolbar, click the **Design** button.

3 In the **Data Type** column, make sure the proper data type is selected for each field in the table, and change it if it isn't.

   For example, if the field has been set to the Number data type but is intended to store an amount of money, you would change the data type setting to Currency.

4 Click the name of each Text or Number field, and in the bottom pane of the window, make sure the **Field Size** property is set properly for the data the field will store. Change it if it isn't.

For a Text field, enter the maximum number of characters you want to allow. For a Number field, enter the most appropriate field size. If you want to store fractional values, be sure to select Single, Double, or Decimal.

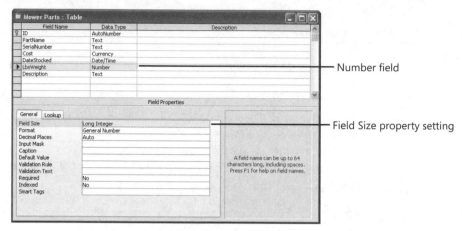

Number field

Field Size property setting

Tip To move between fields quickly, use the DOWN ARROW and UP ARROW keys.

Save

5   When all the settings are correct, click the **Save** button on the Table Design toolbar.

Access converts data types and field sizes to the new settings. If you changed one or more fields to a smaller field size or to a data type that can't store all the existing data, Access warns you that data might be lost.

6   Click **Yes** to convert the data or **No** to preserve the data.

If you choose to continue, Access rounds or deletes data that doesn't fit in the new field settings.

7   If you choose to preserve the data, click **OK** if prompted to acknowledge that the data types were not changed.

8   Close the table.

9   If you chose not to allow Access to convert data and Access asks again if you want to save changes to the table, click **No**.

Practice Exercise

In this exercise, you will open a new table and change data types and field sizes for several fields.

USE the *ChangeType* database in the *My Documents\Microsoft Press\MOS 2003 Study Guide\Access \A03C-1-3* practice file folder.

Open the *ChangeType* database, and acknowledge the safety warning, if necessary. Open the **Mower Parts** table's datasheet. In the **Weight** field of the second record, type **.5** and press **ENTER**. Note that Access changes the value to *0*, indicating that this field doesn't accept fractional values. Switch to Design view, change the data type for the **Cost** field to **Currency**, and change the data type for the **DateStocked** field to **Date/Time**. Save your changes, clicking **Yes** in the message box to continue saving. Change the **Field Size** setting for the **Weight** field from *Long Integer* to **Single**. Then set the **Field Size** property of the **SerialNumber** field to **8**. Save the table again, clicking **Yes** to continue. Switch to the datasheet. In the first record, type **6.25** in the **Cost** field and **3/10** in the **DateStocked** field. In the **Weight** field of the second record, replace 0 with **.5**. Close the **Mower Parts** table, and then close the *ChangeType* database.

Creating a Primary Key Field

Every table in a database should contain a primary key, which is a field (or group of fields) that uniquely identifies each record. Access uses the primary key field to relate tables and to sort records more efficiently.

When you save a new table, Access offers to create a primary key field. If you agree, Access adds an ID field with the AutoNumber data type to the table. You don't have to enter values in this type of primary key; Access fills this field in for every new record.

In some cases, however, the data has its own unique identifier that you want to specify as the primary key. For example, a database of automotive parts might have a field of unique part numbers. In such cases, there's no sense in having a separate primary key.

You can view or change the primary key field setting in the table's Design view. It's a good idea to move the field you'll use as the primary key to the top of the list of fields.

BE SURE TO open a table in Design view before carrying out these steps.

 Tip   To open a table in Design view, click Tables on the Objects bar of the Database window, and then click the Database window's Design button.

To create a primary key:

1   Drag the row selector of the field you want to specify as the primary key to the top of the field list.

   If you want to use more than one field as the primary key, move the other fields below the first. Then when the fields are all in place, select them all by dragging from the first row selector to the last.

 2   On the Table Design toolbar, click the **Primary Key** button.

   The primary key icon appears in the row selector.

3   Save your changes.

   Tip   If the table contains records with duplicate values in the field you select, Access can't create the new primary key. If Access displays errors, close the table, clicking No when Access prompts you to save changes.

4   If you want to delete the old primary key field, click the field, and click **Delete Rows** on the **Edit** menu, clicking **Yes** if Access asks you to confirm the deletion.

Practice Exercise

In this exercise, you will open a table and change its primary key.

USE the *ChangeKey* database in the *My Documents\Microsoft Press\MOS 2003 Study Guide\Access \A03C-1-3* practice file folder.

Open the *ChangeKey* database, and acknowledge the safety warning, if necessary. Open the **Mower Parts** table in Design view. Drag the **SerialNumber** field to the top of the list, and make it the primary key. Delete the **ID** field, clicking **Yes** to confirm the deletion, and then save the table. Close the **Mower Parts** table and the *ChangeKey* database.

Creating a Lookup Field

Minor inconsistencies in the way data is entered might not be important to someone who later reads the information and makes decisions. Most people know that *Arizona* and *AZ* refer to the same state. But a computer is very literal, and if you tell it to create a list so that you can send catalogs to everyone living in *AZ*, the computer won't include anyone whose state is listed in the database as *Arizona*.

When you want to limit the options for entering information in a table, you can use a lookup field. When you create a lookup field, a wizard helps you determine the values that are allowed in the field, and then datasheets and forms display a list or combo box of the allowed values. When you enter data, you can use the list to "look up" a value that is appropriate for the field.

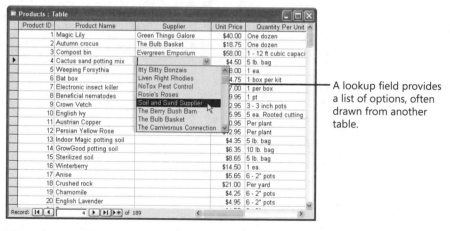

A lookup field provides a list of options, often drawn from another table.

The values in the list for a lookup field often come from a separate table. For example, in a Products table with a field that stores the supplier of the product, the options could come from a Suppliers table. Selecting values from a table or query is recommended, but you must already have a table containing the values you need. When you use the Lookup Wizard to create a field based on another table, Access maintains a relationship between the two tables, querying the table containing the lookup values whenever you enter data in the table containing the lookup field.

BE SURE TO open a table in Design view before carrying out these steps.

 Tip To open a table in Design view, click Tables on the Objects bar of the Database window, and then click the Database window's Design button.

To create a lookup field based on an existing table:

1   In Design view, do one of the following:

- Click the name of the field above which you want to insert the lookup field.

- Click an empty row at the bottom of the list of fields.

2   On the **Insert** menu, click **Lookup Field**.

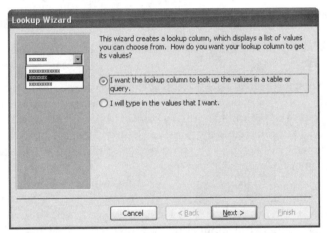

3   Click **Next** to indicate that you want to base the field on an existing table or query.

4   Click the table or query you want to use, and click **Next**.

5   Move the field containing the lookup values from the **Available Fields** list to the **Selected Fields** list, and click **Next**.

6   Click the down arrow, click the lookup field to sort its values in the lookup list, and click **Next**.

7   If necessary, widen the field so that it will hold its longest entry, by dragging the field's column header to the right, and click **Next**.

8   Assign a name to the new lookup field, and click **Finish**.

9   When prompted, click **Yes** to save the table.

The Lookup Wizard creates the field, setting several field properties that allow the field to display its list of values when you enter data in forms and datasheets. You can view and edit these properties on the Lookup tab in Design view.

To create a lookup field with values you type:

1   In Design view, do one of the following:

- Click the name of the field above which you want to insert the lookup field.

- Click an empty row at the bottom of the list of fields.

2   On the **Insert** menu, click **Lookup Field**.

3 Select the **I will type in the values that I want** option, and click **Next**.

4 Click the first row under **Col1**, type a value, press **TAB**, type the next value, and so on, clicking **Next** when you have finished entering values.

5 Assign a name to the new lookup field, and click **Finish**.

6 When prompted, click **Yes** to save the table.

The Lookup Wizard creates the field, setting several field properties that allow the field to display its list of values when you enter data in forms and datasheets. You can view and edit these properties on the Lookup tab in Design view.

Practice Exercise

In this exercise, you will use the Lookup Wizard to add two fields to a table.

USE the *UseLookup* database in the *My Documents\Microsoft Press\MOS 2003 Study Guide\Access \A03C-1-3* practice file folder.

Open the *UseLookup* database, and acknowledge the safety warning, if necessary. Open the **Products** table in Design view. Click the **UnitPrice** field, and start the Lookup Wizard. Use the values in an existing table, and base the lookup field on the **SupplierName** field of the **Suppliers** table. Select **SupplierName** in the top sort order box, and make the field twice as wide as the data shown by dragging the column header to the right. On the final wizard page, type **Supplier** as the field name, and click **Finish**. Save the table if prompted. On the blank row at the bottom of the list of fields, create another lookup field. Specify that you will enter your own values, and in the **Col1** column, type the following values,: **Spring**, **Summer**, **Fall**, **Winter**, **Year-Round**. Name this lookup field **Availability**, and click **Finish**. Switch to the datasheet, saving the table. In the **Supplier** field of the first record, click the down arrow to view the lookup list, and click **Green Things Galore**. Then in the **Availability** field of the first record, click **Summer** in the lookup list. Close the **Products** table and the *UseLookup* database.

Modify Field Properties

A03C-1-4 The skills measured by this objective include the following:

- Setting field properties
- Using an input mask

The Database Wizard or Table Wizard sets a variety of properties for each field that determine what data can be entered in a field and how the data will look on the screen. When you create tables without a wizard, Access applies default property settings to each field. In many cases, you'll want to change these field properties. When you want to change how Access displays numbers, for example, you can set the Format and Decimal Places properties. When you set properties in a table, all the queries, forms, and reports you create based on the table inherit the property settings, so you don't have to set them again.

Setting Field Properties

In Design view, the bottom pane displays properties for the selected field. In some properties, you pick a setting from a drop-down list; in others, you type a value. To help you when setting field properties, you can click each property to see a brief description in the lower-right pane of the window.

Many field properties determine only the appearance or behavior of fields, so you can change them without affecting the data stored in the table. Others can affect existing records in a table, so you should proceed with caution.

These properties affect the data that is allowed in a field:

Property	Use to
Field Size	Limit the number of characters or size of numbers allowed
Validation Rule	Set a rule that data must follow
Validation Text	Provide a message when data rules are broken
Required	Require entry in the field in new records

These properties affect the appearance of a field:

Property	Use to
Format	Display dates and numbers in a selected format
Decimal Places	Display a specified number of digits after the decimal point
Caption	Display a field label other than the field's name

These properties affect the behavior of a field:

Property	Use to
Default Value	Enter a value automatically in new records
Indexed	Increase the speed of searching and sorting
Smart Tags	Cause the field to display a Smart Tag icon, providing a way to use data with other applications

Another property, Input Mask, affects all three aspects of data.

See Also For information about input masks, refer to "Using an Input Mask" later in this section.

BE SURE TO open a table in Design view before carrying out these steps.

 Tip To open a table in Design view, click Tables on the Objects bar of the Database window, and then click the Database window's Design button.

To set field properties:

1   In the top pane, click the field whose properties you want to set.

2   In the bottom pane, click the property you want to set.

A description of the property appears in the lower-right pane of the window.

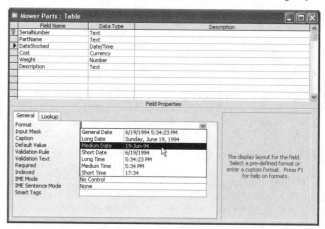

Tip To see a Help topic about any property, click the property and press the F1 key.

3   Do one of the following:

   ■   If a down arrow appears for the property, click it, and then click a setting in the list.

   ■   If the property has no down arrow, type a value.

Build

   ■   If the property has a **Build** button, you can click it to open the Expression Builder to help you set the property.

4   Click other fields in the list to set their properties.

5   When you've finished, save your changes.

6   To test the effect of the property changes, click the **View** button to display the table's datasheet.

View

Practice Exercise

In this exercise, you will open a table and set properties for several fields.

USE the *SetProperties* database in the *My Documents\Microsoft Press\MOS 2003 Study Guide\Access \A03C-1-4* practice file folder.

Open the *SetProperties* database, and acknowledge the safety warning, if necessary. Open the **Mower Parts** table in Datasheet view. Notice a few issues: a part with no name, another with a negative price, weights with different numbers of decimal places, and field names that are hard to read. Switch to Design view. For the **SerialNumber** field, set the **Caption** property to **Serial Number**. For the **PartName** field, set the **Caption** property to **Part Name**, and change its **Required** property setting to **Yes**. (With this setting, Access won't allow new records to be saved without a part name.) Set its **Indexed** property to **Yes (Duplicates OK)**. (With this setting, Access will maintain an index that will help it sort and search for part names efficiently.) For the **DateStocked** field, change the **Format** property to **Medium Date**, and set its **Default Value** property to **=Date()**. (This setting tells Access to use the Date function to automatically provide the current date for new records.) For the **Cost** field, clear the **Default Value** property, set its **Validation Rule** property to **>=0**, and set its **Validation Text** property to **Please enter a non-negative cost**. For the **Weight** field, change the **Format** property to **Standard**, and set its **Decimal Places** property to **2**. Save the table, and click **No** when Access offers to test whether existing data complies with the new rules. To view the effect of these property changes, switch to Datasheet view, and enter a new record. Close the **Mower Parts** table and the *SetProperties* database.

Using an Input Mask

You can use the Input Mask property to control how data is entered in text, number, date/time, and currency fields. When you use input masks in tables and forms, people can easily see the format in which they should make entries and how long they should be. If someone tries to enter a value that doesn't fit the mask, Access rejects the entry.

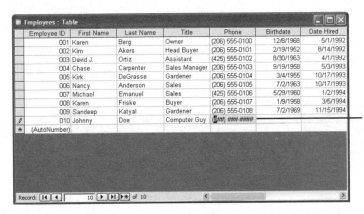

The input mask ensures that every phone number has the same format and number of digits.

The Input Mask Wizard can help you set the property, or you can set it yourself. The Input Mask property setting has three sections separated by semicolons, like this mask for a telephone number:

!\(000") "000\-0000;0;#

The first section contains characters that are used as placeholders for the information to be typed, as well as characters such as parentheses and hyphens. Together, all these characters control the appearance of the entry. The table on the next page explains the purpose of the most common input mask characters.

Character	Description
0	Required digit (0 through 9).
9	Optional digit or space.
#	Optional digit or space; blank positions are converted to spaces; plus and minus signs are allowed.
L	Required letter (A through Z).
?	Optional letter (A through Z).
A	Required letter or digit.
A	Optional letter or digit.
&	Required character (any kind) or a space.
C	Optional character (any kind) or a space.
<	All characters that follow are converted to lowercase.
>	All characters that follow are converted to uppercase.
!	Characters typed into the mask fill it from left to right. You can include the exclamation point anywhere in the input mask.
\	Character that follows is displayed as a literal character.
Password	Creates a password entry box. Any character typed in the box is stored as the character but displayed as an asterisk (*).

The second and third sections of the input mask are optional. Including a 1 or leaving nothing in the second section tells Access to store only the characters entered; including a 0 tells it to store both the characters entered and the mask characters. The character in the third section is displayed in a new record as the placeholder for the characters to be typed. This placeholder defaults to an underscore if the section is omitted.

BE SURE TO open a table in Design view before carrying out these steps.

 Tip To open a table in Design view, click Tables on the Objects bar of the Database window, and then click the Database window's Design button.

To specify an input mask for a field:

1 In the top pane, click the field for which you want to create an input mask.

2 In the bottom pane, click the **Input Mask** property.

3 Click the **Build** button to the right of the cell.

Build

The first page of the Input Mask Wizard appears. (Click Yes if you are prompted to install this feature.)

4   Answer the wizard's questions, clicking **Next** to move between pages.

The wizard lets you specify a placeholder character and whether you want to store the mask symbols in the field. It then enters your specifications as the setting for the Input Mask property.

5   Click **Finish**, and save your changes.

6   To test the input mask, click the **View** button to display the datasheet, and enter data in the field that now has an input mask.

View

Practice Exercise

In this exercise, you will use the Input Mask Wizard to apply an input mask.

USE the *ApplyMask* database in the *My Documents\Microsoft Press\MOS 2003 Study Guide\Access \A03C-1-4* practice file folder.

Open the *ApplyMask* database, and acknowledge the safety warning, if necessary. Open the **Employees** table in Design view. Click the **Phone** field, and use the Input Mask Wizard to create a **Phone Number** mask with the **Placeholder character** set to **#** and the data stored with the symbols in the mask. Save the table, and then switch to the datasheet. Click the blank cell at the bottom of the **Phone** field, and type a phone number to test the input mask. Then close the **Employees** table and the *ApplyMask* database.

Create and Modify One-to-Many Relationships

A03C-1-5   The skills measured by this objective include the following:

■   Creating a relationship between two tables

Many of the powerful features of Access center around its ability to bring together data stored in separate tables. For example, if you store product information in one table and supplier information in another, Access can combine the information in queries, forms, and reports.

Creating a Relationship Between Two Tables

In Access, a relationship is an association between a common field in two tables. For example, a relationship can be established between a Categories table and a Products table if both tables have a CategoryID field. Each product is in only one category, but each category can contain many products, so this type of relationship—the most common—is known as a one-to-many relationship.

Here are a few of the ways Access helps you work with data in related tables:

- A table's datasheet can use a subdatasheet to display related records from another table.
- The results of a query that includes related tables can include data from all of them.
- The Form Wizard and the Report Wizard can create forms and reports that relate records from more than one table.
- Subforms and subreports can display related records from more than one table.

As you create forms and queries, Access might recognize some relationships between the fields in the underlying tables. In fact, if you used the Database Wizard to create tables or the Lookup Wizard to create lookup fields, the database probably already has relationships. However, if you want Access to consistently recognize related data, you can create the relationships in the Relationships window.

Before you can create a one-to-many relationship, the tables you want to relate must contain a common field. The common field often has the same name in both tables, and it must have the same data type. (However, if the field in one table is an AutoNumber field, the other table should contain a Number field with the Field Size property set to Long Integer.) If you want to relate tables that don't have a common field, you will need to add or change a field in Design view to create a common field.

Tip In addition to one-to-many relationships, you can create one-to-one relationships and many-to-many relationships, but they are not as common. In a one-to-one relationship, two related tables have the same primary key field. A many-to-many relationship is really two one-to-many relationships tied together through a third table. For example, in the *AddRecord* database located in the *My Documents\Microsoft Press\MOS 2003 Study Guide\Access\A03C-2-1* practice file folder, the Orders table and the Products table have a many-to-many relationship. The third table that relates the two is Order Details—it includes both the ProductID field and the OrderID field, so it has a one-to-many relationship with both the Products and Orders tables. As a result, every order can include many products, and every product can appear in many orders.

BE SURE TO open the database you want to work with before carrying out these steps.

To create a one-to-many relationship:

Relationships

1 On the Database toolbar, click the **Relationships** button to open the Relationships window.

Show Table

2 If the Show Table dialog box isn't displayed, click the **Show Table** button on the Relationship toolbar.

3   In turn, double-click the two tables you want to relate, and then close the Show Table dialog box.

A list of fields appears in the Relationships window for each table you added.

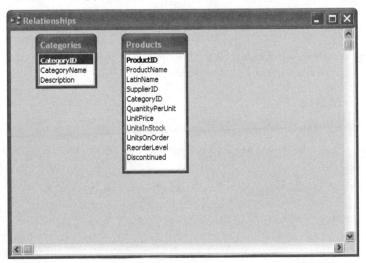

Tip   If either table's field list is too short to display all its fields, you can make it larger it by dragging its lower-right corner. Make sure you can see the field you will use to relate the two tables.

4   Drag the related field from one table—usually the primary key field located at the top of the list—and drop it on the related field in the other table.

Access displays the Edit Relationships dialog box, which lists the fields you have chosen to relate.

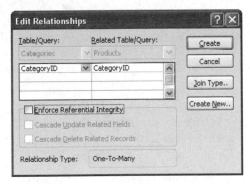

5   Click **Create**.

Access draws a line representing the one-to-many relationship between the two tables.

6   Close the Relationships window, clicking **Yes** when prompted to save the window's layout.

To modfy a one-to-many relationship:

Relationships

1 On the Database toolbar, click the **Relationships** button to open the Relationships window.

2 Do either of the following:

- ■ To change an existing relationship, double-click the line between two fields, make the necessary changes in the Edit Relationships dialog box, and click **OK**.

- ■ To delete a relationship, right-click the line, click **Delete** on the shortcut menu, and click **Yes** to confirm the deletion.

Practice Exercise

In this exercise, you will create a relationship between two tables.

USE the *CreateRelationship* database in the *My Documents\Microsoft Press\MOS 2003 Study Guide\Access \A03C-1-5* practice file folder.

Open the *CreateRelationship* database, and acknowledge the safety warning, if necessary. Display the Relationships window, and use the Show Table dialog box to add the **Categories** and **Products** tables to the window, resizing their field lists as necessary. Drag the **CategoryID** field from one table to the same field in the other table. Create the relationship, and then close the Relationships window, clicking **Yes** when prompted to save the window's layout. Close the *CreateRelationship* database.

Enforce Referential Integrity

A03C-1-6   The skills measured by this objective include the following:

- ■ Setting referential integrity rules

Access uses a system of rules called referential integrity to ensure that relationships between records in related tables are valid and that you don't accidentally delete or change related data. For example, if you have customer records and order records, you would never want to have an order that doesn't have a customer. (To whom would you send the bill?) With referential integrity, you can rest assured that this type of error won't occur.

Setting Referential Integrity Rules

When you create or edit a relationship between tables, you can choose whether to enforce referential integrity. If you do, you cannot change data in a way that invalidates the relationship. For example, if you enforce referential integrity in a relationship between customer records and order records, you cannot delete a customer record that has orders, change customer ID values, or add an order for a customer who doesn't exist.

BE SURE TO open the database you want to work with before carrying out these steps.

To set referential integrity rules:

Relationships

1 On the Database toolbar, click the **Relationships** button to open the Relationships window.

Show All
Relationships

2 If the relationship you want to work with isn't shown, click the **Show All Relationships** button on the Relationship toolbar.

3 Double-click the line between tables that represents the relationship you want to modify.

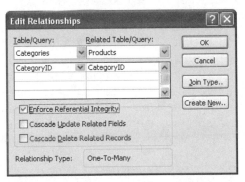

4 Select the **Enforce Referential Integrity** check box, and then click **OK**.

Access makes the line representing the one-to-many relationship between the two tables bold and adds symbols to indicate the type of relationship.

5 Close the Relationships window, clicking **Yes** if prompted to save the window's layout.

Tip Sometimes referential integrity rules prevent you from performing a necessary task. For example, if you want to delete a customer record and its related orders, you would have to locate and delete the orders before deleting the customer record. When the Cascade Update Related Fields check box is selected, changing a primary key value in the primary table automatically updates the matching value in all related records. When the Cascade Delete Related Records check box is selected, deleting a record in the primary table deletes any related records in the related table.

Practice Exercise

In this exercise, you will set referential integrity rules for two tables.

USE the *SetRules* database in the *My Documents\Microsoft Press\MOS 2003 Study Guide\Access\A03C-1-6* practice file folder.

Open the *SetRules* database, and acknowledge the safety warning, if necessary. Open the Relationships window. Double-click the line between **Categories** and **Products**, enforce referential integrity for this relationship, and close the Relationships window, clicking **Yes** if prompted to save the window's layout. Then open the **Categories** table in Datasheet view, and try to delete a record. When Access informs you that deleting a record isn't allowed because of related records in the Products table, click **OK**. Then close the **Categories** table and the *SetRules* database.

Create and Modify Queries

A03C-1-7   The skills measured by this objective include the following:

■ Creating a query by using the Simple Query Wizard

■ Modifying a query in Design view

■ Creating a crosstab query
■ Finding duplicate records
■ Finding unmatched records
■ Updating information with an action query

A query retrieves data from one or more tables and displays the results in a datasheet. A query can sort records, filter records based on criteria, and perform calculations. You can create a query by hand or by using a wizard. Each time you run a query, Access retrieves the records that meet the query's conditions. You can work with the results of a select query in Datasheet view to update records in one or more related tables at the same time. In addition, you can base forms and reports on queries so that the forms and reports aren't limited to the data in a single table.

Creating a Query by Using the Simple Query Wizard

With the Simple Query Wizard, you can add one or more fields from existing tables or queries to the new query. For Access to work effectively with multiple tables, it must understand the relationships between the fields in those tables, so if you include fields from more than one table, the wizard helps you define their relationships.

See Also For information about creating relationships between tables, see A03C-1-5, "Create and Modify One-to-Many Relationships."

BE SURE TO open the database you want to work with before carrying out these steps.

To create a query by using the Simple Query Wizard:

1 On the **Objects** bar, click **Queries**, and then double-click **Create query by using wizard**.
The first page of the Simple Query Wizard appears.

2 In the **Tables/Queries** list, click the table that contains fields for your query.
Fields in the table you've selected appear in the Available Fields list.

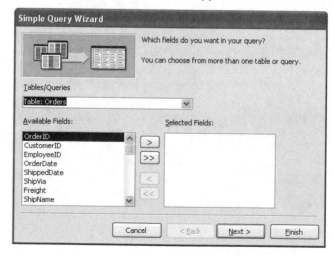

3 Do one of the following:

- For each field that you want to include in the query, click the field name in the **Available Fields** list, and click the **>** button.

- To move all available fields to the **Selected Fields** list, click the **>>** button.

4 Repeat steps 2 and 3 to include fields from other tables, and then click **Next**.

5 If Access asks whether you want a Detail or Summary query, do one of the following, and click **Next**:

- To see all the results retrieved by the query, select the **Detail** option.

- To see the results grouped and summarized—for example, you might want to see the sum or average of a group—select the **Summary** option. Then click **Summary Options**, select the check boxes for the calculations you want Access to include, and click **OK**.

6 Answer any additional questions, clicking **Next** to move between pages.

7 Type a name for the query, and click **Finish**.

Access creates and saves the new query, runs the query to select records from the tables you included, and displays the datasheet.

Tip In most cases, you can edit the data produced by a query. With certain queries, such as Summary queries, some or all fields might be read-only.

8 Close the query.

The new query appears in the Database window, where you can open it later to run the query and view current data.

Practice Exercise

In this exercise, you will use the Simple Query Wizard to create a new query.

USE the *CreateQuery* database in the *My Documents\Microsoft Press\MOS 2003 Study Guide\Access \A03C-1-7* practice file folder.

Open the *CreateQuery* database, and acknowledge the safety warning, if necessary. Start the Simple Query Wizard, and create a new query that uses the **OrderID**, **OrderDate**, and **ShippedDate** fields from the **Orders** table and all the fields from the **Customers** table. Name the query **Orders and Customers**, and then click **Finish**. Close the datasheet and the *CreateQuery* database.

Modifying a Query in Design View

The Simple Query Wizard does a good job of combining tables and fields in a query. However, after you've created and saved a query, you might want to change it. What's more, the wizard doesn't take advantage of many query features that you might want to use.

In Design view, you can add or remove fields, specify sort order, and set criteria for filtering records. In addition, you can perform advanced query tasks, such as changing the way Access joins data between tables.

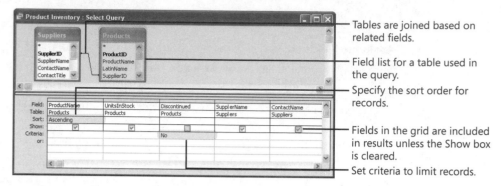

Tables are joined based on related fields.

Field list for a table used in the query.

Specify the sort order for records.

Fields in the grid are included in results unless the Show box is cleared.

Set criteria to limit records.

BE SURE TO open the query you want to work with in Design view before carrying out these steps.

 Design

Tip To open a query in Design view, click Queries on the Objects bar of the Database window, and then click the Database window's Design button.

To add a table or query:

Show Table

1   Click the **Show Table** button on the Database toolbar.

2   In turn, double-click each table or query that you want to add to the open query.

A field list for each table or query appears in the upper pane of the Query window. If the tables are related, a join line appears between them.

Tip You can create your own relationships by dragging a field in one field list to a related field in another field list.

To add a field to the query grid:

● Do either of the following:

■ In the field list in the upper pane of the Query window, double-click each field you want to add.

■ Drag each field from the field list to the query grid to insert it.

Fields in the query grid appear in query results, and you can use them to set criteria or the sort order.

To restrict the set of records the query displays:

1   In the query grid, click the **Criteria** row of the field for which you want to specify criteria.

2   For the first crieria, do either of the following:

■ Type the value you want Access to look for in that field.

■ To look for a range of values, type the >, <, >=, or <= operators followed by a value. For example, to find records with values greater than or equal to 0, type *>=0*.

■ To find records with no value at all, type **Null**. To find all records containing a value, type **Not Null**.

3   To add additional criteria, do any of the following:

■   To find records that meet the first criteria and another criteria, enter additional criteria in other fields in the **Criteria** row.

■   To find records that meet the first criteria or another criteria in the same field, enter additional criteria in the **Or** row, below the existing criteria.

To specify a sort order:

1   In the query grid, click the **Sort** row of the field on which you want to base the sort.

2   Click the down arrow, and click **Ascending** (to sort A-Z or 1-100) or **Descending** (to sort Z-A or 100-1).

To hide a field for which you've set sorting or criteria:

●   In the query grid, clear the **Show** check box for the field you want to hide.

To view query results:

Run

●   Click the **Run** button on the Query Design toolbar.

View

●   Click the **View** button on the Query Design toolbar.

Practice Exercise

In this exercise, you will open a query, add a field, select a sort order, and specify criteria to locate specific records.

USE the *ModifyQuery* database in the *My Documents\Microsoft Press\MOS 2003 Study Guide\Access \A03C-1-7* practice file folder.

Open the *ModifyQuery* database, and acknowledge the safety warning, if necessary. Open the **Product Inventory** query in Design view. In the **Discontinued** field, type **No** in the **Criteria** row to find only records that have not been discontinued. Clear the **Show** check box so that this field will not appear in the results. Indicate that the results should be sorted in ascending order based on the **ProductName** field. Add the **PhoneNumber** field from the **Suppliers** field list to the query grid. Click the **View** button to view the results of your changes. Then close the datasheet, save the changes to the query, and close the *ModifyQuery* database.

Creating a Crosstab Query

A crosstab query calculates and restructures data for easy analysis. It can calculate a sum, average, count, or other type of total for data that is grouped by two types of information—one down the left side of the datasheet and one across the top. The cell at the junction of each row and column displays the results of the query's calculation. For example, you could find each employee's monthly sales totals.

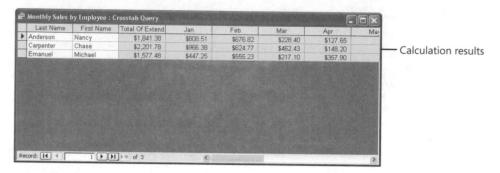

Calculation results

If you want to create a crosstab query that incorporates fields from more than one table, you must first create a query that joins the tables, and then create a crosstab query based on that query.

BE SURE TO open the database you want to work with before carrying out these steps.

To create a crosstab query:

 1 On the **Objects** bar of the Database window, click **Queries**, and then click the Database window's **New** button.

2 In the New Query dialog box, click **Crosstab Query Wizard**, and click **OK**.

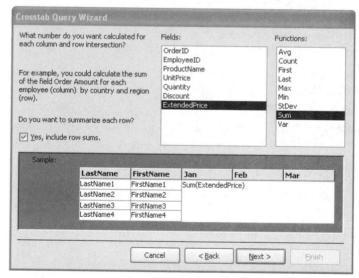

3 Click the table or query on which you want to base the query, and click **Next**.

4 Move up to three of the available fields to the **Selected Fields** list, and click **Next**.

5   Click the field whose values you want to use as column headings, and click **Next**.

As you complete the wizard's pages, the Sample box displays a picture of the row and column structure the current settings will produce.

6   Continue working through the wizard, clicking **Next** to move between pages, until you are asked to select the value that the query will calculate.

7   Click the field whose values will be the basis for the calculation, click the function to be used, and click **Next**.

8   Type a name for the query, and click **Finish**.

The wizard creates the query, runs it, and displays a datasheet with the results.

Practice Exercise

In this exercise, you will create a crosstab query that summarizes monthly sales for each employee based on the date of orders he or she took.

USE the *CreateCrosstab* database in the *My Documents\Microsoft Press\MOS 2003 Study Guide\Access \A03C-1-7* practice file folder.

Open the *CreateCrosstab* database. Display the New Query dialog box, and start the Crosstab Query Wizard. Base the new query on the **Order Details Extended** query, which combines fields from the Employees, Orders, and OrderDetails tables. Move the **LastName** and **FirstName** fields to the **Selected Fields** list. Use the **OrderDate** values as column headings and **Month** as the interval. Base the calculation on the values in the **ExtendedPrice** field, and use **Sum** as the function. Assign the name **Monthly Sales by Employee**, and click **Finish**. The datasheet lists the three employees who take orders, followed by their total sales and monthly breakdowns for each employee. Close the datasheet and the *CreateCrosstab* database.

Finding Duplicate Records

A duplicate query is a form of select query that locates records that have the same information in one or more fields that you specify. For example, you can find the records of customers who have been entered in a table more than once and then delete all but one of the records. The Find Duplicates Query Wizard guides you through the process of specifying the table and fields to use in the query.

BE SURE TO open the database you want to work with before carrying out these steps.

To find duplicate records:

1   On the **Objects** bar of the Database window, click **Queries**, and then click the Database window's **New** button.

2   In the New Query dialog box, click **Find Duplicates Query Wizard**, and click **OK**.

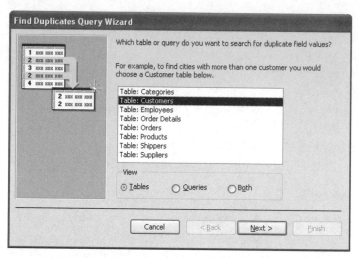

3 Click the table or query on which you want to base the query, and click **Next**.

4 Move the available fields you want to check for duplicates to the **Duplicate-value fields** list, and click **Next**.

5 Specify any additional fields you want to appear in the results, and click **Next**.

6 Name the query, and click **Finish** to create the query and view duplicate records in a datasheet.

Practice Exercise

In this exercise, you will find duplicate records in a table and delete any that don't belong.

USE the *FindDuplicates* database in the *My Documents\Microsoft Press\MOS 2003 Study Guide\Access \A03C-1-7* practice file folder.

Open the *FindDuplicates* database, and acknowledge the safety warning, if necessary. Use the Find Duplicates Query Wizard to create a new query based on the **Customers** table. Search for duplicates in the **FirstName** and **LastName** fields, and also display the **City**, **Region**, and **PhoneNumber** fields in the results. Accept the suggested query name, and click **Finish** to view the datasheet. Of the four records shown, the last two are clearly the same person. Delete the last record in the datasheet, clicking **Yes** to confirm the deletion. Close the datasheet and the *FindDuplicates* database.

Finding Unmatched Records

An unmatched query is a type of select query that locates records in one table that don't have related records in another table. For example, you can locate records in a Customers table that don't have an order in an Orders table. The Find Unmatched Query Wizard guides you through the process of specifying the tables and fields to use in the query.

BE SURE TO open the database you want to work with before carrying out these steps.

To find unmatched records:

1 On the **Objects** bar of the Database window, click **Queries**, and then click the Database window's **New** button.

2 In the New Query dialog box, click **Find Unmatched Query Wizard**, and click **OK**.

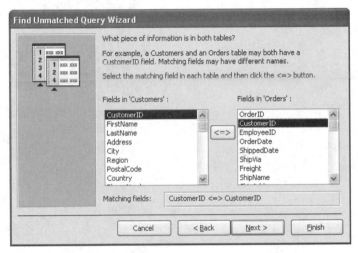

3 Click the table or query on which you want to base the query, and click **Next**.

4 Click the table or query containing the related records, and click **Next**.

5 In the first table's field list, click the common field, and then click the corresponding field in the second table's field list, clicking **Next**, to move to the next page.

6 Specify any additional fields you want to appear in the results, and click **Next**.

7 Name the query, and click **Finish** to create the query and view the results in a datasheet.

Practice Exercise

In this exercise, you will use an unmatched query to find customers who don't have any orders.

USE the *FindUnmatched* database in the *My Documents\Microsoft Press\MOS 2003 Study Guide\Access \A03C-1-7* practice file folder.

Open the *FindUnmatched* database, and acknowledge the safety warning, if necessary. Display the New Query dialog box, and use the Find Unmatched Query Wizard to create a new query based on the **Customers** and **Orders** tables. Look for matches in the **CustomerID** field in both tables. For any unmatched records in the **Customers** table, display all the fields in the datasheet. Accept the suggested query name, and click **Finish** to view the datasheet. Close the datasheet and the *FindUnmatched* database.

Updating Information with an Action Query

An action query updates or makes changes to multiple records in one operation. It is essentially a select query that performs an action on the selected results. Four types of actions are available:

- Update queries, which make changes to records in one or more tables
- Make-table queries, which create a new table from all or part of the data in one or more tables.
- Append queries, which add records from one or more tables to the end of one or more other tables
- Delete queries, which delete records from one or more tables

To create an action query, you first create a select query that returns the records you want to change, delete, or copy to another table. Then you convert the query to an action query and run it to change the records.

Tip When you run an action query, you make changes to the table that can't be undone. You should always create a backup copy of the table before running the query.

BE SURE TO create a query that extracts the records you want to change and then open it in Design view before carrying out these steps.

 Tip To open a query in Design view, click Queries on the Objects bar of the Database window, and then click the Database window's Design button.

To create an update query:

1   With the select query open in Design view, click **Update Query** on the **Query** menu.

The select query is converted to an update query. The only noticeable changes to the design grid are that the Sort and Show rows have been removed and an Update To row has been added.

2   In the **Update To** row under each field that you want to change, do one of the following:

- Type a new value for the field.
- To have Access calculate the new value, type an expression, enclosing field names in brackets.

For example, to increase prices by 10 percent, type *[UnitPrice]*1.1* in the Update To row of the UnitPrice field.

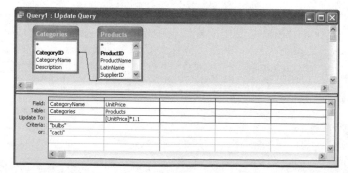

Run

3   On the Query Design toolbar, click the **Run** button.

Access tells you how many records will be affected by the query.

4   Click **Yes** to update the selected records.

5   Close the query, clicking **Yes** when Access prompts you to save changes.

To create a make table query:

1   With the select query open in Design view, click **Make-Table Query** on the **Query** menu.

The select query is converted to a make table query.

2   In the Make Table dialog box, type the name of the table you want to create in the **Table Name** box, and click **OK**.

Run

3   On the Query Design toolbar, click the **Run** button.

Access tells you how many records will be affected by the query.

4   Click **Yes** to copy the selected records to the new table.

5   Close the query, clicking **Yes** when Access prompts you to save changes.

To create an append query:

1   With the select query open in Design view, click **Append Query** on the **Query** menu.

2   In the Append dialog box, click the **Table Name** down arrow, click the name of the table to which you want to append the selected records, and click **OK**.

The select query is converted to an append query.

3   In the **Append To** row, specify fields in the destination table into which you want to append data.

Run

4   On the Query Design toolbar, click the **Run** button.

Access tells you how many records will be affected by the query.

5   Click **Yes** to add the selected records to the end of the specified table.

6   Close the query, clicking **Yes** when Access prompts you to save changes.

To create a delete query:

1   With the select query open in Design view, click **Delete Query** on the **Query** menu.

The select query is converted to a delete query.

2   Enter delete criteria for the fields as appropriate, and click the **Run** button.

Access tells you how many records will be deleted by the query.

Run

3   Click **Yes** to delete the selected records.

4   Close the query, clicking **Yes** when Access prompts you to save changes.

Practice Exercise

In this exercise, you will use an update query to increase the price of selected products by 10 percent.

USE the *UpdateQuery* database in the *My Documents\Microsoft Press\MOS 2003 Study Guide\Access \A03C-1-7* practice file folder.

Open the *UpdateQuery* database, and acknowledge the safety warning, if necessary. Open the **Bulbs and Cacti** query in Design view. Convert the query to an update query. In the **Update To** row of the **UnitPrice** field, type **[UnitPrice]*1.1**. Run the query, clicking **Yes** to acknowledge the warning. Then click the **View** button to display the datasheet, where all the **UnitPrice** values have been increased by 10 percent. Save and close the query. Then close the *UpdateQuery* database.

Create Forms

A03C-1-8   The skills measured by this objective include the following:

- Creating an AutoForm
- Creating a form by using the Form Wizard

A form provides a custom view of the data stored in a table or query. Just as you can view the data in a table or query in Datasheet view, you can view the data in a form in Form view. Forms can include pictures or graphics, fields can be arranged in any order, and special controls can help with data entry or display the result of a calculation.

Creating an AutoForm

Although a form doesn't have to include all the fields from a table, when it is used as the primary method of creating new records, it usually does include all fields. The quickest way to create a form that includes all the fields from a single table is to use an AutoForm.

When you create an AutoForm, Access applies the background style you selected the last time you used the Form Wizard (or the default style, if you haven't ever used the wizard).

BE SURE TO open the database you want to work with before carrying out these steps.

To create an AutoForm:

1   On the **Objects** bar of the Database window, click **Forms**, and then click the Database window's **New** button.

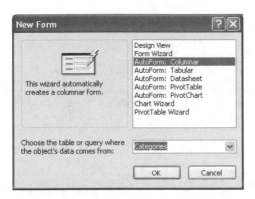

2   Do one of the following:

- ■ To create a form with fields arranged from top to bottom with labels at the left, click **AutoForm: Columnar**.

- ■ To create a form with fields arranged from left to right with labels at the top, click **AutoForm: Tabular**.

3   Click the **Choose the table or query where the object's data comes from** down arrow, and click the name of the table or query on which you want to base the form.

4   Click **OK**.

The dialog box closes, and after a moment, a new form is displayed in Form view.

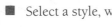
Save

5   On the Form View toolbar, click the **Save** button, type a name for the form (or accept the default name), and click **OK**.

Practice Exercise

In this exercise, you will create an AutoForm.

USE the *CreateAutoForm* database in the *My Documents\Microsoft Press\MOS 2003 Study Guide\Access \A03C-1-8* practice file folder.

Open the *CreateAutoForm* database, and acknowledge the safety warning, if necessary. Display the New Form dialog box, and create an **AutoForm: Columnar** based on the **Categories** table. View the form, and then save it, accepting the default name. Close the form and the *CreateAutoForm* database.

Creating a Form by Using the Form Wizard

The Form Wizard provides many options that aren't available in an AutoForm. When you create a form with the Form Wizard, you can do the following:

- ■ Select the type of field layout you want.
- ■ Select a style, which affects fonts and colors in the form.

575

■ Include only the fields you want. (AutoForms include all the fields in the selected table or query.)

■ Include fields from more than one table. For Access to work effectively with multiple tables, it must understand the relationships between the fields in those tables.

See Also   For information about creating relationships, refer to A03C-1-5, "Create and Modify One-to-Many Relationships."

After you decide what table or query the form will be based on and you know how the form will be used, you can create the basic form with the help of the Form Wizard. Like almost any other object in Access, you can always go into Design view to customize the form after it is created.

See Also   For information about customizing forms, refer to A03C-3-2, "Modify Form Layout."

BE SURE TO open the database you want to work with before carrying out these steps.

To create a form by using the Form Wizard:

1   On the **Objects** bar of the Database window, click **Forms**, and then double-click **Create form by using wizard**.

The first page of the Form Wizard asks you to specify which fields you want the form to display.

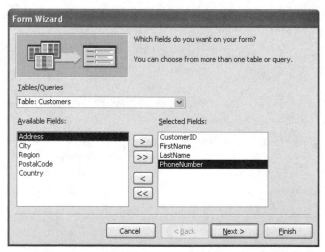

2   In the **Tables/Queries** box, select a table or query.

3   In the **Available Fields** list, do one of the following, and click **Next**:

■ In turn, click the fields you want in the **Available Fields** list, and click **>** to add them to the **Selected Fields** list.

■ To add all the fields, click **>>**.

4   Select a layout for the form, and click **Next**.

5 Select a style, and click **Next**.

6 Assign a name to the form, and click **Finish** to create and open the form.

Practice Exercise

In this exercise, you will create a form in which to view the records in a table.

USE the *AddRecords* database in the *My Documents\Microsoft Press\MOS 2003 Study Guide\Access \A03C-1-8* practice file folder.

Open the *AddRecords* database, and acknowledge the safety warning, if necessary. Start the Form Wizard, and create a form that uses all the fields in the **Customers** table. Select the **Columnar** format and the **Sumi Painting** style. Accept the suggested title, leave the **Open the form to view or enter information** option selected, and click **Finish**. The new Customers form opens, displaying the first customer record in the Customers table. Click the buttons in the record navigator to scroll through a few of the records. Then close the form and the *AddRecords* database.

Add and Modify Form Controls and Properties

A03C-1-9   The skills measured by this objective include the following:

- Setting form and control properties
- Adding controls to a form

Information is displayed on a form in boxes called controls. Some controls display labels that don't change when you move from one record to another, and some display information from the underlying records in the associated table. (This information changes to reflect the record you are currently viewing.) The controls are arranged in sections that determine where the information appears when you view it in Form view. Properties are assigned to each control, each section, and the entire form to control their appearance and the way they work. You can add controls to a form and change the form's properties or layout in Design view.

See Also   For information about changing a form's layout, refer to A03C-3-2, "Modify Form Layout."

Setting Form and Control Properties

When you use the Form Wizard to create a form, the wizard assigns default property settings. There are dozens of form and control properties that control the form's appearance and behavior. You can set most of the formatting properties—for example, the font, color, and alignment properties—by using buttons on the Formatting toolbar. For all other properties, you can open the Properties dialog box (sometimes called the property sheet).

You can modify these properties for the entire form:

Property	Use to
Record Source	Specify the table or query that provides records for the form
Caption	Display text in the form's title bar
Default View	Open the form in a specific view, such as Datasheet view or PivotTable view
Data Entry	Open the form for data entry only, hiding existing records
Allow Edits	Forbid editing data
Allow Deletions	Forbid deleting records
Allow Additions	Forbid adding new records

You can modify these properties for controls:

Property	Use to
Control Source	Specify the field that provides data for the control, or display the result of a calculation in the control
Format	Specify number or date formatting
Decimal Places	Display a specified number of digits for fractions
Enabled	Disable a control so that it can't be edited
Locked	Lock a control so that it can't be edited
Visible	Cause a control to be invisible (except in Design view)

BE SURE TO open the form you want to work with in Design view before carrying out these steps.

 Tip To open a form in Design view, click Forms on the Objects bar of the Database window, and then click the Database window's Design button.

To set font, color, and alignment properties:

1 Click the control whose properties you want to set.

   To set properties for multiple controls at once, click the form's background, and drag to select all the controls you want to change. Small black handles appear around selected controls.

2 Use the buttons on the Formatting toolbar to set the properties you want.

   For example, you can change the font and choose new colors for text, fills, and borders.

   Tip You can copy the formatting of one control to another by using the Format Painter button on the Formatting toolbar.

To set properties in the Properties dialog box:

1 Do one of the following to select the item whose properties you want to set:

- To set form properties, click the form selector box in the upper-left corner of the window (at the junction of the rulers).

- To set section or control properties, click the section or control you want to change.

- To set properties for multiple controls at once, click the form's background, and drag to select all the controls you want to change.

- To set properties for all the controls, click **Select All** on the **Edit** menu.

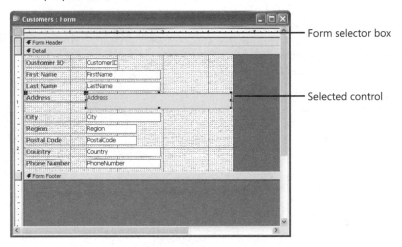

Form selector box

Selected control

Properties

2 If Properties dialog box isn't open, click the **Properties** button.

The dialog box displays all available properties for the control, organized on four tabs (plus the All tab, which includes every property).

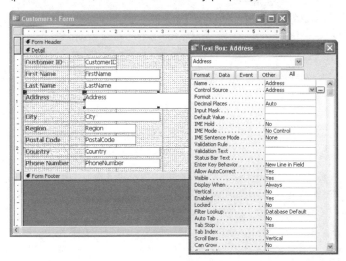

3 At the top of the Properties dialog box, click tabs to find the property you want to set.

579

4 Click the property, and select or type a setting.

Build

If there is a Build button next to the selected property, you can click it to open the Expression Builder to help you set the property.

Tip For information about any property, click its box in the Properties dialog box and press the F1 key.

5 When you've finished setting properties, close the Properties dialog box.

6 To se the effects of the changes, switch to Form view by clicking the **View** button.

View

Practice Exercise

In this exercise, you will edit the properties of a form.

USE the *EditProperties* database and the *tgc_bkgrnd* graphic file in the *My Documents\Microsoft Press \MOS 2003 Study Guide\Access\A03C-1-9* practice file folder.

Open the *EditProperties* database, and acknowledge the safety warning, if necessary. Open the **Customers** form in Design view, and if necessary, maximize its window, moving anything that obstructs your view of the form's controls out of the way. Select all the controls on the form, and change the font to **Microsoft Sans Serif**. (If you don't see Microsoft Sans Serif, click **MS Sans Serif**.) Change the font size to **8** points, and click the **Bold** button. Then with all the controls still selected, open the Properties dialog box. On the **Format** tab, set **Back Style** to **Normal**. Set **Back Color** to pale yellow. (Use the **Build** button to access the color options.) Set **Special Effect** to **Shadowed**, and set **Border Color** to a shade of green by entering a color value such as **32768**. Click the form's **Detail** heading to deselect all the controls. Then select all the label controls on the left (but not the corresponding controls on the right), and in the Properties dialog box, set the **Text Align** property to **Right**. Deselect the labels, and select all the controls on the right. In the Properties dialog box, change the **Left** setting (not Left Margin) to **1.5″** and the **Font Weight** property to **Normal**. Select the entire form, click the **Picture** property, click the **Build** button, and then change the form's background to the **tgc_bkgrnd** graphic located in the *My Documents\Microsoft Press\MOS 2003 Study Guide \Access\A03C-1-9* practice file folder. Close the Properties dialog box and the **Customers** form, clicking **Yes** to save its design. Then close the *EditProperties* database.

Adding Controls to a Form

Labels and text box controls are perhaps the most common controls used in forms. However, you can enhance a form with many other types of controls. For example, you can add groups of option buttons, check boxes, and list boxes to present people with choices instead of making them type entries in text boxes.

The most popular controls are stored in the Toolbox. Clicking the More Controls button in the Toolbox displays a list of all the controls on your computer (many of which are not associated with Access).

You can add controls that are bound to a field so that they display data from the current record, or you can create unbound controls that don't display data from the form's source. You can then put whatever you want in the control. You can format both bound and unbound controls in the usual ways.

See Also   For information about formatting controls, refer to "Setting Form and Control Properties" earlier in this section.

If you no longer need a control, you can easily delete it.

BE SURE TO open a form in Design view before carrying out these steps.

Tip   To open a form in Design view, click Forms on the Objects bar of the Database window, and then click the Database window's Design button.

To add a control that displays data from a field:

Toolbox

1   If the Toolbox isn't displayed, click the **Toolbox** button on the Form Design toolbar.

Field List

2   If the field list isn't displayed, click the **Field List** button on the Form Design toolbar.

The field list displays all the fields from the form's record source.

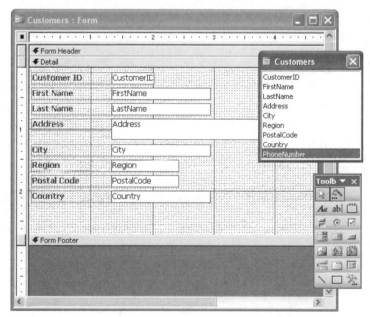

3   In the Toolbox, click the type of control you want to create.

Tip   If you want a wizard to help create the control whenever one is available, make sure the Control Wizards tool is selected.

Control Wizards

4   Drag a field from the field list to the form.

The new control appears on the form with its Control Source property set to the name of the field. If a Control Wizard is available and the Control Wizards tool is active in the Toolbox, the wizard appears to help you create the control.

To add an unbound control:

Toolbox

Control
Wizards

1 If the Toolbox isn't displayed, click the **Toolbox** button on the Form Design toolbar.

2 In the Toolbox, click the type of control you want to create.

> **Tip** If you want a wizard to help create the control whenever one is available, make sure the Control Wizards tool is selected.

3 On the form, do one of the following:

- Click the location where you want to place the control.
- To specify the size of the new control, drag to draw the control's outline on the form.

The new control appears on the form. If a Control Wizard is available and the Control Wizards tool is active in the Toolbox, the wizard appears to help you create the control.

4 Carry out any aditional steps necessary to complete the control.

For example, if you are adding a label, enter text in the control and press ENTER.

To delete a control:

- Click the control you want to delete, and press **DELETE**.

Practice Exercise

In this exercise, you will add a graphic and a caption to a form. You will also replace a text box control with a combo box control.

USE the *AddControls* database and the *tgc_logo2* graphic file in the *My Documents\Microsoft Press \MOS 2003 Study Guide\Access\A03C-1-9* practice file folder.

Open the *AddControls* database, and acknowledge the safety warning, if necessary. Open the **Customers 2** form in Design view, and if necessary, maximize its window, moving anything that obstructs your view of the form's controls out of the way. Use the Toolbox's **Image** tool to drag a rectangle about 1 inch high and 3 inches wide at the left end of the **Form Header** section, and insert the **tgc_logo2** graphic file stored in the *My Documents\Microsoft Press \MOS 2003 Study Guide\Access\A03C-1-9* practice file folder. Use the **Label** tool to drag a rectangle that occupies the remaining space in the **Form Header** section, and type **Customers** in the control. Change the **Font Size** to **18**, and center the text. In the Toolbox, make sure the **Control Wizards** tool is not selected, and use the **Combo Box** tool to drag a rectangle below the current **Country** text box control. Copy the formatting from the **Country** text box to the new combo box control. Set the **Control Source** property for the combo box to **Country**, and then type **SELECT DISTINCT Customers.Country FROM Customers;** in the **Row Source** property. (This is a query that extracts one example of every country in the Country field of the Customers table and displays the results as a list when you click the box's down arrow. Type this query very carefully, using a period instead of a space between *Customers* and *Country* and ending the query with a semicolon.) For the label to the left of the combo box, change the **Caption** property to **Country**. Delete the original **Country** text box and its label. Switch to Form view to test the new controls, and then save and close the form. Close the *AddControls* database.

Create Reports

A03C-1-10   The skills measured by this objective include the following:

- Creating a report by using the Report Wizard
- Creating mailing labels

Reports are custom layouts of information intended for printing. They are often used to summarize groups of data, and they have special features for grouping and printing. Like forms, reports display records from a table or query in controls, and they have properties that determine their appearance and behavior. Although you can preview reports, your primary consideration is the layout of the printed page rather than the way data appears on the screen.

Creating a Report by Using the Report Wizard

When you create a form with the Report Wizard, you can do the following:

- Select the fields and layout you want.
- Select a style, which affects fonts and colors in the report.
- Include fields from more than one table. For Access to work effectively with multiple tables, it must understand the relationships between the fields in those tables.

See Also   For information about creating relationships, refer to A03C-1-5, "Create and Modify One-to-Many Relationships."

- Organize records into groups.
- Summarize data.

Before you begin creating a report with the Report Wizard, you need to know what table or tables it will be based on. (You can also base a report on a query.) Then for each field you specify, the Report Wizard creates a basic layout, attaches styles, and adds a text box control and its associated label. After the report is created, you can customize the report in Design view if it doesn't quite meet your needs.

See Also   For information about customizing the layout of reports, refer to A03C-3-3, "Modify Report Layout and Page Setup."

BE SURE TO open the database you want to work with before carrying out these steps.

To create a report by using the Report Wizard:

1   On the **Objects** bar of the Database window, click **Reports**, and then double-click **Create report by using wizard**.

The first page of the Report Wizard asks you to specify fields you want the report to include.

2   In the **Tables/Queries** box, select a table or query.

3 In the **Available Fields** list, do one of the following, and click **Next**:

■ In turn, click the fields you want in the form, and click **>** to add them to the **Selected Fields** list.

■ To add all the fields, click **>>**.

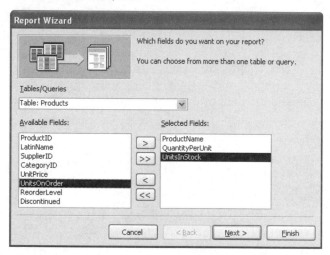

Tip Fields appear in a report in the order in which they appear in the wizard's Selected Fields list. You can save yourself the effort of rearranging the fields in the report if you enter them in the desired order in the wizard. If you select a field in the Selected Fields list, the next field you move from the Available Fields list will appear below the selected field.

4 If you want to group records based on a particular field, double-click the field to add a group heading to the sample box on the right.

For example, you might want to organize customer records by city.

5 If you want to change the default grouping interval, click the **Grouping Options** button at the bottom of the page to display the Grouping Intervals dialog box. Click the **Grouping intervals** down arrow, click the setting you want, and click **OK**. Then click **Next**.

For example, you use this option when you want to group records by the letters of the alphabet.

6 To sort records, click the down arrow, and select the field on which to base the sort, clicking the adjacent button to switch between **Ascending** and **Descending** order.

7 If you want to summarize the records in a particular group, click **Summary Options**, select the check boxes for the calculations you want Access to include, indicate whether you want to show the records and the summary information or just the summary information, and click **OK**. Then click **Next**.

8 Specify the report's layout and orientation, and click **Next**.

9 Click the style you want for the report, and click **Next**.

10 Type a name for the report, and click **Finish** to create and preview the report.

Practice Exercise

In this exercise, you will use the Report Wizard to create a simple report.

USE the *CreateReport* database in the *My Documents\Microsoft Press\MOS 2003 Study Guide\Access \A03C-1-10* practice file folder.

Open the *CreateReport* database, and acknowledge the safety warning, if necessary. Use the Report Wizard to create a report that uses the following fields from the **Products** table: **ProductName**, **QuantityPerUnit**, and **UnitsInStock**. Then click **ProductName** in the **Selected Fields** list to select it, and add the **CategoryName** field from the **Categories** table. View the records **by Products**, and move **ProductName** to the top of the simulated report. To group products by their first letter, display the Grouping Intervals dialog box, and specify **1st Letter** as the interval. Sort the records in **Ascending** order based on the **ProductName** field. Specify **Outline 1** as the layout, **Portrait** as the orientation, and **Compact** as the style. Type **Alphabetical List of Products** as the title, and click **Finish** to preview the report. Then close the Report window and the *CreateReport* database.

Creating Mailing Labels

To create a report that prints mailing labels, you use the Label Wizard. Before you begin creating mailing labels, you need to know which table or query contains the records for which you want to print labels and the dimensions or manufacturer's product number of the labels you are using.

BE SURE TO open the database you want to work with before carrying out these steps.

To create a report that will print mailing labels:

1 On the **Objects** bar of the Database window, click **Reports**, and then click the Database window's **New** button.

The New Report dialog box displays the types of reports you can create.

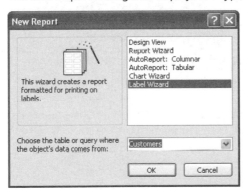

2 Click **Label Wizard**.

3 Click the **Choose the table or query where the object's data comes from** down arrow, and click the name of the table or query on which you want to base the report.

4 Click **OK**.

The wizard displays the types of labels you can create. If the labels you want to use aren't listed, you can specify custom label dimensions.

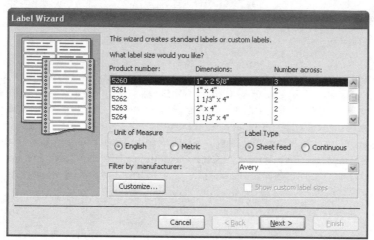

5   Click the product you want to use, and click **Next**.

6   Specify the font, size, weight, and text color, and click **Next**.

7   Move the fields you want to appear on the label to the **Prototype label** box, setting them up exactly the way you want them to appear, and click **Next**.

   For example, you can put multiple fields on the same line, separating them with spaces and punctuation.

8   Indicate the fields on which you want to sort the labels, if any, and click **Next**.

9   Type a name for the mailing label report, and click **Finish** to create and preview the mailing label report.

Practice Exercise

In this exercise, you will use the Label Wizard to create mailing labels for customers.

USE the *CreateLabels* database in the *My Documents\Microsoft Press\MOS 2003 Study Guide\Access \A03C-1-10* practice file folder.

Open the *CreateLabels* database, and acknowledge the safety warning, if necessary. Use the Label Wizard to create a set of mailing labels based on the **Customers** table. You want to use Avery **5260** labels, and the default formatting. Set up the Prototype label as follows:

FirstName LastName
Address
City, **Region PostalCode**
Country

Sort the records by the **LastName** and **FirstName** fields. Accept the suggested name, and click **Finish** to preview the report. If a message warns that some data may not be displayed, click **OK**. Then close the Report window and the *CreateLabels* database.

Add and Modify Report Control Properties

A03C-1-11   The skills measured by this objective include the following:

■ Setting report and control properties

■ Adding controls to a report

You can use the Report Wizard to get a quick start on a report, but you will usually want to use Design view to refine the report and add special touches. Refining a report is an iterative process: you switch back and forth between Design view and Print Preview to evaluate each change you make and to plan the next change.

Setting Report and Control Properties

Every report includes a Detail section that appears once in the report for each record in the underlying data. A report can have other sections, such as a report header, page header, page footer, and report footer. If your report groups records, you can add group header and footer sections that appear once for each group.

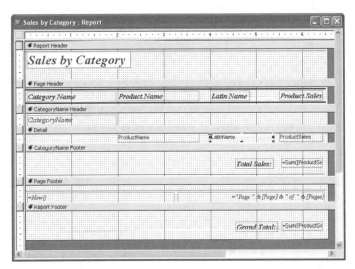

There are dozens of report, section, and control properties that control the report's appearance and behavior. When you use the Report Wizard to create a report, the wizard assigns default property settings. In Design view, you can change these settings to improve the form's appearance or change the way it works. You can set some of the formatting properties—for example, font and alignment properties—by using buttons on the Formatting toolbar. For other properties, you can open the Properties dialog box (sometimes called the property sheet).

You can modify two properties for the entire report:

Property	Use to
Record Source	Specify the table or query that provides records for the report
Caption	Display text in the report's title bar during Print Preview

You can modify these properties for the Detail section or a Group header section:

Property	Use to
Force New Page	Cause the page to break before or after a section
Keep Together	Allow a page break within a section
Can Grow	Allow a section to expand when fields are too large to fit (set property to Yes for section and controls)
Can Shrink	Reduce white space when fields don't fill a section (set property to Yes for section and controls)
Repeat Section (group header sections only)	Repeat the group header at the top of the next page if records in the group span more than one page

You can modify these properties for controls, such as text boxes:

Property	Use to
Control Source	Specify the field that provides data for the control, or display the result of a calculation in the control
Format	Specify number or date formatting
Decimal Places	Display a specified number of digits for fractions
Hide Duplicates	Display a value only once if it repeats from record to record
Can Grow	Allow a field to expand when data doesn't fit (set property to Yes for section and controls)
Can Shrink	Reduce white space when fields don't contain values (set property to Yes for section and controls)
Running Sum	Display a running total for all records up to the current record (for a numeric field)

If your report groups records, you can modify the following properties in the Sorting and Grouping dialog box:

Property	Use to
Group Header	Display a header section for each group
Group Footer	Display a footer section for each group
Group On	Group records in a range of values, such as by month or quarter
Keep Together	Keep records in each group together on one page (whenever possible)

BE SURE TO open the report you want to work with in Design view before carrying out these steps.

Tip To open a report in Design view, click Reports on the Objects bar of the Database window, and then click the Database window's Design button.

To change the text displayed in a label:

1   Click the label whose text you want to change.

Small black handles appear around the selected control.

2   Click the label again, and then select the text you want to change.

3   Type the new text, and press **ENTER**.

Access sets the label's Caption property to the new text. If the label is too small for the text you type, Access resizes the label.

To set font, alignment, and border properties:

1   Click the control whose properties you want to set.

To set properties for multiple controls at once, click the form's background, and drag to select all the controls you want to change. Small black handles appear around selected controls.

2   Use the buttons on the Formatting toolbar to set the properties you want.

To set report, section, or control properties:

1   Do one of the following to select the item whose properties you want to set:

■   To set report properties, click the report selector box in the upper-left corner of the window.

■   To set section or control properties, click the section or control you want to change.

■   To set properties for multiple controls at once, click the report's background, and drag to select all the controls you want to change.

■   To set properties for all the controls, click **Select All** on the **Edit** menu.

Properties

2   If Properties dialog box isn't open, click the **Properties** button on the Report Design toolbar.

The dialog box displays all available properties for the control, organized on four tabs (plus the All tab, which includes every property).

3   At the top of the Properties dialog box, click tabs to find the property you want to set.

4   Click the property, and select or type a setting.

Build

If there is a Build button next to the selected property, you can click it to open the Expression Builder to help you set the property.

5   When you've finished setting properties, close the Properties dialog box.

To set grouping properties:

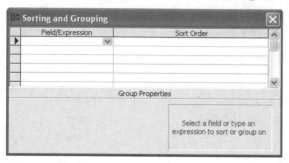

Sorting and Grouping

1   On the Report Design toolbar, click the **Sorting and Grouping** button.

2   In the **Field/Expression** column of each row, select the field you want to sort or group.

3   If you want to sort records in descending order (from Z to A or 100 to 1), click the **Sort Order** down arrow, and click **Descending** in the drop-down list.

4   In the bottom pane of the dialog box, set the group properties.

For example, to display a group header or footer section for the selected group, set the Group Header or Group Footer property to Yes.

5   Close the Sorting and Grouping dialog box.

If you created group headers or footers, the new sections appear in the report. You can add controls to each new section or click to set section properties.

To preview a report:

Print Preview

1   On the Standard toolbar, click the **Print Preview** button.

2   Click the report to zoom in or out.

Practice Exercise

In this exercise, you will open a report in Design view and change fonts, text, and other properties.

USE the *ChangeReport* database in the *My Documents\Microsoft Press\MOS 2003 Study Guide\Access \A03C-1-11* practice file folder.

Open the *ChangeReport* database, and acknowledge the safety warning, if necessary. Open the **Alphabetical List of Products** report in Print Preview, zoom in to view the data, and then switch to Design view. Click the text box control to the right of the **ProductNameBy1st** label, set its font size to **12**, and make it bold. Then delete the label to its left. Display the Properties dialog box for the entire report, and in the **Record Source** property, click the **Build** button to display the Query Builder. Add the **Discontinued** field from the **Products** field list to the field grid, and type **No** in the **Criteria** row of that field. Close the Query Builder, clicking **Yes** to update the property. Close the Properties dialog box. Display the Sorting and Grouping dialog box, and in the bottom pane, set the **Keep Together** property to **Whole Group**. Save your changes, and then preview the report. Close the report and the *ChangeReport* database.

Adding Controls to a Report

If the Report Wizard doesn't include all the information you want on a report—or if you decide to create a report from scratch—you'll need to add controls such as the following:

- You can add labels (text that doesn't change from record to record) and lines. You use the Toolbox to create these unbound controls (so called because they don't display data from the source table or query).

- You can use commands on the Insert menu to add page numbers, dates and times, pictures, and charts.

- You can add controls that display data from the report's underlying table or query. You use the field list to create these bound controls.

- If you want to display the result of an expression, such as the result of an aggregate function or a mathematical calculation, you can create a text box control and specify the expression you want.

Tip An aggregate function is a sum or other value calculated from a group of records. When you use an aggregate function in a group footer, it calculates the total for all records in the group. When you use the same function in the report footer, it calculates the grand total for the report. Examples of aggregate functions are Sum, Avg, and Count.

After you have added controls to a report, you can format them in the usual ways. You can also adjust their layout by moving, alsigning, and sizing them.

See Also For information about formatting controls, refer to "Setting Report and Control Properties" earlier in this section. For information about changing a report's layout, refer to A03C-3-3, "Modify Report Layout and Page Setup."

BE SURE TO open a report in Design view before carrying out these steps.

 Tip To open a report in Design view, click Reports on the Objects bar of the Database window, and then click the Database window's Design button.

To add an unbound control:

Toolbox

Control
Wizards

1 If the Toolbox isn't displayed, click the **Toolbox** button on the Report Design toolbar.

2 In the Toolbox, click the type of control you want to create.

    Tip If you want a wizard to help create the control whenever one is available, make sure the Control Wizards tool is selected.

3 On the report, do one of the following:

- Click the location where you want to place the control.

- To specify the size of the new control, drag to draw the control's outline on the form.

The new control appears on the report. If a Control Wizard is available and the Control Wizards tool is active in the Toolbox, the wizard appears to help you create the control.

4 Carry out any aditional steps necessary to complete the control.

For example, if you are adding a label, enter text in the control and press ENTER.

591

To add a control that displays data from a field:

Toolbox

1 If the Toolbox isn't displayed, click the **Toolbox** button on the Report Design toolbar.

Field List

2 If the field list isn't displayed, click the **Field List** button on the Report Design toolbar.

The field list displays all the fields from the report's record source.

3 In the Toolbox, click the type of control you want to create.

Control Wizards

Tip If you want a wizard to help create the control whenever one is available, make sure the Control Wizards tool is selected.

4 Drag a field from the field list to the report.

The new control appears on the report with its Control Source property set to the name of the field. The new field has an associated label.

To add a control that displays a calculated value:

1 Use the Toolbox to add a text box control to the report.

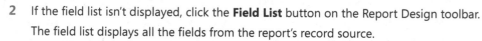

Properties

2 If the Properties dialog box isn't displayed, click the **Properties** button on the Report Design toolbar.

3 In the Properties dialog box, click the **Data** tab.

4 Set the **Control Source** property to an expression that will result in the value you want.

Start the expression with the equal (=) sign, and enclose any field names in square brackets. For example, to display the sum of values in the OrderTotal field, you can place a text box in a group footer or report footer and set its Control Source property to *=Sum([OrderTotal])*.

To use the Expression Builder to set the Control Source property:

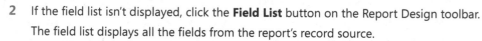

Build

1 In the Properties dialog box, click the **Build** button to the right of the Control Source property box.

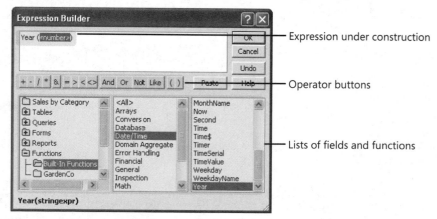

2 In the Expression Builder, double-click fields, functions, operators, and other elements to build the expression you want.

3 Click **OK** to set the property.

Practice Exercise

In this exercise, you will open a report in Design view and add a few controls.

USE the *CreateControls* database in the *My Documents\Microsoft Press\MOS 2003 Study Guide\Access \A03C-1-11* practice file folder.

Open the *CreateControls* database, and acknowledge the safety warning, if necessary. Open the **Sales By Category** report in Design view. Drag **LatinName** from the field list to the **Detail** section, dropping it between the **ProductName** and **ProductSales** controls. Delete the **Latin Name** label to the left of the new text box control. Create a new **LatinName** label in the **Page Header** section, between the **ProductName** and **ProductSales** labels. Create a text box control at the right end of the **CategoryName Footer** section of the report, below the **ProductSales** control. Display the Properties dialog box, and on the **All** tab, type **=Sum([ProductSales])** as the **Control Source** property, and set the **Format** property to **Currency**. Click the control's label, double-click its text, and type **Total Sales**. Use the **Line** tool to draw a line across the bottom of the **CategoryName Footer** section. Save and then preview the report. Close the report and the *CreateControls* database.

Create a Data Access Page

A03C-1-12   The skills measured by this objective include the following:

■ Creating and modifying a data access page

Data access pages are a special type of Web page that you can use to display and edit data in an Access database on the Internet or an intranet. Like forms and reports, data access pages can display records from Access tables or queries, even relating data between tables. In some cases, such as when data comes from a single table and isn't grouped, you can edit the data on a data access page. Unlike Access forms and reports, data access pages can be viewed outside of Microsoft Access in Internet Explorer.

Creating and Modifying a Data Access Page

You can use the Page Wizard to create a data access page that displays records from a table or query. The wizard helps you select the fields to be included on the data access page and set grouping and sorting options.

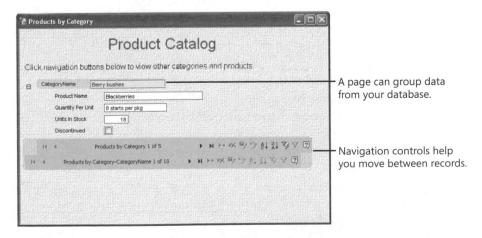

A page can group data from your database.

Navigation controls help you move between records.

Although the Page Wizard can provide a starting point for a data access page, you will probably want to make a few changes in Design view. For example, you might want to do the following:

- Insert text to explain how to use the page
- Add controls, such as an image or hyperlink
- Set properties for a control, a section, or the entire page

Tip To open a data access page in Design view, click Pages on the Objects bar of the Database window, and then click the Database window's Design button.

BE SURE TO open the database you want to work with before carrying out these steps.

To create a data access page by using the Page Wizard:

1 On the **Objects** bar of the Database window, click **Pages**, and then click the Database window's **New** button.

The New Data Access Page dialog box displays options for creating a page.

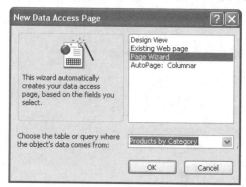

2 Click **Page Wizard**.

3 Click the **Choose the table or query where the object's data comes from** down arrow, and click the name of the table or query on which you want to base the report.

4 Click **OK**.

The first page of the Page Wizard appears.

5 In the **Available Fields** list, do one of the following, and click **Next**:

- In turn, click the fields you want in the form, and click > to add them to the **Selected Fields** list.
- To add all the fields, click **>>**.

6 If you want to group records based on a particular field, double-click the field to add a group heading to the sample box on the right.

7 If you want to change the default grouping interval, click the **Grouping Options** button at the bottom of the page to display the Grouping Intervals dialog box. Click the **Grouping intervals** down arrow, click the setting you want, and click **OK**. Then click **Next**.

8 To sort records, click the down arrow, and select the field on which to base the sort, clicking the adjacent button to switch between **Ascending** and **Descending** order.

9   Type a name for the page.

10   To apply a theme to the page, select the **Do you want to apply a theme to your page?**
     check box, and click **Finish**.

     The wizard creates the page, opens it in Design view, and displays the Theme dialog box.

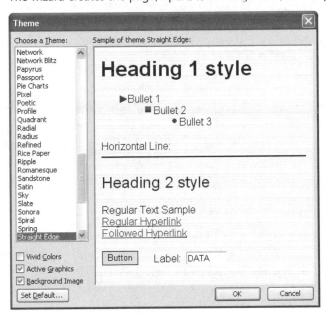

11   Select the theme you want, and click **OK**.

12   At the top of the page, click the **Click here and type title text** placeholder, and type a title
     for the page.

13   Save the page, clicking **OK** if Access displays a warning about absolute and network paths.
     Then close the page.

     Access displays a link to the page in the Database window.

     Tip   Unlike a form or report, which is stored in the database file, a data access page is a sep-
     arate HTML file stored in the same folder as the database. Using Windows, you can locate the
     page and open it in Internet Explorer. To open the page from within Access, double-click
     its link in the Database window.

To test a grouped data access page:

1   If necessary, click the **View** button to change to Page view, and if the window has a vertical
     scroll bar, resize the window until the scroll bar disappears, or maximize the window.

2   On the group navigation bar, click the **Next** button to view the next group.

3   Click the **+** button to the left of group name.

     The view expands to show a record within the group, and a second navigation bar
     is displayed above the first so that you can navigate among the records.

4   On the record navigation bar, click the **Next** button to view the next record in that group.

To add an unbound control:

Toolbox

1 Open the data access page in Design view.

2 If the Toolbox isn't displayed, click the **Toolbox** button on the Page Design toolbar.

3 In the Toolbox, click the type of control you want to create.

Control
Wizards

Tip   If you want a wizard to help create the control whenever one is available, make sure the Control Wizards tool is selected.

4 On the page, do one of the following:

■ Click the location where you want to place the control.

■ To specify the size of the new control, drag to draw the control's outline on the form.

The new control appears on the report. If a Control Wizard is available and the Control Wizards tool is active in the Toolbox, the wizard appears to help you create the control.

5 Carry out any aditional steps necessary to complete the control.

For example, if you are adding a label, enter text in the control and press ENTER.

To add a control that displays data from a field:

1 Open the data access page in Design view, and make sure the Toolbox is displayed.

2 If the field list isn't displayed, click the **Field List** button on the Page Design toolbar.

Field List

The table or query that provides records to the page is expanded to show its fields.

Fields from the underlying table or query for the page

3 In the Toolbox, click the type of control you want to create.

Control
Wizards

Tip   If you want a wizard to help create the control whenever one is available, make sure the Control Wizards tool is selected.

4   Drag a field from the field list to the page.

The new control appears on the page with its Control Source property set to the name of the field. If a Control Wizard is available and the Control Wizards button is active, the wizard appears to help create the control.

To set properties:

1   In Design view, right-click the section or control whose properties you want set, and on the shortcut menu, click **Page Properties**, **Group Level Properties**, **Section Properties**, or **Element Properties**.

The Properties dialog box displays all available properties for the page, group, section, or control, organized on four tabs (plus the All tab, which includes every property).

2   At the top of the Properties dialog box, click tabs to find the property you want to set.

3   Click the property, and select or type a setting.

Build

If there is a Build button next to the selected property, you can click it to open the Expression Builder to help you set the property.

4   When you've finished setting properties, close the Properties dialog box.

View

5   To test your changes, click the **View** button on the Page Design toolbar.

Practice Exercise

In this exercise, you will use the Page Wizard to create a data access page based on a query. You will then make some improvements and preview the page in Internet Explorer.

USE the *CreateDataAccess* database and the *tgc_logo2* graphic file in the *My Documents\Microsoft Press \MOS 2003 Study Guide\Access\A03C-1-12* practice file folder.

Open the *CreateDataAccess* database, and acknowledge the safety warning, if necessary. Use the Page Wizard to create a data access page based on all the fields in the **Products by Category** query. Group the records by **CategoryName**, and sort them in ascending order by product name. Accept the suggested title, select the **Do you want to apply a theme to your page** check box, and click **Finish**. Apply a theme that suggests nature. Change the place-holder at the top of the page to **Product Catalog**, and then click the **View** button to switch to Page view. Use the buttons on the group navigation bar to scroll through the categories. Click the **+** button to the left of **CategoryName**, and use the buttons on the record navigation bar to scroll through the product records in that category. Then use the group navigation bar to move to the next category, and so on. Switch to Design view. In the blank area below the title, type **Click the navigation buttons below to view other categories and products.** Right-click the **Products by Category-CategoryName** header, and click **Group Level Properties** on the shortcut menu. In the Properties dialog box, change the **ExpandedByDefault** setting to **True**, and close the dialog box. Use the Toolbox's **Image Hyperlink** tool to create a hyperlink control in the blank area at the bottom of the page. Insert the *tgc_logo2* graphic file stored in the *My Documents\Microsoft Press\MOS 2003 Study Guide\Access\A03C-1-12* practice file folder, and in the **Address** box of the Insert Hyperlink dialog box, enter **www.msn.thegardencompany.com**. Save the changes to the *Products by Category.htm* file, clicking **OK** to acknowledge the warning. Switch to Page view, and test the navigation controls again. Then close the data access page, and close the *CreateDataAccess* database.

A03C-1 Review

Number	Objective	Mastered
A03C-1-1	Create Access databases	
	Creating a database by using the Database Wizard	❑
	Creating a blank database	❑
A03C-1-2	Create and modify tables	
	Creating a table by using the Table Wizard	❑
	Creating a table by entering data	❑
	Creating and modifying a table in Design view	❑
A03C-1-3	Define and create field types	
	Setting the data type and size of a field	❑
	Creating a primary key field	❑
	Creating a lookup field	❑
A03C-1-4	Modify field properties	
	Setting field properties	❑
	Using an input mask	❑
A03C-1-5	Create and modify one-to-many relationships	
	Creating a relationship between two tables	❑
A03C-1-6	Enforce referential integrity	
	Setting referential integrity rules	❑
A03C-1-7	Create and modify queries	
	Creating a query by using the Simple Query Wizard	❑
	Modifying a query in Design view	❑
	Creating a crosstab query	❑
	Finding duplicate records	❑
	Finding unmatched records	❑
	Updating information with an action query	❑
A03C-1-8	Create forms	
	Creating an AutoForm	❑
	Creating a form by using the Form Wizard	❑
A03C-1-9	Add and modify form controls and properties	
	Setting form and control properties	❑
	Adding controls to a form	❑
A03C-1-10	Create reports	
	Creating a report by using the Report Wizard	❑
	Creating mailing labels	❑

Number	Objective	Mastered
A03C-1-11	Add and modify report control properties	
	Setting report and control properties	❏
	Adding controls to a report	❏
A03C-1-12	Create a data access page	
	Creating and modifying a data access page	❏

A03C-2

Entering Data

The skills tested by this section of the Microsoft Office Specialist Access 2003 Exam all relate to entering data into a database and using forms and datasheets to find or change data. Specifically, the following objectives are associated with this set of skills:

Number	Objective
A03C-2-1	Enter, edit, and delete records
A03C-2-2	Find and move among records
A03C-2-3	Import data to Access

Important Before you can do the practice exercises associated with this skill set, you need to install the practice files from the book's companion CD to their default location. See "Installing the Practice Files" on page xxv for more information.

Enter, Edit, and Delete Records

A03C-2-1   The skills measured by this objective include the following:

- Entering data in a table's datasheet
- Deleting records from a table

In Access, you use tables to store information in structured units called records. For example, each product a company sells might have its own record in a table called Products. The most direct way to enter, edit, and delete records in a table is in its datasheet.

Entering Data in a Table's Datasheet

When you view a table in Datasheet view, you see the table's data in columns (fields) and rows (records). At the bottom is a blank row, where you can enter a new record.

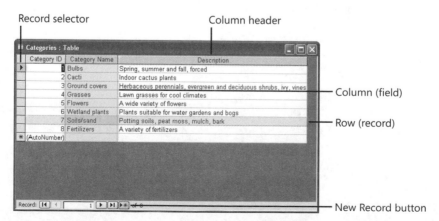

When you click the new record to start entering data, the New Record icon in the record selector (the asterisk) changes to an Edit Record icon (a pencil), indicating that you are working with that record. At the same time, Access adds a row with a New Record icon in its row selector, below the one you are working with. Records with no icon in their row selectors have been saved as part of the table. The record whose selector contains the right-pointing arrow is the active record.

BE SURE TO open a database containing at least one table before carrying out these steps.

To open a table in Datasheet view:

1   In the Database window, click **Tables** on the **Objects** bar.

2   Double-click the table you want to open.

   The table's datasheet appears. If the table contains data, each record is displayed in a row of the datasheet.

To enter a new record:

New Record

1   Click the **New Record** button.

   Access moves the insertion point to the blank record at the bottom of the datasheet, in the column for the first editable field in the table.

   Tip   Most fields in a new record are blank, but some fields might already be filled in. For example, some fields might have a default value that appears automatically in new records. If your table contains an AutoNumber field, that field displays *(AutoNumber)* to indicate that Access enters data in that field automatically.

2   Type a value for the first field in the record.

   The Edit Record indicator appears in the record selector at the left edge of the datasheet. If there is an AutoNumber field, Access enters a unique ID number in that field.

3   To move to the next field, press the **TAB** key.

4   Type values for the other fields in the record, pressing **TAB** to advance to the next field.

To edit an existing record:

1   Click in the field you want to edit.

   If you want to replace all the data in a field, point to the left edge of the field to display the plus pointer, and then click to select all the data.

2   Type your changes in the field.

   When you move to another record or close the datasheet, Access saves your changes.

Practice Exercise

In this exercise, you'll open a table and change an address. Then you'll open another table and add a new record.

USE the *AddRecord* database in the *My Documents\Microsoft Press\MOS 2003 Study Guide\Access\A03C-2-1* practice file folder.

   Open the *AddRecord* database, and acknowledge the safety warning, if necessary. Then open the **Customers** table in Datasheet view. Select the data in the **Address** field of the fourth record (*89 Cedar Way*), and type **251 B St.** Press **ESC** to undo your changes, and then close the **Customers** table. Open the **Categories** table, and note that the new record at the bottom of the datasheet displays (*AutoNumber*) in the **Category ID** column. Click the **Category Name** field of the new record, type **Trees**, press **TAB**, type **Evergreen and deciduous trees**, and then press **TAB** again. Access saves the new record. Close the *AddRecord* database.

Deleting Records from a Table

Over time, some types of information in a database can become obsolete. For example, if a customer doesn't place any orders for a long period of time, you might want to delete that customer's record from the Customers table.

Tip If you want to delete a large number of records matching specific criteria, you can use a special type of query, called a Delete query, to quickly get rid of all of them. For information, search Help for *delete query*.

Before deleting data, it is a good idea to back up your database. After records are deleted from a table, you can't get them back. In certain cases, records in more than one table are affected when you delete data. If the table in which you are deleting records has a relationship with another table and the Cascade Delete Related Records option for that relationship is set, Access will alert you to the possibility that records in the second table will also be deleted.

See Also For information about relationships, refer to A03C-1-5, "Creating and Modifying One-to-Many Relationships."

BE SURE TO open a database containing at least one table before carrying out these steps.

To delete a record:

1 In the Database window, double-click the table or form that contains records you want to delete.

2 Click the record selector at the left edge of the record you want to delete.

   To select more than one adjacent record, drag through their selectors.

Delete
Record

3 Click the **Delete Record** button (or press the **DELETE** key).

4 Click **OK** to confirm the deletion.

Practice Exercise

In this exercise, you will open a table and delete two records.

USE the *DeleteRecord* database in the *My Documents\Microsoft Press\MOS 2003 Study Guide\Access \A03C-2-1* practice file folder.

Open the *DeleteRecord* database, and acknowledge the safety warning, if necessary. Open the datasheet for the **Customers** table. Click the record selector for the record with *BERJO* in the **ID** field, and drag down to select two records. Press the **DELETE** key, and then confirm the deletion. Close the *DeleteRecord* database.

Find and Move Among Records

A03C-2-2   The skills measured by this objective include the following:

- Navigating among records
- Finding a specific record

An Access database is perfect for storing very large numbers of records. As your tables grow, you'll need to know how to navigate among records and find the data you are looking for.

Navigating Among Records

Forms and datasheets have navigation controls similar to the controls on a VCR or media player. The controls tell you the total number of records in the table or recordset, as well as the number of the current record. You can use these controls to navigate among records.

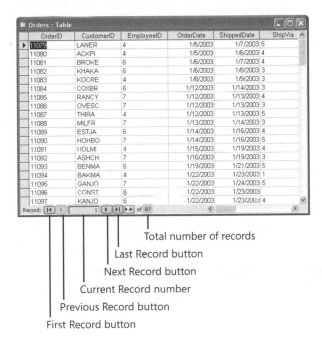

Total number of records

Last Record button

Next Record button

Current Record number

Previous Record button

First Record button

Tip If the total number of records doesn't immediately appear, move to the last record to display the total.

BE SURE TO open the database and table you want to work with before carrying out these steps.

To move among records:

1 Click the **Next Record**, **Previous Record**, **First Record**, or **Last Record** button to move to the corresponding record.

2 To move to a specific record, click the current record number at the bottom of the datasheet or form (or press **F5**), type the record number you want, and press **ENTER**.

Practice Exercise

In this exercise, you'll open a table and move among records.

USE the *NavigateRecords* database in the *My Documents\Microsoft Press\MOS 2003 Study Guide\Access \A03C-2-2* practice file folder.

Open the *NavigateRecords* database, and acknowledge the safety warning, if necessary. Open the **Orders** table in Datasheet view. Note that the navigation area at the bottom of the window indicates that this table contains 87 records and that the active record is number 1. Move the selection one record at a time by clicking the **Next Record** button several times. Then move directly to record **40**. Close the **Orders** table and the *NavigateRecords* database.

Finding a Specific Record

The navigation controls help you move effectively between records, but you have to keep an eye out for the data you need. When you want to locate a record containing a specific value, you can use the Find command.

BE SURE TO open the database and the table, query, or form you want to work with before carrying out these steps.

To find a record containing a specific value:

Find

1   Click the field you want to search.

2   Click the **Find** button on the toolbar (or press **CTRL+F**).

3   In the **Find What** box, type the text you want to find.

4   Do any of the following:

      ▪ To find the text within a field (*Peter* as well as *Peterson*, for example), click the **Match** down arrow, and click **Start of Field** or **Any Part of Field**.

      ▪ To search all fields, click the **Look in** down arrow, and click the name of the table, query, or form.

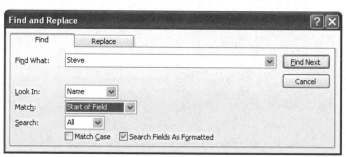

5   Click **Find Next** until you find the record you're looking for.

If the value isn't found in the current field, Access displays a message.

6   Click **Cancel** to close the Find and Replace dialog box.

Tip   To replace one or more instances of the Find What text, use the Replace tab in the Find and Replace dialog box.

Practice Exercise

In this exercise, you'll open a form and find customers whose first names begin with *Steve*.

USE the *FindRecord* database in the *My Documents\Microsoft Press\MOS 2003 Study Guide\Access \A03C-2-2* practice file folder.

Open the *FindRecord* database, and acknowledge the safety warning, if necessary. Open the **Customers** form. Click **Pilar** in the **First Name** field, and then open the Find and Replace dialog box. Specify **Steve** as the **Find What** text, set **Match** to **Start of Field**, and find each record beginning with *Steve* or *Steven* in turn. Then close the **Customers** form and the *FindRecord* database.

Import Data to Access

A03C-2-3   The skills measured by this objective include the following:

- Importing objects from another Access database
- Importing data from other sources

In some cases, you'll need to enter all the data into an Access table by hand. But more often, you'll fill your Access tables with existing information. Fortunately, Access can import data from a variety of sources, such as text files, spreadsheets, web pages, and other databases.

Tip If you want to work with data in Access but leave it in its existing format, you can link tables instead of importing them. For information, search Help for *linking data*.

Importing Objects from an Access Database

When you need to move data from one Access database into another, you can import tables. You can also import other objects: queries, forms, reports, pages, macros, and modules. When importing a table, you have the option of importing just the table definition (the structure you see in Design view) or both the definition and the data. When importing a query, you can import it as a query or you can import the results of the query as a table. However, you have to import the entire object with the same name. You don't have the option of importing selected fields or records. If the active database already has an object of the same name, Access imports the object with a number added to the end of its name.

BE SURE TO open the database you want to work with before carrying out these steps.

To import an object from another Access database:

1   On the **File** menu, click **Get External Data** and then **Import**.
2   In the **Files of type** list, make sure **Microsoft Office Access** is selected.
3   Navigate to the folder containing the database you want to import from, click the database, and then click **Import**.

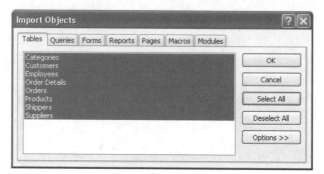

4   Click each table you want to import.

5   To import other types of objects, click the appropriate tab, and then click the object you want.

6   To import menus and toolbars or specify options for the table and queries you import, click the **Options** button, and make your selections.

7   Click **OK** to import the selected objects into your database.

Practice Exercise

In this exercise, you'll import two tables and one form into a database.

USE the *ImportTables* and *Products* databases in the *My Documents\Microsoft Press\MOS 2003 Study Guide \Access\A03C-2-3* practice file folder.

Open the *ImportTables* database, and acknowledge the safety warning, if necessary. Note that the database has only two tables. Import the **Categories** and **Products** tables and the **Enter Products** form from the *Products* database in the *My Documents\Microsoft Press \MOS 2003 Study Guide\Access\A03C-2-3* folder. Verify that the database now contains four tables and one form, and then close the *ImportTables* database.

Importing Data from Other Sources

You can import data from the following sources into Access:

■ Delimited text files—sometimes called tab-separated or comma-separated values— where each field is separated by a tab or comma and each record begins on a new line.

■ Fixed-width text files, where each field and entire record contains the same number of characters. (When data doesn't fill a field, the remaining characters are spaces.)

■ Microsoft Excel workbooks (including worksheets or named ranges within a workbook).

■ Lotus 1-2-3 spreadsheets.

■ HTML files (Web pages) containing tables or lists.

■ XML documents.

■ Files Exchange, Microsoft Outlook, and Microsoft from Microsoft Windows SharePoint Services 2.0.

■ dBASE, Paradox, Microsoft Visual FoxPro, Microsoft SQL Server, and any other database for which you have an ODBC driver.

Depending on the source of your data, Access displays an import wizard or other dialog box to help you import data successfully.

Because of the differences in data formats between programs, importing can be tricky. You might not always get what you expect, or Access might display an error message and fail to import altogether. In some cases, Access imports records but moves some data into an Import Errors table. Here are the most common reasons for import errors:

- Text or spreadsheet data isn't arranged consistently in rows and columns.

- Data in a field isn't all the same type (for example, a field contains a number or date in the first record and text in later records).

- When appending records to an existing table, data doesn't match the existing field structure or contains records with duplicate values in the primary key field.

In some cases, you'll be able to fix errors after importing (the Import Errors table can give you clues). In other cases, you'll need to make changes to the source data and then try importing again. In still others, it is important to specify the right import options. For example, if Access is setting the wrong data type for a field, you can specify the correct data type in the import wizard.

BE SURE TO open the database you want to work with before carrying out these steps.

To import data:

1 On the **File** menu, click **Get External Data** and then **Import**.

2 Click the **Files of type** down arrow, and click the type of file you want to import.

3 Navigate to the folder containing the data file you want to import, click the file name, and then click **Import**.

Access displays additional dialog boxes or the pages of the import wizard appropriate for the format you are importing. For example:

- If the file you are importing contains field names, select the **First Row Contains Field Names** option when importing.

- If the file you are importing has no field names, the wizard applies default field names, such as *Field1*, but you can specify descriptive names if you want.

- If you want to import into an existing table rather than creating a new table, select the **In an Existing Table** option, and specify the appropriate table. (The data types of the data you are importing must exactly match those of the existing table. If you select the **First Row Contains Field Names** option, the imported field names must exactly match as well.)

When you finish specifying options, Access imports data into your database.

Practice Exercise

In this exercise, you will import a comma-delimited text file to create an Employees table in a database. Then, you'll import customer records from a Web page, appending them to an existing table.

USE the *ImportData* database, the *Employees* text file, and the *NewCust* HTML file in the *My Documents \Microsoft Press\MOS 2003 Study Guide\Access\A03C-2-3* practice file folder.

Open the *ImportData* database, and acknowledge the safety warning, if necessary. Display the Import dialog box, and import the **Employees** text file that is stored in the *My Documents\Microsoft Press\MOS 2003 Study Guide\Access\A03C-2-3* practice file folder. On the **Import Text Wizard**'s second page, select the **First Row Contains Field Names** check box, and on the last page, click **Finish** to import the text file. Close the message box, and confirm that nine records were imported. Also confirm that the **Customers** table currently contains 107 records, and then close it. Then import the **NewCust** Web page file into the existing **Customers** table. Close the message box, and confirm that the **Customers** table now contains 110 records. Then close the **Customers** table and the *ImportData* database.

A03C-2 Review

Number	Objective	Mastered
A03C-2-1	Enter, edit and delete records	
	Entering data in a table's datasheet	❑
	Deleting records from a table	❑
A03C-2-2	Find and move among records	
	Navigating among records	❑
	Finding a specific record	❑
A03C-2-3	Import data to Access	
	Importing objects from another Access database	❑
	Importing data from other sources	❑

A03C-3

Organizing Data

The skills tested by this section of the Microsoft Office Specialist Access 2003 Exam all relate to organizing data in an Access database. Specifically, the following objectives are associated with this set of skills:

Number	Objective
A03C-3-1	Create and modify calculated fields and aggregate functions
A03C-3-2	Modify form layout
A03C-3-3	Modify report layout and page setup
A03C-3-4	Format datasheets
A03C-3-5	Sort records
A03C-3-6	Filter records

Important   Before you can do the practice exercises associated with this skill set, you need to install the practice files from the book's companion CD to their default location. See "Installing the Practice Files" on page xxv for more information.

Create and Modify Calculated Fields and Aggregate Functions

A03C-3-1   The skills measured by this objective include the following:

- Adding calculated fields to queries
- Calculating totals in queries

Most of the time, data is taken directly from tables into forms, datasheets, and reports. Sometimes, however, you want Access to perform calculations before displaying data. For example, you might want Access to combine two values in each record or calculate the difference between them. Or you might want Access to aggregate the values in a group of records or an entire table, calculating the sum or average. To perform the same calculation in every record, you use a calculated field. To find a total for a group of records, you create a special type of query that groups records and uses an aggregate function to calculate totals for each group.

Adding Calculated Fields to Queries

In a form or report, it is easy to display the result of a calculation by setting the Control Source property. But whenever you want to use the calculation, you need to set the property again. If you want to perform a calculation in more than one place, you can add a calculated field to a query. After the calculated field is saved in the query, you can use it as if it were a field in the underlying table (except that the value can't be edited in a form or datasheet).

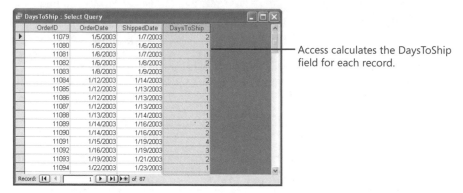

Access calculates the DaysToShip field for each record.

When you want to add a calculated field to a query, you specify an expression in Design view. When Access runs the query and displays records, it calculates the field's value for each record. For example, if you have OrderDate and ShippedDate fields in an Orders table, you can calculate the number of days it took to ship each order. The expression to do this is [ShippedDate] – [OrderDate].

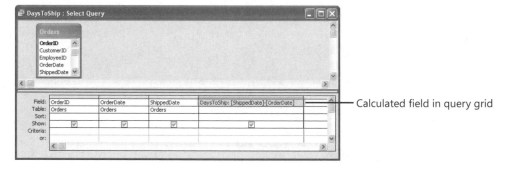

Calculated field in query grid

If the fields involved in the calculation have different data types, the result might not be in the format you expect. If a result doesn't appear in the right format, you can set the Format and Decimal Places properties for the calculated field.

BE SURE TO open a query in Design view before carrying out these steps.

To add a calculated field:

1   In the query grid, do one of the following:

   ■   Click the **Field** box in a blank column. (You might need to scroll to the right.)

   ■   To insert a new field in the query, click a field in the grid, and click **Columns** on the **Insert** menu.

   Tip   If you plan to type a long expression, you can drag the right edge of the column selector to make the field wider.

2   Type a name for the calculated field, followed by a colon (:).

It is important to provide a descriptive name for a calculated field, so that you can later identify the field in forms, reports, or other queries. For example, you might type Days To Ship: in the Field box.

3   Type the expression for the calculated field.

Tip   To use the Expression Builder, click the Build button on the Query Design toolbar and click OK when you're finished.

Build

View

4   To view the result of the calculation in the datasheet, click the **View** button.

Access displays the new field with values calculated for each record.

If the expression causes an error—for example, if you mistyped a field or function name—Access might display an error message or the Enter Parameter Value box, or the field might appear blank or display *#Error* in some records. If this happens, return to Design view and edit the expression.

Tip   In the expression, be sure to enclose table, query, and field names in brackets so that Access won't confuse them with ordinary text. If the query includes more than one table and some field names are used in more than one table, you need to specify the table name along with the field name in the expression. Use the table name, an exclamation point, and then the field name, as in [OrderDetails]![UnitPrice].

To set format properties for a query field:

Properties

1   In the query grid, click the field name, and then click the **Properties** button on the Query Design toolbar.

2   In the Field Properties dialog box, change the setting for the **Format** and **Decimal Places** properties.

For example, for a calculated field resulting in a monetary value, set the Format property to Currency.

3   Close the Field Properties dialog box.

Practice Exercise

In this exercise, you will add a calculated field to a query in a database.

USE the *AddCalcField* database in the *My Documents\Microsoft Press\MOS 2003 Study Guide\Access \A0CS-3-1* practice file folder.

Open the *AddCalcField* database, and acknowledge the safety warning, if necessary. Open the **Order Details Extended** query in Datasheet view, and switch to Design view. In the query grid, click the first blank box in the **Field** row, and enter the following expression:

ExtendedPrice: [Order Details]![UnitPrice]*[Quantity]*(1-[Discount])

Click the expression in the field, click the **Properties** button, and set the **Format** property to **Currency**. Switch to Datasheet view. Save and close the query, and then close the *AddCalcField* database.

Calculating Totals in Queries

You typically use a query to locate all the records that meet some criteria. But sometimes you are not as interested in the details of all the records as you are in summarizing them in some way. For example, you might want to know how many orders have been placed this year or the total dollar value of all orders placed. The easiest way to get this information is to create a query that groups the necessary fields and does the math for you. To do this, you use aggregate functions in the query.

Access queries support the following aggregate functions:

Function	Calculates
Sum	The total of the values in a field
Avg	The average of the values in a field
Count	The number of values in a field, not counting Null (blank) values
Min	The lowest value in a field
Max	The highest value in a field
StDev	The standard deviation of the values in a field
Var	The variance of the values in a field

To use an aggregate function in a query, you display the Total row in the query grid. For each of the fields you want to total, you change the setting in the Total row to an aggregate function. If you want totals for more than one subset of records, you include other fields and use the default Group By setting. For example, in a query that summarizes product records, you can display a single total for all products, or group products by category and display a total for each group.

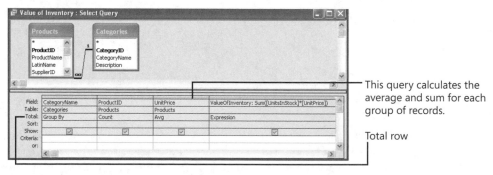

This query calculates the average and sum for each group of records.

Total row

BE SURE TO open the database you want to work with before carrying out these steps.

To create a query that calculates totals:

1 Using Design view or the Simple Query Wizard, create a query that includes the fields you want Access to total.

Totals

2 On the Query Design toolbar, click the **Totals** button.

Access displays the Total row in the query grid and displays *Group By*, the default setting, under each field.

3 Under each field, click **Group By** in the **Total** row, click the down arrow, and then click an aggregate function, such as **Sum** or **Count**.

4 If you want to group records, insert the fields containing values you want to group at the left side of the query grid, keeping the **Group By** setting in the **Total** row.

Run

5 Click the **Run** button.

Access displays totals in the datasheet. The column header for each totaled field indicates the type of total—for example, AvgOfUnitPrice.

Tip If you want to leave some records out of the total, you can add a field to the query grid, click Where in the Total row, and specify criteria for the field in the Criteria row.

Practice Exercise

In this exercise, you will create a query that calculates the total number of products in an inventory, the average price of all the products, and the total value of the inventory. Then you'll modify the query to group records by category, and display these totals for each group.

USE the *CalculateTotals* database in the *My Documents\Microsoft Press\MOS 2003 Study Guide\Access \A0CS-3-1* practice file folder.

Open the *CalculateTotals* database, and acknowledge the safety warning, if necessary. Open the **Value of Inventory** query in Datasheet view. The query displays the UnitPrice field for each product and also calculates the value of current inventory (multiplying price by units in stock). Switch to Design view, and then click the **Totals** button. In the **Total** row under **Product ID**, change the setting to **Count**; under **UnitPrice** change to **Avg**; and under **ValueOfInventory**, change to **Sum**. Switch to Datasheet view. The query calculates that there are 189 products with an average price of $17.81 and a total retail value of $26,815.39.

To group records by category, switch back to Design view, and add the **Categories** table to the query. Add the **CategoryName** field to the left side of the query grid. Run the query. Save and close the query, and then close the *CalculateTotals* database.

Modify Form Layout

A03C-3-2   The skills measured by this objective include the following:

■ Setting control size, alignment, and spacing

■ Modifying form and section layout

Forms are much easier to use—and can hold much more information on the screen—if their controls are well organized and uniform and sections on the form are the right size. That way, you can avoid blank space on forms and make sure the form will fit on the most common screen sizes. You can use the Form Wizard to help you with form layout. If you want to modify the layout of controls on a form, Design view has several features to help you.

613

Setting Control Size, Alignment, and Spacing

In Design view, you can move, resize, and align controls using the mouse. To speed things up, you can select multiple controls and move or resize them all at once. Access also includes keyboard and menu commands that help you resize or align a group of controls.

Before you make changes to controls, you must select them. To select one control, click it. There are several ways to select multiple controls:

- Drag through their outlines on the form.
- Hold down the SHIFT key while clicking each one.
- Drag from one point to another on the horizontal or vertical ruler.
- On the Edit menu, click Select All.

As you work with a form's layout, it is important to pay attention to the shape of the pointer, which indicates the manner in which you can change the selected item. Because a text box and its label sometimes act as a unit, you have to be careful to notice the pointer's shape before making any change. Use the *hand* pointer to move a control with its label, the *pointing finger* pointer to move just a control or its label, and the *double arrow* pointers to resize a control.

Tip To help you align controls, Access lines them up on a grid, which is indicated by dots on the form background. By setting the form's GridX and GridY properties, you can change the divisions in the grid. To prevent Access from lining controls up on the grid, toggle off the Snap To Grid command on the Format menu. To fine-tune the position of a control without regard to the grid, select it, and then hold down the CTRL key while pressing the LEFT ARROW, DOWN ARROW, UP ARROW, or RIGHT ARROW keys.

BE SURE TO open a form in Design view and select the control(s) you want to work with before carrying out these steps.

To move selected controls:

- Point to the controls to display the hand pointer, and then drag the controls to the new location.

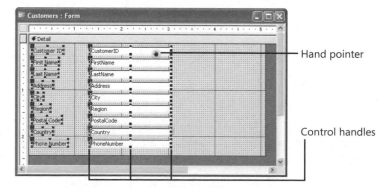

If you move controls outside the border of a form section, the section grows to make room for them.

To move a control or its label independently:

● Point to the control's upper-left corner to display the pointing finger, and then drag to the new location.

To resize selected controls:

● Drag a control handle at the edge of the control to the new size.

To make selected controls the same size:

● On the **Format** menu, click **Size** and then **To Tallest**, **To Shortest**, **To Widest**, or **To Narrowest**.

To make selected controls just big enough to fit text they contain:

● On the **Format** menu, click **Size** and then **To Fit**.

To line up selected controls:

● On the **Format** menu, click **Align** and then **Left**, **Right**, **Top**, or **Bottom**.

To space selected controls evenly from top to bottom or left to right:

● On the **Format** menu, click **Horizontal Spacing** or **Vertical Spacing** and then **Make Equal**.

To change the space between selected controls evenly:

● On the **Format** menu, click **Horizontal Spacing** or **Vertical Spacing** and then **Increase** or **Decrease**.

Practice Exercise

In this exercise, you will open a form, increase its font size, and fine-tune its layout.

USE the *ChangeLayout* database in the *My Documents\Microsoft Press\MOS 2003 Study Guide\Access \A03C-3-2* practice file folder.

Open the *ChangeLayout* database, and acknowledge the safety warning, if necessary. Open the **Customers** form in Design view. Select all the controls on the form, and set the font size to **12**. Use the **Size To Fit** command to resize all the controls, and then increase their vertical spacing evenly. Next, select only the **Address** text box, and drag its right edge to make it twice as wide. Resize the **Region** and **PostalCode** text boxes, making them about as wide as the names they contain. Select the **Region** and **PostalCode** labels and delete them. Move **Region** up next to address and **PostalCode** next to **Region**. If you didn't get them lined up quite right by hand, use menu commands to align them and make their horizontal spacing equal. Move **Country** up underneath **City**. Finally, move the **PhoneNumber** field underneath its label. To test the new layout with data, switch to Form view, and navigate through records. Save and close the form, and close the *ChangeLayout* database.

Modifying Form and Section Layout

Most forms use only the Detail section. Forms also have a Page Header, Form Header, Page Footer, and Form Footer section, which you can display or hide in Design view. The Form Header and Form Footer appear in Form view above and below the Detail section. You can place controls in these sections if you don't want them to move when you scroll up or down in the form. Buttons, hyperlinks, and other controls that don't display data are good candidates for the Form Header or Form Footer. The Page Header and Page Footer are never shown in Form view; they are only used when printing a form.

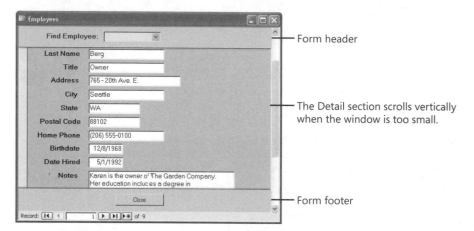

— Form header

— The Detail section scrolls vertically when the window is too small.

— Form footer

You can resize each form section in Design view. Each section has its own height, and the width is shared between all sections. When you add or move controls on a form, sections expand to accommodate them. When you are finished, it is a good idea to resize each section so that it is not much bigger than necessary. Otherwise, the form will display blank space, take up more of the screen than necessary, or waste paper when you print.

BE SURE TO open the database you want to work with in Design view before carrying out these steps.

To view or hide form headers and footers:

● On the **View** menu, click **Form Header/Footer** or **Page Header/Footer**.

To change the height of one section or the width of all sections:

● To change the height of a section, drag its bottom edge.

● To change the width of all sections, drag the right edge of any section.

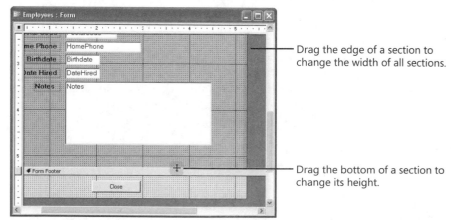

— Drag the edge of a section to change the width of all sections.

— Drag the bottom of a section to change its height.

To change the background color of a section:

1   Click the section you want to change.

2   Click the **Fill/Back Color** down arrow, and click a color.

Fill/Back
Color

Practice Exercise

In this exercise, you will open an existing form, create Form Header and Form Footer sections, and move controls from the Detail section. Then you'll adjust the size of each form section appropriately.

USE the *AdjustSection* database in the *My Documents\Microsoft Press\MOS 2003 Study Guide\Access \A03C-3-2* practice file folder.

Open the *AdjustSection* database, and acknowledge the safety warning, if necessary. Open the **Employees** form in Design view. Display the **Form Header** and **Form Footer**, make each a bit taller, and change their color to make them stand out. Move the **Find Employee** combo box to the left side of the header, and move the **Close** button to the footer. Adjust the width and height of the **Detail** section so it is just a bit larger than the controls it contains. Switch to Form view. Make the window the same width as the form. Save and close the form, and then close the *AdjustSection* database.

Modify Report Layout and Page Setup

A03C-3-3   The skills measured by this objective include the following:

■   Setting control size, alignment, and spacing

■   Modifying report and section layout

When you use the Report Wizard to create a report, it won't always have the layout you want. The report might be spread over too many pages, for example, or some fields might not have enough room for the data they contain. Fortunately, reports are very flexible and include many options for page layout.

Setting Control Size, Alignment, and Spacing

In Design view, you can move, resize, and align controls to improve the layout of a report. You can select multiple controls and move or resize them all at once, and Access offers many commands that help you resize or align a group of controls.

BE SURE TO open a report in Design view and select controls before carrying out these steps.

To move selected controls:

●   Point to the controls to display the hand pointer, and then drag the controls to the new location.

If you move controls outside the border of a report section, the section grows to make room for them.

To move a control or its label independently:

●   Point to the control's upper-left corner to display the pointing finger, and and then drag to the new location.

To resize selected controls:

- Drag a control handle at the edge of the control to the new size.

To make selected controls the same size:

- On the **Format** menu, click **Size** and then **To Tallest**, **To Shortest**, **To Widest**, or **To Narrowest**.

To make selected controls just big enough to fit text they contain:

- On the **Format** menu, click **Size** and then **To Fit**.

To line up selected controls:

- On the **Format** menu, click **Align** and then **Left**, **Right**, **Top**, or **Bottom**.

To space selected controls evenly from top to bottom or left to right:

- On the **Format** menu, click **Horizontal Spacing** or **Vertical Spacing** and then **Make Equal**.

To change the space between selected controls evenly:

- On the **Format** menu, click **Horizontal Spacing** or **Vertical Spacing** and then **Increase** or **Decrease**.

Practice Exercise

In this exercise, you will open a report and increase font size and fine-tune the report's layout.

USE the *AdjustLayout* database in the *My Documents\Microsoft Press\MOS 2003 Study Guide\Access \A03C-3-3* practice file folder.

Open the *AdjustLayout* database, and acknowledge the safety warning, if necessary. Open the **Product List by Category** report in Print Preview. Switch to Design view. Make the **Description** field and its label a bit smaller, and then move the label and field closer together. Move the **Description** field and label up to the right of the **Category Name** field. Align the **Category Name** and **Description** controls, and then move them all down a bit. Resize the blue line above the fields to the exact size of the gray lines in the Report Header. Then select the five detail fields and their column headings (but not the line between them). Move them all halfway to the left margin, and then use the **Increase Horizontal Spacing** command twice to move them further apart. Select only the headings, and size them to fit their text. Then make the **UnitPrice** field narrower by dragging its left side, and make the **QuantityPerUnit** field wider by dragging its right side. Preview the report to see your changes. Save and close the report, and close the *AdjustLayout* database.

Modifying Report and Section Layout

When the layout of a report needs to be refined, the first step is to consider the options for page setup. You can design a report for different page sizes, such as letter or legal, and for portrait (vertical) or landscape (horizontal) page layout. The default margins for a report are 1 inch on all sides, but you can often fit more data on each page by reducing these margins.

If you change these page setup options, you will usually want to change the width of the sections in the report. (All report sections share the same width.) To avoid partial pages—and to use space wisely—make sure that the report section width is the same as the space on the page; that is, the total page width minus the left and right margins. Whenever you change the section width, you also need to adjust the size of any horizontal lines or other wide controls in the report.

Another important consideration in the layout of a report is the height of each section, which determines how much fits on the page and how much blank space appears between lines of information. Some sections repeat on a page but others appear only once, so you need to carefully consider where you want to provide extra space, if any. For example, if its detail section is long, the report will not have room for very many records on the page.

The Report Header appears once at the beginning of the report.

The Page Header appears once per page.

The Group Header appears once for each group of records.

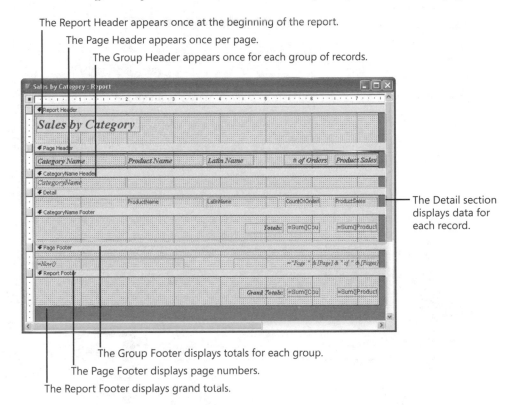

The Detail section displays data for each record.

The Group Footer displays totals for each group.

The Page Footer displays page numbers.

The Report Footer displays grand totals.

With section size and spacing, it is difficult to anticipate the effect of each change. As you adjust section size and control layout, switch back and forth between Design view and Print Preview to evaluate each change.

Although section size and page setup have the most dramatic effect on report layout, you can also affect layout and page breaks by setting report and section properties. For example, the Force New Page, Keep Together, Can Shrink, and Can Grow properties all affect the layout of a report across pages.

See Also   For information on setting properties, see A03C-1-11, "Add and Modify Report Control Properties."

BE SURE TO open a report in Design view before carrying out these steps.

To switch between Design view and Print Preview:

View

● Click the **View** button on the Report Design or Print Preview toolbar.

To change page setup:

1 On the **File** menu, click **Page Setup**.

2 On the **Margins** tab, set **Top**, **Bottom**, **Left**, and **Right** margins.

Depending on your printer, very small margin settings (less than half an inch) might not be available; Access changes an invalid setting to the lowest margin available.

3 On the **Page** tab, click **Portrait** or **Landscape**, and in the **Size** box, select **Letter**, **Legal**, or another paper size.

4 Click **OK**.

The report doesn't look any different in Design view. However, when you preview or print the report, its information might fit across pages in an entirely different way.

To set the width of report sections to match page setup:

1 Calculate the appropriate width by subtracting the right and left margins from the total page width.

For example, for letter-size paper with portrait orientation and .75 inch margins, figure 8.5 − .75 − .75 = 7 inches.

2 If you are making the report narrower, resize and arrange controls in all sections to clear the area to the right of the new section edge.

3 Drag the right edge of any section to the new size (or slightly narrower).

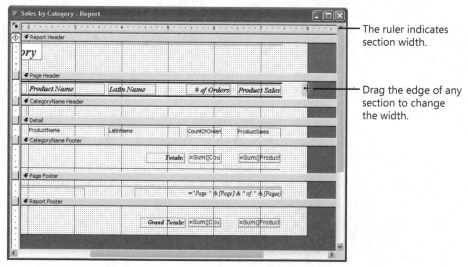

The ruler indicates section width.

Drag the edge of any section to change the width.

4 If necessary, resize and arrange controls to fill space on the right side of the report.

To view or hide header and footer sections:

● On the **View** menu, click **Report Header/Footer** or **Page Header/Footer**.

If you hide these sections, they no longer take up space when you preview or print. If you display them, they take up space even if they contain no controls.

To increase or decrease space between lines of information in a report:

1 In Print Preview, identify which section needs adjustment.

For example, if there is not enough space between the group header labels and the first detail record, the bottom of the Group Header section needs more space. Or, if detail records are taking up too much space on the page, the Detail section is too tall.

2 In Design view, adjust spacing as follows:

■ To change spacing at the beginning of a section, move all its controls closer to or further from the top of the section.

■ To change spacing at the end of a section, drag the bottom edge of the section to adjust section height.

3 Preview the report again.

Changes in one section might make changes necessary in others. For example, if you take out space at the top of a section, the header section above it might need more space.

Practice Exercise

In this exercise, you will increase margins, move controls, and change section height and width in a report.

USE the *AdjustReport* database in the *My Documents\Microsoft Press\MOS 2003 Study Guide\Access \A03C-3-3* practice file folder.

Open the *AdjustReport* database, and acknowledge the safety warning, if necessary. Open the **Sales by Category** report in Print Preview, noticing that it has 28 pages and displays too much white space. Switch to Design view. Adjust the section width to eliminate space on the right. In the Page Setup dialog box, set the left, right, and bottom margins to **.5**, and the top margin to **.75**. Preview the report, which which how has 13 pages. Switch to Design view. Move the **CategoryName** field to the top of its header section, and then make that section as short as possible. Make the **Detail** section as small as possible. Preview the report. Switch to Design view again, and add space at the end of the **CategoryName Footer** section by making the section a bit taller. Preview one more time; there are now just 8 pages. Save and close the report. Close the *AdjustReport* database.

Format Datasheets

A03C-3-4   The skills measured by this objective include the following:

■ Formatting a datasheet

Datasheets are everywhere in Access. Although the data itself is the most important thing in a datasheet, looks are important too. When you want to change the way information is presented, datasheets are easy to customize.

Formatting a Datasheet

You can change the order and width of columns. You can hide some columns altogether, or freeze them so that they always appear at the left side of the datasheet. You can change the font and other aspects of a datasheet's appearance.

When you close a datasheet, Access asks whether you want to save changes to the layout of the object you are working with, so you can view the datasheet with its custom formatting each time you open the object.

BE SURE TO open the table, query, or form you want to work with in Datasheet view before carrying out these steps.

To change the width of a column:

● Click the right edge of the column's selector, and drag to the width you want.

● To change the column width to fit the data in the column, double-click the right edge of the column selector.

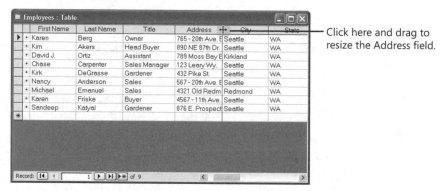

Click here and drag to resize the Address field.

To move columns:

1 Click a column selector.

To select multiple adjacent columns, drag across their column selectors.

2 Drag the columns to the new location.

To hide columns:

1 Click the column you want to hide.

To select multiple adjacent columns, drag across their column selectors.

2 On the **Format** menu, click **Hide Columns**.

To show hidden columns:

1 On the **Format** menu, click **Unhide Columns**.

2 Select the check box next to each column you want to view, and then click **OK**.

To freeze columns:

1 Click the column you want to freeze.

To select multiple adjacent columns, drag across their column selectors.

2   On the **Format** menu, click **Freeze Columns**.

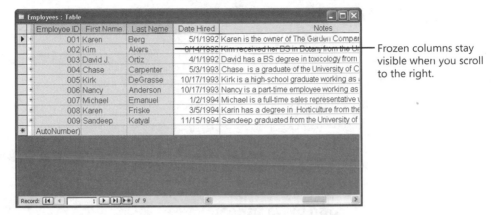

Frozen columns stay visible when you scroll to the right.

To unfreeze columns:

● On the **Format** menu, click **Unfreeze All Columns**.

To change row height:

● Drag the bottom of any row selector to the height you want.

The height of all rows changes. (You can't change the height of individual rows.)

To change the font:

1   On the **Format** menu, click **Font**.

2   Select options in the Font dialog box, and then click **OK**.

To change datasheet color, lines, and effects:

1   On the **Format** menu, click **Datasheet**.

2   Select options in the Datasheet Formatting dialog box, and then click **OK**.

Tip   These procedures affect only the open datasheet. You can also change the default formatting for all datasheets. On the Tools menu, click Options, click the Datasheet tab, and make the changes you want.

Practice Exercise

In this exercise, you will open a table and format its datasheet. You'll change the font, rearrange and resize columns, and freeze columns at the left side so that they are always shown.

USE the *FormatSheet* database in the *My Documents\Microsoft Press\MOS 2003 Study Guide\Access \A03C-3-4* practice file folder.

Open the *FormatSheet* database, and acknowledge the safety warning, if necessary. Open the **Employees** table in Datasheet view. Change the font to 12-point Arial. Freeze the **Employee ID**, **First Name**, and **Last Name** columns. Move the **Home Phone** column between **Title** and **Address**. Resize the **Title**, **Address**, and **Home Phone** columns to fit the data they contain, and make the **Notes** column about three times as wide as the default. Hide the **Photograph** column. Close the table, clicking **Yes** when Access asks if you want to save layout changes. Close the *FormatSheet* database.

Sort Records

A03C-3-5   The skills measured by this objective include the following:

- Sorting records in a form or datasheet
- Sorting records in a report

Sorting information in a specific order helps you organize and find the data you want. You could, for example, sort customer records alphabetically based first on the last name of each customer and then on the first name, like a telephone book.

Sorting Records in a Form or Datasheet

You can sort records in either ascending order—from A to Z or 1 to 100—or in descending order—from Z to A or 100 to 1. Ascending order is most common, but descending order is often useful for numbers and dates, because the most recent date or largest amount (of money, for example) might be of greatest interest.

In Datasheet view, you can sort on more than one field. The fields you want to sort must be adjacent, and they must be arranged in the order in which you want to sort them. Before you sort, move the columns you want to sort to the left side of the datasheet.

Tip   If you store numbers in a field with the Text data type, Access might not sort them in the way you expect. Access sorts text fields alphanumerically (1, 11, 12, ... 2, 21, 22, ...). If you want to sort numbers properly, set the field's data type to Number or Currency in the underlying table.

BE SURE TO open the database you want to work with before carrying out these steps.

To sort records in a datasheet:

1   Click the column that contains data you want to sort.

    To sort multiple adjacent columns, drag across their column selectors.

2   Do one of the following:

Sort
Ascending

- To sort from A to Z or 1 to 100, click the **Sort Ascending** button.

Sort
Descending

- To sort from Z to A or 100 to 1, click the **Sort Descending** button.

    Access sorts the underlying data and moves to the first record in the new order. If you selected more than one column, data in the second column is sorted within each group in the first column, and so on.

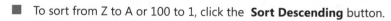

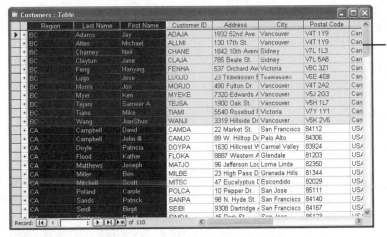

Region is sorted first, and then names are sorted within each region.

To sort records in a form:

1 Click the field that contains data you want to sort.

2 Click the **Sort Ascending** or **Sort Descending** button.

Access sorts the underlying data for the form and moves to the first record in the new order.

Tip After you sort, Access remembers the setting each time you open the form. If you want to return to the form's default sort order, clear the Order By check box for the form.

Practice Exercise

In this exercise, you will open a table in Datasheet view and sort records in different ways.

USE the *SortRecords* database in the *My Documents\Microsoft Press\MOS 2003 Study Guide\Access \A03C-3-5* practice file folder.

Open the *SortRecords* database, and acknowledge the safety warning, if necessary. Open the **Customers** table in Datasheet view. Sort the **Region** column in ascending order, and then reverse the sort order. In turn, freeze the **Region**, **Last Name**, and **First Name** columns. Then select the **Region**, **Last Name,** and **First Name** columns, and sort them. Close the table, clicking **No** when Access asks if you want to save changes. Close the *SortRecords* database.

Sorting Records in a Report

When you create a report with the Report Wizard, you choose the sort order you want. If you want to change sorting in a report, you can use the Sorting and Grouping dialog box.

BE SURE TO open a report in Design view before carrying out these steps.

To sort records in a report:

Sorting and Grouping

1 On the Report Design toolbar, click the **Sorting and Grouping** button.

The Sorting and Grouping dialog box displays one row for each grouping level or sort field. If the report groups records, each group is listed in the dialog box. If you want to preserve existing grouping options, make sure to leave grouping rows as they are.

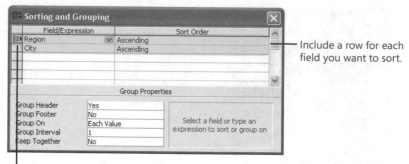

The Grouping icon indicates group levels.

2   In the first row of the **Field/Expression** column—or the first row underneath existing group levels—select the name of the field you want to sort.

3   If you want to sort in descending order, select **Descending** in the **Sort Order** column.

4   To sort additional fields, select their names in subsequent rows.

5   Close the Sorting and Grouping dialog box.

When you preview the report, records appear in the order you specified.

Practice Exercise

In this exercise, you will open a report and change the order in which records appear.

USE the *ChangeOrder* database in the *My Documents\Microsoft Press\MOS 2003 Study Guide\Access \A03C-3-5* practice file folder.

Open the *ChangeOrder* database, and acknowledge the safety warning, if necessary. Open the **Customers by Region** report in Print Preview. Switch to Design view, and display the Sorting and Grouping dialog box. In the section row, change **City** to **Last Name**, and then select **First Name** in the third row. Preview the report to see the result of the change. Save and close the report, and close the *ChangeOrder* database.

Filter Records

A03C-3-6   The skills measured by this objective include the following:

- Filtering records for a selected value
- Filtering records for specified values

Sorting the information in a table organizes it in a logical manner, but you still have the entire table to deal with. With a filter, you see only the records that match a particular pattern. For example, you could quickly create a filter to locate every customer who lives in Seattle, everyone who placed an order on January 13, or all customers who live outside of the United States.

Using a filter is similar to using criteria in a query, except that a filter limits records only temporarily. After you close and reopen the form or datasheet, the filter is no longer applied.

Access remembers the last filter you applied in a table, query, or form, however, so you can reapply it the next time you view records.

Tip When you use a filter, the records that don't match the filter aren't removed from the table; they are simply not displayed.

Filtering Records for a Selected Value

When you view data in a form or datasheet, using a filter is an easy way to limit the data that is displayed. For example, if you want to see only customers from Seattle, you can click Seattle and then filter out all other records. This type of filter is applied to the contents of just one field. You can apply another filter to the results of the first one to further refine the search.

Filtering by selection is very flexible, because you can filter for the entire content of a field or just part of the field. For example, to display only customers from Seattle, you would click any record with *Seattle* in the City field and then apply the filter. To display customers from any city beginning with S, you would select just the S in *Seattle* and then apply the filter.

BE SURE TO open a form or datasheet before carrying out these steps.

To filter by selection:

1   In the column or field you want to filter, do one of the following:

   ■   Click the value for which you want to filter.

   ■   To filter for values that start with, end with, or contain specific text, select that text in the field you want to filter.

Filter By
Selection

2   Click the **Filter By Selection** button.

Access displays records that match your selection. The navigation bar at the bottom of the form or datasheet indicates *(Filtered)* next to the number of records to let you know that you aren't viewing all available records.

To filter excluding a selection:

●   Right-click a field containing the value you want to filter out, and click **Filter Excluding Selection** on the shortcut menu.

Access filters for all values except the one you selected.

627

To remove a filter:

Remove
Filter

● Click the **Remove Filter** button.

Access displays all records in the underlying table or query.

Practice Exercise

In this exercise, you will filter records in a table.

USE the *FilterRecords* database in the *My Documents\Microsoft Press\MOS 2003 Study Guide\Access \A03C-3-6* practice file folder.

Open the *FilterRecords* database, and acknowledge the safety warning, if necessary. Open the **Customers** table in Datasheet view. Click any instance of **Vancouver** in the **City** field, and then filter out the six records for customers who live in that city. Redisplay the rest of the customers. Then select the **M** in *Mary*, and find customers whose first names begin with *M*. Remove the filter, and then find records whose region is **BC**. Without removing this filter, exclude **Vancouver** from the filtered records, noting that the second filter is applied to the results of the first. Close the table, clicking **Yes** when Access asks if you want save it. Close the *FilterRecords* database.

Filtering Records for Specified Values

Although filtering by selection is the simplest way to filter records, it requires you to first find the value you are looking for. With the Filter By Form command, you can type the values you are looking for or select them from a list of existing values, and you can also filter for values in multiple fields at once.

When you use Filter By Form, you see a blank form or datasheet without any records. Each of the blank fields or cells is a combo box with a drop-down list of all the entries that exist in that field. The list under each field makes it easy to filter for the value you want.

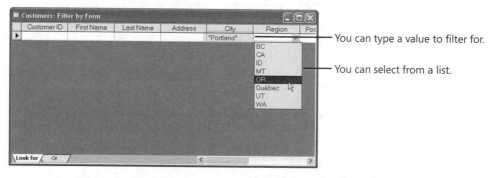

By using wildcards in filter criteria, you can make a filter even more flexible. When you want to find records that match a pattern, or if you aren't sure of exactly what you are looking for, you can use wildcard characters as placeholders for unknown characters in the criteria. The most common wildcards are listed in this table:

Character	Matches	Example
*	Any number of characters	*Co** matches Colman and Conroy
?	Any single alphabetic character	*eri?* matches Eric and Erik
#	Any single numeric character	*1##* matches any number from 100 through 199

You can use all the same features in filter criteria as in queries. For example, if you want to filter excluding a selection, type Not at the beginning of the criteria. If you want a range of records, use >, <, >=, or <=. If you want to filter for records with blank (null) values, type Null or Not Null as the criteria.

BE SURE TO open the database you want to work with before carrying out these steps.

To filter for a specific value in one field:

1 Right-click the field you want to filter, and click **Filter For** on the shortcut menu.

2 Type the value you are looking for, and press **ENTER**.

To filter by form:

Filter By
Form

1 Click the **Filter By Form** button on the Form View, Table Datasheet, or Query Datasheet toolbar.

All data is cleared from the form or datasheet.

2 Type criteria (or select from drop-down lists) in each field you want to filter.

3 If you want to filter for one set of criteria or another, click the **Or** tab at the bottom of the window, and specify additional criteria.

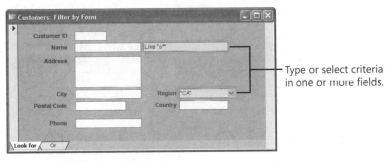

Type or select criteria in one or more fields.

Apply Filter

4 Click the **Apply Filter** button.

Access filters records and displays them in the form or datasheet. The navigation bar at the bottom of the form or datasheet indicates *(Filtered)* next to the number of records. If you want to add or edit criteria in the filter, you can click Filter By Form again.

When you close the form, Access saves the filter in the form's Filter property, but it doesn't apply the filter automatically when you open the form. To apply the filter again, you can click the Apply Filter button.

To remove the filter:

Remove
Filter

- Click the **Remove Filter** button.

  Access displays all records in the underlying table or query.

Practice Exercise

In this exercise, you will use Filter By Form to try to locate a customer's record.

USE the *LocateRecord* database in the *My Documents\Microsoft Press\MOS 2003 Study Guide\Access \A03C-3-6* practice file folder.

Open the *LocateRecord* database, and acknowledge the safety warning, if necessary. Open the **Customers** form in Form view. Use the **Filter By Form** button to display the three records with last names starting with *S* in the **CA** region. Switch back to the filter, click the **Or** tab, and add the records with last names starting with *S* in the **WA** region. Navigate through the six filtered records. Then close the **Customers** form and the *LocateRecord* database.

A03C-3 Review

Number	Objective	Mastered
A03C-3-1	Create and modify calculated fields and aggregate functions	
	Adding calculated fields to queries	❏
	Calculating totals in queries	❏
A03C-3-2	Modify form layout	
	Setting control size, alignment, and spacing	❏
	Modifying form and section layout	❏
A03C-3-3	Modify report layout and page setup	
	Setting control size, alignment, and spacing	❏
	Modifying report and section layout	❏
A03C-3-4	Format datasheets	
	Formatting a datasheet	❏
A03C-3-5	Sort records	
	Sorting records in a form or datasheet	❏
	Sorting records in a report	❏
A03C-3-6	Filter records	
	Filtering records for a selected value	❏
	Filtering records for specified values	❏

A03C-4

Managing Databases

The skills tested by this section of the Microsoft Office Specialist Access 2003 Exam all relate to managing data and objects in an Access database. Specifically, the following objectives are associated with this set of skills:

Number	Objective
A03C-4-1	Identify and modify object dependencies
A03C-4-2	View objects and object data in other views
A03C-4-3	Print database objects and data
A03C-4-4	Export data from Access
A03C-4-5	Back up a database
A03C-4-6	Compact and repair databases

 Important Before you can do the practice exercises associated with this skill set, you need to install the practice files from the book's companion CD to their default location. See "Installing the Practice Files" on page xxv for more information.

Identify and Modify Object Dependencies

A03C-4-1 The skills measured by this objective include the following:

■ Identifying object dependencies

As you work with a database over time, you will probably create many objects—tables, queries, forms, and reports—and all of them will work together and rely on one another. For example, a form relies on a query that supplies its records, and that query in turn relies on its underlying tables.

Before you delete or change an object you haven't used for a while, you should make sure doing so won't affect other objects in the database. If you move or copy an object to another database, you should also move or copy any objects it requires. Fortunately, you don't have to guess which objects are relied on by other objects, because Access can identify object dependencies for you.

Identifying Object Dependencies

For each type of object, there are different dependencies:

Object	Depends on
Table	Related tables
Query	Underlying tables and queries Forms that supply query criteria
Form	Tables and queries that supply records Forms included as subforms
Report	Tables and queries that supply records Reports included as subreports

If you want to change an object that other objects depend on, you can make a copy of the object and make changes to the copy. You could also remove the dependency before making any changes. For example, you could change the Record Source property of a form to remove the dependency on the query you want to change or delete.

BE SURE TO open the database you want to work with before carrying out these steps.

To identify object dependencies:

1 In the Database window, right-click the object you are interested in, and click **Object Dependencies** on the shortcut menu.

The Object Dependencies task pane appears with the name of the object you selected shown at the top.

2 If necessary, click **Objects that depend on me**. Click the expand icon (**+**) next to each object in the list to view the dependencies for that object.

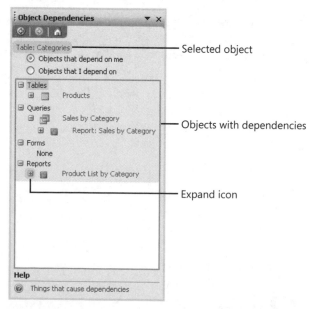

If objects appear in the list, you might not want to change or delete the object you selected (unless you modify the objects so they no longer rely on the selected object).

3   Click **Objects that I depend on**. Click the expand icon (**+**) next to each object in the list to view that object's dependencies.

If objects appear in this list, be aware of them when moving, copying, or modifying the selected object.

4   Close the Object Dependencies task pane.

Practice Exercise

In this exercise, you will view object dependencies in tables and queries in a database.

USE the *ViewDependencies* database in the *My Documents\Microsoft Press\MOS 2003 Study Guide\Access \A03C-4-1* practice file folder.

Open the *ViewDependencies* database and acknowledge the safety warning, if necessary. Display the Object Dependencies task pane for the **Categories** table. With **Objects that depend on me** selected, open the **Product List by Category** report in Print Preview, and then close the report. Then view the dependencies for each query, and delete the **Orders in 2003** query. Check the dependencies of the **Employees** form, and then click **Objects that I depend on**. Close the Object Dependencies task pane, and then close the *ViewDependencies* database.

View Objects and Object Data in Other Views

A03C-4-2   The skills measured by this objective include the following:

■   Using Print Preview and Layout Preview
■   Viewing PivotTables
■   Viewing PivotCharts

You can view all Access objects in Design view. In addition, each object type can be viewed in a variety of other ways. For example, you can display all objects in Print Preview, and you can display reports in Layout Preview. To help you analyze data, you can view tables, queries, and forms in PivotTable and PivotChart view. To get the most from your data, it helps to know about all these views.

Using Print Preview and Layout Preview

Before you print, you can save time and paper by previewing data or objects on the screen. In Print Preview, you can view one to six pages at a time, and you can zoom in and out to examine the details carefully before printing.

In a report, there are two ways to preview: ordinary Print Preview, which formats and displays the entire report, and Layout Preview, which displays a sampling of records in the report. If a report is large or complex, Layout Preview displays the report quicker than Print Preview.

BE SURE TO open the database you want to work with before carrying out these steps.

To preview for printing:

1 If the object you want to preview isn't already open, click its name in the Database window.

Print
Preview

2 Click the **Print Preview** button.

The first page of your object appears as it will be printed.

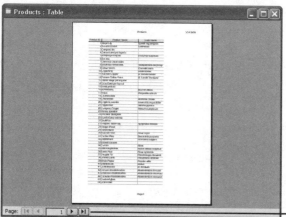

Navigation controls

3 Click anywhere on the page to zoom in. Select a magnification factor in the **Zoom** box to zoom in or out to a particular level.

4 Do any of the following:

Two Pages

■ To display two pages at a time, click the **Two Pages** button.

■ To display more than two pages at a time, click the **Multiple Pages** button.

Multiple
Pages

■ To move between pages, click navigation buttons at the lower left of the window.

■ To move to a specific page, type a number in the **Page** box, and press **ENTER**.

5 When you are finished previewing, click the **Close** button.

To quickly preview the layout of a complex report:

1 Open the report in Design view.

2 On the **View** menu, click **Layout Preview**.

A sample page opens in Print Preview. Because it contains only a few records, the report takes less time to format than it would ordinarily.

Practice Exercise

In this exercise, you will preview a datasheet and a report and zoom in to view various pages.

USE the *PreviewDatasheet* database in the *My Documents\Microsoft Press\MOS 2003 Study Guide\Access \A03C-4-2* practice file folder.

Open the *PreviewDatasheet* database, and acknowledge the safety warning, if necessary. Display the **Products** table in Print Preview. Display two pages at a time, move to page 5, and then zoom in to view the data. Close the table, and display the **Product List by Category** report in Layout Preview. Use the navigation controls to move to the last page of the report. Close the report, and then preview the report in Print Preview. Close the report, and then close the *PreviewDatasheet* database.

Viewing PivotTables

When you display tables, queries, and forms in PivotTable view, you can analyze and summarize data in powerful ways. For example, you can use a PivotTable to organize employee records by title, year hired, or location, and to display the total number in each group.

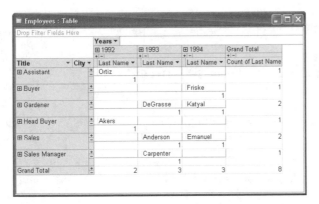

To create a PivotTable layout, you switch to PivotTable view and drag fields from the field list to one of four areas: row, column, detail, and filter. As you add fields, you can see the effect of each change. After you create a PivotTable layout, Access saves it with the table, query, or form so that you can return to view it later.

BE SURE TO open the database you want to work with before carrying out these steps.

To view a PivotTable:

1   If the object you want to preview for printing isn't already open, double-click its name in the Database window.

2   On the **View** menu, click **PivotTable View**.

A blank PivotTable appears and the PivotTable Field List opens.

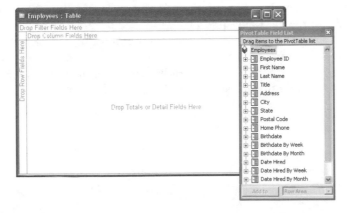

To add fields to the row, column, and detail areas:

● Drag each field you want to add from the **PivotTable Field List** to the row, column, or detail area in the PivotTable.

As you add each field, the PivotTable displays a field selector. To move (or pivot) a field from one area to another—for example, from the row area to the column area—drag its field selector to the new area. You can click the field selector to display a list of the data values in that field.

To add a total field:

1 Click the field selector for the field you want to total.

Σ▾
AutoCalc

2 Click the **AutoCalc** button, and then click the type of total you want, such as **Sum** or **Count**. Totals appear at the end of each group.

⊞
Hide Details

3 To view only totals and no details, click the **Hide Details** button.

To set a filter:

1 If the field you want to filter is not already in the PivotTable, drag it from the field list to the appropriate filter area.

If the field is already in the row, column, or detail area, you can filter it where it is.

2 Click the field selector's down arrow , and deselect the values you don't want to include in the PivotTable.

To remove a field:

● Drag the field selector away from the PivotTable.

Practice Exercise

In this exercise, you will open a table and view its data in a PivotTable.

USE the *ViewPivotTable* database in the *My Documents\Microsoft Press\MOS 2003 Study Guide\Access \A03C-4-2* practice file folder.

Open the *ViewPivotTable* database, and acknowledge the safety warning, if necessary. Open the **Employees** table, and switch to PivotTable view. Drag the **Title** field to the row area, the **City** field to the column area, and the **LastName** field to the detail area. Filter the **Title** field so that it doesn't display *Owner*. Remove the **City** field. In the **PivotTable Field List**, click the expand indicator next to **Date Hired By Month**, and drag the **Years** field to the column area. Click one of the **Last Name** headers, click the **AutoCalc** button, and click **Count**. The PivotTable displays the number of employees hired for each year. To view only the number of employees and not their names, click the **Hide Details** button. Close the **Employees** table, saving layout changes, and then close the *ViewPivotTable* database.

Viewing PivotCharts

When you display a table, query, or form in PivotChart view, you can analyze and summarize data in a graphical way. For example, you can view sales totals in a PivotChart to analyze the sales by various employees.

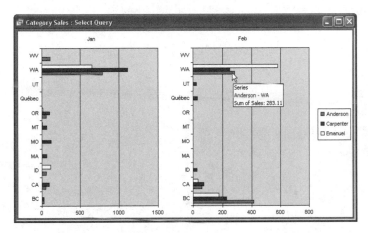

A PivotChart works in nearly the same way as a PivotTable. In fact, when you make changes in PivotChart view, those changes are carried over into PivotTable view and vice versa. After you've created a PivotTable layout, a PivotChart is ready to view as well.

BE SURE TO open the database you want to work with before carrying out these steps.

To view a PivotChart:

1 If the object you want to preview isn't already open, double-click its name in the Database window.

2 On the **View** menu, click **PivotChart View**.

A blank PivotChart appears and the Chart Field List opens.

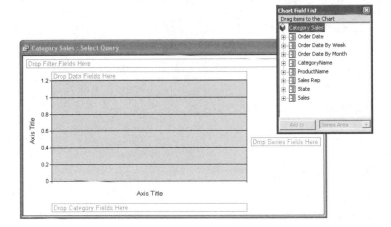

To add fields to the category, series, and data areas:

- Drag each field you want to add from the **Chart Field List** to the category, series, or data area box in the PivotTable.

  As you add each field, the PivotChart displays a field selector. To move (or pivot) a field from one area to another—for example, from the row area to the column area—drag its field selector to the new area. You can click the field selector to display a list of the data values in that field.

To change the chart type:

Chart Type

1 Click the background of the PivotChart, and then click the **Chart Type** button.

Access displays the Properties dialog box.

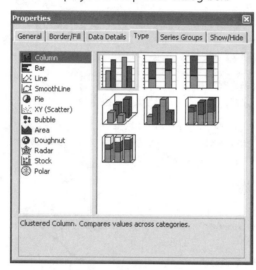

2 Click a chart category (such as **Column**, **Bar**, or **Pie**), click a chart type, and then close the Properties dialog box.

To display a legend for series fields:

Show Legend

- Click the **Show Legend** button on the toolbar.

To view multiple charts:

Multiple Plots

1 Click the **Multiple Plots** button on the toolbar.

The MultiChart Fields area appears at the top of the PivotChart.

2 Drag a field to the **MultiChart Fields** area.

A separate chart appears for each value field.

To view or hide drop areas:

- On the **View** menu, click **Drop Areas**.

  Hiding drop areas provides more room for the chart.

Practice Exercise

In this exercise, you will open a query that calculates sales totals and analyze the data in PivotChart view.

USE the *ViewPivotChart* database in the *My Documents\Microsoft Press\MOS 2003 Study Guide\Access \A03C-4-2* practice file folder.

Open the *ViewPivotChart* database, and acknowledge the safety warning, if necessary. Open the **Category Sales** query, and then switch to PivotChart view. Drag the **State** field to the category area, the **Sales** field to the data area, and the **Sales Rep** field to the series area. Display a legend, and change the chart type to **Clustered Bar**. Click the **Multiple Plots** button. In the **Chart Field List**, click the expand indicator next to **Order Date by Month**, and then drag the **Months** field to the **MultiChart** area. Hide the drop areas to get a better view of the charts. Point to any bar in the chart to display a pop-up box that shows sales figures. Close the query, saving layout changes, and then close the *ViewPivotChart* database.

Print Database Objects and Data

A03C-4-3   The skills measured by this objective include the following:

■   Printing objects and data

Because Access is a Windows application, it interacts with your printer through standard Windows dialog boxes and drivers. This means that any printer that you can use from other programs can be used from Access, and any special features of that printer, such as color printing or duplex printing, are available in Access.

Printing Objects and Data

The Page Setup, Print Preview, and Print commands are available on the File menu when their use is appropriate, which is determined by the object displayed and the current view of that object.

Tip   You can't print the Design view of tables, queries, forms, or reports. If you want to print a list of fields and other settings in a database, you can use the Documenter. The Documenter produces a detailed report of database contents that can be saved and printed. To start the Documenter, click Analyze and then Documenter on the Tools menu.

BE SURE TO open the database you want to work with and turn on your printer before carrying out these steps.

To print with default settings:

1   If the object you want to print isn't already open, click its name in the Database window.

2   Click the **Print** button.

Print

To print with specific options:

1   If the object you want to print isn't already open, click its name in the Database window.

2   On the **File** menu, click **Print**.

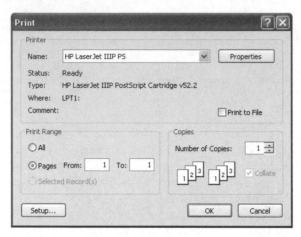

3   Select the options you want, such as the printer, page range, and number of copies, and then click **OK**.

Practice Exercise

In this exercise, you will print employee information in the *PrintData* database. Then you'll print one page of a report.

USE the *PrintData* database in the *My Documents\Microsoft Press\MOS 2003 Study Guide\Access\A03C-4-3* practice file folder.

Open the *PrintData* database and acknowledge the safety warning, if necessary. In the Database window, click the **Employees** table, and then click the **Print** button to send this datasheet to your default printer. Open the **Product List by Category** report in Print Preview, and print just the first page. Close the report, and then close the *PrintData* database.

Export Data from Access

A03C-4-4   The skills measured by this objective include the following:

   ■   Exporting data

When you want to work with data outside of Access, you can export it. For example, you can move data from a table into a Microsoft Excel worksheet.

Exporting Data

You can export Access database objects in a variety of formats. The specific formats available depend on the object you are trying to export. The following table lists the export formats available for each object.

Object	Export Formats
Table or Query	Access, dBASE, Excel, HTML, Lotus 1-2-3, Paradox, Text, SharePoint Team Services, Active Server Pages (ASP), Microsoft Internet Information Server (IIS), Rich Text Format (RTF), Word Merge, XML, Open Database Connectivity (ODBC)
Form	Access, Excel, HTML, Text, ASP, IIS, RTF, XML
Report	Access, Excel, HTML, Text, RTF, Snapshot, XML
Page	Access, Data Access Page (DAP)
Macro	Access
Module	Access, Text

Tip Exporting isn't the only way to use data in other applications. In many cases, programs can link directly to tables or queries in a database. For example, to use Access data in a Word mail-merge document, you could export the data to Word. A better way, however, is to specify the database as the data source for the Word mail-merge operation. That way, Word gets the current data from the database each time you perform the mail merge.

BE SURE TO open the database you want to work with before carrying out these steps.

To export an object and its data:

1 In the Database window, select the object you want to export.

2 On the **File** menu, click **Export**.

3 In the **Save as type** box, select the format you want to export.

4 In the **File name** box, type a name for the exported file.

5 If you are exporting to an existing Access database, click the database to which you want to export.

6 Click **Export**.

Practice Exercise

In this exercise, you will export a table in a format that can be used by Excel.

USE the *ExportData* database in the *My Documents\Microsoft Press\MOS 2003 Study Guide\Access\A03C-4-4* practice file folder.

Open the *ExportData* database, and acknowledge the safety warning, if necessary. Export the **Suppliers** table to the *My Documents\Microsoft Press\MOS 2003 Study Guide\Access\A03C-4-4* practice file folder, selecting **Microsoft Excel 97-2003** as the file type. Close the *ExportData* database. Start Excel, and open the *Suppliers* file from the practice file folder. Then quit Excel.

Back Up a Database

A03C-4-5 The skills measured by this objective include the following:

■ Backing up a database

Your first line of defense against damage or corruption in any kind of file is the maintenance of backups. You should back up a database frequently, especially after making significant changes or before changing the design of objects.

Backing Up a Database

Database files rapidly become too large to conveniently back up to floppy disk, but you have many other options. You can copy the file to another computer on a network, send it as an e-mail attachment to another location, use a tape backup, burn a CD-ROM, or copy it to some other removable media. In some cases, you might want to back up to the same folder that contains the database so that you can return to the earlier version if something goes wrong.

When you create a back up file, Access appends the current date to the file name in the following format: *MyDatabase_2004-04-22.mdb*. You can accept the default, or change the file name to suit your needs.

BE SURE TO **open the database you want to work with before carrying out these steps.**

To back up a database:

1 On the **File** menu, click **Back Up Database**.

Access displays the Save Backup As dialog box and enters a default name for your backup file in the "File name" box.

2 Navigate to the backup folder, such as a network folder or removable disk.

3 If you want to specify a name other than the default, type it in the **File name** box.

4 Click **Save**.

Access creates a copy of the database.

Practice Exercise

In this exercise, you will back up a database.

USE the *BackUpDatabase* database in the *My Documents\Microsoft Press\MOS 2003 Study Guide\Access \A03C-4-5* practice file folder.

Open the *BackUpDatabase* database, and acknowledge the safety warning, if necessary. Back up the database to the *My Documents\Microsoft Press\MOS 2003 Study Guide\Access \A03C-4-5* practice file folder, accepting the default name for the backup. Then close the *BackUpDatabase* database, and use My Computer or Windows Explorer to make sure you can find the backup file.

Compact and Repair Databases

A03C-4-6   The skills measured by this objective include the following:

■   Compacting and repairing a database

In the day-to-day use of an Access database—adding and deleting records, modifying forms and reports, and so on—various problems can develop. This is especially true if the database is stored on a local area network and is accessed by multiple users. It is a good idea to compact and repair a database often.

Compacting and Repairing a Database

Access monitors the health of database files as you open and work with them. If it sees a problem developing, it attempts to fix it. If Access can't fix a problem, it usually displays a message suggesting that you take some action. But Access doesn't always spot problems before they affect the database, and sometimes database performance slows down or becomes erratic. Even if no serious errors creep in, simply using a database causes its internal structure to become fragmented, resulting in a bloated file and inefficient use of disk space. To avoid problems, you can compact and repair the database manually, or you can instruct Access to compact and repair it every time you close it.

BE SURE TO open the database you want to work with before carrying out these steps.

To compact and repair a database:

●   On the **Tools** menu, click **Database Utilities** and then **Compact and Repair Database**.

Access compacts and repairs your database. If your database is large, a meter at the bottom of the window indicates the progress Access is making. If there are any problems with compacting or repairing, Access displays a message. When it finishes compacting, Access reopens the database.

Tip   If you don't have enough space on your hard disk to store a temporary copy of the database, if you don't have appropriate permissions, or if someone else on the network also has the database open, the Compact and Repair Database feature will not run properly.

To compact and repair automatically:

1   On the **Tools** menu, click **Options**.

2   Click the **General** tab, select **Compact on Close**.

3   Click **OK**.

Access compacts each time you close the database (unless another user has the file open at the time).

Practice Exercise

In this exercise, you will compact and repair a database.

USE the *RepairDatabase* database in the *My Documents\Microsoft Press\MOS 2003 Study Guide\Access \A03C-4-6* practice file folder.

Open the *RepairDatabase* database, and acknowledge the safety warning, if necessary. Display the **General** tab of the Properties dialog box for this database, and notice the size of the database (about 800 KB). Then compact the database. When Access reopens the database, view its properties again. The file should be quite a bit smaller (about 500 KB). Close the **RepairDatabase** database.

A03C-4 Review

Number	Objective	Mastered
A03C-4-1	Identify and modify object dependencies	
	Identifying object dependencies	❏
A03C-4-2	View objects and object data in other views	
	Using Print Preview and Layout Preview	❏
	Viewing PivotTables	❏
	Viewing PivotCharts	❏
A03C-4-3	Print database objects and data	
	Printing objects and data	❏
A03C-4-4	Export data from Access	
	Exporting data	❏
A03C-4-5	Back up a database	
	Backing up a database	❏
A03C-4-6	Compact and repair databases	
	Compacting and repairing a database	❏

Part VII
Microsoft Office Specialist Outlook 2003 Exam

This part of the book covers the skills you need to have for certification as a Microsoft Office Specialist in Microsoft Office Outlook 2003. Specifically, you will need to be able to complete tasks that require the following skills:

Number	Skill Set
O03C-1	Messaging
O03C-2	Scheduling
O03C-3	Organizing

You can use these basic skills to send and receive messages, manage calendar appointments, and organize information using Outlook.

Knowledge You Need Before Studying for This Exam

We assume that you have been working with Outlook for a while and that you know how to carry out fundamental tasks that are not specifically mentioned in the Microsoft Office Specialist objectives for Outlook 2003. Before you begin studying for this exam, you might want to scan this section to make sure you are familiar with this information.

Using the Reading Pane

You can display the Reading Pane at the right side or bottom of the screen in any Outlook folder. You can see an item's contents in the Reading Pane without opening the item.

BE SURE TO start Outlook before carrying out these steps.

To display the Reading Pane:

- On the **View** menu, click **Reading Pane** and then **Right** or **Bottom**.

To hide the Reading Pane:

- On the **View** menu, click **Reading Pane** and then **Off**.

To view and interact with items in the Reading Pane:

- With the Reading Pane visible, click the item you want to view.
- To open a message attachment, double-click the attachment at the top of the Reading Pane.
- To respond to a meeting request, click the **Accept** or **Decline** button at the top of the Reading Pane.

Using the Navigation Pane

The Navigation Pane at the left side of the Outlook window displays links to the Outlook folders, the folder structure of a selected message folder, and tools and links pertinent to the selected folder.

BE SURE TO start Outlook before carrying out these steps.

To display or hide the Navigation Pane:

● On the **View** menu, click **Navigation Pane**.

To switch between folders and views:

Mail

● To display the Inbox, click the **Mail** button.

Calendar

● To display the Calendar, click the **Calendar** button.

Contacts

● To display the Contacts folder, click the **Contacts** button.

Tasks

● To display the Tasks folder, click the **Tasks** button.

Notes

● To display the Notes folder, click the **Notes** button.

Folder List

● To display the Folder List, click the **Folder List** button.

Shortcuts

● To display the Shortcuts folder, click the **Shortcuts** button.

Using the Date Navigator

By default, the Date Navigator displayed at the top of the Navigation Pane in the Calendar displays a six-week date range. The days of the selected month are black; days of the previous and next months are gray, but you can still select them in the Date Navigator. Dates with scheduled appointments are bold.

BE SURE TO display your Outlook Calendar before carrying out these steps.

To change the date range displayed in the Date Navigator:

● Click the left arrow to display the previous month or the right arrow to display the next month.

● Click the month heading, and then in the drop-down list, click the month you want to display.

To select dates for display in the Calendar:

● In the Date Navigator, click the specific date to display it in the Calendar.

● In the Date Navigator, click in the margin to the left of a week to display it in the Calendar.

Creating a New Outlook Item

You can create a new message, appointment, contact entry, task, or note from within the appropriate folder by simply clicking the New button in that folder. You can also create Outlook items by using the following alternate methods.

BE SURE TO start Outlook before carrying out these steps.

To create a new item from any Outlook folder:

1   On the toolbar, click the **New** down arrow.

The icon on the New button changes depending on the currently displayed folder.

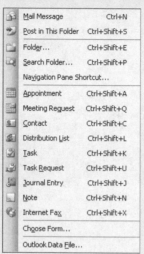

Mail Message	Ctrl+N
Post in This Folder	Ctrl+Shift+S
Folder...	Ctrl+Shift+E
Search Folder...	Ctrl+Shift+P
Navigation Pane Shortcut...	
Appointment	Ctrl+Shift+A
Meeting Request	Ctrl+Shift+Q
Contact	Ctrl+Shift+C
Distribution List	Ctrl+Shift+L
Task	Ctrl+Shift+K
Task Request	Ctrl+Shift+U
Journal Entry	Ctrl+Shift+J
Note	Ctrl+Shift+N
Internet Fax	Ctrl+Shift+X
Choose Form...	
Outlook Data File...	

2   On the drop-down menu, click the item you want to create.

To create an e-mail message from the Address Book:

New
Message

● In the Address Book, select the contact or distribution list to which you want to send the message, and then click the **New Message** button.

To create an appointment, event, or meeting from the Calendar:

● Click the Calendar timeslot in which you want to create the appointment, and then type the appointment subject. To create a longer appointment, drag through the timeslots you want, and then type the subject. Appointments created this way use the default reminder setting and don't include a meeting location. Edit the appointment to change the settings.

To create an appointment, event, or meeting from an e-mail message or task:

1   Drag the originating item to the **Calendar** button in the Navigation Pane.

When you release the mouse button, an Appointment form displaying the subject and content of the e-mail message appears.

2   Add any appointment information you want, and then click the **Save and Close** button.

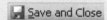

To create a contact from the Contacts folder:

● When displaying your contact entries in a list view, click in the **Click here to add a new Contact** row at the top of the list, and type the contact's information. Press **TAB** to move from one column to the next, and press **ENTER** when you finish.

To create a task from an e-mail message:

1 Drag the message from the Inbox to the **Tasks** button in the Navigation Pane.

When you release the mouse button, a Task form displaying the subject and content of the e-mail message appears.

2 Add any task information you want, and then click the **Save and Close** button.

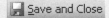

To create a note by dragging text:

1 With Outlook running in the background, switch to the Web page or document from which you want to copy text to a note.

2 Select the text you want, and drag it to the Outlook taskbar button. Don't release the mouse button.

3 When Outlook opens, drag the text to the **Notes** button on the Navigation Pane. When the insertion point changes to a plus sign, release the mouse button.

A new note is created and saved with the selected text. The note is automatically time stamped at the bottom with the current date and time.

4 Make any changes you want, and then close the note.

Setting Your Outlook Options

You can personalize the way Outlook works to best fit your working style.

If you have Microsoft Office Word 2003 installed, Outlook can use Word as its default e-mail editor. Many of Word's powerful text editing capabilities, including styles, tables, and themes, are available to you as you create messages in Outlook. Word will check your spelling as you type, correcting many errors automatically. You can also have Word check the spelling of your message when you send it. If you don't use the buttons on Word's toolbars, you can turn the toolbars off to save space.

Tip The exercises and graphics in this book assume that you are using Word as your default e-mail editor.

BE SURE TO start Outlook before carrying out these steps.

To instruct Outlook to close an open message when you respond to it:

1 On the **Tools** menu, click **Options**, click the **Preferences** tab, and click the **E-mail Options** button.

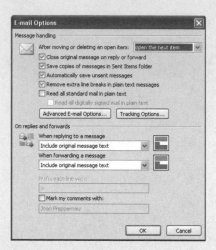

2   Select the **Close original message on reply or forward** check box, and then click **OK** in each dialog box to close it.

To set Word as your e-mail editor:

1   On the **Tools** menu, click **Options**, and then click the **Mail Format** tab.

2   Select the **Use Microsoft Office Word 2003 to edit e-mail messages** check box.

3   Click **OK**.

To turn off Word's Standard or Formatting toolbar in a Message form:

●   On the form's **View** menu, point to **Toolbars**, and then click the toolbar you want to turn off.

O03C-1
Messaging

The skills tested by this section of the Microsoft Office Specialist Outlook 2003 Exam all relate to e-mail and instant messaging. Specifically, the following objectives are associated with this set of skills:

Number	Objective
O03C-1-1	Originate and respond to e-mail and instant messages
O03C-1-2	Attach files to items
O03C-1-3	Create and modify a personal signature for messages
O03C-1-4	Modify e-mail message settings and delivery options
O03C-1-5	Create and edit contacts
O03C-1-6	Accept, decline, and delegate tasks

 Important Before you can do the practice exercises associated with this skill set, you need to install the practice files from the book's companion CD to their default location. See "Installing the Practice Files" on page xxv for more information.

Originate and Respond to E-Mail and Instant Messages

O03C-1-1 The skills measured by this objective include the following:

- Addressing and sending a new e-mail message
- Handling e-mail messages you receive
- Sending and replying to instant messages

With Outlook, communicating by e-mail is quick and easy. You can send messages to people in your office and at other locations regardless of what e-mail software your message recipient is using.

Addressing and Sending a New E-Mail Message

When you address e-mail messages, you can specify different ways of sending the message: directly, as a courtesy copy, or as a blind courtesy copy. In each case, the same message is sent to each recipient. The names of Bcc (blind courtesy copy) message recipients are not visible in the message header; therefore, other message recipients are not aware of them. Message replies are not sent to Bcc recipients of the original message.

If you are working on a network that uses Microsoft Exchange Server, when you send messages to other people on your network, you can type just the part of the address that is to the left of the @ sign. The remaining part of the address identifies the server that handles the e-mail account, so within an organization, the server name is not needed.

Tip By default, Outlook requires that you separate multiple e-mail addresses with semicolons. If you prefer, you can instruct Outlook to accept both semicolons and commas. To do this, click Options on the Tools menu. On the Preferences tab, click the E-mail Options button, and then click the Advanced E-mail Options button. Select the "Allow comma as address separator" check box, and then click OK to close each dialog box.

See Also For information about creating a new e-mail message, refer to "Knowledge You Need Before Studying for This Exam" on page 646.

BE SURE TO open your Outlook Inbox and a new e-mail Message form before carrying out these steps.

To address an e-mail message:

● In the **To** box, type the e-mail address(es) of one or more message recipients, separated by semicolons.

Tip If your recipient's address is in your address book or you've typed it in a message header before, Outlook automatically completes the address for you as you type, and pressing the TAB key inserts the entry. If there are multiple matches, Outlook presents a list of items that match what you've typed so far. Use the arrow keys to select the item you want, and press the ENTER key to insert the entry.

To address a courtesy copy:

● In the **Cc** box, type the e-mail address(es) of one or more people you want to receive copies of the message, separated by semicolons.

To address a blind copy:

1   If the **Bcc** box is not displayed, click the **Options** down arrow on the Message toolbar, and click **Bcc**.

2   In the **Bcc** box, type the e-mail address(es) of one or more people you want to receive blind copies of the message, separated by semicolons.

To send an e-mail message:

1   In the open Message form, enter the message recipient(s), subject, and body of the message.

2   Click the **Send** button.

The Message form closes, and the message is sent to each of the specified recipients.

Practice Exercise

In this exercise, you will send a message to yourself and then look at the results.

NO practice files are required for this exercise.

Create a new e-mail message. Address the message to yourself, add a subject and message text if you want, and send it. When the message arrives in your Inbox, open or preview it so you can see what your message recipients see. Then close the message.

Handling E-Mail Messages You Receive

You can reply to e-mail messages in different ways: You can reply only to the person who sent the message, or you can reply to the person who sent the message and all the people to whom the original message was addressed. Whether you reply to only the sender or to everyone, your reply does not include any files that were attached to the original message.

You can forward a message you have received to any other e-mail user (not only Outlook users). When you forward a message, the message recipient receives the text of the message as well as any files that were attached to the original message.

See Also For information about opening an Outlook item, refer to "Knowledge You Need Before Studying for This Exam" on page 646. For more information about attachments, refer to O03C-1-2, "Attach Files to Items."

BE SURE TO open your Inbox before carrying out these steps.

To reply to only the message sender:

1 Select or open the e-mail message to which you want to reply, and click the **Reply** button on the toolbar.

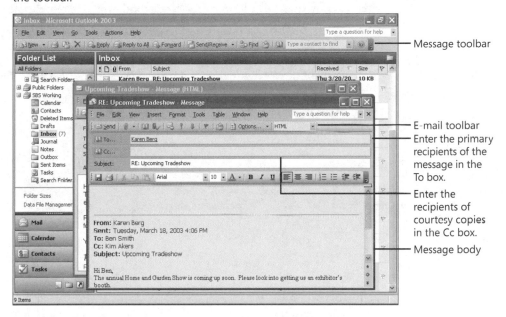

Tip If Microsoft Office Word is your default e-mail editor, the Reply form displays Word's Standard and Formatting toolbars in addition to the regular toolbar.

Note that the To box contains the original message sender's e-mail address, and a prefix, *RE:*, has been added to the subject line. This prefix indicates that this is a response to an earlier message. When you click the Reply button, the reply is sent only to the original sender. Attachments to the original message are not included in the reply.

See Also For information about using Word as your e-mail editor, refer to "Knowledge You Need Before Studying for This Exam" on page 646.

---

2 With the insertion point in the body of the message, type your response to the message.

3 Add any additional message recipients in the **To** or **Cc** boxes.

4 Click the **Send** button.

The reply is sent.

To reply to the message sender and all other recipients:

1 Select or open the e-mail message to which you want to reply, and click the **Reply to All** button on the toolbar.

The Reply Message form appears.

2 With the insertion point in the body of the message, type your response to the message.

3 Add any additional message recipients in the **To** or **Cc** boxes.

4 Click the **Send** button.

The reply is sent to the original message sender and everyone else to whom the original message was addressed.

To forward a message:

1 Select or open the e-mail message you want to forward, and click the **Forward** button on the toolbar.

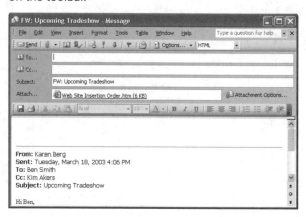

Note that the address lines are blank and that the attachment is included. Note also that a prefix, *FW:*, has been added to the subject line. This prefix indicates to the next recipients that this is a forwarded message.

2 In the **To** box, type the e-mail address to which you want to forward the message.

3 Press the **TAB** key until you get to the message body, and type any additional information you want to include (somewhat like a cover note to the original message).

4 Click the **Send** button.

The message is forwarded to the specified address.

Practice Exercise

In this exercise, you will reply to a message that you received in your Inbox, and then forward a message from your Inbox to another person.

NO practice files are required for this exercise.

Open an e-mail message in your Inbox and send a reply to the original message sender, with a copy to yourself so you can see what the reply looks like. Be sure to add a message in the message body. Then open another e-mail message, preferably one that has an attachment. In the message body, type **Forwarding this message for your information**. Forward the message to a friend, with a copy to yourself so you can see what the forwarded message looks like.

Sending and Replying to Instant Messages

You can communicate with your contacts in real time with instant messages. Instant messaging (IM) is a private online chat method. After you establish a connection with someone who is online and using instant messaging, messages you send to that person appear on his or her screen instantly. Likewise, you see responses from that person instantly on your screen. Instant messaging is especially useful for brief exchanges and can be much more immediate than e-mail. By default, Outlook supports instant messaging using Microsoft Windows Messenger, Microsoft MSN Messenger, and Microsoft Exchange Instant Messaging Service. When Outlook starts, you are automatically logged on to the service you installed.

Before you can use instant messaging, you must obtain the instant messaging addresses of the people you want to communicate with, and add those addresses to the Outlook Contact forms of those people. Then they have to tell their instant messaging programs to accept messages from your address.

After this setup work is done, when you log on to your instant messaging service, you can see whether a contact is online. A contact's online status is displayed in the InfoBar on the Contact form and on any e-mail address associated with the contact.

You can specify how your online status appears to others. For example, if you need to step away from your desk, you can set your status to *Be Right Back* so that any contacts who are online can see that you are temporarily unavailable.

BE SURE TO enlist the help of a co-worker or friend who is using MSN Messenger, Windows Messenger, or Exchange Instant Messaging Service. Have your instant messaging partner log on to his or her IM account before carrying out these steps.

Tip To complete the steps below you must have already added your instant messaging partner to your IM contacts list, and that person must have accepted your request to add him or her. For help with any of these tasks, refer to your IM program's Help file.

To initiate an instant message from the IM program:

1 Start your instant messaging program and start an IM connection to the message recipient.

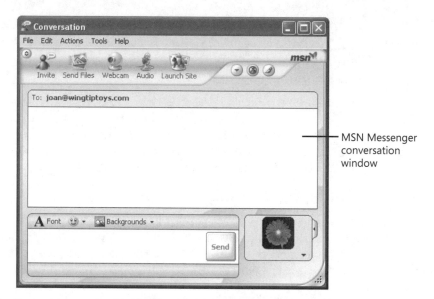

MSN Messenger conversation window

2   Enter the message text in the text box, and then click the **Send** button or press **ENTER**.

The message appears in an IM window on the recipient's screen. On your screen, the status bar indicates when your contact is typing a reply message.

To reply to an instant message:

Tip   It is not necessary to wait until receiving a reply before sending additional instant messages.

● To reply to a message or send additional messages, type the message in the message box, and then click the **Send** button or press **ENTER**.

Practice Exercise

In this exercise, you will create and send instant messages.

NO practice files are required for this exercise.

Sign in to your instant messaging program. Locate a friend or co-worker with an IM address, add that person to your contacts list, and send an instant message to him or her.

Attach Files to Items

O03C-1-2   The skills measured by this objective include the following:

■ Attaching a file to an e-mail message

■ Sending a file through an instant message

When sending e-mail and instant messages to other people, you can include electronic files (such as documents, spreadsheets, graphics, or text files) along with your message. This can be a quick and efficient way of distributing information to other people.

Tip   You can embed a hyperlink to a Web site in an e-mail or instant message simply by including the site's uniform resource locator (URL). To embed a hyperlink, simply type the URL (for example, *www.microsoft.com*) followed by a space. Outlook formats the URL as a link. Your recipients can simply click the link in the message to open the Web page.

When sending file attachments, be sure that your recipients have the software required to open your file. For example, if you are attaching a Word document, your recipients must have Word installed on their computers to open your attachment.

Attaching a File to an E-Mail Message

You can attach any type of file to an e-mail message, but Outlook prevents users from receiving certain types of files that could constitute a security hazard.

Tip   Some system administrators limit the size of individual e-mail Inboxes or prevent e-mail users from receiving certain types of file attachments, such as *.exe* files, which could contain viruses.

The maximum attachment size that your contacts can receive will vary depending on their e-mail systems. The time required to download an e-mail attachment varies depending on the recipient's Internet connection speed.

BE SURE TO open your Inbox and a new e-mail Message form, and have a document, spreadsheet, graphic, or text file available before carrying out these steps.

To attach a file to an outgoing e-mail message:

Insert File

1   On the Message form's toolbar, click the **Insert File** button (not the down arrow to the right of the button).

2   Browse to the file you want to attach, and then click the **Insert** button.

The document appears in the Attach box in the message header.

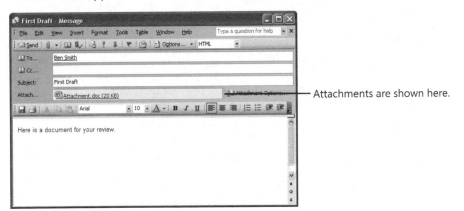

Attachments are shown here.

Practice Exercise

In this exercise, you will attach a file to an e-mail message.

USE the *AttachFile* document in the *My Documents\Microsoft Press\MOS 2003 Study Guide\Outlook \O03C-1-2* practice file folder.

Create a new e-mail message. Address the message to yourself and type **file attachment test** as the subject. Insert the *AttachFile* file to the e-mail message, and send it. When the message arrives in your Inbox, open or preview the message and open the attachment.

Sending a File Through an Instant Message

You can send files to contacts during instant messaging sessions. The files are not actually attached to the message; instead, a link to the file is embedded in the message. Your IM contact can click the link to download the file to his or her computer.

BE SURE TO start an IM session and have a document, spreadsheet, graphic, or text file available before carrying out these steps.

> **Tip** To complete the steps below you must have already added your instant messaging partner to your IM contacts list, and that person must have accepted your request to add him or her. For help with any of these tasks, refer to your IM program's Help file.

To send a file through an instant message:

1 On the toolbar, click the **Send Files** button, or click **Send a File or Photo** on the **File** menu.

2 Browse to the file you want to send, and click the **Insert** button.

Practice Exercise

In this exercise, you will send a file through an instant message.

USE the *AttachFile* document in the *My Documents\Microsoft Press\MOS 2003 Study Guide\Outlook \O03C-1-2* practice file folder.

Sign in to your instant messaging program. Locate a friend or co-worker with an IM address, add that person to your contacts list, and send an instant message asking your contact to help you with this exercise. Send the *AttachFile* document to your contact through the instant messaging program. Then ask your contact to send a small file to you. When you receive the file notification, download and open the file.

Create and Modify a Personal Signature for Messages

O03C-1-3   The skills measured by this objective include the following:

■ Creating and modifying an e-mail signature

■ Specifying unique signatures for multiple e-mail accounts

You can use an e-mail signature to personalize your messages and save time. A signature is a predefined block of text that can be inserted, manually or automatically, at the end of your outgoing messages.

Creating and Modifying an E-Mail Signature

Signatures can include any text you like, but they typically include your name, title, and company name. Signatures can be formatted in the same ways that message text can be formatted.

BE SURE TO open the Inbox before carrying out these steps.

To create a new default e-mail signature:

1 On the **Tools** menu, click **Options**, and then click the **Mail Format** tab.

2 In the Options dialog box, click the **Signatures** button, and then in the Create Signature dialog box, click the **New** button.

3 Type a name for the signature you are creating, and click **Next**.

4 In the **Signature text** box, type the text of the signature block, pressing **ENTER** at the end of each line.

5   Do either or both of the following:

■   Select text that you want to format, click the **Font** button, format the text as you want, and click **OK**.

■   Select paragraphs that you want to format, click the **Paragraph** button, format the paragraphs as you want, and click **OK**.

6   Make any other changes you want, and then click **Finish**.

Your newly created signature is now available in the Create Signature dialog box.

7   Click **OK**.

On the Mail Format tab of the Options dialog box, the signature you just created is selected in the "Signature for new messages" list, and your default account is selected in the "Select signatures for account" list. Outlook will insert your signature into all new e-mail messages you send from this account.

Tip   To automatically insert your signature into forwarded messages and replies, click Options on the Tools menu, and then click the Mail Format tab. Select the account in the "Select signatures for account" list, click the signature you want in the "Signature for replies and forwards" list, and click OK.

8   Click **OK** to close the Options dialog box.

To deselect your default e-mail signature:

1   On the **Tools** menu, click **Options**, and then click the **Mail Format** tab.

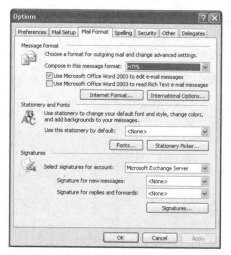

2   In the **Signature for new messages** list, click **<None>**, and then click **OK**.

New messages will now appear without a signature.

Practice Exercise

In this exercise, you will create and modify a personal e-mail signature.

NO practice files are required for this exercise.

Create a new e-mail signature named *Business* that contains the following text: **Regards,** (press **ENTER**) **Your Name** (press **ENTER**) **Your Company Name**. Format the font of the entire signature as blue, 12-point Verdana. Save the signature. Then edit the signature, change the font of your name to bold italic and your company name to bold, and save the signature.

Specifying Unique Signatures for Multiple E-Mail Accounts

You can create multiple signatures for different uses, such as formal business e-mail, casual business e-mail, and personal e-mail. If you use Outlook to access more than one e-mail account (for instance, your work and personal accounts) you can instruct Outlook to attach a specific, unique signature to each account.

BE SURE TO set up two e-mail accounts in Outlook and create two different e-mail signatures before carrying out these steps.

To attach unique signatures to different accounts:

1   On the **Tools** menu, click **Options**, and then click the **Mail Format** tab.

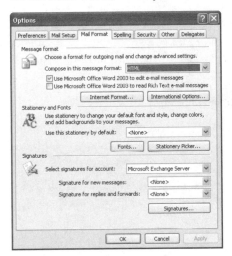

2   In the **Select signatures for account** list, select the first account.

3   In the **Signature for new messages** list, select the signature you want to use with that account.

4   Click **Apply**.

5   In the **Select signatures for account** list, select the second account.

6   In the **Signature for new messages** list, select the signature you want to use with that account.

7   Click **Apply**, and then click **OK**.

Practice Exercise

In this exercise, you will specify default e-mail signatures for two different e-mail accounts.

NO practice files are required for this exercise.

Set up two e-mail accounts in Outlook. (If you don't have a second account, you could create a free Hotmail or Yahoo account.) Create two unique e-mail signatures and attach the appropriate e-mail signature to each account. Then create a new e-mail message in each account, and verify that the appropriate signature appears in each new Message form. Close the Message forms without saving your changes.

Modify E-Mail Message Settings and Delivery Options

O03C-1-4   The skills measured by this objective include the following:

- ■ Flagging an e-mail message for follow-up
- ■ Setting e-mail message formats
- ■ Setting e-mail message importance, sensitivity, and delivery options

You can't always answer every message as soon as you read it, but you can mark messages that require response or action by attaching a follow-up flag. Outlook 2003 features Quick Flags, an easy way to flag messages.

You can send e-mail messages from Outlook in different formats, each designed to fit different needs. To help you manage your e-mail and convey the meaning of your messages more effectively, you can set the importance, sensitivity, and a number of delivery options for e-mail messages.

Flagging an E-Mail Message for Follow-Up

Flags come in six colors; you can use the different colors to indicate different types of follow-up, and you can set a reminder to pop up when the follow-up is due. You can quickly view your flagged messages by using the For Follow-up Search folder.

Each message in your Inbox has a shaded Flag Status icon that indicates whether a message is flagged or completed. You can flag messages in any folder, but the Flag Status icon appears only in active Inbox folders.

BE SURE TO open your Inbox before carrying out these steps.

To flag a received message for follow-up:

- ● Click the inactive **Flag Status** icon next to the message.

  The icon and the flag turn red.

Flag Status
(inactive)

To flag a received message and create a reminder:

Flag Status
(inactive)

1   Right-click the inactive **Flag Status** icon next to the message, and then click **Add Reminder** on the shortcut menu.

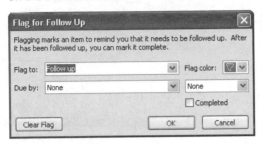

2   In the **Flag to** list, click the type of flag you want.

3   In the **Flag color** list, click the color you want.

4   Click **OK**.

To flag an outgoing message for follow-up:

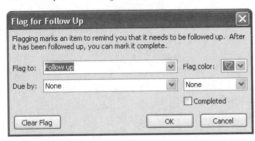

Follow Up

1   On the open Message form's toolbar, click the **Follow Up** button.

2   Click the **Flag to** down arrow, and click **Follow up**, **For Your Information**, **Forward**, **No Response Necessary**, **Read**, or **Reply** in the drop-down list.

3   Click the first **Due by** down arrow, and click the date you want in the drop-down calendar.

4   Click the second **Due by** down arrow, and click the time you want in the drop-down list.

5   Click **OK**.

To mark a flagged message as complete:

Flag Status
(active)

●   Click the active **Flag Status** icon next to the message.

The icon turns white and the flag changes to a check mark to indicate that the task is completed.

To change the current flag color:

●   Right-click the flag, and click the color you want on the shortcut menu.

To change the default flag color:

●   Right-click the flag, point to **Set Default Flag**, and then click the color you want.

To remove a flag:

- Right-click the flag, and then click **Clear Flag**.

To change the flag status of an open message:

Follow Up

1   On the message window's Standard toolbar, click the **Follow Up** button.

2   Set or clear the flag, or mark it as completed, and then click **OK**.

To view all messages flagged for follow-up:

- In the **Favorite Folders** list, click **For Follow Up**.

> **Tip**   If Outlook alerts you that it is unable to open the For Follow Up folder, in the Navigation Pane, click the plus sign next to Search Folders and then click the For Follow Up search folder.

The messages you flagged for follow up are displayed, grouped by flag color.

Practice Exercise

In this exercise, you will flag received messages, update flags, view messages by flag status, and flag a new outgoing message to bring it to the recipient's attention.

NO practice files are required for this exercise.

In your Inbox, use the Quick Flags feature to flag a message for follow-up. To a second message, add a reminder, and then add a blue flag reminding you to reply to the message. Open the message or display it in the Reading Pane to see the *Reply* label at the top of the message. Close the message and then send yourself a message that is flagged for follow up. View the flagged messages in the For Follow Up folder. Return to your Inbox and using the method of your choice, mark both flagged messages as completed.

Setting E-Mail Message Formats

E-mail messages are sent in one of three formats: HTML, Plain Text, or Outlook Rich Text Format (RTF). Outlook supports all three formats. Other e-mail programs might be able to work with only some of them.

- HTML is the default Outlook message format. HTML supports text formatting, numbering, bullets, pictures and backgrounds in the message body, styles, and stationery. Most popular e-mail programs support HTML messages.

- Outlook Rich Text Format supports a host of formatting options including text formatting, bullets, numbering, background colors, borders, and shading.

- Plain Text is supported by all e-mail programs, but as the name implies, messages in Plain Text do not include any formatting.

For the most part, the HTML message format will meet your needs. When you send an HTML message to someone whose e-mail program doesn't support HTML format, the message is displayed as Plain Text in the recipient's e-mail program. Outlook automatically converts RTF messages you send over the Internet into HTML format. When you reply to or forward a message, Outlook uses the format of the original message by default. However, you can choose the format for any message you send.

When sending messages in HTML format, you can enhance the appearance of your messages by using stationery and themes. When you use stationery, you can specify the background, fonts, bullets, images, and other elements you want to use in outgoing e-mail messages. You can choose from a collection of predefined stationery that comes with Outlook, customize one of the patterns, create new stationery, or download new patterns from the Web. If you use Microsoft Office Word as your e-mail editor, you can choose from additional patterns available as Word themes.

See Also   For information about using Word as your e-mail editor, refer to "Knowledge You Need Before Studying for This Exam" on page 646.

BE SURE TO open your Inbox before carrying out these steps.

To set the default e-mail message format:

1   On the **Tools** menu, click **Options**, and click the **Mail Format** tab.

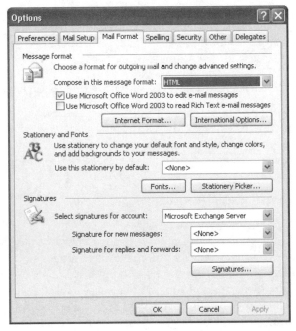

2   In the **Message format** area, click the **Compose in this message format** down arrow, click **HTML**, **Rich Text**, or **Plain Text**, and then click **OK**.

The Options dialog box closes. The default message format for new messages is now set to the format you specified.

To set the format for an individual e-mail message when Word is your e-mail editor:

HTML ▼
Message
format

1   In the Message form, click the **Message format** down arrow, and then click **HTML**, **Rich Text**, or **Plain Text**.

2 If a message box appears prompting you to confirm the change, click **Continue**.

> **Tip** To bypass this warning in the future, select the "Don't show this dialog box again" check box before continuing.

To set the format for an individual e-mail message when Outlook is your e-mail editor:

1 In the Message form, click **HTML**, **Rich Text**, or **Plain Text** on the **Format** menu.

2 If a message box appears prompting you to confirm the change, click **Yes**.

Practice Exercise

In this exercise, you will set the default message format to HTML, and then format an individual message as Plain Text.

NO practice files are required for this exercise.

Display the Mail Format tab of the Options dialog box, and set the default message format to HTML. Open a new Message form and in the message body, type **Roses are red, violets are blue.** Format the font of the entire sentence as 14-point, black Lucida Sans. Format the word *red* as red text and the word *blue* as blue text. Then change the message format to Plain Text. Close the Message form without saving it.

Setting E-Mail Message Importance, Sensitivity, and Delivery Options

You can set a message to *High*, *Normal*, or *Low* importance. Messages sent with High importance are indicated by a red exclamation point. Messages that were sent with Normal importance have no special indicator. Messages that were sent with Low importance are indicated by a blue downward-pointing arrow. These indicators appear in the Importance column in the Inbox.

You can also set message sensitivity to *Normal*, *Personal*, *Private*, or *Confidential*. Messages marked as Private cannot be modified after they are sent.

To help you manage messages you receive, you can choose to have replies to your messages sent to another e-mail address. For example, you might have replies sent to a new e-mail address as you transition from one to another. To help you manage messages you send, you can choose whether to save copies of your sent messages and in which folder they should be saved. You can also specify when a message will be delivered, and expire messages after a certain date and time. When a message expires, the sender and receipt information are "crossed out" in the recipient's Inbox to indicate that he or she does not need to read the message.

BE SURE TO start Outlook and create a new e-mail message before carrying out these steps.

To set the importance of a message:

Importance:
High Low

● On the Message form's toolbar, click the **Importance: High** or **Importance: Low** button.

> **Tip** To reset a message to Normal importance, click the Importance: High or Importance: Low button again to toggle it off.

To set the sensitivity of a message:

1 On the Message form's toolbar, click the **Options** button.

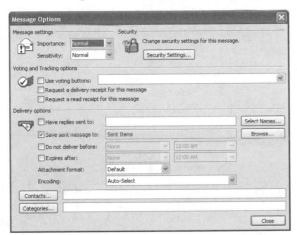

2 In the **Message settings** area, click the **Sensitivity** down arrow, and click **Normal**, **Personal**, **Private**, or **Confidential** in the drop-down list.

3 Click **Close**.

To specify the address to which a message's replies will be sent:

1 On the Message form's toolbar, click the **Options** button.

2 In the **Delivery options** area, select the **Have replies sent to** check box, delete the text that appears in the adjacent box, and type the e-mail address where you want replies sent.

3 Click **Close**.

To specify the folder in which a sent messages will be saved:

1 On the Message form's toolbar, click the **Options** button.

2 In the **Delivery options** area, select the **Save sent message to** check box, and click the **Browse** button.

3 In the **Folders** list, browse to the folder in which you want to save sent messages, and then click **OK**.

4 Click **Close**.

To specify the time at which a message will be sent:

1 On the Message form's toolbar, click the **Options** button.

2 In the **Delivery options** area, select the **Do not deliver before** check box.

3 Select the date and time you want the message to be sent.

4 Click **Close**.

After you send the message it will be held in your Outbox until the specified date and time.

To delete an unread message from the recipient's Inbox at a certain time:

1 On the Message form's toolbar, click the **Options** button.

2 In the **Delivery options** area, select the **Expires after** check box.

3 Select the date and time you want the message to be deleted from the recipient's Inbox.

4 Click **Close**.

Practice Exercise

In this exercise, you will set the importance of a message and schedule it to be sent at a future date and time.

NO practice files are required for this exercise.

Open a new Message form. Click the **Importance: Low** button to indicate to the recipient that the message is not urgent. Click the **Options** button. In the Message Options dialog box, select the **Do not deliver before** check box. In the drop-down boxes to the right, specify that the message should be delivered to the recipient at 9:00 AM tomorrow, and then click **Close**. Close the Message form without saving your changes.

Create and Edit Contacts

O03C-1-5   The skills measured by this objective include the following:

■ Creating and updating contact entries

■ Creating instant messaging contact entries

Think of your Outlook Contacts list as a powerful electronic Rolodex, where you can store all the information you need to stay in touch with contacts. For each contact entry, you can store the following types of information:

■ Name, job title, and company name

■ Business, home, and other addresses

■ Business, home, fax, mobile, pager, and other phone numbers

■ E-mail, Web page, and instant messaging addresses

You can also store the following details for each contact entry:

■ Professional information, including department, office, profession, manager's name and assistant's name

■ Personal information, including nickname, spouse's name, birthday, anniversary, and the title and suffix to use in correspondence

■ The directory server and e-mail alias to use for online meetings

■ The address of the contact's free/busy information server

Creating and Updating Contact Entries

You can create an entry for a contact with as little as a name, or as much information as you want. You can add general notes and track all the Outlook activities that are connected with each contact. You can add to or change the information for a contact at any time. To save time, you can create contact entries for people who work for the same company based on an existing contact from that company.

If you have Person Names smart tags enabled, you can add contact entries to your Outlook Contacts list from an e-mail message form or from the Reading Pane.

See Also For information about creating a contact entry or using the Reading Pane, refer to "Knowledge You Need Before Studying for This Exam" on page 646.

BE SURE TO open your Contacts folder before carrying out these steps.

To create a new contact entry:

1 Open a new Contact form.

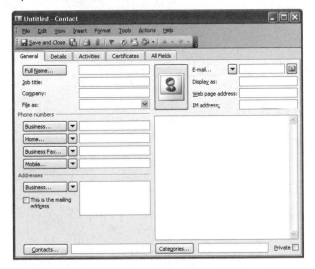

2 In the **Full Name** box, type the contact's first and last name, and press the **TAB** key.

Outlook completes the "File as" box, indicating that the contact entry will be filed by the person's last name.

3 Enter the additional contact information you want.

Tip The first time you enter a phone number in a Contact form, Outlook might open a dialog box and prompt you to enter your own country and area code. This information allows Outlook to set up dialing rules. You must enter your area code in the dialog box and then click OK; you can't close the dialog box without entering the requested information.

Tip Outlook automatically checks addresses for standard elements such as street address, city, state, and zip code. If Outlook cannot identify these elements, the Check Address dialog box appears, prompting you to enter each item in its own box. You can also open the Check Address dialog box by clicking the Address button.

4 If you want to enter further details, click the **Details** tab.

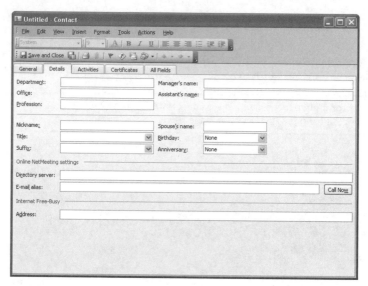

5   Enter the additional information you want.

6   Click the **Save and Close** button.

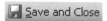

The Contact form closes. Your Contacts folder is displayed, containing the new address card.

To create a new contact entry based on an existing contact entry:

1   In the Contacts folder, double-click the contact entry on which you want to base the new entry.

2   On the **Actions** menu, click **New Contact from Same Company**.

A new Contact form opens, already containing the company name, address, phone number, and Web page address.

3   Enter the contact's name and any additional information you want.

4   Click the **Save and Close** button in each of the open forms.

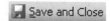

The Contact forms close, and the Contacts folder is displayed.

To edit a contact entry:

1   In the Contacts folder, double-click the entry you want to edit.

The Contact form opens.

2   Change the contact information you want.

3   Click the **Save and Close** button.

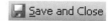

The Contact form closes, saving the updated information, and the Contacts folder is displayed.

To add a contact entry from an e-mail message:

Person
Names

1   Open the message or preview it in the Reading Pane.

2   Click the **Person Names** smart tag next to the contact's name, and then click **Add to Outlook Contacts** in the drop-down list.

3   In the new Contact form, add any information you want and then click the **Save and Close** button.

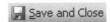

Practice Exercise

In this exercise, you will create a new e-mail contact entry and create a contact entry based on an existing entry.

NO practice files are required for this exercise.

Open a new Contact form. Enter your own information including your company name and contact details. Save and close the Contact form and re-open it. Create a new contact entry based on your existing contact form. In the new Contact form that is created, enter real or fictitious information for another person from your company. Save and close the new entry.

Creating Instant Messaging Contact Entries

If you use Windows Messenger or MSN Messenger, you can create contact entries directly in your instant messaging program, or add them from your Outlook Contacts list to your Messenger contact list.

BE SURE TO start MSN Messenger before carrying out these steps.

To manually add a contact entry to MSN Messenger:

1   On the MSN Messenger **Contacts** menu, click **Add a Contact**.

2   Select the **Create a new contact by entering their e-mail address or sign-in name** option, and then click **Next**.

3   Type the instant messaging address of the person you want to add, and then click **Next**.

4   Click **Finish** to close the wizard.

To add a contact entry to MSN Messenger from your Outlook address book:

1   On the MSN Messenger **Contacts** menu, click **Add a Contact**.

2   Select the **Choose from a list of my existing address book contacts** option, and then click **Next**.

    Your address book is displayed in the wizard's window.

3   Select the person you want to add, and then click **Next**.

4   Click **Finish** to close the wizard.

Practice Exercise

In this exercise, you will add a contact's instant messaging address to your Windows Messenger or MSN Messenger contact list.

NO practice files are required for this exercise.

Have the IM address of a friend available. Start your instant messaging program and add your friend as a contact.

Accept, Decline, and Delegate Tasks

O03C-1-6   The skills measured by this objective include the following:

■   Handling task assignments

When another Outlook user assigns a task to you through Outlook, you become the temporary task owner. You then have three options:

- You can accept the task. When you accept a task, it is added to your Outlook Tasks list. If the original task owner requested it, a copy of the task is kept in his or her Tasks list so he or she can see your progress.

- You can decline the task. If you do so, the task is returned to the original task owner, who can reclaim or reassign the task.

- You can delegate the task to another person. If that person accepts the task, he or he becomes the task owner. If not, the task is returned to you.

See Also   For information about assigning tasks, refer to O03C-2-4, "Create, Modify, and Assign Tasks."

Handling Task Assignments

When you receive a task request, you must accept or decline the task in the same way that you would accept or decline a meeting.

See Also   For information about using the Reading Pane, refer to "Knowledge You Need Before Studying for This Exam" on page 646.

BE SURE TO have another Outlook user assign one or more tasks to you before carrying out these steps.

To accept a task:

1   Open the task request or preview it in the Reading Pane.

2   In the open Message form or in the Reading Pane, click the **Accept** button.

3   In the Accepting Task dialog box, select one of the following options:
- **Edit the response before sending**
- **Send the response now**

4   Click **OK**.

5   If you selected the first option, the Task form opens as an e-mail message. Make any changes to the task and/or enter additional information if you want, and then click **Send**.

The Task form closes and the task request disappears from your Inbox. The new task is added to your Tasks list, and a notice of your acceptance is sent to the requester.

To decline a task:

1 Open the task request or preview it in the Reading Pane.

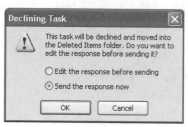

2 In the open Message form or in the Reading Pane, click the **Decline** button.

3 In the Declining Task dialog box, select one of the following options:

- ■ **Edit the response before sending**
- ■ **Send the response now**

4 Click **OK**.

5 If you selected the first option, the Task form opens as an e-mail message. Make any changes to the task and/or enter additional information if you want, and then click **Send**.

The Task form closes and the task request disappears from your Inbox. A notice that you have declined the request is sent to the requester.

To delegate a task:

1 Open the task request, and on the Message form's toolbar, click the **Assign Task** button.

The Task form opens as an e-mail message.

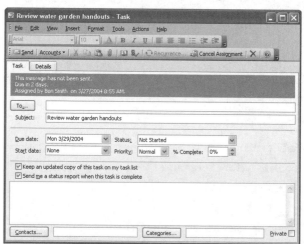

2 In the **To** box, enter the name or e-mail address of the person to whom you are delegating the task.

3 Make any changes to the task and/or enter additional information if you want, and then click **Send**.

The Task form closes and the task request disappears from your Inbox.

Practice Exercise

In this exercise, you will view and decline a task assignment.

NO practice files are required for this exercise.

Ask another Outlook user to assign a task to you. When you receive the task assignment in your Inbox, open or preview it to see what it looks like. Accept the task, and then change to Tasks view to verify that the task is added to your Tasks list.

O03C-1 Review

Number	Objective	Mastered
O03C-1-1	Originate and respond to e-mail and instant messages	
	Addressing and sending a new e-mail message	❑
	Handling e-mail messages you receive	❑
	Sending and replying to instant messages	❑
O03C-1-2	Attach files to items	
	Attaching a file to an e-mail message	❑
	Sending a file through an instant message	❑
O03C-1-3	Create and modify a personal signature for messages	
	Creating and modifying an e-mail signature	❑
	Specifying unique signatures for multiple e-mail accounts	❑
O03C-1-4	Modify e-mail message settings and delivery options	
	Flagging an e-mail message for follow-up	❑
	Setting e-mail message formats	❑
	Setting e-mail message importance, sensitivity, and delivery options	❑
O03C-1-5	Create and edit contacts	
	Creating and updating contact entries	❑
	Creating instant messaging contact entries	❑
O03C-1-6	Accept, decline, and delegate tasks	
	Handling task assignments	❑

O03C-2
Scheduling

The skills tested by this section of the Microsoft Office Specialist Outlook 2003 Exam all relate to the Outlook Calendar. Specifically, the following objectives are associated with this set of skills:

Number	Objective
O03C-2-1	Create and modify appointments, meetings, and events
O03C-2-2	Update, cancel, and respond to meeting requests
O03C-2-3	Customize Calendar settings
O03C-2-4	Create, modify, and assign tasks

Create and Modify Appointments, Meetings, and Events

O03C-2-1   The skills measured by this objective include the following:

- Adding an appointment or event to the Outlook Calendar
- Inviting people and resources to a meeting

Adding your time commitments to a calendar can help you manage your daily schedule. You can use Outlook's Calendar to schedule appointments (which typically last just part of a day) or events (which typically last all day). For example, you might create an appointment in your Outlook Calendar for the time you will spend seeing your doctor, and you might schedule an event for an all-day seminar you plan to attend. You can also schedule meetings and meeting resources. When you schedule a meeting, you send an invitation to each attendee. If your meeting attendees use Outlook, the meeting is placed in their Calendars unless declined.

Adding an Appointment or Event to the Outlook Calendar

Both appointments and events can be recurring, meaning they occur repeatedly at regular intervals—for example, daily, weekly, or monthly. You can specify a subject and location for each Calendar item as well as the date and time. You can indicate your availability as available, tentative, busy, or out of the office during the scheduled time, and you can choose to receive a reminder of an appointment or event. Reminders are displayed in a small dialog box that appears as the time of the appointment or event approaches.

Outlook must be open for you to receive reminders.

See Also   For information about creating new appointments and events, refer to "Knowledge You Need Before Studying for This Exam" on page 646.

BE SURE TO open the Calendar before carrying out these steps.

To schedule an appointment:

1   Open a new Appointment form.

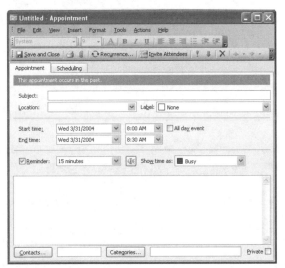

2   In the **Subject** box, enter the appointment name you want to appear in your Calendar.

3   In the **Location** box, enter the appointment location.

    In the Calendar, this text will appear in parentheses following the appointment subject.

4   Click the first **Start time** down arrow, and in the drop-down list, click the appointment date.

5   Click the second **Start time** down arrow, and in the drop-down list, click the appointment starting time.

6   Click the second **End time** down arrow, and in the drop-down list, click the appointment ending time.

7   If you want a reminder to appear prior to the appointment, select the **Reminder** check box and specify the reminder time.

8   In the **Show time as** drop-down list, click **Free**, **Tentative**, **Busy**, or **Out of Office** to indicate how you want the time to appear (to yourself and others who view your Calendar remotely) in your Calendar.

9   If you want to hide appointment details from other Outlook users who view your Calendar remotely, select the **Private** check box.

    Tip   In your Calendar, a key icon next to an item indicates that an item is marked as Private.

10 Complete any additional information you want, and then click the **Save and Close** button.

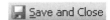

    The appointment appears in the Calendar.

To schedule a multi-day event:

1 Open a new Appointment form.

2 In the **Subject** box, enter the event name you want to appear in your Calendar.

3 In the **Location** box, enter the event location.

In the Calendar, this text will appear in parentheses following the event subject.

4 Click the first **Start time** down arrow, and in the drop-down list, click the event start date.

5 Click the first **End time** down arrow, and in the drop-down list, click the event end date.

6 Select the **All day event** check box.

7 If you want a reminder to appear prior to the event, select the **Reminder** check box and specify the reminder time.

8 In the **Show time as** drop-down list, click **Free**, **Tentative**, **Busy**, or **Out of Office** to indicate how you want the time to appear (to yourself and others who view your Calendar remotely) in your Calendar.

9 If you want to hide event details from other Outlook users who view your Calendar remotely, select the **Private** check box.

> **Tip** In your Calendar, a key icon next to an item indicates that an item is marked as Private.

10 Complete any additional information you want, and then click the **Save and Close** button.

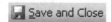

The event appears in the Calendar.

To make an appointment or event recurring:

1 Create the appointment or event.

2 On the Appointment form toolbar, click the **Recurrence** button.

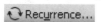

The Appointment Recurrence dialog box appears.

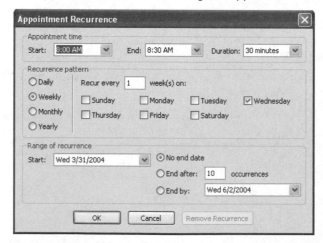

3   In the **Recurrence pattern** area, select the **Daily**, **Weekly**, **Monthly**, or **Yearly** option, and then set the specific recurrence frequency.

4   In the **Range of recurrence** area, select the **No end date**, **End after**, or **End by** option, and then set the specific number of occurrences or the end date if required.

Tip   By default, the start date is set to the appointment or event date. To change the start date, click the Start down arrow, and select a new start date in the drop-down calendar.

5   Click **OK**.

The recurrence settings are shown in the Appointment form.

6   In the Appointment form, click the **Save and Close** button.

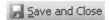

The recurring appointment appears in your Calendar. Circling arrows indicate the recurrence.

Practice Exercise

In this exercise, you will add an appointment to your Outlook Calendar.

NO practice files are required for this exercise.

Display your Calendar and create a recurring event on your birthday. Set a reminder to appear two weeks ahead of the event to give you time to plan a celebration!

Inviting People and Resources to a Meeting

You can use Outlook to schedule meetings and invite attendees—both those who work for your organization and those who don't. To choose a date and time for your meeting, you can check the availability of attendees and resources by viewing their free/busy information. When inviting attendees from within your organization, you can automatically see their Outlook Calendar information. You can see free/busy information for people outside of your organization only if they make this information available over the Internet.

You can choose the meeting time, or to have Outlook select it for you, you can provide a list of attendees and indicate whether the attendance of each invitee is required or optional. Outlook uses this information to search for available meeting times, prioritizing times that work for all required attendees and most optional attendees.

After you have selected a time, you send a meeting request—a type of e-mail message—to each invited attendee and requested resource. Responses from attendees and those responsible for scheduling the resources you requested are tracked as you receive them.

See Also   For information about creating new meetings, refer to "Knowledge You Need Before Studying for This Exam" on page 646.

If you are working on a network that uses Microsoft Exchange Server and your system administrator includes resources (such as conference rooms, audiovisual equipment, or meeting supplies) in the organization's Global Address List, you can reserve those resources by inviting them to the meeting. Your meeting request is sent to the person who manages the schedule for the resource. That person responds to your meeting request based on the availability of the resource.

BE SURE TO have an available meeting resource before carrying out these steps.

To schedule a meeting:

1 Open a new Meeting Request form.

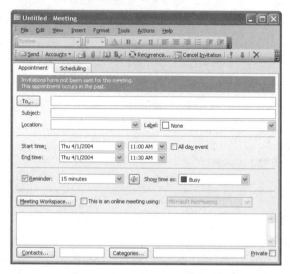

2 In the **To** box, enter the names or e-mail addresses of the people you want to invite to the meeting.

Check
Names

3 If necessary, click the **Check Names** button on the toolbar to validate the invitees' contact information.

4 In the **Subject** box, enter the text you want to appear in the Calendar.

5 In the **Location** box, enter the meeting location.

In the Calendar, this text will appear in parentheses following the meeting subject.

6 Click the first **Start time** down arrow, and in the drop-down list, click the meeting date.

7 Click the second **Start time** down arrow, and in the drop-down list, click the meeting starting time.

8 Click the second **End time** down arrow, and in the drop-down list, click the meeting ending time.

9 If you want a reminder to appear prior to the meeting, select the **Reminder** check box and specify the reminder time.

10 In the **Show time as** drop-down list, click **Free**, **Tentative**, **Busy**, or **Out of Office** to indicate how you want the time to appear in the Calendar.

11 If you want to hide meeting details from other Outlook users who view your Calendar remotely, select the **Private** check box.

Tip In your Calendar, a key icon next to an item indicates that an item is marked as Private.

12   Complete any additional information you want on the **Appointment** tab, and then click the **Scheduling** tab.

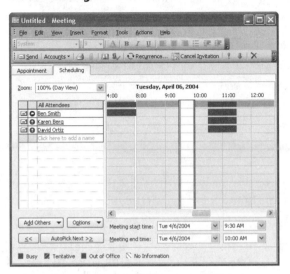

13   Add attendees or resources or adjust the meeting date or time as you want. When you are satisfied with the meeting details, click the **Send** button.

The meeting requests are sent and the meeting appears in the Calendar.

To schedule a resource while creating a meeting request:

1   In the Meeting form, click the **Scheduling** tab.

2   Click the **Add Others** button, and then click **Add from Address Book**.

3   In the **Name** list, select the resource or resources you want to add.

Tip   To select multiple resources, click the first resource, press CTRL, and then click the additional resource(s).

681

4   Click the **Resources** button, and then click **OK**.

5   Complete the remaining meeting information, and then click the **Send** button.

To schedule a resource for an existing meeting:

1   Open the Meeting form, and click the **Scheduling** tab.

2   Click the **Add Others** button, and then click **Add from Address Book**.

The Select Attendees and Resources dialog box appears.

3   In the **Name** list, select the resource or resources you want to add.

4   Click the **Resources** button, and then click **OK**.

5   Click the **Send Update** button.

Practice Exercise

In this exercise, you will schedule a recurring meeting.

NO practice files are required for this exercise.

In your Outlook Calendar, schedule a meeting from 11:30 A.M. to 12:30 P.M. on the first Tuesday of each month, starting next month. Set a reminder to occur 30 minutes before each meeting, and then send meeting requests to your co-workers.

Update, Cancel, and Respond to Meeting Requests

O03C-2-2   The skills measured by this objective include the following:

- Responding to a meeting request
- Updating or canceling a meeting

Scheduling a meeting sends a meeting request e-mail message to each attendee and places the meeting on each attendee's Outlook Calendar, as well as on your own. Meeting requests give the attendee the option to accept or decline the meeting, or propose a new meeting time. The number of attendees who have accepted or declined your meeting request is visible in the meeting form on your Calendar.

As the meeting organizer, you can update a meeting or cancel it at any time from your Calendar.

Responding to a Meeting Request

Just as you can send meeting requests, other people can send them to you. When you receive a meeting request, you can respond in one of four ways:

- You can accept the request and inform the meeting organizer that you will attend. Meetings that you accept are entered in your Calendar.
- You can tentatively accept a request, indicating that you might be able to attend the meeting. Meetings that you accept tentatively are also entered in your Calendar, but your free/busy information will show you as only tentatively scheduled for that time.

■ You can propose a new meeting time, in which case the request is referred to the meeting organizer for confirmation. Your Calendar shows the proposed new meeting time as tentatively scheduled.

■ You can decline a meeting, in which case the request is deleted and no entry is made in your Calendar. When you decline a meeting, you can choose whether Outlook notifies the person who sent the request.

If you prefer, you can choose to respond to meeting requests automatically. Outlook will process meeting requests and cancellations as you receive them, responding to requests, adding new meetings to your Calendar, and removing cancelled meetings. If you choose, Outlook will automatically decline meeting requests that conflict with existing items on your Calendar. You can also choose to automatically decline any request for a recurring meeting.

BE SURE TO have a friend or co-worker send you one or more meeting requests before carrying out these steps.

To view a meeting in your Calendar before responding to the request:

1   Open the meeting request, and click the **Calendar** button.

Your Calendar appears in a new window, displaying the date of the requested meeting. For recurring meetings, the date of the first meeting is displayed. The requested meeting has a blue-striped bar at the left, which means it is tentatively scheduled.

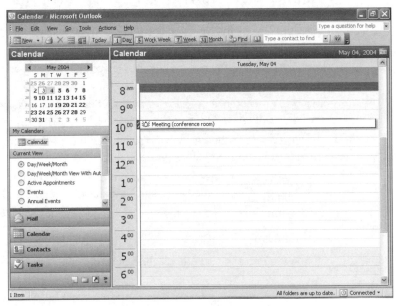

Close

2   In the open Calendar window, click the **Close** button.

The Calendar closes and you return to the Meeting form.

To accept a meeting request:

1 Open the meeting request, and click the **Accept** button.

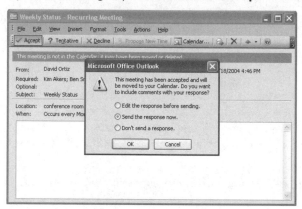

Tip When accepting or declining a meeting, you can choose to send a standard response, send a response that you compose yourself, or send no response. If you do not send a response to the meeting organizer, your acceptance will not be tallied in the Meeting form. The organizer and other attendees will not know whether you are planning to attend the meeting.

2 Select the option you want:

- To send a personalized acceptance message to the meeting organizer, select the **Edit the response before sending** option, and then click **OK**. In the Meeting Response form that opens, enter the message you want in the message body area, and then click the **Send** button.

  Your response is sent to the person who requested the meeting and the meeting appears on your Calendar.

- To send a blank acceptance message to the meeting organizer, select the **Send the response now** option, and then click **OK**.

  Your response is sent to the person who requested the meeting, the Meeting form closes, and the meeting appears on your Calendar.

- To accept without sending a response, in which case your acceptance will not be tallied in the Meeting form, select the **Don't send a response** option, and then click **OK**.

  The Meeting form closes and the meeting appears on your Calendar.

To decline a meeting request:

1 Open the meeting request, and click the **Decline** button.

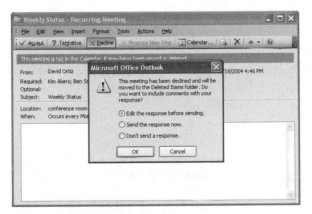

2   Select the option you want:

- ■ To send a personalized declination message to the meeting organizer, select the **Edit the response before sending** option, and click **OK**. In the Meeting Response form that opens, enter a message in the message body area, and then click the **Send** button.

    Your response is sent to the person who requested the meeting and the meeting is removed from your Calendar.

- ■ To send a blank declination message to the meeting organizer, select the **Send the response now** option, and then click **OK**.

    Your response is sent to the person who requested the meeting, the Meeting form closes, and the meeting is removed from your Calendar.

- ■ To decline without sending a response, in which case your declination will not be tallied in the Meeting form, select the **Don't send a response** option, and then click **OK**.

    The Meeting form closes and the meeting is removed from your Calendar.

To propose a new meeting time:

1   Open the meeting request, and click the **Propose New Time** button.

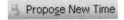

The Propose New Time dialog box appears.

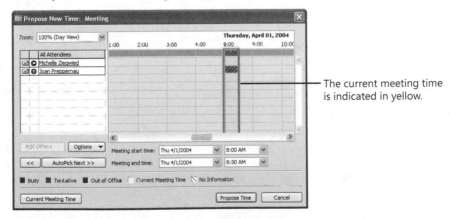

The current meeting time is indicated in yellow.

2 Drag the green and red start time and end time markers, or change the **Meeting start time** and **Meeting end time** settings, to change the proposed meeting date and/or time.

3 Click the **Propose Time** button.

The Propose New Time dialog box closes, and a Meeting Response form appears. The subject of the response indicates that you are proposing a new time for the meeting.

4 Add any personalized message you want in the message body area, and then click the **Send** button.

Your response is sent, and the Meeting form closes. The meeting is added to your Calendar as tentatively scheduled for the original meeting time.

To instruct Outlook to automatically respond to meeting requests:

1 On the **Tools** menu, click **Options**, and then click the **Preferences** tab.

2 In the Options dialog box, click the **Calendar Options** button, and then click the **Resource Scheduling** button.

3 Select the **Automatically accept meeting requests and process cancellations** check box.

4 Select the **Automatically decline conflicting meeting requests** and/or the **Automatically decline recurring meeting requests** check boxes if you want Outlook to do this.

5 Click **OK** to close each open dialog box.

Practice Exercise

In this exercise, you will respond to a meeting request.

NO practice files are required for this exercise.

Ask a friend or co-worker to send you a meeting request. When the meeting request arrives, open the message, view the meeting in your Calendar, and then propose a new meeting time.

Updating or Canceling a Meeting

People's schedules can shift on a daily basis. Outlook makes it easy to update or cancel meetings as your needs change. For example, an important attendee might be sick or delayed, or have other plans come up that take precedence over your meeting. In this case, you can change the date or time of the meeting or cancel the meeting altogether. You can also add people to or remove people from the list of attendees.

Tip You can update or cancel only those meetings for which you are the meeting organizer.

BE SURE TO open your Calendar before carrying out these steps.

To update a scheduled meeting:

1. Open the scheduled meeting, and click the **Scheduling** tab.

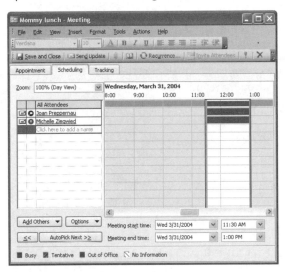

2. Drag the green and red start time and end time markers, or change the **Meeting start time** and **Meeting end time** settings, to change the proposed meeting date and/or time.

3. On the toolbar, click the **Send Update** button.

An updated meeting request is sent to each invited attendee.

To remove an invited attendee:

1. Open the scheduled meeting, and click the **Scheduling** tab.
2. In the **All Attendees** list, click the name of the person you want to remove.
3. Press the **DELETE** key, and then press **TAB**.

   The attendee is removed from the list.

4. On the toolbar, click the **Send Update** button.

A meeting cancellation is sent to the removed attendee.

To cancel a scheduled meeting:

1. Open the scheduled meeting.
2. On the **Actions** menu, click **Cancel Meeting**.

A message box appears, prompting you to send a cancellation notice to the attendees.

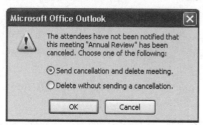

3   With the **Send cancellation and delete meeting** option selected, click **OK**.

4   On the toolbar, click the **Send** button.

The cancellation notice is sent to all remaining attendees, the Meeting form closes, and the meeting is removed from your Calendar.

Practice Exercise

In this exercise, you will update the time and attendee list for a meeting that you schedule.

NO practice files are required for this exercise.

Schedule a meeting and invite two friends or co-workers. Then change the meeting start time, and remove one of the people you invited from the attendee list.

Customize Calendar Settings

OO3C-2-3   The skills measured by this objective include the following:

■   Setting your Outlook Calendar options
■   Defining your available time

The Outlook Calendar is a versatile tool. You can quickly display traditional calendar pages for a variety of time periods. You can also display the calendar items in list format, grouped by type or category.

Using the Work Week option, you can specify the time periods during which you are generally available for work-related events. This helps people who are scheduling meetings with you to make them at a suitable time.

Setting Your Outlook Calendar Options

To help you stay on top of your schedule, you can view your Calendar for a variety of time periods:

■   Day view displays one day at a time, separated into half-hour increments.
■   Work Week view displays your defined work week in columnar format.
■   Week view displays one calendar week at a time.
■   Month view displays five weeks at a time. This is the default Calendar view.

To help you find the Calendar items you are looking for, Outlook offers a number of Calendar view modes:

- Day/Week/Month displays a calendar-like view of appointments, events, and meetings for the period of time you specify. This is the default view, and it includes the Date Navigator.

- Day/Week/Month With AutoPreview is the Day/Week/Month view with the addition of the first line of comment text for each Calendar item.

- Active Appointments displays a list of appointments and meetings scheduled for today and in the future, showing details in columns.

- Events displays a list of events, showing details in columns.

- Annual Events displays a list of annual events, showing details in columns.

- Recurring Appointments displays a list of recurring appointments, showing details in columns.

- By Category displays a list of all items, grouped by category, showing details in columns.

BE SURE TO display your Outlook Calendar before carrying out these steps.

To view only one day in the Calendar:

- On the toolbar, click the **Day** button.

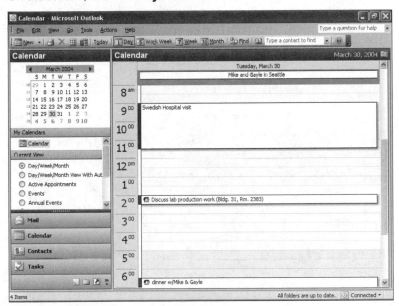

To view the current day in the Calendar:

- On the toolbar, click the **Go to Today** button.

Today

Go to Today

To view your defined work week in the Calendar:

● On the toolbar, click the **Work Week** button.

The Calendar displays the schedule for your currently defined work week. The work week is shaded in the Date Navigator.

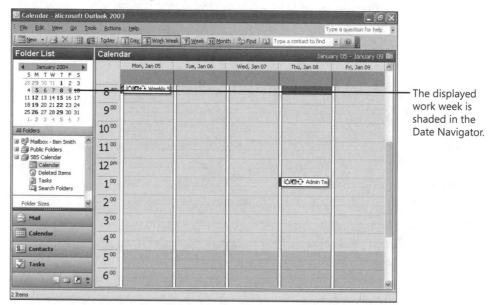

The displayed work week is shaded in the Date Navigator.

To view one week in the Calendar:

● On the toolbar, click the **Week** button.

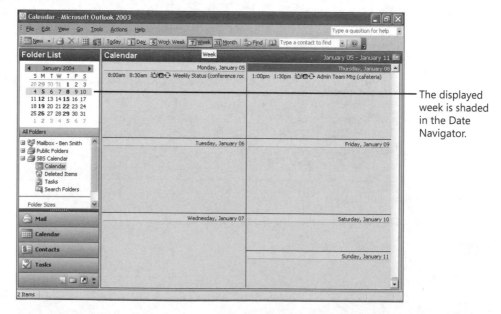

The displayed week is shaded in the Date Navigator.

To view one month in the Calendar:

● On the toolbar, click the **Month** button.

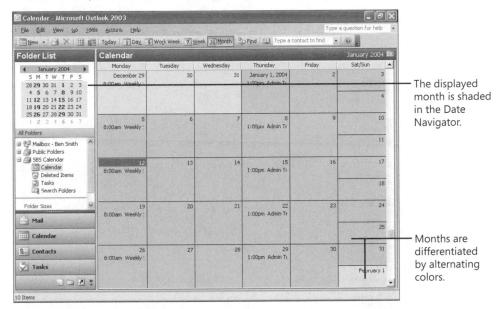

The displayed month is shaded in the Date Navigator.

Months are differentiated by alternating colors.

To display a specific day or week:

● In the Date Navigator:

■ Click the left and right arrows to scroll the month.

■ Click in the margin to the left of a specific week to display it.

■ Click a specific day to display it.

To display two months in the Date Navigator:

1 Point to the vertical frame divider between the Navigation Pane and the Calendar.

2 When the pointer changes to a double-headed arrow, drag the frame to the right.

To select the view mode:

● On the **View** menu, click **Arrange By**, **Current View**, and then **Day/Week/Month**, **Day/Week/Month With AutoPreview**, **Active Appointments**, **Events**, **Annual Events**, **Recurring Appointments**, or **By Category**.

Practice Exercise

In this exercise, you will look at different Calendar options.

NO practice files are required for this exercise.

In the Calendar, display the current month. Use the Date Navigator to display only the current week. Then change the Calendar view to display all the events on your Calendar. Depending on your installation, your country's holidays might be shown here. When you finish looking at the events, return to Day/Week/Month view and display today's schedule.

Defining Your Available Time

You can tell Outlook what your work schedule is so that other people can make appointments with you only during the times when you plan to be available. This defined time is called your work week. The work week is colored differently on your Calendar, and by default is the only time displayed to other people on your network who look at your Calendar.

By default, Outlook defines the work week as Monday through Friday from 8:00 A.M. to 5:00 P.M. You can change this to suit your needs—for instance, if you work a late shift or weekends.

Tip Outlook doesn't allow you to define a workday that crosses midnight, or to define different start and end times for different days.

BE SURE TO open your Outlook Calendar before carrying out these steps.

To define your default work week:

1   On the toolbar, click the **Work Week** button and scroll the calendar page so you can see the beginning and end of the work day.

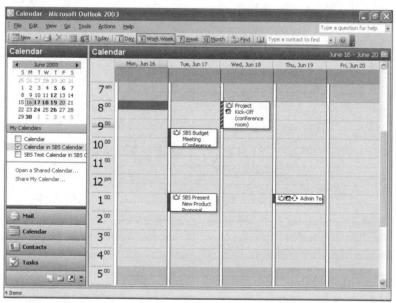

The Calendar displays your current work week. The working hours are shaded differently from the rest of the day.

2   On the **Tools** menu, click **Options**, and then click the **Preferences** tab.

3   In the Options dialog box, click **Calendar Options**.

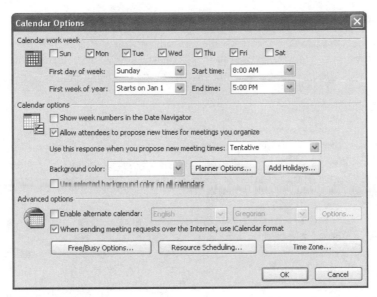

4   In the **Calendar work week** area, select the check boxes for the days you work, and clear the check boxes for the days you don't work.

5   Click the **Start time** down arrow, and click the time you start work.

6   Click the **End time** down arrow, and click the time you finish work.

7   Click **OK**, and in the Options dialog box, click **OK** again.

The Calendar displays your new default work week.

Practice Exercise

In this exercise, you will define your work week to reflect a schedule of four 10-hour days (with an hour for lunch).

NO practice files are required for this exercise.

In the Outlook Calendar, display your current work week and note the available times shown. In the Calendar Options dialog box, set your work week to Tuesday through Friday from 7:00 A.M. to 6:00 P.M. Save your settings and then redisplay the work week to confirm that your available times are updated.

Create, Modify, and Assign Tasks

O03C-2-4   The skills measured by this objective include the following:

■   Creating and modify a task

■   Assigning a task

You can create and store a list of tasks for any activity that you want to remember and track to completion. The tasks can be your own, or you can delegate them to other people.

See Also   For information about accepting and declining tasks, refer to O03C-1-6, "Accept, Decline, and Delegate Tasks."

Creating and Modifying a Task

For each task, you can specify a due date and a start date. A task is displayed in your Tasks list beginning on the start date. A task that is incomplete past its due date is displayed in red to indicate that it is overdue. You can also set the priority of a task—High for urgent tasks, and Normal and Low for less important tasks. And you can choose to set a reminder for a task, much like reminders for appointments.

Tip If you set reminders for tasks, you will start receiving reminder messages as task due dates approach. When a reminder pops up on your screen, you can respond in one of three ways. Clicking the Dismiss button closes the task, and you will receive no further reminders for this task. Clicking the Snooze button sets the reminder to appear again in a specified amount of time. You can also open the item, which closes the reminder.

Tasks can recur either at regular intervals or at intervals based on the date on which you mark the task complete. For example, you might create a task to review the status of a project every seven days. If you perform your review on a Friday and mark the task as complete, Outlook creates the next instance of the task as due on the following Friday. If you perform your next review on a Thursday, Outlook creates the next instance of the task as due on the following Thursday. A task that you create to recur at a regular interval will be regenerated at that interval regardless of the status of earlier instances of the task. For example, you might create a task for submitting your employees' expense reports to the finance department on the fifth of each month. When you mark the task as complete, regardless of the day, Outlook creates the next instance of the task and marks it as due on the fifth of the next month.

As you complete your tasks, you will want to remove them from your to-do list. You might find that some tasks are unnecessary and can be deleted. You might also acquire new tasks that other Outlook users assign to you, asking that you report back on your progress. Outlook makes it easy to manage changes to your tasks.

You can create and modify tasks in the Tasks folder or in the TaskPad that appears in the default Calendar view.

See Also For information about creating new tasks, refer to "Knowledge You Need Before Studying for This Exam" on page 646.

BE SURE TO display the Tasks folder before carrying out these steps.

To populate a task form:

1   Create a new task, and in the **Subject** box, type the task description.

2   If the task must be completed by a specific date, click the **Due date** down arrow, and then click that date.

3   If work on the task should start on a specific date, click the **Start date** down arrow, and then click that date.

4   Click the **Save and Close** button.

   🖫 Save and Close

The Task form closes. The new task appears in the Tasks folder.

To mark a task as recurring:

1 Open the Task form, and click the **Recurrence** button on the toolbar.

The Task Recurrence dialog box appears.

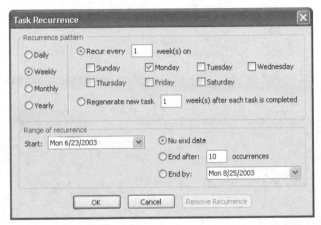

2 In the **Recurrence pattern** area, select the frequency and pattern of recurrence.

3 In the **Range of recurrence** area, select the **No end date**, **End after**, or **End by** option, specify the number of occurrences or the end date if appropriate, and then click **OK**.

4 Click the **Save and Close** button.

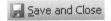

The Task form closes. The new task appears in the Tasks folder.

To set a reminder:

1 In the Task form, select the **Reminder** check box.

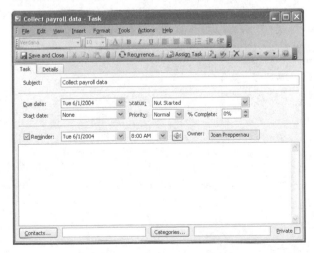

2 Type the date you want the reminder in the adjacent box, or click its down arrow and select the date.

3 Type the time you want the reminder in the next box, or click its down arrow and select the time.

Tip If you would like to select a special sound for your reminder, click the sound button, browse to the sound file you want to use, and then click OK.

To mark a task as complete:

Mark
Complete

● Open the Task form, and click the **Mark Complete** button on the toolbar.

● In the Simple List view of the **Tasks** list, or in the TaskPad, select the check box that appears to the left of the task.

Tip When you mark a recurring task as complete, the next instance of the task is added to your Tasks list.

To stop a task from recurring:

1 Open the Task form, and click the **Recurrence** button on the toolbar.

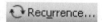

2 In the Task Recurrence dialog box, click the **Remove Recurrence** button.

3 On the Task form's toolbar, click the **Save and Close** button.

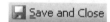

To delete a task:

1 In the **Tasks** list, click the task you want to delete.

Delete

2 On the toolbar, click the **Delete** button.

To delete a recurring task:

1 In the **Tasks** list, click the task you want to delete.

Delete

2 On the toolbar, click the **Delete** button.

3 In the message box, select the **Delete all** or **Delete this one** option, and click **OK**.

To change the due date of a task:

1   Open the Task form.

2   Click the **Due date** down arrow.

    The current due date is indicated in the Calendar by a yellow box.

3   In the drop-down calendar, click the revised due date.

    Tip   Click the arrow to the left or right of the month name to change the displayed month.

To update the status of a task:

1   Open the Task form.

2   Click the **Status** down arrow, and then click the revised status.

To change the date of a task reminder:

1   Open the Task form.

2   Be sure the **Reminder** check box is selected.

3   Click the first **Reminder** down arrow, and then click the date on which you want the reminder.

4   Click the second **Reminder** down arrow, and then click the time at which you want the reminder.

5   Click the **Save and Close** button.

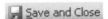

    The Task form closes. The updated task appears in the Tasks folder.

Practice Exercise

In this exercise, you will create a task, create a recurring task, and set a task reminder.

NO practice files are required for this exercise.

Create a new task called **Order new brochures**. Make the task due tomorrow. Create a new recurring task called **Submit timesheet**. Make it due every Friday at 5:00 P.M. from now on, with no end date. Set a reminder for the task to appear at 4:30 P.M. every Friday.

Assigning a Task

You can create a task in Outlook and assign it to someone else for completion. You might delegate a task to your assistant, or when your project depends on receiving something from another department, you might assign a task to your contact in that department.

Although you can update the tasks you create for yourself, when you assign a task to someone else, only that person can update it. However, you can keep a copy of the task in your Tasks list, and your copy will be updated as the other person updates the tasks. For example, if the other person changes the status or the percent complete, your copy of the task will be updated. You can also specify that you want to receive status reports for the task. Status reports are special e-mail messages that reflect the current status of a task.

Tip If you assign a task to more than one person, you cannot keep a copy of the task in your Tasks list. To be able to track the progress of tasks assigned to more than one person, create duplicate tasks, and assign each of them to one person.

BE SURE TO open your Outlook Tasks folder before carrying out these steps.

To assign a task while creating the task item:

1 Create a new task, and populate the task information you want.

2 On the toolbar, click the **Assign Task** button.

The Task form changes to include a To box.

3 In the **To** box, type the e-mail address of the person to whom you want to assign the task.

Tip The "Keep an updated copy of this task on my task list" and "Send me a status report when this task is complete" options are selected by default.

4 On the toolbar, click the **Send** button. If a message notifies you that the task reminder has been turned off, click **OK**.

The task request is sent. You will be notified when the assignee accepts or declines the task.

Practice Exercise

In this exercise, you will assign a task to a contact.

NO practice files are required for this exercise.

Create and populate a new task. Assign the task to a co-worker or friend (be sure to include a note to let the person know what you are doing).

O03C-2 Review

Number	Objective	Mastered
O03C-2-1	Create and modify appointments, meetings, and events	
	Adding an appointment or event to the Outlook Calendar	❏
	Inviting people and resources to a meeting	❏
O03C-2-2	Update, cancel, and respond to meeting requests	
	Responding to a meeting request	❏
	Updating or canceling a meeting	❏
O03C-2-3	Customize Calendar settings	
	Setting your Outlook Calendar options	❏
	Defining your available time	❏
O03C-2-4	Create, modify, and assign tasks	
	Creating and modifying a task	❏
	Assigning a task	❏

O03C-3

Organizing

The skills tested by this section of the Microsoft Office Specialist Outlook 2003 Exam all relate to ways you can organize your information with Outlook. Specifically, the following objectives are associated with this set of skills:

Number	Objective
O03C-3-1	Create and modify distribution lists
O03C-3-2	Link contacts to other items
O03C-3-3	Create and modify notes
O03C-3-4	Organize items
O03C-3-5	Organize items using folders
O03C-3-6	Search for items
O03C-3-7	Save items in different file formats
O03C-3-8	Assign items to categories
O03C-3-9	Preview and print items

Create and Modify Distribution Lists

O03C-3-1   The skills measured by this objective include the following:

- Creating a distribution list
- Modifying a distribution list

Address book entries can be for an individual contact or for a distribution list—a group of individual addresses stored as a single entity. For example, to facilitate communication within a team, you might create a distribution list including the addresses for all the people working on a particular project.

Creating a Distribution List

You can create a distribution list from existing contact entries, or you can add contact information directly to the distribution list. In this way, you can maintain a distribution list of people to whom you wouldn't necessarily send e-mail messages on a regular basis, thus keeping your Contacts folder smaller and easier to manage.

See Also   For information about creating new address book entries, refer to "Knowledge You Need Before Studying for This Exam" on page 646.

BE SURE TO create address book contact entries to add to your distribution list before carrying out these steps.

To create a distribution list of existing contact entries:

1 Click the **New** down arrow, and then click **Distribution List**.

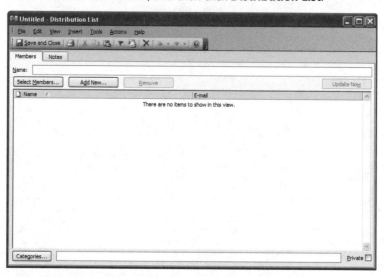

2 In the **Name** box, type a name for the new distribution list, and then click the **Select Members** button.

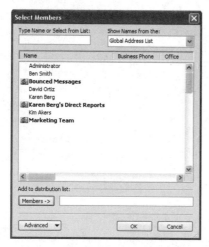

3 If necessary, click the **Show Names from the** down arrow, and click the address book from which you want to add the distribution list members.

4 In the **Name** list, double-click each name you want to add to the distribution list; or, select the names you want to add, and then click the **Members** button.

Tip To add multiple names to the distribution list simultaneously, click a name in the Name list, hold down the CTRL key, click any additional names you want to add, and then click the Members button.

5 Click **OK** to close the Select Members dialog box.

6 In the Distribution List form, click the **Save and Close** button.

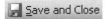

To create a distribution list of new contact entries:

1 Click the **New** down arrow, and then click **Distribution List**.

2 In the Distribution List form, type a name for the new distribution list in the **Name** box, and then click the **Add New** button.

3 Complete the information in the Add New Member dialog box:

- In the **Display name** box, type the new contact's name as you want it to appear in the distribution list.

- In the **E-mail address** box, type the contact's e-mail address.

- If you want to specify the format in which e-mail messages are sent to the contact you're adding, click the **Internet format** down arrow, and then click **Send Plain Text only** or **Send using Outlook Rich Text Format**. Otherwise, accept the default **Let Outlook decide the best sending format** option.

- If you want to add the new contact to your Contacts list (and automatically create an individual contact entry) select the **Add to Contacts** check box.

4 Click **OK** to close the Select Members dialog box.

The new contact is added to the distribution list, and to your Contacts list if you selected the Add to Contacts option.

5 For each additional distribution list member you want to add, click the **Add New** button and repeat step 3.

6 In the Distribution List form, click the **Save and Close** button.

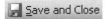

Tip You can create e-mail messages to a distribution list from the Address Book or from the Distribution List form, or you can type a distribution list name in the To or Cc box of a message just as you would for an individual e-mail address. Outlook matches what you type with the name in your address book and displays the name as bold and underlined to indicate that the name represents a distribution list rather than an individual address.

Practice Exercise

In this exercise, you will create a distribution list and send a message to it.

NO practice files are required for this exercise.

Open a new Distribution List form. Create a distribution list named **Important People**. Using the **Select Members** or **Add New Members** option, add three (or more) friends or co-workers to your new distribution list. Save and close the Important People distribution list, and then send a message to it, with a copy to yourself so you can see what your friends see when they receive your message.

Modifying a Distribution List

You can add members to an existing distribution list, delete members from a distribution list, or change distribution list member contact information at any time by opening the distribution list form. You can also remove distribution list member from specific e-mail messages—for example, if a person is on vacation and you don't want to clutter up his or her Inbox, or if you want to let the rest of the group know about an event (such as a surprise birthday party).

To modify a distribution list:

Address
Book

1 Click the **Address Book** button to open the Outlook address book.

2 If necessary, click the **Show Names from the** down arrow, and click **Contacts** (or the address book in which the distribution list is saved).

Properties

3 In the **Name** list, click the distribution list you want to modify, and then click the **Properties** button.

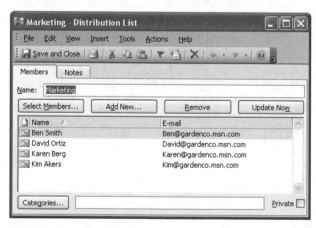

4 Make the modifications you want:

- ■ To add a contact entry from an address book, click the **Select Members** button, double-click the entry you want to add, and then click **OK**.

- ■ To add a contact that is not in an address book, click the **Add New** button, type the contact's display name and e-mail address, and then click **OK**.

- ■ To delete an entry, select the entry in the list, and then click the **Remove** button.

5 In the Distribution List form, click the **Save and Close** button.

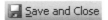

To temporarily modify a distribution list while sending a message:

1 Create a new message to the distribution list.

See Also For information about creating new messages, refer to "Knowledge You Need Before Studying for This Exam" on page 646.

Check
Names

2 If necessary, click the **Check Names** button to resolve the distribution list name.

3 Click the plus sign to the left of the distribution list name to expand the distribution list. If you see a warning like the one shown here, click **OK**.

4 In the expanded list of members, select the recipient who should not receive this e-mail message, and then click **Delete**.

Practice Exercise

In this exercise, you will modify a distribution list while creating a message.

NO practice files are required for this exercise.

> Create a distribution list, if you haven't already. Open a new Message form, and type the name of the distribution list in the **To** box. Then click the **Check Names** button to validate the address. Click the plus sign to the left of the distribution list name, and click **OK** if you see the warning that the list can't be compressed. When the list expands to display all the list members, delete a recipient's name. Then close the message without sending it.

Link Contacts to Other Items

O03C-3-2   The skills measured by this objective include the following:

■ Linking an Outlook item to a contact entry

Keeping track of what's been done or needs to be done in connection with a particular contact can be challenging. You can link contact entries to other Outlook items including appointments or events, journal entries, notes, and e-mail messages.

Linking an Outlook Item to a Contact Entry

You can use Outlook Notes to record information about your dealings with contacts. For example, after a phone call with a client, you might link a note you created during that call to the contact information for that client. You can also forward that note to a co-worker who is working with the same client.

BE SURE TO create the contact entry to which you want to link before carrying out these steps.

To link a message to a contact entry:

1 Right-click the message you want to link, click **Options** on the shortcut menu, and then click the **Contacts** button.

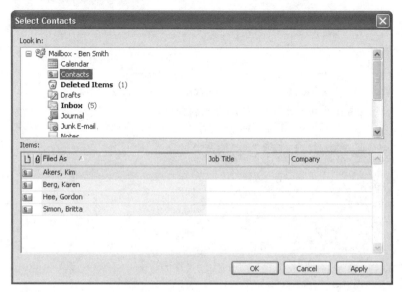

2 In the **Items** list, click the contact entry to which you want to link, and then click **OK**.

Tip To select multiple contacts, click the first contact entry, hold down the CTRL key, and click the additional entries.

The contact's name appears in the Message Options dialog box, indicating that this message is linked to the contact entry.

3 In the Message Options dialog box, click the **Close** button.

Tip E-mail messages sent to a contact are automatically linked to that contact entry.

To link a calendar item to a contact entry:

1 Open the appointment, event, or meeting, and click the **Contacts** button in the lower-left corner.

2 In the **Items** list of the Select Contacts dialog box, click the contact entry to which you want to link, and then click **OK**.

3 Close the appointment, event, or meeting.

To link one contact entry to another:

1 Open the contact entry, maximize the window if necessary, and click the **Contacts** button in the lower-left corner.

2 In the **Items** list of the Select Contacts dialog box, click the contact entry to which you want to link, and then click **OK**.

3 Close the contact entry.

To link a task to a contact entry:

1   Open the task, and click the **Contacts** button in the lower-left corner.

2   In the **Items** list of the Select Contacts dialog box, click the contact entry to which you want to link, and then click **OK**.

3   Close the task.

To link a note to a contact entry:

1   Open the note you want to link.

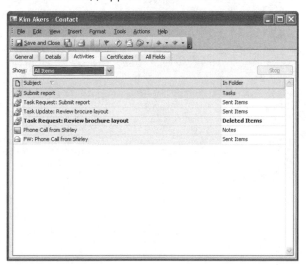

Note icon

2   In the upper-left corner of the note, click the **Note** icon, and then click **Contacts** in the drop-down list.

3   In the Contacts for Note dialog box, click the **Contacts** button.

4   In the **Items** list of the Select Contacts dialog box, click the contact entry to which you want to link, and then click **OK**.

5   In the Contacts for Note dialog box, click the **Close** button.

6   Close the note.

To view the items linked to a contact entry:

● Open the contact entry, and click the **Activities** tab.

   The linked item(s) appear in the Activities list.

Practice Exercise

In this exercise, you will link items to a contact entry.

NO practice files are required for this exercise.

Create a contact entry for yourself if you haven't already done so, or open your Contact form if you already have one. Click the **Details** tab and enter your birth date in the **Birthday** box. Then click the **Activities** tab. Wait for the list of activities to generate (the list might be quite long if you have been using Outlook for a while). Note that your birthday appears in the **Activities** list—it is automatically linked as an activity when you enter it on the **Details** tab. Click the **Show** down arrow, and then click **Notes**. Without closing your Contact form, open the Notes folder and create a new note. Type **Remember to study for the Microsoft Office Specialist Outlook exam!** Link the note to your own contact entry, and then save and close it. Return to your Contact form to verify that the note appears in the filtered list on the **Activities** tab. Close your Contact form when you're done.

Create and Modify Notes

O03C-3-3 The skills measured by this objective include the following:

■ Creating and editing notes

You can use Outlook's Notes feature to record questions, ideas, reminders, messages, or anything else that you might otherwise write down. Because you can leave notes open on your screen even while Outlook is minimized, they are especially useful for storing small bits of information that you might need as you work. For example, you might open a Note form to record your notes during a phone conference, or you might use a note to jot down useful references you find while doing research on the Web.

Creating and Editing Notes

You can create notes from scratch or by dragging information to the Notes icon in the Navigation Pane.

See Also For more information about creating new notes, refer to "Knowledge You Need Before Studying for This Exam" on page 646.

BE SURE TO open the Notes folder before carrying out these steps.

To create a new note:

1 Open a new Note form, and type the information you want to save in the note.

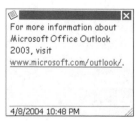

Tip If your note includes a Uniform Resource Locater (URL) or Web site address, a corresponding hyperlink is created so you can click the URL to open the Web site.

2 To save your note, click the **Close** button.

Close

Your note is saved in the Notes folder, and the first line appears as the note's title.

To edit an existing note:

Close

- Open the note, make whatever changes you want, and then click the **Close** button.

To delete a note:

- Select the note, and press the **DELETE** key.

Practice Exercise

In this exercise, you will create and edit a note.

NO practice files are required for this exercise.

Open a new Note form. In the body of the note, type **Monday Conference Call**, press **ENTER** twice, and then type **Attending: Stan, Jane, Joanne, and Barbara**. Press **ENTER** and then type **Agenda: What are this week's sales goals?** Close and save the note. Open the **Monday Conference Call** note, click at the end of the second line of text, press **ENTER** to insert a new line, and type **Absent: Joanne**. Then remove Joanne from the list of attendees. Press **CTRL+END** to move the insertion point to the end of the note contents. Press **ENTER** and type **Top salesperson this week wins a trip!** Then close the note and save your changes.

Organize Items

O03C-3-4   The skills measured by this objective include the following:

- Adding and deleting fields from folder views
- Sorting Outlook items
- Filtering messages
- Organizing Outlook items by using colors
- Organizing e-mail messages by using rules
- Organizing Outlook items by using views

If you use Outlook on a regular basis, it won't take long for you to accumulate a variety of information. Outlook includes a number of methods for personalizing the way you view and sort information so that you can more easily find what you're looking for. You can change the information that is displayed in individual folders, change the way it is displayed, and manually or automatically sort and label items.

Adding and Deleting Fields from Folder Views

You can collect a large amount of information in an Outlook item. Not all the information is displayed by default in every folder view. You can customize the information shown by adding or removing fields from the folder view.

Tip   To change the order of columns in any view, simply drag the column headings to the locations you prefer. While you are dragging a column heading, red arrows indicate where the column will appear when you release the mouse button.

BE SURE TO open the folder view you want to change before carrying out these steps.

To add a field to a folder view:

1 On the **View** menu, click **Arrange By**, **Current View**, and then **Customize Current View**.

2 In the Customize View dialog box, click the **Fields** button.

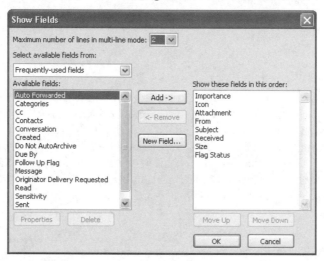

3 In the **Available fields** list, click the field you want to add, and then click the **Add** button.

4 In the **Show these fields in this order** list, drag the fields into the order you want, and then click **OK**.

5 In the Customize View: Messages dialog box, click **OK**.

To remove a field from a folder view:

1 On the **View** menu, click **Arrange By**, **Current View**, and then **Customize Current View**.

2 In the Customize View dialog box, click the **Fields** button.

3 In the **Show these fields in this order** list, click the field you want to remove, click **Remove**, and then click **OK**.

4 In the Customize View: Messages dialog box, click **OK**.

To remove a field from a folder view by dragging:

● Drag the heading of the column you want to remove downward, and release the mouse button when a large black X appears over the heading.

Practice Exercise

In this exercise, you will customize the information displayed in your Contacts folder.

NO practice files are required for this exercise.

Open your Contacts folder and view it as a phone list. Remove extraneous headings to display only the *Full Name*, *Company*, *Business Phone*, and *Business Fax* fields. Then add the *Mobile Phone* field back to the display.

Sorting Outlook Items

Regardless of the view you choose, you can group and sort your Outlook items by any column simply by clicking the column heading. By default, messages in your Inbox are grouped by the received date in descending order—the most recent messages appear at the top of the list. Messages you received this week are grouped by day. Earlier messages are grouped by weeks or longer periods. You can sort columns in either ascending or descending order. You can also group your messages by the contents of any column—by the sender of the message, for instance, or by the subject.

A downward-pointing arrow in a column header indicates that the folder items are sorted in descending order by that column. An upward-pointing arrow indicates that items are sorted in ascending order.

When items are grouped, the total number of items and the number of unread items in each group is indicated in parentheses following the conversation subject.

BE SURE TO open the folder of items you want to sort before carrying out these steps.

To sort Outlook items in a list view:

- Click the heading of the column by which you want to sort. Click the heading again to reverse the sort order.

Practice Exercise

In this exercise, you will sort the messages in your Inbox.

NO practice files are required for this exercise.

Open your Inbox and send yourself a new message. Sort your messages by the date they were received so that your new message appears at the top of the list. Then sort your received messages by sender and locate the message you sent to yourself.

Filtering E-Mail Messages

As messages accumulate in your Inbox, it can be a challenge to find specific messages or groups of messages. To make locating individual messages easier, you can filter your messages to display only those messages that meet common criteria, helping you identify a specific collection of messages.

BE SURE TO open your Inbox before beginning this exercise.

To manually filter messages:

1 On the **View** menu, click **Arrange By** and then **Custom**. Then click the **Filter** button.

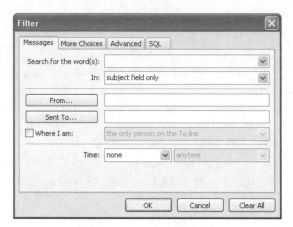

2   In the **Search for the word(s)** box, type the word or words contained in the messages you want to display.

3   Click the **In** down arrow, and then click **subject field and message body** to search the full text of each message.

   Tip   If you want to filter on items other than text, select those options now.

4   Click **OK** in the Filter dialog box, and then click **OK** in the Customize View dialog box.

   The folder displays only those messages meeting the specified criteria.

To define a new view to filter messages:

1   Display the view on which you want to base your filtered view.

2   On the **View** menu, click **Arrange By**, **Current View**, and then **Define Views**.

3   In the Custom View Organizer dialog box, click the **Copy** button.

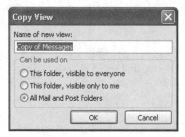

4   In the **Name of new view** box, type a name for the new view, such as *Filtered for Show*, and click **OK**.

5   In the Customize View dialog box, click the **Filter** button.

6   In the **Search for the word(s)** box, type the word or words contained in the messages you want to display, and click **OK**.

7   In the Customize View dialog box, click **OK**.

8   In the Custom View Organizer dialog box, with the new view selected in the **View Name** list, click the **Apply View** button.

To remove the filter:

● On the **View** menu, click **Arrange By**, **Current View**, and then click the view you want.

Practice Exercise

In this exercise, you will apply a filter to your Inbox.

NO practice files are required for this exercise.

Open your Inbox. Apply a filter so that only messages containing the word *help* are displayed. If the filter shows no results, send yourself a message with the subject line **Help me find this message!** and watch it appear in the filtered view when it is received. Then remove the filter.

Organizing Outlook Items by Using Colors

There are many ways to use color to organize your Outlook items:

■ You can display e-mail message header information in any of the 16 system colors to help you easily distinguish messages with certain characteristics. For example, you might show all messages from your boss in red, and all messages from the finance department in green. You can also choose to have messages that were sent only to you displayed in a different color than messages sent to multiple recipients.

■ You can color-code appointments, meetings, and events, choosing from one of ten colors. Each color is identified with a preset label: None, Important, Business, Personal, Vacation, Must Attend, Travel Required, Needs Preparation, Birthday, Anniversary, and Phone Call. If the default labels don't fit your needs, you can edit them to suit.

■ You can change the color of notes from the default yellow to white, pink, green, or blue. There are no default meanings associated with the colors, but you can create your own system; for example, coloring business-related notes yellow, finance-related notes green, and personal notes pink.

BE SURE TO open the appropriate folder before carrying out these steps.

To color-code messages:

1   On the **Tools** menu, click **Organize**.

Tip   The Ways to Organize pane is available for the Mail, Calendar, Contacts, Tasks, and Notes folders. The available options vary by folder.

2   In the Ways to Organize pane, click **Using Colors**.

3   To change the color of messages sent to or from specific people, in the **Color Messages** area:

- Click the first down arrow, and then click **from** or **sent to**.

- In the second box, type the name or e-mail address of the message sender or recipient whose messages you want to color-code.

- Click the second down arrow, and click the color you want to apply to the specified messages.

- Click the **Apply Color** button.

Messages to or from the specified recipient or sender are now displayed in the selected color. New messages meeting the criteria will automatically have the color applied.

4   To change the color of messages with no other recipients, click the **only to me** down arrow, select the color you want the messages to appear, and then click **Turn on**.

To view the applied color-coding rules:

● In the Ways to Organize pane, click the **Automatic Formatting** button.

To color-code a note:

● Right-click the note whose color you want to change, click **Color** on the shortcut menu, and then click **Blue**, **Green**, **Pink**, **Yellow**, or **White**.

To organize notes by color:

● On the Notes folder **View** menu, click **Arrange By**, **Current View**, and then **By Color**.

To manually color-code a Calendar item:

● In the Calendar, right-click the item you want to label, click **Label** on the shortcut menu, and then click the label you want.

Calendar
Coloring

● Select the appointment, event, or meeting you want to label, click the **Calendar Coloring** button, and then click the label you want.

To change the label associated with a calendar color:

Calendar
Coloring

1 In the Calendar folder, click the **Calendar Coloring** button, and then click **Edit Labels**.

2 In the Edit Calendar Labels dialog box, select the label you want to change, replace the text, and then click **OK**.

To automatically color-code Calendar items:

Calendar
Coloring

1 In the Calendar folder, click the **Calendar Coloring** button, click **Automatic Formatting**, and then click **Add**.

2 In the Edit Calendar Labels dialog box, select the label you want to change, replace the text, and then click **OK**.

Practice Exercise

In this exercise, you will change the color of messages sent only to you.

NO practice files are required for this exercise.

Open your Inbox, and then open the Ways to Organize pane. On the **Using Colors** tab, instruct Outlook to color-code the header text of all messages sent only to you as red, so they stand out in your Inbox.

Organizing E-Mail Messages by Using Rules

You can instruct Outlook to evaluate your e-mail messages in the same way that you would evaluate them, and to make corresponding decisions about what to do with them. These instructions are called rules. You can create rules that process messages as they arrive or as you send them; checking for names, words, attachments, categories, or other message conditions on which you might base processing decisions. After the messages are evaluated, Outlook can automatically move, copy, delete, forward, redirect, reply to, or otherwise process messages that meet the criteria you set.

Rules that are applied to messages as they are received or processed by the Exchange server are called server rules. Rules that are applied to messages on your computer are called client rules.

Tip You cannot use Outlook rules to filter messages to an HTTP e-mail account.

BE SURE TO open your Inbox and have an active connection to your Exchange server before carrying out these steps.

To create a rule to move messages to a folder:

Tip You can create many different types of rules. Adapt the specific selections shown here to suit your needs.

1 On the **Tools** menu, click **Rules and Alerts**.

2 In the Rules and Alerts dialog box, click the **New Rule** button.

3   In the **Select a template** list, click **Move messages from someone to a folder**, and then click **Next**.

4   In the **Select condition(s)** list, select the check box(es) of the condition(s) for which you want the rule to be applied, clear all others, and then click **Next**.

The "Edit the rule description" box is updated to reflect the change. The underlined words in the description are values that you must specify to complete the rule.

5   In the **Edit the rule description** box, click each underlined word or phrase, supply the requested information, and then click **Next**.

6   In the **Select action(s)** list, select the check box(es) of the action(s) you want the rule to invoke under the specified condition(s) and clear all others. In the **Edit the rule description** box, click any new underlined word or phrase, supply the requested information, and then click **Next**.

7   In the **Select exception(s)** list, select the check box(es) of the exception(s) to the rule and clear all others. In the **Edit the rule description** box, click any new underlined word or phrase, supply the requested information, and then click **Next**.

8   Select the **Run this rule now on messages already in "Inbox"** check box, and then click the **Finish** button.

9   In the Rules and Alerts dialog box, click **OK**.

The rule is now active, and Outlook applies it to the messages in the Inbox.

Practice Exercise

In this exercise, you will create a rule that alerts you to incoming messages.

NO practice files are required for this exercise.

Open the Rules and Alerts dialog box. Create a new rule that alerts you with a sound when you receive an e-mail message from yourself. While you're creating the rule, have a look at the other available rule and alert options. Send yourself a message to test the alert, and then modify the rule so a sound alerts you to all incoming messages. Wait to receive one or more new messages to test the rule. When you want to, delete the rule.

Organizing Outlook Items by Using Views

You can choose different ways of displaying the items stored in each Outlook folder to make the information contained therein most accessible to you. If you change views frequently, you can display a list of available views in the Navigation Pane so you can quickly switch between them.

Tip   You can customize the existing contact views or define your own view from scratch. To get started, on the View menu, click Current View and then Customize Current View or Define Views.

BE SURE TO open the appropriate folder before carrying out these steps.

To display the Current View list:

●   On the **View** menu, click **Arrange By** and then **Show Views In Navigation Pane**.

Tip   The Current View list for each folder lists only the views available for that folder.

To organize messages by using views:

●   With the Inbox or other Mail folder displayed, on the **View** menu, click **Arrange By**, **Current View**, and then **Messages**, **Messages with AutoPreview**, **Last Seven Days**, **Unread Messages in This Folder**, **Sent To**, or **Message Timeline**.

●   In the **Current View** list, select the view option you want.

To organize calendar items by using views:

- With the Calendar folder displayed, on the **View** menu, click **Arrange By**, **Current View**, and then **Day/Week/Month**, **Day/Week/Month View With AutoPreview**, **Active Appointments**, **Events**, **Annual Events**, **Recurring Appointments**, or **By Category**.

- In the **Current View** list, select the view option you want.

To organize contact entries by using views:

- With the Contacts folder displayed, on the **View** menu, click **Arrange By**, **Current View**, and then **Address Cards**, **Detailed Address Cards**, **Phone List**, **By Category**, **By Company**, **By Location**, or **By Follow-up Flag**.

- In the **Current View** list, select the view option you want.

To organize tasks by using views:

- With the Tasks folder displayed, on the **View** menu, click **Arrange By**, **Current View**, and then **Simple List**, **Detailed List**, **Active Tasks**, **Next Seven Days**, **Overdue Tasks**, **By Category**, **Assignment**, **By Person Responsible**, **Completed Tasks**, or **Task Timeline**.

- In the **Current View** list, select the view option you want.

To organize notes by using views:

- With the Tasks folder displayed, on the **View** menu, click **Arrange By**, **Current View**, and then **Icons**, **Notes List**, **Last Seven Days**, **By Category**, or **By Color**.

- In the **Current View** list, select the view option you want.

To return to the default view:

1. On the **View** menu, click **Arrange By**, **Current View**, and then **Define Views**.
2. In the Define Views dialog box, click the **Reset** button, click **OK**, and then click **Close**.

Practice Exercise

In this exercise, you will customize your view of each of the main Outlook folders to ensure that you have the information you want available.

NO practice files are required for this exercise.

Open your Inbox and display the **Current View** list. Select each view option in turn and note the information available. Then select your favorite option. Repeat this for the Calendar, Contacts, Tasks, and Notes folders.

Organize Items Using Folders

O03C-3-5   The skills measured by this objective include the following:

- Organizing messages in folders
- Archiving Outlook items

Creating folders to organize your messages helps you avoid an accumulation of unrelated messages in your Inbox. For example, you can create a folder for each project you're working on and store all messages regarding a particular project in its own folder.

Tip To manage a list of many tasks, you can organize your tasks in folders. To move a task to a folder, simply drag it from the Tasks list to a Task Items folder in the Folder List. (If you drag the task to a Mail, Calendar, Contact, or Note Items folder, a Message, Meeting, Contact, or Note form opens with the task's subject entered in the form.)

See Also For information about creating and deleting Search Folders, refer to O03C-3-6, "Search for Items."

Organizing E-Mail Messages in Folders

After you create the folder structure in which you want to organize your messages, you can move messages to the folders manually or have Outlook move them for you.

See Also For information about creating new folders, refer to "Knowledge You Need Before Studying for This Exam" on page 646. For more information about automatically moving messages, refer to O03C-3-4, "Organize Items."

BE SURE TO open your Inbox before carrying out these steps.

To create a new folder:

1　On the **File** menu, click **New** and then **Folder**.

2　In the Create New Folder dialog box, type the name of your new folder in the **Name** box.

3　In the **Select where to place the folder** list, click the folder in which you want to create the new folder (usually the Mailbox or Inbox), and then click **OK**.

To move a message to a folder:

● Open the folder in which the message appears, and drag the message to the destination folder in the Navigation Pane.

● Right-click the message, click **Move to Folder**, and in the Move Items dialog box, click the destination folder.

To move a folder:

● Drag the folder to the destination (parent) folder.

To rename a folder:

● Right-click the folder, click **Rename**, type the new name, and press **ENTER**.

Delete

To delete a folder:

1　Click the folder, and then click the **Delete** button.

2　When Outlook asks you to confirm that you want to delete the folder, click **Yes**.

   Tip When you delete a folder, any messages contained within that folder are also deleted.

Practice Exercise

In this exercise, you will organize messages by moving them to a folder.

NO practice files are required for this exercise.

In your Inbox, create a new folder named **Practice Folder**. Send yourself an e-mail message. When you receive the message, drag it to the new folder. Rename the folder **Messages From Me**. Then delete the folder and the message inside it.

Archiving Outlook Items

As messages accumulate in your Inbox and other message folders, you might need to consider other ways to store them to reduce the storage space you're using. For example, you might want to archive all messages sent or received before a certain date. Archiving messages in a separate Outlook message file helps reduce clutter and the size of your primary message file, while still allowing easy access to archived messages from within Outlook.

You can archive messages manually or automatically. When archived messages are moved to a separate message file, the messages are removed from their original folder. By default, Outlook automatically archives messages in all folders at regular intervals to a location determined by your operating system. You can change the default global settings for the AutoArchive function and specify varying archive settings for specific folders. Archive settings selected for a specific folder override the global settings for that folder. If you don't specify AutoArchive settings for a folder, Outlook uses the global settings.

BE SURE TO open your Inbox before carrying out these steps.

To view and change the automatic archive settings for your mailbox:

1   On the **Tools** menu, click **Options**, and then click the **Other** tab.

2   In the Options dialog box, click the **AutoArchive** button.

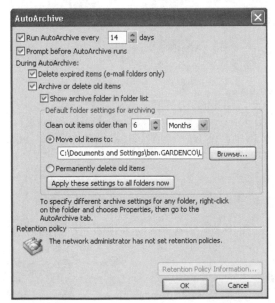

3 Review your AutoArchive default settings—particularly note the interval at which the archive will happen, the age at which items will be archived, and the location in the **Move old items to** box.

4 Change any settings you want, click **OK** to close the AutoArchive dialog box, and then click **OK** to close the Options dialog box.

To modify the automatic archive settings for an individual folder:

1 Right-click the folder you want to change, and then click **Properties** on the shortcut menu.

2 In the Properties dialog box, click the **AutoArchive** tab.

3 Select the **Do not archive items in this folder**, **Archive items in this folder using the default settings**, or **Archive this folder using these settings** option.

4 If you selected the **Archive this folder using these settings** option, change any settings you want:

   ■ In the **Clean out items older than** box, specify the number of months, weeks, or days of the oldest item you want in the folder.

   ■ Select the option for the way you want to handle old items.

5 Click **OK** to close the dialog box and apply your changes to the individual folder.

Practice Exercise

In this exercise, you will adjust your AutoArchive settings.

NO practice files are required for this exercise.

Open the AutoArchive dialog box and direct Outlook to archive your account every two weeks. Then change the AutoArchive settings for your Sent Items folder to archive your sent mail every seven days.

Search for Items

OO3C-3-6   The skills measured by this objective include the following:

■ Finding messages
■ Using Search Folders

If you don't know the particulars of a message that you're looking for, such as the sender, subject, or date received, or if you don't know what folder the message is stored in, it can be difficult to find a specific message by sorting. When you don't know precisely what you're looking for, Outlook's Find feature helps you search with a minimum amount of information.

If you frequently need to find messages that share certain characteristics, you can create virtual Search Folders that are automatically updated.

Finding E-Mail Messages

If you are having trouble locating a particular message in your Inbox or another message folder, you can search for it using Outlook's Find or Advanced Find features. You can look for messages in a single folder, a group of folders you select, or all your folders. You can instruct Outlook to search through the text of every message or only the Subject field.

BE SURE TO display your mailbox before carrying out these steps.

To display the Find pane:

- On the toolbar, click the **Find** button.

  The Find pane appears above the folder contents.

To find Outlook items containing specific text:

1 Display the Find pane.

2 In the **Look for** box, type the word or phrase contained in the items you want to find.

3 Click the **Search In** down arrow, and click the folder you want to search; if the folder is not shown in the drop-down list, click **Choose Folders**, select the check boxes of the folders you want to search, select the **Search subfolders** check box if you want, and then click **OK**.

4 Click the **Find Now** button.

To find Outlook items assigned to a category:

1 Display the Find pane.

2 Click the **Options** button, and then click **Advanced Find** in the **Options** drop-down list.

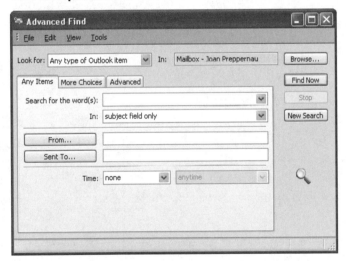

3 Click the **Look for** down arrow, and then click **Any type of Outlook item**, **Appointments and Meetings**, **Contacts**, **Files**, **Journal entries**, **Messages**, **Notes**, or **Tasks**.

  The available options change depending on your selection.

4 Click the **More Choices** tab, and then click the **Categories** button.

5 In the Categories dialog box, select the check box in the **Available categories** list of the category you want to find, and then click **OK**.

  The Categories dialog box closes, and you return to the Advanced Find window. Your category appears in the Categories box.

721

6   Click the **Find Now** button.

Outlook searches your messages and displays the matching items in a list at the bottom of the Advanced Find window.

Practice Exercise

In this exercise, you will find a message using the Find feature, and then revise your search using the Advanced Find feature.

NO practice files are required for this exercise.

Use the Find pane to locate all the messages you've sent that contain the phrase *thank you*. If you don't get any results, try a different phrase that you commonly use. Then revise the search to display only the messages sent in the past week.

Using Search Folders

Search Folders, like Outlook's Find feature, show all the files that match a set of search criteria, and can show files from different folders together in one place. Unlike a search conducted using the Find feature, when you create a Search Folder, it becomes part of your mailbox and is always kept up to date.

The default Outlook 2003 installation includes three Search Folders:

■ The *For Follow Up* folder displays messages flagged for follow-up.

■ The *Large Mail* folder displays messages larger than 100 kilobytes (KB), grouped by size as *Large (100 – 500 KB)*, *Very Large (500 KB – 1 MB)*, *Huge (1 – 5 MB)*, and *Enormous (> 5 MB)*.

■ The *Unread Mail* folder displays messages that are marked as unread.

Although Search Folders look like any other Outlook folders, they are actually virtual folders. Each message in your mailbox is stored in only one Outlook folder (such as your Inbox), but it might appear in many Search Folders. Changing or deleting a message in a Search Folder changes or deletes the message in the Outlook folder where it is stored.

BE SURE TO open your Outlook mailbox before carrying out these steps.

To view a default Search Folder:

● In the **All Mail Folders** list, click the plus sign next to *Search Folders*, and then click **For Follow Up**, **Large Mail**, or **Unread Mail**.

● In the **Favorite Folders** list, click the **Unread Mail** or **For Follow Up** folder.

Tip   Depending on your previous use of Outlook, the default Search Folders might be empty.

To create a new Search Folder:

1   In the **All Mail Folders** list, right-click **Search Folders**, and then click **New Search Folder** on the shortcut menu.

2   In the **Select a Search Folder** list, click the type of mail you want to show in the new folder.

Depending on your selection, a text box and Choose button might appear in the Customize Search Folder area at the bottom of the dialog box.

3   If appropriate, click the **Choose** button and specify the necessary criteria.

4   When the information in the New Search Folder dialog box is complete, click **OK**.

To change the parameters of an existing Search Folder:

1   Right-click the Search Folder you want to change, and then click **Customize this Search Folder** on the shortcut menu.

2   To change the folder name, select the existing text in the **Name** box, press **DELETE**, and type the new name.

3   To change the criteria of the search, click the **Criteria** button.

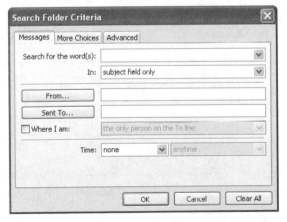

4   Enter the search criteria you want on the **Messages**, **More Choices**, and **Advanced** tabs, and then click **OK**.

5 To change the mail folders included in the search, click the **Browse** button.

6 In the Select Folder(s) dialog box, select the check boxes of the folders you want to include, and then click **OK**.

7 In the Customize dialog box, click **OK**.

To delete a Search Folder:

● Right-click the Search Folder you want to delete, and then click **Delete** on the shortcut menu.

    Tip Deleting a Search Folder does not delete the contents of the folder.

Practice Exercise

In this exercise, you will use and create Search Folders.

NO practice files are required for this exercise.

Use the default Search Folder to locate all the unread e-mail messages in your Outlook mailbox. Create a new, custom Search Folder called **Small Messages** displaying all e-mail messages smaller than 5 KB. Display the folder, and on the status bar in the lower-left corner of the Outlook window, note the number of items in the folder. Then change the name of the folder to **Really Small Messages** and change the search criteria to display messages smaller than 2 KB. Again, display the folder and note the number of items shown.

Save Items in Different File Formats

O03C-3-7   The skills measured by this objective include the following:

■ Saving Outlook items in different file formats

Sometimes a message will contain information that you want to save or use in another program. You can save messages, calendar items, contact entries, tasks, and notes to your computer as individual files.

Saving E-Mail Messages in Other Formats

You can save a message as a plain text file, which most programs can open or import. Or you might save a message as an HTML document, which would make it easier to post it to a team portal or Web site.

BE SURE TO locate or create the folder to which you want to save the Outlook item before carrying out these steps.

To save an Outlook item as a file:

1 Select the message you want to save, and on the **File** menu, click **Save As**.

    Tip Your Save As dialog box will show your My Documents folder or the last folder in which you saved an Outlook item. If you have file extensions turned on, the name in the File Name box will include the extension (for example *Order status.htm*).

2 Browse to the folder in which you want to save the item.

3 In the **File name** box, specify the name for the file.

Tip By default, the file name is the same as the item's name or subject.

4   Click the **Save as type** down arrow, and click the type of file you want (available file types vary based on the original item format).

5   Click **Save**.

Practice Exercise

In this exercise, you will save a contact entry as a file on your computer.

NO practice files are required for this exercise.

Create a contact entry for yourself if you haven't already done so. Save your Contact form as a Rich Text Format file in your My Documents folder. Then in Windows Explorer, browse to the file and open it.

Assign Items to Categories

O03C-3-8   The skills measured by this objective include the following:

■   Assigning Outlook items to categories

Another way to organize and find items is to assign them to categories. With categories, you group items by a common characteristic. Outlook includes a set of predefined categories, and you can also create your own. For example, you might assign all messages about invoices and payments to the Finance category, or you might create a Payroll category for all messages related to timesheets and paychecks.

Assigning Outlook Items to Categories

You can assign all types of Outlook items to categories. There are many ways to assign items to categories, but there is one simple process that applies to all types of items.

BE SURE TO open the appropriate folder before carrying out these steps.

To assign an Outlook item to an existing category:

1   Right-click the item, and click **Categories** on the shortcut menu.

2   In the **Available categories** list, select the check box of the category you want, and then click **OK**.

To assign an Outlook item to a new category:

1   Right-click the item, and click **Categories** on the shortcut menu.

2   In the **Item(s) belong to these categories** box, type the name you want for the new category, and then click the **Add to List** button.

The category is added to the "Available categories" list and selected.

3   In the Categories dialog box, click **OK**.

To organize Outlook items by categories:

●   On the **View** menu, click **Arrange By**, **Current View**, and then **By Category**.

Practice Exercise

In this exercise, you will assign contact entries to a category and then view them.

NO practice files are required for this exercise.

Open your Contacts folder. Create contact entries for yourself and for one or more of your relatives if you haven't already done so. Create a new category called **Family** and assign the contact entries for you and your family members to the new category. Then view your Contacts folder by category, and locate the contact entries for your family members.

Preview and Print Items

O03C-3-9   The skills measured by this objective include the following:

- Previewing and printing an e-mail message
- Previewing and printing your Outlook Calendar
- Previewing and printing contact information

Many Outlook users manage a large amount of information in Outlook: e-mail messages, contact information, calendar information, general notes, and task lists. In addition to having information available electronically on a desktop, laptop, or handheld computer, it is sometimes necessary or desirable to have a hard copy, or printout, of the information stored by Outlook.

Previewing and Printing an E-Mail Message

There might be occasions when you need a hard copy, or printout, of an e-mail message. For example, you might need to print the directions to the location of an appointment or distribute copies of a message at a meeting. With Outlook, you can print your e-mail messages in much the same way you would any other document.

Depending on the format (HTML, Rich Text, or Plain Text) of the message you want to print, you can set a number of page setup options, including paper size, margins, and orientation. You can also use Print Preview to see how a message will appear when printed.

BE SURE TO install a printer before carrying out these steps.

To see how an e-mail message will look when printed:

- On the **File** menu, click **Print Preview**.

    Tip   Print Preview is not available for Outlook items formatted as HTML.

To change the page setup before printing:

1   On the message window's **File** menu, click **Page Setup** and then **Memo Style**.

2   Change any settings you want:

- In the **Paper** area, select the paper size and source.
- In the **Headers and Footers** area, type any text you want to appear at the top or bottom of the message printout.
- In the **Orientation** area, select the **Portrait** or **Landscape** option.
- In the **Margins** area, change the **Left**, **Right**, **Top**, or **Bottom** margin.

3   Click **OK** to close the Page Setup dialog box and save your changes.

4   On the toolbar, click the **Print** button.

Print

To change the print options:

1   On the message window's **File** menu, click **Print**.

2   Change any settings you want:

- In the **Select Printer** area, click the printer you want to use.
- In the **Page Range** area, select **All** to print the entire message, or select **Pages** and type the page or pages in the **Pages** box.
- In the **Number of copies** box, click the arrows or select the current entry and type a new number to change the number of copies that will print.

3   Click **Print**.

To print a message using the default print options:

Print

- On the toolbar, click the **Print** button.

Practice Exercise

In this exercise, you will change the page setup for a message and then print it.

NO practice files are required for this exercise.

Open the Inbox, and then open a received message. Preview the message and adjust the page settings to print the message in Landscape format, with a header reading **IMPORTANT MESSAGE**. Then print the message and confirm that your settings worked.

Previewing and Printing Your Outlook Calendar

When your schedule is full and you find yourself running from one appointment to the next, you might not always be able to check your Outlook Calendar. By printing your Calendar, you can take your schedule with you. You can print your Calendar in a variety of formats, called print styles. You can select from the following pre-defined print styles:

- Daily Style prints the selected date range with one day per page. Printed elements include the date, day, TaskPad and reference month calendars, along with an area for notes.

- Weekly Style prints the selected date range with one calendar week per page, including reference calendars for the selected and following months.

- Monthly Style prints a page for each month in the selected date range. Each page includes the six-week range surrounding the month, along with reference calendars for the selected and following months.

- Tri-fold Style prints a page for each day in the selected date range. Each page includes the daily schedule, weekly schedule, and TaskPad.

- Calendar Details lists your appointments for the selected date range, as well as the accompanying appointment details.

You select the date or range of dates to be printed each time you print.

BE SURE TO install a printer and open the Calendar folder before carrying out these steps.

To print your Outlook Calendar:

Print

1 On the toolbar, click the **Print** button.

The Print dialog box appears with the displayed time period automatically selected.

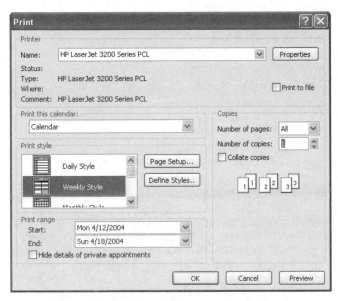

2 In the **Print style** list, click **Daily Style**, **Weekly Style**, **Monthly Style**, **Tri-fold Style**, or **Calendar Details Style**.

3 In the **Print range** area, select the start and end dates of the time period you want to print.

4 Click **Preview**.

5 To make changes to the format, paper, header, or footer, click the **Page Setup** button.

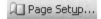

The Page Setup dialog box appears.

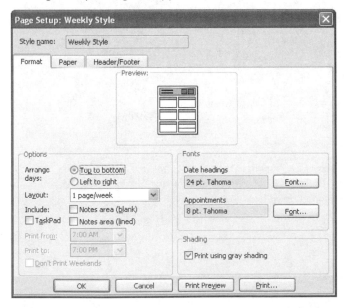

6 Make the changes you want, and then click **Print Preview**.

7 When the calendar appears as you want to print it, click the **Print** button in the Print Preview window and then click **OK** in the Print dialog box.

Practice Exercise

In this exercise, you will print two different views of your Calendar.

NO practice files are required for this exercise.

Open the Calendar folder. Display your schedule for today and then print it. Then open the Print dialog box, and print a calendar of the entire month.

Previewing and Printing Contact Information

To make it easy to take contact information with you while you are away from your computer, you can print your Contacts list. You can print contact information from any of the available views, and for the Address Card views, you can select from a number of print styles. You can define your own print styles for all views, specifying the layout, the margins, orientation, and more. The print options available to you vary based on the view selected when you chose to print.

BE SURE TO install a printer and open the Contacts folder before carrying out these steps.

To preview and print a phone list of contacts:

1 On the **View** menu, click **Arrange By**, **Current View**, and then **Phone List**.

The contact entries are displayed in a columnar list.

2 Display and arrange the columns as you want to print them.

■ Right-click any column header to display your options, and click the option you want.

■ Drag a column header to the left or right to move that column (the new location is indicated by red arrows).

3 If you don't want to print all the contact entries, select the row(s) you want to include in the phone list.

> **Tip** To select multiple rows, click the first row, hold down the CTRL key, and click each additional row.

Print

4 On the toolbar, click the **Print** button.

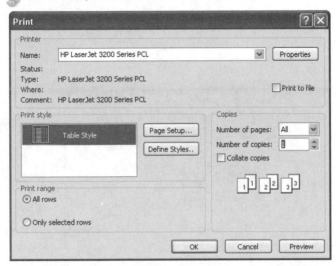

5 In the **Print range** area, select the **All rows** or **Only selected rows** option, and click **Preview**.

6 To make changes to the format, paper, header, or footer, click the **Page Setup** button.

7 Make the changes you want, and then click **Print Preview**.

8 When the phone list appears as you want to print it, click the **Print** button in the Print Preview window and then click **OK** in the Print dialog box.

To preview and print an address book of contact entries:

1 On the **View** menu, click **Arrange By**, **Current View**, and then **Address Cards**.

The contact entries are displayed as address cards.

2 If you don't want to print all the contact entries, select the contact entry(ies) you want to include in the phone list.

> **Tip** To select multiple contact entries, click the first row, hold down the CTRL key, and click each additional contact entries.

Print

3 On the toolbar, click the **Print** button.

4   In the **Print style** list, click **Card Style**, **Small Booklet Style**, **Medium Booklet Style**, or **Phone Directory Style**.

Tip   Small Booklet Style and Medium Booklet Style are designed for double-sided printing. Select these options only if your printer can print double-sided.

5   In the **Print range** area, select the **All items** or **Only selected items** option, and click **Preview**.

6   To make changes to the format, paper, header, or footer, click the **Page Setup** button.

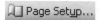

The Page Setup dialog box appears.

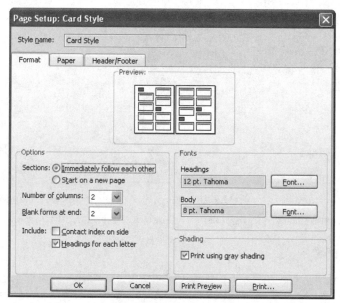

7   Make the changes you want, and then click **Print Preview**.

8   When the phone list appears as you want to print it, click the **Print** button in the Print Preview window and then click **OK** in the Print dialog box.

Practice Exercise

In this exercise, you will print contact information to take with you.

NO practice files are required for this exercise.

Open your Contacts folder. Print a phone list of all your contacts. Then select an individual contact entry, and print an address card for that entry.

O03C-3 Review

Number	Objective	Mastered
O03C-3-1	Create and modify distribution lists	
	Creating a distribution list	❏
	Modifying a distribution list	❏
O03C-3-2	Link contacts to other items	
	Linking an Outlook item to a contact entry	❏
O03C-3-3	Create and modify notes	
	Creating and editing notes	❏
O03C-3-4	Organize items	
	Adding and deleting fields from folder views	❏
	Sorting Outlook items	❏
	Filtering e-mail messages	❏
	Organizing Outlook items by using colors	❏
	Organizing messages by using rules	❏
	Organizing Outlook items by using views	❏
O03C-3-5	Organize items using folders	
	Organizing messages in folders	❏
	Archiving Outlook items	❏
O03C-3-6	Search for items	
	Finding messages	❏
	Using Search Folders	❏
O03C-3-7	Save items in different file formats	
	Saving Outlook items in different file formats	❏
O03C-3-8	Assign items to categories	
	Assigning Outlook items to categories	❏
O03C-3-9	Preview and print items	
	Previewing and printing an e-mail message	❏
	Previewing and printing your Outlook Calendar	❏
	Previewing and printing contact information	❏

Index

Numerics

3-D effects, 478
  adding to shapes, 479
3-D Style button (PowerPoint
  Drawing toolbar), 479

A

absolute positioning of graphics in
  Word, 143
absolute references in Excel
  formulas, 267
Accept button (Outlook), 673, 684
Accept Change button (Word
  Reviewing toolbar), 104
accepting meeting requests, 682, 684
  automatically, 686
  tentatively, 682
accepting changes, in Excel, 396
accepting changes, in
  PowerPoint, 498–99
accepting changes, in Word, 104
Accepting Task dialog box
  (Outlook), 673
accepting tasks, 673
Access
  entering data, 600
  records. *See* records (Access)
  security, changing level, 538
action buttons (PowerPoint), 511–14
  background color, adding, 513
  borders, adding, 513
  creating, 511, 513
  formatting, 513
  hyperlinks, attaching, 513
  hyperlinks, to hidden slides, 515
  sounds, adding, 511
  text, adding, 513
Action Buttons command
  (PowerPoint), 512
action queries (Access), 572–74
  append queries, 571–73
  backing up tables before
    running, 572
  creating, 572

delete queries. *See* delete queries
  (Access)
  make-table queries, 571–73
  update queries, 571–73
Action Settings command
  (PowerPoint), 461, 508
Action Settings dialog box
  (PowerPoint), 461, 508, 512
Active Appointments view (Outlook
  Calendar), 689
ActiveX controls, 210
Actual Page button (Word Reading
  Layout toolbar), 168
Add a Contact command (MSN
  Messenger), 671
Add a Contact Wizard
  (Outlook), 671
Add Constraint dialog box
  (Excel), 344
Add New Member dialog box
  (Outlook), 701
Add Reminder command
  (Outlook), 663
Add Scenario dialog box
  (Excel), 335
Add Style dialog box (Word), 138
Add Text command
  (PowerPoint), 513
Address Book button
  (Outlook), 702
address books (Outlook)
  adding contacts to distribution
    lists from, 702
  creating e-mail messages from, 648
  distribution lists. *See* distribution
    lists (Outlook)
  printing, 731
addressing e-mail messages, 651–52
adjusting shapes, 452
adjustment handles, 452
Advanced Filter dialog box
  (Excel), 328
advanced filtering (Excel), 328–29
Advanced Find dialog box
  (Outlook), 721
Advanced Layout dialog box
  (Word), 144
aggregate functions (Access), 612–
  13. *See also specific function
  names*

Align Bottom button (PowerPoint
  Tables and Borders
  toolbar), 440
Align button (Word Tables and
  Borders toolbar), 158
Align command (Access), 615
Align Left button
  Excel Formatting toolbar, 281
  PowerPoint Formatting toolbar,
    471
  Word Formatting toolbar, 75
Align Right button
  Excel Formatting toolbar, 281
  PowerPoint Formatting toolbar,
    471
  Word Formatting toolbar, 75
Align Top button (PowerPoint
  Tables and Borders
  toolbar), 440
aligning
  controls, in Access, 578, 614, 615
  graphics, in Word, 143–45
  graphics, in PowerPoint, 476–78
  page numbers, in Word, 88
  paragraphs, 73–76
  text, 75, 470–71
  text, in PowerPoint tables, 440
  text, in Word tables, 158
  worksheet cells, 280–81
All Connecting Lines command
  (Word), 31
Allow Additions form property
  (Access), 578
Allow Deletions form property
  (Access), 578
Allow Edits form property
  (Access), 578
Allow Multiple Pages button (Word
  Reading Layout toolbar), 127,
  168
Allow Users to Edit Ranges dialog
  box (Excel), 384
Analysis ToolPak (Excel), 339
analyzing data in Excel, 339
Angle Counterclockwise button
  (Graph Formatting
  toolbar), 446
angling chart text in
  PowerPoint, 446

animating slides, 485–86. *See also* animation schemes (PowerPoint)

animation effects. *See* animation effects

animation effects (PowerPoint). *See also* transition effects (PowerPoint)
applying, 485
applying, to entire presentation, 486
custom, adding, 486
in Web presentations, 525

animation schemes (PowerPoint), 485

Animation Schemes command (PowerPoint), 485, 486

annotating Word documents, 198–202

annotating slide shows, 519–20
erasing all markup, 520
highlighter tool, 520

Annual Events view (Outlook Calendar), 689

append queries (Access), 572–74

Append Query command (Access), 573

Apply All Changes command (PowerPoint), 499

Apply button (PowerPoint Reviewing toolbar), 499

Apply Design Template dialog box (PowerPoint), 483

Apply Filter button (Access), 629

Apply to All Slides button (Slide Transition task pane), 516

applying
animation effects, 485
animation effects, to entire presentation, 486
animation schemes, 485
color schemes, in PowerPoint, 469
grayscale, to PowerPoint graphics, 475
styles, in Word, 67
templates, in PowerPoint, 483–84
text effects, in Word, 70–71
transition effects, 486–87

Appointment Recurrence dialog box (Outlook), 678

appointments (Outlook), 676–82
color-coding, 711
creating, from Calendar, 648
creating, from e-mail messages/tasks, 648

hiding, 677, 678
linking to contacts, 704
location, setting, 677
organizing by category, 725
private, 677, 678
recurring, 676, 678
reminders. *See* reminders (Outlook)
scheduling, 676–79
start date, changing, 679

archiving (Outlook), 719–20
AutoArchive, 719
changing settings for individual folder, 720
viewing settings for, 719

arguments (Excel), 352

arithmetic operators (Excel), 263

arithmetic, in Excel, 263–64

Arrange All command
PowerPoint, 506
Word, 128

Arrange By command (Outlook), 716, 717

Arrange By/Current View command (Outlook), 711

Arrange By/Current View/Active Appointments command (Outlook), 691

Arrange By/Current View/Address Cards command (Outlook), 731

Arrange By/Current View/Annual Events command (Outlook), 691

Arrange By/Current View/By Category command (Outlook), 691, 725

Arrange By/Current View/By Color command (Outlook), 712

Arrange By/Current View/Customize Current View command (Outlook), 708

Arrange By/Current View/Day/Week/Month command (Outlook), 691

Arrange By/Current View/Day/Week/Month With AutoPreview command (Outlook), 691

Arrange By/Current View/Define Views command (Outlook), 710

Arrange By/Current View/Events command (Outlook), 691

Arrange By/Current View/Phone List command (Outlook), 730

Arrange By/Current View/Recurring Appointments command (Outlook), 691

Arrange By/Custom command (Outlook), 709

Arrange By/Show Views In Navigation Pane command (Outlook), 716

Arrange command (Excel), 305, 310

arranging windows
in Excel, 309–10
in Word, 128–30

arrays (Excel), 342

arrow pointer, displaying in slide shows, 519

arrows, adding to organization chart lines
in Excel, 381
in Word, 31

Assign Task button (Outlook), 674, 698

assigning tasks, 697–98

attaching templates to existing Word documents, 108

attachments, e-mail, 657–58

Attributes dialog box (Word), 180

auditing worksheets, 355–56

authentication (Excel). *See* digital signatures (Excel)

authentication (Word). *See* digital signatures (Word)

AutoArchive (Outlook), 719

AutoArchive dialog box (Outlook), 719

AutoCalc button (Access), 636

AutoComplete (Excel), 241
entering text with, 242

AutoContent Wizard, 427–29

AutoCorrect, 16–17

AutoCorrect dialog box (Word), 16, 17

AutoCorrect Options button (Word), 16

AutoCorrect Options command (Word), 16

AutoFill (Excel)
copying formulas with, 245–46
custom lists and, 245

AutoFilter (Excel), 259. *See also* filtering (Excel)

Autoformat button
Excel Organization Chart
toolbar, 272, 380
PowerPoint Organization Chart
toolbar, 448
Word Organization Chart
toolbar, 31
AutoFormat command (Excel), 282
AutoFormat dialog box (Excel), 282
AutoFormats (Word), 49
AutoFormats (Excel), 281–82
AutoForms (Access), 574–75
Automatic Formatting dialog box
(Outlook), 713
Automatic Layout Options button
(PowerPoint), 462
automatic repagination, 89
automating tasks. *See* macros
AutoNumber data type
(Access), 548
AutoShape command
Excel, 381
Word, 32
AutoShapes
adding, 453
inserting, 28
positioning, 29
sizing, 29
AutoShapes button (PowerPoint
Drawing toolbar), 453, 477,
507
AutoSum button
Excel Standard toolbar, 264
Word Tables and Borders toolbar,
156
AutoSummarize (Word), 162–63
AutoSummarize dialog box
(Word), 162
AutoText, 17–18
AutoText command (Word), 17
Avg function (Access), 612

B

Back button in presentations. *See*
action buttons (PowerPoint)
Back Up Database command
(Access), 642
Background command
PowerPoint, 480, 481, 482
Word, 188, 190

Background dialog box
(PowerPoint), 480
backgrounds, document, 188–91
color, changing, 188
fill effects, applying, 189
watermarks, 189–90
backgrounds, slide
coloring, 480–82
fill color, adding, 480
graphics, adding, 478
graphics, changing, 482
patterns, adding, 478
shading, 480–82
textures, adding, 481
backing up
databases, in Access, 642
tables, before running update
queries, 572
balloons for displaying comments/
tracked changes. *See*
comment balloons
Bcc Field command (Outlook), 652
Beginning button in presentations.
See action buttons
(PowerPoint)
blank presentations. *See* templates
(PowerPoint)
blind courtesy copies, 652
Bold button
Excel Formatting toolbar, 278
PowerPoint Formatting toolbar, 466
Word Formatting toolbar, 63
bolding text, 466
Bookmark command (Word), 165
Bookmark dialog box (Word), 165
bookmarks (Word), 165–66
deleting, 165
vs. hyperlinks, 165
inserting, 165
jumping to, 166
naming, 165
Border button (Word Formatting
toolbar), 47, 77
borders (Excel)
adding to worksheet cells, 279
formatting, 379
borders (PowerPoint)
adding to action buttons, 513
borders (Word)
applying, 76–78
custom, creating, 77
Borders and Shading command
(Word), 47, 48, 76, 77, 78

Borders and Shading dialog box
(Word), 47, 48, 77, 78
Borders button (Excel Formatting
toolbar), 279
borders, table (Word), 46
adding, 47
complex, 47
formatting, 47
bound controls (Access), 580, 591
Break command (Word), 82, 90
Break dialog box (Word), 82, 90
breaking bullet points, 432
breaks
column, 82
page. *See* page breaks
section, 89, 90
brightness, graphic
changing, in Excel, 373–74
changing, in PowerPoint, 475
changing, in Word, 142–43
Browse to Web button (Word), 58
browsers, selecting for Web
presentations, 525
Build button (Access), 556, 558, 611
bullet points (PowerPoint), 430
adding, 431, 433
breaking, 432
color, changing, 491
deleting, 432
formatting, 491
replacing, 431
selecting, 425
size, changing, 491
subpoints, 430, 433
bulleted lists (PowerPoint). *See*
bullet points (PowerPoint)
bulleted lists (Word), 50–52. *See
also* numbered lists (Word)
converting paragraphs to, 50
converting, to outlines, 54
creating, 50–52
customizing, 50–52
sorting, 153–54
styles, 137–38
styles, changing, 68
styles, clearing, 68
Bullets and Numbering command
PowerPoint, 492
Word, 51, 53, 54, 55, 68, 137
Bullets and Numbering dialog box
PowerPoint, 492
Word, 51, 53, 55, 68, 137
Bullets button (Word Formatting
toolbar), 50

buttons, toolbar (Excel)
customizing, 411–13
displaying/hiding, 412
resetting, 412
buttons, toolbar (Word)
customizing, 230–31
displaying/hiding, 230
resetting, 230
By Category view (Outlook Calendar), 689
Byte field size (Access), 549

C

calculated fields (Access)
adding to queries, 609–11
creating, 610
naming, 610
calculating
subtotals, in Excel, 326–27
totals, in queries, 612–13
calculations (Access)
performing in multiple locations. *See* calculated fields (Access)
Calendar (Outlook), 676–713
Active Appointments view, 689
Annual Events view, 689
appointments. *See* appointments (Outlook)
By Category view, 689
closing, 683
color-coding, automatically, 712–13
creating items from, 648
customizing, 688–93
Day view, 688
Day/Week/Month view, 689
displaying, 647
displaying specific dates in, 647
displaying specific day/week, 691
Events view, 689
events. *See* events (Outlook)
meetings. *See* meetings (Outlook)
Month view, 688
previewing, 728–30
print styles, 728
printing, 728–30
Recurring Appointments view, 689
view, changing, 691
views, 688
Week view, 688
Work Week view, 688
work week, 692

Calendar button (Outlook), 647, 683
Calendar Coloring button (Outlook), 713
Calendar Details style, printing Outlook Calendar in, 728
Can Grow control property (Access), 588
Can Grow section property (Access), 588
Can Shrink control property (Access), 588
Cancel button (Excel worksheets), 240
Cancel Meeting command (Outlook), 687
canceling meetings, 687
Caption dialog box (Word), 200
Caption property (Access), 555, 577, 586
captions (Word), 200–201
cascading updates (Access), 563
categories (Word)
assigning, 220
searching by, 220
categories (Outlook), 725
Categories command (Outlook), 725
cc messages. *See* courtesy copies
Cells command (Excel), 243, 278, 281, 283, 298, 370
cells, datasheet, 443
cells, table (PowerPoint)
colors, changing, 440
formatting, 439
merging, 441
moving between, 439
selecting, 439
splitting, 441
cells, table (Word), 39
borders. *See* borders, table (Word)
merging, 43, 44, 157–58
referencing in formulas, 156
selecting, 43
shading, 46, 48
splitting, 44, 157–58
text position, changing, 158
cells, worksheet (Excel)
absolute references, 267
adding to Watch Window, 358
aligning, 280–81
borders, adding, 279
centering, 280
clearing contents of, 247–48
clip art, inserting, 254

comments, 292–93
copying formatting, 284
data type, setting, 282–84
deleting, 298
deleting contents, 247
editing, 247–49
filling ranges of, 245
finding and replacing formatting, 250
finding contents of, 249
formatting, 277–80
inserting, 298
jumping to, 360
left-aligning, 280
locking, 384
moving, 298
naming, 360–61
navigating, with Go To command, 251–52
password protecting, 384
pasting options for, 301
preformatting, 280
protecting, 383–86
referencing in formulas, 266–67
relative references, 266
right-aligning, 280
shading, 279
styles, 285–86
text, formatting, 278
values, displaying formats, 283
watching, 358–59
wrapping text in, 286
Center button
Excel Formatting toolbar, 281
PowerPoint Formatting toolbar, 471
Word Formatting toolbar, 75
Center Vertically button (PowerPoint Tables and Borders toolbar), 440
centering
table text, 440
text, 75
worksheet cells, 280
change markers, 496. *See also* tracked changes
change tracking (Excel), 394–95. *See also* tracked changes (Excel)
change tracking (PowerPoint). *See* tracked changes (PowerPoint)
change tracking (Word), 102–5. *See also* tracked changes (Word)
changing. *See* editing; modifying

character count, checking in Word documents, 111–13

character formatting, 62–65
  clearing, in Word, 64
  combinations, changing multiple simultaneously, 64
  copying, 65
  in Excel, 277–80
  finding and replacing, 65–66
  spacing, 71–72

character spacing, 71–72

character styles (Word), 67
  applying, 67

characters, non-printing, 125

Chart command (Excel), 274

chart objects (Excel), 377
  formatting, 379
  optional, turning off, 378
  positioning, 379
  sizing, 379

chart objects (PowerPoint), 443

chart objects (Word), 33

Chart Objects button (Chart toolbar), 379

Chart Options command
  Excel, 378
  PowerPoint, 446
  Word, 35

Chart Options dialog box
  Excel, 378
  PowerPoint, 446
  Word, 35

Chart Type button
  Access, 638
  Excel Chart toolbar, 350, 377
  Graph Standard toolbar, 34, 445

Chart Type command
  Excel, 350, 377
  PowerPoint, 444

Chart Type dialog box
  Excel, 377
  PowerPoint, 444

chart types (Excel). *See also individual chart types*
  changing, 376, 377
  custom, 377

chart types (PowerPoint), 444

chart types (Word), 33, 34. *See also individual chart types*

Chart Wizard (Excel), 274

Chart Wizard button
  Excel PivotTable toolbar, 349
  Excel Standard toolbar, 274

charts. *See also diagrams; Graph*
  axes, 378

datasheets. *See datasheets*
  legends, 443
  organization. *See organization charts*
  pivot. *See PivotCharts*

charts (Excel), 273–75
  adding data to, 275
  adding notes to, 379
  borders, 379
  data markers, 379
  deleting, 275
  formatting, 275, 376–80
  gridlines, adding, 378
  legends, formatting, 378, 379
  moving, 275
  objects in. *See chart objects (Excel)*
  plotting, 274
  sizing, 275
  text, attaching to axes, 378
  titles, adding, 378
  types of. *See chart types (Excel)*
  updating, 275

charts (PowerPoint)
  animating, 485
  creating, 442–46
  data markers, 443
  font size, changing, 445
  formatting, 443
  gridlines, formatting, 446
  importing data into, 444
  inserting, 442–46
  text, rotating, 446
  types, changing, 444

charts (Word)
  copying data into, 150
  creating by importing data, 149–50
  formatting, 33–36
  importing data, 149
  inserting, 33–36
  linking to external data, 150–51
  modifying imported data, 150
  modifying links in, 151
  objects, 33
  positioning, 34
  sizing, 34
  types of, 33, 34

chatting. *See instant messages*

Check Address dialog box (Outlook), 669

Check Box Form Field button (Word Forms toolbar), 185

Check Box Form Field Options dialog box (Word), 185

Check Names button (Outlook), 680, 703

check-box form fields (Word), 184

checking
  grammar. *See grammar, checking*
  spelling. *See spelling, checking*
  styles, in PowerPoint, 437
  worksheets, for errors, 356–57

Choose an XML Transform dialog box (Word), 181

Choose Files to Merge with Current Presentation dialog box (PowerPoint), 502

Circle Invalid Data button (Excel Formula Auditing toolbar), 357

circling invalid data, in Excel, 357–58

Circular Reference toolbar (Excel), 356

circular references (Excel), tracking down, 356

citations, marking in Word, 195

Clear Flag command (Outlook), 664

Clear Formatting command (Word), 64

Clear Validation Circles button (Excel Formula Auditing toolbar), 358

Clear/All command (Excel), 249

Clear/Comments command (Excel), 249, 294

Clear/Contents command (Excel), 249

Clear/Formats command (Excel), 249

clearing
  cell contents, in Excel, 247
  formats/comments, from Excel worksheets, 248
  formatting, in Word, 64
  styles, from bulleted or numbered lists in Word, 68
  styles, from Word tables, 69
  tab stops, in Word, 80

client rules (Outlook), 714. *See also rules (Outlook)*

clip art, 25
  color, changing, 475
  coloring, in PowerPoint, 475
  inserting, 25
  inserting, in Excel, 254
  inserting, in slides, 449–51
  online gallery, 449
  searching for, 25
  searching for, by keyword, 450

Clip Art task pane
(PowerPoint), 450, 460
opening, 453
Clip Organizer, inserting sounds
from in slides, 460
Clipboard task pane (Excel), 300
Clipboard. *See* Office Clipboard
Close and Return to Microsoft Excel
command (Excel), 419
Close and Return to Microsoft Word
command (Word), 227
Close button
Outlook Calendar, 683
Outlook, 706
PowerPoint Rehearsal toolbar, 517
Close command (PowerPoint), 524
Close Grayscale View button
(PowerPoint Grayscale View
toolbar), 530
Close Preview button (PowerPoint
Print Preview toolbar), 529
closing
Calendar, in Outlook, 683
comments, in PowerPoint, 501
databases, 537
e-mail messages, after responding
to, 649
Reviewing pane, in Word, 209
Web presentations, 524
Collapse button (Word Outlining
toolbar), 56
Collapse Subdocuments button
(Word Outlining
toolbar), 203
collapsing
outlines, in Word, 56
subdocuments, in Word, 203
worksheet outlines, 329
Color button
Excel Picture toolbar, 373
PowerPoint Picture toolbar, 475
Word Picture toolbar, 143
Color dialog box (PowerPoint), 469
color schemes (PowerPoint), 468
applying, 469
changing, 469
creating, 469
customizing, 468, 469
editing, 469
color slides, previewing before
printing, 528
Color/Grayscale button
(PowerPoint Standard
toolbar), 530

color-coding
appointments/events/
meetings, 711–14
e-mail messages, 711–14
notes, in Outlook, 711–14
Outlook Calendar,
automatically, 713
Outlook Calendar, manually, 712
viewing applied rules, 712
coloring
action buttons, in PowerPoint, 513
backgrounds. *See* shading
bullet points, 491
clip art, 475
form backgrounds, 617
graphics, in PowerPoint, 474–76
organization chart lines, in
Excel, 381
organization chart lines, in Word, 31
shadows, 479
shapes, 476
slide backgrounds, 480–82
table cells, in PowerPoint, 440
text, in PowerPoint, 468–70
text, in Word, 63
Word document backgrounds, 188
column breaks (Word), 82
Column/AutoFit Selection
command (Excel), 287
Column/Standard Width command
(Excel), 287
Column/Width command
(Excel), 287
Column/Width dialog box
(Excel), 287
columnar forms (Access)
columns (Outlook), reordering, 707
columns (Word), 81–83
flowing selected text in, 82
formatting, 83–84
inserting, 81–83
sizing, 83
Columns button (Word Standard
toolbar), 81, 82
Columns command
Access, 610
Excel, 289
Word, 81, 84
Columns dialog box (Word), 84
columns, datasheet (Access), 622–23
columns, table (PowerPoint)
deleting, 440
inserting, 440
selecting, 439

columns, table (Word)
changing width, 44
deleting, 43
inserting, 43
selecting, 43
totaling, 156
columns, worksheet (Excel)
deleting, 289
determining number of, 350–52
displaying hidden, 288
freezing, 309
hiding, 288
inserting, 288–89, 298
sizing, 286–88
unfreezing, 309
width, adjusting, 287
Comma Style button (Excel
Formatting toolbar), 283
commands (Word), adding/
removing from
menus, 227–29
comma-separated files, 606
comment balloons
setting options for, 208–9
turning off, 208
Comment command
Excel, 292
PowerPoint, 500
comments (Excel)
attaching to worksheet
cells, 292–93
clearing, 248
deleting, 293, 294
displaying, 293
editing, 293
hiding, 293
positioning, 293
sizing, 293
comments (Outlook), adding to
tasks, 697
comments (PowerPoint)
closing, 501
deleting, 501
displaying, 497, 501
editing, 501
hiding, 501
inserting, 500
opening, 501
reviewer name, changing, 501
user information, changing, 501
comments (Word), 100–102
deleting, 101–2
editing, 101–2
hiding, 101
inserting, 100–101

comments (Word) (*continued*)
moving among, 100
responding to, 101, 102
reviewing, 100–101
ScreenTips and, 100
viewing, in versions of Word documents, 213
compacting databases (Access), 643–44
Compare and Merge Documents command (Word), 98
Compare and Merge Documents dialog box (Word), 98
Compare and Merge Presentations command (PowerPoint), 502
Compare and Merge Workbooks command (Excel), 394
comparing presentations, 502–3
comparing Word documents, 97–99
comparing workbooks, 393–94
compiling
indexes, in Word, 192, 194
readability statistics, in Word documents, 163–64
completing worksheet entries, 240
condensing character spacing, 72
conditional formatting (Excel), 372–73
Conditional Formatting command (Excel), 372
Conditional Formatting dialog box (Excel), 372
connecting graphics (PowerPoint), 476–78
connection points (PowerPoint), 476, 477
Consolidate command (Excel), 407
consolidating data from multiple worksheets, 407–8
contact views (Outlook), 716
contacts (Outlook), 668–71
adding, 669
adding, from e-mail messages, 671
adding, to distribution lists, 700
address checking, 669
creating, from Contacts folder, 649
creating, from existing contacts, 670
displaying, 647
editing, 670
for instant messages, 671–72
linking items to, 704–5
organizing, with views, 717
phone numbers, entering, 669
previewing, 730–32
printing, 730–32

selecting multiple, 704
viewing linked items, 705
Contacts button (Outlook), 647
contrast, graphic
changing, in Excel, 373–74
changing, in PowerPoint, 475
changing, in Word, 142–43
control boxes, 443
Control Source property (Access), 577, 587, 592
controls (Access)
adding to forms, 580–82
adding to reports, 591–93
aligning, 578, 614, 615
bound, creating, 591
bound, vs. unbound, 580
calculated values, displaying with, 592
color, changing, 578
copying formatting, 578
deleting, 582
displaying list of, 580
field data, adding to data access pages, 596
fonts, changing, 578
incrementally positioning, 614
moving, 614
moving independently from label, 615
properties, 577–80, 587–90
resizing, 615
selecting, 614
sizing to fit, 615
sizing to match other selected control, 615
spacing evenly, 615
unbound, adding to data access pages, 596
unbound, adding to forms, 582
unbound, creating, 591
Convert Text to Table dialog box (Word), 42
Convert/Text to Table command (Word), 41
converting lists
into Word outlines, 54
into Word paragraphs, 53
converting text (Word)
into bulleted lists, 50
into numbered lists, 53
into tables, 41–42
Copy button
Excel Standard toolbar, 299
PowerPoint Standard toolbar, 453
Word Standard toolbar, 11, 185

Copy command
Excel, 267, 299, 400
Word, 10, 11, 37, 150
Copy View dialog box (Outlook), 710
copying
check boxes, from check-box form fields in Word, 184
drawing guides, in PowerPoint, 477
entries, in worksheets, 299
formatting, 65
formatting, in Excel, 284
formulas in Excel worksheets, with AutoFill, 245–46
shapes, 453
text, 10–12
Count function (Access), 612
courtesy copies, 652
Create New Folder button
Excel, 318
PowerPoint Save As dialog box, 523
Word, 113
Create Signature dialog box (Outlook), 659
Create Subdocument button (Word Outlining toolbar), 203
criteria ranges
creating, 328
filtering with, 328–29
Crop button
Excel Picture toolbar, 375
PowerPoint Picture toolbar, 473
Word Picture toolbar, 141
cropping graphics
in Excel, 375
in PowerPoint, 472–74
in Word, 141
Cross-reference dialog box (Word), 201
cross-references in indexes, 194
cross-references in Word documents, 201–2
inserting, 201
updating, 202
crosstab queries (Access), 567–69
Crosstab Query Wizard (Access), 568
currency, formatting Excel values as, 283
Currency data type (Access), 548
Currency Style button (Excel Formatting toolbar), 283
Current View list (Outlook), 716

Custom Animation command
    (PowerPoint), 486
custom chart types (Excel), 377
Custom Dictionaries dialog box
    (Word), 234
custom dictionary (Word), 233–34
custom lists (Excel)
    creating, 246
    fill handles and, 245
custom number formats
    (Excel), 370–71
Custom Shows command
    (PowerPoint), 510
Custom Shows dialog box
    (PowerPoint), 510
custom slide shows, 510–11
    adding slides to, 510, 511
    creating, 510
    deleting slides from, 511
    editing, 511
    modifying, 511
    publishing as Web
        presentations, 526, 527
    rearranging slides in, 511
Customize Bulleted List dialog box
    (Word), 51
Customize command
    Excel, 412, 414
    Word, 228, 230
Customize dialog box
    Excel, 412, 414, 415
    Word, 228, 229, 231
Customize Numbered List dialog
    box (Word), 53, 55
Customize this Search Folder
    command (Outlook), 723
customizing
    borders, in Word, 77
    bulleted lists, in Word, 50–52
    Calendar, in Outlook, 688–93
    chart types, in PowerPoint, 444
    color schemes, in PowerPoint, 468,
        469
    contact views, in Outlook, 716
    Excel, 411–15
    menus, in Excel, 413–15
    menus, in Word, 227–29
    numbered lists, in Word, 52–54
    Search Folders, in Outlook, 723
    slide shows. See custom slide shows
    tab stops, in Word, 79
    toolbars, in Excel, 411–13
    toolbars, in Word, 230–31
    transition effects, 487
    Word, 223–231

Cut button
    Excel Standard toolbar, 299
    Word Standard toolbar, 11
Cut command
    Excel, 299
    Word, 10, 11
cutting and pasting, 10
    in Excel, 301–2
    multiple worksheet entries, 300

D

Daily Style, printing Outlook
    Calendar in, 728
data (Access)
    entering, 600–610
    linking to, vs. importing, 605
data (Excel)
    analyzing, 339
    consolidating from multiple
        worksheets, 407–8
    formatting, 277, 370
    invalid, circling, 357–58
data access pages (Access), 593–97
    adding field data controls, 596
    control properties, setting, 597
    creating, 593–97
    grouped, testing, 595
    modifying, 594–97
    opening in Internet Explorer, 595
    section properties, setting, 597
    unbound controls, adding, 596
data analysis (Excel), 339
    Goal Seek. See Goal Seek (Excel)
Data Analysis command
    (Excel), 339
Data Analysis dialog box
    (Excel), 339
Data Connection Wizard
    (Excel), 399
Data Entry form property
    (Access), 578
Data Form dialog box (Word), 170
data maps (Excel), 362–64
data markers, 443
    formatting, in Excel charts, 379
data series, 443
data source (Excel), 399
data source (mail merge), 169–72
    creating labels with. See mailing
        labels
    editing, 170
    filtering, 171

    merging into form letter, 174
    sorting, 171
    specifying, 169
data tables (Excel), 340–43
    multiple variables in, 342
data types (Access), 548–51. See also
    individual data types
data validation (Excel), 331–32
Data Validation dialog box
    (Excel), 332
database functions (Excel), 352–53
Database Utilities/Compact and
    Repair Database command
    (Access), 643
Database window (Access), 536
Database Wizard (Access), 539–41
databases (Access), 536–37
    backing up, 642
    closing, 537
    compacting, 643–44
    creating, blank, 541–42
    creating, with Database
        Wizard, 539–41
    importing objects from, 605–6
    managing, 631
    object dependencies, 632–33
    objects. See objects, database
    opening, 536
    organizing data in, 609–613
    primary keys, 551–52
    referential integrity, 562–63
    repairing, 643–44
    saving, 538
    security warning, 538
    structuring, 539
Datasheet command (Access), 623
Datasheet view (Access), 546
datasheets (Access), 33, 443
    cells, 443
    changing color, lines, and
        effects, 623
    columns, freezing/unfreezing,
        622–23
    columns, hiding/unhiding, 622
    control boxes, 443
    default formatting, changing, 623
    displaying total number of
        records, 603
    entering data into, 443, 600–602
    finding records in, 604–5
    font, changing, 623
    formatting, 622–24
    importing data into, 444
    navigating, 34, 603

datasheets (Access) *(continued)*
  opening, 601
  rows, changing height, 623
  selecting, 33
  sorting records in, 624–25
datasheets (Word). *See* tables
Date and Time command
  (Word), 19
Date and Time dialog box
  (Word), 19
date and time functions (Excel), 269
Date Navigator (Outlook), 647
  date range in, changing, 647
  displaying two months in, 691
  navigating in, 691
  selecting dates in, 647
Date/Time data type (Access), 548
dates (Excel), 242
  entering series of, 245
dates (Word), 19–20
Day button (Outlook), 689
Day view (Outlook Calendar), 688
Day/Week/Month view (Outlook
  Calendar), 689
dBASE files, importing Access data
  from, 606
Decimal field size (Access), 549
Decimal Places property
  (Access), 555, 577, 587
Decline button (Outlook), 674, 684
declining
  meeting requests, 683, 684, 686
  task requests, 674
Declining Task dialog box
  (Outlook), 674
Decrease Decimal button (Excel
  Formatting toolbar), 283
Decrease Font Size button
  (PowerPoint Formatting
  toolbar), 466
decreasing font size, 466
Default Value property
  (Access), 555
Default View form property
  (Access), 578
defaults (Excel), modifying, 420–21
Define Custom Show dialog box
  (PowerPoint), 510
Define Name dialog box
  (Excel), 361
delegating tasks, 674
Delete All Markup command
  (PowerPoint), 499

Delete button
  Access, 537
  Outlook, 696, 718
Delete command
  Excel, 289, 298
  Outlook, 724
  PowerPoint, 447
Delete Comment button
  Excel Reviewing toolbar, 294
  PowerPoint Reviewing toolbar,
  499, 501
Delete Comment command
  Excel, 294
  PowerPoint, 501
  Word, 101
Delete dialog box (Excel), 298
delete queries (Access), 572–74
  creating, 573
  running, 601
Delete Query command
  (Access), 573
Delete Rows button (Access Table
  Design toolbar), 547
Delete Rows command
  (Access), 551
Delete Sheet command (Excel), 305
Delete Slide command
  (PowerPoint), 506
Delete/Columns command
  (Word), 43
Delete/Rows command (Word), 43
deleting
  bookmarks, in Word, 165
  bullet points, 432
  cell contents, in Excel, 247
  charts, in Excel, 275
  comments, in Excel, 293, 294
  comments, in PowerPoint, 501
  comments, in Word, 101–2
  conditional formatting, in
    Excel, 372
  controls, in Access, 582
  data maps, in Excel, 364
  database objects, 537
  database records, 602. *See also*
    delete queries (Access)
  distribution list entries, 702
  e-mail messages, unread, 668
  Excel macros, 417
  fields, from Outlook folder
    views, 708
  filters, from e-mail messages, 711
  filters, in Access, 628
  filters, in Excel, 259
  flags, from e-mail messages, 664

folders, 319
folders, in Outlook, 718
folders, in Word, 114–15
header and footer
  information, 494
hyperlinks, 60–61
hyperlinks, in Excel, 304
macros, in Excel, 417
macros, in Word, 223–26
manual page breaks, in Excel, 314
markup, in PowerPoint, 499
meeting attendees, 687
meetings, 687
menus, in Excel, 414
menus, in Word, 228
notes, in Outlook, 707
page breaks, in Word, 89–91
passwords, in Excel, 388
passwords, in Word, 216
placeholders, in
  PowerPoint, 491–93
recurring tasks, 696
relationships, in Access, 562
rows, in Access, 547
Search Folders, in Outlook, 724
slides, 506–7
slides, from custom slide
  shows, 511
subdocuments, in Word, 204
tab stops, in Word, 79
table columns/rows, in
  PowerPoint, 440
table columns/rows, in Word, 43
tasks, 696
text, 430
text, in Word, 9–10
toolbars, in Excel, 413
toolbars, in Word, 231
tracked changes, in
  PowerPoint, 499
unread e-mail messages from
  recipient's Inbox, 668
versions of Word documents, 213
Word documents, 114–15
Word macros, 223–26
workbooks, 319
worksheet cells, 298
worksheet columns/rows, 289
worksheets, 305
delimited text files, 606
delivering presentations, 504–21
  without PowerPoint installed, 521.
    See also PowerPoint Viewer
delivering slide shows, 518–19

Demote button
    PowerPoint Outlining toolbar, 433
    Word Outlining toolbar, 56
demoting
    outline headings, in Word, 56
    PowerPoint text, 433–34
dependencies, object (Access), 632–33
dependents (Excel), 355
deselecting text objects, in PowerPoint, 426
Design button (Access), 547, 549
design templates. *See* templates
Design view (Access), 546
    modifying queries in, 565–67
    modifying tables in, 546–48
    opening tables in, 551
    printing, 639
Diagram Gallery dialog box
    Excel, 271
    PowerPoint, 447
    Word, 30
diagrams. *See also* **charts**
    creating, 30, 447–49
    organization charts. *See* organization charts
diagrams (Excel), 271–73
    organization charts. *See* organization charts (Excel)
    sizing, 273
dictionaries (Word)
    adding custom, 233–34
    specifying new default, 233
digital signatures (Excel), 386–87
    attaching to workbooks, 387
    viewing, 387
digital signatures (Word), 218–19
    attaching to documents, 219
    viewing, 219
Display for Review button (Word Reviewing toolbar), 99, 104
displaying
    comments, in PowerPoint, 497, 501
    drawing guides, in PowerPoint, 477
    Find pane, in Outlook, 721
    formatting, in Word, 6
    gridlines, in PowerPoint, 477
    Handout Master, 490
    hidden slides, 515
    hidden text, in Word, 6
    hidden workbooks, 311
    Navigation Pane, in Outlook, 647
    Notes Master, 490

    Reading Pane, in Outlook, 646
    rulers, in PowerPoint, 492
    Slide Master, 489
    Title Master, 489
    toolbar buttons, in Excel, 412
    toolbar buttons, in Word, 230
    tracked changes, in PowerPoint, 497
    tracked changes, in Word, 99, 104
    workbooks, hidden, 311
    worksheet columns/rows, hidden, 288
    worksheets, hidden, 290–91
distribution lists (Outlook), 699–703
    adding contacts to, 700
    adding contacts to, from address books, 702
    adding multiple names simultaneously, 700
    addressing messages to, 701
    creating, 699–702
    creating, from new contacts, 701
    deleting entries from, 702
    modifying, 702–3
    modifying, for single message only, 703
Document Map (Word), 166–69
    navigating with, 167
Document Map button (Word Standard toolbar), 167
documents (Word)
    annotating, 198–202
    attaching templates to, 108
    attaching XML schemas to, 178
    authenticating, 218–19
    backgrounds. *See* backgrounds, document
    categories, assigning, 220
    collaborating on, 94
    comparing, 97–99
    creating from templates, 106–9
    cross-references, creating, 201–2
    deleting, 114–15
    digital signatures, 218–19
    displaying as they will be printed. *See* Print Layout view (Word)
    editing, 9–10
    e-mailing for review, 94–97
    formatting, 106, 183
    hyperlink base, assigning, 219, 220
    hyperlinks. *See* hyperlinks (Word)
    indexes. *See* indexes (Word)
    keywords, assigning, 220
    managing, 106

    master documents. *See* master documents (Word)
    merging, 97–99
    merging, with tracked changes, 98–99
    moving in, 3
    navigating, 23
    opening in new window, 129
    organizing in Outline view, 56
    outlines, dynamic. *See* Document Map (Word)
    password-protected, opening, 215
    previewing as Web pages, 122–23
    previewing before printing, 121–22
    printing, 118–19
    properties, viewing, 109
    readability statistics, 163–64
    read-only access, setting, 214
    renaming, 114–15
    restricting changes to, 216–18
    saving, as Web pages, 116–17, 209–12
    saving, as templates, 107
    saving, in new folders, 113–14
    saving, in other formats, 115–16
    saving, new versions of, automatically, 212
    searching, by category or keyword, 220
    selecting, 2
    structured, saving as XML, 180
    summarizing, 109–11, 219–21
    summarizing, with AutoSummarize, 162–63
    summarizing, with custom information, 221–22
    switching between, 128–30
    themes, 191
    tracking changes to. *See* change tracking (Word); tracked changes (Word)
    version management. *See* versions of Word documents
    watermarks, 189–90
    white spaces between pages, hiding, 125
    word count, checking, 111–13
    XML structure, applying, 180
documents (XML), saving with invalid structure, 180
Double field size (Access), 549
drag-and-drop editing, 10
Draw button (PowerPoint Drawing toolbar), 476

Draw Table button
  PowerPoint Tables and Borders
    toolbar, 441
  Word Tables and Borders toolbar,
    39, 41, 44, 158
drawing canvas, 29
drawing guides (PowerPoint)
  aligning graphics with, 476
  copying, 477
  displaying, 477
  moving, 477
  turning off, 477
drawing shapes, 27
  in slides, 452–54
drawing tables, in Word, 39, 41
drawing tools (PowerPoint), 452
drop areas (PivotCharts), 638
Drop Areas command (Access), 638
Drop Down Form Field Options
    dialog box (Word), 186
drop shadows, 478–79
Drop-Down Form Field button
    (Word Forms toolbar), 186
drop-down form fields (Word), 185
duplicate queries (Access), 569–70

E

Edit Calendar Labels dialog box
    (Outlook), 713
Edit Color Scheme dialog box
    (PowerPoint), 469
Edit Comment button (Excel
    Reviewing toolbar), 293
Edit Comment command
  Excel, 293
  Word, 102
Edit Hyperlink command
  Excel, 304
  Word, 60
Edit Hyperlink dialog box
    (Word), 60
Edit in Formula Bar command
    (Excel), 355
Edit Movie Object command
    (PowerPoint), 463
Edit Relationships dialog box
    (Access), 561, 563
Edit WordArt Text dialog box
    (PowerPoint), 455
editing
  color schemes, in PowerPoint, 469
  comments, in Excel, 293

comments, in PowerPoint, 501
comments, in Word, 101–2
contacts, in Outlook, 670
custom slide shows, 511
data source (mail merge), 170
database records, 601
embedded objects, in
    PowerPoint, 459
Excel macros, 418–19
Excel worksheets, 247–49
hyperlinks, 60–61
hyperlinks, in Excel, 304
macros, in Excel, 418–19
macros, in Word, 226–27
mailing label text, in Access, 589
movies, in slides, 463
notes, in Outlook, 707
organization charts, in
    PowerPoint, 447
preventing, in Word, 216
redoing, 9
redoing, multiple actions, 10
relationships, in Access, 562
repeating action, 10
shared workbooks, 392
subdocuments, in Word, 203
text placeholders, in
    PowerPoint, 507
text, in Word, 9
text, on slides, 430–32
tracking changes. *See* change
    tracking (Word); tracked
    changes (Word)
undoing, 9
undoing, multiple actions, 10
Web pages, in Word, 210
Word documents, 9–10
Word macros, 226–27
Word tables, in PowerPoint, 458–59
WordArt text, 454
workbook templates, 406
worksheets, 247–49
edits, tracking. *See* tracked changes
effects
  adding to shapes, 478–79
  animation. *See* animation effects
  fill. *See* fill effects
  text, 70–71
  transition, 486–87
em dashes, 7
e-mail attachments, 657–58
e-mail addresses
  hyperlinks to, inserting, 59
  setting replies to different, 666,
    667

E-mail button (Word Standard
    toolbar), 95
e-mail messages
  adding contacts from, 671
  address separators,
    configuring, 652
  addressing, 651–52
  addressing to distribution
    lists, 701
  archiving. *See* archiving (Outlook)
  assigning to categories, 725
  attachments, 657–58
  automatic address
    completion, 652
  closing after responding to, 649
  color-coding, 711–14
  courtesy copies, 652
  creating tasks from, 649
  creating, from address books, 648
  deleting unread from recipient's
    Inbox, 668
  delivery time, specifying, 667
  editing with Word, 649
  expiration date, setting, 668
  filtering, 709–11, 714–16
  filters, removing, 711
  finding, 720–22
  finding, with Search
    Folders, 722–24
  Flag Status icon, 662
  flagging. *See* flagging e-mail
    messages
  format, setting, 664–66
  forwarding, 654
  forwarding, automatically inserting
    signatures when, 660
  grouping, 709
  HTML format, 664
  hyperlinks, embedding in, 657
  importance, setting, 666
  linking to Outlook contacts, 704
  margins, setting, 726
  moving to folders, 718
  organizing, by category, 725
  organizing, in folders, 718–19
  organizing, with views, 716
  Outlook Rich Text format, 664
  page setup, changing, 726
  Plain Text format, 664
  Plain Text format, setting as
    default, 665
  previewing, 726
  print options, 727
  printing, with default options, 727
  replying to, 653

replying to all recipients, 654
replying to, with Microsoft
      Word, 653
rules, filtering with, 714–16
saving, as files, 724
saving, in other formats, 724–25
sending, 652
sensitivity, setting, 666, 667
sent, specifying folder for saving
      in, 667
setting replies to different
      address, 666, 667
signatures. *See* signatures, e-mail
sorting, 709
stationery, 665 (Outlook)
themes, 665
turning off Word toolbars in, 650
URLs, embedding in, 657
E-mail Options dialog box
      (Outlook), 649
e-mailing Word documents, 94–97
embedded fonts, including when
      packaging presentations for
      CD, 521
embedded objects
      (PowerPoint), 459
editing, 459
formatting, 460
embedded objects (Word), 147
modifying, 148
Enabled control property, 578
End button in presentations. *See*
      action buttons (PowerPoint)
endnotes (Word), 198–200
enforcing referential integrity,
      562–63
Enter button (Excel
      worksheets), 240
entries (Excel)
copying, 299
moving, 299
pasting multiple, 300
envelopes, printing in
      Word, 119–21
Envelopes and Labels dialog box
      (Word), 119
printing from, 120
equations. *See* **formulas**
Eraser button
PowerPoint Tables and Borders
      toolbar, 441
Word Tables and Borders toolbar,
      44, 158

erasing
borders, in Word tables, 44
lines, in PowerPoint tables, 441
lines, in Word tables, 157
slide show markup, 520
Error button (Excel), 354
Error Checking (Excel), 356–57
Error Checking command
      (Excel), 357
Error Checking dialog box
      (Excel), 357
error messages (Excel), 354–55
errors in Access when importing
      data, 607
errors in Excel
fixing, 354–55
tracing, 355
Evaluate Formula dialog box
      (Excel), 359
evaluating formulas, in
      Excel, 359–60
events (Outlook), 676–82
color-coding, 711–14
creating, from Calendar, 648
creating, from e-mail messages/
      tasks, 648
linking to contacts, 704
multi-day, scheduling, 678
organizing, by category, 725
private, 678
recurring, 676, 678
reminders. *See* reminders
      (Outlook)
scheduling, 676–79
start date, changing, 679
Events view (Outlook
      Calendar), 689
Excel
collaboration, 383
customizing, 411
defaults, modifying, 420–21
importing data, 399, 400–401
opening file created in another
      program, 399
outline mode, leaving, 331
Exchange files, importing Access
      data from, 606
Expand button (Word Outlining
      toolbar), 56
Expand Subdocuments button
      (Word Outlining
      toolbar), 204
expanding
character spacing, 72
outlines, in Word, 56

subdocuments, in Word, 204
worksheet outlines, 329
expiration date, setting for e-mail
      messages, 668
Export command (Access), 641
Export To dialog box (Access), 641
exporting from Access, 640–41
exporting from Excel, 402
exporting from
      PowerPoint, 532–33
Expression Builder (Access), 592,
      611
expressions (Access), 611
external data source (Excel), 399

F

fancy text. *See* **WordArt**
felt tip pen tool, in slide shows,
      519–20
Field command (Word), 19, 161
field data controls (Access), 596
Field List button
Access Form Design toolbar, 581
Access Page Design toolbar, 596
Access Report Design toolbar, 592
Field Settings button (Excel
      PivotTable toolbar), 348
Field Size property (Access), 555
fields (Access)
adding to query grid, 566
arranging in reports, 584
calculated. *See* calculated fields
      (Access)
data types, 548–51
default values in, 601
deleting, 547
entry formats, restricting. *See* input
      masks (Access)
hiding, 567
input masks. *See* input masks
      (Access)
inserting, 547
inserting, in queries, 610
lookup. *See* lookup fields (Access)
moving, 547
moving quickly between, 550
naming, 544, 546
number fields, 549
primary key, 551–52
properties, 555–57
query fields, 611
renaming, 547

restricting to specific options. *See* lookup fields (Access)
size, restricting, 549
structure, changing, 547
updating automatically when primary table is changed, 563
fields, form (Word). *See* **form fields (Word)**
figures (Word)
captions, 200–201
table of, 195–98
File command (Word), 211
files
default location, changing, 232–33
hyperlinks to, inserting, 57, 508
importing into Excel, from other applications, 398–400
inserting graphics from, 25
inserting, in e-mail messages, 657
saving e-mail messages as, 724
sending, via instant messages, 658
Fill Color button
Excel Formatting toolbar, 279
PowerPoint Drawing toolbar, 476, 478
PowerPoint Tables and Borders toolbar, 440
Fill command (Excel), 245
fill effects, 478
applying to Word document backgrounds, 189
Fill Effects dialog box
PowerPoint, 480, 481, 482
Word, 189
fill handles (Excel)
custom lists and, 245
entering cell content with, 245–46
Fill/Back Color button (Access), 617
filling Excel ranges, 245
fills
background, adding, 480
textured, applying to slides, 481
Filter By Form button (Access), 629
Filter By Form command (Access), 628
Filter By Selection button (Access), 627
Filter dialog box (Outlook), 709
Filter Excluding Selection command (Access), 627
Filter For command (Access), 629
Filter/Advanced Filter command (Excel), 328

Filter/AutoFilter command (Excel), 259
Filter/Show All command (Excel), 329
filtering data source for mail merge, 171
filtering (Access)
deleting filters, 628
by form, 629
by selection, 627–28
by specified values, 628–30
wildcard characters, 628
filtering (Excel). *See also* **AutoFilter (Excel)**
advanced, 328–29
creating custom filters, 260
criteria ranges for, 328–29
PivotChart display, 349
PivotTable reports, 346
in PivotTables, 348, 636
removing, 259
rows, 259
filtering e-mail messages, 709–11
defining new view for, 710
manually, 709
with rules, 714–16
financial functions (Excel), 269–70
Find and Replace dialog box
Access, 604
Excel, 248, 249
Word, 20, 21, 22, 23, 66, 166
Find button
Access, 604
Outlook, 721
Find command
Excel, 250
Word, 21
Find Duplicates Query Wizard (Access), 570
Find Format dialog box (Excel), 250
Find Now button (Outlook), 722
Find pane (Outlook), displaying, 721
Find Unmatched Query Wizard (Access), 571
finding and replacing (Access), 603–4
finding and replacing (Excel), 247, 249–51
cell formatting, 250
multiple entries, 247
specific cell content, 249
finding and replacing text, 20–22. *See also* **searching**

all occurrences, 21
with Find command, 21
fonts, 471–72
formatting, 21, 65–66
homophones, 21
matching case when, 21
with Replace command, 22
whole words only, 21
wildcard characters, 21
First Line Indent marker (Ruler), 74, 493
Fit Text button (PowerPoint Organization Chart toolbar), 448
fitting slides to page, 505
fixed-width text files, importing Access data from, 606
Flag for Follow Up dialog box (Outlook), 663
Flag Status icon (Outlook), 662
flagging e-mail messages, 662–64
creating reminders when, 663
displaying flagged messages only, 664
flag color, changing, 663
Flag Status icon, 662
flag status, changing, 664
marking as complete, 663
outgoing, 663
removing flags, 664
flipping graphics, in PowerPoint, 476, 478
Folder List (Outlook), 647
Folder List button (Outlook), 647
folder views (Outlook), 707–8
fields, adding/removing, 708
folders
creating, 718
creating, to save presentations in, 523
creating, to save Word documents in, 113–14
creating, to store workbooks in, 318–19
deleting, 114–15, 319
organizing tasks in, 718
renaming, 114–15, 319, 718
folders (Outlook)
creating new items from, 648
deleting, 718
moving, 718
moving e-mail messages to, 718
organizing e-mail messages in, 718–19
Follow Up button (Outlook), 663

Font button
Excel Formatting toolbar, 278
PowerPoint Formatting toolbar, 466
Word Formatting toolbar, 63
Font Color button
Excel Formatting toolbar, 278
PowerPoint Formatting toolbar, 468
Word Formatting toolbar, 64
Font command, 46
Access, 623
PowerPoint, 466, 513
Word, 46, 64, 71, 72, 235
Font dialog box
Excel, 278
PowerPoint, 466
Word, 64, 71, 72, 235
Font Size button
Excel Formatting toolbar, 278
Graph Formatting toolbar, 445
PowerPoint Formatting toolbar, 466
Word Formatting toolbar, 63
fonts
attributes, 62. *See also* character formatting
bolding, 466
changing, in datasheets, 623
changing, in PowerPoint, 466
changing, in Word, 63
color, 63
color, changing, 468
color, changing in Word, 63
default, changing in Excel, 420–21
default, changing in Word, 234–35
effects, 63
embedded, including when packaging presentations for CD, 521
finding and replacing, in PowerPoint, 471–72
italicizing, 466
size, 62
size, changing, 466
size, changing in PowerPoint charts, 445
size, changing in Word, 63
style, 63
style, changing, 466
style, changing in Word, 63
TrueType, 521

TrueType, including when packaging presentations for CD, 521
underlining, 466
footers. *See* **headers/footers**
Footnote and Endnote dialog box (Word), 199
footnotes (Word), 198–200
formatting, 199
inserting, 199
Force New Page section property (Access), 588
Form Field Options button (Word Forms toolbar), 184
form fields (Word), 183
check-box, 184
drop-down, 185
formatting, 187
frames, adding, 187
help text, adding, 185
moving, 187
properties, changing, 187
setting properties, 183
sizing, 187
text in, 184
Form Fields Options button (Word Forms toolbar), 185, 186
Form Header/Footer command (Access), 616
form letters, 172–73
merging, 174
preparing, 172
Form Wizard (Access), 575–76
Format AutoShape command (PowerPoint), 513
Format AutoShape dialog box
Excel, 381
PowerPoint, 467, 513
Word, 32
Format Cells command (Excel), 384
Format Cells dialog box (Excel), 278, 281, 283, 370, 385
adding borders and shading with, 279
Format command (Graph), 35
Format control property (Access), 578, 588
format of e-mail messages, setting, 664–66
Format Painter button
Excel Standard toolbar, 284
Word Formatting toolbar, 65
Format Picture button (Word Picture toolbar), 144

Format Picture command
Excel, 256, 374
Word, 142
Format Picture dialog box
Excel, 256, 374
PowerPoint, 473, 474
Word, 144
Format property (Access), 555
Format Text Box command (Excel), 379
Format WordArt button (WordArt toolbar), 456
Format WordArt dialog box (PowerPoint), 456
formatting
action buttons, in PowerPoint, 513
automatically. *See* AutoFormats
borders, in worksheet cells, 279
bullet points, 491
cells, in Excel worksheets, 277–80
characters. *See* character formatting
charts, in Excel, 275, 376–80
charts, in Graph, 443
charts, in Word, 33–36
check-box form fields, in Word, 184
clearing, in Word, 64
columns, in Word, 83–84
conditional, in Excel, 372–73
copying, 65
copying, in Excel, 284
data markers, in Excel charts, 379
data, in Excel, 277, 370
datasheets, 622–24
displaying, in Word, 6
drop-down form fields, in Word, 185
embedded objects, in PowerPoint, 460
endnotes, in Word, 199
Excel worksheets, in PowerPoint, 460
expressions, in Access, 611
footnotes, in Word, 199
form fields, in Word, 187
forms, in Access, 577
graphics, in Excel, 374–76
gridlines, in PowerPoint charts, 446
headers/footers, in Excel, 316
hiding, in Word, 6
index entries, in Word, 193
numbers, as text in Excel, 243

formatting (*continued*)
  organization chart box text, in
    Excel, 273
  organization chart box text, in
    PowerPoint, 448
  organization charts, in
    Excel, 380–81
  organization charts, in
    PowerPoint, 447
  organization charts, in
    Word, 30–32
  page numbers, in Word, 87–89
  paragraphs, in Word, 67
  phone numbers, in Excel, 243
  placeholders, in
    PowerPoint, 491–93
  pre-defined. *See* AutoFormats
  query fields, 611
  revealing, in Word, 63
  social security numbers, in
    Excel, 243
  table borders, in Word, 47
  table cells, in PowerPoint, 439
  table paragraphs, in Word, 46
  table text, in PowerPoint, 440
  table text, in Word, 46
  tables, in Word, 46–48, 68, 157
  text form fields, in Word, 184
  text, in PowerPoint, 465–68
  text, in worksheet cells, 278
  values, in Excel, 282–84
  Word documents, 106, 183
  WordArt text, 454
  worksheets, with AutoFormats,
    281–82
  ZIP codes, in Excel, 243
Formatting Restrictions dialog box
  (Word), 216
forms (Access)
  AutoForms, 574
  backgrounds, coloring, 617
  columnar, creating, 574
  controls, adding, 580–82
  creating, 574
  creating, with Form
    Wizard, 575–77
  creating, with Report
    Wizard, 583–85
  exporting, 640
  finding records in, 604–5
  formatting, 577
  headers/footers, hiding/
    displaying, 616
  layout, modifying, 615–17
  navigation controls, 603

  pointer shape, 614
  properties, 577–80
  sections of. *See* sections, form
    (Access)
  sorting records in, 624–25
  styles, applying, 574
  tabular, creating, 574
forms (Word), 183–88
  creating, 183
  help text, adding, 185
  modifying, 187–88
  protecting, 213–14
  setting up, 183–87
Forms toolbar (Word), 183
Formula Auditing command
  (Excel), 355
Formula Auditing Mode
  (Excel), 355
Formula Auditing/Evaluate Formula
  command (Excel), 359
Formula Auditing/Remove All
  Arrows command
  (Excel), 356
Formula Auditing/Show Watch
  Window command
  (Excel), 358
Formula Auditing/Trace
  Dependents command
  (Excel), 355
Formula Auditing/Trace Error
  command (Excel), 355
Formula Auditing/Trace Precedents
  command (Excel), 355
formula bar (Excel), changing entry
  in, 247
Formula command (Word), 156
Formula dialog box (Word), 156
formulas (Excel)
  cell references in, 266–67
  cells/ranges in, replacing with
    names, 362
  checking for errors, 356–57
  copying, with AutoFill, 245–46
  database functions in, 352–53
  date and time functions in, 269
  dependents, 355
  entering, 263
  entering, from scratch, 265
  entering, with Insert Function
    button, 265
  evaluating, 359–60
  financial functions in, 269–70
  functions in, 264–66
  hiding, 385
  logical functions in, 270–71

  names in, 361–62
  operators, 263
  precedents, 355
  range references in, 266–67
  reusing in same worksheet, 267
  statistical functions in, 268
formulas in Word tables, 156–57
Forward button (Outlook), 654
forwarding e-mail messages, 654
  automatically inserting signatures
    when, 660
frames pages, 211–12
Frames/New Frames page command
  (Word), 211
framing graphics, 451
Freeze Columns command
  (Access), 623
Freeze Panes command (Excel), 309
freezing
  datasheet columns, 622
  worksheet columns/rows, 309
Function Arguments dialog box
  (Excel), 266, 353
functions (Access) . *See also specific*
  function names
  aggregate, 612–13
functions (Excel)
  capitalizing, 265
  database, 352–53
  date and time, 268–69
  financial, 269–70
  in formulas, 264–66
  logical, 270–71
  Lookup, 350–52
  PMT, 270
  Reference, 350–52
  searching for, 265
  statistical, 268
  SUM, 264
  VLOOKUP, 350, 352
functions in Word tables, 156

G

General format (Excel), 282
Get External Data/Import command
  (Access), 605, 607
Go To command
  Excel, 251–52
  Word, 23, 166
Go To dialog box (Excel), 251
Go to Slide command
  (PowerPoint), 515

Go To Special dialog box
(Excel), 252
Go to TOC button (Word Outlining
toolbar), 196
Go to Today button (Outlook), 689
Goal Seek (Excel), 339–40
finding unknown values with, 340
Goal Seek command (Excel), 340
Goal Seek dialog box (Excel), 340
grammar, checking (Word), 12–14
Graph, 30, 442–46. *See also* charts
activating within Excel, 377
activating within Word, 34
data series, 443
datasheets. *See* datasheets
graphics (Excel)
adding to worksheet
backgrounds, 290
brightness, changing, 373–74
contrast, adjusting, 373–74
cropping, 375
formatting, 374–76
height/width, changing, 374
inserting, 254–55
positioning, 254–55
restoring original formatting, 373
rotating, 376
scaling, 375
sizing, 255–56, 374
washout effect, 373
graphics (PowerPoint)
adding to notes, 507
aligning, 476–78
background color, changing, 474
background, adding, 478
background, changing, 482
brightness, changing, 475
color, changing, 474–76
connecting, 476–78
connection points, 476, 477
contrast, changing, 475
cropping, 472–74
flipping, 476, 478
framing, 451
grayscale, 475
height, setting, 473
inserting, in slides, 451–52
resetting, 472, 475
restoring original colors, 475
restoring original size, 472
rotating, 476–78
scaling, 473
sizing, 472–74
width, setting, 473

graphics (Word)
absolute positioning, 143
aligning with surrounding
text, 143–45
brightness, adjusting, 142–43
captions, 200–201
contrast, adjusting, 142–43
cropping, 141
inserting, 24–26
inserting, from files, 25
positioning, 24–26
relative positioning, 143
repositioning visually, 26
restoring to original format, 143
rotating, 142
scaling, 141
sizing, 24–26, 141
sizing visually, 26
text wrapping around, 143–45
as watermarks, 190
graphs (Excel). *See* charts (Excel)
grayscale (PowerPoint), 475, 529
previewing, 530
settings, changing, 530
Greeting Line dialog box
(Word), 173
grid (Access), 614
Grid and Guides command
(PowerPoint), 477
Grid and Guides dialog box
(PowerPoint), 477
gridlines (PowerPoint)
aligning graphics with, 476
formatting, 446
snapping shapes to, 477
turning on/off, 477
Group and Outline/Auto Outline
command (Excel), 330
Group and Outline/Clear Outline
command (Excel), 331
Group and Outline/Group
command (Excel), 330
Group and Outline/Settings
command (Excel), 330
Group Footer group property
(Access), 588
Group Header group property
(Access), 588
Group On group property
(Access), 588
grouping
database records, 590
e-mail messages, 709
shapes, 29
guides. *See* drawing guides
(PowerPoint)

H

handles, shape, 452
Handout Master, 489. *See also*
masters (PowerPoint)
displaying, 490
layout, changing, 490
number of slides per page,
setting, 490
handouts (PowerPoint)
formats, 532
headers and footers, adding, 494
masters for. *See* Handout Master
Hanging Indent marker (Ruler), 74,
493
hanging indents
adjusting, 492
creating, 74
Header and Footer command
PowerPoint, 493
Word, 85, 86, 87, 88
Header and Footer dialog box
(PowerPoint), 493, 494
headers/footers (Access)
hiding/displaying, on forms, 616
hiding/displaying, in reports, 621
headers/footers (Excel), 315–16
headers/footers
(PowerPoint), 493–94
headers/footers (Word)
creating, 85–87
different in different sections, 85
different on first page, 86
different on odd and even
pages, 87
displaying, 86
modifying, 85–87
navigating, 86
showing next, 86
switching between, 85
height of table rows, changing in
Word, 44
Help button in presentations. *See*
action buttons (PowerPoint)
Help on this error command
(Excel), 354
help text, adding to form fields in
Word, 185
hidden slides, 514–15
displaying, 515
hiding/unhiding, 514
hyperlinks to, creating, 515
hidden text (Word), 5, 125
displaying, 6

Hide Columns command
(Access), 622
Hide command (Excel), 288, 311
Hide Comment command
(Excel), 293
Hide Details button (Access), 636
Hide Duplicates control property
(Access), 588
Hide Slide button (Slide Sorter
toolbar), 515
Hide Slide command
(PowerPoint), 514
hiding
comments, in Excel, 293
comments, in PowerPoint, 501
comments, in Word, 101
datasheet columns, 622
drawing guides, in
PowerPoint, 477
formatting, in Word, 6
formulas, in Excel, 385
gridlines, in PowerPoint, 477
index entries, in Word, 192
Navigation Pane, in Outlook, 647
Reading Pane, in Outlook, 646
slide formatting, in Slide Sorter
view, 506
slides. See hidden slides
toolbar buttons, in Excel, 412
toolbar buttons, in Word, 230
tracked changes, in Word, 99, 104
white space between pages, in
Word, 125
workbooks, 311
worksheet columns/rows, 288
worksheets, 290–91
hierarchical level of text, changing
in PowerPoint, 433–34
Highlight button (Word Formatting
toolbar), 70
Highlight Changes dialog box
(Excel), 392, 395
highlighter, annotating slide shows
with, 520
highlighting text, 70
highlighting pointer (Word), 70
Home button in presentations. See
action buttons (PowerPoint)
Horizontal Spacing command
(Access), 615
HTML
e-mail messages, 664
hyperlinks. See hyperlinks
presentations. See Web
presentations

HTML command (Outlook), 666
HTML files, importing Access data
from, 606
hyperlink base, assigning to Word
documents, 220
Hyperlink command
Excel, 303
Word, 58
Hyperlink data type (Access), 548
hyperlinks (Excel)
deleting, 304
editing, 304
inserting, 302–3
ScreenTips, adding to, 303
hyperlinks (PowerPoint), 508–9
action buttons, attaching to, 513
creating, with Insert Hyperlink
dialog box, 509
to files, 508
to hidden slides, 515
inserting, 508
to other slides, 508
to Web sites, 508
hyperlinks (Word)
deleting, 60–61
editing, 60–61
to e-mail addresses, 59
embedding in e-mail
messages, 657
to files, 57
inserting, 57–60
to Web pages, 58

illustrations. See figures (Word)
Import Data dialog box (Excel), 399
Import Data Options dialog box
PowerPoint, 444
Word, 149
Import External Data/Import Data
command (Excel), 399
Import File button (Graph Standard
toolbar), 149, 444
Import File dialog box (Word), 149
Import Objects dialog box
(Access), 606
Import XML Data button (Excel List
toolbar), 367
Importance button (Outlook), 666
importing
Access data, 606–7
Access tables, vs. linking to, 605

database objects, into
Access, 605–6
datasheet data, into PowerPoint
charts, 444
Excel data, 399
Excel data, from Web pages, 400–
401
files, into Excel, 398–400
text files, into Access, 606
XML data file, into structured
worksheet, 367
Inbox (Outlook), displaying, 647
Increase Decimal button (Excel
Formatting toolbar), 283
Increase Font Size button
(PowerPoint Formatting
toolbar), 466
indent markers (PowerPoint), 491.
See also indents (PowerPoint)
moving, 492
indent markers (Word), 73
indenting paragraphs, 73–76
indents (PowerPoint) . See also
indent markers
changing, 492
hanging, adjusting, 492
moving, 491
Index and Tables dialog box
(Word), 194, 196, 197
index entries (Word), 192
cross-references, creating, 194
formatting, 193
hiding, 192
marking, 192, 193
subentries, 192
Indexed property (Access), 555
indexes (Word), 192–95
compiling, 192
compiling, on separate page, 194
marking entries, 192, 193
updating, 194
Information button in
presentations. See action
buttons (PowerPoint)
initials, changing, 501
ink color of pen tool in slide shows,
changing, 520
input errors, avoiding in Excel,
331–32
input masks (Access), 557–59
characters in, 557
creating, 558
Insert Address Block dialog box
(Word), 172
Insert button (Outlook), 657, 658

Insert Chart icon (PowerPoint), 443
Insert Clip Art button (Word Drawing toolbar), 25
Insert Clip Art icon (PowerPoint), 450
Insert Columns command (PowerPoint), 440
Insert command (Excel), 289
Insert Comment button
  PowerPoint Reviewing toolbar, 500
  Word Reviewing toolbar, 100, 102
Insert Diagram or Organization Chart button
  Excel Drawing toolbar, 271
  PowerPoint, 447
  Word Drawing toolbar, 30
Insert dialog box (Excel), 298
Insert File button (Outlook), 657
Insert Frame button (Word Forms toolbar), 188
Insert Function button (Excel formula bar), 265, 268, 269, 270, 351, 353
Insert Function dialog box (Excel), 265
Insert Hyperlink button
  PowerPoint Standard toolbar, 509
  Word Standard toolbar, 57, 58
Insert Hyperlink dialog box
  Excel, 303
  PowerPoint, 509
  Word, 57
Insert Media Clip icon (PowerPoint), 461, 462
Insert mode, 5
Insert New Slide Master button (Slide Master View toolbar), 490
Insert New Title Master button (Slide Master View toolbar), 490
Insert Object dialog box (PowerPoint), 458
Insert Picture button (Word Drawing toolbar), 25
Insert Picture dialog box (Word), 25
Insert Picture icon (PowerPoint), 451
insert rows (Excel), 333
Insert Rows command (PowerPoint), 440
Insert Rows button (Access Table Design toolbar), 547

Insert Shape button
  Excel Organization Chart toolbar, 272
  PowerPoint Organization Chart toolbar, 447
Insert Table button (Word Standard toolbar), 39, 40
Insert Table dialog box
  PowerPoint, 439
  Word, 40
Insert Table icon (PowerPoint), 439
Insert WordArt button (Drawing toolbar), 454
Insert/Columns command (Word), 43
Insert/Rows command (Word), 43
Insert/Table command (Word), 39, 40
inserting
  AutoShapes, 28
  bookmarks, in Word, 165
  captions, in Word, 200
  charts, in PowerPoint, 442–46
  charts, in Word, 33–36
  check-box form fields, in Word, 184
  clip art, 25
  clip art, in Excel, 254
  clip art, in slides, 449–51
  column breaks, 82
  columns, in Word, 81–83
  columns, in worksheets, 298
  comments, in PowerPoint, 500
  comments, in Word, 100–101
  cross-references, in Word, 201
  dates, in Word, 19–20
  drop-down form fields, in Word, 185
  endnotes, in Word, 199
  fields, in Access, 547
  fields, in queries, 610
  files, in e-mail messages, 657
  footnotes, in Word, 199
  frames, in text form fields, 187
  frames, into frames pages, 211
  graphics, from files, 25
  graphics, in Excel, 254–55
  graphics, in slides, 451–52
  graphics, in Word, 24–26
  hidden text, in Word, 5
  hyperlinks, 57–60
  hyperlinks, in Excel, 302
  hyperlinks, in PowerPoint, 508
  hyperlinks, to e-mail addresses, 59
  hyperlinks, to files, 57
  hyperlinks, to Web pages, 58

  linked objects, in PowerPoint slides, 459
  masters, in PowerPoint, 490
  movies, in slides, 460–63
  objects, in Word, 145–48
  organization chart boxes, in Excel, 272
  organization chart boxes, in PowerPoint, 447
  organization charts, in Excel, 271
  organization charts, in PowerPoint, 447
  organization charts, in Word, 30–32
  page breaks, before paragraphs in Word, 140
  page breaks, in Word, 89–91
  page numbers, in Word, 87–89
  photo albums, in slides, 451
  PowerPoint text, from Word, 434–35
  rows, in worksheets, 298
  section breaks, in Word, 90
  shapes, 27–30
  shapes, simple, 28
  signatures, automatically in e-mail forwards/replies, 660
  Slide Master, 490
  sounds, in slides, 460–63
  special characters, in Word, 7–8
  stock quotes, in Excel, 253
  subordinate boxes, in Excel organization charts, 272
  subordinate boxes, in PowerPoint organization charts, 447
  symbols, in Word, 7–8
  table columns/rows, in PowerPoint, 440
  table of authorities, in Word, 197
  table of contents, in Word, 196
  table of figures, in Word, 197
  table columns/rows, in Word, 43
  tables, in PowerPoint, 439
  tables, in Word, 39–41
  text boxes, in Word, 26–27
  text form fields, in Word, 184
  text, in Word, 5–6
  time, in Word, 19–20
  Title Master, 490
  Word outlines, in PowerPoint presentations, 435
  Word tables, in PowerPoint slides, 458–59
  worksheet cells, 298
  worksheet columns/rows, 288–89
  worksheets, 305

insertion point, moving, 3
installing
    Analysis Toolpak, in Excel, 339
    Solver, in Excel, 343
instant messages, 651, 655–56
    contacts, creating, 671–72
    online status, specifying, 655
    replying to, 656
    sending, 655
    sending files with, 658
    setting up, 655
Integer field size (Access), 549
Italic button
    Excel Formatting toolbar, 278
    PowerPoint Formatting toolbar,
        440, 466
    Word Formatting toolbar, 63
italicizing text, 466

J

jumping
    to bookmarks, in Word, 166
    to named cells, 360
    to a specific item in Word, 23–24
Justify button (Word Formatting
      toolbar), 75
justifying text, 75

K

Keep Together property
      (Access), 588
keyboard shortcuts (Excel), 416
keyboard shortcuts
      (PowerPoint), 518
    demoting/promoting text
      with, 433
keyboard shortcuts (Word), 3
    assigning to macros, 224
keywords
    assigning to Word documents, 220
    searching clip art by, 450
    searching Word documents
      by, 220

L

Label Options dialog box
      (Word), 175
Label Wizard (Access), 585–86
labels (Access), moving
      independently from
      control, 615
labels, mailing (Access). *See* mailing
      labels (Access)
labels (Word). *See* mailing labels
      (Word)
Landscape button (PowerPoint Print
      Preview toolbar), 529
landscape orientation, 91
Language/Thesaurus command
      (Word), 15
layout, slide. *See* slide layout
Layout button
    Excel Organization Chart
      toolbar, 273
    PowerPoint Organization Chart
      toolbar, 449
Layout Preview (Access), 633–35
layouts, applying to slides, 429
Left Indent marker (Ruler), 74, 492
left-aligning
    table text, in PowerPoint, 440
    worksheet cells, 280
legends, chart, 443
Less Brightness button
    Excel Picture toolbar, 373
    PowerPoint Picture toolbar, 475
    Word Picture toolbar, 143
Less Contrast button
    Excel Picture toolbar, 373
    PowerPoint Picture toolbar, 475
    Word Picture toolbar, 143
Letters and Mailings/Envelopes and
      Labels command (Word), 119
Letters and Mailings/Mail Merge
      command (Word), 169, 172,
      174, 175
Line Color button (PowerPoint
      Drawing toolbar), 476
line spacing, adjusting in Word, 74
lines, selecting, 2
lines of text, keeping together in
      Word, 140
Link to Previous button (Word
      Header and Footer
      toolbar), 86
linked charts (Word), 150–51
linked files (PowerPoint), 521

linked objects (PowerPoint), 459
linked objects (Word), 147
    modifying, 148
linking to tables in Access, vs.
      importing, 605
Links dialog box (Word), 151
links. *See* hyperlinks
List/Convert to Range command
      (Excel), 334
List/Create List command
      (Excel), 333
List/Resize List command
      (Excel), 333
lists (Excel), 333–34
    converting into ordinary ranges, 334
    creating, 333
    custom. *See* custom lists (Excel)
    insert rows, 333
    modifying, 333
    resizing, 333
    rows, inserting, 334
    sorting, 261–63
    total rows, 333
    total rows, adding, 334
lists (Word). *See* bulleted lists
      (Word); numbered lists
      (Word)
Locked control property
      (Access), 578
locking forms, in Word, 213–14
locking Excel cells and ranges, 384
logical functions (Excel), 270–71
Long Integer field size (Access), 549
long values in Excel worksheets, 240
Lookup Field command
      (Access), 553
lookup fields (Access), 552–54
Lookup functions (Excel), 350–52
    VLOOKUP. *See* VLOOKUP
      function (Excel)
looping movies, in slides, 463
Lotus 1-2-3 spreadsheets, importing
      Access data from, 606

M

Macro/Macros command
    Excel, 417, 418
    Word, 225, 226
Macro/Record New Macro
      command
    Excel, 416
    Word, 224

Macro/Security command
  Access, 538
  Excel, 389
  Word, 223
macros (Access), exporting, 640
macros (Excel), 388–89, 416
  adjusting security level, 389
  deleting, 417
  editing, 418–19
  keyboard shortcuts, assigning, 416
  recording, 416
  running, 417
macros (Word)
  creating, 223–26
  deleting, 223–26
  editing, 226–27
  editing, with VBA, 226
  keyboard shortcuts, assigning, 224
  recording, 224
  running, 224
  security, setting, 223
Macros dialog box
  Excel, 417, 418
  Word, 225
magnifying. *See* **zooming**
Mail button (Outlook), 647
mail merge
  data source. *See* data source (mail
    merge)
  form letters. *See* form letters
Mail Merge Recipients dialog box
  (Word), 170
mailing labels (Word), 175–77
  printing, 119–121, 175
mailing labels (Access), 585–86
  printing, with reports, 585
  text, editing, 589
mailing lists. *See* **distribution lists**
  (Outlook)
Make Table Query command
  (Access), 573
make-table queries
  (Access), 572–74
managing
  databases, 631
  versions of Word
    documents, 212–13
  Word documents, 106
  workbooks, 296 398
manual page breaks in Word, 89
many-to-many relationships
  (Access), 560
margins, setting
  in Access, 620
  in Excel, 313

  in Outlook, 726
  in Word, 91–92
Mark Complete button
  (Outlook), 696
Mark Index Entry dialog box
  (Word), 193
marking
  citations, in Word, 195
  cross-references, in Word
    indexes, 194
  e-mail messages. *See* flagging e-mail
    messages
  index entries, in Word, 192, 193
  tasks, as complete, 696
marking up slide shows. *See*
  annotating slide shows
markup. *See* **tracked changes**
master documents (Word), 202–4
  creating, 203
  modifying subdocuments from
    within, 204
  subdocuments, 203–4
  view, changing, 204
Master Layout command
  (PowerPoint), 491
Master view (PowerPoint), 505
Master/Handout Master command
  (PowerPoint), 490
Master/Notes Master command
  (PowerPoint), 490
Master/Slide Master command
  (PowerPoint), 489
masters (PowerPoint)
  changing, 489–91
  Handout Master. *See* Handout
    Master
  headers and footers in, 493–94
  inserting, 490
  multiple, 489
  Notes Pages Master, 489
  placeholders in. *See* placeholders
    (PowerPoint)
  templates, applying, 490
  Title Master. *See* Title Master
Max function (Access), 612
Maximize button (Word), 129
maximizing windows, 128
Media Clip dialog box
  (PowerPoint), 462
media clips. *See* **movies**
  (PowerPoint); sounds
  (PowerPoint)
meeting requests (Outlook), 679
  accepting, 682, 684
  accepting, automatically, 686

  accepting, tentatively, 682
  declining, 683, 684
  declining, automatically, 686
  proposing new time, 683
  responding to, 682–86
  responding to, automatically, 683
meetings (Outlook), 676–82
  attendees, removing, 687
  canceling, 687
  color-coding, 711–14
  creating, 648
  deleting, 687
  linking to contacts, 704
  meeting requests. *See* meeting
    requests (Outlook)
  organizing, by category, 725
  proposing new time, 685
  requests. *See* meeting requests
    (Outlook)
  scheduling, 679–82
  scheduling resources for, 681–82
  updating, 687
  viewing, 683
Memo data type (Access), 548
menus (Excel)
  creating, 413
  customizing, 413–15
  deleting, 414
  moving, 414
  renaming, 413
  resetting, 415
menus (Word)
  adding commands to, 228
  creating custom, 228
  customizing, 227–29
  deleting, 228
  moving, 228
  resetting, 229
Merge Cells button
  PowerPoint Tables and Borders
    toolbar, 441
  Word Tables and Borders toolbar,
    157
Merge Cells command (Word), 43
Merge Scenarios dialog box
  (Excel), 337
Merge to Printer dialog box
  (Word), 176
merging
  form letters, 174
  presentations, 502–3
  scenarios, in Excel, 336–37
  table cells, in PowerPoint, 441
  table cells, in Word, 43, 44,
    157–58

merging Word documents, 97–99
tracked changes, 98–99
merging workbooks, 393–94
Message Format button
(Outlook), 665
messages
e-mail. *See* e-mail messages
instant. *See* instant messages
Microsoft Access. *See* Access
Microsoft Excel. *See* Excel
Microsoft Graph. *See* Graph
Microsoft Outlook. *See* Outlook
Microsoft Visual Basic for
Applications, editing Word
macros with, 226
Microsoft Word. *See* Word
Min function (Access), 612
misspellings. *See* spelling, checking
Modify Location dialog box
(Word), 233
Modify Style dialog box (Word), 135
modifying
custom slide shows, 511
distribution lists, 702–3
distribution lists, for single
message only, 703
embedded objects, in Word, 148
font, in PowerPoint, 466
forms, in Word, 187–88
linked chart data, in Word, 151
linked objects, in Word, 148
lists, in Excel, 333
objects, in Word, 145–47
PivotTable reports, 348
shared workbooks, 392
slide layout, 482–83
subdocuments in Word, from
master document, 204
tables, in Access Design
view, 546–48
templates, in Word, 107
Web pages, in Word, 210
work week, in Outlook, 692
worksheet cell styles, 285–86
modules (Access), exporting, 640
Month button (Outlook), 691
Month view (Outlook
Calendar), 688
Monthly style, printing Outlook
Calendar in, 728
More Brightness button
Excel Picture toolbar, 373
PowerPoint Picture toolbar, 475
Word Picture toolbar, 143

More Contrast button
Excel Picture toolbar, 373
PowerPoint Picture toolbar, 475
Word Picture toolbar, 143
Move Down button (Word Outlining
toolbar), 56
Move Up button (Word Outlining
toolbar), 56
Movie Options dialog box
(PowerPoint), 463
movies (PowerPoint)
default slide layout, changing, 462
editing, 463
inserting, 460–63
inserting, from files, 462
inserting, with content layout, 462
looping, 463
pausing, 462
playing, 462
Movies and Sound/Movie from File
command (PowerPoint), 462
Movies and Sounds/Sound from
Clip Organizer command
(PowerPoint), 460
moving
charts, in Excel, 275
controls, in Access, 614
datasheet columns, 622
drawing guides, in
PowerPoint, 477
fields, in Access, 547
folders, in Outlook, 718
form fields, in Word, 187
indents, in PowerPoint, 491, 492
menus, in Excel, 414
menus, in Word, 228
slides, 506
slides, from other
presentations, 506
sounds, in slides, 461
tab stops, in Word, 80
tables, in Word, 45
text, 10–12
to a specific item in Word, 23–24
Web pages, 116
Web presentations, 524
WordArt, 456
worksheet cells, 298
worksheet entries, 299
worksheets, 305–6
worksheets, to different
workbook, 305
MSN Messenger, 671

Multiple Pages button
Access, 634
Print Preview toolbar, 122
Multiple Plots button (Access), 638

N

Name/Define command
(Excel), 361
Name/Paste command (Excel), 362
naming. *See also* renaming
bookmarks, in Word, 165
calculated fields, in Access, 610
fields, in datasheets, 544, 546
worksheet cells, 360–61
worksheet ranges, 360–61
worksheets, 289–90
navigating
Access records, 603–4
comments, in Word, 100
datasheets, 34
Date Navigator, in Outlook, 691
Excel, with Go To
command, 251–52
headers/footers, in Word, 86
presentations, 426
slide shows, 518
tables, in Word, 39
tracked changes, in
PowerPoint, 497
tracked changes, in Word, 99, 104
Web presentations, 525
Word documents, 167–68
Word documents, with Go To
command, 23
Word documents, with Select
Browse Object button, 23
Navigation Pane
(Outlook), 646–47
New button
Access Database toolbar, 540, 541,
542
Outlook, 648, 700
New command
Excel, 405
Word, 107
New Contact from Same Company
command (Outlook), 670
New Data Access Page dialog box
(Access), 594
New Folder dialog box
Excel, 318
Word, 113

New Form dialog box (Access), 575
New Frame Left button (Word Frames toolbar), 211
New Message button (Outlook), 648
New Presentation task pane (PowerPoint), 429
New Range dialog box (Excel), 384
New Record button (Access), 601
New Report dialog box (Access), 585
New Rule button (Outlook), 714
New Search Folder command (Outlook), 722
New Search Folder dialog box (Outlook), 722
New Slide button (PowerPoint Formatting toolbar), 429
New Style dialog box (Word), 134, 136
New Table dialog box (Access), 542
New Web Query dialog box (Excel), 401
New Window command (Word), 129
New Workbook task pane (Excel), 297
New/Folder command (Outlook), 718
Next button
    PowerPoint Rehearsal toolbar, 517
    Word Reviewing toolbar, 99, 100, 104
    Word scroll bar, 24
Next button in presentations. See action buttons (PowerPoint)
Next Item button (PowerPoint Reviewing toolbar), 497
Next Page button (PowerPoint Print Preview toolbar), 529
Next Record button (Mail Merge task pane), 174
Normal command (Word), 124
Normal style (Word), 67
Normal template, 67, 106
Normal view (PowerPoint), 424, 505
Normal view (Word), 123
    comparing with Print Layout view, 124
Normal View button (Word), 124
Note icon (Outlook), 705
notes (Excel), adding to charts, 379
notes (Outlook), 703-6, 706-7
    color-coding, 711-14

creating, 706
creating, by dragging text, 649
deleting, 707
displaying, 647
editing, 707
including URLs in, 706
linking to contacts, 705
organizing, by color, 712
organizing, with views, 717
saving, 706
notes (PowerPoint), 507-8. See also Notes Page view (PowerPoint)
    adding, 507
    entering non-text information, 507
    exporting to Word, 532-33
    graphics, adding, 507
    headers and footers, adding, 494
    masters for, 489
    viewing all, 507
Notes button (Outlook), 647
Notes Master, displaying, 490
Notes Page command (PowerPoint), 507
Notes Page view (PowerPoint), 505, 507. See also notes (PowerPoint)
Notes Pages Master, 489. See also masters (PowerPoint)
Number data type (Access), 548
number fields (Access), 549
numbered lists (Word), 52-54. See also bulleted lists (Word)
    converting paragraphs to, 53
    converting, into outlines, 54
    converting, into paragraphs, 53
    creating, 52-54
    customizing, 52-54
    overriding autonumbering, 54
    sorting, 153-54
    style, changing, 68
    styles for, 137-38
    styles, clearing, 68
Numbering button (Word Formatting toolbar), 53
    entering as text, 242
    entering sequentially, with interval greater than 1, 245
    formatting as text, 243
numbers (Excel), 241-45
    creating custom formats, 370-71
    entering as text, 242
    entering sequentially, with interval greater than 1, 245
    formatting as text, 243

O

Object command
    PowerPoint, 458, 459
    Word, 146, 147
object dependencies (Access), 632-33
Object Dependencies command (Access), 632
Object dialog box (Word), 146, 147
objects (Access), 536-37
    deleting, 537
    exporting, 640-41
    importing, 605-6
    opening, 537
    printing, 639-40
    renaming, 537
objects (Excel), chart. See chart objects (Excel)
objects (PowerPoint), 425. See also shapes
    chart, 443
    embedded. See embedded objects (PowerPoint)
    linked, 459
    text. See text objects (PowerPoint)
objects (Word)
    chart, 33
    embedded. See embedded objects (Word)
    inserting, 145-47
    inserting, from files, 147-48
    linked vs. embedded, 147
    modifying, 145-47
    opening source program for, 146
Office Clipboard, 10
    copying shapes to, 453
OLE Object data type (Access), 548
one-to-many relationships (Access), 560-62
    common field for, 560
    modifying, 562
one-to-one relationships (Access), 560
Open button
    Access, 536
    Excel Standard toolbar, 319, 399
    PowerPoint Standard toolbar, 435
    Word Standard toolbar, 114, 210, 215
Open command
    Excel, 319
    Word, 114

Open dialog box (Word), 210
opening
    Clip Art task pane, in
        PowerPoint, 453
    Clipboard task pane,
        automatically, 300
    comments, in PowerPoint, 501
    database objects, 537
    databases, 536
    file created in another program, in
        Excel, 399
    Mark Index Entry dialog box
        (Word), 193
    password-protected Word
        documents, 215
    presentations, on computers
        without PowerPoint, 521–22.
        See also PowerPoint Viewer
    tables, in Access, 601
    tables, in Access Design view, 551
    Web pages, in Word, 210
    Word documents, in new
        windows, 129
    Word documents, password-
        protected, 215
    Word outlines, in PowerPoint, 435
operators (Excel), 263
Options button (Outlook), 667
Options command
    Access, 623, 643
    Excel, 387, 420
    Outlook, 650, 652, 659, 661, 665,
        686, 692, 719
    PowerPoint, 437, 501, 525
    Word, 116, 125, 163, 208, 214,
        219, 232, 233
Options dialog box
    Excel, 246, 420
    Outlook, 650, 660, 661, 665, 686,
        693
    PowerPoint, 437, 501
    Word, 163, 214, 232, 233
Options/Preferences/E-mail
    Options command
    (Outlook), 649
Organization Chart Style Gallery
    (Excel), 380
Organization Chart Style Gallery
    dialog box
    Excel, 272
    PowerPoint, 448
organization charts (Excel)
    arrows, adding to lines, 381
    autoformatting, 272
    boxes, 272–73

connecting lines, selecting, 381
formatting, 380–81
formatting, with predefined
    styles, 380
inserting, 271
layout, changing, 273
lines, coloring, 381
positioning, 273
sizing, 273
style, changing, 272
organization charts
        (PowerPoint), 447–49
    autoformatting, 448
    boxes, formatting text in, 448
    boxes, inserting, 447
    boxes, selecting all at same
        level, 448
    boxes, subordinate, 447
    editing, 447
    fitting to contents, 448
    formatting, 447
    inserting, 447
    layout, changing, 449
    positioning, 448
    sizing to fit contents, 448
    style, changing, 447, 448
organization charts (Word), 30
    arrows, adding to lines, 31
    connecting lines, selecting, 31
    formatting, 30–32
    formatting, with predefined
        styles, 31
    inserting, 30–32
    lines, coloring, 31
    positioning, 32
    sizing, 32
Organize command (Outlook), 711
organizing
    data, in Access, 609
    data, in Excel, 325
    Outlook, 699
    Outlook notes, by color, 712
    slides, 506–7
    Word documents, in Outline
        view, 56
orientation (Word), 91–92
orientation, slide, 484–85
orphans. *See* widows/orphans
Outline tab (PowerPoint), adding
        text in, 431
Outline view (Word), 54, 123
    organizing documents in, 56
Outline View button (Word
        document window), 56

outlines (PowerPoint), exporting to
        Word, 532–33
outlines (Word), 54–56. *See also*
        Document Map (Word)
    collapsing, 56
    converting bulleted/numbered
        lists into, 54
    creating, 54
    creating PowerPoint presentations
        from, 435
    expanding, 56
    headings, demoting/
        promoting, 56
    headings, moving, 56
    inserting in PowerPoint
        presentations, 435
outlining worksheets, 329–31
Outlook
    automatic address completion
        in, 652
    importing Access data from, 606
    options, setting, 649–50
    organizing, 699
    organizing with colors, 711
    personalizing, 649–50
Outlook Rich Text Format, 664
Overtype mode, 5
overtyping text, 430
    in Word, 5, 9

P

Package for CD command
        (PowerPoint), 521
Package for CD dialog box
        (PowerPoint), 521
packaging presentations for
        CD, 521–22
    embedded fonts, including, 521
    PowerPoint Viewer, including, 521
    unpacking and delivering, 522
Page Break command (Excel), 314
page breaks (Excel), 314
page breaks (Word) . *See also*
        section breaks (Word)
    deleting, 89–91
    inserting, 89–91
    inserting before paragraphs, 140
    manual, 89
    preventing within paragraphs, 140
    soft, 89
Page Header/Footer command
        (Access), 616, 621

page margins. *See* margins
Page Number Format dialog box
  (Word), 88
page numbers (Word)
  aligning, 88
  formatting, 87–89
  inserting, 87–89
  positioning, 87, 88
  starting number, changing, 88
  style, changing, 88
Page Numbers command
  (Word), 88
Page Numbers dialog box
  (Word), 88
page orientation (Excel), 312
  changing, 312
page orientation (Word), 91–92
Page Setup
  Card Style dialog box
    (Outlook), 732
  Weekly Style dialog box
    (Outlook), 729
page setup (Access)
  changing, 620
  reports and, 618
page setup (Outlook), 726
page setup (PowerPoint), 530
Page Setup button
  Outlook, 729, 731
  Word Header and Footer toolbar,
    86
Page Setup command
  Access, 620
  Excel, 312, 315
  PowerPoint, 484
  Word, 91, 92
Page Setup dialog box
  Excel, 312, 315
  Outlook, 726
  PowerPoint, 484, 531
  Word, 86, 91
Page Setup/Memo Style command
  (Outlook), 726
pages (Access), exporting, 640
pages (Word)
  displaying as thumbnails, 127
  white spaces between, hiding, 125
pagination (Word), 139–40
Paradox files, importing Access data
  from, 606
Paragraph command (Word), 47,
  75, 76, 139, 140, 166
Paragraph dialog box (Word), 75,
  139

paragraph styles (Word), 67
paragraphs
  aligning, 73–76
  borders. *See* borders (Word)
  converting numbered lists into, in
    Word, 53
  converting to bulleted lists, in
    Word, 50
  converting to numbered lists, in
    Word, 53
  creating styles for, in Word. *See*
    styles (Word)
  formatting, in Word, 67
  formatting, in Word tables, 46
  indenting, 73–76
  indenting, first lines of, 74
  indenting, with hanging indent, 74
  indenting, with rulers, 74
  inserting page breaks before, in
    Word, 140
  keeping together, in Word, 140
  selecting, 2
  shading. *See* shading
  spacing, 73–76
Password dialog box (Word), 215
password protection
  (Excel), 387–88
  applying to worksheet cells and
    ranges, 384
  password guidelines, 388
  removing, 388
password protection
  (Word), 214–16
  opening documents with, 215
  removing, 216
passwords (Excel), 388
passwords (Word)
  deleting, 216
  guidelines for, 215
  setting, 214–16
Paste button
  Excel Standard toolbar, 299
  PowerPoint Standard toolbar, 453
  Word Standard toolbar, 11, 185
Paste command
  Excel, 267, 400
  Word, 10, 11
Paste Link command (Word), 150
Paste Special command
  (Excel), 301–2
Paste Special dialog box (Excel), 301
pasting. *See* cutting and pasting
patterns, background, 478
pausing movies, in slides, 462

pen tool, in slide shows, 519
  color, changing, 520
  erasing all marks made by, 520
  highlighting with, 520
Person Names smart tag
  (Outlook), 671
phone numbers, in Excel, 243
Photo Album dialog box
  (PowerPoint), 451
photo albums, 451
Picture command (PowerPoint), 507
Picture/Chart command
  (Word), 33, 149, 150
Picture/Clip Art command
  Excel, 254
  PowerPoint, 450
  Word, 25
Picture/From File command
  PowerPoint, 451
  Word, 25
Picture/New Photo Album
  command (PowerPoint), 451
pictures. *See* graphics
PivotChart View command
  (Access), 637
PivotCharts, 637–39
  adding fields to, 638
  changing type, 350
  chart type, changing, 638
  drop areas, viewing/hiding, 638
  filtering display, 349
  legends, displaying, 638
  plotting, 349–50
  viewing, 637
  viewing multiple, 638
PivotTable and PivotChart Report
  command (Excel), 347
PivotTable Field dialog box
  (Excel), 348
PivotTable View command
  (Access), 635
PivotTables, 635–36
  adding fields to, 636
  calculation, changing type of, 348
  fields, removing, 636
  filtering in, 348
  filters, setting, 636
  plotting, 349–50
  reports, creating, 345–49
  reports, filtering, 346
  reports, modifying, 348
  updating, 348
  total fields, adding, 636
  viewing, 635

Placeholder command
    (PowerPoint), 467
placeholders (PowerPoint), 489
    adding, 491–93
    deleting, 491–93
    formatting, 491–93
    formatting text in, 491
    replacing text in, 430
    text. *See* text placeholders
        (PowerPoint)
placeholders (Word), 107
Plain Text command (Outlook), 666
Plain Text format (Outlook), 664
    setting as default, 665
playing
    movies, in slides, 462
    sounds, in slides, 461
plotting PivotTables, 349–50
plotting charts in Excel, 274
PMT function (Excel), 270
Pointer Options/Ballpoint Pen
    command (PowerPoint), 519
Pointer Options/Erase All Ink on
    Slide command
    (PowerPoint), 520
Pointer Options/Eraser command
    (PowerPoint), 520
Pointer Options/Felt Tip Pen
    command (PowerPoint), 519
Pointer Options/Highlighter
    command (PowerPoint), 520
Pointer Options/Ink Color
    command (PowerPoint), 520
pointer, in slide shows. *See* pen tool,
    in slide shows
Portrait button (PowerPoint Print
    Preview toolbar), 529
portrait orientation, 91
positioning
    AutoShapes, 29
    chart objects, in Excel, 379
    charts, in Word, 34
    comments, in Excel, 293
    drawing canvas, 29
    graphics, in Excel, 254–55
    graphics, in Word, 24–26
    organization charts, in Excel, 273
    organization charts, in
        PowerPoint, 448
    organization charts, in Word, 32
    page numbers, in Word, 88
    shapes, 27–30
    tab stops, in Word, 79
    text boxes, in Word, 26–27

PowerPoint
    delivering presentations on
        computers without, 521. *See
        also* PowerPoint Viewer
    slides. *See* slides
PowerPoint Viewer, 521
    including when packaging
        presentations for CD, 521
    opening presentations with, 522
precedents (Excel), tracing, 355
pre-defined formats. *See*
    AutoFormats
preformatting worksheet cells, 280
presentations
    blank. *See* templates (PowerPoint)
    checking spelling. *See* spelling,
        checking (PowerPoint)
    collaborating on, 496
    comments. *See* comments
        (PowerPoint)
    comparing/merging, 502–3
    consistent design, applying. *See*
        templates (PowerPoint)
    creating, from Microsoft Word
        outlines, 435
    creating, with AutoContent
        Wizard, 427–29
    creating, with templates, 429–30
    delivering, 504
    exporting, to Word, 532–33
    headers and footers, 493–94
    hidden slides, 514–15
    masters. *See* masters (PowerPoint)
    moving around, 426
    navigating, 426
    notes. *See* notes (PowerPoint)
    opening, on computers without
        PowerPoint, 521. *See also*
        PowerPoint Viewer
    opening, with PowerPoint
        Viewer, 522
    packaging for CDs. *See* packaging
        presentations for CD
    previewing, 528–30
    previewing, as thumbnails, 505.
        See also Slide Sorter view
        (PowerPoint)
    printing, 530–32
    publishing as Web pages. *See* Web
        presentations
    rehearsing. *See* rehearsing
        presentations
    saving, 523
    saving, as templates, 488

saving, as Web pages. *See* Web
    presentations
sending to Word, 532–33
templates. *See* templates
    (PowerPoint)
unpacking, 522
viewing on computers without
    PowerPoint, 521. *See also*
    PowerPoint Viewer
views in, 505–6
presenting slide shows, 518–19
preventing editing/formatting, in
    Word, 216
previewing. *See also* Print Preview
    animation schemes, 485
    color slides, for printing, 528
    contacts, in Outlook, 730–32
    e-mail messages, 726
    grayscale, in PowerPoint, 530
    layout, in Access, 633–35
    Outlook Calendar, 728–30
    presentations, 528–30
    presentations, as thumbnails, 505.
        See also Slide Sorter view
        (PowerPoint)
    reports, in Access, 590
    tracked changes, in
        PowerPoint, 498
    Web presentations, 524
    Word documents, as Web
        pages, 122–23
    Word documents, before
        printing, 121–22
    workbooks, as Web pages, 307
    worksheets, before
        printing, 306–7
Previous button
    Word Reviewing toolbar, 99, 101,
        104
    Word scroll bar, 24
Previous Item button (PowerPoint
    Reviewing toolbar), 497
Previous Page button (PowerPoint
    Print Preview toolbar), 529
Primary Key button (Access Table
    Design toolbar), 551
primary keys, 551–52
Print Area/Clear Print Area
    command (Excel), 312
Print Area/Set Print Area command
    (Excel), 312
Print button
    Access, 639
    Excel Standard toolbar, 316
    Outlook, 727, 728, 731

PowerPoint Standard toolbar, 531
Word Print Preview toolbar, 118
Word Standard toolbar, 118
Print command
  Access, 640
  Excel, 317
  Outlook, 727
  PowerPoint, 531
  Word, 118
Print dialog box
  Excel, 317
  Outlook, 729, 731
  PowerPoint, 531
  Word, 118
Print Layout command (Word), 125
Print Layout view (Word), 123, 124–26
  comparing with Normal view, 124
Print Layout View button (Word), 125
Print Preview (Access), 633–35
  zooming in, 634
Print Preview (Excel), 306–7
Print Preview (Outlook), 726
Print Preview (PowerPoint), 528–30
  for color slides, 528
  grayscale, 529
  switching to, 528
Print Preview button
  Access, 634
  Access Standard toolbar, 590
  Excel Standard toolbar, 306
  PowerPoint Standard toolbar, 528
  Word Standard toolbar, 121
Print Preview command (Outlook), 726
Print Preview window, 121
Printed Watermark dialog box (Word), 190
printers, switching, 118
printing
  Access data, 639–40
  address books (Outlook), 731
  color slides, previewing before, 528
  contacts, in Outlook, 730–32
  Design view, in Access, 639
  e-mail messages, 727
  envelopes, in Word, 119–21
  grayscale, in PowerPoint, 529
  labels, in Word, 119–21
  mailing labels, 175
  orientation, 91
  Outlook Calendar, 728–30

Outlook Calendar, selecting number of days per page, 728
  presentations, 530–32
  settings, changing, 118
printing Word documents, 118–19
  with custom settings, 118
  with default settings, 118
  to different printer, 118
  multiple copies, 118
  previewing before, 121–22
printing worksheets
  all in workbook, 317
  clearing print area, 312
  page orientation, changing, 312
  partial, 311
  scaling during, 313
  specific pages, 317
  specifying print area when, 311–12
  with default settings, 316
  with specified settings, 317
Promote button
  PowerPoint Outlining toolbar, 433
  Word Outlining toolbar, 56
promoting
  outline headings, in Word, 56
  PowerPoint text, 433–34
Properties button
  Access, 579
  Access Query Design toolbar, 611
  Access Report Design toolbar, 598, 592
  Outlook, 702
Properties command
  Excel, 408
  Outlook, 720
  Word, 109, 111, 115, 220, 221
Properties dialog box
  Access, 579, 589, 597
  Excel, 409
  Word, 109, 110, 111, 220, 221
Propose New Time button (Outlook), 685
Propose New Time dialog box (Outlook), 685
Propose Time button (Outlook), 686
Protect Document command (Word), 216
Protect Document task pane (Word), 216
Protect Form button (Word Forms toolbar), 214
Protect Shared Workbook dialog box (Excel), 391

Protect Sheet dialog box (Excel), 385
protecting
  Excel documents, 383–86
  forms, in Word, 213–14
  Word documents, with passwords. *See* password protection (Word)
Protection/Allow Users to Edit Ranges command (Excel), 384
Protection/Protect Shared Workbook command (Excel), 391
Protection/Protect Sheet command (Excel), 385
Publish as Web Page dialog box
  Excel, 403
  PowerPoint, 527
publishing
  custom slide shows, as Web presentations, 526, 527
  Web presentations, 527
  Web presentations, from selected slides, 527
  worksheets, as Web pages, 403–4
punctuation, checking in PowerPoint, 437

Q

queries (Access)
  action. *See* action queries (Access)
  adding, 566
  adding criteria, 566
  aggregate functions in, 612–13
  append, 571–73
  calculated fields, adding to, 609–11
  calculating totals in, 612–13
  creating, with Simple Query Wizard, 564–65
  crosstab, 567–69
  delete, 571–73
  detailed, 564
  duplicate, 569–70
  editing data produced by, 565
  excluding records from, 613
  exporting, 640
  hiding fields, 567
  inserting fields in, 610
  make-table, 571–73

queries (Access) *(continued)*
   modifying in Design
      view, 565–67
   opening in Design view, 566
   running, 572
   sorting, 567
   summarized, 564
   update, 571–73
   viewing results, 567
query fields (Access), 611
query grids, adding fields to, 566
Query Options dialog box
   (Word), 171

R

ranges (Excel)
   converting lists into, 334
   criteria, setting, 331–32
   determining number of columns,
      rows, or areas in, 350–52
   filling, 245
   list. *See* lists (Excel)
   locking, 384
   naming, 360–61
   password protecting, 384
   referencing in formulas, 266–67
Read button (Word Standard
   toolbar), 127
Readability Statistics dialog box
   (Word), 164
readability statistics, for Word
   documents, 163–64
Reading Layout command
   (Word), 127
Reading Layout view (Word), 123,
   126–27
Reading Pane (Outlook), 646
read-only Word documents, 214
Reapply Layout command
   (PowerPoint), 483
rearranging slides, 506–7. *See also*
   slide layout
   in custom slide shows, 511
Recolor Picture button (PowerPoint
   Picture toolbar), 475
Recolor Picture dialog box
   (PowerPoint), 475
Record Macro dialog box
   Excel, 416
   Word, 224
Record Source property
   (Access), 578, 587

recording macros
   in Excel, 416
   in Word, 224
records (Access)
   default field values in, 601
   deleting, 602
   deleting, with queries, 571–73
   duplicate, finding, 569–70
   editing, 601
   entering, 601
   excluding from queries, 613
   filtering by form, 629
   filtering by selection, 627–28
   filtering by specified
      values, 628–30
   filtering with wildcard
      characters, 628
   finding, 604–5
   grouping, 590
   grouping interval, changing, 583
   navigating, 603–4
   sorting, 624–25
   total number of, displaying, 603
   unmatched, finding, 570–71
records (Excel), displaying with
   specific criteria, 260
Recount button (Word Count
   toolbar), 112
Recurrence button (Outlook), 678,
   695, 696
Recurring Appointments view
   (Outlook Calendar), 689
recurring appointments/events
   (Outlook), 676
   creating, 678
recurring tasks (Outlook)
   creating, 695
   deleting, 696
   stopping recurrence, 696
Redo button (Word Standard
   toolbar), 9
Redo command (Word), 9
redoing, 9
   multiple actions, 10
Reference functions
   (Excel), 350–52
Reference/Caption command
   (Word), 200
Reference/Cross-reference
   command (Word), 201
Reference/Footnote command
   (Word), 199
Reference/Index and Tables
   command (Word), 193, 194,
   196, 197

references (Excel)
   circular, tracking down, 356
   replacing with names, 362
referential integrity
   (Access), 562–63
Refresh Data button (Excel
   PivotTable toolbar), 348
Refresh Data command (Excel), 348
Rehearse Timings button
   (PowerPoint Slide Sorter
   toolbar), 517
rehearsing presentations, 516–18
   repeating rehearsal for slide, 517
   starting over, 517
Reject Change/Delete Comment
   button (Word Reviewing
   toolbar), 104
rejecting changes
   in Excel, 396
   in PowerPoint, 498–99
   in Word, 104
relationships (Access)
   deleting, 562
   displaying, 562
   ensuring validity of, 562–63
   many-to-many, 560
   one-to-many, 560–62
   one-to-one, 560
Relationships button (Access
   Database toolbar), 560, 562
relative positioning of graphics in
   Word, 143
relative references in Excel
   formulas, 266
reminders (Outlook), 676
   creating, when flagging e-mail
      messages, 663
   setting, 677
   for tasks, 694
   for tasks, setting, 695, 697
Remove Filter button (Access), 628,
   630
Remove Hyperlink command
   Excel, 304
   Word, 60
Remove Page Break command
   (Excel), 314
Remove Recurrence button
   (Outlook), 696
Remove Split command
   Excel, 308
   Word, 129
Remove Subdocument button (Word
   Outlining toolbar), 204
removing. *See* deleting

Rename command
  Access, 537
  Excel, 319
renaming. *See also* naming
  database objects, 537
  fields, in Access, 547
  folders, 319, 718
  folders, in Word, 114–15
  menus, in Excel, 413
  Word documents, 114–15
  workbooks, 319
repagination, automatic, 89
repairing databases, in
    Access, 643–44
Repeat button (PowerPoint
    Rehearsal toolbar), 517
Repeat command, 9
Repeat Section section property
    (Access), 588
repeating editing, 10
Replace command (Word), 22, 65
Replace Font dialog box
    (PowerPoint), 471
Replace Fonts command
    (PowerPoint), 471
replacing
  bullet points, 431
  text. *See* finding and replacing text
  titles, in PowerPoint, 431
Reply button (Standard
    toolbar), 653
Reply to All button (Outlook), 654
replying to e-mail messages, 653
  to all recipients of, 654
  automatically inserting signatures
    when, 660
  with Microsoft Word, 653
replying to instant messages, 656
Report Header/Footer command
    (Access), 621
Report Wizard (Access), 583–85
reports (Access)
  arranging fields in, 584
  controls, adding, 591–93
  controls, modifying, 617–18
  creating, with Report
    Wizard, 583–85
  exporting, 640
  grouping interval, changing, 583
  headers/footers, hiding/
    displaying, 621
  layout, modifying, 618–21
  mailing labels, printing, 585
  page setup and, 618

previewing, 590
properties, 587–90
section width, changing to match
  page setup, 620
sorting records in, 583, 625–26
spacing, changing, 621
summarizing records in, 583
reports (PivotTable)
  creating, 345–49
  filtering, 346
  modifying, 348
Required property (Access), 555
Research command
  Excel, 253
  Word, 37
Research Service, 36–37
Research task pane
  PowerPoint, 438
  Word, 15, 36
Research tool (Excel), 253–54
Reset All Page Breaks command
    (Excel), 314
Reset Toolbar command
  Excel, 412
  Word, 230
resetting
  graphics, in PowerPoint, 472, 475
  menus, in Excel, 415
  menus, in Word, 229
  page breaks, in Excel, 314
  slide layout, 482, 483
  slide timings, 517
  toolbars, in Excel, 412
  toolbars, in Word, 230
resizing. *See* sizing
Resolve Conflicts dialog box
    (Excel), 392
resources (Outlook), scheduling,
    681–82
responding
  to comments, in Word, 101, 102
  to meeting requests, 682–86
  to task reminders, 694
restoring
  Word graphics, 143
  PowerPoint graphics, 472, 475
  slide layout, 482, 483
restricting entries, in Excel, 331–32
Return button in presentations. *See*
    action buttons (PowerPoint)
Reveal Formatting command
    (Word), 64, 65
revealing formatting in Word, 63–65

Reviewers button (PowerPoint
    Reviewing toolbar), 497
reviewing
  comments, in Word, 100–101
reviewing changes. See change
    tracking, 196
Reviewing pane (Word)
  closing, 209
  resizing, 209
Reviewing Pane button (Word
    Reviewing toolbar), 209
Reviewing toolbar (Word), 103
revision marks (Word), 102. *See also*
    change tracking (Word
Revisions task pane
    (PowerPoint), 497
Rich Text command (Outlook), 666
Rich Text Format (Outlook), 664
Right Indent marker (Ruler), 74
right-aligning
  table text, in PowerPoint, 440
  worksheet cells, 280
rotating
  chart text, in PowerPoint, 446
  graphics, in Excel, 376
  graphics, in PowerPoint, 476–78
  graphics, in Word, 142
  shapes, 452
  WordArt, 456
rotating handles, 452
Row Height dialog box (Excel), 287
Row/Height command (Excel), 287
Rows command (Excel), 289
rows, datasheet (Access), changing
    height, 623
rows, table (Access), 547
rows, table (PowerPoint)
  deleting, 440
  inserting, 440
  selecting, 439
  selecting multiple, 439
rows, table (Word)
  changing height, 44
  deleting, 43
  inserting, 43
  selecting, 43
  totaling, 156
rows, worksheet (Excel)
  deleting, 289
  determining number of, 350–52
  displaying hidden, 288
  displaying specific, 258–60
  displaying, with certain
    criteria, 260
  filtering, 259

rows, worksheet (Excel) *(continued)*
hiding, 288
insert rows, 333
inserting, 288–89, 298
sizing, 286–88
summary, changing default
location, 330
total rows, 333–34
unfreezing, 309
Ruler command (PowerPoint), 492
rulers (PowerPoint), 492
rulers (Word)
changing margins with, 92
indenting paragraphs with, 74
tab stops. *See* tab stops (Word)
rules (Outlook), 714–16
client vs. server, 714
moving messages to folders
with, 714
**Rules and Alerts command
(Outlook), 714**
Rules Wizard (Outlook), 714
**Run button (Access Query Design
toolbar), 573, 613**
running
Excel macros, 417
queries, 572
Word macros, 224
running slide shows, 518–19
**Running Sum control property
(Access), 588**

S

**Save and Close button
(Outlook), 670, 677, 694,
701, 703**
Save As command
Excel, 318, 320, 367, 387, 402,
405, 406
Outlook, 724
PowerPoint, 488, 523, 533
Word, 113, 115, 180, 181
**Save As dialog box
(PowerPoint), 523, 526**
Save as Web Page command
Excel, 321, 403
PowerPoint, 526, 527
Word, 117
Save button
Access, 538
Access Form View toolbar, 575

Access Table Datasheet toolbar,
545
Access Table Design toolbar, 547,
550
Excel Standard toolbar, 318, 392
PowerPoint Standard toolbar, 523
Word Standard toolbar, 113
Save command
PowerPoint, 523
Word, 211
**Save Options dialog box
(Excel), 388**
**Save Record command
(Access), 538**
saving
databases, 538
e-mail messages, in other
formats, 724–25
frames pages, 211
notes, in Outlook, 706
presentations, 523
presentations, as templates, 488
sent e-mail messages, specifying
folder for, 667
slides, 523
slides, as graphics, 523–24
templates, in PowerPoint, 488
templates, in Word, 107
versions of Word
documents, 212–13
Word documents, as Web
pages, 116–17, 209–12
Word documents, as XML, 177
Word documents, in new
folders, 113–14
Word documents, in other
formats, 115–16
Word documents, new versions of,
automatically, 212
workbook templates, 405
workbooks, to use in other
programs, 320
worksheets, as Web pages, 321
XML data files, in Excel, 402
XML documents, with invalid
structure, 180
XML worksheets, 362–64
**Scale Drawing button (Word
Drawing Canvas toolbar), 29**
scaling
graphics, in Excel, 375
graphics, in PowerPoint, 473
graphics, in Word, 141
worksheets during printing, 313

scenarios (Excel), 334–38
creating multiple, 335
merging, 336–37
PivotTables, printing, 337
reports, creating, 337
showing, 336
**Scenarios command (Excel), 335,
336, 337**
scheduling
appointments/events, 676–79
meetings, 679–82
multi-day events, 678
resources, 681–82
Schema Library, 178
**Schema Library dialog box
(Word), 178**
schemas, XML, 177–82
adding to Schema Library, 178
attaching to Word documents, 178
data maps, 362–64
**scientific notation, in Excel
worksheets, 240**
**ScreenTips, adding to hyperlinks in
Excel, 303**
scroll bars, 3
Search command (Word), 220
**Search Folder Criteria dialog box
(Outlook), 723**
Search Folders (Outlook), 722–24
changing parameters, 723
creating, 722
customizing, 723
deleting, 724
modifying messages in, 722
viewing default, 722
searching. *See also* **finding and
replacing**
for clip art, 25
for clip art, by keyword, 450
for functions, in Excel, 265
searching (Outlook), 720–24
for e-mail messages, 720–22
for e-mail messages assigned to a
category, 721
for e-mail messages with specific
text, 721
section breaks (Word), 89. *See also*
page breaks (Word)
inserting, 90
**sections (Word), different headers/
footers in, 85**
sections, form (Access)
background color, changing, 617
properties, setting, 589
resizing, 616

sections, report (Access)
    layout, modifying, 618–21
    width, changing to match page
        setup, 620
security (Access), changing level
    of, 538
Security dialog box (Excel), 389
security warning in Access
    databases, 538
Select All button (datasheets), 33
Select All command
    Access, 579, 614
    Word, 139
Select Attendees and Resources
    dialog box (Outlook), 681
Select Browse Object button (Word
    scroll bar), 23
Select button
    Excel Organization Chart
        toolbar, 273, 381
    PowerPoint Organization Chart
        toolbar, 448
    Word Organization Chart toolbar,
        31
Select Changes to Accept or Reject
    dialog box (Excel), 396
Select Files to Merge Into Current
    Workbook dialog box
    (Excel), 394
Select Members button
    (Outlook), 700
Select Members dialog box
    (Outlook), 700
Select Picture dialog box
    (PowerPoint), 450
select queries (Access). See
    duplicate queries; unmatched
    queries
Select Table button (tables), 43
Select/Table command (Word), 43
selecting
    bullet points, 425
    controls, in Access, 614
    datasheets, 33
    documents, 2
    Excel organization chart boxes, of
        same level, 273
    in PowerPoint, 425
    lines, 2
    organization chart boxes of same
        level, 448
    organization chart connecting
        lines, 31, 381
    paragraphs, 2
    sentences, 2

slides, all, 487
table cells, in PowerPoint, 439
table cells, in Word, 43
table columns, in PowerPoint, 439
table columns/rows, in Word, 43
table rows, in PowerPoint, 439
tables, in PowerPoint, 439
tables, in Word, 43
text objects, in PowerPoint, 425
text, with specific formatting, 65
words, 2
words, in PowerPoint, 425
selection area, 2
selection boxes (PowerPoint), 425
Send button (Outlook), 652, 654,
    656, 686, 688, 698
Send Files button (Outlook), 658
Send To Microsoft Office Word
    dialog box (PowerPoint), 533
Send To/Mail Recipient (as
    Attachment) command
    (Word), 96
Send To/Mail Recipient (for Review)
    command (Word), 94, 95
Send To/Microsoft Office Word
    command (PowerPoint), 533
Send Update button (Outlook), 687
sending
    e-mail messages, 652
    instant messages, 655
    presentations, to Word, 532–33
    Word documents, for review,
        94–97
Sensitivity button (Outlook), 667
sentences, selecting, 2
server rules (Outlook), 714. See also
    rules (Outlook)
Set Default Flag command
    (Outlook), 663
Set Target Frame dialog box, 58
setting
    height/width of graphics, in
        PowerPoint, 473
    passwords, in Word, 214–16
    slide timings. See slide timings
    tab stops, in Word, 78–81
Setting button (PowerPoint
    Grayscale View toolbar), 530
setting up
    forms, in Word, 183–87
    instant messages, 655
    XML worksheets, 364–68
SGML, 177

shading, 76–78
    slide backgrounds, 480–82
    table cells, in Word, 48
    tables, in Word, 46
    worksheet cells, 279
Shading Color button (Word Tables
    and Borders toolbar), 48
Shadow Color button (PowerPoint
    Shadow Settings
    toolbar), 479
Shadow On/Off button (PowerPoint
    Shadow Settings
    toolbar), 479
Shadow Style button (PowerPoint
    Drawing toolbar), 457, 479
shadows, 478–79
shapes
    3-D effects, 478–79
    adjusting, 452
    animating, on slides, 485
    AutoShapes. See AutoShapes
    color, changing, 476
    connection points, 476–77
    copying, 453
    drawing, 27
    drawing, in slides, 452–54
    effects, adding, 478–79
    equal height/width, drawing, 28
    grouping, 29
    handles, 452
    inserting, 27–30
    pasting, 453
    positioning, 27–30
    rotating, 452
    shadows, 478–79
    simple, inserting, 28
    sizing, 27–30, 452
    sizing handles, 452
    snapping to gridlines, in
        PowerPoint, 477
    textures, adding, 478
Share Workbook command
    (Excel), 390
Share Workbook dialog box
    (Excel), 390
shared workbooks (Excel), 391–93
    creating, 390
    editing, 392
    history, viewing, 392
    requiring tracked changes, 391
Sheet/Background command
    (Excel), 290
Sheet/Hide command (Excel), 290
Sheet/Unhide command
    (Excel), 290

shifting worksheet cells, 298
shortcut keys, 3
Shortcuts button (Outlook), 647
Shortcuts folder (Outlook), 647
Show All Relationships button (Access Relationship toolbar), 563
Show button (Word Reviewing toolbar), 99, 101, 104, 207, 208
Show Calculation Steps command (Excel), 354
Show Drawing Canvas Toolbar command (Word), 29
Show Fields dialog box (Outlook), 708
Show First Line Only button (Word Outlining toolbar), 204
Show Large Previews command (PowerPoint), 429
Show Legend button (Access), 638
Show Level button (Word Outlining toolbar), 56
Show Next button (Word Header and Footer toolbar), 86
Show Picture Toolbar command (Excel), 375
Show Table button (Access Relationship toolbar), 560, 566
Show/Hide ¶ button (Word Standard toolbar), 5, 6, 125, 172, 194
Show/Hide Comments command (Excel), 293
Show/Hide Markup button (PowerPoint Reviewing toolbar), 501
signatures, digital. See digital signatures
signatures, e-mail, 659–61
   creating, 659
   creating multiple, 661–62
   deselecting default, 660
   in forwards/replies, inserting automatically, 660
   removing, 660
   specifying for multiple e-mail accounts, 661–62
Simple Query Wizard (Access), 564–65
Single field size (Access), 549
Size command (Access), 615

sizing
   AutoShapes, 29
   bullet points, 491
   chart objects, in Excel, 379
   charts, in Excel, 275
   charts, in Word, 34
   columns, in Word, 83
   comments, in Excel, 293
   controls (Access), 615
   diagrams, in Excel, 273
   drawing canvas, 29
   form fields, in Word, 187
   form sections, in Access, 616
   frames, in frames pages, 211
   graphics, in Excel, 255–56, 374
   graphics, in PowerPoint, 472–74
   graphics, in Word, 24–26, 141
   lists, in Excel, 333
   organization charts, in Excel, 273
   organization charts, in Word, 32
   organization charts, to fit contents, 448
   Reviewing pane, in Word, 209
   shapes, 27–30, 452
   tables, in Word, 44
   text boxes, in Word, 26–27
   text objects, in PowerPoint
   text, in PowerPoint, 466
   WordArt, 456
   worksheet columns/rows, 286–88
sizing handles, 452
skipping slides. See hidden slides
slanted-line selection boxes (PowerPoint), 425
Slide Design button (PowerPoint Formatting toolbar), 469, 483, 490
Slide Design task pane (PowerPoint), 429
slide layout
   changing, 482–83
   default for objects, changing, 462
   reapplying original, 482
   resetting, 482, 483
   restoring original, 482, 483
   switching, 483
Slide Layout command (PowerPoint), 483
Slide Layout task pane (PowerPoint), 429
Slide Master, 489. See also masters (PowerPoint)
   design template, applying, 490
   displaying, 489
   inserting, 490

   multiple, 489
   template, applying, 490
slide navigation controls on Web presentations, 525
Slide pane (PowerPoint), 430
Slide Show button (PowerPoint), 462
Slide Show view (PowerPoint), 505
   navigating, 518
   popup toolbar, 518
slide shows, 505
   creating different versions of. See custom slide shows
   customizing. See custom slide shows
   delivering, 518–19
   drawing on slides. See annotating slide shows
   hiding slides in. See hidden slides
   movies. See movies (PowerPoint)
   navigating, 518
   pointer, changing to felt tip pen, 519
   pointer, displaying, 519
   sounds. See sounds (PowerPoint)
   timing, setting. See slide timings
   transition effects, 486–87
Slide Sorter view (PowerPoint), 505
   hiding slide formatting in, 506
slide timings, 515–16
   applying to all slides, 516
   rehearsing. See rehearsing presentations
   resetting for single slide, 517
   setting automatically. See rehearsing presentations
   setting, for single slide, 516
Slide Transition button (PowerPoint Slide Sorter toolbar), 516
Slide Transition command (PowerPoint), 487
Slide Transition task pane (PowerPoint), 516
slides
   adding to custom slide shows, 510, 511
   advancing automatically, 516
   animating, 485–86
   animating different levels separately, 485
   applying layouts to, 429
   backgrounds. See backgrounds, slide
   clip art. See clip art
   deleting, 506–7

deleting, from custom slide
shows, 511
displaying entire page in
window, 505
editing text. *See* text objects
(PowerPoint)
headers and footers, 493–94
hiding formatting, in Slide Sorter
view, 506
hiding. *See* hidden slides
hyperlinks to, creating, 508
layout. *See* slide layout
movies. *See* movies (PowerPoint)
moving, 506
notes in. *See* notes (PowerPoint)
objects, 425
organizing, 506–7
orientation, setting, 484–85
previewing, in grayscale, 530
rearranging, 506–7
rearranging, in custom slide
shows, 511
saving, 523
saving as graphics, 523–24
selecting all, 487
size, setting, 484–85
sounds. *See* sounds (PowerPoint)
subtitles, adding, 430
timings. *See* slide timings
titles. *See* titles (PowerPoint)
transition effects, 486–87
unhiding, 515
Slides from Outline command
(PowerPoint), 435
Smart Tags property (Access), 555
Snap To Grid command
(Access), 614
social security numbers, in
Excel, 243
soft page breaks, 89
Solver (Excel), 343–45
installing, 343
Solver command (Excel), 344
Solver Parameters dialog box
(Excel), 344
Solver Results dialog box
(Excel), 344
Sort Ascending button
Access, 624
Excel Standard toolbar, 261
sort codes (Excel), 261
adding, 262

Sort command
Excel, 262
Word, 154, 155
Sort Descending button
Access, 624
Excel Standard toolbar, 261
Sort dialog box
Excel, 262
Word, 155
sort order, restoring in Excel, 261
Sort Text dialog box (Word), 154
sorting
data source (mail merge), 171
e-mail messages, 709
in Excel, 261
lists, in Excel, 261–63
lists, in Word, 153–54
in Outlook, 709
records (Access), 624–25
tables, in Word, 154
worksheets, on multiple
columns, 261–63
worksheets, on one column, 261
worksheets, restoring order
after, 261
Sorting and Grouping button
(Access Report Design
toolbar), 590, 625
Sorting and Grouping dialog box
(Access), 590, 626
sounds (PowerPoint)
action settings, changing, 461
attaching to action buttons, 511
inserting, 460–63
inserting, from Clip Organizer, 460
inserting, with content layout, 461
moving, 461
playing, on mouse over, 461
spacing
Access controls, evenly, 615
in Access reports, 621
paragraphs, 73–76
spacing, character, 71–72
spacing, line, 74
speaker notes (PowerPoint). *See*
notes (PowerPoint)
special characters (Word), 7–8
Spelling and Grammar button
(Word Standard toolbar), 13,
14, 164
Spelling and Grammar dialog box
(Word), 13
Spelling button (PowerPoint
Standard toolbar), 436

Spelling dialog box
(PowerPoint), 436
spelling, checking
(PowerPoint), 436–38
spelling, checking (Word), 12–14
adding words to the dictionary, 13
entire document, 12
individual words, 12
Split Cells button
PowerPoint Tables and Borders
toolbar, 441
Word Tables and Borders toolbar,
157
Split Cells command (Word), 44
Split Cells dialog box (Word), 44
Split command
Excel, 308
Word, 129
splitting
table cells, in PowerPoint, 441
table cells, in Word, 44, 157–58
windows, in Excel, 308–9
windows, in Word, 128–30
SQL Server files, importing Access
data from, 606
Standard Column Width dialog box
(Excel), 287
Standard Generalized Markup
Language (SGML), 177
Start enforcing protection dialog
box (Word), 217
Start Searching button
Excel Thesaurus, 253
Research task pane, 37
stationery (Outlook), 665
statistical functions (Excel), 268
statistics, compiling for Word
documents, 163–64
status bar indicator, 240
StDev function (Access), 612
stock quotes, inserting in Excel, 253
Stop Recording button
Excel Stop Recording toolbar, 417
Word Stop Recording toolbar, 224
structuring XML worksheets, 365
structuring databases, 539
Style button (Word Formatting
toolbar), 67
style checker, 437
Style command (Excel), 285
Style dialog box (Excel), 285
styles (Access), applying to
forms, 574
styles (Excel), 285–86

styles (Word), 67–70
    applying, 67
    of bulleted lists, clearing, 68
    changing all of similar type, 68
    character, 66
    creating, 133–36
    creating, for tables, 49
    creating, from existing styles, 134
    creating, from formatted text, 134
    creating, from scratch, 135
    of lists, changing, 68
    Normal, 67
    of tables, 136–37
    of tables, changing, 68
    of tables, clearing, 69
    paragraph, 67
    viewing applied, 67
Styles and Formatting command
    (Word), 67, 68, 134, 199
stylized text. See WordArt
subdocuments (Word)
    collapsing, 203
    creating, 203
    deleting, 204
    editing, 203
    expanding, 204
    hiding, 203
    modifying, from master
        document, 204
subordinate chart boxes, 447
subpoints, adding, 433
Subtotal command (Excel), 326
Subtotal dialog box (Excel), 326
subtotals (Excel),
        calculating, 326–27
Sum function (Access), 612
SUM function (Excel), 264
summarizing
    with AutoSummarize, 162–63
    Word documents, 109–11, 219–21
    Word documents, with custom
        information, 221–22
    worksheet data, 407–8
Switch Between Header and Footer
    button (Word Header and
    Footer toolbar), 86
switching
    between Word
        documents, 128–30
    printers, 118
    views, in PowerPoint, 505
    views, in Word, 123

Symbol command
    Excel, 243
    Word, 7
Symbol dialog box (Word), 7, 8
symbols (Excel), 241–45
symbols (Word)
    inserting from Symbol dialog
        box, 7
    inserting with keyboard
        shortcuts, 8
synonyms. See thesaurus

T

Tab button (Ruler), 79
Tab Color command (Excel), 290
tab leaders (Word), 79
tab stops (Word)
    adjusting interval between, 80
    clearing all, 81
    custom, clearing, 80
    custom, moving text to, 80
    deleting, 79
    moving, 80
    positioning, 79
    setting, 78–81
    setting custom, 79
Table AutoFormat command
    (Word), 49, 69, 136
Table AutoFormat dialog box
    (Word), 49, 69
Table button (PowerPoint Tables
    and Borders toolbar), 440
Table command
    Excel, 342
    PowerPoint, 440
Table dialog box (Excel), 342
table of authorities (Word), 195–98
    inserting, 197
table of contents (Word), 195–98
    inserting, 196
    updating, 196
table of figures (Word), 195–98
    inserting, 197
Table Properties command
    (Word), 45, 160
Table Properties dialog box
    (Word), 43, 45, 159, 160
Table Wizard (Access), 542–44

tables (Access)
    adding, 566
    backing up, before running action
        queries, 572
    creating, from scratch, 544–45
    creating, with Table
        Wizard, 542–44
    data types in, 548–51
    datasheets. See datasheets (Access)
    deleting records from, 602
    editing records, 601
    exporting, 640
    fields. See fields (Access)
    importing data into, 607
    linking to, vs. importing, 605
    modifying, 546–48
    opening, in Datasheet view, 601
    opening, in Design view, 551
    pivot. See PivotTables
    primary keys, 551–52
    records. See records (Access)
    relationships between. See
        relationships (Access)
    structure, changing, 547
    views, 546
tables (Excel), looking up
    information in, 351
tables (PowerPoint)
    columns. See columns, table
        (PowerPoint)
    creating, 439–42
    entering text in, 439
    fill color, changing, 440
    filling in, 439
    inserting, 439
    lines, erasing, 441
    rows. See rows, table (PowerPoint)
    selecting, 439
    text, aligning, 440
    text, formatting, 440
tables (Word). See also datasheets
    AutoFormats, 49
    borders. See borders, table (Word)
    captions, 200–201
    cells. See cells, table (Word)
    character formatting, applying, 46
    converting text to, 41–42
    drawing, 39, 41
    editing, in PowerPoint, 458–59
    entering data in, 41
    erasing borders, 44
    erasing lines, 157
    fields, inserting, 160–61
    formatting, 46–48, 157
    formatting, with styles, 68

formulas in, 156–57
functions in, 156
headings, changing direction
    of, 158
inserting, 39–41
inserting in PowerPoint
    slides, 458–59
modifying, 43–46
moving, 45
moving, incrementally, 45
navigating, 39
paragraphs, formatting, 46
properties, adjusting, 45
properties, modifying, 159–60
selecting, 43
shading, 46
sizing, 44
sorting, 154
structure, changing, 43–46
styles, 136–37
styles, changing, 68
styles, clearing, 69
styles, creating, 49
text in, aligning, 158
text in, changing position, 158–59
totaling columns/rows, 156
Tables and Borders button
    PowerPoint Standard toolbar, 440
    Word Standard toolbar, 41
Tabs command (Word), 80, 81
Tabs dialog box (Word), 80
**tabs, worksheet, changing color,
    290**
tab-separated files, 606
tabular forms (Access), 574
Task Pane command (Excel), 300
**Task Recurrence dialog box
    (Outlook), 695**
TaskPad (Outlook), 694
tasks, 693–98
tasks (Outlook)
    accepting, 673
    assigning, 697–98
    assigning, to multiple people, 698
    comments, adding, 697
    creating, 694
    creating, from e-mail
        messages, 649
    declining, 674
    delegating, 674
    deleting, 696
    displaying, 647
    due date, changing, 697
    due date, setting, 694

linking to contacts, 705
marking as complete, 696
organizing, by category, 725
organizing, in folders, 718
organizing, with views, 717
recurring, creating, 695
recurring, deleting, 696
reminders. *See* reminders
    (Outlook)
removing recurrence, 696
sending as e-mail, 698
updating, 697
viewing, 695
Tasks button (Outlook), 647
Tasks list (Outlook), 694
**templates (Access), displaying
    available, 540**
templates (Excel)
    creating workbooks from, 296–97,
        405
    editing, 406
    saving, 405
templates (PowerPoint)
    applying, 483–84
    applying, to masters, 490
    creating presentations
        with, 429–30
    saving, 488
    saving presentations as, 488
templates (Word), 67
    attaching to existing
        documents, 108
    default storage location,
        changing, 232–33
    font settings, changing, 235
    modifying, 107
    Normal, 67, 106
    placeholders in, 107
    predefined, 107
    saving, 107
**Templates and Add-Ins command
    (Word), 178**
**Templates and Add-Ins dialog box
    (Word), 179**
Templates dialog box
    Excel, 297
    Word, 107
**testing grouped data access
    pages, 595**
text (Excel)
    entering, 241–45
    entering, with AutoComplete, 242
    entering numbers as, 242
    wrapping, 286

text (PowerPoint)
    adding to action buttons, 513
    adding to slides, 430–32
    adding, in Outline tab, 431
    adding, in Slide pane, 430
    aligning, 470–71
    animating, on slides, 485
    bolding, 466
    colors, changing, 468–70
    deleting, 430
    editing, 430–32
    entering, in tables, 439
    fonts. *See* fonts
    formatting, 465–68
    formatting, on action buttons, 513
    formatting, with Font dialog box
        (PowerPoint), 466
    inserting, from Word, 434–35
    italicizing, 466
    overtyping, 430
    placeholders, 489, 507
    promoting/demoting, 433–34
    selecting, 425
    sizing, 466
    in tables, formatting, 440
    underlining, 466
text (Word)
    adding to frames pages, 211
    aligning, 75
    centering, 74
    character spacing, 71–72
    coloring, 63
    converting tables to, 41–42
    converting, to bulleted list, 51
    converting, to numbered list, 53
    copying, 10–12
    creating styles for. *See* styles
        (Word)
    deleting, 9–10
    deselecting, 3
    editing, 9–10
    effects, 70–71
    fancy. *See* WordArt
    finding. *See* finding and replacing
        text
    fonts. *See* fonts
    formatted, creating styles
        from, 134
    formatting in tables, 46, 49
    formatting as columns. *See*
        columns (Word)
    hidden, displaying, 5, 6, 125
    highlighting, 70
    inserting, 5–6

text (Word) *(continued)*
justifying, 74
moving, 10–12
overtyping, 5, 9
replacing. *See* finding and
replacing text
selecting, with particular
formatting, 65
size, changing, 63
style, changing, 63
styles, applying, 67
styles, changing all of similar
type, 67
stylized. *See* WordArt
in tables. *See* tables (Word), text
viewing applied styles, 67
wrapping around
graphics, 143–45
**Text Box button (Word Drawing
toolbar), 26**
text boxes (Word)
inserting, 26–27
positioning, 26–27
positioning, visually, 27
sizing, 26–27
sizing, visually, 27
Text data type (Access), 548
**Text Direction – Table Cell dialog
box (Word), 159**
**Text Direction command
(Word), 159**
text effects (Word), 70–71
text files, importing into Access, 606
**Text Form Field button (Word
Forms toolbar), 184**
**Text Form Field Options dialog box
(Word), 184**
text form fields (Word)
formatting, 184
frames, inserting, 187
inserting, 184
text objects (PowerPoint), 425
color, changing, 470
deselecting, 426
dotted selection boxes, 426
editing text in, 425
selecting, 425
sizing, to fit text, 467
text placeholders (PowerPoint), 489
editing, 507
**textured backgrounds, applying to
slides, 481**
textures, adding to shapes, 478

Theme command (Word), 191
Theme dialog box (Word), 191
themes (Outlook), 665
themes (Word), 191
Thesaurus (Excel), 252–53
thesaurus (PowerPoint), 438
thesaurus (Word), 15
**Thesaurus command
(PowerPoint), 438**
thumbnails (PowerPoint)
changing size, 429
previewing presentations as, 505.
See also Slide Sorter view
(PowerPoint)
thumbnails (Word)
displaying, 168
displaying pages as, 127, 166–69
navigating with, 168
**Thumbnails button (Word Reading
Layout toolbar), 127, 168**
tiling workbooks, 310
time (Excel), 242
time (Word), inserting, 19–20
timing slides. *See* slide timings
Title Master, 489. *See also* masters
(PowerPoint)
creating, 489
design template, applying, 490
displaying, 489
inserting, 490
multiple, 489
template, applying, 490
titles (PowerPoint)
adding, 430
masters for. *See also* Title Master
replacing, 431
**Toggle Total Row button (List
toolbar), 334**
Toolbar Options button, 230, 412
toolbars (Excel)
buttons. *See* buttons, toolbar
(Excel)
creating, 412
customizing, 411–13
deleting, 413
resetting, 412
sorting with, 261
switching between one row and
two, 411
toolbars (Word)
creating custom, 230
customizing, 230–31
deleting, 231

resetting, 230
switching between one row and
two, 230
Toolbars/Reviewing command
PowerPoint, 501
Word, 103
**Toolbars/Revisions command
(PowerPoint), 497, 498**
**Toolbars/Word Count command
(Word), 112**
Toolbox (Access), 581
Toolbox button
Access Form Design toolbar, 581
Access Page Design toolbar, 596
Access Report Design toolbar, 591
Tools button
Excel, 319, 387
Word, 114
Tools button (Word), 114
total rows (Excel), 333
adding, 334
**totaling table columns/rows, in
Word, 156**
**totaling values with SUM function
in Excel, 264**
**Totals button (Access Query Design
toolbar), 613**
tracing errors, in Excel, 355
**tracing precedents/dependents, in
Excel, 355**
**Track Changes button (Word
Reviewing toolbar), 103**
**Track Changes dialog box
(Word), 207, 208**
**Track Changes/Accept or Reject
Changes command
(Excel), 396**
**Track Changes/Highlight Changes
command (Excel), 392, 395**
tracked changes (Excel), 396. *See
also* change tracking (Excel)
tracked changes (PowerPoint). *See
also* change tracking
(PowerPoint)
accepting, 498–99
accepting all, 499
change markers, 496
deleting all, 499
displaying, 497
navigating, 497
previewing, 498
rejecting, 498–99
rejecting all, 499

tracked changes (Word) . *See also* change tracking (Word)
  accepting, 104
  balloon options, 208–9
  colors, specifying, 207
  displaying particular reviewer's, 207
  hiding/displaying, 99, 104
  hiding/displaying formatting, 99
  managing, 103–5
  in merged documents, 98–99
  moving among, 99, 104
  rejecting, 104
  reviewer options, 206–7
tracking word count, in Word Count toolbar, 112
transforms, 177–78
transition effects (PowerPoint). *See also* animation effects (PowerPoint)
  applying, 486–87
  customizing, 487
transporting presentations. *See* packaging presentations for CD
Tri-fold style, printing Outlook Calendar in, 728
TrueType fonts, including when packaging presentations for CD, 521
turning off
  balloons for tracked changes, in Word, 208
  checking spelling as you type, 436
  drawing guides, in PowerPoint, 477
  gridlines, in PowerPoint, 477
  optional chart objects, in Excel, 378
  password protection, in Excel, 388
  password protection, in Word, 216
  rulers, in PowerPoint, 492
  shadows, 479
turning on Reviewing toolbar, in Word, 103
Two Pages button (Access), 634
typeface. *See* fonts

U

Unapply All Changes command (PowerPoint), 499
Unapply button (PowerPoint Reviewing toolbar), 499
unbound controls (Access), 580
  adding to data access pages, 596
  adding to forms, 582
  creating, 591
Underline button
  Excel Formatting toolbar, 278
  PowerPoint Formatting toolbar, 440, 466
  Word Formatting toolbar, 63
underlining text, 466
Undo button
  PowerPoint Standard toolbar, 478
  Word Standard toolbar, 9
Undo command (Word), 9
undoing, 9
  multiple actions, 10
Unfreeze All Columns command (Access), 623
Unfreeze Panes command (Excel), 309
unfreezing worksheet rows/columns, 309
Unhide Columns command (Access), 622
Unhide command (Excel), 288, 311
unhiding slides, 515
Uniform Resource Locaters. *See* URLs
unmatched queries (Access), 570–71
unpacking presentations, 522
Update Field command (Word), 202
update queries (Access), 572–74
Update Query command (Access), 572
Update TOC button (Word Outlining toolbar), 196
updating
  charts, in Excel, 275
  cross-references, in Word, 202
  indexes, in Word, 194
  meetings, 687
  PivotTables, 348
  table of contents, in Word, 196
  tasks, 697

URLs
  in e-mail messages, 657
  including in Outlook notes, 706
user information, changing, 501

V

validating XML worksheets, 366
validation (Excel), 331–32
Validation command (Excel), 332
Validation Rule property (Access), 555
Validation Text property (Access), 555
Validation/Clear All command (Excel), 332
values (Excel)
  displaying with commas, 283
  displaying with decimals, 283
  finding unknown, 340
  formatting, 282–84
  formatting as currency, 283
  long, 240
  totaling, 264
  totaling, with SUM function, 264
Var function (Access), 612
variables (Excel), using data tables with multiple, 342
VBA, 226
Versions command (Word), 212
Versions dialog box (Word), 212
versions of Word documents
  comments, viewing, 213
  creating, 212
  deleting, 213
  displaying, 213
  managing, 212–13
  saving, 212–13
Vertical Spacing command (Access), 615
View button (Access), 547, 556, 559, 580, 611, 620
View Datasheet button (Graph Standard toolbar), 150, 151
viewing. *See* displaying
views (Access), switching between, 620
views (Outlook), 716–17
  contact, 716
  default, returning to, 717
  defining new, to filter messages, 710
  displaying current, 716

views (Outlook) (*continued*)
folder, 707–8
organizing contacts with, 717
organizing messages with, 716
organizing notes with, 717
organizing tasks with, 717
switching between, 647
views (PowerPoint), 505–6
views (Word), switching between, 123
viruses, and Word macros, 223
Visible control property (Access), 578
Visual Basic Editor, 226, 416, 419
Visual Basic for Applications, 416
Visual FoxPro files, importing Access data from, 606
VLOOKUP function (Excel), 350
looking for exact match with, 352

W

washout effect, adding to graphics, 373
Watch Window (Excel), 358–59
adding cells to, 358
watching worksheet cells, 358–59
watermarks (Word), 189–90
creating, 190
graphics as, 190
Web browsers
specifying, when converting Word documents to Web pages, 116
Web documents (Word), 116–17, 209–12
Web Layout command (Word), 117
Web Layout view (Word), 117, 123
Web Layout View button (Word), 122
Web Options dialog box
PowerPoint, 525
Word, 116
Web Page Preview command
Excel, 307
PowerPoint, 524
Word, 122
Web pages
editing, in Word, 210
frames pages, 211–12
hyperlinks. *See* hyperlinks
importing Access data from, 606
importing Excel data from, 400–401

modifying, in Word, 210
moving, 116
opening, in Word, 210
previewing Word documents as, 122–23
previewing workbooks as, 307
publishing worksheets as, 403–4
saving Excel documents as, 321
saving Word documents as, 116–17, 209–12
Web presentations, 524–28
animation, displaying, 525
closing, 524
custom slide shows, publishing as, 526, 527
moving, 524
navigating, 525
options, setting, 525
previewing, 524
publishing, 526, 527
publishing selected slides as, 527
slide navigation controls on, 525
target browser, selecting, 525
Web sites, creating hyperlinks to in PowerPoint, 508
Week button (Outlook), 690
Week view (Outlook Calendar), 688
Weekly style, printing Outlook Calendar in, 728
white space between pages in Word, hiding, 125
widows/orphans, controlling in Word, 139
width
of columns in Word, changing, 83
of table columns, changing in Word, 44
wildcard characters, 21
windows (Excel)
arranging, 309–10
removing splits, 308
splitting, 308–9
windows (Word)
arranging, 128–30
maximizing, 128
splitting, 128–30
Word
as default e-mail editor, 649
customizing, 223
exporting presentations to, 532–33
inserting PowerPoint text from, 434–35
word count (Word documents)
checking, 111–13

displaying, 111
tracking, in Word Count toolbar, 112
Word Count command (Word), 112
Word Count dialog box (Word), 112
Word Count toolbar (Word), 112
Word documents. *See* documents (Word)
word wrap, 5
WordArt, 454–57
character spacing, changing, 455
editing text, 454
moving, 456
position, changing, 456
rotating, 456
shadow, adding, 457
shadow, changing style of, 457
shape, changing, 455
sizing, 456
text, formatting, 454
WordArt Character Spacing button (WordArt toolbar), 455
WordArt Gallery dialog box (PowerPoint), 454
WordArt Shape button (WordArt toolbar), 455
words
selecting, 2
selecting, in PowerPoint, 425
work week (Outlook), 692
Work Week button (Outlook), 690, 692
Work Week view (Outlook Calendar), 688
workbooks (Excel), 296–97
authenticating, 386–87
collaborating on, 292
comparing, 393–94
creating folders to store in, 318–19
creating, from templates, 296–97, 405
default storage location, changing, 420
deleting, 319
digital signatures, 386–87
displaying hidden, 311
hiding, 311
importing Access data from, 606
macro settings, adjusting, 389
merged, viewing changes, 394
merging, 393–94
moving worksheets between, 305
password protecting, 387–88
previewing as Web pages, 307

properties, viewing/
    changing, 408–10
protecting, 383–86
publishing as Web pages, 403
read-only access, 387
renaming, 319
saving, as Web pages, 321
saving, for use in other
    programs, 320
shared. *See* shared workbooks
    (Excel)
summary information, viewing/
    changing, 408–10
templates for. *See* templates (Excel)
tiling, 310
tracking changes to, 394–95
Worksheet command (Excel), 305
**Worksheet Object/Edit command
    (PowerPoint), 460**
worksheets (Excel)
    auditing, 355–56
    AutoFormats, 281–82
    background graphics, adding, 290
    calculating subtotals in, 326–27
    cells in. *See* cells, worksheet
    checking for errors, 356–57
    clip art, inserting, 254
    comments in, 293
    completing entries in, 240
    conditional formatting, 372–73
    conditional formatting, deleting, 372
    consolidating data from
        multiple, 407–8
    data maps, adding, 363
    data tables, 340–43
    dates, entering series of, 245
    dates/times, entering, 242
    deleting, 305
    displaying specific records
        in, 258–60
    editing, 247–49
    error messages, 354–55
    expanding/collapsing
        outlines, 329
    filling ranges in, 245
    formatting, in PowerPoint, 460
    formulas in. *See* formulas (Excel)
    headers/footers, 315–16
    headings, repeating, 314
    hiding/revealing, 290–91
    inserting, 305
    inserting in PowerPoint
        slides, 459–60
    lists. *See* lists (Excel)
    moving, 305–6

moving, between workbooks, 305
    naming, 289–90
    navigating, with Go To
        command, 251–52
    numbers, entering, 241–45
    numbers, entering as text, 242
    numbers, entering sequentially,
        with interval greater than
        1, 245
    outline mode, leaving, 331
    outlining, 329–31
    page breaks in, 314
    pasting data into, 301
    phone numbers, formatting, 243
    preventing changes, 385
    previewing, before printing, 306–7
    print margins, changing, 313
    printing, 312–17
    protecting, 383–86
    publishing as Web pages, 403–4
    reusing formulas in, 267
    rows in. *See* rows, worksheet
        (Excel)
    saving, as Web pages, 321
    saving, in XML, 362–64
    scenarios. *See* scenarios (Excel)
    social security numbers,
        formatting, 243
    sort codes, adding, 262
    sort columns, adding, 262
    sorting, on multiple columns, 261–
        63
    sorting, on one column, 261
    stock quotes, inserting, 253
    summarizing data in, 407–8
    summary rows, changing default
        location, 330
    symbols, entering, 241–45
    tabs, changing colors, 290
    text, entering, 241–45
    text, entering with
        AutoComplete, 242
    totaling values in, 264
    unfreezing rows/columns, 309
    XML. *See* XML worksheets
**wrapping text in worksheet
    cells, 286**

X

x-axis, 378
XML, 177–181

elements, assigning attributes
    to, 180
invalid, saving documents
    with, 180
saving structured Word
    documents as, 180
saving Word documents as, 177
schemas. *See* schemas, XML
structure, adding to Word
    documents, 180
transforms, 181–82
XML worksheets
    entering data, 364
    importing data file, 367
    saving, 364
    setting options/properties, 366
    setting up, 364–68
    structuring, 365
    validating, 366
XML data files, 402
**XML documents, importing Access
    data from, 606**
**XML Map Properties button (Excel
    List toolbar), 366**
**XML Map Properties dialog box
    (Excel), 367**
XML Maps dialog box (Excel), 363
**XML Options dialog box
    (Word), 179**
XML/Export command (Excel), 402
**XML/XML Source command
    (Excel), 363**

Y

y-axis, 378
Yes/No data type (Access), 548

Z

ZIP codes, in Excel, 243
Zoom button
    Access, 634
    PowerPoint Standard toolbar, 505
    Word Standard toolbar, 125
zooming
    in PowerPoint, 505
    in Print Preview, 306
    in Word, 125